SHADOW KING

Also by Lauren Johnson

FICTION

The Arrow of Sherwood

NON-FICTION

*So Great a Prince: England and
the Accession of Henry VIII*

SHADOW KING

The Life and Death of
HENRY VI

LAUREN JOHNSON

An Apollo Book

This is an Apollo book, first published in the UK in 2019 by Head of Zeus Ltd

9 7 5 3 1 2 4 6 8

A catalogue record for this book is available from
the British Library.

ISBN (HB): 9781784979638
ISBN (E): 9781784979621

Typeset by Adrian McLaughlin

Printed and bound in Great Britain by
CPI Group (UK) Ltd, Croydon CRO 4YY

Head of Zeus Ltd
First Floor East
5–8 Hardwick Street
London EC1R 4RG

WWW.HEADOFZEUS.COM

For Mum, Dad & Joe
– for everything

Contents

PART II

ADULT RULE

PART II

'A KINGDOM DIVIDED AGAINST ITSELF'

Note on names, dates and money

The fifteenth century was an age of woefully unimaginative forenames and complex titles, so in naming the key players in Henry's life I have striven for clarity, occasionally at the expense of strict historical accuracy (e.g. 'John Beaufort' rather than 'John Beaufort, third earl of Somerset / first duke of Somerset'). For those of non-English origin I have used their original names instead of anglicized versions (e.g. François not Francis), with two notable exceptions: Joan of Arc and Margaret of Anjou. Since both are well-known historical figures in British history, for clarity I have used the anglicized version of their names.

Although the fifteenth-century calendar dated the new year from Lady Day (25 March) or, in the case of civic records, sometimes from the date of a mayor's election, I have followed modern convention and dated all years from 1 January.

Both English and French currency in this period were divided into denominations, sometimes labyrinthine in their complexity. The key denominations are given below:

English

12 pennies = 1 shilling
20 shillings = 1 pound

1 mark = two-thirds of a pound (13s 4d or 160 pence)

French

12 *deniers* = 1 *sol*

20 *sols* = 1 *livre tournois*

Distances between two locations are based on Google Maps walking directions.

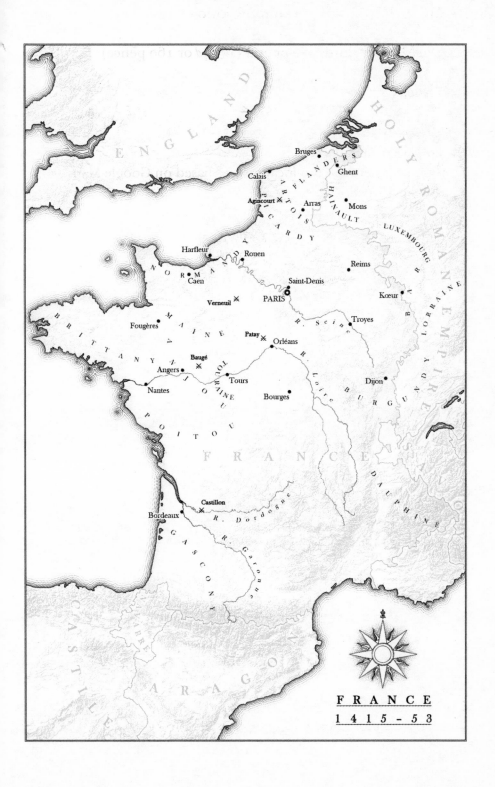

ENGLAND

HOLY ROMAN EMPIRE

Bruges

Calais

Ghent

FLANDERS

Agincourt ✕

Arras

Mons

HAINAULT

ARTOIS

PICARDY

LUXEMBOURG

Harfleur

Rouen

Reims

NORMANDY

Caen

Saint-Denis

Kœur

Verneuil ✕

PARIS

R. Seine

Troyes

BAR

LORRAINE

Fougères

MAINE

Patay ✕

Orléans

Baugé
✕

Angers

Dijon

Tours

TOURAINE

BURGUNDY

Nantes

ANJOU

Bourges

R. Loire

BRITTANY

POITOU

FRANCE

DAUPHINÉ

Castillon
✕

Bordeaux

R. Dordogne

GASCONY

R. Garonne

CASTILE

NAVARRE

ARAGON

FRANCE
1415 - 53

Royal Franchise

Ecclesiastical Private Franchise

Lay Private Franchise

The March of Wales

LANCASTRIAN ESTATES

YORKIST ESTATES

NOBLE LANDHOLDINGS

IN ENGLAND AND WALES

THE WARS OF THE ROSES
1455-71

House of Lancaster

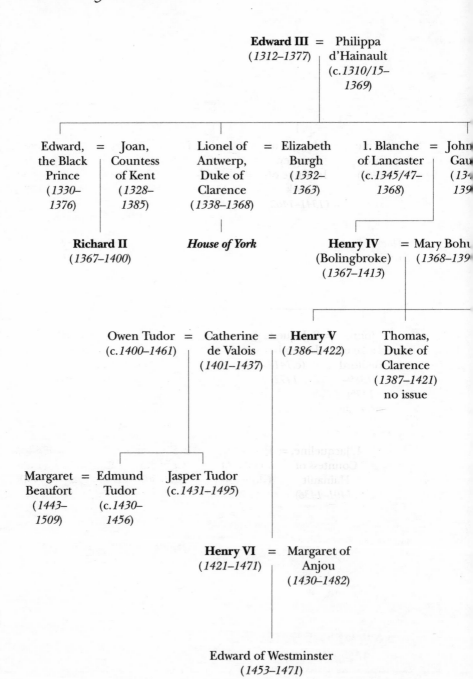

Edward III = Philippa
(*1312–1377*) d'Hainault
(c.*1310/15–
1369*)

Edward, = Joan,   Lionel of = Elizabeth   1. Blanche = John
the Black   Countess   Antwerp,   Burgh   of Lancaster   Gau
Prince   of Kent   Duke of   (*1332–*   (c.*1345/47–*   (*134*
(*1330–*   (*1328–*   Clarence   *1363*)   *1368*)   *139*
1376)   *1385*)   (*1338–1368*)

Richard II   *House of York*   **Henry IV**   = Mary Bohu
(*1367–1400*)   (Bolingbroke)   (*1368–139*
                           (*1367–1413*)

Owen Tudor = Catherine = **Henry V**   Thomas,
(c.*1400–1461*)   de Valois   (*1386–1422*)   Duke of
           (*1401–1437*)   Clarence
                               (*1387–1421*)
                               no issue

Margaret = Edmund   Jasper Tudor
Beaufort   Tudor   (c.*1431–1495*)
(*1443–*   (c.*1430–*
1509)   *1456*)

Henry VI = Margaret of
(*1421–1471*)   Anjou
              (*1430–1482*)

Edward of Westminster
(*1453–1471*)

```
···· =  3. Katherine        Edmund of  =  Isabella of          Thomas of   =   Eleanor
          Swynford          Langley,         Castile              Woodstock,         Bohun
          (1350–1403)       1st Duke of     (1355–               1st Duke of      (c.1365/6–
                            York            1392)                Gloucester          1399)
                            (1341–1402)                          (1355–1397)


              see House of                                            House of
              Beaufort                                                Stafford


  1. Anne of  =  John,     =  2. Jaquetta of                 Blanche  =  Louis III,
     Burgundy     Duke of       Luxembourg                    (1392–      Elector
     (1404–       Bedford       (c.1416–                       1409)      Palatine
     1432)        (1389–        1472)                                     (1378–
                  1435)                                                    1436)
                  no issue


              1. Jacqueline, =  Humphrey, =  2. Eleanor       Eric,      =  Philippa
                 Countess of     Duke of        Cobham         King of       (1394–
                 Hainault        Gloucester     (c.1400–       Denmark,      1430)
                 (1401–1436)     (1390–         1452)          Sweden
                                 1447)                         and
                                 no issue                      Norway
                                                              (c.1381–
                                                               1459)
```

House of Beaufort

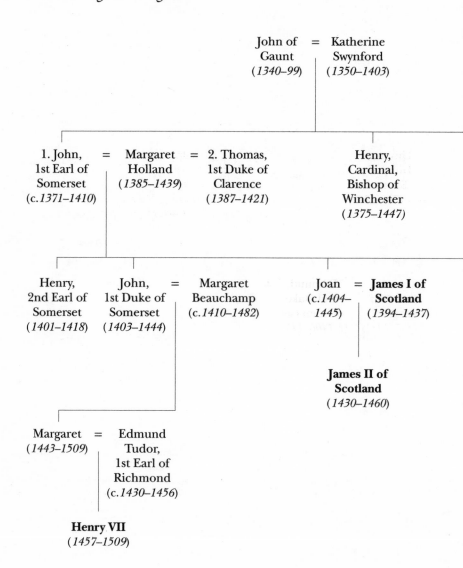

John of Gaunt (*1340–99*) = Katherine Swynford (*1350–1403*)

1. John, 1st Earl of Somerset (c.*1371–1410*) = Margaret Holland (*1385–1439*) = 2. Thomas, 1st Duke of Clarence (*1387–1421*)

Henry, Cardinal, Bishop of Winchester (*1375–1447*)

Henry, 2nd Earl of Somerset (*1401–1418*)

John, 1st Duke of Somerset (*1403–1444*) = Margaret Beauchamp (c.*1410–1482*)

Joan (c.*1404–1445*) = **James I of Scotland** (*1394–1437*)

James II of Scotland (*1430–1460*)

Margaret (*1443–1509*) = Edmund Tudor, 1st Earl of Richmond (c.*1430–1456*)

Henry VII (*1457–1509*)

Thomas,   Joan   = Ralph Neville,
Duke of   Beaufort   Earl of
Exeter   *(1379–*   Westmorland
(c.*1377–1426*)   *1440*)   ***House of Neville***
                            (*1364–1425*)

Thomas,   Edmund, =   Eleanor   Margaret = Thomas
Count of   2nd Duke   Beauchamp   Beaufort   Courtenay,
Perche   of Somerset (*1408–1467*)   (c.*1409–*   13th Earl
(*1405–1431*) (c.*1406–1455*)   *1449*)   of Devon
                                          (*1414–1458*)

House of York

Edward III = Philippa
(1312–1377) d'Hainault
(c.1310/15–1369)

Edward, = Joan,   Lionel of = Elizabeth   John of
the Black   Countess   Antwerp,   Burgh   Gaunt
Prince   of Kent   Duke of   (1332–1363)   (1340–1399)
(1330–1376)   (1328–1385)   Clarence
                         (1338–1368)

Richard II   Philippa, = Edmund
(1367–1400)   Countess of   Mortimer, 3rd
                       Ulster   Earl of March
                       (1355–1382)   (1352–1381)

Elizabeth = Henry   Roger = Alianore
Mortimer   'Hotspur'   Mortimer,   Holland
(1371–1417)   Percy   4th Earl of   (1370–1405)
          (1364–1403)   March
                       (1374–1398)

Anne = Richard of Conisburgh,
Mortimer   3rd Earl of Cambridge
(1390–1411)   (1385–1415)

Isabel = Henry,   Richard Plantagenet, = Cecily
of York   Viscount   4th Earl of   Neville
(1409–1484)   Bourchier,   Cambridge,   (1415–1495)
          Earl of Essex   3rd Duke of York
          (c.1404–1483)   (1411–1460)

Anne = Henry   Edward,   Edmund,   Elizabeth = John de
(1439–   Holland,   Earl of   Earl of   (1444–   la Pole,
1476)   3rd Duke   March, later   Rutland   1503)   Duke
        Exeter   **Edward IV**   (1443–   of Suffolk
        (1430–   (1442–   1460)   (1442–
        1475)   1483)   1492)

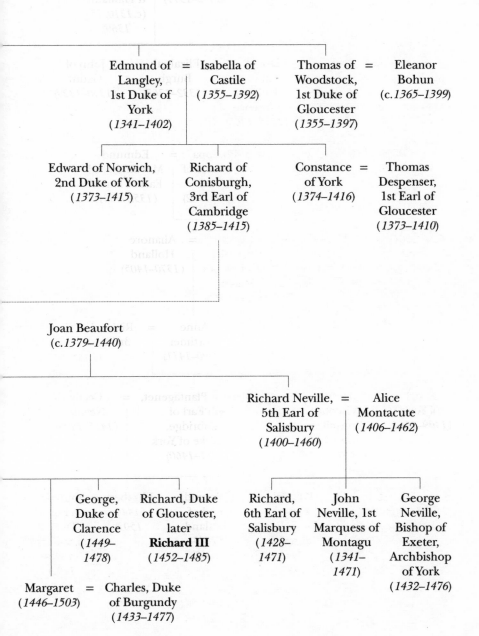

Prologue

'Woe to thee, o land, whose king is a child'[1]

London
5 November 1422

The funeral procession reached London as the church bells struck one. Throughout its journey from France, this was the sound that had accompanied the body of the dead king: a distant, dull tolling that rose to welcome him into each new settlement where his cortege paused, and underneath it the familiar rhythmic chanting of the Office of the Dead. From the castle of Bois de Vincennes, southeast of Paris, the mournful incantations of monks had echoed across the contested territories of the king of France, into the duchy of Normandy, over the sea to Kent and all the way to the capital of England itself.[2]

The cortege took a route that had been well known to the king in life. He had made such ceremonial entries into London when he was crowned, when he returned as a conquering hero of the wars with France and brought the city its new queen as hostage to peace. But now the subjects who had heralded victory with drunken shouts and triumphant music watched the procession pass in eerie silence. The only sounds were bells, chanting, and the rough footfall of those who marched with the dead sovereign.

The king's place was easy to find in this pageant of grief: his coffin lay swathed in black velvet and golden silk on a carriage pulled by five horses. All around him the banners of his patron saints fluttered: St Edward of England, St George, St Edmund, the Virgin Mary and the Holy Trinity. As it processed to Westminster Abbey for burial the following day, his coffin would be topped with a life-size image of the king himself, crafted from leather that had been boiled and then painted. The face would still look young, for the king had only been thirty-six when he died. Instead of the armour of a warrior, so familiar to those who had known him in life, the mannequin would wear all the regalia of monarchy: velvet robes and crown, a golden orb and sceptre in his painted hands.

Around the dead king flocked the warrior lords who had accompanied him to France, mounted on horses draped in black. In stark contrast, the figures who walked before the funeral car wore newly made white gowns, torches blazing in their hands. Despite their lustre, these men and women were poor, their clothes a charitable donation to keep once the funeral was over. Between these two extremes of wealth and rank came the religious and the guilds. The king had been famed for his piety in life, so it was only right that everywhere the eye turned a priest or bishop could be seen, a mitred abbot or poor friar. And, since London was at heart a merchant city, the thirty-one trade guilds who dealt in everything from silk to pins had the honour of accompanying the king on his final journey through their streets. So vast was the procession that, when the king's body reached the doors of St Paul's Cathedral to rest overnight, the mourners at its rear, including Queen Catherine, had still not crossed London Bridge, 2 miles (3 km) behind. Catherine was barely in her twenties, only two years married, a new mother and now a widow.

Within the 2-mile (3 km) radius encircling the dead king, all the peoples of England were represented, from queen to commoner. Royal counsellors, pages in training, silkwomen, paupers, foreign-born merchants, sailors, priests. But one person, as custom dictated, was absent from this vast funeral procession: the new king who had inherited his father's realm. His reign had begun at the moment of the late king's death and every single person bowing their heads before the funeral car was now his subject. His lands stretched far beyond London, beyond the shores even of England and Wales. Like his ancestors, he claimed lordship over the duchies of Normandy and Gascony. For the first time in history, he was not merely rightful king of England, but king of France as well. He was now King Henry VI. And he was not yet one year old.

Fifty years later, in May 1471, the city of London was again the scene of a royal funeral procession. But this one was not carried out with the elaborate ritual of a reigning monarch. Soldiers surrounded the bier, bearing halberds instead of torches, as it made its journey from the Tower of London through the cramped and sombre streets to St Paul's Cathedral. There had been no time to make a funeral effigy – indeed, the corpse was barely cold, death having taken place a matter of hours before, around midnight, within the Tower walls. Though the body was embalmed with wax and oil, and wrapped in fine linens, the dead man's long face was left exposed, its small, puckered lips and wide-set gaze familiar to the citizens of London. Curious eyes peered through the defensive ring of soldiers to catch a glimpse of the man as he passed. When it finally reached the cathedral, the body was set up on the pavement near the altar. Now bystanders were able to stare with impunity at the corpse of the king. Ominously, as it lay in the holy sanctuary of the cathedral, the body was seen to bleed afresh. For two days the corpse was displayed in this manner – time enough to demonstrate, definitively, that this man's life was over. That the reign of Henry VI had come to an end.

Half a century separates these funeral processions. Fifty years that saw English fortunes slide inexorably from the peak of victory to the depths of ignominious defeat. Henry's French realm was lost, with neither battle nor peace treaty able to save it. The vast patrimony that had belonged to his father was, by 1471, a thin strip around the pale of Calais. Even worse than this, England itself descended into civil war.

The reign of Henry VI is rightly remembered as a nadir in national history – and the king's shadow fell across his realms for years after he was deposed. This was the age of England's defeat in the Hundred Years War and the Wars of the Roses. Conflict was to be Henry's principal legacy. Yet Henry himself, the child king who became a martyred holy man, was no tyrant. He loved peace before war. He treated his wife and child with affectionate respect. He rewarded his friends, remembered past kindnesses and strove to avoid bloodshed and cruelty at all costs. How did a man with such good intentions cause such an outpouring of blood and horror? The answer lies in Henry himself. In an age of personal monarchy, the character of the ruler was of vital importance, and Henry's proved to be his reign's fatal flaw. For a medieval king, good intentions in themselves were of no use whatsoever. What mattered was the ability to turn intention into action. What mattered was royal will, and in that respect, Henry showed himself to be singularly lacking.

Henry has long been the 'shadow on the wall' described by his contemporary Georges Chastellain, looming darkly over our image of the fifteenth century.[3] Yet like a shadow he has been intangible in history and literature, seeming to disappear in the bright glow of the large characters who surrounded him – the indefatigable Margaret of Anjou; his bellicose uncle, the 'good duke of Gloucester'; the proud and ambitious Richard, duke of York. In the contrasting portraits drawn by his contemporaries, it is difficult to discern Henry's true outline. Was he the pious saint-in-waiting, too godly and innocent for the cruel vagaries of politics, as his hagiographer John Blacman would have us believe? Was he the half-witted cuckold depicted in Yorkist propaganda? Or was he the weak-willed ruler decried by his rebellious subjects as being too easily swayed by bad counsel?

In recent history Henry the man has been overshadowed by Henry the political symbol – his government and kingship have been reassessed but Henry himself has not received the same personal attention. In the past thirty years, biographies of Henry have presented him as everything from an actively malign force in politics to an inert figurehead propped up by desperate advisers. But there has been little attempt to chart Henry's development from infant ruler through adulthood, mental collapse and captivity, or to present these events empathetically as happening to a real person – flawed, certainly, but still potentially redeemable. It is my intention here to explore Henry VI as an evolving individual struggling in an extraordinary situation. In short, to consider him as a man.

The terrible bloodshed that Henry inadvertently unleashed on his people – and, in the end, on his own family – was not inevitable. It was the result of a tragic combination of nature and nurture: weak will subverted into indolence by the strife of his upbringing, the absence of a father and the overweening presence of too many uncles. Henry developed into a complex and contradictory man: someone who abhorred violence, fled conflict and was inclined to pardon violent offenders, but who still arbitrarily condemned dissenting subjects to grisly deaths and spurned those whose loyalty he mistrusted. A generous and merciful young man who failed to consider the consequences of his actions and was later held hostage by paranoia. A man who exhibited perfect health until he collapsed into a catatonia so complete he did not even recognize his wife and son – and then emerged from it as if no time had passed.

It is only by exploring Henry's own life, by observing his evolution from a child for whom everything was possible, through troubled adolescence, conflicted adulthood and a middle age beset with mental health troubles that we can understand this shadowy figure. By understanding Henry himself, we can see how things went so terribly wrong for his kingdom.

PART I

Child King

1

'That divine king your father'[1]

King Henry V arose to a dreary dawn. It had been a miserable night, full of autumn rain, and the scene that confronted him did little to cheer the spirits. Stretching away from him in all directions was a vast open plain of cropland. The fields had recently been sown, and stubby stalks of wheat struggled through the mud towards daylight. As he strode out among his army, the muddy ground beneath the king's feet was treacherous: clogging beneath the heels and dragging his heavy feet deeper into the mire, then slippery and over-yielding, threatening to send him sprawling. There was at least some comfort to be had in the sight of the soldiers yawning their way into the morning. For two months these men had marched and fought beside King Henry, risking their lives in pursuit of the French crown. The English campaign had begun with glorious victory in a siege of the coastal fortress of Harfleur, but progress stalled thereafter as Henry's army was reduced by disease. As they attempted to retreat towards the English-held stronghold of Calais, their passage over the River Somme was continually blocked by numerically superior French forces. Now, weakened by dysentery and hunger, their bodies aching from the ceaseless march, the English were forced to test the justness of their cause in battle. This day Henry V put his claim into God's hands.[2]

It was the feast day of two lowly martyr-saints, Crispin and Crispinian, the patrons of shoemakers, saddlers and tanners. Perhaps that was a good omen for the English army, which was heavily weighted in favour of low-born archers rather than high-born horsemen. Less reassuringly for King Henry's cause, both these saints had been French.* Such ill omens were not to be dwelt on. King Henry had insisted that the men put themselves in readiness for battle as soon as the watery sun rose, the bustle of preparing arms, kicking out fires and dressing for battle distracting them from the inevitable feelings of anxiety. There was not even time to eat a proper meal. The king heard Mass in his battle dress, the weight of the gleaming plate harness lying heavy across his shoulders as he knelt in prayer. It would have been a sensation he was used to; although he was only twenty-nine years old, Henry V was already a seasoned veteran. He had first fought in battle at Shrewsbury when he was just sixteen, an experience that had marred his good looks with a livid scar, the gory memory of an arrow that had embedded itself 6 inches into the soft flesh of his face.[3]

King Henry was accompanied by noble commanders who ran the full gamut of military experience, from fifty-eight-year-old Sir Thomas Erpingham, who had fought beside the Black Prince in the earlier days of the Hundred Years War, to Henry's youngest brother Humphrey, duke of Gloucester, who was twenty-five and facing combat for the first time. King Henry's long military experience was clear today, as his army – the largest English invasion force deployed in over fifty years – had the same distinctive composition as those that had fought so successfully in his teenage years. For every one man-at-arms,

---

* Strictly speaking, Crispin and Crispinian were Gauls, beheaded on the orders of the Roman emperor Diocletian.

who would fight on foot armed with sword, spear or axe, King
Henry had brought three archers to battle. English archers
were justly feared in combat, able to shoot ten arrows a minute
over distances up to 230 metres (250 yards). At close range, the
steel-tipped arrows loosed from their longbows could pierce
plate armour.[4]

These archers, who were likely to have been at least 5,000 in
number, moved towards the field of battle, the king riding among
them on a small grey horse. Henry was easily identifiable amid
the throng of longbowmen, for his helmet was encircled with a
rich gold crown studded with fleur-de-lys – a visual reminder of
what he saw as his right to the French crown. Around the king
fluttered his five royal banners: the royal coat of arms reflected
his claims to the thrones of both England and France, alongside
standards dedicated to the Trinity, the Virgin Mary, St George
and St Edward the Confessor. No trumpets blasted as the English army moved into position, drawing up their lines in three
'battles', the vanguard and rearguard on each flank and King
Henry in the main battle at the centre.* With inferior numbers
and exhausted men, King Henry chose his position carefully to
maximize his chances of success. His men were arranged between
two sheltering copses, the muddy plain widening in front of them
so that their enemy would be funnelled into a narrower gap, their
advantage in numbers thus minimized as they advanced. Bristling
to either side and interspersed between the three battles were
the English archers, protected by sharpened stakes, taller than
a man, that they plunged into the mud in front of them as an
anti-cavalry device. King Henry commanded his baggage train to
be brought up behind them to protect the rear of his troops and,
perhaps, to enable a swifter retreat if the day turned against them.

King Henry had resolved to fight on foot, among his men, but

---

* This was the customary arrangement for combat: the three 'battles'
or 'wards' were comprised of a middle 'main battle' directly opposite the
enemy, a 'vanguard' to the right and a 'rearguard' to the left.

before dismounting for battle he rode up and down his battle line addressing his soldiers. The fifteen-year-old Burgundian noble Jean de Waurin was at Agincourt on the French side, and he reported how King Henry inspired his men:

saying that he had come to France to recover what was rightful inheritance, telling them that they should remember that they had been born in England where their fathers and mothers, wives and children were at this moment. Because of that they ought to exert themselves so that they could return there in great honour and glory.[5]

Having rallied his troops, King Henry stepped down from his horse and stood ready, battle axe in hand, before the might of the French army. Because the French had called King Henry to battle, it was their right to begin proceedings. Across the distant plain, the king could make out the whirling preparations of the French forces, constantly jostling and reorganizing their ranks. Henry's scouts had informed him that the French intended to make a devastating cavalry charge on his front line, concentrating their forces against his archers. The mass of French knights and noblemen wheeled on their mounts, eager to place themselves in the increasingly bloated vanguard for the first charge. The disarray and confusion in French ranks arose from the lack of a single clear point of command. While King Henry had united his noblemen, and his nation, behind his invasion and had fostered bonds of leadership and respect through privations shared during the last two months of campaigning, the French commanders were deeply divided. For twenty years the country had torn itself apart in civil war.

The French wars had begun in summer 1392 when the young French king, Charles VI, had succumbed to the first episode of what was to be a recurrent mental illness. Already physically drained by anxiety and over-exertion, King Charles had been riding at the head of his army towards Brittany to put down a rebellion when, after hours under the beating sun, he was seized by an attack of violent paranoia. As he spurred his horse towards the front of his army, a careless attendant dropped his lance on to the gleaming helmet of a soldier in front of him and, in the sudden clamour, Charles thought he was being attacked by his own men. He drew his sword and swung it wildly at his soldiers, who looked on in horror, unable to defend themselves for fear of hurting their king. Charles's kinsmen made unavailing attempts to calm the king, but by the time they managed at last to over-power him, he had killed six men, including his bodyguard, and almost murdered his own brother. Dragged from his horse and transferred to a sickbed, after a few days Charles seemed to recover. However, such scenes of royal mania would become all too familiar in the years that followed.⁶

Charles's wife, Queen Isabeau, and his kinsmen had tried to help him rule but his episodes of illness became more frequent and the periods of good health in between grew shorter. For months at a time he was scarcely able to take care of himself, never mind the country. During one attack he refused to be washed or changed, fouling his silken gowns until eventually the soiled and stinking garments were forcibly peeled from him to reveal lice-riddled flesh beneath. He would tear through the corridors of his palaces, imagining assassins at his heels, so the doors had to be bricked up to prevent him dashing straight out into the streets. Although seven of the twelve children Isabeau bore him were conceived after his first episode of madness, he sometimes did not recognize them – or anyone else – and became enraged when he saw Isabeau's heraldry in his chambers. Once, he wept in the faces of his advisers, ordering them to take away his knife lest he injure them, or himself. He begged whoever had bewitched him with this sickness to release him from it and let him die.⁷

In the absence of firm royal rule and with ambitious noble-men eyeing the seat of power for themselves, there was only so much Isabeau and her allies could do to bind the fraying seams of government together. Soon, blue blood spattered across the streets of Paris and full civil war broke out between factions supporting two cadet branches of the French royal family: the House of Orléans (the Armagnac faction) and the House of Burgundy (the Burgundian faction). The turmoil arising from the bitter struggle between these rival French parties presented King Henry V of England with an enticing opportunity: he asserted his own right to the French crown, a claim that had been made repeatedly by his predecessors since Edward III began the Hundred Years War in 1337. As many as 12,000 Englishmen flocked to France in 1415 in support of Henry's title and around 9,000 were still with him as he stood ready to fight on the field of Agincourt.[8] His ailing rival, Charles VI, was absent from the battlefield, so the chief prince of blood royal present was the French King's nephew Charles, duke of Orléans. Orléans was only twenty years old, with no military experience, and had only arrived at Agincourt the previous day. A number of dukes and their retinues had still not arrived by the morning of 25 October, which was partly why the French hung back instead of giving battle.

By ten o'clock, King Henry could wait no longer – if the French would not advance by choice, he would force their hand. A small party emerged from the English ranks, clustered around a figure on horseback, pausing some way in front of their line. Sir Thomas Erpingham, the grizzled veteran who had command of the English archers, threw a baton high into the air, crying, 'Now strike!' Banners were raised and English voices roared as King Henry and his men marched forward. The French forces looked around in amazement. Another English shout split the air, unleashing a volley of arrows that darkened the morning sky as they flew towards the enemy. It was impossible for the French to delay any longer. At last, their cavalry charged.

The plain shuddered with the thunder of the French advance and another volley of arrows rained down. Arrows punctured the iron barding of the horses and pierced the visors of their riders. Men tumbled to the earth and were trampled. Horses, their eyes wild with panic, fought against their bridles as the field narrowed between the flanking woodland, compressing the French front line and making the French knights easy prey for the English longbowmen. Those who made it to the English front line unhurt were driven on to the stakes in front of the archers.

As the cavalry reared and panicked, the French men-at-arms advanced. The recent rain had turned the field into a quagmire that sucked at the soldiers' legs, pulling them in up to their knees. The cavalry's advance and retreat over the same ground had churned the mud still further. Positioned at the rear, the French archers and crossbowmen looked on in confusion, the distant English screened by the sea of French soldiers in between. Despite the exhaustion of their march across the muddy battle-field, the French men-at-arms broke over the English front line with such force that the English fell back almost 4 metres (12 ft).

Iron sounded on iron as the English and French struggled hand to hand, blades slicing at legs and slashing at faces. Amid the melee, King Henry fought 'not so much as a king but as a knight... offering an example in his own person to his men by his bravery'.[9] A cry rang out – the king's brother Humphrey, duke of Gloucester had fallen, wounded in the groin. King Henry lunged forward to defend his brother, but the next moment was forced to his knees himself. A swingeing axe-blow to the head dizzied him and broke a piece from his crown, sending it glinting into the mud. But Gloucester was dragged to safety and Henry recovered his footing.

The brutality and chaos of the battle was reaching its peak. There was no time to take prisoners, and cries for mercy went unheeded. The duke of Alençon reached out his hand to surrender himself to Henry only to be hacked to death by the king's bodyguard. The tide was turning against the French. They were crushed so tightly in the channel between the flanking copses that some could scarcely raise their arms to defend them-selves. Seeing their enemy penned in, English archers who had loosed all their arrows cast their bows aside and seized discarded

swords and lead-covered mallets to press home the attack.
Lightly armoured and nimble, they struck wherever they saw a
break in the line, felling their opponents with single blows to
the head. The French dead began to pile on top of one another,
impeding the progress of those who came behind. An English
priest, watching the carnage from the baggage train,* described
how

> the living fell on top of the dead, and others falling on top
> of the living were killed as well, with the result that, in each
> of the three places where the strong contingents guarding
> our standards were, such a great heap grew of the slain and
> of those lying crushed in between that our men climbed
> up those heaps, which had risen above a man's height, and
> butchered their enemies down below.[10]

After three hours of vicious combat, the French vanguard was
broken and in flight and the sacred banner of the French army,
the oriflamme, fell. So many French princes had been butchered
or captured that the rearguard was left virtually leaderless, looking on in bewilderment, torn between the urge to flee and
the duty to fight on. It seemed that King Henry must emerge
victorious. But all at once a shout went up in the English forces:
the French rearguard were regrouping. The English baggage
train had been attacked. Confusion and panic set in among the
English. It was feared that the French prisoners, their courage
fortified by the apparent reanimation of their cause, might
attempt to rearm themselves. The order 'Kill the prisoners!'
reverberated through the line. The unarmed Frenchmen at the
field edge, some of them wounded and all defenceless, were
massacred – their throats cut, their bodies set aflame by burning
brands tossed into their midst.[11]

---

* The anonymous author of *Gesta Henrici Quinti* wrote of his experiences
as a priest in the English army in *c.*1417.

This decisive act of brutality on King Henry's part ended French resistance. The French rearguard withdrew and their herald Montjoie came to tell King Henry that he was victorious. The nominal commander of the French army, Charles, duke of Orléans, was found beneath a pile of French dead as the English stripped their enemies of their arms and armour. Battered and bloodied, Orléans was dragged into imprisonment. He was fortunate to have survived; thousands of his compatriots had been killed, including a far higher than usual quota of noblemen. The English death toll was much lower and only two of Henry's noble followers were killed, the duke of York and earl of Suffolk.[12] Gloucester limped home with his brother: his heroic role in the events of 25 October would expand in the retelling. The English had gained a staggering victory against the odds. God had smiled on King Henry's cause.

But Henry V had won the day in a manner that demonstrated the brutality as well as the glory of war. The English priest wrote in his report of the battle shortly after:

Our England, therefore, has reason to rejoice and reason to grieve. Reason to rejoice [in] the victory gained and the deliverance of her men, reason to grieve for the suffering and destruction wrought in the deaths of Christians.[13]

Troyes, France
21 May 1420

Surrounded by soldiers, noblemen and courtiers, Catherine of Valois stepped from her chariot into the sacred grounds of the cathedral of St Peter and St Paul. For years, this princess of France had been exiled with the French court inside the walled city of Troyes, unable to leave for fear of the gangs of outlaws and thieves who stalked the roads radiating out into the countryside of Champagne. Today marked a change, not only in the course of Catherine's life but in that of French and English history. For today she would become the queen of England and by her marriage to King Henry V, she would bind their two nations together in peace at last.*

Though she was still only eighteen, Catherine's marriage to Henry V had been openly discussed for a decade. The pair had met only three times, but Henry had been so impressed by a painting of Catherine that he had promised to marry her without a dowry, which was just as well since the ravages of war had drained the French royal treasury. Catherine had inherited the wide, deep-set eyes and high cheekbones of her mother, Queen Isabeau, and it was to be hoped that she had also inherited some of her mother's political acumen.

Queen Isabeau arrived with her daughter at the cathedral in a golden chariot, draped in fine fabrics. A display of magnificence was expected of a queen, but Isabeau took her appreciation of finery to the extreme, revelling in cloth of gold, silvery-blue squirrel fur and jewel-encrusted headdresses, including one that glittered with ninety-three diamonds and numerous sapphires, rubies and pearls.[14] Such lavish ornamentation befitted Isabeau's status not only as royal consort but as one of the three architects of the Treaty of Troyes. Since King Charles was again 'in his illness', it had been left to Isabeau and her ally Philippe, duke of Burgundy, to represent French interests in the vexed negotiations with Henry V.† The twenty-four-year-old Duke Philippe accompanied Catherine and Isabeau into the cathedral, cutting an altogether more sombre figure in funereal black velvet, limiting his ostentation to his remarkable sleeves, which were so long that they brushed the earth even when he

---

* As was traditional, Catherine was known as 'queen of England' from the time of her formal betrothal, even though she and Henry V did not marry until June.

† Philippe was one of the many members of a cadet branch of the Valois royal family. His lands extended beyond the duchy of Burgundy (in northeastern France) to encompass Flanders, Artois and Franche-Comté.

rode on horseback.[15] While Isabeau's focus that day might be on achieving the longed-for peace and Catherine's on her imminent marriage to a virtual stranger, Philippe's mind was bent wholly on revenge.

Despite the devastating blow that the Battle of Agincourt had dealt to the French nobility, it had taken King Henry another five years of relentless campaigning to force them to accept his terms for peace; five years of creeping English advances through Normandy and northern France while the French aristocracy continued to tear itself apart. The feud between Burgundians and Armagnacs had grown bloodier as the rival factions grappled for control of the royal family and the capital city of Paris. The leader of the Burgundians had been Duke Philippe's father, Jean 'the Fearless' of Burgundy, who had saved himself from the slaughter of Agincourt by simply staying away. The Armagnacs were led by the last remaining son of King Charles VI and Queen Isabeau, the adolescent Dauphin Charles.* Charles was an unprepossessing young man: short, skinny and ungainly with small hooded eyes and a long, bulbous nose. He also had a curiously unbalanced body: his legs were weak and his shoulders too broad for his frame. His contemporary the Burgundian chronicler Georges Chastellain observed that Charles did not like to fight – indeed, that he lacked courage by nature – but he made up for his innate deficiencies with intelligence and good sense. Charles's early exposure to the harsh realities of warfare and political intrigue made him mistrustful and changeable. It also left him paranoid to the point that among his many phobias in later life were a fear of strangers, eating in front of others and crossing wooden bridges on horseback.[16] Although Charles had presided over councils and meetings of the Estates General since the age of fourteen, he had become increasingly isolated

---

* In an age of high infant mortality, Charles and Isabeau were particularly unfortunate; in 1421 only five of their twelve children were still alive. Dauphin Charles inherited his title from his older brother in 1417.

from the Burgundian-dominated court. Isabeau and the citizens of Paris had turned to Jean the Fearless as a guiding light in the endless wars, and with Jean's hand on the tiller of government, the dauphin had withdrawn with his Armagnac allies to establish a rival court at Bourges in Berry, central France.[17]

By 1419 it seemed that at long last there were hopes of peace: in May, King Henry negotiated with Jean and Isabeau in the fields of Meulan, 25 miles (40 km) northwest of Paris, meeting Catherine for the first time. When those talks proved fruitless, in July the forty-eight-year-old Jean and fifteen-year-old Dauphin Charles drew up a treaty of peace, binding one another with promises of friendship that swore French unity against English aggression. To conclude further details, Charles invited Jean to meet him at the fortified town of Montereau-sur-Yonne, 45 miles (72 km) southeast of Paris, in September. Despite their mutual protestations of amity, Jean was reluctant to put himself at the mercy of his long-term enemies. Charles attempted to assuage his anxieties, insisting that they meet on the many-arched bridge that spanned the River Yonne between the town on one bank and its castle on the other, even granting custody of the fortress to Jean's Burgundian supporters as a sign of his sincerity. On Sunday 10 September 1419, Jean strode on to the bridge with a handful of attendants and met the dauphin inside a wooden palisade, which was locked to prevent either party bringing in their soldiers. As protocol dictated, Jean greeted the ungainly adolescent who would be his next king with a respectful bow, doffing his black velvet hat. But before he could rise, Charles made a signal and the Armagnac Thanguy du Châtel brought an axe crashing down into Jean's skull. This ruthless political assassination changed the French political landscape completely.[18]

Jean's son and heir, twenty-three-year-old Philippe, inherited the title of duke of Burgundy and with it control of the French royal family. Philippe went into ostentatious mourning, publicly proclaiming his determination to take revenge. There could now be no reconciliation between Armagnac and Burgundian, nor between the dauphin and his long-suffering parents, who were so appalled by Charles's actions that they disinherited him. As an anonymous 'Bourgeois' of Paris observed in his journal: 'It was therefore necessary, however distressing, to negotiate with the English king, France's ancient enemy, because of the Armagnacs' barbarity.'[19] The abortive negotiations with England were revived and on 21 May 1420 Henry, Isabeau, Catherine and Philippe came together at Troyes to bind themselves to the twin objectives of restoring peace to France under Henry's rule and bringing the dauphin to justice for the murder of Jean the Fearless.

Inside Troyes Cathedral, English, Burgundian and French looked on as Queen Isabeau and King Henry ascended the steps to the high altar. There, in the holiest part of the church, the terms of the Treaty of Troyes were read aloud for all to hear. Charles VI's rule was to be set aside in place of a regency under Henry V, and once Charles was dead – an event which, given his current condition, no one believed could be very far off – Henry would inherit his throne as king of France. Henry, Isabeau and Philippe swore never to make an alliance with Dauphin Charles without first gaining the consent of each other and of the 'three estates' of England and France.* Isabeau and Henry pressed their royal seals into hot wax to confirm the treaty, swearing to uphold its terms. Duke Philippe set the example for 15,000 Frenchmen to follow the next day by promising to abide by the treaty. Then, as regent and heir of France, King Henry took Catherine's hands and they pledged their union to each other.[20]

Catherine and Henry's official wedding took place two weeks later, celebrated with the blare of trumpets and shimmer of rich fabrics. The bride and her mother arrived in a chariot drawn by eight white horses, a gift from her new husband. Such romantic gestures were in short supply in the days that followed. Henry

---

*   In England, this meant parliament, and in France the Estates General.

cancelled the customary tournaments that should have been fought the next day, loudly announcing his intention to besiege Sens, 40 miles (65 km) to the west. 'There', he said, 'we may all tilt and joust and prove our daring and courage, for there is no finer act of courage in the world than to punish evildoers.'[21] Henry was keenly aware that half of the territory supposed to be in his power as regent was still in the clutches of Dauphin Charles. The day after their wedding, Henry bade Catherine farewell and rode with King Charles and Duke Philippe to wage war on the dauphin.[22]

King Henry's attention in those honeymoon days was focused purely on wresting back control of the area south of Paris from Catherine's brother. Sens fell within a week, but other fortresses proved more recalcitrant. The siege of Melun, begun immediately after Sens fell, did not end until October. Catherine joined her husband at Melun, attended by a small household carefully selected by the king himself. Every evening King Henry had the royal musicians play music to his wife, perhaps as a necessary diversion from the miseries of warfare so close at hand.[23]

By the end of 1420, with Melun vanquished, Henry determined that the war was proceeding well enough for him to accompany his bride back to England for her coronation. On 27 December 1420, Catherine bade farewell to her parents at Paris. 'It was a sad parting,' reported the Bourgeois of Paris, 'especially between the king of France and his daughter.'[24] Given the state of King Charles's health it must have been far from certain that father and child would ever meet again. Catherine also had to leave behind almost all of her own servants, keeping only three French ladies and two maids. The rest of her royal entourage would now be entirely English.

After a leisurely progress through northern France and Normandy, Catherine and Henry arrived in England early in February 1421, and Catherine began her new life as queen. By the time spring blossom had appeared on the trees, it was clear that Henry and Catherine's union had borne fruit: Catherine was pregnant. The future of the dual monarchy of England and France seemed assured.

Westminster
23 February 1421

From her seat at the end of Westminster Hall, Catherine looked out over a table laden with the choicest delicacies that the Lenten season would allow: roast porpoise and powdered whelks, crabs and savoury custards, trout, lampreys, jellies, shrimp and lobster were all laid before her, each of the three courses of her coronation banquet accompanied by a sugar sculpture 'subtlety' of the queen's namesake, St Catherine of Alexandria,* in different guises. This martyr-saint was an exemplar of virginity and self-sacrifice, a fitting patron for the queen.[25]

The feast that followed Catherine's coronation in Westminster Abbey afforded the new queen of England the opportunity to observe her husband's most important subjects. Custom dictated that King Henry did not attend, but the hall nonetheless glittered with the greatest men and women of his realm. The highest-born of Catherine's attendants was James I, king of Scots. The twenty-six-year-old King James had lived in honourable captivity at the English court since being taken hostage by pirates and delivered up to the English in 1406. He was sufficiently trusted by Henry V that he had recently accompanied the English army to France, acting as a figurehead to undermine the loyalty of the considerable Scottish forces who had gone into French service.

Sitting on the right-hand side of the queen in the hall, also reserved a position of honour, was a man who had a chequered history with Henry V, but whose wealth made him indispensable

---

* St Catherine was a Christian martyr tortured to death in particularly bloody fashion by the Roman emperor Maxentius in the early fourth century AD.

to the cash-strapped king. Henry Beaufort, bishop of Winchester, was Henry's uncle of the half-blood. Where Henry V's Lancastrian line was descended legitimately from Edward III's third surviving son, John of Gaunt, the Beauforts were the result of an illegitimate union between Gaunt and his lover, Katherine Swynford.* Bishop Beaufort was a formidably intelligent political player and, just as important, phenomenally rich. At the height of his powers he had a fortune of £50,000, making him the wealthiest English bishop of the late Middle Ages, and he expended vast sums in the service of the crown, providing endless loans for Henry's French campaigns. He had also served in the chief political office of the land as chancellor for both his half-brother, King Henry IV, and his nephew.

However, Bishop Beaufort's relationship with Henry V had never fully recovered from his appointment as cardinal in 1417. King Henry perceived this promotion by Pope Martin V as a conspiracy between his uncle and the Roman church to undermine royal authority in English religious affairs. He had forbidden Bishop Beaufort to exercise his authority as cardinal under threat of legal action. For several years Bishop Beaufort had been out of favour, but his position of honour at Catherine's coronation suggested that King Henry had grudgingly forgiven him and might once more admit his uncle to a position of political influence.

Bishop Beaufort was not the only representative of the Lancastrian family present at Catherine's coronation. Two of Henry V's three brothers were also in attendance: John, duke of Bedford and Humphrey, duke of Gloucester. One of the strengths of the Lancastrian dynasty was that Henry, as the the eldest of four sons, was able to lead armies overseas while his siblings offered military support or watched over the affairs of England. And were he to be killed on campaign, there were three immediate

---

* They were legitimized after the fact in 1397, but barred from inheriting the throne.

heirs – all of them experienced in military and governmental matters – available to inherit the throne. This family fecundity had not yet carried over into the next generation as, unusually for their age and status, only two of the Lancastrian princes were currently married: Henry and the second eldest, Thomas, duke of Clarence, who was away fighting in France in February 1421 and was therefore the only one of Henry's brothers not to be feasting with Queen Catherine at Westminster on 23 February. Only a year younger than Henry, the impetuous and brave Clarence had been their father's favourite, but he had always been overshadowed by his elder brother. While he lacked Henry's intellect, he shared his zeal for soldiering and during Henry's absence in England, it was he who had taken command of the campaign against Dauphin Charles. Clarence's wife Margaret Holland had, since Catherine's marriage, become one of the queen's principal English companions. The couple had no offspring of their own but Margaret had several children from her first marriage, to John Beaufort, earl of Somerset. Two of the Beaufort boys were serving alongside Clarence in France.

Representing the family in Clarence's place was Henry's middle brother John, duke of Bedford, who had served as keeper of England while Henry fought overseas. Bedford was a capable and loyal lieutenant, and if he lacked the king's charismatic qualities he shared his energy and devotion to duty. He had been at Henry's side when the Treaty of Troyes was sealed and had campaigned with him against the Armagnacs throughout 1420. The chronicler Thomas Basin, who as bishop of Lisieux in Normandy had dealings with Bedford, esteemed him to be 'brave, humane and just'.[26] A man with expensive tastes, Bedford had also sired two illegitimate children, and was steadily amassing a treasure trove of artistic and literary works.

Standing bareheaded in Westminster Hall and serving as 'overlooker' of the feast was the youngest of Henry's brothers, Humphrey, duke of Gloucester. Gloucester owed his life to King Henry's protection at Agincourt – he was considered more of

a scholar than a warrior. Gloucester shared the family taste for
literature and learning, and his interest in classical and chivalric literature was evident in the names of his two illegitimate
children, Arthur and Antigone. Among the writers Gloucester
patronized was Titus Livius, an Italian humanist whose works
praised the duke as a charismatic military leader respected by
his peers and supported by the people of England. The future
Pope Pius II appraised Gloucester more critically,* claiming that
he preferred pleasure and reading to feats of arms, and cared
more about his life than his honour.[27] This uneasy dichotomy
between Gloucester's perception of himself and others' lower
opinion of his abilities was to become a running theme in the
decades ahead.

Although a number of noblewomen attended Catherine for
her coronation, royal women were noticeably absent. Henry V's
sisters were long since married and dispersed to the foreign realms
of their husbands and his mother had been dead for decades.[†]
Henry's stepmother, the dowager queen Joan of Navarre, was
very much still alive but currently languishing in prison at Leeds
Castle.[‡] In 1419 Joan's confessor, Friar Randolph, had accused
her of attempting to bring about Henry V's death by witchcraft.
Henry V had been only too happy to detain his stepmother
on this charge, less out of any personal malice than because
it enabled him to confiscate her substantial dowry to bolster
the royal coffers. With the French wars a constant drain on his
treasury, finding money was a perennial challenge.

Yet for all the apparent strength of the Lancastrian family,
it was not entirely forgotten that this was a new dynasty – and
a usurping one at that. Henry V's French wars had united the

---

* In 1435, when Pius was Aeneas Silvius Piccolomini, he visited the English court en route to and from a diplomatic mission to Scotland.
† Mary de Bohun, first wife of Henry V's father Henry IV, died giving
birth to her daughter Philippa in 1394.
‡ Henry IV married his second wife, Joan of Navarre, in 1403. Their
marriage was childless.

country around his regime, but Catherine knew only too well that the foundations of his authority were shallow. Almost three decades earlier, Catherine's elder sister Isabella had presided over just such a banquet on the day of her own coronation as queen of England. Isabella, then only seven years old, had been the second wife of the thirty-year-old King Richard II, a former child ruler whose reign descended into tyranny. In 1399, Richard had been overthrown by his cousin Henry, duke of Lancaster who thus became Henry IV.* The main casualty of this relatively bloodless change of dynasty had been Richard himself, who is thought to have starved to death in Pontefract Castle. Richard was deeply unpopular with both commons and nobility, and he had no sons to carry grudges into the next generation, so although Henry IV had struggled to assert his control over the crown, his eldest son, Henry V, had inherited his throne peacefully. Barring one traitorous plot led by his kinsman Richard, earl of Cambridge – uncovered and swiftly quashed just as the king was about to leave the realm for his Agincourt campaign – the reign of Henry V had been largely free of rebellion.

Which is not to say that the country at large was content. As Catherine and Henry set off on a progress around England to display the new queen to her people, there were dark clouds on the horizon. Although Henry's treaty at Troyes formally declared perpetual peace, in reality all it did was guarantee further war, since it committed Henry to fighting for his French crown until Dauphin Charles was brought to heel. The English people knew that foreign war demanded English money to pay for it, and English service overseas as well. In the past six years, taxation had fallen heavily on Henry's subjects, and now that England and France were officially at peace they were very reluctant to grant yet more taxes. When Henry appealed to parliament to support his next military campaign, in May 1421, they refused.

---

*   Henry IV was the son of John of Gaunt and grandson of Edward III.

He was forced instead to rely on loans, largely from his wealthy uncle Bishop Beaufort. Worse, some English believed that the dual monarchy proclaimed by the Treaty of Troyes threatened to put a French overlord on the English throne, since the future king of England would also be king of France and there was no certainty future generations of monarchs would be raised in their lands. The victors of Agincourt found the prospect of such foreign sovereignty distasteful in the extreme. Catherine's progress was a public relations exercise to win over her new subjects and allay their fears – and ideally to encourage them to open their purses in support of the war.[28]

Amid these concerns, news of Catherine's pregnancy offered welcome cause for celebration. However, Henry would not be in England for the birth of his first child. In April 1421, he received news that his commander in France, his brother Thomas, duke of Clarence, had been killed in a battle with Franco-Scottish forces at Baugé, east of Angers. Clarence had entered the fray against the advice of his lieutenants and paid for the mistake with his life – his two Beaufort stepsons had been captured and would remain prisoners until the vast sums demanded for their release were paid. This was a serious reversal of English fortunes and Henry could not risk delaying and incurring further losses. In June 1421 he returned to France, leaving his brother John, duke of Bedford, to govern as keeper of the realm in his absence.

As autumn turned to winter Catherine approached her eighth month of pregnancy. Custom dictated that she spend the last weeks before her child's birth in confinement, and Windsor Castle was chosen as the location. A later tale claimed that the king had warned against giving birth in Windsor, because of a prophecy that the child 'born at Windsor shall long reign and all lose'.[29] In reality, Henry must have discussed and agreed the venue of his first child's birth with Catherine before she was confined.

Henry learnt that Catherine had taken to her chambers while he was laying siege to the fortified town of Meaux, 30 miles (48 km) east of Paris. A major obstacle to control of the River

Marne, Meaux had already held out for two months, and a lengthy winter siege seemed inevitable. As the king shivered outside Meaux, Catherine made one last preparation for her confinement, having a holy relic called the 'Silver Jewel', the foreskin of the infant Jesus, sent to her from France.[30] The couple's first – and, it transpired, their only – child would be born before the year was out.

2

'In infant bands crowned king'[1]

Windsor Castle
6 December 1421

Henry and Catherine's child entered the world in the shadowed cold of deepest winter. He was born at four o'clock in the afternoon on 6 December, the sky already dark outside the single open window in Queen Catherine's chamber. The whole royal apartment was gloomy, all other windows shuttered, every surface covered in carpet and tapestry, the flickering of candle flame and firelight casting shadows over the golden drapes of her bed. It was the feast day of St Nicholas, patron saint of children, a good day for a royal prince to enter the world. As was customary, during her confinement Catherine had been attended solely by women, her male servants having to hand over any business for her at the great chamber door. It was into the waiting arms of one of these women that the little prince was passed, to be swaddled in layers of linen, fur and silk, as bells rang out and bonfires leapt in celebration at the news of his birth. It had been a bitterly cold winter, mill wheels freezing in place and the streets of Paris flooded. At the French castle of Meaux, Henry V relentlessly pursued his siege of Armagnac forces in driving winter rains as sickness spread through the English camp. He 'rejoiced greatly' when he heard the news that his first-born child was a son, and no doubt by prior arrangement the boy was named in his honour, the third generation of the Lancastrian line to be called Henry.[2]

Now, amid the drudgery of war and winter, there was a bright spark of hope. At Windsor, 200 candles were brought to surround the precious child as he was borne along the route from the queen's chamber to the chapel. Henry had the most illustrious godparents available. They assembled at the door to the queen's chambers, although Catherine herself would not attend the baptism, nor any court duties for a month after the birth. Prince Henry was carried in the arms of Duchess Jacqueline of Hainault, a strong-willed and courageous young noblewoman from the Low Countries who had taken refuge in England to escape a loveless marriage and civil war in her territories. Behind Jacqueline, carrying the long, scarlet, fur-trimmed train of the prince's gown, came Prince Henry's uncle, John, duke of Bedford, while the last of his godparents, Bishop Henry Beaufort, awaited him at the font. At the moment of baptism, all 200 candles in the chapel were lit at once, illuminating the cloth of gold that decked the walls in a sudden blaze of light. Then Prince Henry was carried to the nursery that had been prepared for him, and laid in a 'cradle of estate' under a coverlet of ermine-furred cloth of gold. The royal arms were emblazoned above his head, a reminder to all who looked on him that this was their future king. No one realized, then, quite how soon he would be inheriting that position.

In the new year, preparations were soon underway for Queen Catherine to leave her son and rejoin the king in France in the hope that they could add another child or two to the royal nursery. On 12 January 1422, when Catherine emerged from the confinement of her chambers at Windsor, a team of servants was already in place to attend to the prince's needs and by mid-March he had a full household to take care of him in his mother's absence. Prince Henry had a wetnurse, as was usual among the nobility, and a team of female 'rockers' to watch over his cradle. One of Queen Catherine's ladies, Elizabeth Ryman, was appointed to see to his care, and a physician to monitor his feeding sessions, while yeomen, grooms, sewers and pantlers attended to everything else he required. A lifetime of attendance had begun. Prince Henry would never have to dress or undress himself. He would never be alone.[3]

In early May 1422, everything was ready for Catherine's departure. The king's brother, the duke of Bedford, was instructed to accompany Queen Catherine on her journey through the restless northern French territories. To take his place as keeper of England, King Henry dispatched their youngest brother Humphrey, duke of Gloucester. By St George's Day Gloucester had reached Windsor, presumably meeting his little nephew in the ornate carved cradle before presiding over a chapter of the Knights of the Garter.* Taking a leisurely route through Normandy, Catherine and Bedford were reunited with her parents and husband at the castle of Bois de Vincennes outside Paris on 26 May. After seven months of fierce resistance, Meaux had finally submitted to King Henry's forces, allowing him to leave the fortress and join his wife. They had just celebrated their second wedding anniversary.

As a symbol of their unity, and in defiance of Armagnac plots swirling around the capital, the entire royal family entered Paris in state on Whitsun Eve, 29 May. Queen Catherine impressed onlookers with her 'splendid escort of knights and ladies', two ermine cloaks being carried in front of her litter as a sign of her royal status in both England and France. After paying their respects at the Cathedral of Notre Dame, King Henry and Queen Catherine retired to the Louvre palace to celebrate Whitsun. They sat crowned in state, surrounded by 'English princes, dukes, knights and prelates'. The citizens of Paris were enthralled by the

---

* Members of a chivalric order established by Edward III in imitation of King Arthur's mythical knights of the round table. Their patron saint was St George.

'most precious diadems' and 'rarest viands' served up, but less impressed when the English king failed to provide the traditional gift of meat and drink for the populace.[4]

In spite of the lavish display of loyalty to their English regent, which included putting on a mystery play about St George for his entertainment, some citizens grumbled about Henry V's rule. In June 1422 an Armagnac plot to hand Paris to Dauphin Charles was uncovered, the traitors rounded up and executed. The French were alarmed at how little pomp and ceremony the ailing King Charles VI seemed to enjoy within his own court. In the city, food and drink remained expensive in spite of the truce with England. Henry's military activities around Meaux meant that farmers could neither plough the land nor sow their crops. Grim stories circulated of wolves roaming the countryside, eating women and children and digging up newly buried corpses, even swimming across the Seine to leap up at the remains of traitors impaled over gateways. With the dauphin's men still in control of swathes of northern France and the reality of English rule starting to bite, the optimism of the Treaty of Troyes seemed a distant memory.[5]

The uneasy family reunion of Valois and Lancaster proved to be brief. On 12 June King Henry escorted his wife and in-laws to Senlis, a small cathedral town 25 miles (40 km) northeast of Paris, and it was there that he received an urgent request for assistance from Philippe of Burgundy. The dauphin's forces had attacked the town of Cosne, on the upper Loire, hoping to sever communications between Philippe's headquarters at Dijon in the duchy of Burgundy and King Henry's base at Paris. The fortress's commander had declared that it could not hold out, and that unless a relieving army arrived, he would surrender on 12 August.

Henry gathered his forces from around Paris and promised to lead his men personally against the dauphin. King Henry's drive and focus seemed undiminished, despite months of siege warfare and an oppressively warm summer. In the heat of June and July, the vegetable gardens around Paris became so parched and dusty that labourers could pull the harvest of oats and barley from the earth with their bare hands. The hot weather had also encouraged the spread of disease. In the cities of France, small-pox was cutting a swathe through the citizenry, particularly affecting children, leaving those who survived disfigured and blind. Even King Henry was not immune to illness.[6]

Henry set out from Senlis intending to relieve Cosne, but early in his journey he was suddenly halted by an acute fever. It seemed to be a recurrence of an illness that he had suffered during the siege of Meaux, where dysentery had been rife. His strength diminished and his bowels were in such turmoil that his doctors feared to give him any internal medicines. Too ill to ride his horse, he had to be carried in an invalid's litter to Corbeil, south of Paris. It had taken him days to cover the short distance from Senlis and his condition only worsened. Realizing he could neither lead his men nor risk losing Cosne to the Armagnacs, he appointed his brother Bedford to command the men and lingered at Corbeil in hope of recovery. For two weeks he waited. A physician, John Swanwyth, was summoned from England. All across northern France processions were held and prayers said for his restoration to health and for the peace of the kingdom. Clearly, the two were intimately linked in the minds of the citizens.[7]

Throughout his illness, Henry continued to oversee government, considering a treaty with the bishop of Liège from his sickbed. Eventually, however, it became clear that he was not fit to rejoin his army. He turned back towards Paris, taking a boat up the Seine and then – still unable to ride – was carried to Bois de Vincennes in a litter, reaching the fortress on 13 August.

Meanwhile, Bedford had ridden on and united his forces with Philippe's. Together their armies reached Cosne, but when confronted by the might of the Anglo-Burgundian force in battle readiness, the dauphin's troops simply withdrew. Cheated of a decisive battle, Philippe returned to Burgundy, and Bedford retired towards Troyes. On the march his journey was interrupted by an urgent message. The king had gone into a steep decline. Bedford had to reach Bois de Vincennes as quickly as possible.

Leaving the army at a gallop, Bedford and a few faithful servants hastened back to their king. Despite the warning, Bedford was shocked when he saw his brother. He 'found him worse than had been told'.[8] The royal physicians were loath to admit it, but it was clear that King Henry was not going to recover. His trusted advisers had been summoned to hear his last wishes.

Alongside Bedford at Henry V's deathbed were noble comrades in arms who had dedicated themselves to Lancastrian service. Among them was Edmund Mortimer, earl of March, a distant cousin of Henry's and Bedford's – another direct descendant of Edward III whose name had occasionally been whispered in connection with treasonable plots against the Lancastrians. Despite his rival royal blood, March had proved a loyal commander for Henry, enduring with him the misery of the siege of Meaux. With him was Henry and Bedford's uncle Thomas Beaufort, duke of Exeter, the brother of Bishop Beaufort and another long-term military companion – he had fought alongside Henry since his very first battle as a teenaged prince of Wales at Shrewsbury in 1403. While Exeter distinguished himself with the ruthlessness of his campaigning, his fellow veteran Richard Beauchamp, earl of Warwick, was famed for his chivalry – he was a part-time poet whose fluency in French had earned him a leading role in the negotiations at Troyes. This was a brotherhood in arms, united by the blood they had shed with and for their king, and Henry was duly appreciative. 'For the good services done to me in these years,' he told his former comrades in arms as he lay, hollow-cheeked, in his bedchamber, 'I give thanks to you and all my fellow knights.'[9] Absent from King Henry's bedside was Queen Catherine. Perhaps there was anxiety about infection. Or perhaps their relationship had never really been much of a partnership. The preparations Henry made for her future life suggest that he did not expect her to play much of a political role: she was to live in their son's household, but not to have a position of any real authority. King Henry preferred to vest his power in the Englishmen he had grown up and served with.

Henry V had never been a man to leave things to chance, and even as he lay dying he refused to relinquish his influence over his two kingdoms. Although he had anticipated his own death on campaign, King Henry had not imagined that his sickly father-in-law King Charles VI would outlive him. Now his infant heir faced the prospect of becoming not only king of England but also regent of France, where civil war still raged. Like many of his fellow soldiers, before leaving for war Henry had drawn up his will – three of them, to be precise, the most recent on 10 June 1421, after he had married Catherine but before Prince Henry was born. To provide for his son's future Henry insisted on adding a codicil to this last will. He explained his wishes to the circle of trusted brothers in arms at his deathbed.[10] 'On the loyalty and love you have ever expressed for me,' he said, 'I beseech you... that you show the same loyalty and affection to my son.'[11]

It would be necessary, of course, for adults to oversee the rule of France and England during Prince Henry's infancy, and the king wished the regency of France to be offered first to Philippe of Burgundy and then, if he refused the position, to the duke of Bedford, with specific provisos. 'My good brother,' he said to Bedford, 'I beseech you... that so long as you shall live, you do not suffer [my son] to conclude any treaty with our adversary [the dauphin] Charles, and that on no account whatever the duchy of Normandy be wholly restored to him.'[12] As well as demanding that the French prisoners taken at Agincourt remain imprisoned until the prince's majority, Henry gave a final word of warning. The English counsellors must 'avoid all quarrels and dissensions with our fair brother of Burgundy'. The Anglo-Burgundian agreement was the lynchpin of their hold over the French crown, and if, 'God forbid', that was severed, Dauphin Charles could all too easily step into the breach.

As for the prince himself, Henry appointed his brother Gloucester to have his *tutelam et defensionem principales* (principal guardianship and defence), while the reliable old Thomas Beaufort, duke of Exeter, was given responsibility for the prince's education and household. He was to be supported by Henry's household servants Lord Fitzhugh and Sir Walter Hungerford, who were commanded always to be in attendance on the prince. It is a remarkable sign of the king's undiminished energies that he made these provisions only five days before his death.[13]

Having finalized his worldly affairs, King Henry turned his mind to the spiritual, expressing his regret that he had never made it to Jerusalem for a final crusade. He received the last rites clutching a crucifix tightly in his hands as his chaplains chanted psalms over him. An hour or two after midnight on the last day of August 1422, he died. 'Thus ended the life of King Henry,' lamented the Burgundian chronicler Enguerrand de Monstrelet, 'in the flower of his age.'[14]

Exactly what brought down this mighty king 'in the flower of his age' is uncertain. As the story spread, the cause of death varied. In Paris it was believed he had died of smallpox; in Normandy it was said to be leprosy. Hostile sources claimed that his death was divine punishment for attempting to move the relics of St Fiacre* to England from the defeated castle of Meaux. In vengeance, St Fiacre had given him the disease named after him – a conclusion perhaps born of the fact that St Fiacre's Day was 30 August, Henry's last day of life. A generation later, French sources would develop this story into a tale of a hermit who had warned Henry that, as the instrument of God, he ought to fight the Infidel, not the French. Ignoring the hermit's advice, Henry died by divine displeasure. The English chronicler Thomas Walsingham was probably closest to the truth when he claimed that Henry had 'acute fever and overpowering dysentery'. His living conditions at the prolonged siege of Meaux had been far more comfortable than most of his men's but he had still spent the hot summer of 1422 fighting and travelling, drinking ale

---

* A famed healer and the patron saint of gardeners, St Fiacre was a seventh-century Irish saint who had lived as a hermit in France under the protection of the bishop of Meaux.

or wine instead of the sometimes suspect water available, and thereby exacerbating with dehydration any intestinal problems from which he was suffering.[15]

In England, the cause of King Henry's death was less important than the fact of it. How was the country to cope when its rallying point – the man who had provided firm and decisive leadership for almost a decade – was replaced with a baby who could not yet even walk or talk? Joy at the birth of Prince Henry had been transformed, within nine months, into fear for the future of this child and his entire realm.

Windsor Castle
28 September 1422

As the sun set at the hour for Vespers, the evening prayer, the interim council of King Henry VI crowded into his chamber at Windsor. More than a dozen of the senior lords of his father's council were there, including the venerable archbishop of Canterbury, Henry Chichele, and Henry Beaufort, bishop of Winchester. They huddled around the little figure of their king as he performed his first royal duty. Still not quite a year old, Henry reached out his pudgy fingers to take a white leather purse from the hands of his father's chancellor, Thomas Langley, bishop of Durham. Contained within the purse was the golden seal with which all royal documents were authenticated. With his uncle Humphrey, duke of Gloucester acting as puppet master, Henry passed the purse to the keeper of the chancery rolls, who would then deliver it to the royal treasury until a new chancellor could be appointed. It was more than a fortnight since news of Henry V's death had reached England and politics had been in stasis. All the appointments made by the late king were held to be void at his death, and without a ruling government preparations could not even be made for his funeral, never mind for government by his infant successor. This transfer of the seal, trivial though it might appear at first sight, was a vital first step in establishing the minority rule of Henry VI.[16]

Henry's participation in the ceremony of the great seal demonstrated that, young as he was, he was visibly reigning. It did not mean, though, that he would actually be ruling – and certainly not that he would be ruling two countries, which soon became the reality facing his interim government. For on 21 October 1422 Henry's grandfather, the sickly Charles VI, died. Under the terms of the Treaty of Troyes, Henry V's heir succeeded him. The governing elite around Henry VI now had to rule both France and England on his behalf until he was old enough to do so himself. This was not, however, the first minority that either country had faced. There were precedents available for the men in Henry's chamber for the ceremony at Vespers – and beyond, serving as his caretakers in government in France – to follow as they waited for the king to grow up. Here, the machinery of government helped them, for the support structures of English rule were becoming increasingly sophisticated. By 1422 it was legally possible for a council, parliament and – if necessary – regent to assist an underage monarch in the daily business of governing. Since William the Conqueror every English king – except, notably, Henry's grandfather Henry IV – had gone overseas to administer territory and expand or defend international borders, so government by deputies in a king's absence was a familiar concept to the English. It was a pattern that Henry V had continued in recent years – his endless campaigning in France meant he had barely set foot in England since 1415. As a result, there was a large pool of experienced administrators and commanders available to assist Henry VI in 1422. The English political establishment had watched France tear itself apart as desperate factions conducted a bitter struggle for supremacy around an inert king during the reign of Charles VI and they knew that England was at its most vulnerable now it had lost its champion in Henry V. The greatest hope for peace, internally and externally, lay in uniting behind the infant king.

Such impulses had guided previous minorities. Between 978 and 1216 there had been no child monarchs in England, but since that date Henry VI was the fourth such to accede. In 1216, nine-year-old Henry III had inherited the throne from his father, King John, in the midst of a civil war. In 1377 the Plantagenet Richard II had succeeded his grandfather, Edward III, at ten years old. Edward III himself had been only fourteen when he took power. With the reign of Henry VI, though, England faced the longest minority in its history – and that was assuming he survived, which was far from certain for children in the fifteenth century. Henry could not really be expected to rule until he approached adolescence, meaning that a decade loomed in which the king could barely even fulfil the ritual elements of his role. Edward III and Richard II had both been old enough to open parliament personally, but the first parliament of Henry's reign would have to be summoned as soon as possible to make arrangements for the future – and they could hardly call on a child who was not yet a year old to open it. Instead, an interim government was appointed, with the men who had been present at the passing of the great seal summoning parliament while Gloucester – who since May had been acting as keeper of England – opening it as commissioner on Henry's behalf.[17]

So far, the political elite around Henry had acted with admirable cooperation. But when it came to questions of exactly what form government should take for the next decade, and who should lead it, consensus broke down. It soon became clear that Gloucester expected the leading role in government to go to him. With the duke of Bedford necessarily remaining in France to ensure the smooth transition from the rule of Charles VI to Henry VI,* Gloucester was the closest blood relative of the new king in England. He had twice served as keeper in his brother's

---

* Henry VI is not counted among the kings of France. If he had a regnal number it would be 'Henry II', but that title is usually given to the king who ruled France 1547–59.

absence and Henry V had given him the *tutelam et defensionem principales* (principal guardianship and defence) of Henry VI in the codicil to his will. Gloucester understood this title to confer on him powers similar to those of a regent, or at the very least to entail greater powers than he had enjoyed as keeper.

Unfortunately for Gloucester, he was alone in this belief. A party of noblemen, led by his uncle Bishop Henry Beaufort, believed that the role Henry V had intended for Gloucester was limited to guardianship of Henry VI's property. Explicit control of the body of the king was beyond his remit, since Henry V had granted that to their uncle, Thomas Beaufort, duke of Exeter. Even if the late king had intended a regency for Gloucester, there was no precedent in English law for a dead king to determine the future rule of the country as Gloucester suggested. The preference of Bishop Beaufort and his allies was for Henry VI's minority government to be a council in which Gloucester would have an equal voice with a number of other lords of church and state. There was a precedent for such a minority council in the reign of Richard II, when a 'continual council' of twelve men discharged government business on his behalf, occasionally joined by Richard's royal uncles to consider weightier matters at great councils. For an adult king, royal councils assisted in the daily grind of government – scrutinizing royal grants, communicating with foreign envoys and hearing disputes between the nobility – but when the king was a child, a regency council would be expected to carry out all the business of government by itself. It was a collective way to rule. But it was not at all what the ambitious Gloucester wanted.[18]

The issue was not merely a question of regency versus conciliar government, it was a matter of personality. The experienced politicians on the late king's council harboured serious doubts about Gloucester's suitability to govern. He was a bluff and choleric young man, ruled more by his passions than by political good sense. There was too much at stake to trust to Gloucester's leadership alone.

Most damningly for Gloucester's ambitions, one of the leading opponents to his rule was his own brother, the duke of Bedford. On 26 October Bedford wrote a letter to the mayor and citizens of London reminding them that as the eldest surviving brother of Henry V, according to the 'laws and ancient usage and custom' of England, he should take precedence in governmental decisions over Gloucester. He assured them that if given authority over the realm he would not misuse it for his own benefit – insinuating that Gloucester would. By late October, Bedford had clearly heard whispers of Gloucester's ambitions – probably from Bishop Beaufort – and was eager to cut them off quickly. He had to appeal to the Londoners directly because while Gloucester's abilities were not appreciated by his colleagues in government, the people of England loved him. The duke was to prove time and again in the decades to come that he had an enviable common touch. His outspoken militarism (and sometimes outright xenophobia) chimed with the prevailing feelings of the citizens of London. If Gloucester could motivate this support in his favour, it might win him dominance in government. It was therefore vital for Beaufort, Bedford and their supporters to act before he could do so.[19]

The first step to undermine Gloucester's bid for power had come only the day after the passing of the great seal at Windsor, when the caretaker council sent out summons to convene parliament as soon as legally possible – within six weeks. Among the summonses that went out was one addressed 'to Humphrey, duke of Gloucester'.[20] The significance of this summons was enormous, if not immediately grasped by Gloucester himself. While serving as 'keeper' of the realm, neither he nor Bedford had been summoned to a parliament, for the simple reason that the keeper was the king's representative in parliament – it was he who opened and closed the session and therefore he who did the summoning. By submitting to his summons without challenge, Gloucester was implicitly accepting that his time as keeper was over, and therefore that the political decisions of the late Henry V were at an end. All his subsequent authority would have to be held in conjunction with the council or parliament, so, although he was given a commission to open parliament on Henry's behalf, his powers were greatly reduced from when he was keeper. Once he realized his mistake, Gloucester took the offensive. On or about 31 October, Henry V's funeral cortege finally reached England. Within a week, Gloucester had asserted his right to lead his nephew's government.[21]

For three weeks, Gloucester's status was debated by the Lords in parliament. Bishop Beaufort continued to lead the opposition to Gloucester's independent authority and his cause was bolstered by the return of those veterans of the French wars who had stood at Henry V's bedside and escorted his body back to England for burial. The duke of Exeter and earls of March and Warwick all favoured conciliar rule, reminding their colleagues in parliament that during the last minority, fifty years earlier, Richard II's uncles had not ruled for him. Indeed, his eldest uncle John of Gaunt had not even been an ordinary member of the regency council.

Gloucester countered with the precedent of 1216, when rule on behalf of the nine-year-old Henry III had been exercised by a *rector regis et regni* (governor of the king and kingdom). On that occasion, the *rector* had not even been a blood relative of the king, yet his rule had been supported. How much more suitable, then, must Gloucester be to fulfil such a role, since he was King Henry's own uncle? As the days trickled past, Gloucester must have started to worry whether he would be given any power during Henry VI's minority at all.

Eventually, on 5 December 1422, a compromise was reached. Henry VI's minority government would be administered by a council, but Gloucester was named 'protector and defender of the realm' and chief councillor of the king. For his services he was awarded a salary of 8,000 marks (over £5,300). However, two major limitations were imposed on Gloucester's authority. Firstly, the protector had no right of veto, instead having to rule

alongside the council; and secondly, he was only to hold the
position at the king's pleasure – crucially – when Bedford was
abroad. Whenever Bedford returned, Gloucester would be supplanted by his older brother.[22] As the articles determining the
rule of the council were pronounced, in English, before the
Commons in parliament, Gloucester must have silently seethed.
All of the efforts he had made to ensure his own supremacy
during his nephew's infancy had been subverted to the benefit
of his brother.

For now, the matter rested. Henry's council was given wide-
ranging powers – most of the powers an adult king would exercise
– but it was also closely monitored and held accountable for its
decisions. The clerk of the council had to record the names
of all those in attendance and a full quota was required for
all important decisions. The advice of Bedford or Gloucester
would be sought for issues about which the king would usually
be consulted. A number of measures were also put in place to
discourage corruption and to keep council intelligence con-
fidential. Thus was the government that would administer
Henry's realm until he could rule for himself established. But
Gloucester's pride had been wounded, and a worrying faultline
revealed in his relationship with his brother Bedford and uncle
Bishop Beaufort. This division within Henry's family was to rear
its head time and again in the years ahead, overshadowing his
childhood and the peaceful governance of his realm. The legacy
of Henry V might appear at first to have been unity among his
lords and loyalty to his son, but behind that façade lay a darker
reality of blighted ambition and fractured allegiance, which
would engender years of conflict and mistrust. Henry's infancy
would be far from easy.[23]

3

'The universal joy
and comfort of us all'[1]

Staines
14 November 1423

A t an inn on the road to London, Henry VI was being readied for his first visit to parliament. He had still not reached his second birthday, and the 28-mile (45 km) journey from his winter base at Windsor Castle to the seat of government at Westminster had been carefully planned by Queen Catherine and the attendants of his household to take place in short stages. However, as his mother and servants tried to bundle him from their lodgings at Staines out into the cold of the queen's carriage on the second morning of their journey Henry 'cried and screamed and would not be carried further'. Attempts to entice the king back on to the road failed completely. Eventually he was taken back into the inn and allowed to stay one more night. When Queen Catherine tried again on Monday morning, Henry was in better spirits and allowed his mother to take him as far as Kingston.[2]

Henry's childhood was in some ways not so different from that of other noble boys of his generation. Many children grew up with absent or dead fathers, thanks to the ongoing wars with France and the necessity for lords to attend parliament and great councils far from their homes. Although Henry had never met his father, his mother was a constant presence. Throughout the first seven years of his life Queen Catherine lived in his household, contributing some of the £2,300 allowance she received yearly from the exchequer towards the living expenses of their attendants and homes. Together, Catherine and Henry travelled between the royal palaces of the Thames Valley. At Christmas, they were joined by the great and good, often at Eltham Palace or Catherine's manor at Hertford, enjoying 'mummings' by travelling players.[3] Easter and St George's Day they usually spent together at Windsor Castle, the chivalric base of the Knights of the Garter, and in the summer months Henry was escorted over dusty roads, distracted by his entourage of minstrels and accompanied by a pair of portable organs, to his mother's manors of Wallingford and Hertford. Catherine's dower lands were remarkably widespread, stretching all the way from Yorkshire to Devon, and from Flintshire to northern France.[4]

Catherine not only lived with Henry, she also kept a close watch on his household servants, and many of Henry's attendants had existing connections to the queen. A leading knight of his chamber, Sir Walter Beauchamp, was Catherine's chief steward in 1421 and a later chamberlain was the Hainault-born Louis Robessart, so famed for his chivalrous military service that he had been Henry V's standard bearer. Robessart had also played a key part in the negotiations for the Treaty of Troyes and had accompanied Queen Catherine to her marriage.[5]

Apart from the ceremonial occasions when he opened parliament or processed through London, Henry spent most of his childhood out of the public gaze. His entourage of attendants was largely female, led by Lady Alice Botiller, an old servant of Queen Catherine's chosen for her wisdom and experience and probably also for her relation to great lords like the earl of Warwick. Alice's son Ralph had been one of Henry V's companions in France and by 1423 was serving as a royal councillor. Alice was amply rewarded for her service as, effectively, governess and financial director of Henry's household. She received a salary of £40 a year, which was increased by an additional 40 marks in 1426 and converted into a pension. However, Alice's position was a delicate one. She needed to teach Henry courtesy and discipline, and, as the incident at Staines demonstrated, toddlers were not always willing to do as their governesses commanded. Usual practice with recalcitrant children was, as the early fifteenth-century advice poem *How the Good Wife Taught Her Daughter* put it, to 'take a smart rod and beat them'.[6] But raising your hand against the king of England was fraught with danger, so Alice was given a special dispensation by the council to 'reasonably chastise him from time to time, as the case requires'.[7] Supporting Alice in bringing up Henry were a number of servants who, to judge by Henry's later kindnesses to them, he must have remembered fondly. His chief nurse was Joan Asteley, whose husband Thomas was also in royal service. Joan received a grant for life of £40 a year in 1438, long after she had left Henry's service. At any one time Henry was attended by Joan, along with a day nurse – sometimes Rose Chetewynd, sometimes Matilda Forbroke – and two chamberwomen.[8]

But while his upbringing with his mother and the women of his household was normal, Henry could never be allowed to forget that the entire future of two realms depended on him. As the speaker of the Commons expressed it to Henry when the king finally arrived at parliament on Thursday 18 November, 1423, clasped on his mother's lap, a king was 'the root, well and shield of our worldly comfort and protection'. It gave the Commons 'such a feeling of comfort and gladness', the speaker continued, 'to see your high and royal person sitting and occupying your own rightful seat and place in your parliament'.[9] Whether or not Henry understood much of the lengthy speech recited before him, it was clear to everyone else in the chamber that he was the slender thread holding the fabric of the political realm together. In 1423, there was good cause for parliament to need the reassurance of Henry's presence before them. For even as his infant eyes stared down at the speaker, a plot was unfolding to take his crown and perhaps even to end his short life.

At the heart of this plot was Sir John Mortimer of Hatfield in Hertfordshire, who had been a prisoner in the Tower of London on and off since 1418. His past crimes included treasonable conspiracy and absconding with heretics, but by early 1424 he had a more far-reaching plot in mind. He intended to escape from the Tower, rendezvous with his kinsman Edmund Mortimer, earl of March, and raise an army on the borders of Wales. Together, they would overthrow the government, 'slay the duke of Gloucester, cutting off his head, and the heads of all the lords, especially that of [Henry Beaufort] the bishop of Winchester, for Mortimer would make merry with the bishop's money'.[10] With Henry's leading councillors dead, Mortimer's army would replace the infant king with the earl of March and Mortimer would be appointed his heir. If need be, Mortimer was prepared even to join forces with Dauphin Charles and recruit French troops to his cause. All of this was revealed to a servant of the lieutenant of the Tower, William King, in an attempt to gain his support for the conspiracy. It seemed that Mortimer had succeeded in winning King over, for on 23 February King helped Mortimer escape his cell. Mortimer made it all the way to the Tower wharf, beyond the fortress walls. Here the River Thames offered him a route to freedom. But Mortimer had been betrayed; King had reported everything he had heard to the lieutenant of the Tower and no sooner was Mortimer on the wharf than he was ambushed, 'foul wounded and beat' and thrown back in his cell. Three days later this sorry, battered figure was dragged before parliament, where Gloucester acted as Henry's commissioner, to answer for his crimes.[11]

Mortimer's scheme was far-fetched, but it contained a discomforting kernel of menace to Gloucester and Henry's other councillors: the claim that the earl of March had a better right to the crown than the House of Lancaster. The Mortimers, Lancastrians and Richard II were all related through the sons of Edward III: Richard II was the only child of Edward's eldest son, the Black Prince; the Mortimers were the heirs of King Edward's second son Lionel, duke of Clarence; and the Lancastrians were descended from his third, John of Gaunt, duke of Lancaster. Henry IV's usurpation of Richard II in 1399 had effectively leap-frogged both the superior lines, and the Mortimer claim had been a thorn in his side throughout the 1400s. Even Henry V had not been immune from the Mortimer challenge – on the eve of his departure for the Agincourt campaign in 1415 Henry had uncovered a treasonable plot to usurp his throne and replace him with the earl of March.

In recent years March had seemed fully reconciled to the Lancastrian regime: he bore the sceptre for Queen Catherine at her coronation; he had fought alongside Henry V at the siege of Meaux and served as his lieutenant in Normandy; he had even been at the king's bedside in his last days. Since his return from France in October 1421, March had served as Henry VI's councillor. Would he really have risked his life and honour with the madcap scheme of John Mortimer? Perhaps there was still a lingering suspicion as to March's loyalties among some of Henry VI's relatives. A contemporary cleric claimed that March's arrival at parliament in October 1423 with a considerable body of men had aroused the suspicions of the duke of Gloucester.*

However, if March was involved in Mortimer's plot at all, it was as a willing stooge on behalf of the House of Lancaster. For, unbeknown to Mortimer, he had been set up. King's notes about his prisoner's plot had been reported to parliament, where Gloucester and his fellow lords had carefully monitored the progress of the scheme, allowing him just enough rope to hang himself while taking no chances that he would actually escape.

---

* This was the anonymous author of *Chronicon Angliae*. Giles, p. 6.

They were going to use Mortimer as a warning to any other would-be traitors against the regime of Henry VI that conspiracy would not be tolerated. By the time Mortimer appeared before Henry's parliament on 26 February 1424 his fate was already sealed. Even as he had been plotting his escape, parliament had drawn up a new statute that made it proof of treason for anyone accused of conspiring against the crown to attempt to escape prison. This new law ensured that even if there was not enough evidence to condemn Mortimer for his intended rebellion, he could still be found guilty of treason and executed.

When the bruised and bloodied Mortimer staggered into the parliament chamber at Westminster he must have realized his life was forfeit. He was confronted by Gloucester, the lay lords and the commons, but not a single bishop or archbishop. The religious lords had absented themselves because they were forbidden to shed blood, and Mortimer was already certain to face a traitor's death. Sure enough, that very day he was condemned and dragged on a hurdle from the Tower of London through the frozen streets of the capital. Outside the city walls, at the gallows in Tyburn, he was hauled to his feet. There, he was hanged until almost dead before being, as the parliamentary record reports,

> stretched out on the ground, and his head cut off, and his intestines burnt, and his body divided into four parts, and his head placed on the gate of London Bridge, and the said four parts of his body... put separately on the other four gates of London.[12]

By autumn of 1424, the earl of March had left the country for Ireland. He had been appointed lieutenant there back in March 1423 and his decision to belatedly take up the role may have been inspired by the events surrounding his kinsman. Within a matter of months, March was dead. Contemporary chronicles agreed that he died of plague rather than from any nefarious cause, but his death was probably something of a relief to Henry VI's councillors. His heir was his nephew Richard, duke of York, a thirteen-year-old orphan.* The Mortimer legacy was to leave its mark on the boy in a way that would impact not only on his own life, but on Henry's – and, ultimately, on the entire realm.

Winchester Palace, Southwark
12 February 1424

The inky waters of the River Thames rippled and slid beneath the wherrymen's oars. In places the peaks of the waves glistened, light falling from the windows of Winchester Palace as bursts of laughter and music echoed out. Bishop Henry Beaufort's magnificent London residence was the setting for a royal marriage, one of several unions forged in recent years to strengthen the dual monarchy of Henry VI. Today the couple resplendent in cloth of gold in the great hall were James I, king of Scots, strong-limbed and clear-eyed, and Joan Beaufort, niece of Bishop Henry Beaufort, as cunning as she was fair. James later memorialized his first sighting of Joan in a poem called *Kingis Quair*, claiming that he had looked out from the tower where he was held captive and seen Joan walking in the springtime garden below. The reality of their courtship was more prosaic. In the fifteenth century the marriage of princes was a political decision, not a matter of the heart, and even if James did consider Joan to be 'The fairest or the freshest young flower / That ever I saw', what enticed him to marry her was the promise that by so doing he could finally leave English captivity and return to Scotland after almost twenty years. Joan and James's union was one condition of an Anglo-Scottish treaty agreed in late 1423. The treaty had the advantage to Henry's regime that it cut off Scottish

---

* Richard, duke of York, was the son of the earl of March's sister, Anne Mortimer, and Richard, earl of Cambridge.

military support to the dauphin – James swore not to permit any further aid – and it filled the royal coffers with £40,000, which James paid to cover his 'expenses' during imprisonment. For Joan's uncle, Bishop Beaufort, the union also elevated his family into the realms of legitimate royalty. In April 1424, James was allowed to return to Scotland at last, taking his new bride to a land that he scarcely knew, and which was not altogether pleased by his return. In the anxious years that followed, he came to rely increasingly on Joan as an ally in Scottish politics.[13]

The marriage of James and Joan Beaufort was the latest in a number of international alliances that had been contracted with English royalty (or, in Joan's case, semi-royalty). Since Henry's succession, his uncles Gloucester and Bedford had also finally married. In choosing their brides, the relative importance each man placed on self-interest or English diplomatic concerns revealed their very different personalities. When John, duke of Bedford married Anne of Burgundy in March 1423, foremost in his thoughts were the needs of the dual monarchy of France and England. He remembered Henry V's deathbed warning that the alliance with Philippe of Burgundy must be maintained at all costs, 'for should any coolness subsist between you, which God forbid, the affairs of this realm... would soon be ruined'.[14]

Bedford spent the early years of his regency in France trying to ensure that the toil of fighting for Henry VI's rights in France did not exhaust the Burgundians' loyalty. In April 1423 his efforts were rewarded with a triple alliance sealed at Amiens. This was not merely a political alliance, but a chivalric brotherhood cemented by bonds of marriage between the three key participants: John, duke of Bedford, Philippe, duke of Burgundy and Jean, duke of Brittany. Just as Burgundian support protected the eastern borders of Henry's French crown, Breton aid was vital to expand his western frontiers. Unfortunately Jean of Brittany and Philippe of Burgundy were a slippery, self-serving pair concerned first and foremost with their own rights and territories, and neither had proven wholly loyal to England in the past. The Treaty of Amiens was intended to change that, for it made the men family: Philippe's sisters, Anne and Marguerite, were betrothed to the duke of Bedford and Jean's brother Arthur de Richemont respectively. In honour of this union, the three dukes swore at Amiens 'to be and to remain as long as we shall live, in fraternity, good love and union'.[15] They would fight for each other whenever one of them had need of their help and restore peace to their lands in order to relieve the misery of their subjects.

Despite the political motivation for their marriage, the duke and duchess of Bedford proved to be well matched, sharing luxurious tastes and an inclination towards carefully considered diplomacy. Anne was reported by the Bourgeois of Paris 'to be livelier than all the other ladies of her day'.[16] After their marriage she and Bedford were seldom apart. They enjoyed music and rich furnishings, turning their homes in Paris and Rouen into opulent centres of artistic patronage. Anne was the glue that bound her brother and husband together through sometimes very rocky periods in their relationship. Her skills as a diplomat were soon put to the test by the duke of Gloucester's marriage.

Unlike Bedford, Gloucester had chosen a bride who suited his own desires, not those of his family. In autumn 1422 he had married Henry's godmother, Jacqueline of Hainault, a young woman of renowned intelligence, beauty and spirit. The only trouble was, she was already married. As heir to the territories of Hainault (south of Flanders), and Holland and Zeeland (to the north of it), Jacqueline had been wed at sixteen to her cousin, Johan of Brabant.* The couple's lands abutted each other but their geographical proximity was about all they had in common. When war broke out between them and their uncle, Johann

---

* Johan of Brabant was Jacqueline's second husband. She had earlier been married to Jean of Touraine, older brother of the future Charles VII, who had died in April 1417.

'the pitiless' of Bavaria,* Jacqueline and her husband wanted
to pursue very different strategies. The impotent and cowardly
Johan was unwilling to fight their fearsome kinsman and in
1419 he accepted a humiliating truce that mortgaged almost
the entirety of Jacqueline's inheritance to her enemy. Unable to
accept such a humiliating concession, Jacqueline repudiated her
marriage and fled to England in the hope of eliciting military
aid from Henry V. In this she was disappointed: although she
was treated as a respected guest and given a £100 annuity, she
received little material assistance for her war. The accession
of Henry VI changed the landscape completely, positioning
Jacqueline in the orbit of the ambitious Gloucester. Enticed
equally by Jacqueline and her inheritance, Gloucester was all
too willing to assume the role of her champion and protector.
In England his ambitions and military interests were frustrated,
but the possibility of a war to regain Jacqueline's territories gave
him renewed purpose. The future Pope Pius II claimed that
Gloucester had won Jacqueline over by assuring her that

> a woman was a fool who married one who was not a man
> or, when she found out he was impotent, continued a union
> which could be no marriage; and he offered himself as her
> husband if she did not scorn... a man in the prime of life and
> of such attractions as she could see for herself.[17]

Jacqueline and Gloucester were married, notwithstanding the
unfortunate Johan of Brabant, and as 'Count of Hainault, Zeeland and Holland' Gloucester announced early in 1424 that
he would wage war against Johann 'the pitiless' to reclaim his
wife's inheritance. To do so, Jacqueline and Gloucester had to
march an army through the dominions of Philippe of Burgundy,
so Gloucester notified his ally of his intentions as a matter of

---

* So named because he had drowned a number of ecclesiastics who
rebelled against him in 1408.

courtesy. To his astonishment, Philippe refused to allow Gloucester access to his territories.

Philippe of Burgundy had been hawkishly watching the struggle over Jacqueline's land for years. Not only was his own county of Flanders flanked by Jacqueline's patrimony, but as cousin to both her and Johan of Brabant he expected to be named their heir. As long as their union produced no child – which, it had become clear, it was very unlikely to do – he had every hope of inheriting their territories after they died. Jacqueline's marriage to Gloucester threw all of Philippe's schemes into disarray. Where Johan of Brabant was 'cold and impotent', Gloucester was hot-blooded and already had two bastards. There was a very real danger that this union might produce an heir to oust Phillippe completely. Now Gloucester had either to defy Philippe and endanger the Anglo-Burgundian alliance, or abandon his war for Jacqueline's territories.

These tensions in Anglo-Burgundian relations occurred at the worst possible time for Henry's French realm. The spring campaigning season was just beginning, and Bedford needed all the support he could muster as he launched a major push against the dauphin's forces on the frontiers of Normandy. Charles's cause had just been refreshed by a substantial grant from his subjects, and an influx of 6,000 Scottish soldiers under the earl of Douglas.* It was imperative to keep Philippe of Burgundy's support as the war between Bedford and Dauphin Charles recommenced in earnest.[18]

Verneuil, Normandy
17 August 1424

The men of the duke of Bedford's army emerged blinking

---

* The earl had indented to fight for Dauphin Charles before James I sealed the Anglo-Scottish treaty in 1423.

and breathless from the shadows of the forest of Piseux. Eight thousand strong, they had been marched at speed across the borderlands of Normandy. It was a hot day in mid-August but the sight that met their eyes as they adjusted to the brightness was enough to chill the blood. A vast plain stretched before them, the ramparts of the fortress of Verneuil just visible in the distance. Between that fortress and them was the entire strength of the French army, outnumbering them by as much as two to one, and shimmering along its front line was a mass of heavily armoured cavalry – the most intimidating soldiers of the fifteenth century.[19]

From horseback, the familiar beaked profile of the duke of Bedford surveyed the scene. He looked every inch the chivalric knight, his armour covered by the blue velvet cloak of a Knight of the Garter and emblazoned with the red and white crosses of England and France. But he and his men were coated in dust, red-faced and sore-footed from the forced march they had made to reach Verneuil. Bedford's second in command was an old comrade in arms, the thirty-six-year-old Thomas Montagu, earl of Salisbury, a man justly famed for his courage and calm under pressure. When Bedford's brother Clarence had been butchered by superior Franco-Scottish forces at Baugé, it had been Salisbury who rallied his panicking army and recovered Clarence's body from the battlefield to bring it home for burial. As experienced soldiers, Bedford and Salisbury knew that in the coming battle, the odds were stacked against them – already, their exhausted force of English, Norman and Picard soldiers had been diminished by desertions. But it was too late to turn back now. Wills had been written, last letters sent to their wives and a mass grave prepared for the inevitable casualties. Bedford and his men were prepared to face their deaths on the field of Verneuil.

None of this was how Bedford had planned it. He had intended to fight the dauphin's men near the border castle of Ivry two days earlier, with the support of their Burgundian allies. A vital fortress in the frontier territory between Anglo-Burgundian and Armagnac strongholds, Ivry had been at the centre of fierce fighting for months. When the fortress could hold out no longer, a *journée* was set for 15 August – an official date on which Bedford's men would face the dauphin's to decide Ivry's fate.* There, Bedford had had time to arrange matters to his strategic advantage, even parading before his men to inspire them with the justness of their cause. They were the defenders of the Treaty of Troyes, the protectors of the rights of King Henry VI. God would surely favour them.

But when the dauphin's scouts reported the strength of Bedford's position to Charles's commanders, the Franco-Scottish army headed for Ivry diverted instead towards an easier target: the neighbouring English-held fortress of Verneuil. There, by daubing their Scottish soldiers in blood and having them cry out in English, the French convinced the garrison that they were Bedford's men and that the English had been defeated in battle. Unwittingly, Verneuil opened its gates and let the enemy in.[20] When Bedford received news of the dauphin's deceit, he hastily reorganized his forces into marching formation. They must retake Verneuil before news of its bloodless fall infected the morale of other English garrisons. But before he set out, Bedford dismissed the Burgundian soldiers, depriving himself of almost 2,000 men.

Why did Bedford make such an apparently foolhardy decision? The alliance between Bedford, Burgundy and Brittany that had been cemented with Bedford's marriage to Anne of Burgundy had started to come undone almost as soon as it was agreed. Within five days of their treaty at Amiens, the dukes of Burgundy and Brittany had made a secret agreement that if one of them was reconciled with Dauphin Charles in the future, the other would remain their ally – in other words, they were already

---

* The *journée* was a chivalric protocol that appointed an agreed day of battle in what amounted to a 'judicial duel' between two armies.

considering the possibility of cutting Bedford out of their alliance
and uniting instead with his enemy. By August 1424, rumours
that Philippe had secretly negotiated an agreement with the
dauphin reached Bedford's ears. Burgundian loyalty was now
suspect, and Bedford was not prepared to harbour potential
traitors in his midst.

When he arrived before Verneuil and was confronted with
the fighting strength of the enemy Bedford may have ques-
tioned the wisdom of his decision to release 2,000 fighting
men. Dauphin Charles's forces were bolstered by 2,000 heavily
armoured Lombard cavalry – horsemen from northern Italy
who were feared throughout Europe. The previous September
a few hundred of them had devastated Burgundian forces at
the Battle of La Buissière. The Lombards were at the cutting
edge of military technology, pioneering the use of horse armour
to protect their mounts from English longbow attack, and of
helmets that allowed the wearer greater visibility. They were
shock troops, intended to punch into their enemies' lines with
devastating effect. This was the first time the English had faced
them at first hand.

Hurrying to ready his forces for battle, Bedford deployed his
men as best he could to shield his army from the Lombards'
onslaught. He anticipated that the cavalry would try to outflank
him, and with little protection afforded by the terrain he moved
his lightly armoured reserve forces to defend the rear. A 'horse-
wall' was created by tying the army's horses together by the
halters and tails, three or four deep alongside the baggage train.
As a last resort, pages – who would not usually fight in battle –
were posted on top of these horses to repel enemy cavalry. Just
as at Agincourt a decade before, the English archers hammered
wooden stakes into the earth in front of them. The rest of the
army was arranged in a single unit between the archers and the
baggage train, with the wood behind.

Having done everything possible in the short time available,
Bedford and Salisbury took up their positions beneath their

standards. They fought alongside their men on foot, Bedford armed with a great poleaxe. Among those fighting with the English that day was the Burgundian chronicler Jean de Waurin, who later wrote a lengthy description of his experience in the battle. 'I saw the assembly at Agincourt,' he recorded, 'where there were many more princes and troops... but certainly that at Verneuil was of all the most formidable and the best fought.'[21]

With a great shout and blast of trumpets, the two armies advanced. 'The one side cried *St Denis*,' reported Waurin, 'and the other *St George!* And so horrible was the shouting that there was no man so brave or confident that he was not in fear of death.'[22] The parched earth trembled as the Lombard cavalry charged at Bedford's forces, not splitting to attack its flanks as anticipated but ploughing straight into the English position, punching all the way through and out the other side. The English army was split within a matter of moments into two separate forces. Men-at-arms sprawled on the ground, falling against their comrades, or dropped to their knees and simply let the Lombard cavalry ride over them. As the Lombards reached the rear of Bedford's forces and began to plunder the baggage train, the English reserve forces – around 500 men – fled the field, spreading panic through the Norman countryside as they clamoured for sanctuary in neighbouring garrisons. The Lombards gave chase.

Bedford's army was in complete disarray. His men wavered between competing impulses to protect their possessions in the baggage train, to fight on, or to try and save themselves by fleeing the field. Seeing his men falter, and at any moment fearing the return of the Lombard cavalry, Bedford advanced in front of his army. He called on the men 'not... to break nor remove their array for winning or keeping worldly goods, but only to win worship in the right of England that day'.[23] Inspired by his example, Bedford's forces regrouped and a fierce melee set in. In the thick of battle, Salisbury was so hard pressed that he renewed a vow to go on pilgrimage to Jerusalem if he survived the day. The English battle standard tumbled – usually a sure sign of defeat – but a Norman knight plunged into the enemy line to retrieve it. The English rallied again.

Remarkably, with the Lombard cavalry still plundering the baggage train and chasing the fleeing reserve forces, the English began to gain the upper hand. The French and Scottish forces fell out of alignment. With another shout of 'St George!' Bedford's men surged forward and the French line broke. They ran, hollering, towards the fortress of Verneuil a mile away, begging to be let in. But the garrison kept its gates firmly closed. The dauphin's men tumbled desperately into the ditches surrounding the town, and there the English fell on them. Waurin recalled the slaughter with the words: 'Mercy had no place there.'[24]

By the time the Lombard cavalry returned, the battle was over. Six thousand of Dauphin Charles's men fell, including the Scottish and French commanders. English vengeance on the Scots was particularly savage – payback for the English defeat at Baugé. After the battle, 200 high-born Frenchmen were taken prisoner.

Bedford's victory at Verneuil was justly compared with Henry V's success at Agincourt. Bedford's fellow soldier, John Hardyng, memorialized the duke's courage in his chronicle: 'The regent was there that day a lion.'[25] When he returned to Paris in the wake of battle Bedford was greeted like a conquering Roman emperor. The citizens flocked to him in crimson gowns, celebrating with pageants and bonfires, processions, shouts of 'Noel!' and acrobats tumbling in the city streets.[26] In England, news of the battle reaffirmed national self-belief, bolstering the dedication of Henry's beleaguered subjects to the dual monarchy.

By September 1424, thanks to Bedford's victory at Verneuil and alliance with Philippe of Burgundy, Henry VI controlled nearly half the landmass of France, from the Low Countries in the north to Gascony in the south. The dauphin's territories were sandwiched between the rivers Loire and Garonne, his base established in the cathedral city of Bourges, virtually in the centre of France. With the ongoing support of Bedford's ally Jean of Brittany, it should have been possible for Bedford to open a route from Normandy into Maine and Anjou, regaining domains that had been held by kings of England in centuries past. But in order for Henry's existing French lands to remain secure, and especially to take advantage of the success at Verneuil, Bedford relied more than ever on the support of Philippe of Burgundy to keep up pressure on the dauphin from the east. And Gloucester's hotheadedness was stretching that alliance to breaking point. Even as Bedford revelled in his victory, he learnt that his brother had defied him. Gloucester and Jacqueline were preparing an army of invasion, and it was headed for Philippe of Burgundy's lands.

Calais

16 October 1424

In the English Channel, the storms raged so fiercely that for over a fortnight ships had been stranded in port. The soldiers and merchants who lived in Calais were accustomed to such periods of inactivity. For almost a century the port city in the coastal flatlands of northern France had been in English hands, and through it passed goods bound for the cloth markets of Antwerp and luxury markets of London. It might take a matter of hours to make the crossing, or, if the wind turned against you, you could be stranded at sea for weeks. On the afternoon of 16 October 1424, if the wool factors of Calais had glanced beyond their harbour walls and sandbanks, they would have seen a mighty fleet struggling towards them: forty-two ships, white sails flashing above the breakers, bringing with them a force 5,000 strong. Jacqueline of Hainault and Humphrey of Gloucester had come to claim her domains.

The couple and their army had been held hostage by the bad weather at Dover since 29 September, but when at last the winds changed they reached Calais within six hours.[27] After a fortnight, they were joined by further men, and on 18 November their forces set off towards Mons, the capital of Jacqueline's territories. To reach Hainault, their army had to traverse Philippe of Burgundy's county of Artois and, since Philippe was still denying them permission to do so, it was a fraught undertaking. In a futile attempt to court Philippe's favour, Gloucester ordered his army to pass through the duke's territory peaceably, suffering 'no disturbance to be made except lodgement for his men, and the taking of victuals and drink courteously'.[28]

Philippe's resistance to Gloucester and Jacqueline's war had only increased since he learnt of their marriage. In April, Jacqueline's enemy, the childless Johann 'the pitiless', had made Philippe heir to his Dutch estates, giving Philippe yet more incentive to oppose the couple's campaign to regain her lands. Indeed, as they took up residence in Mons that autumn, Gloucester and Jacqueline might well have felt the world was united against them. Pope Martin V refused to recognize the validity of their marriage, although the matter was still being debated among the cardinals in Rome. The lords of Henry's government in both England and France advised Gloucester against acting in any way that would offend Philippe. Gloucester did not even have the full support of Jacqueline's subjects. As the contemporary memoirist, Pierre Fenin of Artois, put it succinctly: 'There were many great cities and forts who gave obedience to them, and others who did not obey them at all.'[29]

Worst of all for his ambitions, Gloucester's brother Bedford opposed his war. So concerned was Bedford to maintain the faltering Anglo-Burgundian alliance that as soon as he heard of Gloucester's fleet assembling in the Channel he called a summit with Philippe in Paris, relying on his wife Anne to use all her diplomatic skills to mediate with the 'wonderfully displeased' duke. But when Philippe and Bedford worked out a means of resolving the conflict between Jacqueline and her ex-husband Johan of Brabant, Gloucester and Jacqueline promptly rejected it. Philippe was outraged, as the Burgundian chronicler Jean de Waurin reported: 'He said plainly to... [Bedford] that since he saw that his brother of Gloucester would not condescend to any reasonable argument, he would aid with all his power Duke Johan of Brabant.'[30]

In December, Philippe commanded his subjects throughout the Low Countries to join the campaign against Gloucester and Jacqueline.[31] Gloucester was seriously affronted by Philippe's interference, and as their troops clashed, the dukes engaged in a war of words. Letters whipped back and forth between Mons and Dijon, the two men asserting ever more hotly the gross offences done to their honour until finally, in March 1425, as their forces collided in a bloody siege at the fortress of Braine-le-Comte, Philippe challenged Gloucester to a duel. 'Enough,' he wrote, 'and indeed too much, for me is the dishonour and outrage which you have done to me.'[32] The 'mortal enemies' called off their forces and retreated to their own territories to ready themselves for single combat. With heavy symbolism, Gloucester chose St George's Day (23 April) 1425 as the date for their duel.

While Philippe retired to Hesdin Castle in Artois to commission elaborate new armour, Gloucester readied his forces to return to England for his own preparations. The people of Hainault appealed for Jacqueline to stay behind when Gloucester left, and while he agreed, she was decidedly reluctant. 'She had great fear,' according to Waurin, 'that she would not remain there in peace.' Her anxiety can have been little allayed by the fact that when Gloucester departed, he took with him the bulk of his English army (5,000–6,000 soldiers), leaving Jacqueline dependent on the ambiguous loyalty of her subjects for protection. More personally concerning for Jacqueline was the realization that Gloucester had also taken one of her ladies-in-waiting, a 'marvellously fair and pleasing' young Englishwoman called Eleanor Cobham. Gloucester's enthusiasm for both his wife and her war had cooled considerably during his time in Hainault.[33]

Despite their continued loathing for each other, Gloucester and Philippe delayed and eventually cancelled their duel. Both Bedford and the pope had forbidden it, which enabled the two men to withdraw from the fight without doing damage to their honour. However, Gloucester's war in Hainault had proved to be a personal and political disaster. He had been perfectly willing to antagonize Henry VI's chief ally in the French wars, but his peers back in England were more alive to the wider political danger of so doing. The duke's initial attempts to raise military aid for the continuation of the Hainault campaign in England yielded little result, and he soon abandoned it altogether.

When Jacqueline's second husband Johan of Brabant finally died in 1427 and Jacqueline and Gloucester's legally dubious marriage could at last be validated, Pope Martin V ruled that their union was illegal, and Gloucester chose to wed Eleanor Cobham instead. By then he had abandoned his first wife to her fate. Ironically, many of Gloucester's compatriots continued to champion Jacqueline years after he had left Hainault. In March 1428 a delegation of London women from the Stocks Market brought an open letter to parliament reproaching Gloucester for abandoning his wife's cause because 'his love for her had gone cold'. [34] Jacqueline proved just as dogged in her determination to regain control over her territories: she plotted with her mother, made a daring escape from Burgundian imprisonment disguised as a man and resisted more than one siege, but all was to no avail. After Gloucester married Eleanor Cobham, Jacqueline finally bowed to the inevitable. In July 1428 she signed over her territories to Philippe of Burgundy's guardianship. One of the conditions of her agreement with Philippe was that she must not remarry without his consent. True to form, she defied this stricture and took a fourth husband, Frank van Borselen, in 1432. For her defiance, Philippe imprisoned her new husband until Jacqueline was forced to abdicate. What Jacqueline lacked in political shrewdness, she more than made up for in courage.

As for Gloucester, he returned to England in spring 1425

humiliated but not chastened, expecting to take up his position as protector at the head of government once more. Although he had been frustrated in his continental ambitions, he could at least settle back into his position of dominance in English politics. Or so he thought. In the five months of his absence, however, his place at the heart of government had been supplanted by his uncle Bishop Beaufort and Gloucester returned to find his own authority diminished. Already smarting from one affront to his pride, Gloucester was not prepared to suffer another. His angry reaction opened a new rift in the politics of England and the dynamic of Henry's family. Control of Henry himself was about to become a battleground.

4

'The serpent of division'[1]

London
27 April 1425

I n the closing days of April King Henry processed through the streets of London on Queen Catherine's lap. If the journey from Windsor had been the occasion for further royal tantrums, chroniclers remained silent on the subject. At the west door of St Paul's Cathedral the little figure in magnificent robes and gilded chains was lifted from his mother's chair by the firm hands of his uncle Gloucester. Impressing onlookers, the three-year-old Henry walked unsupported into the body of the church and then, as one London chronicler noted proudly, 'went upon his feet from the west door to the stairs' to make an offering at the altar to St Paul, patron saint of the city of London. Even more impressively, on his return journey to his palace at Kennington, south of London, Henry rode on a courser – a tall horse – through Cheapside and over London Bridge, to show himself to his subjects.[2]

Three days later, the king took his seat in the Painted Chamber at Westminster, for the first time overseeing the opening of his parliament. Henry sat before his Lords and Commons and listened as his great-uncle Henry Beaufort, bishop of Winchester and now chancellor of England, made the traditional opening sermon. 'Glory to God in the highest,' Beaufort cried to the hundreds gathered in the chamber, 'and on earth peace, good will toward men'.* Under the circumstances this message was ironic in the extreme, for the streets through which King Henry passed that spring day crackled with tension.

For months, the capital had been on edge. The duke of Gloucester's war for Jacqueline's lands had stirred up the anti-immigrant feeling that always bubbled close to the surface in fifteenth-century England, particularly in London. Although England and the Low Countries had a long history of trade links, the relationship between them had seldom been easy. Dutch and Flemish merchants (usually known generically by the English as 'Flemings') were the main markets for English wool, the backbone of the national economy. If Gloucester's campaign to seize Hainault, Holland and Zeeland had been successful English merchants would have gained control of a lucrative market for English cloth. But the territories were so economically dependent on each other that political disagreements almost always resulted in punitive economic measures and, in the wake of his war with Gloucester, Philippe of Burgundy had banned English cloth in his domains. English traders feared that if the situation continued that ban might be extended throughout the entire Low Countries. There were also fears about Flemish reprisals on English shipping, which could be disastrous for an island nation dependent on the sea for its exports.[3]

Rather than blaming Gloucester for these troubles, the English blamed the Flemings, especially those living in England. From the start of Gloucester's war, xenophobic hostility had increased markedly. Even foreign-born servants working in the

---

* Beaufort then moved on to suggest that parliament should be more like an elephant, whose good memory, lack of enmity and capacity for reflection were an admirable example for human counsellors to follow. PR, 1425, items 2–3.

households of the dowager queens of England were not above suspicion: the widow of Henry's grandfather Henry IV, Joan of Navarre, was accused in parliament of harbouring foreign spies within her household, who 'reveal the advice given to the king to his enemies overseas'.[4] A member of Queen Catherine's household also sought denization in this parliament, suggesting that anxieties about being foreign-born prevailed even within the upper echelons of court.*

On 13 February 1425 pamphlets attacking Flemings were pinned all over London and its suburbs. Some were placed, pointedly, at the gates of the residence of Bishop Beaufort. If Gloucester was seen as the avenger of Flemish wrongdoing, Beaufort was viewed suspiciously as their champion. Fleeing increased physical and verbal abuse, Flemings started to leave the capital in droves. As chancellor, Beaufort attempted to regain control of the situation before a riot broke out, putting the Tower into the keeping of Richard Woodville, a veteran of ten years' service in France and the chamberlain of the duke of Bedford. In the cramped streets of London, men suspected of violence and pamphleteering were rounded up and imprisoned. Beaufort's actions restored a measure of calm, but won him little love from the Londoners. Rumours circulated that he had employed a crooked 'appealer' to condemn innocent men of treason, and his unwillingness to assist Gloucester in his war against Philippe of Burgundy was recast as the behaviour of a traitor to the national interest.[5]

In this heightened atmosphere, Gloucester's return in April 1425 with 5,000 soldiers at his back was incendiary. His failures in Hainault and his displacement at the heart of English government by Beaufort made him extremely sensitive to affronts to his honour. When he went to lodge at the Tower of London, Richard Woodville denied him entry, saying his orders from the council were to 'suffer no man to be allowed into the Tower who

---

* Denization gave someone born outside the king's dominions the same rights and privileges as an English subject.

was [militarily] stronger than himself, unless he had the special charge or command of the king and by the advice of the council'.[6] Gloucester saw Beaufort's hand in this public demonstration of disrespect, and perhaps Bedford's too – in the past twelve months his brother's interference in his plans had become a source of constant irritation.

Rumours soon reached Bishop Beaufort's ears that Gloucester had been making dire threats against him and he was advised to stay away from parliament or risk physical harm. Emboldened by Gloucester's overt hostility against the chancellor, the Londoners' angry chatter grew louder. A mob assembled on the wharves opposite Beaufort's magnificent bankside palace to exchange 'bills and language of slander and menace' against him. Grim jokes about teaching Beaufort 'to swim with wings' (i.e. drown him in the Thames) echoed across the water.[7]

If little King Henry's presence at the opening of parliament was supposed to inspire harmony among those attending, it failed. The entire session was dominated by the Commons' desire to control the immigrant population and the Lords' conflicting requests for money to fund either Gloucester's war or Bedford's French campaigns. With cash perennially tight, the Commons held the Lords to ransom to extract its demands, refusing direct taxation and only giving grants on condition that stringent controls were placed on the 'alien' traders operating in England. But despite the strictures laid down in parliament, Bishop Beaufort continued to support immigrant merchants. He failed to enforce the new rules against 'aliens' and insisted that foreign-born subjects of Henry VI should be protected from seizures of their shops and goods. After a vexed ten-week session, Beaufort and Gloucester retired from parliament to their London residences, both unwilling to leave the volatile capital. Beaufort resided in the bishop's palace at Southwark on the south bank of the river, while Gloucester stayed at Baynard's Castle on the north, and there they sat glowering at each other across the Thames as the heat rose.[8]

Henry was kept cloistered from his fractious relatives in the tranquility of Eltham Palace, 9 miles (14 km) from the fumes and noise of London. But it was lost on neither Gloucester nor Beaufort that physical control of the young king could turn the political tide in their favour. In a personal monarchy, proximity to the king – no matter what his age – increased a person's authority and influence. In recent months, with Gloucester out of the country, Beaufort had gained greater access to Henry. This was an alarming development for Gloucester, but even more so were the whispers that Beaufort's alluring young nephew, Edmund Beaufort, had been enjoying a secret liaison with Henry's mother, Queen Catherine. Catherine was still only twenty-four years old and the anonymous clerical author of the *Chronicon Angliae* reproved her for being 'unable fully to curb her carnal passions'.[9] It was rumoured that she wished to marry the nineteen-year-old Edmund, who was probably living at the time in the household of Thomas Beaufort, duke of Exeter, the man Henry V had appointed guardian of the infant king. As such, Edmund would have been in close contact with both Catherine and Henry VI. For Gloucester the possibility of Henry's mother remarrying introduced a dangerous new element into politics, for any stepfather of the king would have easy access to the monarch as he grew up and his influence over the boy could soon come to rival that of his uncles. Even worse, if Catherine's second husband was a Beaufort, the bishop's control of the political realm would be assured. Gloucester needed to loosen Henry from his enemies' snares before it was too late.

London
29 October 1425

On the evening of 29 October the newly elected mayor of London, John Coventry, sat down to a traditional celebration dinner with his aldermen. They had barely put knife to plate when a summons from the duke of Gloucester ended the meal. The men rushed to Baynard's Castle, where Gloucester charged the mayor with an urgent mission: he must deploy the citizens to keep a 'strong watch' over the city that night, for Bishop Beaufort had been gathering men from Lancashire and Cheshire to serve as his personal army. Beaufort's nefarious intention, Gloucester told the mayor, was to march on Eltham Palace and seize King Henry in order to rule through the infant king himself. The citizens' opinion of Bishop Beaufort was so low that Gloucester's claims were all too readily believed and soon the darkened streets flared with roving torches and the heavy footfall of armed men.[10]

The next morning brought no calm to London. Gloucester had commanded the citizens to muster at eight o'clock and first light brought 300 Londoners pouring from all corners of the city to congregate on the north side of London Bridge. Beyond the jumble of stalls and houses that comprised this, the only river crossing for more than 20 miles (32 km), stood Bishop Beaufort's palace on the south bank of the Thames. But Southwark Palace had been fortified overnight; soldiers stood ready at the chambers within and crossbowmen were positioned at the windows. As the bell tolled nine, Beaufort's men drew up chains and dragged barricades into place at the south end of London Bridge.[11]

Word spread through the city, fast as fire, that Bishop Beaufort had prepared for a siege. Traders shut up their stalls as more and more citizens rushed to the gates of London Bridge to stand beside the duke of Gloucester. Had the Londoners been able to surge across the bridge into Bishop Beaufort's palace, blood would have been spilt in the streets. However, the new mayor stood his ground on the north bank and the arrows glinting from Southwark Palace were never loosed.

Ordinarily, such violent contests between the nobility would be resolved by the arbitration of the king, but three-year-old Henry could hardly play the mediator when the twin pillars of his regime were on the brink of war with each other. In the absence of Bedford, who was acting as Henry's regent in France, negotiations

to restore concord were left to other representatives of the
Lancastrian regime: Henry Chichele, archbishop of Canterbury;
Humphrey Stafford (later the duke of Buckingham);* and Pedro,
prince of Portugal, a grandson of John of Gaunt who happened
to be visiting England at the time. As kinsman to Bishop Beaufort,
Gloucester and the king, Pedro led the peace envoys eight times
as they travelled back and forth across London Bridge to negotiate between the two camps. Eventually, order was restored, but
the feud between Beaufort and Gloucester was far from over.

Bishop Beaufort was not prepared to sit idle and await further
attacks by Gloucester. Two days later, he wrote to the duke of
Bedford in France, appealing for him to return to England
and deal with Gloucester. 'As ye desire the welfare of the king
our sovereign lord,' he wrote anxiously, 'and of his realms of
England and of France, and your own weal and ours also, haste
you hither, for by my troth [if] ye tarry, we shall put this land
in aventure with a field [i.e. a battle]. Such a brother you have
here. God make him a good man.'[12]

Eltham Palace
Christmas 1425

For Henry, Christmas 1425 was a brief interval of family harmony in what was to become a distressingly familiar cycle of
hostility. On 5 November, in a symbolic reassertion of royal
control over the uneasy capital, he had left the tranquility of
Eltham Palace to parade through the streets of London with
the duke of Gloucester, Prince Pedro, Mayor Coventry and the
leading citizens. Bishop Beaufort's absence from this ritual procession suggests the chancellor was still not fully reconciled

---

* Humphrey Stafford had the title 'earl of Stafford' in this period and
was only created duke of Buckingham in 1444. However, to avoid confusion I have used his ducal title throughout.

with either Gloucester or the Londoners. Henry may not have known the reason for his procession but he might well have sensed the lingering unease in the capital. When Bedford answered Beaufort's appeal for aid and returned to England in December – accompanied, as always, by his duchess, Anne of Burgundy – his first act was to summon a parliament far from London. Political consensus was desperately needed and that could not be guaranteed close to the volatile capital. Instead, Bedford commanded parliament to assemble in the new year in the heartland of the Lancastrian dynasty at Leicester.[13]

Before addressing the division between his relatives, Bedford spent Christmas with his wife, King Henry and Queen Catherine at Eltham. The duke would have observed his young nephew with interest. He and Henry had not met since the boy was five months old; now he was just past his fourth birthday, Henry must have been starting to show glimmers of his developing personality. Secure inside the moat and battlements of the palatial retreat of Eltham, the family enjoyed a Christmas 'mumming' in the great hall. It may have been for Bedford's visit that the poet-monk John Lydgate composed a rhyming ballad to be performed before the king, in which Henry's rights to France and England were upheld by classical gods and Christian patriarchs. Bedford would certainly have agreed with the optimistic sentiment of Lydgate's promise that war would soon be supplanted by peace:

> Mars that is most furious and mad,
> Causer of strife and disobedience,
> Shall cease his malice, and God that is good
> Of unity shall send all sufficiency.[14]

Bedford's hope that peace would triumph in English affairs must, however, have seemed a forlorn one in the early days of 1426. Gloucester kept his distance from his brother, skulking with Eleanor Cobham at his estate at Devizes. Bedford's arrival meant Gloucester could no longer enjoy the title and authority of protector, so he brooded on his misfortunes and made excuses not to attend when Bedford summoned him to St Albans to mediate a resolution with Bishop Beaufort.

Gloucester's wariness was not wholly unwarranted. From the first it was clear that Bedford's sympathies lay more with his uncle than his brother. On 10 January 1426 the duke and duchess of Bedford made a ceremonial entry into London, with Bishop Beaufort pointedly given pride of place at their side. To ensure his safety and as a sign of respect, the couple then took up lodgings next door to Beaufort in Westminster 'to right great grievance of the people'. It was evident that if Bedford found fault with anyone for the recent strife, it was with the Londoners themselves. When the mayor of London presented Bedford with silver gilt basins and 1,000 marks as a welcoming gift, he 'had but little thanks'.[15]

By February, Gloucester's recalcitrance was becoming an embarrassment. He steadfastly refused to attend council meetings at St Albans and Northampton, even though Bedford offered him the opportunity to present his complaints against Beaufort and 'be eased as towards his griefs'. Gloucester insisted that he would only attend if Beaufort was absent or removed from his position as chancellor. Both demands were rejected as unreasonable. In the end Bedford used the trump card he held as protector – he announced that Henry would personally open parliament in Leicester on 18 February. When the king demanded his attendance, Gloucester could not disobey.[16]

Thus in the great hall of Leicester Castle, four-year-old King Henry perched on his throne to preside over a bitterly contested parliament chamber. Bedford had taken additional measures to keep the peace, with the noble retinues attending their masters ordered to arrive unarmed, but they found increasingly ingenious means of evading the strictures, as *Gregory's Chronicle** relates:

---

* Named for William Gregory, a London mayor who was believed to be its author. In fact, the work is a continuation of an earlier chronicler, probably compiled by a London cleric before 1470.

Every man was warned and cried through the town that they should leave their weapons in their inns, that is to say their swords and bucklers, bows and arrows. And [so] the people took great bats in their necks... The next day they were charged that they should leave their bats at their inns, and then they took great stones in their bosoms and their sleeves, and so they went to the Parliament with their lords.[17]

Because of the array of concealed weaponry that was smuggled into the great hall as Henry opened proceedings at Leicester, the parliament earned the nickname 'the parliament of bats'.[18]

Perhaps Henry's presence acted as a pacifier, for despite the surfeit of sticks and stones hidden in men's clothing, violence was averted. That did not mean, of course, that unity reigned. Having finally deigned to attend parliament, Gloucester was determined not merely to air his grievances but to humble Bishop Beaufort. He had expanded his complaints against his uncle from usurpation of the protector's authority to assertions that fell only just short of accusations of treason. According to Gloucester, Bishop Beaufort had 'kept the said Tower [of London held] against him ungoodly and against reason' and 'proposed and disposed him to set hands on the king's person and to remove him from Eltham, the place where he was, to the intent to put him in such governance as him [wished]'.[19] These accusations were inflammatory enough, but Gloucester went further, claiming that his late brother, Henry V, had suspected Bishop Beaufort of plotting to murder him and usurp his father Henry IV. The details of the bishop of Winchester's alleged scheme to kill Henry V were particularly sensational:

At a time when our sovereign lord [Henry V] being prince was lodged in the palace of Westminster in the green chamber, by the [barking] of a spaniel there was one night espied and taken behind a tapestry of the same chamber a man [who...] confessed that he was there by the excitation and procuring of my said lord of Winchester, ordained to have slain the said prince there in his bed.[20]

The attempted assassin, Gloucester concluded, had been tied in a sack and drowned in the River Thames.

Unsurprisingly, when accused of plotting against three generations of his own family, Bishop Beaufort vociferously denied these charges, insisting that 'he never purposed treason or untruth against any of their persons'. As proof of his innocence Beaufort reminded parliament of 'the great wisdom truth and manhood that all men knew in [Henry V]'. The king would hardly have 'set in my said lord the chancellor so great trust as he did if he had found or [believed] in him such untruth'.[21] The bishop insisted he had never plotted to seize Henry VI and had only armed himself at London Bridge because a number of people had told him that 'Gloucester purposed him bodily harm'.

It took over a fortnight for Bedford and his fellow peers to resolve the feud between Beaufort and Gloucester. During that time, Henry was absent from parliament but on 7 March 1426 he returned to the great hall of Leicester Castle to see his uncles 'take either other by the hand... in sign and token of good love and accord'. Beaufort assured Gloucester that he had 'never imagined [nor] purposed [any]thing that might be hindering or prejudice to your person, honour or estate', while Gloucester promised to 'be good lord to my said lord of Winchester and have him in love and affection as his kinsman and uncle'. Each swore not to trouble 'the adherents, councillors and favourers of that other'.[22] A carefully balanced settlement had been reached: although Bishop Beaufort was declared innocent of any treason, Gloucester succeeded in having him removed from power. On 17 March Beaufort resigned the chancellorship and his seat on the royal council. In May he was given permission to go on pilgrimage overseas and he left for Calais in early 1427. There, Beaufort was finally granted the cardinalate that Henry V had denied him and Bedford personally placed the cardinal's hat on his uncle's head. Thus, although Bishop Beaufort's English ambitions had been sacrificed to appease Gloucester, his aspirations within the Roman church were rewarded.*

Henry's recollection of the events at Leicester, impressionistic as a four-year-old's memory was, must have been of the success of royal reconciliation – how even apparently serious noble quarrels could be resolved with a handshake and professions of love. His uncles had arrived at the opening of parliament as inveterate rivals, their men armed with cudgels and stones. By the time Henry returned to Leicester Castle, all enmity had been publicly put aside. 'Love and accord' had triumphed over discord and envy. The unresolved tensions and adult ambitions that survived this public declaration were probably not apparent to the king at the time. In terms of how Henry believed conflict could be resolved in his future career, the reconciliation at Leicester was a crucial first impression.

The other memory that must have been forged for Henry at Leicester was the ceremony that concluded his time there. On Whitsunday (19 May) 1426, the four-and-a-half-year-old king knelt before his uncle the duke of Bedford and was dubbed a knight. Then he turned to the young men and boys who surrounded him within the chamber and knighted thirty-eight lords with his own hand. Among the newly created knights were Richard, duke of York; John Mowbray, the heir of the duke of Norfolk; and John de Vere, earl of Oxford, who rather spoiled the occasion by slipping and breaking his leg.[23] Henry's elevation to knighthood and bestowal of that rank on others was the first step towards a change in his status. It marked his entry into the warrior class of England, a prelude to Henry taking up arms himself in the future. Young as he was, thoughts were already turning to Henry's rule as king.

---

* Beaufort had been named cardinal by Pope Martin V in 1417 but Henry V had refused to allow him to exercise the rank.

5

'Virtues and teachings convenient for the royal person'[1]

Windsor
1 June 1428

The English summer of 1428 was not an auspicious one. It rained virtually every day from Lady Day (25 March) to Michaelmas (29 September) and there was such a scarcity of wheat, beef and mutton that Henry's subjects complained of inflated prices until harvest time.[2] For Henry, though, this was a season of transformation. He was approaching his seventh birthday and the end of his 'tender age'. The care of women and childhood toys were laid aside. Where once he had played with a silver gilt ship on wheels, and probably with wooden castles and lead knights, now the royal armoury provided him with training swords and little coats of armour.[3] At Windsor Castle, where he spent his summers, a 'supreme academy' of noble youths had been established to keep Henry company. All the heirs of baronial rank in royal wardship had been ordered to join Henry, growing up with him in a tumble of ages and personalities that was customary for fifteenth-century aristocrats.[4] Among them were boys beginning a lifetime of service to their king, including James Butler, future earl of Wiltshire, who was only a year older than Henry; and John Beaumont, Richard, duke of York, and John de Vere, earl of Oxford, who had more than a decade on him. Henry was also appointed a team of knights and esquires of the body to act as his royal escort and bodyguard.

Watching over all of these youths, tasked with ensuring Henry was schooled in 'good manners, letters, language, nurture and courtesy' was Richard Beauchamp, earl of Warwick. On 1 June 1428, he replaced Henry's governess Alice Botiller as head of Henry's household, becoming his 'master'. The king's formal education for kingship had begun. Henry would be trained in the martial arts, horse riding and hunting, and learn French and Latin as well as studying English literary works. Warwick was chosen for this task because of his 'loyalty, wisdom, good breeding, prudence and discretion'.[5] His family had almost been destroyed by Richard II and Warwick had proven a lifelong servant of the House of Lancaster, particularly close to Henry V. Like the boys now attending Henry VI at Windsor, Warwick had grown up with his king, and been rewarded for his faithful service. As a royal councillor from 1410 and captain and emissary in Henry's French wars from 1417, Warwick had practical experience of diplomacy, politics and warfare to share with his young charge.

Warwick's appointment was decided on by Henry's council in agreement with the dukes of Bedford and Gloucester but, as was standard practice, the official record was written as if by King Henry himself. Warwick was thus assured that 'if we refuse to learn or commit wrongdoings or are naughty' he could 'reasonably chastise us... in the manner of other princes of our age' without being 'stopped, molested or prevented'. Warwick also had the power to remove bad influences from around the king, and move him from one manor to another if any sudden 'pestilence or aventure' required it. For taking on this 'authority, licence, charge and command, above all others' Warwick was rewarded with 250 marks a year, around four times as much as Alice Botiller had been paid.[6]

Warwick was assisted in the task of educating King Henry by Dr John Somerset, who had been appointed Henry's physician a year earlier. Somerset's experience teaching as the master of a grammar school qualified him to serve as Henry's primary tutor, helping him learn to read and recite religious texts using his primer or prayer book. Henry was a diligent student, and by March 1428 John Kempe, archbishop of York and Bishop Beaufort's successor as chancellor of England, proudly reported that the king had 'perfectly' learnt Matins, the litanies, the hours of the Blessed Virgin, the six penitential psalms and was beginning on his psalter. Such ability, said Kempe, had never been seen before in a person of such tender years.[7]

As well as religious works, Henry was taught using 'mirrors for princes' and histories: books in which the stories of saints and kings from 'times passed' were presented as exemplars or warnings. Among the ideal kings he encountered were the Anglo-Saxon kings Alfred and St Edmund the Martyr,* and his French forebear St Louis – rulers associated with learning and chastity, as well as self-sacrifice and self-regulation.† St Louis appeared on an illuminated page in Henry's psalter, where he presented an infant Henry to the Virgin Mary and baby Jesus.[8] The psalter had once been owned by Charles VI's eldest son, and probably came down to Henry through his mother Queen Catherine. Such visual and literary examples were supposed to encourage Henry to imitate the virtues and avoid the vices of his ancestors. They were particularly important for a boy growing up without a flesh and blood example of kingship to observe and learn from.[9]

---

* King Edmund of East Anglia (d. 869) was martyred by the pagan Vikings while Alfred 'the Great' of Wessex (d. 899) won a number of victories over them. Alfred was remembered in Henry's day more for his wisdom and promotion of education than his martial exploits.
† St Louis (1214–70) was King Louis IX of France, a crusader king remembered for his piety.

The living role models available to Henry were more problematic. His uncles Bedford and Gloucester continued to play out their disagreements in public. The duke of Bedford was diligent and authoritative, but his presence in England during 1425–7 had not laid to rest any of the inherent problems in Henry's royal council and had only exacerbated the duke of Gloucester's frustration at his thwarted ambitions. Bedford was determined that before he returned to France to take up his duties as regent, he would force Gloucester to acknowledge the authority of the royal council. On 28 January 1427, in the Star Chamber at Westminster, Bedford made a formal submission to the council. With tears in his eyes and a book of gospels in his hand, Bedford swore to be 'advised, demesned and ruled by the lords of the council and obey unto... them... with all his heart'.[10] Gloucester absented himself from this meeting with the excuse that he was 'diseased with sickness' but the next day the councillors called his bluff by visiting him at home, where they insisted that he take the same oath. At first Gloucester refused, saying

> that if he had done anything that touched the king his sovereign lord's estate, thereof would he not answer unto no person alive, save only unto the king when he came to his age... 'Let my brother govern as he lust whilst he is in this land', he added, 'for after his going over into France I will govern as me seemeth good'.[11]

When the council pointed out that as protector, Bedford had set a precedent for obeying conciliar rule, Gloucester was grudgingly forced to swallow his hot words and swear the oath as well.

However, he would not let the matter rest. When Bedford and Bishop – now Cardinal – Beaufort left the country together in spring 1427 Gloucester became protector once more. He insisted that 'his power and authority... be made fully certain' in parliament and refused to fulfil his duties until the issue was resolved. His fellow lords curtly responded that this matter had already been settled, in 1422, and if the duke of Bedford was happy with the authority he held as protector when he was in England, then Gloucester ought to be too. 'We are amazed with all our hearts,' the lords told Gloucester, 'that... you should in any way be prompted or moved not to be content with this'. Gloucester was once again forced to back down. However, the rivalry between him and Bedford, smouldering over the past two years in England, now sparked a flame that threatened to engulf Henry's French realm.[12]

In July 1427, the veteran commander Thomas Montagu, earl of Salisbury, returned to England to raise an army to fight in France. Salisbury and Gloucester were natural allies – both proud, bellicose and militarily experienced noblemen, united by a personal vendetta against Philippe of Burgundy. Salisbury had held a grudge against Philippe ever since a Parisian wedding in 1424 when the duke had made lascivious advances towards Salisbury's beautiful wife Alice. By 1428, Salisbury also shared Gloucester's frustration with the duke of Bedford over the progress of the war in France. Salisbury had spent the past fifteen years campaigning and had fought beside Bedford at Verneuil. Since that day he had proved himself a remarkable military leader, pushing the boundaries of Henry's French realm beyond the duchy of Normandy into Maine and Anjou. In 1424 he took thirty-six 'strong towns and castles' from the dauphin, including Le Mans, capital of Maine. Now, however, he and Bedford found themselves espousing two irreconcilable strategies for the advancement of the war. While the duke of Bedford favoured a cautious approach, involving an assault on the city of Angers, which would safeguard his own lands in Maine and Anjou, Salisbury believed the English army should proceed up the River Loire to the heavily defended fortress town of Orléans and batter it into submission with heavy artillery. Not only would this seriously threaten Dauphin Charles and open up a route into his territory, it had the attraction for Salisbury of allowing him to seize for himself the lands he captured there. Gloucester shared Salisbury's belief that a more vigorous military campaign was needed to make headway in France and while Salisbury was in England the pair connived to ensure that Bedford's military strategy was sidelined and the next French campaign followed Salisbury's plan instead. To further undermine Bedford's honour, when Salisbury left for the Loire at the head of his army in March 1428 he was given unprecedented independence from Bedford's authority as regent.[13]

Salisbury's campaign was to have far-reaching consequences for Henry. When the earl left England the intention of Henry's councillors seems to have been to crown their young king within a few years, perhaps when he was ten, as Richard II had been at his coronation. The chancellor, Archbishop Kempe, hinted as much to parliament in March 1428: 'It may please the grace of God for [King Henry] to assume his own royal power within a few years.'[14] But within months, their hand had been forced. 1428 was to prove a crisis point for Henry's rule in France, the start of a serious decline. The regency of the duke of Bedford was no longer enough. It would soon be imperative for Henry to go, in person, to the defence of his French realm.

Orléans, France
27 October 1428

A fortnight into the siege of the fortified city of Orléans, the earl of Salisbury surveyed a scene of devastation. The besieged Armagnac forces had torn down the suburbs of the town – churches, chapels, even the magnificent houses of the rich had all fallen to their hooks and fire.[15] A cratered wasteland had been left between the city's defences – its eight gates, more than thirty towers, its thick stone walls – and the English attackers on the south side of the Loire. Fierce fighting had secured the great tower of Les Tourelles for the English. It was one of the few tall buildings that survived, looming over the ruined arches of the bridge across the river. Salisbury had ordered cannons to be moved into the Tourelles, to batter the city walls into submission. He had confidence that given another month or two, he could bring the Armagnacs to heel with the old besieger's arsenal of firepower and famine.[16]

From his vantage point on the second floor of Les Tourelles Salisbury had a good view of the destruction being wrought. The English had pressed their attack far into the belly of the dauphin's territory, pushing towards his base in Bourges beyond the Loire. They had already taken Jargeau, Meaux and Beaugency, the forts that flanked Orléans along the Loire. If they could seize control of the mighty city of Orléans, the other garrisons of the valley would surely fall with hardly a crossbow shot, just as Salisbury had watched the fortifications of Anjou and Maine topple like dominoes before his artillery in 1425.

With a sudden burst of flame, a cannon was fired within the walls of the city, its gunner's sight focused on Les Tourelles. Hearing the sound, Salisbury retreated across the chamber, away from the window. A captain who had been standing near him was slower to react, and was killed instantly. Salisbury was not so fortunate. The massive cannonball struck the window, sending fragments of iron and stone hurtling into the chamber. A piece of shrapnel shattered Salibury's jaw and tore away his cheek and one of his eyes. His men rushed to carry their stricken commander out of the tower, away from the siege to the safe city of Meaux. It took Salisbury eight agonizing days to die.[17]

The loss of the earl of Salisbury was a body blow to the English cause. Every chronicler who spoke of his death – French, Burgundian, English – praised him as a strong and chivalrous captain. But in his absence the siege of Orléans had to continue. Ten days after Salisbury's death the duke of Bedford appointed the thirty-two-year-old William de la Pole, earl of Suffolk, to take Salisbury's place as commander. But for all his years of military experience, Suffolk was not the charismatic, ruthless captain that Salisbury had been. And having suffered such a blow to their military confidence, the English now chose to pursue less aggressive tactics: they would no longer pound Orléans with men and mortars but would instead attempt to starve it into submission. The English army thus had to encircle the entire city in an attempt to strangle its supply lines. With winter setting in, the besiegers could expect a long, miserable campaign.

The siege of Orléans marked a turning point in English fortunes in France. Bedford had always opposed the strategy of taking the city as too risky and, as time passed, his reservations proved to be well founded. The siege had to be conducted from south of the Loire, making it difficult to resupply the English army from their base at Paris, 80 miles (129 km) to the northwest across the river. Ironically, in the light of their intention to blockade the city into submission, it was failure to prevent supplies from entering Orléans that would prove fatal to the English cause. For, accompanying a convoy of provisions, a secret weapon penetrated the city. She came in gleaming new armour, commissioned at the dauphin's expense, riding on horseback, beneath a white standard bearing an image of Jesus Christ in judgement. For all she was dressed like a knight, the origins of this seventeen-year-old lay in the poor farming lands of Domrémy near Lorraine. The French called her *la Pucelle*, the maid. The English used more abusive terms. She came to liberate Orléans, force the English out of France and crown Dauphin Charles king in Henry VI's place. Her name was Joan of Arc.

The arrival of Joan of Arc at the siege of Orléans on 29 April 1429 was the death knell of the English campaign. The fact that she had got into the city at all through the ring of English earthworks, cannons and soldiers was regarded by the citizens as nothing short of a miracle. Her campaign against the English was as much moral as military. She railed against the English, emphasizing Dauphin Charles's divinely appointed right to the French throne and the patriotism of his cause. One of the many messages she sent to the English commanders to intimidate them was tied around an arrow and shot into their camp. 'You men of England, who have no right in this kingdom of France,' she wrote, 'the king of Heaven orders and commands you through me, Joan the Pucelle, to abandon your strongholds and go back to your own country. If not, I will make a war cry that will be remembered forever.' The English responded by mocking her as a whore and a witch. One of the captains who had cursed her the loudest subsequently fell into the Loire in full armour and drowned. Her allies cried that this was divine punishment. The English called it sorcery.[18]

Joan revived the spirit of the exhausted defenders of Orléans. In one daring raid after another she rallied the French to odds-defying victories. In one such attack, on 7 May, she was struck in the shoulder with an arrow. Despite the shaft penetrating 6 inches into the flesh above her breast, she fought on until nightfall. What impressed her soldiers was not only her ability to withstand considerable pain but also hunger. Men marvelled at how she fought all day and slept all night in her armour, ready for action, yet survived on a little toast dipped in watered-down wine. To the French she increasingly appeared to be 'a prophetess and a worthy goddess'.[19]

Little more than a week after Joan's arrival, following a series of successful French sorties, the siege of the city was lifted and the English were in retreat, hounded as they fled by Joan and the Armagnac forces. The earl of Suffolk headed for the fortified city of Jargeau 11 miles (18 km) away but suffered a crippling defeat there barely a month later, in early June. One of his brothers was killed, another was captured and Suffolk himself was taken prisoner. Days later the fortress of Beaugency, the river crossing to the west of Orléans, also fell. Finally, at Patay on 18 June, an English army led by some of its most respected commanders – including the veterans Lord John Talbot and Sir John Fastolf – was decisively crushed by Joan's forces. Talbot was taken prisoner and Fastolf fled the field, an act that did irreparable harm to his reputation. The eyewitness chronicler Jean de Waurin reported that 2,000 English soldiers were killed.[20]

Joan of Arc's mission had always been to crown the dauphin in order to resurrect the French cause and drive out the English, and the Battle of Patay opened up the route to Reims, where the kings of France were traditionally crowned. Now, through summer fields, the dauphin and Joan marched their army north-east in a triumphal progress that saw city after city bow before them. On 17 July 1429, with Joan of Arc holding her white standard beside him at the altar – and her shepherd parents, presumably rather bemused by their changed circumstances, somewhere among the crowds – the dauphin was crowned King Charles VII in Reims Cathedral. All of the French royal regalia, even the crown, were still in the English-held abbey of St Denis so Charles had to make do with an anointing. Fortunately, the holy oil of Clovis – which, legend told, had been delivered to St Remi by an angel in the form of a dove* – was kept in Reims, so this sacred ritual could be carried out.[21]

No sooner was Charles VII crowned than his forces marched west to lay siege to St Denis and Paris. Already, on 16 July, Philippe of Burgundy had fled the capital in fear of imminent Armagnac attack, taking his sister, Anne, duchess of Bedford, with him. The Armagnac cause now had an anointed king at its head and renewed certainty in the legitimacy of its cause. Bedford believed that the only way to undermine French confidence was to crown Henry in turn. He had first appealed for Henry to be crowned king in France in April 1429, when the first English

---

* According to tradition, in AD 496 St Remi, bishop of Reims, used oil from a small glass vial known as the *Sainte Ampoule* ('Holy Ampulla') to baptize Clovis, the first Frankish king to convert to Christianity. The *ampoule* later came to light in the abbey of Saint-Remi and was used for the coronation of Louis VII in 1131 – and for the coronation of every French king down to Louis XVI in 1774.

forts had started to fall. The English council, alarmed at the pro-
jected cost and logistical challenge of escorting their seven-year-
old king to France, had prevaricated. Now, however, there was
no question of their demurring. Whether he was ready for it or
not, Henry would be crowned. He would be the king of England
and of France in more than just name.[22]

Westminster

6 November 1429

On a bright clear winter's day, the seven-year-old Henry was
carried into Westminster Abbey in the arms of his master, the
earl of Warwick, for the first of his two coronations. The crowds
pressed in so eagerly to see the infant king in his silken shift
and furred scarlet cloak that some bystanders stumbled and
were crushed to death in the throng. It was the feast day of St
Leonard, patron saint of prisoners, although this fact did little
good to the cutpurses and pickpockets who were dragged from
Westminster to the pillory to have their ears cut off.[23]

    To allay English anxieties about being ruled over by a king of
France, it had been decided to crown Henry in England before
he proceeded to his French coronation. Already something of
a veteran of public ceremonies, despite his tender years, Henry
behaved with suitable decorum. Raised up on a special platform
that had been constructed in the nave of the abbey, dwarfed by
the looming stone columns that towered above him, Henry sat
on his throne 'beholding the people all about sadly and wisely'.
Turning to all four corners of the abbey in turn, the archbishop
of Canterbury called out to the assembled throng. 'Sirs,' he cried,
'here comes Henry, King Henry V's son, humbly… asking the
crown of this realm by right and descent of heritage. If ye hold you
well pleased with all and will be pleased with him, say you now ye!
And hold up your hands'. 'And then,' as a Londoner chronicler
reported, 'all the people cried with one voice, "Ye! Ye!"'[24]

But before Henry could be crowned he had to endure a lengthy series of ceremonies, offering at the high altar, lying prostrate, taking of oaths and – most importantly – anointing with holy oil. To make this sacred ritual easier, Henry had been dressed in a silk shift that unlaced at the shoulders, breast and elbows. The archbishop of Canterbury brought forth holy oil in a golden eagle and ampulla, to dab at each of these places, and also on the infant king's back, head and palms. The oil was said to have been given by the Virgin Mary herself to a previous arch-bishop of Canterbury: the martyred St Thomas Becket. Before the oil could cool on Henry's skin, pieces of linen were bound in place and his shirt was retied. Finally, the archbishop daubed a sign of the cross on his head with the oil, and then a linen coif was tied over it. The oil would remain uncleansed for eight days before being ceremonially removed with warm white wine, and the anointed linen bindings burnt. Towards the end of the ceremony, Henry was finally clothed in royal vestments and the great crown of St Edward was brought for him.* It had to be held above his head by two bishops standing on either side of him, since 'it was over heavy for him, for he was of a tender age'.[25]

Once the ritual of coronation was over every bishop and lord in England and Wales lined up before Henry in the abbey and knelt in homage, promising to be his liegeman. The ceremony must have had a profound impact on such a serious and pious child as Henry. The thundering voices of his people, acclaiming him as their king, echoing from the ancient stones of Westminster Abbey where his forefathers had been so acknowledged, must have reinforced his sense of duty and destiny as sovereign lord of two nations. Henry's status as rightful king of two realms was proclaimed even in the food on the table as he sat beside Cardinal Beaufort in Westminster Hall for his coronation banquet. The sweet 'subtleties' that accompanied every course emphasized

---

* This crown, believed to have belonged to St Edward the Confessor, was used at all royal coronations from 1220 until the seventeenth century.

Henry's dual crown. In one St Edward the Confessor and St
Louis stood armed, flanking a sugar representation of Henry
himself. In another, the Virgin Mary and an infant Jesus offered
up crowns to both St George and St Denis, the twin patron saints
of Henry's realms.

In Henry's French territories, the duke of Bedford had ensured
that propaganda was disseminated that emphasized Henry's
right to the French crown. The walls of French churches were
decorated with ornate banners displaying poetry and images that
broadcast Henry's dual descent. Even the coins in his French
subjects' purses reinforced this message, showing an angel holding the shields of both nations in its hands, combining the heraldic symbols of the English leopard with the French fleur-de-lys.
The message Bedford was determined to disseminate was that
Henry was rightful king and the newly crowned Charles VII a
murderous usurper who threatened French lives and livelihoods.
In the proclamations issued on Henry's behalf, Bedford refused
to describe Charles as 'dauphin' or his troops as 'French', since
that might have appeared to recognize Charles's right to the
throne or encourage patriotic partisanship to his cause. Instead,
Charles's soldiers were referred to only by their factional name
in the civil war: 'Armagnacs'.[26]

On 20 December 1429 Henry addressed his subjects in Paris,
Rouen and other French towns through a letter signed by his
council. He declared that although he was young he had been
given one sacred coronation and was on his way to his second, in
order to ensure that they, his beloved and loyal subjects, would
be protected from the wicked Charles Valois and allowed to live
and work in peace and tranquility.[27] But making this promise
and keeping it were two very different matters. The difficulty
of the task facing Henry and his council was apparent almost as
soon as he arrived in Calais in April 1430.

6

'The throne of his kingdom will be established'[1]

Calais

23 April 1430

Between ten and eleven o'clock on the morning of St George's Day 1430, the small, pale figure of King Henry VI stepped onto French soil for the first time. Already crowned king of England, he was now headed for his second coronation at the head of a vast army: over 300 men formed Henry's personal entourage, and the total English force that sailed for France in 1430 numbered almost 8,000, the largest army assembled so far in Henry's eight-year reign. Accompanying the king as he arrived in France were twenty-one of the leading peers of his English realm. The fifteen-year-old earl of Devon, Thomas Courtenay, had been knighted on the eve of Henry's English coronation, but he was not the youngest nobleman in attendance; James Butler, the future earl of Wiltshire, was only nine and brought with him a small escort of two men-at-arms and six archers, a symbol of the new nobility mustering to their king's war banner just as their parents had for Henry V.[2] Guiding these young nobles by example were the old guard of the Lancastrian court, chief among them Cardinal Henry Beaufort, who was to be a near-constant presence as Henry travelled through his French territories. In the Norman capital of Rouen, Bedford and his wife Anne of Burgundy awaited his arrival; Gloucester remained behind in England as Henry's protector of the realm.

Spring had come early to France that year and white roses were already in flower as Henry and his attendants rode through the streets of Calais to hear Mass and give thanks for his safe arrival at the church of St Nicholas. It was surely a sign of divine favour that Henry had landed in France on the feast day of St George, patron saint of England, his untroubled passage across the Channel seeming to demonstrate the conspicuous rightness of his claim to the French crown. The complex logistics of ferrying thousands of men across the sea meant that most of his forces followed a week later. When they arrived many of them would be housed outside the city walls, since the fortified port of Calais could not contain them all.[3]

It was intended that Henry's coronation would take place in Reims, in the county of Champagne. But the task of getting him there would be far from easy, as the city was still firmly in the hands of Charles VII. Henry's forces would somehow have to gain control of 165 miles (265 km) of hostile territory before he could reach Reims cathedral.

The first English attempts to drive back the Armagnacs surrounding Paris ended in humiliating failure. On Wednesday 16 April 1430, one of his commanders, Thomas, Lord Roos, arrived in Paris 'with more ceremony than any knight ever did', bugles and trumpets blasting triumphantly. As son-in-law of the respected earl of Warwick, great things were expected of him.* But two days after his arrival, while pursuing a pack of Armagnacs attempting to rustle cattle across the River Marne, Roos missed

---

* Lord Roos was married to Eleanor Beauchamp, the earl of Warwick's second daughter and co-heiress. Before 1436 Eleanor remarried Edmund Beaufort, duke of Somerset.

the ford, fell into the river and drowned. It was an ignominious beginning to Henry's coronation expedition.[4]

More seriously, there was disagreement among Henry's leading advisers about how best to get the king to his place of coronation. Philippe, duke of Burgundy, believed that Henry should proceed as swiftly as possible to Reims and take it by brute force. Henry's English councillors, however, were aware of how damaging to Henry's authority a protracted (and potentially unsuccessful) siege of Reims would be – to say nothing of the attendant danger to the king's person. Although the English knew a long campaign might be necessary to secure Henry's French throne – the soldiers on the coronation expedition had indented for a year's military service, rather than the customary six months – Henry's commanders did not want to get bogged down besieging a single city, potentially for several months, when other areas also needed suppressing. They wanted to focus their campaign on clearing the route to Reims by taking the forts of Laon, Soissons and Compiègne, driving Charles VII into retreat.[5]

Never a man to take the impugning of his dignity lightly, Philippe had to be persuaded to override his council's advice and give up his strategy. Once again, Cardinal Beaufort applied his considerable diplomatic skills to the situation, relying in part on a new family relationship he had with the mercurial duke. In January 1430, the twice-widowed Philippe had married Beaufort's niece, Isabella of Portugal, in a lavish eight-day celebration in Bruges. To reward his investment in retaking the county of Champagne, Philippe was to be granted the territory once the Armagnacs had been cleared from it and would also receive a payment of 12,500 marks for supplying 1,500 soldiers. Still grumbling about English strategy, Philippe duly set off to besiege the mighty fortress of Compiègne.[6]

Dominating the single bridge crossing the River Oise, this vital fortified town was protected by thick stone walls, forty-four towers and a moat. It lay at a crossroads between Henry's Norman capital at Rouen in the west, Charles's cathedral city of Reims to the east, Paris to the south and Calais far in the north. The town had surrendered to Charles VII a month after his coronation, but according to the terms of an earlier agreement with Philippe it was supposed to be under Burgundian control. Philippe of Burgundy sent one of his trusted commanders, Jean de Luxembourg, to besiege the town. His English counterpart was John Fitzalan, earl of Arundel, who had sworn a chivalric oath of honour never to cover his head until he had brought Normandy to heel.[7] Two knights of Henry's household, Sir John Montgomery and Sir John Steward, joined the ranks of Englishmen surrounding Compiègne, enduring heavy bombardment from artillery on the walls. They were there on 23 May, Ascension Eve, when the Anglo-Burgundian forces were attacked by a sortie of Armagnac soldiers. Leading this force, shouting encouragement from horseback as a banner daubed with images of God and the angels danced above her, was Joan of Arc.

The fighting across the bridge at Compiègne was fierce. Twice, Arundel and Jean de Luxembourg's soldiers were forced all the way back to their encampment. Men tumbled into the river below, the weight of their armour dragging them to their deaths, while above the clash of steel echoed in the gathering darkness. Montgomery and Steward were among the many English soldiers injured: Montgomery's arm was cut in two and Steward shot in the thigh by a crossbow quarrel. But at last their forces pressed Joan's Armagnac soldiers so close to the town that, fearing the enemy would surge inside and put the citizens to the slaughter, the captain of Compiègne barred the gates against his own allies. Trapped between the great walls and the resurgent Anglo-Burgundian army, Joan tried to spur her horse across the fields and escape but she was dragged from her saddle by her enemies. She was now a Burgundian captive.[8]

Jean de Luxembourg had Joan escorted to his castle, where a curious Philippe of Burgundy interviewed the shepherdess who had caused him so much trouble. He dispatched news of his victory far and wide across the territories loyal to him and Henry. 'Joy, comfort and consolation!' he announced. 'The woman known as the Maid has been captured.'[9] It was not the end of resistance to Henry's rule – it was not even the end of resistance at Compiègne, which held out until November 1430 – but it was a significant morale boost for his cause. Such victories were badly needed at a time when disgruntlement was rife among Henry's French subjects. The English soldiers in France did little to endear themselves to the French. The Bourgeois of Paris complained that they jeered at the local populace and looted holy sites, tipping sacred relics out of silver reliquaries just to get at the precious metal casing. In Paris, the impoverished citizens even grumbled at having to light bonfires to celebrate Henry's arrival; firewood was expensive and people had doubts as to whether he had really come at all.[10]

Their scepticism was understandable: even after Joan of Arc's capture Henry's advance through his French kingdom proceeded at a snail's pace. By July 1430, the fall of the mighty Château Gaillard on the Seine south of Rouen – its rippling shell-like keep created by Henry's ancestor Richard the Lionheart in the twelfth century – allowed Henry and his entourage to move as far as the Norman capital. In one summer month, twelve forts around Paris were retaken by the dukes of Norfolk and Buckingham, but with so many battles to fight to get Henry to Reims, men and money were stretched to breaking point.[11]

Rouen
23 December 1430

On the day before Christmas Eve a ragged-haired woman entered Rouen through the Beauvoisine gate. Joan of Arc was escorted through streets full of soldiers and shadowed by the half-timbered merchants' homes and distinctive pitched roofs of the city. The hostile military presence would have made her heart sink. She had often said that she would rather die than be imprisoned by the English, and now she was entering the centre of English power in Normandy as their prisoner, purchased by Henry's government from Philippe of Burgundy for the princely sum of 10,000 *livres tournois*. Emblazoned on the chests of the soldiers were red crosses on blue or white backgrounds – the symbols of St Andrew and St George, of Burgundy and England. For months such heraldry had surrounded her as she journeyed from one castle prison to another, under the curious gaze of the people. Now Joan of Arc had been brought to her last captivity. The champion of Henry's enemy would not leave Rouen alive.

Although Rouen was the seat of Henry's government in Normandy, it had an ambiguous relationship with its English overlords. In 1418–19 Henry V had bombarded and starved the defiant city into submission, maintaining a six-month siege that left its citizens skeletal and corpses lying in the streets. When Bedford took up his post as regent in 1422 he learnt that the English had 'committed many wrongs, abuses and excesses... Churches are broken down, married women and others are taken and raped, and the poor people are beaten inhumanly'. Under Bedford's governance, conditions had improved. The city had been rebuilt, law and order prevailed and the Rouennais had largely come to terms with English occupation – at least for now.[12]

The castle at the northeastern edge of the city was the centre for law and government and it was here that Joan of Arc was brought. She was to be tried by the church for religious heterodoxy. Joan was bound with chains and locked in a room in one of the many round towers that punctuated the walls of Rouen Castle. From her window she could see the fields and chalk hillsides that extended north of the city – a tantalizing glimpse of liberty that she would never again enjoy.

In another part of the castle, the king she had defied was preparing to celebrate Christmas. There was no possibility of Henry VI coming into contact with a woman the English condemned as a sorceress and heretic, although a number of his companions in France knew her well enough. His master, the earl of Warwick, oversaw Joan's imprisonment and arranged for a doctor to attend her when she was ill – he warned the man to be careful with his knife when bleeding her, since she had already tried to escape more than once. Cardinal Beaufort was prominent in his crimson robes when Joan abjured her sins in front of Saint Ouen Abbey on 24 May 1431. Henry's aunt Anne, duchess of Bedford, even oversaw an inspection of *la Pucelle*'s virginity. But this adult world of sexuality and violence was concealed from Henry, who had only just celebrated his ninth birthday.[13]

For Henry, this strange Christmas at the court of Rouen was probably most significant for being the first time he had spent the festive season away from his mother. Queen Catherine was at Waltham Abbey, in Essex, where Cardinal Beaufort visited her on a brief return to England. Perhaps he conveyed messages between mother and son as he travelled. Henry was not without family and familiarity, however. The duke and duchess of Bedford remained with him in Rouen over Christmas and the earl of Warwick and his daughter Margaret, Lady Talbot, acted as hosts to various visiting dignitaries.* Henry's cousin, Bedford's illegitimate daughter Mary, lived with him in Rouen and probably spent some time with him. Despite its threatening exterior, Rouen Castle had been transformed by Bedford and Anne into a sumptuous palace with its own library, suites of private apartments and chapels. Henry's court in Rouen was a royal household overseas with twelve minstrels to entertain it and, to attend to Henry's physical and spiritual well-being, four surgeons, two chaplains, a confessor and a physician on the royal payroll. No fewer than 138 valets and pages catered to the needs of the court.[14]

---

* Margaret Talbot was a formidable woman who, like Henry, abhorred swearing. She punished anyone who swore in her house, including her children, with a diet of bread and water.

Bedford's Rouen base was an artistic and literary centre, producing works like the magnificently illuminated book of hours
that Anne gave Henry as a new year gift in 1431. It contained
portraits of the duke and duchess of Bedford, kneeling in their
finest gilded and embroidered clothing before their patron
saints. The book still survives,* an opulent reminder of how the
mystical and the domestic intermingled in the fifteenth-century
imagination.[15] It was no contradiction for a man like Bedford
to be intelligent, cosmopolitan and worldly, and also to believe
that a teenage shepherdess was a limb of Satan and represented
a greater threat to Henry's kingdom than a hundred French
soldiers.

Beyond Rouen, the war continued unabated and it cannot
have left Henry wholly untouched. His household servants
were occasionally dispatched to take musters or ferry messages
to the front lines. Warwick and Bedford both undertook military missions alongside their visits to Henry's court. Henry's
Master of the Horse, Sir John Steward, had been wounded at
Compiègne when Joan of Arc was captured, and some familiar
faces who left Henry's service during his time in Rouen would
never return. Prominent among the fallen was Louis Robessart,
a Hainault-born knight who had been a stalwart Lancastrian
servant, numbering among the trusted few who stood at Henry
V's deathbed. He had played a crucial role in forging the Treaty
of Troyes, even escorting Queen Catherine to her marriage.
Having served as the late King Henry's standard bearer, he was
a man of unquestioned loyalty and chivalry, and became Henry
VI's chamberlain for a time. On 27 November 1430 he and
Cardinal Beaufort's nephew Thomas Beaufort were bringing
4,000–5,000 troops to Philippe of Burgundy's aid when they
were overtaken by a force of French and Scots. Caught out in
the open, Robessart told Thomas to ride with as many men as

---

* See images 4 and 7 in first plate section.

possible to a neighbouring castle while he held off the French. Preferring to 'die honourably [rather] than to live censured and dishonoured in this mortal world', Robessart was cut down by the enemy. Thomas Beaufort and the vast majority of their men survived. Tales of Robessart's death would still have been fresh in the minds of Henry's courtiers at Christmas 1430. His chivalrous actions won him praise and fame, perhaps being held up as an example of military heroism to the young king.[16]

Robessart's death was a necessary price to pay for the continuing loyalty of Duke Philippe. During a relentlessly windy and wet winter, Philippe's irritation with the demands of Henry's cause had increased. In spite of the capture of Joan of Arc, the siege of Compiègne had been a miserable failure, with too few men and too little money to successfully take the town. By November 1430, despite Philippe's pleas, the English forces abandoned Compiègne. Observing the widening rift in the relationship between Burgundy and England, Charles VII had begun focusing his attacks on Philippe's territories, hoping that self-interest might drive the duke from Henry's service. Philippe complained vociferously to Henry about the situation, particularly when promised English funds for his military service fell months into arrears. 'My very redoubtable lord,' he wrote in November 1430,

at your urgent request I have employed myself in the business of your war of France, and on my part I have done and accomplished until this present time all that I have agreed and promised... [but] I cannot support nor continue for my part without your good provision... and also without having payment for that which is due to me from you.[17]

By alienating their most vital ally, the English were playing with fire.

Henry's stay in Rouen proved to be considerably longer than anticipated. The protracted inquisitions, examinations and

denouncements of Joan of Arc were concluded months before
he was able to leave. Cardinal Beaufort was a prominent figure
throughout the proceedings, which began in January 1431 under
the auspices of a church court led by Pierre Cauchon, bishop
of Beauvais. Although Henry's English regime was behind Joan's
trial, the court was dominated by French clergymen, most of
them from the University of Paris.* The outcome of the trial
that took place in the chapel of Rouen Castle was never really in
doubt. After discrediting Joan by forcing her publicly to abjure
her 'crimes and errors' – which included having her 'hair cut in
a circle in a masculine fashion... [and] cruelly desiring the shedding of human blood'[18] – she was goaded into renouncing her
words. In the miserable conditions of her imprisonment, harassed
by her guards and kept in chains, she put on men's clothing and
retreated into visions of St Michael, St Catherine and St Margaret
again. Her renunciation sealed her fate.

On the morning of 30 May 1431 Joan was led to the marketplace of Rouen and tied to a stake on a platform built of plaster. On
her shaved head was a mitre that read 'heretic, relapse, apostate,
idolator', condemnations that were repeated by Bishop Cauchon
as he addressed the assembled crowd. Then, as Joan pressed a
small wooden cross to her breast, the royal executioner, Geoffroi
Thérage, set fire to the platform. She died crying out 'Jesus!' over
and over. At Cardinal Beaufort's insistence her ashes were thrown
in the Seine to prevent their veneration – or, as the Bourgeois of
Paris believed, 'for fear of enchantments that they might have
been used for'.[19] To undermine Armagnac morale, messages were
sent out in Henry's name announcing Joan's execution to the
bishops and great towns of France and far beyond: to the pope,
the Holy Roman Emperor and foreign princes. The letters, which
dwelt on the justness of her death, and the 'formality and due

---

* Beaufort was one of only 8 Englishmen out of 131 judges, assessors and
other clergy involved in Joan's trial. Vale, M. G. A., *Charles VII* (London,
1974), p. 48.

gravity' of her trial, upheld Henry's government in France as that of a true Christian prince – and Charles's, by contrast, as based in idolatry and injustice.[20] The Armagnacs, who had abandoned Joan long before her death, found a new mystic to replace her: a shepherd called William who rode side-saddle like a woman and was said to exhibit stigmata. He, too, ended up a prisoner in Rouen late in 1431.[21]

In Paris, the citizens were less concerned about alleged sorcery than they were with their dwindling supplies. An Armagnac blockade put a stranglehold on food arriving by river, and carters attempting to fetch in the harvest had been butchered by Charles's soldiers. Philippe of Burgundy, Parisians said bitterly, 'did not care a farthing for Paris' and was too concerned with his new wife Isabella of Portugal to come to their aid.[22] Instead, the duke of Bedford had to negotiate swollen rivers and Armagnac ambush to bring more than sixty vessels stuffed with victuals down the Seine to relieve the city in January 1431. Keeping the citizens of Paris happy was vital, as it was becoming increasingly clear that it was here that Henry would be crowned, Reims having proved impossible to wrest from Charles's grasp. It was October 1431 before the route to the capital city was cleared with the fall of the strategically important town of Louviers, south of Rouen, which had resisted the English since May. During the course of the siege the English commander Thomas Beaufort, Cardinal Beaufort's nephew, was killed. Louviers had defected to Charles in 1429, and in retribution the English razed the walls to the ground. Henry's second coronation could at last take place.[23]

St Denis, English-controlled France
30 November 1431

On the feast day of St Andrew, Henry arrived at the abbey of St Denis, 6 miles (10 km) north of Paris. Two thousand soldiers waited outside as the king paid his respects at the marble tombs of his mother's ancestors. English control of St Denis meant that Henry enjoyed one benefit that was denied his rival Charles VII: he could be crowned with the French regalia. Henry and his entourage paused at St Denis for two days, awaiting the arrival of Philippe of Burgundy. Bedford and his fellow councillors hoped that Philippe would publicly acknowledge Henry as his king at the forthcoming coronation, and they may have timed their arrival outside Paris to appeal to the mercurial duke, for St Andrew was the patron saint of Burgundy. But even the saints could not force Philippe to commit himself definitively to a cause that he was no longer certain was in his best interests. While Henry prayed at the altars of St Denis, Philippe prevaricated and stayed away. On the first day of Advent, Sunday 2 December 1431, Henry advanced towards Paris without him.

As tradition and civic pride demanded, the citizens of Paris had organized a spectacular welcome for their young king. At La Chapelle, halfway between the city and St Denis, Henry was met by a vast throng led by the provost of Paris, Sir Simon Morhier, and the first of numerous pieces of civic theatre was performed. Gathered in their furred and crimson satin doublets, fine blue hoods at their neck, Sir Simon and the city officials introduced a pageant of nine male worthies and nine warrior queens on horseback: here Henry could recognize mythical heroes and heroines from his books, the Amazonian Queen Hypolita, David who slew Goliath, Alexander the Great and Charlemagne, leapt from the page to vivid life. The eighteen worthies rode ahead of Henry as he proceeded across fields towards the bristling spires of Paris, trumpets blasting to herald his approach. According to the Burgundian chronicler Enguerrand de Monstrelet, 'as they advanced, [the citizens] made their reverences to the king, each according to his rank... With regards to the common people, they were numberless'.[24]

At the city gates Henry found a silver-covered ship set over the stonework, so large that six people were able to stand inside it, representing the different officers of Paris. Three blood-red hearts hanging over the ship opened as Henry rode up to the gate, releasing a flock of white doves. As he passed beneath the shadows of the gateway, another heart opened and violet petals fluttered down on him. The Bourgeois of Paris remembered the scene:

> As soon as the king entered the town they put a great azure canopy over him, all starred with golden fleur-de-lis; the four aldermen carried it over him, just as is done for Our Lord at Corpus Christi, and more, for everyone shouted *Noel!* as he went by.*

Henry rode slowly through the city streets, processing along the great Rue St Denis, on to the Île de la Cité and then back over the river onto the north bank of the Seine, as far as the palatial Hôtel les Tournelles† in the east. The entire city had been scrubbed clean and decked out with precious tapestries so that the stone buildings could barely be seen. Linen cloths and straw dulled the clatter of horses' hooves and prevented them slipping in the morning frost. Wherever the streets widened, at bridges and gateways or in front of churches, Henry paused to watch a pageant performed by the citizens. At the little bridge of St Denis performers dressed as mermaids swam in a fountain of wine while others disguised as 'wild men' performed tricks ('everyone liked watching this,' observed the usually grouchy Bourgeois of Paris). On a scaffold stretching from the church of St Sauveur‡ to the Queen's Fountain, scenes from the nativity of the Virgin Mary were played out 'in dumb show... especially

---

* Corpus Christi ceremonies at midsummer often involved the procession of a consecrated eucharist – believed to be the real body of Christ – under a canopy. *Parisian Journal*, p. 269.

† This is now in the fourth arrondissement, close to Place des Vosges in the Marais.

‡ Long demolished, this church lay in what is now the second arrondissement.

well acted'. There were tales of the martyrdom of St Denis and a stag hunt in the streets. At Le Châtelet, where the scaffold was decked in cloth of gold and arras, Henry met his own reflection, in a pageant representing himself and his most important advisers. A boy of Henry's age and build was dressed in a furred scarlet robe, two crowns suspended above his head. On the boy's right hand a figure representing Philippe of Burgundy knelt to present 'Henry' with the coat of arms of France, flanked by other French lords, while on his left representations of Bedford, Warwick and other English lords recognizable by their coats of arms presented the shield of England.[25]

As he passed the Hôtel Saint-Pol* towards the end of the day, Henry paused at the sight of a woman in a window above, surrounded by ladies-in-waiting. It was his grandmother, Queen Isabeau of France, and this was the first time the pair had ever laid eyes on each other. Henry lowered his hood and bowed respectfully. In return, Isabeau reverenced her grandson and king. Then she 'turned away in tears'.[26] For decades her family had torn itself apart fighting for control of the French crown, and with Henry's coronation a third generation of the Valois bloodline had entered the conflict.

No doubt to Henry's relief, a fortnight separated this day-long pageant of welcome from the ritual of his coronation. During that time he lodged at the Castle of Bois de Vincennes, where his father had died nine years earlier. Compared with his magnificent entry into the city, Henry's coronation on 16 December, ten days after his tenth birthday, was a shabby and disorganized affair. Although he processed in 'great pomp' from the palace on the Île de la Cité to the steps of Notre Dame, the ceremony of coronation and the celebration afterwards seemed designed to offend Henry's French subjects. The customs of France were ignored. Cardinal Beaufort insisted on chanting Mass and

---

* This was a royal residence of the Valois used by Charles VI and Isabeau in what is now the fourth arrondissement.

personally crowning Henry, 'to the great displeasure of the bishop of Paris, who said that that office belonged to him'.[27] Not content with alienating the bishop, the English also angered the canons of the cathedral by purloining a silver gilt wine jug that was rightfully a French perquisite. 'There was a small tournament the day after his consecration,' wrote the Bourgeois of Paris, 'but, really, many a time a Paris citizen marrying his child has done more.' Worst of all was the banquet in the great hall of the Palais Royal. 'The food was shocking, no one had a good word for it,' and such was the disorganization that the commons of Paris surged into the hall before the city's officials could take their places. Respectable representatives of the university and *parlement* were forced to sit at the lowly end of the great hall, surrounded by 'cobblers, mustard-sellers, packers, winestall keepers [and] stonemasons' lads'. It seemed a poor return for the grand welcome the city had given Henry.[28]

On 21 December 1431, during a hard frost, Henry attended his first – and only – session of the French *parlement*. Curiously, he addressed the representatives in English, which the earl of Warwick translated. It is possible that he had been instructed to do so by his advisers as a demonstration to the French of his 'Englishness' as monarch. He was certainly capable of speaking French, having been brought up in the company of his French mother and schooled by Warwick, who was a renowned linguist. Eighteen months later Henry was able to converse quite comfortably in French with a Burgundian ambassador.[29] Perhaps he was exhausted by the several public appearances he had made in Paris. Or it may be that Henry's initial willingness to please his French subjects had soured; only three days before Henry's coronation, Philippe of Burgundy had agreed a truce with Charles VII. News of the agreement would have reached the king not long after, in a letter sent by Philippe himself, in which he placed the blame for his change of heart squarely on the English. 'By default of your said succour,' he wrote, 'and in order to [avoid] the destruction of my said countries and

subjects, I have been constrained to consent [to] certain truces...
with your said enemies and mine.' Philippe asked Henry 'not to
conceive of any suspicion or evil surmise' in him, assuring him
of his continuing willingness to please him, but the harsh truth
was that Henry's ally had betrayed him.[30]

As soon as Christmas Day was over, on 26 December 1431,
Henry left Paris. His court had not endeared itself to its French
hosts: 'All [the English] cared about was how soon they could get
[things] over and done with'.[31] Little more than a month later,
Henry was in Calais, preparing to sail back to England. After
almost two years of intense struggle to secure Henry his French
coronation, his departure was startlingly abrupt. Perhaps Henry
harboured few warm feelings for France, a country riven by war,
in which he had lived virtually under house arrest in one great
city after another. He certainly made little impression on his
French subjects. The main comment that was made about him
was that he was young. The Bourgeois of Paris believed him to
be 'nine years old or thereabouts' and observed that in the wake
of his sudden departure 'not a soul, at home or abroad, was
heard to speak a word in his praise – yet Paris had done more
honour to him than to any king both when he arrived and at his
consecration'.[32]

Henry's departure from France was overshadowed by yet
another conflict between his uncles. In general, his time outside
England and English politics – especially away from Gloucester's
divisive presence – had been a peaceful one for the young king,
but Henry's new status as crowned king of the dual monarchy
unsettled the political status quo in both his realms, effectively terminating the positions of protector and regent held
by Gloucester and Bedford. In Henry's presence, Bedford and
Cardinal Beaufort quarrelled bitterly when Beaufort insisted that
Bedford's regency must no longer be considered his birthright
but must instead be granted as a commission from the council –
a commission that could be revoked whenever it pleased the king
and his advisers. To Bedford this diminishing of his authority

appeared to be part of a wider Beaufort scheme to sideline him and take the leading role in Henry's French government for himself. During the coronation expedition, Beaufort had served as president of the Grand Council, overseeing the government and administration of Henry's continental territories, while Bedford was assigned to a purely military role. As president, Beaufort had not been a shining success. He had changed the system of wage-payment so that soldiers were paid individually instead of through their captains, leaving wages seriously in arrears. He had also gifted French captaincies to Englishmen who were not best placed to serve in such roles – although they often served Beaufort's interests. Yet despite these issues, Cardinal Beaufort preferred to remain on the continent after Henry returned to England. After all, the only thing waiting for him in English politics was further wrangling with his nephew Gloucester.[33]

During Henry's time in France he had fallen under Beaufort's influence and their bond had been strengthened rather than weakened by the king's coronations. It had been the cardinal who crowned Henry king of France, forging a unique religious connection that Beaufort commemorated by giving his great-nephew a ruby ring. By now Bedford had had the opportunity to get to know Henry better and he may have been disturbed be what he saw, for the boy was pliable and easily led. Bedford might easily have come to believe that Henry had been manipulated by Cardinal Beaufort into altering the terms of Bedford's appointment as regent, a realization that would have done little to foster familial harmony or confidence in Henry's future rule. However, with king and council united on the issue of Bedford's commission, he was forced to accept Cardinal Beaufort's primacy and this latest family quarrel seemed to have been resolved.

If Henry hoped that his return to England would bring a more peaceful environment, he was to be sorely disappointed. In the absence of his chief rivals, Gloucester had been plotting the means by which he could reassert his control over the young king on his return. The Lancastrian family was about to be torn apart by infighting. All this awaited Henry as he stepped aboard ship in Calais early in February 1432, having spent less than two years in his French realm. He would never return.

7

'Earthly goods'[1]

Sandwich
6 February 1432

In the darkness of the harbour mouth, lights flashed and glared. Above the low creak of ships' timbers, men's voices punctured the frosty stillness of the night. Occasionally there came a low thump of coffers hitting the decking. A groan. A cricked back. And then the great chests lifted again, edged closer, step by heavy step, towards the tilting flank of a ship called *Mary of Winchelsea*. Within these coffers lay a princely trove of treasure: twenty golden drinking vessels, ninety-nine gold cups, candlesticks, chalices, an entire chest filled with parcels of gold, their glister hidden within careful cloth wrappings. In total, this treasure, the accumulated wealth of Cardinal Beaufort, was worth £20,000.[2]

At the port of Sandwich, the duke of Gloucester watched the men loading their precious cargo on board the ship. He and his retinue were waiting for the moment to strike. Gloucester had ridden in haste from Dover, where the officials and councillors waited for the foaming tide to bring their twice-crowned king back from France. When he heard that the cardinal was attempting to smuggle his wealth out of the country to join him on the continent, Gloucester had been determined to catch the ship before it could make sail. It was short work for the duke and his men to halt the loading, prise open the great coffers and search inside. Gloucester immediately confiscated the treasure to the crown. Cardinal Beaufort would be notified that his wealth was now forfeit, the product of an illegal attempt to export precious metal from England without licence, denuding a poverty-stricken country of its gold in order to restock his own coffers. At last, Gloucester believed, he had found the means to bring down his rival, once and for all.

During King Henry's absence Gloucester had ruled England with the powers he had been seeking for almost a decade. As Henry's appointed keeper of the realm, he had more authority than he had ever enjoyed as protector. In 1431, when a group of Lollards* were discovered to be plotting a rising that encompassed Coventry, London and Salisbury, Gloucester had acted quickly and decisively, hunting down the offenders and executing them. Although the focus of the Lollard rising was the English church, the fact that they were led by a man calling himself 'Jack Sharp', who claimed to come from the marcher heartlands of the Mortimer family, was ample cause for the council to fear a wider conspiracy against the Lancastrian regime. In gratitude for his swift repression of the rising the council awarded Gloucester a 50 per cent pay rise. But despite his praiseworthy efforts, Gloucester knew that when Henry returned, his new-found authority as keeper would end. From now on Gloucester – and Bedford, when he was in England – would be his nephew's chief councillor, nothing more. Neither Gloucester nor Bedford resented Henry's increasing authority – they had always accepted that the young king was their overlord – but what Gloucester could not abide, what he may even have feared, was the return of

---

* Lollards were followers of the religious reformer John Wycliffe (d. 1384), who advocated the translation of the Bible into English. Lollardy was a forerunner of the Protestant Reformation.

Henry's entourage. In particular, Gloucester was anxious about the influence Cardinal Beaufort and his allies would hold over the king after nearly two years in his company.[3]

Now that Henry was crowned king, the potential power of those close to him was increased. It was an accepted fact of monarchy that the closest attendants of a king were also his advisers, and often his cherished friends. He would be guided by, and in turn reward, these men (only later, with a wife or mistress, would women be added to this inner circle). They would control access to the king and surround him at all hours of the day and night. As he grew into adolescence and adulthood, the potential influence of such attendants would increase and eventually they might supplant his relatives and his councillors as his most trusted and powerful advisers. If this was true for most kings, it was doubly so for Henry. The boy was biddable, obliging, and he felt the debts he owed to others keenly, even if he did not always fully think through the consequences of his actions. In 1428 when he wanted to give a gift to a Prussian ambassador, he had taken a gold chain still warm from the neck of his attendant, the nineteen-year-old earl of Oxford, and presented it to the ambassador, much to Oxford's bemusement. This impetuous act of childish generosity revealed a great deal about Henry's character. When asked for something, he gave it. It was left to others to deal with the consequences.[4]

To regain his own influence over Henry after twenty-two months of separation, Gloucester needed to infiltrate the circle around the king and, ideally, control it himself. Within a few weeks of Henry's return to England, Gloucester oversaw a sweeping change of personnel in the royal household. He justified this action with the need to integrate households that been split between England and France, and waited until Henry was back in the country to give his actions legitimacy, but the changes were entirely self-serving.

Out went the aged John, Lord Tiptoft and into his position as steward went the veteran soldier and servant of Lancaster,

Sir Robert Babthorpe. Ralph, Lord Cromwell, was ejected as chamberlain in favour of Sir William Philip. After Archbishop John Kempe retired as chancellor on 25 February John Stafford, bishop of Bath and Wells, took his place. Even Henry's almoner and dean of the chapel were replaced, part of a drive by Gloucester to surround Henry with the most firmly orthodox religious influences possible. The most partisan change was the treasurership: Sir Walter Hungerford was supplanted by Gloucester's ally John, Lord Scrope, who had proposed the duke's wage increase in November 1431. All of the new appointments were instructed to present themselves before Gloucester to receive their commissions.[5]

On 21 February 1432, Henry and Gloucester entered London together, riding through streets lined with celebratory pageants to rival those presented for Henry's Paris coronation. Giants bent their heads to them amid an array of magnificently dressed women – testament more to Gloucester's interests than Henry's, perhaps. The women appeared as empresses in girdles that shone like sapphires to represent Nature, Grace and Fortune; celestial virgins with golden tresses meekly saluting as 'heavenly creatures'; virgins adorned with gold stars who presented Henry with gifts including a 'girdle of love and perfect peace'; and 'glorious virgins' drawing wine from a well over the conduit in Cheapside to offer to the king. With the changes to Henry's household and this splendid public parade through the streets of the capital, Gloucester had dramatically reasserted control over his young nephew. He felt confident at last to proceed against Cardinal Beaufort.[6]

Gloucester had laid the groundwork for Cardinal Beaufort's downfall months before Henry returned to England. At a council meeting on 6 November 1431 questions were raised about Beaufort's unprecedented status as both bishop and cardinal – questions behind which it is easy to see Gloucester's influence.

All previous English bishops had resigned their dioceses on being made cardinal, but Beaufort still held the see of Winchester four years after his promotion. It was suggested that perhaps Beaufort ought to surrender his bishopric, an action that would cost 'the rich cardinal' dearly, for Winchester was the basis of his immense fortune, and through it his political influence. Not only Beaufort's wealth was at stake, however, as at this same meeting concerns were raised about the fact Beaufort had asked the pope to exempt him from the jurisdiction of Canterbury. This, it was argued, contravened the 1393 Statute of Praemunire.* Beaufort was accused of bypassing the jurisdiction of English authorities in favour of the pope. In short, Cardinal Beaufort had broken the law.[7]

According to the law of praemunire, once summoned to answer the charge, Cardinal Beaufort would have two months' grace in which to appear, and out of respect for his close kinship to the king, the council delayed issuing Beaufort's summons until Henry had returned to England in February. The council anticipated that Beaufort would return with Henry, but the cardinal must have heard whispers about Gloucester's move against him; when Henry set sail for Dover, Beaufort headed instead for the Burgundian court at Bruges. Philippe of Burgundy was a prickly character but Beaufort was a master of diplomacy and the two seem to have enjoyed a happier relationship than Philippe did with either of the cardinal's nephews. Their good terms were reinforced by Philippe's marriage to Beaufort's niece Isabella of Portugal[†] in 1429. Shortly after his arrival in Bruges Cardinal Beaufort was named godfather to Isabella and Philippe's son.

Cardinal Beaufort's intention seems to have been to forge a

---

* The statute had been introduced under Richard II during an ongoing dispute between crown and papacy to give the king of England power to prevent the pope from interfering in various matters relating to the English church.
† Isabella was the sister of Pedro of Portugal, who had brokered peace between Gloucester and Beaufort in 1425.

new career in Europe, perhaps even one day to aspire to the
papacy. He might be fifty-seven, but he still had reserves of energy
and ambition to spare. All of this, however, required money, so
once Cardinal Beaufort was safely in the asylum of Philippe's
territories he sent for his treasure from England. It was this
treasure that Gloucester had impounded at Sandwich. In the
long term, this would prove a costly mistake on the duke's part.
The accusation of praemunire might have kept the cardinal out
of England for good, giving Gloucester unrivalled dominance
over Henry. Instead, the duke's vengeful seizure of the treasure
at Sandwich and rumour-mongering about treason had forced
Beaufort to return and answer the charges laid against him.
Gloucester had overreached himself, and in so doing he would
bring Henry's influence to bear on proceedings in a way that
would not be to his advantage.[8]

In June 1432 the first parliament since Henry's return assem-
bled at Westminster, with both Gloucester and Cardinal Beaufort
ready for a trial of strength.[9] Neither lacked supporters and
Gloucester's dismissal of Henry's household officers had brought
Beaufort a number of new allies, including Lord Ralph Cromwell.
The rival factions eyed one another across the chamber while
King Henry sat soberly in their midst. Beaufort addressed parlia-
ment, explaining that he had been forced to return after learning

> both by letters sent to him and from rumours circulating that
> he had been charged and accused of treason here in England.
> For which reason the same cardinal, wishing to preserve
> unharmed his name, reputation and honour more than any
> of his earthly goods, personally returned to come before our
> aforesaid lord king, humbly beseeching his highness for a
> declaration of his faithfulness and innocence to be made.[10]

If anyone wished to accuse Beaufort of treason, he appealed for
them now to 'declare his accusation in the presence of the lord
king himself' and he would make his answer. Beaufort's challenge

went unanswered. Neither Gloucester nor any of his allies chose to formally accuse the cardinal. Instead, further discussion of the matter was ended 'at the command of the lord king himself... It was answered that no one had accused the cardinal himself of any treason, nor knew of anyone who wished to accuse him'.

In the six years since Bedford had been forced to mediate between Beaufort and Gloucester at the 'parliament of bats', Henry had grown into his kingship. In 1426 he had mutely observed the peacemaking between his relatives, but now, at ten years old, he was capable of speaking out himself. He insisted before Gloucester and the lords that he 'held, considered and declared the aforesaid cardinal himself as his true and faithful liegeman'. Beaufort's innocence of treason was thus assured – although the cardinal took the precaution of having the fact 'confirmed in letters issued under the great royal seal'. It was the second time that Gloucester and Beaufort had opposed one another before Henry – and the second time that Beaufort had walked free. Whereas previously Gloucester could blame the duke of Bedford's interference for protecting Cardinal Beaufort, this time Henry's own sympathies had carried the day. Despite his control over Henry's household, Gloucester had not succeeded in wresting the king from Beaufort's influence.[11]

But Gloucester had not given up hope of humbling his rival. The matters of Beaufort's seized treasure and the possible prae-munire charge – which could mean the forfeiture of all the cardinal's lands and offices – remained. Without his wealth, Cardinal Beaufort's authority would be seriously weakened and Beaufort was sufficiently concerned that on 9 June he made a gift of all his goods and chattels to his nephew, Edmund Beaufort, and to his allies Archbishop Kempe of York and Lord Ralph Cromwell. Both Kempe and Cromwell had lost office in Gloucester's coup in March and were ready to help Beaufort however they could. Most of the victims of Gloucester's coup had submitted quietly but the proud Lord Cromwell was determined to put up a fight. As he saw it, he had done nothing to warrant being dismissed from office, especially as he had been attending Henry in France when Gloucester plotted his downfall. If anyone had acted wrongly, Cromwell believed, it was Gloucester, whose sweeping changes were against the articles drawn up to protect council members in 1429. In revenge, Cromwell was determined to undermine Gloucester's campaign against Cardinal Beaufort and his allies. On 16 June Cromwell declared to the lords in parliament that his dismissal had 'denigrated, diminished and damaged' his reputation – a serious concern for this honour-minded warrior class – and demanded that his innocence of any wrongdoing should be officially declared. In support of his appeal he presented letters from the duke of Bedford and recited his years of military service. A 'declaration of his innocence and good name and reputation' was duly written into the parliament roll, an implicit criticism of Gloucester's recent actions.[12]

Cromwell's defiance was an augury of Beaufort's triumph. Cardinal Beaufort was as shrewd as he was rich and he channelled all his energies into currying favour with parliament, so that by the time the session at Westminster ended, popular opinion had swung firmly in his direction. 'Piously having compassion for the poverty' of Henry's subjects, on 3 July Beaufort offered to loan £6,000 to King Henry, with another £6,000 being given as a deposit for the restoration of his treasure, on the condition that when Henry was sixteen, Beaufort would demonstrate his innocence of the charges of illegally exporting it. The cardinal's generosity was deeply appreciated by the Commons, who other-wise faced increased taxation to support the French war. At the appeal of the Commons, the charges of praemunire against Beaufort were dropped. Duly thanked for his 'most praiseworthy, exceptional, lavish and fruitful services' for England, Beaufort was restored to his former position of authority.[13]

The lesson Gloucester learnt in this bruising encounter with parliament was not that Beaufort was his tactical superior, but that Henry himself was starting to demonstrate the first signs of royal will. It was will, admittedly, still vulnerable to the manipulation of those around him – his loyalty to those nearest to him was all too plain in his assertion of Beaufort's innocence – but if anything, that made Henry all the more useful to Gloucester's ambition. He saw now that the best means of maintaining his primacy in English politics was by encouraging Henry's first glimmers of assertiveness, while simultaneously increasing his hold over the boy's affections. Gloucester's encouragement of Henry's precocity was far from welcome to the king's other advisers.

In November 1432, shortly before Henry's eleventh birthday, the earl of Warwick sent an impassioned plea to the lords of the council to 'firmly and truly assist him in his charge' as the young king was starting to chafe against his master's discipline. 'The king is grown in years and stature of his person,' wrote Warwick, 'and also conceit and knowledge of his high and royal authority and estate, the which naturally causes him... more and more to grudge with chastising and to loath it.' Warwick asked the council to remind the king that he was acting on their instruction, for Henry's own good. He also, tellingly, asked for – and was granted – the power to keep undesirable people (those 'not behoveful nor expedient to be about the king') out of Henry's presence. Warwick complained that in recent times, some people had been speaking to Henry in private about 'divers matters not behoveful' and repeating 'malicious and untrue... informations' about Warwick himself in Henry's hearing. He asked that in future either he or one of the four knights of the body be present whenever Henry held an audience.[14]

Warwick was not alone in fearing the consequences of too early an adoption of royal authority or of unfettered access to him by men like Gloucester. Even two years later, in 1434, the council reported that although it was believed that Henry was 'endowed... with as great understanding and feeling as ever they saw or knew in any prince or other person of his age' he was still 'in his tender age' and lacking in the 'feeling, knowledge and wisdom' of mature experience.[15] In 1432, Warwick's fellow councillors responded to his appeal with a promise to support him. Notwithstanding his two coronations, Henry must accept chastisement from his master and the council until he had gained the necessary experience to rule alone. It was agreed by the council that 'when the king cometh next to London all his council shall come to his presence and there this shall be declared to him'.[16]

Gloucester failed to undermine Warwick's authority over Henry in 1432, but he succeeded in maintaining his private access to the king. Although the council acquiesced to Warwick's request that he be present for all meetings between Henry and his advisers, an exception was made in cases where the visitors were 'such persons as for nighness of blood... [should] speak with the king'. In other words, men such as Gloucester, Bedford and Beaufort. Unsurprisingly, top of the list of signatories to that caveat was the duke of Gloucester himself.[17]

For Henry, the division within his council and among his guardians must have led to some profoundly confusing mixed messages. On the verge of adolescence, he had been assured that he was intellectually advanced and pushed into coronation years before his council had originally planned, yet he was given no independent authority and when he attempted to exercise his powers of kingship he was warned that he was not yet ready, even that he might make decisions 'prejudicial, perilous or harmful to him or to his people'.[18] He was pushed back to his books and his theoretical lessons on kingship with Warwick. The council's position was understandable – the authoritarian streak of the last child king, Richard II, had developed into tyranny – but the sensitive young Henry was left chastened by this contradictory guidance, lacking trust in his own judgement.

It cannot have helped that on his return from France there was further personal upheaval for Henry and his household. As a logical extension of his removal into the company of men as he grew up, Henry's household had separated from his mother's on his return from France. However, there was a little more to Queen Catherine's removal from her son's company than first appeared. Probably under the aegis of the duke of Gloucester, the parliament of 1427 had put a stop to Catherine's romance with Edmund Beaufort by enacting a statute that made it a crime for any man to marry a dowager queen without the king's permission, and until the king was of 'the age of discretion'.[19] The penalty for such actions was forfeiture of the man's estate. Edmund Beaufort was a notoriously mercenary nobleman, and the threat to his estates had quickly cooled his ardour for the 'carnal' queen.[20] It had not, however, prevented Catherine seeking affection elsewhere. During Henry's absence in France, if not before, the queen had become involved with one of her servants, a Welshman called Owen ap Meredudd ap Twdwr. The English knew him simply as Owen Tudor.

The story of how Owen and Catherine fell in love has been embroidered over the centuries. One sixteenth-century Welsh source related how the queen watched her servant bathing naked and was enticed by his beauty. Another tale claimed that Owen danced so vigorously at a celebration that he fell into the queen's lap. However their romance began, and exactly when, are still obscured by these myths, but the outcome of their relationship is not in question. Owen and Catherine married secretly. Owen had less to lose than Edmund Beaufort, or possibly cared less about his worldly goods. Over the course of their relationship the couple had four children together: three sons and one daughter.[21] The daughter died young and the third son went into the church, but the two eldest boys, Edmund and Jasper, may have grown up in their mother's household. Owen and Catherine's marriage seems to have been an open secret. Edmund and Jasper were born at the manors of important bishops and Henry himself never criticized his mother's relationship.* When he was a little older, Henry watched over his half-siblings, providing for their education and bringing them to

---

* Edmund Tudor was born in the bishop of London's estate of Much Hadham, and Jasper at Hatfield, part of the bishop of Ely's estate.

court; they rewarded him with unfailing loyalty. In 1432 perhaps the one thing Henry would have regretted about his mother's new family was that it deprived him of her company. They saw each other only rarely in the remaining years of her life. But then perhaps that would always have been the case. Kings had to move out of their mothers' pockets eventually.[22]

Surrounded by competing factions as he neared adolescence, it is perhaps little wonder that Henry bridled at the constraints imposed by his master Warwick. Yet Warwick's concern about his precocity was not entirely misplaced, given the challenges facing the dual monarchy at the time. England might be largely at peace, but Henry's coronation expedition had done nothing to tighten his hold on France. The first year of Henry's reign as crowned king was to prove disastrous for his French realm.

8

'Mother of mercy, save both realms'[1]

The winter of 1432 brought misery to Paris. Armagnacs were at the gates trailing slaughter in their wake, storms had battered their harvests and, as well as enduring bitingly cold weather, the city was ravaged by plague. Children and the young were particularly affected, dying in great numbers in the city streets. One of the afflicted was Anne, duchess of Bedford, who took to her bed in the Hôtel de Bourbon near the Louvre. In an effort to save her, Bedford ordered the relics of St Germain to be carried in procession through Paris, appealing to the saint to intercede for her. His efforts were in vain; two hours after midnight on 13 November, Anne died. She was only twenty-eight years old. Anne was buried in the convent of the Célestins the following Saturday, surrounded by the citizens of St Germain and priests in their black stoles bearing candles. As her body was lowered into the grave, the English in attendance sang 'most movingly by themselves, in the fashion of their own country'.[2] When her funeral rites were celebrated the following January, Bedford gave 14,000 paupers money to pray for the soul of his beloved wife. He 'was sorely afflicted at her death, as were many of his party'. The Bourgeois of Paris remembered Anne as 'the most delightful of all the great ladies then in France, for she was good and beautiful... The Parisians loved her.' But the citizens of Paris, and Bedford's comrades, did not weep solely for Anne herself. They feared what her death would mean for relations between her brother and her husband. She had been the glue binding England and Burgundy together, the symbol and agent of lasting peace between the uneasy allies. 'With her', wrote the Bourgeois, 'died most of the hope that Paris had'.[3]

Anne's death came in the midst of a year of trouble for Henry's French realm. In February 1432, only weeks after Henry had left Rouen, the castle where he had stayed was overrun by Armagnac forces. The English commander, the twenty-four-year-old earl of Arundel, had been woken early in the morning by the news that the Armagnacs had clambered into the ditch below the castle and scaled the walls. A traitor in the garrison had allowed them to reach right to the heart of the castle, the great tower. The Anglo-Norman garrison had to escape over the walls, the earl of Arundel lowered from the top of his tower to the castle ditch in a basket. Fierce resistance by the Rouennais and siege engines sent urgently up the Seine by Bedford from Paris eventually regained Rouen Castle, but so humiliating had been its loss that Bedford took bloody vengeance on its attackers. In March 1432 over a hundred Armagnac soldiers were executed in Rouen marketplace in a single day. Their executioner was the same Geoffroi Thérage who had burnt Joan of Arc to ashes there a year earlier. The decomposing quarters of the traitor who had allowed the Armagnacs to gain the castle were still speared over the city gateways when the next wave of disasters befell Bedford's regime.[4]

In April, as the buds were blackened by spring frosts, the cathedral city of Chartres fell to subterfuge. Carts filled with Armagnac soldiers hidden inside barrels of salt and fish were rolled through the city gates, and the bishop was butchered in the streets as he tried to defend his flock. In the first week of June a plot was discovered to deliver the town of Pontoise, 30 miles (48 km) northwest of Paris, to the Armagnacs, and in August Paris itself was almost betrayed by the abbess of St-Anthoine and her nuns. That summer Bedford tried to take the fight to the Armagnacs by besieging Lagny, east of Paris on the River Marne, but the elements conspired against him. August was unusually hot, drying the corn around Paris to a papery crisp. Already out-numbered five to one, the English at Lagny succumbed in large numbers to the heat. Even Bedford collapsed from exhaustion. Following a summer storm, the River Marne broke its banks and flooded the English camp. Bedford abandoned the siege; in his hurry to be gone he left his artillery and food 'all cooked and waiting' in the field.[5]

In early 1433, the English stronghold of Calais was rocked by rebellion. For a hundred years, this port had been a vital trading and military outpost for the English, an entry point not only to France, but to the rich markets of the Low Countries. As was the case in many English military outposts, the wages of the soldiers in Calais were consistently in arrears and the dispute over pay escalated as the soldiers' frustration came to focus on Bedford's deputy, Sir William Oldhall. In February 1433 the exasperated soldiers seized woolsacks from the wharves in lieu of their over-due wages and threw Oldhall out of the gates, keeping his wife behind as a hostage. Bedford restored order but the price was the heads of four of the mutineers and the banishment of more than 200 others. The garrison never forgave him.[6]

It was becoming clear that Henry's councillors needed to seri-ously rethink their policy towards the dual monarchy. Henry's coronation expedition had not bound his French and Norman subjects closer to him. In order to secure his crown, either his councillors needed to lead an aggressive campaign of conquest to defeat Charles VII in the field, or they had to consider making peace with the Valois. It would be years before Henry VI could personally lead an army against King Charles and years of constant warfare had already drained the treasuries of both

England and Normandy. In May 1431, under pressure from the new pope, Eugenius IV,* the English council had first discussed the possibility of a truce with Charles VII. Eugenius was a fervent proponent of peace, hoping to unite the warring Christian princes so that together they could crush heresy in Europe. To this end he had sent Cardinal Niccolò Albergati to mediate between France, England and Burgundy. In November 1432, an English delegation met with Albergati and the French, but little was achieved. The following spring, they tried again.

In April 1433, for once, Henry's fractious uncles united in the cause of peace. Gloucester, Bedford and Cardinal Beaufort led an English embassy to Calais, which for the first time in a decade seriously considered defying Henry V's will. Henry V's wishes had cast a long shadow over his son's early reign. On his deathbed the late King Henry had demanded that his relatives refuse to treat with Charles VII and that they keep the French princes captured at Agincourt imprisoned until Henry VI was of age. Now the English suggested their willingness to ignore both of these stipulations. By sending its senior representatives, the Lancastrian government was clearly demonstrating its willingness to negotiate with Charles, and their readiness to consider releasing the French prisoners – even the commander of the French forces at Agincourt, Charles, duke of Orléans – was such that they brought the captives to Dover to fulfil a potential role as bargaining chips. Unfortunately, these conciliatory moves came to nothing. The English embassy loitered in the pale of Calais for a month but Charles's representatives never appeared. By June peace talks had once again been abandoned.[7]

The one demand that Henry V had made which was still just about upheld was his insistence on Anglo-Burgundian unity, but that too was strained almost to breaking point by Gloucester's war on Hainault and Philippe's desertion of Henry VI during his

* Eugenius was consecrated pope in March 1431.

coronation expedition. The death of Anne of Burgundy severed a last critical link between Philippe and Bedford, and deprived the alliance of one of its most important mediators. Without Anne's quiet but assured diplomacy to bind them together, Philippe and Bedford soon fell out. On 20 April 1433 Bedford remarried, to a young woman twenty-three years his junior and considered by the Burgundian chronicler Enguerrand de Monstrelet to be 'handsome, well made and lively'.[8] Philippe, the thrice-married father of fifteen bastards, could hardly begrudge Bedford his marriage, but he could find fault with the way the marriage had been arranged. Bedford's second wife was the seventeen-year-old Jaquetta of Luxembourg, the niece of Bedford's trusted ally Louis of Luxembourg. Since 1424 Louis had been chancellor of France for Henry VI, and was also a member of the Norman council. Jaquetta's family had remained fiercely loyal to the Anglo-Burgundian cause, and they also had links to the Holy Roman Emperor, Sigismund. However, Jaquetta's father, the count of St Pol, was a vassal of Philippe of Burgundy and should have sought the duke's permission before arranging his daughter's marriage. To add insult to injury, the wedding had taken place inside Burgundian territory, in the county of Artois.[9]

In May 1433, Cardinal Beaufort tried to reconcile the squabbling dukes at a conference at St Omer in the Pas-de-Calais. The town lay in Philippe's territories, so he expected Bedford to visit him first as a mark of respect. Bedford, as the regent of France, expected to have similar respect shown to him by Philippe. Since neither would make the first move, they both left St Omer without ever once meeting. They never saw each other again.[10]

Despite the strain on his relationship with Bedford, the duke of Burgundy was still willing to consider a rapprochement with Henry VI's regime if peace looked to be in his interests. To consider his possibilities, in summer 1433 he sent an ambassador, the Anglophile Hue de Lannoy, to England to report on the mood of the English council, and also on the young king himself. As he had refused to meet Henry during his coronation expedition, Philippe did not have much sense of how the boy was developing.

Lannoy met with Henry at his hunting lodge at Guildford, where he was enjoying 'a hunting and pleasure excursion' in June. He arrived early in the morning, catching Henry on his way from Mass. Lannoy thought the eleven-year-old Henry 'a very beautiful child and well grown'. With the good manners of a boy schooled in kingship since birth, Henry asked after Philippe in French, and he and Lannoy had 'some gracious conversation' before turning to the business at hand. They retired to a chamber where Henry's noblemen knelt around him as Lannoy read out letters from his master. Gloucester, Warwick and the new steward of Henry's household, William de la Pole, earl of Suffolk, all listened carefully. Perhaps also in attendance was Henry's ten-year-old cousin, Gilles of Brittany, who had joined the king's 'supreme academy' a year earlier. Gilles had been invited as an expression of English goodwill towards his father, Duke Jean V of Brittany, in the hope that Duke Jean would acknowledge Henry as king of France, and Henry had grown so attached to his cousin that the boy had stayed on at royal expense.[11]

Lannoy was able to report to Philippe of Burgundy that although nothing had yet been agreed, a number of senior English nobles had hopes of concluding a peace with France. He had 'heard it said' that a marriage between Henry VI and one of Charles VII's daughters was 'hurried on by certain people' in order to bring about 'general peace'. A likely source of these whispers was the earl of Suffolk, who told Lannoy that he had 'greater hope of a general peace [than he] ever had before'.[12] Now nearing forty, Suffolk had faithfully served the Lancastrian cause in France for most of his life. He had lost a brother and father in Henry V's Agincourt campaign – where he was himself injured – and been taken prisoner by Joan of Arc's army at Jargeau in 1429. After buying his freedom, Suffolk had retired from warfare and moved into politics, where he had demonstrated sufficient diplomatic skill to maintain good relations with both Bedford and Gloucester. In his early political career, Suffolk had a major asset in his wife, Alice Chaucer, widow of the earl of Salisbury who had died at Orléans and granddaughter of the poet Geoffrey Chaucer. Alice and Suffolk were well matched, both ambitious, cunning and charming but willing to be ruthless if necessary. They would come to be the leading influences of Henry's adolescence. For now, however, Suffolk was most noticeable to Lannoy as one of the few unstintingly friendly councillors at the English court. English feelings towards Philippe of Burgundy had soured since he made his treaty with Charles VII. Many 'harsh words' were 'heard daily... menacing [Philippe] and his lands.' Warwick, who was noticeably cool with Lannoy, explained that, 'we English, to tell you the truth, are exceedingly displeased and disappointed that whilst the king was in France, my lord of Burgundy, your master, has neither seen him nor visited him.'[13]

Even the usually diplomatic Cardinal Beaufort was 'somewhat stranger than before'. The hostility of the English lords was less revealing to Philippe, however, than the information contained at the end of Lannoy's report. As he was returning from England through Calais Lannoy happened to meet an emissary coming from Charles VII's court who told him that Charles refused to consider peace with England unless the imprisoned duke of Orléans was released and Henry gave up his French crown. 'On this point [Charles] would admit of no compromise.'[14]

Here was the insurmountable problem preventing peace between England and France. The English would not negotiate a peace that cost Henry his French crown and the French would not consider one that allowed him to keep it. Now that both Henry and Charles had been crowned, it was impossible for a treaty to be negotiated without one of them losing face. Philippe realized this uncomfortable truth far sooner than his fellow princes. And he resolved that if peace with both England and France proved untenable, he would ally with whichever of them served his interests better. His ties of kinship with Bedford were gone, and as 1434 dawned, he started building a closer

relationship instead with relatives loyal to Charles. The loss of
Anne of Burgundy would have serious long-term repercussions
for Henry's changeable ally.

On the eve of the duke of Bedford's return to England, in the
company of his new wife, there was a solar eclipse. Two days
before midsummer 1433, in the afternoon, the skies darkened
and 'people doubted and were sore afraid'.[15] It was a sinister
omen at a time when both England and France were beset with
troubles. Around Paris smallpox raged throughout the summer,
with a death rate so high it brought back memories of the Black
Death of 1348. The neighbouring town of St Marcel was taken
by Armagnacs and denuded of its citizens, the living carted away
to be ransomed, 'leaving hacked corpses and burning churches
behind them'. Armagnac fires blazed across France and into
Artois, and no farmers or cattle seemed safe. Meanwhile, England
was enduring a spate of lawlessness that unleashed 'murders,
homicides, rapes of women, robberies, arsons and numerous
other misdeeds' on its population.[16]

Bedford had come to England to gather support for another
campaign to regain control over Henry's French realm. If the
abortive peace talks with Charles recommenced, it was essential
that England was able to negotiate from a position of strength,
and if no truce was forthcoming, then they would have to fight
with renewed vigour to overcome Charles's growing advantage.
But there was another reason behind Bedford's return. His
friends in England had told him that rumours were being spread
against him, claims that his military mismanagement had placed
Henry's French crown in danger. This was an affront to Bedford's reputation that he could not let stand, especially when
the source of these rumours was almost certainly his brother
Gloucester.

Gloucester and Bedford had worked together as members of
the English embassy sent to Calais in the spring of 1433, but

little had fundamentally changed in the dynamic of their relationship. Gloucester still sniped jealously at his elder brother
and yearned for the superior power he possessed. Bedford was
as sensitive as ever to Gloucester's criticisms of his regency. He
confronted Gloucester on the now familiar Lancastrian family
battleground: across the parliament chamber. On 13 July, Henry
sat watching his uncles in the Painted Chamber of Westminster
Palace, as Bedford reported

> how a false and perverse belief was being put about and
> spread among very many people in the realm of England,
> namely that the damage and loss which our aforesaid lord
> king had sustained in his realm of France and in his duchy
> of Normandy must have resulted from the negligence and
> carelessness of [Bedford] himself, which was to the scandal of
> his person and to the grave damage of his name, reputation
> and honour.[17]

This matter so closely touched his honour that Bedford demanded that if any man wished to accuse him of such treasonable
mismanagement he should stand now and do so to his face.
'According to what the law of arms demands,' Bedford would
fight his accuser in single combat, even 'if the person should be
of equal or similar rank and birth'. As Bedford's words echoed
in the chamber the Lords and Commons shifted uneasily, more
than one eye surely coming to rest on Gloucester. Would the
relentless dispute between the two brothers finally end in blood?
But just as he had sat silently when challenged by Beaufort two
years earlier, Gloucester again refused to respond. The lords of
the council insisted 'that such profane and scandalous words
concerning the duke of Bedford have not previously come to'
their hearing. Henry, cast in the role of mediator once again,
added that he had 'always considered and held the aforesaid
duke of Bedford as his true and faithful liege and his dearest
uncle' and thanked him for his service as regent.[18]

Deprived of vengeance on Gloucester, Bedford contented himself with visiting retribution on his brother's allies. He replaced Gloucester's appointments in Henry's household with men more to his liking, among them the earl of Suffolk (who became Henry's steward) and Lord Cromwell, who was made treasurer in place of Gloucester's particular friend Lord Scrope. Any joy Cromwell felt at his new appointment would have been short-lived. On 18 October 1433 he came before the Lords of parliament grim-faced, asking them to inspect the books of accounts. The crown was not only seriously in debt – to the tune of £165,000 – but it was also running at a deficit of £22,000. There was not enough money in the royal treasury to cover Henry's annual household expenses, never mind fund the war with Charles VII.[19]

Cromwell's revelation left the lords struggling to find a solution to England's intractable economic problems but for Henry, the dire financial situation impacted on him only in that it forced a change from his usual Christmas residence at Eltham. To save the exchequer the regular festive expenses incurred in maintaining Henry's household, for four months he and his household lived at the expense of the abbot of Bury St Edmunds in Suffolk. He arrived in state on Christmas Eve 1433, his entourage so vast it stretched a mile along the road. He was escorted to the abbey by 500 local townspeople in red livery before being greeted by the monks of the abbey in their best robes. Through a mist of incense and holy water, he processed inside as an antiphon for St Edmund was sung, to pray at the martyr's shrine.

Until he left to celebrate St George's Day, as tradition dictated, at Windsor Castle, Henry lived on the abbot's generosity. And it was some generosity. To enable his various lodgings to be cleaned and refitted, Henry's household moved every few weeks between the best buildings in the precinct: the bishop's palace, a manor house 10 miles (16 km) outside of town and the prior's lodging. Henry had easy access to open country to amuse himself with hunting or fishing, and there were ponds to admire and enclosed vineyards to amble through. From time to time he would have gone inside the abbey in his furred robe, to escape the winter frost, and knelt on a luxurious carpet placed by his attendants before the shrine of St Edmund, the abbey's patron saint. In an illuminated image in a manuscript copy of John Lydgate's *The Lives of St Edmund and Fremund* Henry appears in this pose, hands clasped in prayer and eyes lost in the heavens while one of his attendants – perhaps Gloucester – languidly leans his sword against his shoulder. The poem was commissioned by the abbot, a copy of it created by the monks and presented to Henry as a memento of the king's time with them. It was yet another theoretical work that sought to teach Henry how to rule by the example of long-dead monarchs. Before they left Bury, his uncle Gloucester was admitted to the fraternity of the monastery and Henry asked if he, too, could be enrolled, although he was too young. A special ceremony was laid on in his honour in the chapter house.[20]

Henry's time at Bury was to prove an oasis of calm in yet another season of strife between his uncles. Shortly before he set off for the abbey, the Commons presented a petition to Henry in parliament pleading for Bedford to remain in England a while longer, claiming that since his arrival 'the peaceful rule and governance of this realm has... greatly grown'. Their appeal was a blow to the duke of Gloucester, for as long as Bedford remained in England, he took precedence as Henry's chief councillor. Moreover, as the price of staying longer than anticipated, Bedford was able to negotiate an extension of his powers. He was granted the authority to nominate councillors personally, and to prevent any councillor from being dismissed without his permission, even once he returned to France – a clear effort to stymie any future attempts by Gloucester to pack the council with his own supporters. As a sop to popular opinion, Bedford took a pay cut of almost a quarter and insisted that funds be set aside to care for a number of ageing Lancastrian retainers in their old age. That all of this was granted within a month, while

Gloucester had been wrangling over such issues for more than a decade, must have done little to improve fraternal relations.[21]

Gloucester's reaction to Bedford taking his place in England was to attempt to usurp his brother in France. On 26 April 1434, a matter of days after Henry had left the calm of Bury St Edmunds, Gloucester put a plan before the great council in Westminster for a massive attack on Charles VII. His intention was to raise an army from £50,000 in loans, using the crown jewels as security. He would then lead this army to France himself. The scheme was unrealistic and wholly impractical, as the lords of Henry's council must have realized. But Bedford saw Gloucester's suggestion as yet another attack on his regency, and Gloucester read Bedford's appalled reaction as a slight on his honour. On 8 May Henry appeared in council himself to settle the dispute. Although he was still only twelve, such feuds between princes of the blood royal could only be resolved by the monarch. Henry's uncles had prepared speeches and documents in support of their arguments but Henry refused to let them present them, demanding that they hand the papers over to him for destruction. He insisted that neither of them had had their honour besmirched and that their dissension must end 'so that love and friendship could reign'. He felt respect and gratitude for both his uncles, he told them, and that must be the end of the matter.[22]

This was, in essence, the same tactic that Bedford had used in the 'parliament of bats' after Gloucester and Beaufort had torn London apart with their feud. Henry appeared to cherish a child-like belief that ambitious and powerful men would put aside their quarrels and suppress all rancour simply because he told them to. No more was heard of Gloucester's plan, although Bedford was sufficiently stung by his brother's criticism that he presented articles to the council in June to discharge him of any blame in the wars since 1422. In early July 1434, Bedford left England to resume his campaign in Normandy. Essential though the Commons considered his presence to be to the maintenance of law and order in England, Bedford believed the needs of the dual monarchy were more immediate.[23]

In his brother's absence, Gloucester was once again embold-ened to encourage Henry to assert his right to greater authority. If he was sufficiently trusted to resolve his uncles' dispute, Henry might well feel, then surely he should be trusted with further powers of kingship – the authority to guide policy, perhaps, and make binding royal grants. But still his council resisted. Without Gloucester present, they appeared en masse before Henry at Cirencester in November 1434 to warn him not to be misled by the 'stirrings and motions' of others into assuming his governance too early. A lengthy 'protestation' was read 'word for word' by the chancellor, John Stafford, bishop of Bath and Wells, advising Henry that he still lacked the necessary 'foresight and discretion to depart and choose, namely in matters of great weight and difficulty' and that 'until by cognition and by hearing, seeing and experience he be further grown and increased in feeling and knowledge of that that belongeth to good rule and governance' he ought not to seek to assume greater responsibility.[24]

As the council were all too aware, if Henry had chosen to overrule them and demand unfettered power, even at twelve years old, he could do so; but instead, having listened solemnly to the protracted lecture on his immaturity, Henry bowed to conciliar rule and agreed to submit to their government a while longer. This in itself demonstrated that Henry was not yet capable of exerting independent authority, for it confirmed the council's suspicion that the real impetus behind Henry's apparent desire for power had come not from the king himself, but from Gloucester. Without his uncle to shore up his resolve, Henry easily gave in. This was a source of grave concern to his noblemen. The vital ingredient of medieval kingship was royal will – the ability to take counsel from a number of sources but ultimately to commit to a policy of one's own and impose it on others. Susceptibility to influence and mutability such as Henry was demonstrating suggested a worrying lack of willpower. And a firmness of royal will would be sorely needed in the months ahead, for the dual monarchy was about to face the greatest threat of Henry's reign so far.

9

'Treason walking'[1]

Arras, Burgundian Artois
6 September 1435

As rain lashed against the stones of St Vaast Abbey, Cardinal Beaufort and an escort of Englishmen hurried from the colonnades, their faces darker than the lowering skies. They mounted their horses swiftly, the downpour drenching their expensive vermilion livery. On the sleeves of Beaufort's men, the word 'honour' flashed as they rode away. What had begun as a peace conference between representatives of England, Burgundy and France had ended in bitter recriminations and cries of betrayal. For months Beaufort and his English embassy had striven to make peace, to protect King Henry's French realm, but all their efforts had been in vain. Now Philippe of Burgundy was resolved to ally with their enemy, Charles VII. Barely four years since Henry's coronation in Paris, the foundation of his rule in France had been destroyed.

Despite Philippe's mounting discontent with his English allies, neither Beaufort nor Henry had seen this coming. Yet Philippe had been laying the groundwork for his abandonment of Henry's cause for almost two years. Since the murder of his father, Jean the Fearless, by Charles's men on the bridge at Montereau in

1419, Philippe had largely dedicated his services to campaigning with the English. But he had never forgotten that he came from a line of French princes. Recently he had forged new connections with his relatives among the French aristocracy, many of whom were eager to mediate between Philippe and Charles, to unite the French armies – and expel the English from their lands. Family gatherings had provided an ideal cover for diplomatic talks, particularly with Philippe's brothers-in-law Charles, duke of Bourbon, and Arthur de Richemont. Bourbon, who was married to Philippe's sister Agnes, had inherited his title on his father's death in February 1434. The late duke of Bourbon had been one of the unfortunate French princes taken prisoner at Agincourt, and he had ended his days in English captivity almost twenty years later. Philippe's older sister Marguerite had married the Breton Arthur de Richemont as part of the tripartite alliance negotiated with Bedford at Amiens in 1423. From the outset, however, Richemont had proved an unreliable ally to Bedford, choosing to fight the English in the army of Joan of Arc at the Battle of Patay. It had been at the wedding of another relative of Philippe's by marriage, the son of the duke of Savoy,* in February 1434 that a Franco-Burgundian alliance was first seriously discussed.

By January 1435 the conversation had grown more intense, and the duke of Bourbon, Richemont and Philippe reunited at Nevers in Philippe's territories. This time, the trio were joined by Charles VII's chancellor, Regnault de Chartres, a leading advocate of peace with Burgundy. Charles knew that Philippe was growing frustrated with the relentless expense and effort of supporting the English in their war, when his own interests lay to the north, in uniting the Low Countries under his sovereignty. Through Regnault, Charles offered his adversary the opportunity for a lasting peace between them. If Philippe became his ally,

---

* The duke of Savoy was married to Philippe's aunt Marie.

and the English refused to come to terms, then Philippe could hold a vast sweep of lands that Charles had previously claimed for the French crown: from Ponthieu and the major towns along the River Somme to the north, to Auxerre and the Mâconnais further south. Although these lands would be held in homage, Philippe would not have to bend his knee as vassal to Charles in his own lifetime. On the thorny issue of the murder of Jean the Fearless, Charles was willing to make public atonement and reparation. All of this was enough to convince Philippe that his interests now lay in an alliance with Charles. He notified Henry VI that he was going to meet Charles's representatives in a formal conference at Arras on 1 July 1435, and if the English could not also agree a truce with Charles then he would renounce his English allegiance and make a treaty with him alone.[2]

By now Philippe was publicly promoting the House of Burgundy as the champion of peace. In Easter 1435 he visited Paris with his wife Isabella, their infant son and a handful of 'very good-looking youngsters not born in marriage'. During the stay, a large gathering of women from the city appeared before Duchess Isabella and begged her to 'take the kingdom's peace under her own protection'. 'My dear friends,' the duchess replied, 'it is one of the things that I most long for in this world.'[3] The people of Paris had good reason to make such an appeal, having borne the brunt of the wars in France for thirty years, but the women's visit may not have been as spontaneous as it appeared. It was probably a set piece to add weight to Philippe's self-representation as mediator and pacifier in the Anglo-French war. He was doing everything possible to ensure that he emerged from the congress at Arras as peacemaker. If that meant that England must appear the villain, then so be it.

At first, Henry's advisers were so offended at the news that Philippe planned to make a treaty with Charles VII that they were inclined to stay away from Arras altogether. It went completely against the terms of the Treaty of Troyes for Philippe to make an agreement unilaterally, without the permission of Henry and the Three Estates of England. But as summer approached, it became clear that they would have little choice but to attend. Pope Eugenius IV chastised the English for not showing better willingness to conciliate and sent two of his cardinals to Arras: Niccolò Albergati, cardinal priest of Santa Croce, and Hugues de Lusignan, cardinal of Cyprus. Representatives from Sicily, Spain, Portugal, Denmark, Poland and Italy were also invited to the meeting, so by 5 July 1435 the English council reluctantly agreed to send their own delegation. John Kempe, archbishop of York, led the ecclesiastical contingent to Arras, while the English lords in attendance were all experienced in French affairs, having commanded armies against the Armagnacs in the past: John Holland, earl of Huntingdon; William de la Pole, earl of Suffolk; and Walter, Lord Hungerford. Cardinal Beaufort joined the embassy late in the day, arriving on 23 August. The fact that even as negotiations went on, the English and French were fighting for control of St Denis did little to suggest their desire for reconciliation.[4]

Negotiations proceeded in a fog of mistrust and ill will, the pope's cardinals scurrying back and forth between the delegations with offers and counter-offers. It proved impossible even to have the French and English in the same room for divine service, so sensitive were the issues of honour and precedence that would have to be overcome first. Who would enter the chamber first? Where would they stand? Who should kneel to whom? As representatives of Kings Henry and Charles, the English and French ambassadors could not yield on the slightest point of honour until an agreement had been reached. That was, if one could be reached at all.

The first offer made by the French delegation under Arthur de Richemont, Charles of Bourbon and Regnault de Chartres was risible. They offered the English the same terms that had been rejected by Henry V in July 1415, before he won the Battle of Agincourt: Henry VI must do homage to Charles VII for the lands he held in France, including the duchy of Normandy. Since this would make Henry the vassal of his enemy, the English rejected it outright. The English delegation in turn demanded that Charles surrender the kingdom to Henry as the true king of France, a request that was never going to be accepted. It was expected that the French and English would start with absurdly optimistic demands and chip away at each other until a compromise was reached, but the tone of proceedings suggested that no deal would ever satisfy both parties. Every offer made was met with mockery and derision, the French delegation turning from the table in disgust, the English laughing in contempt. Lord Hungerford said one French proposal was like 'being offered an apple by a child'.[5] Cardinal Albergati observed that both sides claimed everything for themselves and wanted to give away nothing.[6]

Cardinal Beaufort valiantly attempted to salvage something from the conference in its dying days, defying diplomatic protocol to hold a private interview with Philippe of Burgundy. He pleaded so fervently with the duke that sweat beaded on his forehead. It made no difference: the final French offer was still too partisan for the English to accept. Charles would allow Henry to hold Normandy and some parts of Picardy in homage, and arrange his marriage to a French princess. In return, Henry must release the duke of Orléans and wholly renounce his French crown. It was impossible for the ambassadors to accept such conditions. Beaufort and the English delegates left Arras on 6 September. As Beaufort rode away he swore that he would now commit his vast resources to fighting for Henry's rights in France.[7]

Once the English had abandoned the talks, Philippe of Burgundy was free to renounce his loyalty to Henry and make an alliance with Charles VII. The pope's cardinals absolved him of the obligations attached to the Treaty of Troyes, since to abide by it would endanger his soul and commit him to further bloodshed. Henry's regime was condemned as unreasonable and antagonistic. On 21 September 1435, at four minutes past seven in the evening, Philippe made his treaty with Charles. The Anglo-Burgundian alliance was dead.[8]

In England, Henry VI received confirmation of the treaty in a letter from Philippe himself. Henry read it in front of his councillors, with Cardinal Beaufort and Gloucester present. When he saw that the letters addressed him only as king of England, not as Philippe's sovereign lord, Henry realized he had been betrayed and burst into tears. He announced to Gloucester and the councillors nearby that he saw that Philippe was disloyal now, and he feared 'that his dominions in France would fare the worse for it'. Henry's family reacted, characteristically, by turning on each other. Beaufort and Gloucester 'abruptly left the council much confused and vexed... and collected in a small knot and abused each other as well as the duke of Burgundy'.[9] Twenty years later, the memory of Burgundian betrayal still stung Henry. In 1456 he confided to a French ambassador that Philippe was the only man he would like to make war on, and he intended to do it, 'because he abandoned me in my boyhood, despite all his oaths to me, when I had never done him any wrong'. For a man who sometimes forgave too easily, Henry's lingering resentment of Philippe shows how keenly he felt this abandonment.[10]

Henry was not alone in feeling bitterness towards Philippe and his countrymen. His subjects were outraged at Philippe's perfidy for making an alliance with their enemy. The Burgundian chronicler Enguerrand de Monstrelet described the violent revenge Englishmen took on his compatriots and other foreigners:

> No one... was sparing of the grossest abuse against the duke of Burgundy and his country. Many of the common people collected together, and went to different parts of [London] to search for Flemings, Dutchmen, Brabanters, Picards, Hainaulters and other foreigners, to use them ill... Several were seized in the heat of their rage and murdered.[11]

Ambassadors sent by Philippe to Henry heard similar expressions of anger everywhere they went, and they received little of 'that civility they used formerly' to enjoy from the English. In parliament the chancellor, John Stafford, bishop of Bath and Wells, railed against the faithless duke of Burgundy in his opening address. War, he suggested, was imminent.[12]

There was some justification in English accusations of Burgundian double-dealing. After Burgundy and France agreed peace terms the men and women of the Burgundian party who had argued most vehemently for the alliance received large payments from the French crown. Among their number was the duke's closest adviser and favourite, Anthoine, lord of Croy, who received 10,000 gold *saluts*.* Even Isabella, duchess of Burgundy, had not been inspired to argue for a French alliance solely out of her desire for peace or the appeals of the women of France. When the treaty was agreed, she received an annual payment of £4,000 in thanks.[13] The Burgundians were handsomely rewarded for turning their coats.

The architect of the Anglo-Burgundian alliance never learnt the full details of their ally's betrayal. The week after the English ambassadors abandoned the congress at Arras, before three o'clock on the morning of 14 September, the duke of Bedford died in Rouen, worn down by the efforts of defending Henry's French crown. In accordance with his wishes, he was buried on the north side of the choir of Rouen Cathedral, near the high altar and the royal tombs of his Norman ancestors. As executors of his will he named his trusted allies: Cardinal Beaufort, Louis of Luxembourg and Ralph, Lord Cromwell. The name of his brother Gloucester was conspicuously absent.[14]

Bedford's death was followed, ten days later, by that of Queen Isabeau of France. Henry's grandmother had spent the last years of her life 'in great poverty' in the Hôtel de Saint-Pol, Paris. English victory in the siege of St Denis, which was captured in early October, meant that her body could be buried in the

* A gold *salut* was worth about a third of a pound.

French royal tomb at the abbey, but the proximity of Armagnac forces made the roads too dangerous to travel, so Isabeau had to be conveyed to her resting place by boat along the River Seine.[15]

The victory at St Denis was a solitary ray of light in a year that saw Henry's realm gripped by the deepest crisis of his reign so far. The commander of the English forces, the twenty-seven-year-old earl of Arundel, was killed trying to quash a rebellion in Normandy, his leg shot to pieces by an Armagnac gun and amputated in an unsuccessful attempt to stop the wound festering. West of St Denis, the vital bridge town of Meulan was lost, cutting off a supply route between Normandy and Paris. As autumn gave way to winter, the Armagnacs breached Norman defences, capturing the seaports of Dieppe in late October and Harfleur the day after Christmas. By early 1436 Armagnac and Burgundian forces moved to take two of the last remaining lynchpins of Henry's rule: the capital city of Paris and the vital staple port of Calais. With French forces resurgent, Bedford dead and the Anglo-Burgundian alliance in tatters, a ruling king had never been needed more. The rising threat to Henry's French realm demanded a tangible head of state to rally his subjects to the defence of the dual monarchy. Despite the misgivings of the council and the earl of Warwick, the needs of his two realms demanded that Henry finally take up the reins of government for himself. The minority of Henry VI was coming to an end.[16]

10

'The royal crown
is in the hand of God'[1]

Canterbury
26 July 1436

'Stir the hearts' of the people, the commissioners had been told as they radiated across the counties of England in the early summer of 1436, eager for loans of men and money: remind listeners 'what a precious jewel the said town of Calais is to the realm, what profit and refreshing growth' it provided and what 'dishonour, rebuke, slander and shame' would attach itself to England if the town was lost. It had been announced that the English forces protecting Calais would be led, for the first time, by King Henry himself. He would imitate his warrior father and ride with his forces to war. The commissioners did their jobs well. Unprecedented sums flooded into the royal treasury from loyal Englishmen and women, eager to give their money to the cause. Along the coast of Kent the fruits of these loans rocked at anchor in the Channel ports: aboard these ships of war a vast force of 8,000 soldiers, archers and sailors geared themselves for the defence of Calais. A few hours away, across the Channel, an army commanded by the perfidious Philippe of Burgundy was advancing through the sand dunes and marshes towards Calais.[2]

As he sat within his comfortable chambers at Canterbury, in the midst of these military preparations, Henry took up pen and ink. With a scratching flourish he wrote his name, 'Henry', on a piece of vellum – a simple gesture that had enormous significance. The document was a release of 5,000 marks to his uncle Gloucester, and it was the first grant Henry had made on his personal authority alone. Now by the mere act of signing his name, Henry had the power to bestow titles, estates, marriages and sums of money. He was no longer ruling through his council. The adult rule of Henry VI was beginning at last.[3]

The fourteen-year-old king was by now growing tall and strong, with the long limbs and auburn hair of his Plantagenet ancestors, though he still had a pale, wide face that made him appear younger than he really was. Around this time Henry was visited by a papal diplomat called Piero da Monte who left a sketch of his impressions of the king on the verge of adulthood. Da Monte was impressed by Henry's quiet dignity and wisdom beyond his years, and particularly struck by the teenage king's concern for religious matters. He found him 'not to be a king or worldly prince' but 'more religious than a man of religion'.[4] Henry greeted all representatives of the church respectfully, calling them 'father', and took due care and attention with his religious devotions. Unlike many of his subjects, who would wander about the church during Mass, making jokes or talking business, Henry arrived early at church, knelt in prayer and kept his eyes and hands upturned throughout, his lips moving instinctively with the priest's liturgy.[5]

It is little surprise that, as he grew up, Henry's enjoyment of religious ritual outstripped that of most of his contemporaries. His time at Mass was one of the few occasions when he could legitimately be alone with his thoughts. For his entire life, his private moments had been interrupted by the demands of government: at Eltham, a duke knocking at his door as he was immersed in reading; at Windsor, his study interrupted by a councillor. Henry did not often express annoyance, but he 'complained heavily' when he was not allowed to be at peace with himself in his own palace. 'They do so interrupt me,' he told his confessor and later biographer John Blacman, 'that by day or night I can scarcely snatch a moment to be refreshed by reading of any holy teaching without disturbance.' His temper tantrum as an infant when he was dragged from a roadside inn to parliament was only unusual in that Henry put up such noisy resistance. In general, the king was notably quiet even when irritated, using 'very brief speech' and trying 'always to speak truth' – which, in the flattering and divisive world of politics, may be one and the same impulse. He was notable for abhorring swearing, and the strongest oath he used was the mild 'Forsooth and forsooth'.[6]

When he indulged his leisure hours, Henry generally prefer-red solitary activities, although reports that he disliked hunting and plays are demonstrably false. John Blacman claimed Henry 'despised as trifling' 'vain sports and pursuits'. Piero da Monte suggested in 1437 that he hated 'scurrilous pageants... mimes and plays' but Henry watched plays and disguisings throughout his life, and the king's accounts demonstrate that he enjoyed hunting. He spent the summer of 1435 hunting in Rockingham Forest in Northamptonshire, staying at Higham Ferrers castle until Michaelmas 1435, and between 1435 and 1446 there was extensive renovation of the royal hunting lodge of Clipstone in Sherwood Forest.[7]

The time Henry spent cloistered with books of history and religion had left him with a serious-minded piety, and an unusual degree of prudishness for an adolescent prince. Da Monte noted that the gawky teenager 'flees the sight and speech of women'. John Blacman agreed that Henry 'was chaste and pure from the beginning of his days. He eschewed all licentiousness in word or deed while he was young; until he was of marriageable age', utterly avoiding 'the unguarded sight of naked persons' and 'never look[ing] unchastely upon any woman'. One Christmas a nobleman brought 'young ladies with bared bosoms who were to dance in that guise before the king' but Henry 'spurned the delusion and very angrily averted his eyes, turned his back upon them and went out to his chamber saying *Fy fy for shame forsooth ye be to blame*. Although Henry's reaction at first seems excessive, it is likely that the women were not merely dancers, but prostitutes stripping 'off their clothes as they danced'. In that context, his rejection of the lord's dancing girls makes more sense. They were an inappropriate and unwanted diversion for a young king disturbed by the lascivious sexuality of the court, and it is tempting to see the duke of Gloucester's hand behind such a dangerously impolitic entertainment.[8]

Henry's concern for chastity may have been a result of over-zealous education on the part of the earl of Warwick and Dr John Somerset. Books of education were full of advice to avoid lechery and 'fleshly love'. According to the works of Vegetius and the didactic text, *Secreta Secretorum*, both of which were popular educational texts for medieval nobility, lechery was the root of vice:

> Fleshly love engenders avarice, avarice engenders desire of riches, desire of riches makes a man without shame; man without shame is proud and without faith; man without faith draws to theft; theft brings a man to endless shame, and so comes a man to captivity and to final destruction of his body.[9]

Henry set more store by these lessons than most of his contemporaries. Sexual licence in aristocratic men was permitted to the extent that even Henry's great-uncle, Cardinal Beaufort, had an illegitimate daughter. Sumptuary legislation* allowed sexually suggestive clothing that showed off a man's buttocks, crotch and legs for the nobility only. Perhaps Henry was inspired by his father's example. While all of Henry V's brothers had illegitimate

---

* Sumptuary laws regulated clothing that might be worn according to social status.

children, the king noticeably did not. Nor had he allowed women any real authority within his court. Henry VI was not instinctively militaristic as his father had been, but he could imitate the late king's virtue with his chastity.[10]

Henry's behaviour as described by da Monte in 1437 largely accorded with the expected demeanour of a prince, although the king's naivety and excessive piety might have raised eyebrows. Kings ought to be chaste, gentle and devout, but not to the detriment of their authority. Kings also needed to bear children, lead armies and dispense justice, all of which required more energy and strength of will than Henry demonstrated. According to the contemporary theory that linked celestial phenomena with the four humours that made up all human bodies, none of this was surprising.* Born in the depths of winter, when the sun was weakest and the watery moon at its most influential, Henry was a classic phlegmatic, inclined to be internally wet and cold. Temperamentally, the planetary conditions and his humoral imbalance meant he would be lethargic, vacillating, too quick to forgive and inattentive. The influence of the moon made him feminine and unwarlike, and potentially even inclined him to mental instability. Henry was a healthy adolescent, and his physicians would have tailored his diet and exercise regime to counter his natural inclination towards these gentle and unmanly qualities, but some of Henry's personal traits were already worryingly close to the negative stereotype of a phlegmatic.[11]

It was precisely because Henry was easily led and occasionally absent-minded that his council had been unwilling to allow him to rule until Bedford's death and the collapse of the Anglo-Burgundian alliance made it essential. As recently as November

---

* Humoral theory held that all humans were made up of four humours: blood, phlegm, black bile, and choler (also known as yellow bile). An imbalance in one of these humours would cause illness of the mind and body.

1434 the idea of him taking control of government for himself
had been such a concern to the council that they had confronted him at Cirencester to explain why he was still too young to
rule autonomously.[12] Yet within a year of this intervention, on
1 October 1435, Henry attended his first council meeting with
Cardinal Beaufort, Warwick and Gloucester. Two months after
that it was announced in a letter to the Norman estates that
Henry was attending to affairs of state himself. By May 1436
the earl of Warwick was dismissed as Henry's master, and Henry
assumed control of the privy seal used to authenticate royal
decisions. The council continued to take responsibility for most
state business, but the power of royal grace – to grant lands and
money by seal or, increasingly, by signature alone – was now fully
in Henry's hands.[13]

In the summer of 1436 Henry was approaching his fifteenth
birthday, an age at which many young men of status went to
war and exercised authority. But although Henry had a strong
theoretical grasp of what a king should be, he had no real
experience to match, as the council had been at pains to point
out to him in 1434. Yet how was he to gain such experience
unless he was given some authority? Henry grew up watching a
team of older, more experienced figures rule for him. He never
saw kingship in action. Even when Bedford mediated the feud
between Gloucester and Beaufort in 1426, he was careful to do so
in Henry's presence and couched in language that made it clear
he was acting *for* the king. It was statesmanlike behaviour, but it
was not kingship. The closest Henry ever came to witnessing the
exercise of kingly power was by reading about the deeds of dead
kings in his books. Even as he was given more power, the central
contradiction of his childhood – that, as king, he was held up as
ultimate authority and yet wielded no actual influence, was not
resolved. He was encouraged to mistrust his own judgement and
delegate authority to others even while his councillors made it
clear they expected him to grow up to be a man like his father:
strong-willed, authoritative and fair-minded – but ruthless when

necessary. To be held to the standard of someone whose exploits he could only ever know second hand was yet another challenge that Henry's upbringing imposed on him.

For most aristocratic young men, their most formative experience would be going to war. Henry's father and uncles Bedford and Clarence all had military experience by the time they were sixteen and Henry V had accompanied the retinue of Richard II on a military campaign to Ireland when he was only eleven. Their grandfather, John of Gaunt, had been a mere ten years old when he watched the bloody Battle of Winchelsea from aboard his father Edward III's ship in 1350. Charles VII, who saw his enemy Jean the Fearless butchered in front of him at sixteen, had ridden at the head of his army in full armour as a teenager, displaying his device of an armoured hand grasping a naked sword. Educational works advised that youths should learn the art of warfare in their mid-teens, although it was common for military training to take place earlier among the warrior class of the aristocracy. Henry's military training had probably begun in 1428, when the earl of Warwick took over his household; at that time 'little cote armours' were made for him. When he went on his coronation expedition, aged eight, he took a newly commissioned suit of armour, garnished with gold. Many of the lay lords serving on Henry's council in 1436 had been to war while in their late teens, or only just out of them.[14]

For Henry to lead an army to France in his early teens was not, then, unthinkable and by 1436 it looked like it might be highly necessary. The whole coastline of upper Normandy and Picardy had been lost. The Pays de Caux* had rebelled and additional forces had to be sent to strengthen the Norman capital Rouen, 'for,' as a contemporary London chronicler lamented, 'there was so much treason walking' that even the capital of the duchy was not safe.[15] How far English fortunes had fallen became clear

---

* The Pays de Caux is a chalk plateau in northern Normandy between the Seine estuary and the Channel coastline.

in April when Paris fell to Armagnac and Burgundian forces, a matter of weeks after the citizens had sworn an oath 'on pain of their souls' damnation to be true and loyal to King Henry of England'. The Parisians threw ladders over the walls for the enemy to enter, tore the red crosses of St George from their clothing and exchanged them for the St Andrew's cross. To rub salt in the wound, one of the commanders who took the capital was the Burgundian Lord de l'Isle-Adam, who had only recently defected from service with the English.[16] Even England itself was not safe. In February 1436 James I of Scotland took advantage of his neighbour's weakness to besiege Roxburgh Castle on the border. The fortress was bombarded for twelve days before James turned back in the face of an approaching English army.[17]

By spring 1436 the town of Calais was an isolated English outpost surrounded by Armagnac forces with the seas left in the care of privateers – lawless men whose sole qualification was the possession of a ship. In March 1436 Henry learnt that Philippe of Burgundy was marching on Calais with 60,000 men and a formidable force of siege engines. The news sparked a wave of xenophobic violence in London, where the government demanded that Flemings take an oath of fealty to Henry in return for protection. Despite the oaths, attacks on immigrant merchants continued and in London Flemish brewers were boycotted for brewing beer that was 'poisonous, not fit to drink and caused drunkenness'.[18]

To protect Calais was essential, but the financial problems that had dogged Henry's minority had not abated. In order to gather sufficient forces to defend the town from Philippe of Burgundy's army, a considerable outlay of money would be needed. This was why the council had appointed commissioners to gather loans and why, to bolster support from a nation 'so tired of war that they are more or less desperate', Henry was named captain of the Calais forces.[19] Whether born of anxiety about losing Calais or concern for their young king, the loans yielded an astonishing amount of money. Between April and July 1436 sixty-three individual loans raised more than £4,000 while the total raised between Michaelmas (29 September) 1435 and Easter 1436 was more than £48,000. With this sum the English were able to field their largest army of the decade.[20]

In spite of the council's promise, when the English army set sail for Calais Henry was not at its head. It had been decided in the end that the risk to his person would be too great. Although he would have acted solely as a figurehead, and remained safely behind the front line, on campaign Henry might still fall ill or into enemy hands. His father had fought in battle at sixteen, but his father had been one of four sons, whereas Henry's only heir was his forty-five-year-old uncle Gloucester. If misadventure befell Henry in his first campaign, it would redouble Armagnac and Burgundian faith in their own cause and deal a crushing blow to English morale. His life, in the end, was too precious a commodity to imperil. Instead, Gloucester gained the command he had long sought and was put in charge of the enormous English army sent to fight his old nemesis Philippe of Burgundy.

It took time to assemble Gloucester's army, which would form the core of English resistance, so in May 5,000 men accompanied the newly appointed lieutenant-general of Normandy, Richard, duke of York, and the earls of Salisbury and Suffolk to retake fortresses in the Pays de Caux. Earlier the same month 2,000 men under Cardinal Beaufort's nephew Edmund Beaufort had been diverted from Maine to hold Calais until Gloucester's army arrived. As Gloucester's force of 8,000 men was mustering in Kent, Henry made his first grant to his uncle, following it on 30 July with a grant of the county of Flanders, an over-optimistic piece of patronage given that the territory was still in the possession of Philippe of Burgundy. Two days later, Gloucester's vast forces crossed the Channel, only to find that the siege was already over.[21]

When Gloucester stepped ashore on 2 August he saw a trail of wine barrels and canvas scattered along the coastline, and siege engines grounded on the sand dunes, but the Burgundian army had fled after only three weeks. Although Philippe of Burgundy had managed to blockade Calais on its landward side, it had proved impossible to stop supplies from arriving by sea. Philippe's fleet arrived too late, and his attempt to prevent English vessels from reaching port by scuttling ships at the harbour mouth failed when the boats grounded on the sands at low tide. The grateful citizens of Calais ran out with axes under the eyes of their besiegers and pillaged the defenceless vessels for firewood. Philippe himself almost lost his life when a cannon shot close to him killed a trumpeter and three horses. In Gloucester's absence, Edmund Beaufort had sapped Burgundian morale with pillaging raids and a daring attack on an enemy tower, which was celebrated in triumphalist newsletters sent back to England. The advance forces of Gloucester's massive fleet, under Lord Welles, had appeared on 28 July, making such a display of might that Philippe's troops believed the entire English army had arrived ahead of schedule, and promptly mutinied. Philippe was forced to chase after his own men as they retreated from Calais.[22]

Gloucester was thus denied the opportunity for a glorious battle against his enemy. Not content to let a good army go to waste, Gloucester launched an eleven-day raid into west Flanders, pillaging, burning down settlements and generally disseminating panic through Philippe's domains. It was an inglorious endeavour, but such were Gloucester's powers of self-promotion that by the time the story of his exploits reached London he had become the hero of the siege. Xenophobic rhymes swirled around the city, mocking the 'false foresworn' Philippe and his cowardly countrymen, and praising the English lions and their warrior captain. The nation had united around the defence of Calais, and all the other English losses were briefly forgotten.

In the parliament that met in 1437 Gloucester was praised for his military exertions. Although Henry had not, in the end, blooded himself at Calais, his progression to independent rule was celebrated with a literary flourish in the chancellor's opening speech. John Stafford, bishop of Bath and Wells, interpreted the crown on Henry's head, adorned with gold and metal flowers, and decorated with precious jewels, as 'the symbol of government and public affairs of the realm': Henry's subjects were the gold, and the flowers represented the royal dignity. Stafford advised Henry that 'prudence should be placed at the front of the crown... adorned with three jewels, to wit, recollection of the past, circumspection of the present, and foresight of the future'. Henry's advisers had spent the past decade and a half recalling the legacy of his father, and cautiously working day to day to maintain his authority in his two realms. But now it was time to look to the future.[23]

At the feast of All Saints (1 November) 1437, Henry appeared before his court at Merton Priory in a crown-wearing ceremony, the golden fleur-de-lys on his coronet glistening. His old master, the earl of Warwick, was in the chamber that day, observing what may have been a formal assumption of power by the young king. In a similarly cloistered environment, at the Hospital of St John in Clerkenwell, London, on 12 November, Henry's council were formally re-appointed and granted powers based on the council established for his grandfather in 1406. Their authority was decreased – from now on no matters of weight were to be decided without the king's advice. Any disputes between the lords were henceforward to be referred directly to Henry to settle. Nineteen councillors were given new commissions by the king, Gloucester and Cardinal Beaufort's names at the top of the list. At one month shy of sixteen, Henry was finally stepping out of the shadow of his council and beginning his reign as an adult.[24]

PART II

Adult Rule

11

'A fixed purpose'[1]

Sheen Palace
11 October 1440

The crenellated keep of Windsor Castle stood serene above a scene of intense activity. In a quarry beneath the palace, chalk and flint were hewn from the earth to be banked into white-hot furnaces nearby, steadily spewing out lime to set between the clay-red bricks fired in vast ovens 2 miles (3 km) across the river. Windsor Park was no quieter. Here, as throughout the forested reaches of the Thames Valley, axe and chisel strikes echoed as timber fell, a cacophony of noise greeting the barges plying their way upriver. The ships came weighted down with Newcastle sea-coal and Derbyshire lead, even with the famed white stone of Normandy. Local roads were ground into ruts by the pressure of the traffic pouring over them. The focus of this activity was what had once been a poor parish church at Eton in the shadow of Windsor. All this – furnace fires, quarries, smithies, ships – was set in motion by Henry, as his nineteenth birthday neared, with the scratch of his signature on to the page of a charter of foundation, a legacy in brickwork and stone to celebrate Henry's assumption of adult power.[2]

As Henry wrote in the charter that prompted this flurry of

architectural activity, he had 'carefully revolved in our mind how, or in what manner, or by what royal gift' he could commemorate having 'now taken into our hands the government of both our kingdoms'. When he reached his 'riper age' – as the serious-minded king considered his late teenage years – he came to a decision:

> At length, while we were thinking over these things with the most profound attention, it has become a fixed purpose in our heart to found a college, in honour and in support of that our Mother [the Virgin Mary], who is so great and so holy, in the parochial church of Eton near Windsor, not far from our birthplace.[3]

Henry's plan for Eton was to convert a local parish church dedicated to the Assumption of the Virgin Mary into a college of priests with an adjoining almshouse and school, catering in all to the needs of seventy men and boys. The new foundation would be known as the 'Royal College of the Blessed Mary at Eton near Windsor', and in return for Henry's beneficence, all those supported at the college would pray for the souls of Henry's parents.[4]

English kings had always been builders, whether of fortresses, abbeys or palaces. Sheen Palace, where Henry signed his charter founding Eton College, stood as a vivid testament to this fact: Richard II had first enriched and then destroyed the palace in the late fourteenth century, tearing it down in despair when his queen died, for reminding him too painfully of happier times. In the next century Henry V had spent more than £8,000 restoring Sheen to its former glory, importing brick on a huge scale from Calais to create an innovative moated palace where the king could enjoy privacy. Henry VI put his own stamp on the palace, installing his coat of arms and heraldic beasts in the great and privy chambers.[5] Such expressions of royal magnificence were expected of a monarch, but no king of England before Henry had built an educational establishment – never mind two. Six months after creating Eton, Henry himself laid the foundation stone for another college in Cambridge. Dedicated to the Virgin Mary and St Nicholas (the saint on whose feast day Henry had been born), what was eventually to be known as 'King's College' would provide education to twelve poor scholars to improve the church and help rid England of heresy.

Henry's childhood interest in learning and profound piety had found a natural expression in these educational projects, but the colleges also expressed a distinctly Lancastrian family concern for religion and literature. Henry's grandfather Henry IV had inculcated bibliomania in his descendants, building a library to house his books at Eltham Palace and appointing a special keeper to watch over them. On one visit to Bardney Abbey he had relaxed by 'reading for as long as he wished' in the monastic library, a leisure pursuit that Henry VI would have dearly loved to indulge had the business of government not kept intervening. Henry V and his brothers the dukes of Bedford and Gloucester all had substantial libraries: Henry V had so many books to bequeath in his will that they were left not only to his son and kinsmen, but also to the monastic houses of Sheen and Syon (which he had founded). He stipulated that the houses must not be given duplicates of the same works. Henry VI had probably visited Bedford's specially constructed library in Rouen Castle, where 800 volumes that had once belonged to King Charles VI were only a portion of his possessions. Henry's uncle Gloucester had a sufficiently large library to donate more than 200 books to Oxford University in his lifetime as well as commissioning a number of new works by humanist scholars.[6]

In his unique manner of commemorating his accession Henry VI demonstrated that he had inherited not only a love of learning, but also a profound concern for his subjects' souls. In 1439 William Bingham, the rector of St John Zachary in London and founder of God's House College, Cambridge,* appealed to

---

* The original name for what is now known as Christ's College.

Henry to remedy the shortage of grammar schools in the country, claiming that in his region alone more than sixty schools had recently closed. This was, he said, leading to a decline in the understanding of Latin, which imperilled the 'wisdom, cunning and governance of the kingdom'.[7] It also endangered English souls, for Latin was the language of the church and widespread ignorance of religious teachings threatened to keep Henry's subjects from salvation. Henry was disturbed at the possibility that his inertia might place his people in spiritual jeopardy.

Where his uncle Gloucester combatted religious heterodoxy with military action, Henry chose a more pacific route. The pious youth was growing up with a strong sense of Christian responsibility.[8] Henry saw his educational foundations, fundamentally, as devotional works, in the manner of other charitable endeavours of his age: Henry Chichele, archbishop of Canterbury, had founded All Souls College in Oxford on the provision that its fellows must pray not only for the souls of its founders but also for all those killed in the Hundred Years War,* and the earl and countess of Suffolk had founded their own almshouse and school at Ewelme in Oxfordshire.

To provide income for Eton and King's College, Henry petitioned Pope Eugenius IV for an array of papal indulgences to draw in pilgrims, whose thanksgiving offerings or donations for intercession could yield a lavish bounty.† By 1442 no fewer than four of Henry's envoys were at work in the papal curia endeavouring to win these indulgences. Further grants of rights and land to both colleges were confirmed in parliament. As well as ensuring 1,000 marks were vouchsafed to Eton annually from the duchy of Lancaster estates, Henry also endowed them with a range of relics to entice pilgrims: first came the finger-bone and part of the spine of John 'the confessor' of Bridlington, and later

---

*   Henry VI granted All Souls its foundation charter in 1438.
†   A papal indulgence gave its purchaser remittance from the penalties owed for committing sin.

the 'Tablet of Bourbon',* which was said to contain the blood of Jesus Christ, Mary, St Nicholas and St Catherine, as well as shards of the True Cross.[9]

The financial underpinning that allowed building work to begin on Henry's cherished project was an endowment of alien priory lands,† which Henry enfeoffed‡ to a dozen trusted servants in 1440.§ These twelve men represented the leading figures in Henry's government but also in his affections, and while councillors like Archbishop Henry Chichele of Canterbury and Bishop John Stafford of Bath and Wells had long been pillars of Henry's regime, there were new names who represented the rise of an influential coterie closer to Henry himself. Power was no longer vested predominantly in Henry's council. Now that the teenage king had assumed independent control of government, political influence resided with the men who were most frequently attendant on him: the servants and companions who accompanied him as he travelled between his homes and protected and advised him at all hours of the day. These were the men of his household: John Somerset, James Fiennes, Bishop Aiscough and especially William de la Pole, earl of Suffolk.

A royal household was divided into two parts. The 'below stairs' household of over 250 people attended to the material needs of the court under the watchful eye of the steward, the earl of

---

*   This highly valuable French reliquary had been acquired by the crown as part of the ransom for a member of the Bourbon family during the Hundred Years War.

†   Alien priories were religious houses in England under the control of monastic orders outside the country. Henry V had appropriated the revenues of these priories to crown control in 1414.

‡   Enfeoffment was a means of transferring property that bypassed legal restrictions. In this case, the feoffees received the alien priory lands with which Eton was to be endowed.

§   The twelve men were Archbishop Chichele; Bishops Stafford, Lowe and Aiscough; the earl of Suffolk; John Somerset; Thomas Beckington; Adam Moleyns; John Hampton; Richard Andrewe; James Fiennes and William Tresham. Watts, pp. 169–70.

Suffolk, and various financial officers. 'Above stairs', monitored by Henry's chamberlain, contained a similar number of higher-ranking attendants who made up the royal 'court'. Ministering to Henry's spiritual needs were his confessor and dean of the chapel, while a large array of officers, knights and esquires dressed him, served his food and provided him with a suitably impressive escort. Until Henry had a wife with her own royal household, it was the men of this upper household, with their frequent, informal access to the king, who wielded political influence unchecked.[10]

Chief among the men of the new household was William de la Pole, earl of Suffolk. Suffolk had been Henry's steward and therefore a constant presence in his household since the king was eleven years old. As Henry matured into adulthood, Suffolk became a mentor to him, perhaps even something of a father figure. The earl had a disarming ability to win confidence and influence without causing offence. Although Suffolk inherited the earl of Warwick's ascendant position, Henry did not chafe against his guidance as he had against his old master. Suffolk was a shrewd diplomat, astute enough to find a middle way between the warring uncles of Henry VI, and besides his personal abilities he had the considerable benefit of being married to Alice Chaucer. Alice was unlucky with husbands – her first, Sir John Phelip, died fighting for Henry V at Harfleur in 1415, and her second, the earl of Salisbury, was killed by cannon fire at the siege of Orléans in 1429. Despite this unhappy history, Suffolk had eagerly married Alice in 1430 to gain her political connections. Alice's father, Thomas Chaucer, was Cardinal Beaufort's cousin and chief ally on the royal council. Chaucer took Suffolk in virtually as an adopted son, and on his death in 1434 left Alice and Suffolk an extensive Oxfordshire estate, which supplemented Suffolk's own East Anglian holdings. In administering these estates, as well as in matters of high politics, Suffolk depended on his wife's political acumen. 'Above all the earth,' he later wrote, 'my singular trust is most in her.'[11] The king's trust, meanwhile, was increasingly vested in Suffolk.

Suffolk's allies were a prominent presence both in Henry's household and among the feoffees to whom he entrusted his educational projects. Among them was the polymath Adam Moleyns, bishop of Chichester,* clerk of the council and (from 1444) keeper of the privy seal. Moleyns played a vital role in confirming Henry's grants of patronage and was often in attendance either at court or council, although he maintained an impressive international reputation as a correspondent and diplomat. The Kentishman James Fiennes pursued a very different path into Henry's esteem, becoming a favoured esquire of the body after undertaking military service in France. Fiennes was a ruthless political operator intent on building a powerful regional affinity for himself, but that did not prevent him from winning Henry's favour and rising through the ranks at court. By 1447 he would be chamberlain of Henry's household, controlling access to the king in concert with Suffolk.

Among Henry's many spiritual advisers William Aiscough, bishop of Salisbury, was perhaps pre-eminent. In 1438, the forty-three-year-old Aiscough had become Henry's confessor. A staunch opponent of religious heterodoxy, the Yorkshire-born Aiscough was a near-constant presence at Henry's court throughout the next decade, working closely with his fellow ecclesiastic John Kempe, archbishop of York. An ambitious and highly capable man, Kempe's closest colleague on the council was Cardinal Beaufort, whose patronage helped him to be named a cardinal in 1439, despite the fierce opposition of the archbishop of Canterbury, Henry Chichele. Kempe was thus only the second cardinal in English history to retain his bishopric.

Henry's transition to adult rule had been a halting, tentative process, but with the foundation of Eton College the king saw himself acting on his own initiative and in his own divinely appointed power. He started to move away from the narrow

---

* Moleyns was named bishop of Chichester in 1445.

geographical boundaries in which he had spent most of his childhood. While he continued to pass much of his time in the Thameside palaces, close to the seat of government, Henry also embarked on annual progresses, spending the summer months riding between hunting lodges and religious centres, moving every few days in the company of his courtiers and advisers. In 1437 he had been particularly active, travelling north from London in July through wooded and enclosed lands via Barnet and St Albans to visit the Midlands. On reaching the sandstone crags and forests of Nottinghamshire he had turned south, following a lengthy return loop that took him through his estates in the open country of Leicestershire and Warwickshire, before skirting the edge of the Cotswolds and Berkshire Downs to return to London in November. Everywhere he travelled he was accompanied by his household. They increasingly came to represent a new form of family for him, especially as during Henry's teenage years many of the formative influences of his youth had passed away.[12]

Early in 1437, both Henry's step-grandmother, the dowager queen Joan of Navarre, and his mother, Queen Catherine, had died.* Catherine had been unwell for some time and expired at Bermondsey Abbey, south of London, on 3 January, only two days after Henry had sent her a beautiful piece of engraved gold in the image of a crucifix. Perhaps it had been intended to comfort her in her last hours.[13] Henry's half-siblings Edmund and Jasper Tudor (Catherine's children by Owen Tudor) were sent to live with Katherine de la Pole, abbess of Barking, sister of the earl of Suffolk, and there they would remain until they were old enough to come to court. Later that year the earl of Warwick, who had governed Henry's childhood as master of his household, had reluctantly agreed to take on Bedford's responsibilities in France as lieutenant-general and governor. Having sailed from England

---

*   Joan of Navarre died in her palace at Langley in July 1437.

with his countess, he died in France in 1439. By 1440 Henry's only immediate family members still living were the duke of Gloucester, his duchess Eleanor and Cardinal Beaufort.

With the royal family so streamlined – little more than a king, a royal uncle and a great-uncle of the half-blood – Henry entered his majority with an embarrassment of landed riches. The territories which ordinarily would have been occupied by a queen, vast swathes of the duchy of Lancaster and Cheshire, were in his possession. The estates usually gifted to a king's son – the duchy of Cornwall, the principality of Wales, the earldom of Chester – were his too. Some of Bedford's estates had already been divided up and parcelled out to others, but much of his land was still under crown control. Although Henry could not permanently alienate lands in the royal demesne, he could grant the keeping of these manors, forests and tenants, or the offices attached to them, to his chosen recipients. The generous-spirited Henry was happy to share his wealth with his surviving family and friends and those nearest at hand were swift to respond to the resulting opportunities for personal aggrandizement.[14]

The earliest expression of Henry's favour, his first royal grants, had been made to his uncles Gloucester and Cardinal Beaufort. But Henry's family now increasingly gave way to the representatives of his household in Henry's affections and as recipients of his patronage. Between 1438 and 1441 Henry made around seventy grants a year to household members, with some of the most prominent officers receiving two or three each.[15] At around the time Henry established his colleges he elevated two of his long-term attendants to unprecedented heights. In 1440, his childhood friend John Beaumont was made the first ever English viscount. Beaumont and Henry had grown up together at court after John's father Henry, Baron Beaumont, died when he was four years old. This shared upbringing, and perhaps also shared experience of fatherlessness, created a deep bond between the pair, and despite achieving little of military or political note Beaumont was lavishly rewarded by the king. Among his many royal grants were the county of Boulogne, the vicomté of Beaumont in Maine, extensive life interests in royal lands in Norfolk and Lincolnshire, the Order of the Garter, the office of Lord Great Chamberlain and marriage to Katherine Strangways, dowager duchess of Norfolk, who held a life interest in the vast East Anglian duchy estates. Henry's generosity was not misplaced. Beaumont was to prove one of the most steadfast Lancastrian courtiers, even in the most troubled days of Henry's reign.[16] A year after Beaumont's elevation, Henry rewarded another long-term attendant, Ralph Botiller, son of Henry's old governess Alice. Ralph had fought alongside both Henry V and the duke of Bedford in France before serving as a knight of the body during Henry VI's coronation expedition to France. His service to the king earned him the stewardship of the royal estate of Kenilworth and Henry's first new baronage: Ralph was created Lord Sudeley in 1441.[17]

To these men – and many more – within Henry's household, the king proved unfailingly generous; so generous, in fact, that the council soon grew anxious. As early as November 1436 council minutes included a note to advise 'the king that he give office to such persons as the office were convenient to, not [granting] to high estate a small office, neither to low estate a great office'.[18] In February 1438 there was a flurry of conciliar reminders to speak to the king about his grants: he must be told not to appoint receivers for life,* he should remember that over-generous pardons materially disadvantaged him and that crown lordships should not be given away. A council clerk named Henry Benet was appointed to have a serious discussion with Henry about his levels of patronage after the king lost the crown 3,000 marks in just two grants.[19] As late as 1444 measures were being put in place by the council to ensure that individuals did not receive

---

* A receiver was a government-appointed officer who received rents, tolls or other money due.

the same monetary grant twice over, and that petitioners were clearly named. By then Henry was twenty-two.

Henry seemed unwilling or unable to be guided by the council. He remained all too happy to hand over manors and pardons on little more than a petitioner's request. In 1441 he granted Thomas Daniel, a squire of the body, a manor rent-free for life after being told it was only worth £20 a year. Smelling a rat, the council investigated further and discovered the manor was worth considerably more. Far from being angry at his body servant's deception, Henry granted Daniel the same £20 a year for life for his 'good service'.[20] And it was not just that Henry was easily manipulated; he was also inattentive, sometimes accidentally granting the same office to two different petitioners. In February 1438, he bestowed the alien priory of St James, near Exeter, to two men on consecutive days, causing the first of them – as was expressed with considerable forbearance in letters patent a year later – 'much inconvenience'.[21]

Not all Henry's grants were so extensive. He also remembered past kindnesses with small gifts. In December 1437, he granted a life pension and two tuns of wine a year to Alice Botiller, his old governess, 'in consideration of the good service done to the king during his minority'. His old nurse Joan Asteley was one of a number of his childhood attendants rewarded with an annuity of £40 in July 1438.[22] However, even small grants of patronage, when doled out to a household that was ballooning in size and cost, soon became an issue. By November 1439 parliament had grown alarmed at the swelling cost of Henry's household and successfully demanded reform to cover its expenses.[23] Nonetheless, Henry's 'above stairs' household continued to expand, rising from 360 servants when he entered his majority to more than 400 within a decade. In 1437–9 there were more than 270 valets and esquires of the hall or chamber alone.[24]

In 1440, Henry had begun to establish the sort of king he wished to be. The educational foundations that he intended to serve as his legacy were an expression of his upbringing, showing that he had learnt well the lessons that he must be pious, compassionate and magnificent as monarch. But he also believed he should be openhanded and receptive, without subjecting those impulses to the necessary checks of circumspection and discretion. The criticisms levelled at his early majority were exactly those that his council had raised after his coronations in the early 1430s: he lacked foresight and judgement, he was too easily influenced by those around him. But in 1440 he was still only eighteen – there remained the possibility that he would outgrow his youthful naivety. After all, his martial father Henry V had been a very different man in his youth, but when he acceded to the throne he sloughed off indulgence and vice in favour of military action, self-restraint and strong kingship.[25]

In 1440, what could not be doubted was that Henry was seeking a very different form of kingship from that exercised by his father. Government had remained in stasis since 1422, the will of the dying Henry V maintaining its vice-like grip on the policy of his kinsmen and councillors. Warfare had been its defining characteristic. This was a course that Henry VI could no longer follow. Now that he had full authority over his two kingdoms and the support of a coterie of new advisers within his household, he was determined to pursue a policy of peace.

12

'To the counsellors of peace is joy'[1]

Westminster Abbey
28 October 1440

Dwarfed by the ribbed marble columns of the sanctuary, Charles, duke of Orléans, approached the high altar of Westminster Abbey. Up the steps and across the intricately tiled floor, its mosaics glistening, lay freedom. For twenty-five years Orléans had been a prisoner of the English, ever since the day he had been dragged, broken and defeated, from beneath a pile of French corpses on the battlefield of Agincourt. His wife and only child had died while he languished in prison and he had sought consolation in poetry, writing more than 500 works during his captivity. Now at last, this pawn in the interminable game of Anglo-French diplomacy would be released. All he had to do was swear that he would not raise his sword against his liege lord King Henry of England and France. He must promise to aid the English in their negotiations with his kinsman Charles VII, so that a lasting peace could be negotiated that brought shame to neither nation. As he laid his hand on the altar, Orléans took his oath gladly. Within a week, Henry had put his seal to the duke's release. The result of years of hard bargaining, not just between England and France but within English politics, it had been bought at no small cost to the relationship between Henry and his surviving uncles.

Since the betrayal of Arras in 1435, the war with France and Burgundy had rumbled on like some grotesque machine of annihilation, constantly demanding fresh supplies of men and money be churned out of England to control the deteriorating situation across the Channel. The war for Henry's French crown was supposed to be self-funding, the money extracted from his French estates, but his continental subjects were suffering more than ever from the pestilence, famine and destruction that stalked in the wake of war. From the start of Henry's reign, the English parliament had been reluctant to grant taxes to fund the war and raising loans from church and state was a relentless grind. Even Cardinal Beaufort's generosity had started to falter.[2] By the time Henry entered his personal rule it had become clear that the only way to end the war was either with one last mighty push or by negotiating a peace with Charles VII. Each policy had its supporters: the duke of Gloucester was firmly in favour of investing everything in one major assault, while Cardinals Beaufort and Kempe led the calls for a diplomatic solution.* However, this was no longer a government in which Henry sat idly by and let his advisers determine policy. The king now had an agenda of his own, and he was firmly of the opinion that negotiated peace was the better policy.

A 'plain declaration' disseminated by Henry's council around the time Orléans was released made his feelings on the matter clear: 'It is thought to the king not [only] expedient but necessary to him to intend to the peace.' 'The war that hath long continued and endured, that is to say a hundred years and more... [must] cease and take end.' After a century of conflict 'there hath be done all the labour and diligence that could be done... with great and long labour and loss of many men's lives

---

* John Kempe, archbishop of York, was not made a cardinal until 18 December 1439, but for clarity I have used his new title throughout.

and with great and grievous cost [to] the king and of this land.' As his advisers had been at pains to make clear, English finances were in disarray and the expense of the war could no longer be supported. In parliament the Commons consistently complained of their poverty in the face of crown demands for tax. Henry's subjects on both sides of the Channel were impoverished by the 'great and grievous cost' of the conflict. But worse – far worse to Henry's sensibility – was the 'importable sorrow and misery of this war', which was reported to him in desperate appeals from his continental subjects.[3]

More men had been killed in this century of war, it was claimed, than were alive now in both realms.[4] To Henry, this was particularly offensive at a time when the Catholic Church was torn apart by infighting. For years there had been conflict between the pope and his council, but by 1439 the situation had deteriorated to the point that the Council of Basel deposed Pope Eugenius IV and elected an anti-pope, Felix V, in his place. Henry could not bear to be part of a divisive war between Christians at a time when the papacy was in schism, heresy was on the rise and the threat of the Muslim Ottoman empire to the east was ever increasing. All Christian princes, he believed, should do all in their power to protect their church and work to end the papal schism 'with one will and one heart'. Peace with France was 'the greatest means earthly to the appeasing of the said trouble of the Church'.

In favouring a policy of peace Henry did not see himself as betraying his father's legacy. Henry V, like Edward III before him, had negotiated for peace when it became necessary to do so. The fundamental difference between the two Henrys, though, was that Henry VI never showed any inclination to lead an army in battle. In part this was because he was still unmarried and lacked an heir, leaving his kingdom vulnerable if he died on campaign, but it seems also to have been a personal choice. Henry was content to let others fight on his behalf. Ideally, he would have preferred them not to have to fight at all.

In his abhorrence of continuing the war, Henry was not alone.

The earl of Suffolk and Cardinal Beaufort had been proponents of peace before the Congress of Arras, and once their anger at the Burgundian betrayal of 1435 had cooled they reverted to their pacific stance. They became fervent advocates of Henry's peace policy, shoring up his conviction that diplomacy was the best means of concluding the war, even if he had to defy the wishes of Gloucester and the will of Henry V to achieve it.

In the summer of 1439 it had at first seemed that there was a realistic hope, if not of long-term peace, then at least of fruitful negotiation with the French. The duke of Brittany was encouraging and Isabella, duchess of Burgundy, offered her services as intermediary for negotiations between England and France, replacing her unpopular husband. It was settled that embassies from France and England would meet at Oye, in the Calais pale, in June 1439, with Isabella acting as mediator. The English envoys, led by Cardinal Kempe, were given their formal instructions by Henry at his manor of Kennington outside London on 21 May. His demands appeared uncompromising: the English embassy was to insist on maintaining Henry's title as king of France, permit no marriage alliance unless peace was agreed, and demand a truce to endure, ideally, for fifty years. As a concession, Henry agreed that Charles VII could hold the lands beyond the River Loire (barring Poitou and Gascony) as his vassal. Such forceful bargaining would probably have been acceptable even to Gloucester.[5]

But four days later Henry held a secret meeting with Cardinal Beaufort in which he 'opened and declared all his intent in this matter'. Although Beaufort was officially acting as a 'stirrer to the peace' – an impartial mediator – he was now tasked by Henry with a further mission.[6] If it seemed that the negotiations would 'fall to rupture', Beaufort was given royal authority to make a number of further concessions, which were left out of the formal instructions given to the other members of the embassy. Such secrecy was necessary because Henry was willing to concede points that his subjects, and especially his councillors, would strongly oppose. As long as he could retain Normandy and Gascony in full sovereignty, Henry was willing to give up his title as king of France. He was also prepared to bow to the demand that had been made repeatedly in negotiations with the French over the years, and free the duke of Orléans. As a sign of good faith, Orléans was allowed to travel with the English embassy as a mediator.[7]

The Anglo-French talks began, as usual, with unrealistic demands and acrimonious exchanges. The French proposals, reported Henry's secretary, Thomas Beckington, were 'full of wormwood and snares'.[8] But eventually, after weeks of debate, a compromise was reached. In return for a truce to last between fifteen and thirty years, Henry could hold the territories he already controlled in France – Gascony, Calais and most of Normandy. During this period of peace, Charles would not insist on his sovereignty over any of these territories but nor could Henry use the title 'king of France'. As a first step, Orléans was to be released from prison without paying his ransom. The English embassy accepted these terms in theory, but they would not commit themselves to signing off on the agreement until they were certain of the king's mind. Even Cardinal Beaufort may have suspected that this hard-won agreement was too unpalatable for the English without the king's public acceptance. With the talks in danger of rupturing, Beaufort dispatched Kempe back to England for further instructions, to buy some time while he continued the negotiations at Oye.

At Windsor Castle, Kempe presented the prospective treaty to Henry and his council. To ensure peace, Henry was quite willing to consider the suggested terms, which were not unlike those he had already conceded to Beaufort, but his council were not so pliant. Gloucester, in particular, was appalled. He rejected outright the notion that Henry could give up his title to the crown of France:

[This is] the greatest sign of infamy that ever fell to you, my redoubted lord, or to your noble progenitors since they first took on the said title and right of your said realm and crown of France... I would never agree to this, and would rather die.[9]

While not expressing things in quite such dogmatic terms, the rest of Henry's council tended to share Gloucester's opinion. They did not trust Charles VII to abide by such a truce, suspecting he would use it as a cover to continue his military expansion. Their suspicions appeared to be confirmed when word arrived that even as peace talks had been ongoing, a force of Frenchmen commanded by Arthur de Richemont had taken the English-held fortress of Meaux. This castle had been one of those that Beaufort had been negotiating to exchange for the more valuable French-occupied towns of Harfleur, Mont St Michel and Dieppe. Now the English had lost an important bargaining chip, and been given apparent proof that the French looked on peace with contempt.

Although Kempe 'made all the persuasions' he could, Henry's council were not willing to sign an agreement that denied Henry his title in France. It would 'show too great a simpleness and lack of foresight in him that accepteth', and set a precedent that would 'hurt the opinion of [Henry's] right and claim' to France, not to mention suggesting a 'lack of might or of right or of courage' in the king.[10] Faced with such overwhelming opposition, Henry bowed to conciliar pressure and rejected the terms Kempe presented. By the time Kempe returned to Calais with the news, the French had abandoned the talks. Cardinal Beaufort was only able to secure one small concession: in September 1439, he agreed a commercial treaty with Burgundy that re-opened trade routes and exports of English wool from Calais.

Henry had been thwarted in his first attempt to broker peace, but his belief in the moral justification for his policy was unwavering. Moreover, French arguments in favour of Orléans's release had convinced him that to keep the duke prisoner so long was contrary to the law of arms. He believed that if Orléans was freed he could prove a vital intermediary in future negotiations with France, perhaps at last tipping the scales in favour of an enduring peace. At the very least, his release would show English willingness to conciliate, and thereby encourage the French to compromise in turn. At heart, Henry was an optimist. He had deep reserves of sympathy and forgiveness, which had rarely been confronted with the reality of worldly corruption. Philippe of Burgundy's betrayal at Arras was one of the few times his faith in his fellow man had been fundamentally challenged. By the end of the year, his mind was made up: Orléans would be freed.

But Henry had reckoned without the duke of Gloucester. Gloucester was as disturbed by the suggestion of Orléans's release as he was by the threat to Henry's title in France. He believed that the king was being manipulated into a reckless and futile act of concession by Cardinals Kempe and Beaufort, and that freeing Orléans made both the English cause and Henry himself appear weak. Early in 1440, Gloucester appealed to parliament to undermine the cardinals' hold over the king. He insisted that Cardinal Beaufort was the agent behind Orléans's release and that this was only the latest 'fraudulent' attempt by the cardinal to usurp Henry's authority. Gloucester attacked Beaufort from every angle he could, criticizing his diplomacy (the money for embassies like Arras would have been better spent on armies), his loans (from which 'little benefit, or none' had come), his family (whose members Beaufort raised to high rank and advantageous marriage at the expense of better men) and even his wealth, which 'great lucre' Gloucester suggested Beaufort had achieved by defrauding the crown. The old complaint was raised about Beaufort holding a bishopric and a cardinalate at the same time – Gloucester pointedly reminding parliament that Henry V had forbidden the bishop of Winchester to accept the papal appointment – and concerns about the release of King James I of Scotland were resurrected almost twenty years after the fact, reinterpreted as a traitorous act forced through for Beaufort's own nefarious ends. Worst of all, Gloucester accused Beaufort of monopolizing the king to such an extent that he was 'estranged' from his natural counsellors, including Gloucester himself, the archbishop of Canterbury and lords of the blood such as the duke of York.[11]

For all the duke's rhetoric, the reality was that Gloucester was out of step with his nephew's regime. He clung to the martial legacy of Henry V even as Henry VI strove to discard it. The men whose stars were in the ascendant at Henry's court – men like the earl of Suffolk and Adam Moleyns – understood that supporting Henry's peace policy was a surer means of establishing their authority than harping on old grievances. Gloucester and his ilk were relics of a rejected past. Henry VI treated the latest skirmish in Gloucester's twenty-year campaign to undermine Cardinal Beaufort with the respect he felt it deserved: he ignored it, not even calling for Beaufort and Kempe to respond to Gloucester's accusations. Cardinal Beaufort would not be put under investigation, and Orléans's release would proceed as intended.

In June 1440, Gloucester demanded that his opposition to this course of action be officially recorded under the great seal. 'I never was,' Gloucester's protest recited, 'am, nor never shall be consenting, counselling, nor agreeing' to Orléans's release.[12] By then his increasingly public expressions of defiance were beginning to infect Henry's subjects. There was soon such general 'grudging' that Henry was forced to issue a manifesto explaining the reasons for his decision. Henry reassured his subjects that he had not resolved to free Orléans out 'of simpleness, nor of self will, nor without notable causes'. He had acted out of 'the sovereign and singular desire that he hath, and always had had… [for] peace'. His subjects were not all convinced. Some, indeed, suspected that Gloucester was right and that Henry had been manipulated into this folly by his advisers. This suggestion also had to be quashed in the manifesto issued on Henry's behalf:

He [wishes] not that any charge should be laid therefore at any times hereafter upon any other person, but wills that it be openly felt and plainly known that [what] he hath done in this said matter he hath done of himself and of his own advice and courage... moved and stirred of God and of reason as he trusteth fully.[13]

Whether Henry's manifesto convinced his subjects or not, he had his wish. On 2 July the terms of Orléans's release were agreed: the duke must pay a ransom of 40,000 nobles and a further 80,000 within six months.* If he failed to arrange peace within that time, his ransom would be cancelled, and if he could not raise the necessary sums he was honour-bound to return to captivity.[14] As if to emphasize Henry's resolve to distance himself from the war, on the same day that he sealed the terms of Orléans's release he appointed a new lieutenant-general and governor of France to replace the late earl of Warwick. As the new appointment was for five years it was evident that Henry had no intention of personally leading the military efforts in France in the near future. Perhaps as a sop to his disaffected uncle Gloucester, Henry did not choose Cardinal Beaufort's preferred candidate, his nephew John Beaufort, but gave the post to their twenty-eight-year-old kinsman Richard, duke of York.

In the long term, Gloucester's misgivings about Orléans's release were to prove prescient. Charles VII showed little inclination to heed Orléans's advice in peace negotiations, or even to meet him when he returned from imprisonment. Instead, Orléans headed for the Burgundian court, where he was lavishly received, inducted into the chivalric Order of the Golden Fleece and married to Philippe of Burgundy's niece, Marie of Cleves. The forging of such close ties with Burgundy served only to increase Charles's suspicion of his returned kinsman. The next three years saw little return on Henry's investment in Orléans's freedom. His ransom went unpaid, he did not return to prison when he failed to secure a peace treaty, and he actively alienated

---

* A noble was worth 80 pence (a third of a pound), meaning in total Orléans's ransom was £40,000.

Charles by joining with other French princes in a revolt called the *Praguerie*. So much for Henry's high hopes.[15]

The realization of his suspicions would have been little comfort to Gloucester, however. It was hard for such a proud man to forget the injuries done to him by Henry in 1440. The boy who had once been so easily bent to Gloucester's will had dismissed his counsel and ignored his warnings. Cardinal Beaufort was still in as dominant a position after Gloucester had accused him in parliament as he had been before.[16] On 28 October 1440, as the sacred singing of priests in Westminster Abbey accompanied the oath that guaranteed Orléans's release, Gloucester made a public demonstration of defiance. As Mass began, he stormed from the abbey and on to his barge, refusing to be present at a ceremony he opposed. The event underlined the rift that had developed between Henry and his uncle in recent years. Gloucester might be heir to the throne, but there was little beyond blood kinship to bind them otherwise.[17]

Such divisions in the royal family could have serious consequences. For while Gloucester had been attempting to use parliament to gain political dominance, his wife Eleanor had turned to more direct methods of influencing events. As 1441 dawned, treason wormed its way into the very heart of the royal family.

13

'Instruments of necromancy'[1]

London
25 July 1441

As Henry left the sweltering city of London to seek peace in his countryside manor of Kennington, the summer calm was shattered by a sudden thunderstorm. Lightning split the air, and rain and hail pounded against the roofs of London market stalls. 'Well was him that was within house', the *Brut* chronicle observed. This storm, it was believed, was no natural phenomenon. It had been conjured up by the same malevolent forces that were abroad across London – 'wicked fiends and spirits [raised] out of hell by conjuration, for to disturb the people in the realm, and to put them to trouble, dissension and unrest.' These fiends, it was asserted, had been conjured for Eleanor Cobham.[2]

A month earlier, on 28 June 1441, Eleanor, duchess of Gloucester, had entered London in state. As befitted the wife of the heir to the throne, the aldermen and mayor went out to meet her, escorting her across London Bridge and into the city with every possible sign of deference. She lodged at the King's Head in Cheapside. That night, or the next, as she was sitting down to dinner in the inn, Eleanor received disturbing news. Gloucester's servant, and Eleanor's personal clerk, Roger Bolingbroke, had been arrested.[3]

Accusations against any of the duchess's household servants would have been cause for alarm, but in Bolingbroke's case there was especial reason to worry. For the clerk knew the intimate details of Eleanor's life and was privy to her most secret ambitions. 'A great and cunning man in astronomy',[4] he had been commissioned by Eleanor to draw a horoscope for the king. Working with Eleanor's physician, Dr Thomas Southwell, the pair had divined that Henry's death was imminent. According to their calculations Henry would sicken in his twentieth year, enduring a wasting disease that would strike him first with fever and cold, then with an unnatural heat. By summer at the latest, he would be dead. The horoscope did not include details of what would happen next, but Eleanor knew it well enough. Henry's heir was the duke of Gloucester, her husband. With Henry in his grave, she and Gloucester would take the throne.[5]

But Bolingbroke's work on Eleanor's behalf had been uncovered, and he was charged with committing acts of necromancy. He was accused of going into various churches around London with Southwell and Eleanor's chaplain, John Home, with the purpose of hastening Henry's death with unholy rituals. The three men had been provided with a waxen image of the king by Margery Jourdemayne, also known as 'the Witch of Eye', which, on melting, would bring about the death of the king.

On Sunday 23 July, Bolingbroke publicly abjured his necromancy at St Paul's Cross.[6] Raised on a stage in the city churchyard, he listened while the bishop of Rochester recited a sermon on his sins. A jostling press of people – not only from London, but 'aliens of other strange lands beyond the sea' – came to stare as Bolingbroke sat in a painted chair 'wherein he was wont to sit when he wrought his craft'. It was a weird piece of apparatus, to each of whose four corners a sword inscribed with copper images was fixed. Bolingbroke himself held a sword and sceptre in each hand, and to make it clear that he had transgressed the natural order with his treasonable plot, he was topped with a mocking paper crown. In the crowd representatives of royal government, including Cardinal Beaufort and the archbishop of Canterbury, watched proceedings alongside the aldermen of London.[7]

For Eleanor, the public condemnation of her servant was a stark warning. On Monday 24 July, fearing her own arrest, she fled into sanctuary at Westminster Abbey. That very day she was called to appear before the bishops and priests of the royal council. The presence of her husband's rival, Cardinal Beaufort, would have been particularly concerning for her as she stood before the high altar of St Stephen's chapel in Westminster to deny the twenty-eight charges of necromancy, treason and heresy made against her. Both treason and heresy were punishable by death, and for a woman that meant being burnt at the stake like Joan of Arc.

Eleanor's contemplation of the succession was not in itself either surprising or necessarily treasonous. At nineteen years old, Henry was still unmarried and childless, and as the duke of Gloucester had been increasingly sidelined in recent years, it was natural for him and his duchess to seek reassurance about their futures. What was potentially treasonable was for Eleanor to attempt to ascertain the exact date and cause of Henry's death. Moreover, as the indictment against Eleanor expressed it, by spreading a belief in Henry's imminent mortality, the duchess had fomented unrest, encouraging his subjects to turn from their 'cordial love' of the king.[8]

While Eleanor's trial progressed throughout the summer and autumn of 1441, Henry's council endeavoured to discredit her accomplices' alarming horoscope, according to which the king's death could come any day. To dismiss the validity of these claims, and perhaps to allay Henry's own concerns, a new horoscope was commissioned and presented to him at Sheen Palace on 14 August 1441. The new horoscope carefully contradicted the calculations of Eleanor's accomplices Southwell and Bolingbroke. Like many of his contemporaries, including his uncles Charles VII of France and the duke of Gloucester, Henry saw no contradiction between his conventional Catholic piety and the use of prognostication. But there was a difference between the science of astrology and the dark art of necromancy, and it was the latter that Eleanor and her accomplices were suspected of.[9]

On Monday 23 October 1441, Eleanor was convicted with all her accomplices. When pressed in her second examination, she had confessed to five of the twenty-eight counts of felony and treason, but she insisted that she had not sought Henry's death, and that the wax images which the court interpreted as intended for his destruction were actually part of a fertility ritual, 'for to have borne a child by her lord, the duke of Gloucester'.[10] This more innocent use of magic did not save her from condemnation, however. By her own admission, she was a traitor and must be punished.

Did Henry suspect Gloucester of complicity in Eleanor's crimes? Contemporaries were unanimous in attaching the blame for this affair to Eleanor alone, emphasizing her excessive pride for betraying her into sin. 'As Lucifer fell down for pride,' recited the ballad, *Lament of the Duchess of Gloucester*, '[she] fell from all felicity.'[11] It was easy to cast the comparatively low-born Eleanor in the guise of a modern Jezebel. The fact that she had enticed Gloucester away from Jacqueline of Hainault, his high-born and popular first wife, resurfaced during the course of the trial, and Eleanor was accused of having used love potions to get her man.

However, Eleanor's actions could not be completely divorced from her husband. Theirs was a love match and they were known to share interests and to participate in a number of activities together. They were, for instance, joint members of the fraternity of St Alban's Abbey; but, rather more disquietingly, both husband and wife had a demonstrable curiosity about – and family connections with – the worlds of necromancy and astrology. Among Gloucester's vast library of manuscripts were a number of ancient texts that referred to astrology and wax image magic. He and Eleanor had also maintained an affectionate and long-standing relationship with his stepmother, Joan of Navarre, herself a condemned royal witch. In 1419 Joan had been arrested, imprisoned and declared guilty of using necromancy to compass Henry V's death. Joan's confessor, and alleged accomplice, Friar John Randolph, also had links to Gloucester. The friar had drawn up a set of astrological tables for Gloucester and, it was alleged, the duke had attempted to free Randolph from imprisonment at the Tower of London during the period when he and Cardinal Beaufort were wrangling over control of the fortress in 1425. Friar Randolph had been killed in a brawl with a mad priest in the Tower in 1429, but Joan lived on until 1437, pardoned of her alleged crimes and enjoying respectable retirement at various royal castles. Gloucester and Eleanor had frequently been guests at her dinner table.[12]

On 6 November 1441, Gloucester's colleagues on the council – including his hated rival Cardinal Beaufort – annulled his marriage to Eleanor on the grounds that it been brought about by sorcery. Stripped of her rank as duchess, Eleanor was condemned to do public penance. On three consecutive market days, when the streets of London would be teeming with wide-eyed gawkers, she was to walk barefoot, dressed in black, with nothing covering her hair but a plain kerchief, through the city. On 14 November, Eleanor was met at the dank river steps by the aldermen and mayor of London. In a mortifying inversion of her entry into the city in June, the aldermen walked in a ring around her as she processed through the streets, a one-pound taper of wax burning in her hands. On her first day of penance, this taper was presented to the altar of St Paul's Cathedral. On the following days two further churches would receive a candle from her hands. The citizens of London were ordered not to molest her, but they were also warned not to regard her with sympathy.

Once Eleanor had completed her three days of penance she was taken under guard to be imprisoned at Leeds Castle, where her custodian was Thomas Stanley, the controller of Henry's household. So eager was Henry to have his aunt removed from London after her penance that Stanley was instructed not to delay their departure 'for sickness or any dissimulation in her'.[13] Leeds Castle had once been the prison of Joan of Navarre, but where dowager queen Joan enjoyed comfortable house arrest with 1,000 marks a year granted towards her custody, Eleanor's custodians had to make do with 100. Joan had never been forced to endure public penance, and she was pardoned and released within three years. Eleanor, however, would remain a prisoner until her death, spending most of her time incarcerated in fortresses in distant corners of Henry's realm.[14]

As she was rowed away from London for the last time in January 1441 Eleanor might have consoled herself with the knowledge that her fate was comparatively merciful. Her low-born accomplices were condemned to death for their complicity in her treason. Thomas Southwell predicted that 'he should die in his bed and not by justice', and indeed he passed away in the Tower the night before his execution. Given that Southwell was a physician, it is likely that, to avoid the torments of a traitor's death, he took matters into his own hands. The 'Witch of Eye' was not so fortunate. For producing her waxen images, Margery Jourdemayne was burnt at the stake at Smithfield on 27 October 1440. Roger Bolingbroke went to his death still insisting he was innocent. On 18 November he was dragged from the Tower to Tyburn and there hanged, drawn and quartered. His head was speared on London Bridge and his quartered corpse sent to four cities associated with the heresy of Lollardy: Bristol, Cambridge, Oxford and Hereford.[15]

Whether Gloucester was innocent of complicity in Eleanor's actions or not, these events cast a long shadow over his relationship with his nephew. Henry now had good reason to suspect the motivations of his overbearing uncle, and he certainly neither forgot nor forgave Eleanor's crimes, remaining sensitive about mentions of his aunt long after the date predicted for his death had passed. In 1444 a common-born woman berated Henry on Blackheath for keeping Eleanor imprisoned rather than releasing her to return to her husband. When arrested for using 'ungodly language' towards the king, the woman refused to enter a plea in court and was, as a punishment, crushed to death with iron weights.* Where Eleanor was concerned, neither Henry nor his council were inclined to mercy. Even after she was imprisoned, the uncomfortable truth was that the succession was still in danger. Gloucester now had no heir *and* no wife, and as long as he was Henry's successor the Lancastrian line hung by an alarmingly slender thread.[16]

With the annulment of his marriage to Eleanor, Gloucester's importance to the line of succession had effectively been neutralized. Despite two marriages – both apparently motivated by a degree of sexual attraction – he had no legitimate children.† Now that Gloucester was divorced and reaching advanced middle age, the likelihood of him bearing any further children was extremely slim. Henry was already making preparations in anticipation of Gloucester's heirless death, with parcels of his estates being promised to the king's chosen few from 1440 onwards.

The lack of rival claimants to the throne would, on the face of it, seem to be a major advantage to Henry VI, but as Eleanor Cobham's downfall had shown, where there was dynastic insecurity, political anxiety and unrest were sure to follow. Henry was now almost twenty, and on his shoulders rested the entire future of the Lancastrian dynasty. In 1404, his grandfather Henry IV had carefully vested the dynasty's succession in the heirs of Henry V – if Henry V's line failed, the crown would pass

---

* This was the standard punishment for failing to enter a plea.
† Like his brother Bedford, Gloucester had two illegitimate children, Arthur and Antigone.

to one of Henry IV's three younger sons, the dukes of Clarence, Bedford and Gloucester, and then to their heirs general. Henry IV could hardly have foreseen that all three dukes would fail to sire a legitimate heir, nor that Henry V would marry so unusually late that he would produce only one son before his untimely end. Henry VI's heir in 1441 remained his fifty-year-old uncle Gloucester. After that, the line ran out. Or at least, it ran out of direct Lancastrian claimants. For there was a large pool of noblemen with royal blood in their veins from other branches of the wider Plantagenet family.[17]

Henry was always conscious of his blood kinship to his own nobility, and rewarded his many distant cousins as their rank demanded. Positions of vice-regal honour – lieutenancies of France and Ireland, governorships of Normandy – went first and foremost to his relatives, which was exactly what the fifteenth-century worldview expected. There was a particular need for high-born individuals to represent Henry's monarchy in France, defending his title and asserting his authority, while Henry himself remained safely remote from danger. Foremost among these deputies was Richard, duke of York. Ten years older than Henry, York was the first appointee to French rule after the death of the duke of Bedford. In 1436 he was made lieutenant-general and governor of France. In the duke's royal commission Henry explicitly said that it was York's nearness of blood that had recommended his 'dear cousin' to this position.[18] This conveniently sidestepped the fact that York arguably had a stronger claim to the throne than Henry did. The Lancastrian line was descended from Edward III's third son, John of Gaunt, but York could claim double descent from Edward III: his grandfather was that king's fourth surviving son, Edmund; while his mother was descended from the king's *second* son Lionel, duke of Clarence. Henry IV's seizure of the throne from Richard II had displaced these 'Yorkists' from the line of succession.

This royal lineage had caused serious problems for a number of York's forebears: his father Richard, earl of Cambridge, had been executed for trying to depose Henry V in 1415, and his uncle, the otherwise impeccably loyal earl of March, had been implicated in the traitorous plot of John Mortimer in 1423. Having grown up at the royal court from the age of seventeen York had thus far proven himself as devoted to Lancastrian service as his uncle. He had also managed to straddle the Gloucester–Beaufort division at court, making himself reasonably acceptable to both men. He had been named among the high-born lords Gloucester felt had been unduly sidelined by Henry in 1440, suggesting a sense of shared interests between them, but he had been brought up by Cardinal Beaufort's sister Joan, countess of Westmorland, and married to her daughter Cecily Neville. As such York could also be considered a Beaufort associate. In contrast to the unhappy procreative history of the Lancastrians, the duke and duchess of York were merrily repopulating the royal family at a rate of knots: they had eight sons and four daughters between 1439 and 1455, although not all survived infancy.[19]

The Beauforts were the king's other prominent royal cousins. Like Henry, they were descended from John of Gaunt, but they were the illegitimate offspring of Gaunt's third marriage to Katherine Swynford. After Cardinal Beaufort, the chief representatives of the family were his nephews, John and Edmund Beaufort. This pair had a further connection to the royal family, as their stepfather had been Henry V's younger brother Thomas, duke of Clarence. John Beaufort had been captured by the French and suffered the indignity of seventeen years' imprisonment at their hands. He was only able to return to England after considerable diplomatic effort on his mother's part and the payment of a heavy ransom of £24,000. Since his release from captivity John had led two cardinal-funded expeditions to Normandy in 1439 and 1440. He was determined to make his military mark again. Meanwhile, John's younger brother Edmund had been campaigning in France almost unceasingly since 1427, most famously representing English interests at the Siege of Calais in 1436. In 1443 John Beaufort was made duke of Somerset, one of a number of promotions Henry granted to his kinsmen in this period.

Another branch of family who were particularly singled out in the 1440s were the Staffords, who were descended from Edward III's granddaughter, Anne of Woodstock.* The head of the family, Humphrey Stafford, was once infamous for his temper. During Joan of Arc's interrogation in 1431 he had tried to stab her. Despite such tendencies, he was elevated to the dukedom of Buckingham in September 1444, a suitable reward for a man who had spent the past two decades either governing in England or fighting for Henry in France. Buckingham's high position in Henry's favour was promoted by the fact that despite his considerable military experience and occasional violent outbursts, he had become a leading proponent of peace with France. He had joined Cardinal Beaufort at Calais in 1439 and was mellowing into a mediatory figure in English politics.

The last branch of the extended royal family was the Hollands. Their head was John Holland, son of Henry IV's sister Elizabeth and a kinsman of Richard II. Like York, Holland's father had been executed for plotting against the Lancastrian kings and, again like York, his own road to restoration lay through war in France. As earl of Huntingdon he had captained the English forces at Compiègne, where Joan of Arc was captured. Holland was another of those lords of the blood that Gloucester claimed had been wrongfully excluded from Henry's council in 1440 but he was always considered a reliable military commander and in January 1444 he was elevated to the duchy of Exeter.

This surfeit of relatives was all well and good, but what Henry really needed was a son and heir, and that could only be achieved through marriage. Henry's strong sense of sexual continence meant he was not going to complicate matters with illegitimate children. He regarded chastity as a cardinal virtue and almost

---

* Anne was the daughter of Thomas of Woodstock, youngest son of Edward III.

certainly remained a virgin until he married. The first steps towards his marriage had been taken in 1429, when Alfonso of Aragon had suggested a marriage between the eight-year-old Henry and one of Queen Blanche of Navarre's daughters. This potential Spanish alliance had been rejected by the English council, who felt it imperative that Henry choose his wife for himself. The matter was laid to rest until 1438, when the death of England's old ally, the Holy Roman Emperor Sigismund, led Henry to consider a marital alliance with a relative of Sigismund's successor, Albrecht II of Austria. Unfortunately, Albrecht died before the plans could be brought to fruition. In 1442–3 a Portuguese union was considered, then rejected in favour of a French match. A possible marriage to one of Charles VII's daughters was mooted in various peace negotiations but was never brought close to being realized. In all of these cases matters of international diplomacy intervened to put a halt to proceedings.[20]

By 1442, Henry was finally ready to seriously consider marriage. The count of Armagnac had offered an alliance with one of his daughters as part of a wider plot by the French princes of the blood royal to unite against Charles VII and replace him with his teenage son, Dauphin Louis. The count of Armagnac approached Henry on the advice of a triumvirate of dukes: Brittany, Alençon and Henry's former prisoner Orléans, who seemed at last to be rewarding Henry's faith in him. This marriage had the potential to solve the two major challenges facing Henry's regime in one fell swoop: it would ensure the succession and end the wars with France.

Armagnac offered the choice of his three daughters and Henry dithered over which would suit him best. For all his concern for chastity, he was not willing to take a wife to whom he was not physically attracted. Characteristically late in the day, and having already dispatched his ambassadors – who had got as far as Plymouth – Henry decided it would be prudent to inspect all three young women before making his decision. He wanted an artist appointed to paint the ladies 'in their kirtles simple' – that is, in their under-dresses without their expensive and concealing gowns over the top – so that he could 'see their stature and their beauty and colour of skin and their countenances, with all manner of features' and then decide 'which him liketh' best. So great was Henry's concern that he signed his new instruction 'of our own hand, the which as ye [know] well we be not much accustomed for to do in other cases'.[21]

Unfortunately for Henry his embassy's arrival in Gascony coincided with a renewal of Charles VII's military efforts there. Far from being able to report on the charming ladies of Armagnac, Henry's ambassadors, Sir Robert Roos and Thomas Beckington, had to send panicked messages back to king and council, reporting alarming French gains and requesting as a matter of urgency that an English army be sent to check Charles's progress. The envoys were so concerned that intelligence about the dire English military situation might fall into enemy hands that they had a secret letter sent to England sewn inside the hem of a pilgrim's garment.[22]

With Charles's army blocking the ambassadors' path to Armagnac and letters sometimes taking a month to arrive at their destination, the marriage negotiations proceeded at a snail's pace. Even the weather turned against them: Hans, the artist dispatched to paint Henry's prospective brides, complained that in the winter cold his paints could not be mixed and applied.[23] By the beginning of 1443 he had completed only one portrait while the count of Armagnac offered temporizing assurances about his continued commitment. Since his son was fighting in Charles's French army at the time, Roos and Beckington were understandably sceptical. They left Bordeaux to report back to Henry in January 1443. A few months later Charles's son, Dauphin Louis, invaded the Armagnac lands and took the count and his family prisoner. With so little progress made and such misfortune heaped on the negotiations, it is little surprise that Henry decided to allow the idea of an Armagnac marriage to be quietly dropped.[24]

★

The abortive negotiations with Armagnac had at least belatedly roused Henry into taking action to protect Gascony. For years the duchy had been left almost to its own devices, with English military attention focused predominantly on Normandy and the pale of Calais. Now fears for the crucial trading cities of Bayonne and Bordeaux convinced the English government that military intervention was vital. But how to pay for it when Normandy was also under constant threat? In May 1443, Henry asked his treasurer, Lord Ralph Cromwell, to produce a report on the financial situation so that a plan could be formulated. Its conclusions were profoundly troubling: there was simply not enough money to fund a war on two fronts. The treasury could only afford to dispatch one sizeable army to the continent, so it must go either to Gascony or to Normandy.[25] Henry was faced with the unsavoury prospect of losing one of his hard-won French territories. Gascony had been in English hands since the mid-twelfth century and was an indispensable trade partner. But Normandy's connection to England went back even further, having been attached to the crown since the Norman Conquest, although it had been lost for 200 years from 1204. Losing either of these territories would be disastrous.

Fortunately, a saviour seemed to be at hand. In autumn 1442 Cardinal Beaufort's nephew John Beaufort nominated himself to command a major offensive against Charles VII, with the generous financial backing, naturally, of the cardinal. Noble enthusiasm for campaigning in France had waned considerably in recent years so Henry eagerly accepted his cousin's offer. But before the final indenture for service could be drawn up, John Beaufort had a number of demands. Under the circumstances, they were considerable. He wanted to be made a duke, so he was duly invested as duke of Somerset on St George's Day 1443. More problematically, John wanted his brother Edmund's governorship of Anjou and Maine* to be transferred to him when its terms ended, and for it to come to him under the English seal – in other words, for its authority to be completely independent of the duke of York, the lieutenant-governor of Normandy. Somerset demanded that any new territories he conquered were also to be held independently. Finally, he demanded the authority to act in military matters according to 'his own will and intent', rather than being under the command of the duke of York.[26] All of this Henry granted. The only one of John Beaufort's demands that was not fully met was a requested grant of land worth 1,000 marks, which was reduced by a third.[27]

In return for this unprecedented level of autonomy, John Beaufort's plan was to land neither in Gascony nor Normandy, but instead to face Charles VII head on, crossing the Loire into his heartland 'and there use most cruel and mortal war' against the French.[28] This, it was hoped, would divert Charles's attention from his Gascon offensive and provide a 'shield' for Normandy. If Charles fled, John Beaufort had the authority to seek him out 'wherever he be'. The financial heft of the Beaufort expedition was considerable and the army to be assembled was the largest since Henry's coronation expedition – the first two quarters' wages for the men cost over £26,000.[29]

In his eagerness to dispatch John Beaufort with his army, Henry had failed properly to consider the impact of the new duke of Somerset's independent authority on the lieutenant-general and governor of Normandy, Richard, duke of York. York was informed about John Beaufort's powers in a letter from Henry which asked the lieutenant-general to 'give [John] all comfort, succour and help that may be to him possible'. The affront to York's office was bad enough, but Henry also informed him that payment of the next instalment of his salary would be delayed as crown finances were already devoted to John Beaufort's

---

* Anjou and Maine were largely English-held territories bordering Normandy.

expedition. To appeal to the king to reconsider John's unparalleled powers, York dispatched a committee of delegates from his Norman council. Despite their remonstrations, Henry would not be moved.

Henry's faith in John Beaufort proved to be woefully misplaced. Following the lengthy haggling process over the terms of his preferment the duke of Somerset suddenly fell ill, so although his forces were urgently needed in France in spring 1443, John Beaufort and his army were still in England in the summer. When he was finally well enough to coordinate his departure, problems persisted. He could not entice high-born men to join his army and had to request that they were replaced with archers.[30] He also proved unreliable, twice missing his intended muster date. Where musters did take place there were rumours of malpractice and unruly behaviour. By 9 July 1443 Henry had to send commissioners to chastise John Beaufort and order him to leave immediately. 'He marvelleth greatly,' Henry told the commissioners, 'and not without cause the long abode of his said cousin on this side [of] the sea and the many great and long delays of his passage, to the king's full great hurt, harm and charge in many and sundry wises.' The delays were by then costing £500 a day.[31]

It was an ignominious beginning to a campaign that was to prove an abject failure. John Beaufort failed to draw Charles's army to battle, leaving the English army bumbling around the Breton–Angevin borderlands for several months before retreating back to Normandy by December. One of John Beaufort's rare successes was his seizure of the fortified town of La Guerche, but even this was not without its issues. Although part of the estate of the French duke of Alençon, the town lay within Breton territory and the new duke of Brittany, François I, was enraged at the violation of his borders. John Beaufort's actions were particularly embarrassing as, at the time La Guerche was taken, Breton ambassadors – including Henry's old friend and the duke's brother, Gilles of Brittany – were at Henry's court on a diplomatic mission.[32]

After John Beaufort disbanded his army in early January 1444 he returned to a cold reception in England. All that Somerset had achieved – at huge expense to the crown and with no military progress to show for it – was to seriously offend both an important international ally and Henry's lieutenant-general and governor in France. The high expectations invested in John Beaufort's expedition, and the level of rewards he had demanded to undertake it, served only to render yet more unpalatable an already disastrous outcome. As it was, he returned to England and immediately went into political exile. When Henry would not receive him at court, John Beaufort retreated to his West Country home in Wimborne, where he died, aged only forty, on 27 May 1444. There were rumours that 'being unable to bear the strain of so great a disgrace', he took his own life.[33]

With the failure of John Beaufort's expedition in 1443 it had become clear that, for the good of his realm, Henry would have to make peace with France as soon as possible. Even if major concessions were demanded, the war could simply no longer be supported financially or militarily. Fortunately for Henry, the last few years had been as unkind to Charles VII as they had been to the king of England. In the *Praguerie* of 1440 Charles had faced a rebellion by his royal kinsmen which attempted to install his son Louis, the dauphin, as regent of France. Relentless campaigning against both the English and his own rebellious subjects had eventually worn the French king down, and induced in him an unaccustomed desire for reconciliation.

In May 1443 Charles had finally met the duke of Orléans, in company with their kinsman René of Anjou. It was around this time that Charles first made overtures for peace through Gilles's Breton embassy to the English court. Henry's 'very dear and well-beloved cousin' Gilles of Brittany, younger brother of the new duke, 'several times expressed' the desire of Duke François to mediate a truce with France.[34] Knowing that Henry was both inclined to peace and seeking a bride, Charles made overtures to assist him – and by extension, of course, help himself. Thus, in

May 1444, another peace conference was scheduled to be held at Tours, in France. To cement the alliance, Charles suggested a royal marriage. This time Henry was to be the groom, and the suggested bride was Charles's niece, Margaret of Anjou.

14

'Welcome... Princess, our lady sovereign' [1]

Tours, Charles's French territory
24 May 1444

The city of Tours was no stranger to royal weddings, nor to child brides and grooms. It was here that the ten-year-old Charles VII had been betrothed to Marie of Anjou in 1413, and here that their adolescent son, Dauphin Louis, wed Princess Margaret of Scotland in 1436. Now the king and queen, and the dauphin and dauphine, gathered their courts to watch Marie's fourteen-year-old niece, Margaret of Anjou, marry Henry VI. The Angevin princess, dark-haired and good-looking, entered the basilica of St Martin under the shadow of its five looming turrets and walked the 100 metres from one end of the building to the other on the arm of her uncle Charles. Her parents looked proudly on amid the press of watching French and English nobility. At the altar, Charles doffed his hat respectfully and handed his niece to the papal legate officiating at the ceremony. Although Margaret was marrying Henry, it was not he who slipped a wedding ring on to her finger or spoke the marriage vows, but the fifty-something William de la Pole, earl of Suffolk, acting as the king's proxy. News of the marriage was greeted on both sides of the Channel with delighted cries of 'peace, peace!'. At long last it seemed there was hope of a real and lasting union between adversaries who had waged bitter war for more than a century.[2]

Suffolk's role as proxy king was a visible sign of his ascendancy in Henry's affections and government. Since the ostracizing of Gloucester and the humiliating failure of the Beaufort expedition in 1443, Suffolk had become Henry's chief adviser, constantly in attendance on the young king or seeing to his concerns in council. He knew Henry's mind well, and when talk turned seriously to a marriage alliance with France, Henry insisted that Suffolk lead the negotiations. Charles VII himself had proposed Suffolk's pre-eminent role in the English embassy, a fact that was sufficiently concerning to the earl that he asked Henry to indemnify him against any charges of misconduct if the talks were not successful. Perhaps he feared a repeat of the personal attack that Gloucester had launched on Cardinals Beaufort and Kempe in the wake of the failed 1439 negotiations. He may also have been mindful of the concessions Henry was willing to contemplate in order to bring about peace. In return for sovereignty over Normandy and Gascony, Henry was prepared to give up his claim to the French throne. Suffolk would have to tread carefully to avoid committing Henry to a peace that Gloucester and his 'grudging' supporters could paint as traitorously opposed to English interests. Having been both a prisoner of war in France and the keeper of the duke of Orléans, Suffolk was an easy target for such ire.[3]

In March 1444, Suffolk had left for France at the head of an embassy that included a number of Henry's trusted household attendants. Among them were Adam Moleyns, the keeper of the privy seal; Henry's secretary Richard Andrewe; and one of his esquires, John Wenlock. These men were trusted with a particularly delicate mission. As Henry's close personal interest in the Armagnac princesses had shown, he was not willing to commit himself to an unhappy marriage for the cause of peace. Having some knowledge of the king's personality and tastes, Suffolk and his fellow household men were tasked with vetting Margaret of Anjou as a suitable consort for the king.

Margaret was the youngest surviving child of Isabelle, duchess of Lorraine, and René of Anjou, titular king of Sicily and Jerusalem. Her father was a famed patron of literature, art and chivalrous endeavours who, in his later years, amused himself with elaborate tournaments and a menagerie of exotic animals for whom his tailors embroidered costumes. During Margaret's childhood René was often absent on campaign, or enduring imprisonment by his enemies. As a result she had grown up at the court of her grandmother, Yolande of Aragon. The cultured Yolande was a respected force in French politics, and trusted adviser to her son-in-law Charles VII. Charles had spent his adolescence in her court and occasionally returned to visit during Margaret's youth. From the turrets of Saumur Castle above the River Loire, Yolande had exercised authority over territories that stretched from Maine to Provence and Lorraine to Italy. Margaret's mother, Isabelle of Lorraine, had been just as steadfast in defence of her and René's rights, once leading a fleet to Naples on her husband's behalf. Margaret had thus grown up in an atmosphere of educational and imaginative expression, watching women protect their family's interests with the same capability as their male relatives.[4] As for her appearance, although a Milanese ambassador described Margaret as 'somewhat dark' for medieval tastes,* he also praised her as 'a most handsome woman... wise and charitable' and the Norman chronicler Thomas Basin reported that at the time of the embassy's visit Margaret was 'a good-looking and well-developed girl... mature and ripe for marriage'.[5]

Margaret impressed the English envoys sufficiently that – from

---

* In an illumination that appears in the Talbot Book of Hours, which was presented to her c.1444/5 by Lord John Talbot, Margaret is portrayed according to contemporary ideals of queenly beauty, with blond hair and pale skin. This cannot, however, be taken for a true likeness.

her arrival in Tours on 4 May – it took only three weeks for the marriage with Henry to be agreed and effected. Henry's envoys were preoccupied not only by Margaret's personal charms but by the political aspects of the union. In English eyes, a signifi- cant diplomatic advantage of rapprochement with the Angevins was that they stood high in Charles's favour in the wake of the *Praguerie*, with René's brother, Charles of Maine, a particular royal favourite.* Marriage into the House of Anjou was less prob- lematic to the English than previously suggested unions with Charles VII's daughters. In 1444 Charles VII's marriageable daughters were still only children, and Henry needed an heir to fortify his dwindling dynasty as quickly as possible. For their own reasons, both Charles and Henry's advisers were concerned about the long-term implications of a union between Valois and Lancaster. On the English side, there was anxiety about seeming to legitimize a line that had been disinherited in the Treaty of Troyes; and on Charles's, a concern that it might bolster Henry's claim to his French territories. Marriage with Margaret suited all parties better. Admittedly, her dowry was pitiful – 20,000 francs and a meaningless endowment of Majorca and Minorca, both currently under the control of a rival – but the union offered the prospect of children for Henry, peace with France and allies in the House of Anjou now that the old Burgundian alliance had withered and died.

On 28 May 1444, in the wake of the proxy marriage at St Martin's, the first truce between England and France in more than twenty years was sealed. Henry had hoped it would be an everlasting peace, or at least one that would endure several decades, but all Suffolk was able to negotiate was a twenty-three- month truce, with the possibility of extension. The questions of sovereignty and the French throne were put on hold until a larger embassy could meet in England the following year. In

---

* The *Praguerie* was led by Charles, duke of Bourbon, and Dauphin Louis. René of Anjou and Charles of Maine had not been involved.

his desire for peace – any peace – perhaps Suffolk had fulfilled the concerns of his critics and failed to press the French hard enough for advantageous terms. His most fundamental error was not realized until later: in the terms for the Anglo-French truce, he had allowed François of Brittany to be listed as a vassal of King Charles, despite the fact that François was allied with England. This error was to rear its head with damaging consequences for Henry's interests in the years ahead. However, if Henry was disappointed in his chief minister's efforts, he gave no indication of it. When Suffolk returned to England to confirm with the king the terms of the truce and his marriage, Henry elevated him to a marquessate as reward for his services. He also granted him the wardship of the infant heiress of the late duke of Somerset, Margaret Beaufort, a considerable financial and political boon.[6]

While Henry prepared for his queen's arrival with costly restoration and building work on the royal palaces, Margaret remained with her family in Lorraine.* In the end, she did not leave them until March 1445, eventually making the journey from Nancy through Armagnac-controlled France with a considerable escort of musicians, courtiers and servants. Margaret's brother, Jean of Calabria, accompanied her with a French escort as far as St Denis, then the duke of Orléans took his place as representative of the French princes. At Pontoise, on the ancient road from Paris to Rouen, her French escort left her altogether and she was delivered into the care of the English. Henry had spent more than £5,000 providing his queen with a suitably impressive entourage, 300 strong, for her journey, but the strain of endless travel and the transformation in her situation started to take its toll on Margaret. She had only

---

* As well as modifications to Westminster and the Tower of London, an entire new hall, scullery and saucery had been built for the queen at Eltham, as well as a waterbridge, 'great quadrangle with a gatehouse' and brick garden tower at Sheen Palace in Richmond. POPC, VI, pp. 31–2.

just turned fifteen and had still never met the man for whom she was leaving her family and friends to begin a new life in England. Her physician's bills mounted, Dr Francis mixing up 'diverse spices, confections and powders' to make her medicine while a yeoman toiled in the kitchen to try to restore her to health with nourishing dishes. It did not help. Margaret was so ill by the time she reached Rouen that the sumptuous chariot draped in cloth of gold that Henry had sent for her formal entry into the city had to be occupied by a proxy.* Suffolk's wife, Alice Chaucer, played the part of 'queen' while the sickly Margaret languished in Rouen Castle.[7]

On 3 April, Margaret was rowed out to the *Cock John* off Cherbourg, one of a fleet of ships arranged to convey her to England. As the ship sailed along the coast between Portsmouth and Southampton she was serenaded from two Genoese galleys. The music failed to soothe her. Margaret blamed the crossing for the sickness she suffered on arriving in England, but as she was still ill a week after setting foot on dry land, the 'pox' that afflicted her sounds more like the result of anxiety. Whatever her private worries may have been, there was no turning back now. Her life as princess of Anjou was over. She was now queen of England.[8]

London
29 May 1445

It was twenty-three years since England had had a queen. Twenty-three years of warfare and heavy taxation, of disrupted trade and piracy, when the heavy footfall of armies on city streets and the blaze of beacons on clifftops had become commonplace. The

---

* Her chief attendant may have been Cecily, duchess of York, for, although she was the wife of Henry's representative in Normandy, Cecily did not attend the entry into Rouen.

arrival of Margaret of Anjou promised to end those troubles. She was the harbinger of peace, 'causer of wealth, joy and abundance'.[9] As she entered London for her coronation at the end of May 1445, Margaret was greeted with almost hysterical optimism. The citizens crowded from the streets to the roofs and windows of buildings to snatch a sight of her. Tavern signs and roof tiles had been tightened and gutters cleared so that daredevil spectators could risk their necks to greet their new queen. The aldermen of London had spent weeks debating what colour robes they ought to wear – saffron or red? – to make the best first impression, and vast expense had been put into decking the streets through which Margaret would pass with tapestries and sumptuous cloth. In the back of her chariot, weighed down by innumerable pearls and a jewel-studded collar, Margaret of Anjou bore the attention well.[10]

What did Margaret expect her role to be when she arrived in England? Probably very much what it had been for previous queens, almost all of whom since the Norman Conquest had been foreign-born.* She would protect her own servants and estates, act as intercessor for her subjects to appeal for peace and mercy from the king, and she would have lots of children as swiftly as possible. Margaret might also have been prepared for occasions when her authority as queen would be expanded, and a more overtly political role would be expected of her. She had, after all, watched two generations of her own female relatives exercising their authority, so she knew from first-hand experience that although active queenship was unusual, when necessary, women were capable of it.

What she made of Henry was a different matter. She must have considered it a good sign that during the eleven months between their wedding and their first meeting, Henry showered her with thoughtful, chivalrous gifts. Her wedding band was the

---

* The sole exception was Henry I's wife Edith, also known as Matilda, who was of Anglo-Scottish heritage and grew up in Hampshire.

same ruby ring that Henry had worn at his French coronation, an item that must have held tremendous significance for him as a symbol of commitment to his French subjects. When Henry learnt that Margaret liked riding, he sent her a horse and saddle; when she arrived in England in need of new clothing, he commissioned Margaret Chamberlayne, the duchess of York's 'tyremaker', to deck the queen in expensive gowns. For Margaret's coronation, he had the keeper of his jewels deliver his 'right entirely well-beloved queen' a range of jewel-studded brooches and an ornamental collar dripping with rubies, sapphires and pearls. Perhaps Henry had heard about René of Anjou's interest in the exotic; as a wedding gift, he presented Margaret with a lion from the Tower of London.[11]

Margaret's arrival stirred Henry to previously unsuspected flights of chivalrous imagination. Imitating the famed romantic gestures of Margaret's Angevin forebears, Henry visited his new bride for the first time disguised as a lowly squire. With the marquess of Suffolk's collusion, Henry delivered Margaret a letter from 'the king' and knelt humbly before her as she read through it. When Henry had left, Suffolk revealed the squire's true identity and Margaret said she 'was vexed... because she had kept him on his knees'. For all her protestation, it is more likely that Margaret knew exactly what she was doing in this game of courtly inversion, acting the innocent lady and pretending to pay no heed to her suitor. In her childhood she must have heard of how, when her grandfather Louis of Aragon first met her grandmother Yolande, he kissed her hand dressed as a simple knight; or how Yolande's father, King Juan of Aragon, disguised himself as a troubadour to present his future queen with a ring.[12]

Such charades aside, Henry showed a touching concern for his new wife. He cancelled his attendance at the traditional celebration of St George's Day at Windsor so he could stay with his 'most dear and best-beloved wife' while she was unwell. The couple could easily converse in French, making Margaret's acclimatization to her new home a little easier. Perhaps she might have found her husband, who was eight years her senior, a little childish and easily led, but for a teenager away from home for the first time that was not necessarily a bad thing.[13]

On 22 April 1445, Margaret had recovered enough for the couple to be married at Titchfield Abbey in Hampshire by Henry's confessor, William Aiscough, bishop of Salisbury, and on 29 May Margaret processed from the Tower of London through thronged city streets to her coronation in Westminster Abbey. The jewelled collar that Henry had given her glittered across her shoulders, and as was traditional her long hair was loose over a gleaming white gown. Tradition also dictated that Henry absented himself publicly from the coronation, but he watched Margaret's progress through London from the windows of the house of the goldsmith William Flour. Goldsmiths' stalls clustered around Cheapside, the area through which Margaret passed after pausing at Leadenhall and Cornhill to watch two of the eight pageants put on by the city in her honour. The fifth pageant was performed at the conduit on Cheapside (no doubt flowing with free wine for the occasion), so Henry's rented lodgings might have been chosen for their view of the scene.[14]

In these pageants, which combined spoken text with static tableaux for what may have been the first time in English history, Margaret was imagined as the white 'dove that brought the branch of peace'. 'Peace between England and France', it was claimed, had been achieved 'by means of Margaret'. In reality, time was running out for an Anglo-French peace settlement: the realm was already a year into the truce agreed at Tours, with barely eleven months left to run. It remained to be seen if Henry and Margaret could turn their marriage into the means by which lasting peace could be achieved.

15

'Stretch forth the hand'[1]

As Christmas approached, and frost rimed the gardens of Sheen Palace, Margaret took up quill and parchment and set out to convince King Charles VII of her ongoing dedication to peace. 'Most high and powerful prince, our very dear uncle,' she wrote to him, 'we pray sweet Jesus Christ that he keep you in his blessed protection.' It was an appropriate time to encourage goodwill to all men, and although Margaret had not long been queen, she had already learnt to imitate her husband's emollient approach to the conduct of international relations. 'No greater pleasure can we have in this world', she assured Charles, 'than to see an arrangement for a final peace between [Henry] and you, as well for the nearness of lineage in which you stand the one to the other, as also for the relief and repose of the Christian people, which has been so long disturbed by war.' She promised to 'stretch forth the hand, and employ ourselves herein... for your pleasure the best that we can do, as we have always done'. The new queen of England would need to do all she could, for the reality was that despite Henry's best efforts the peace talks begun at Tours in May 1444 were already faltering.[2]

In July 1445 the largest and most important foreign embassy to come to England in thirty years had arrived to treat with King Henry. So vast was the entourage that disembarked beneath the white cliffs of Dover that it took eleven days for them all to travel from Calais to Dartford, with more than 300 horses drafted in to carry the visitors to London for the talks. As testament to the seriousness of these negotiations, the embassy included senior figures from Charles's court – the master of his household, Louis, prince of Bourbon; Jacques Jouvenel des Ursins, archbishop of Reims; Charles's master of requests, the diplomat Guillaume Cousinot. Charles's chamberlain, Bertrand de Beauvau, lord of Précigny, was an intimate friend and servant of Margaret's father René and had escorted Margaret on her journey from Nancy to the English court eight months earlier. His presence must have been welcome to the new queen, enabling her to hear news from her family. There were also representatives of the ruling families of Castile, Brittany, Alençon and Anjou. Noticeably absent from this vast international delegation were any ambassadors from Philippe of Burgundy. Although officially this was down to issues with their safe conduct, the real reason was that Charles wanted to sideline his old rival.

To symbolize the amicable tone of these talks, the French envoys entered London side by side with their English counterparts. Men who had faced one another in battle now rode through the city streets together, resplendent 'in cloth of gold, and silk, and goldsmiths' work', even 'their horses [having] trappings of silver gilt, and of goldsmiths' work and some of cloth of gold'. 'A great multitude of people' came out to watch this display of amity, and as far as the French could tell they all 'appeared to have joy thereat'. After a century of international war, it was not only Henry who desired peace.[3]

As at Tours, Suffolk was again a key intermediary, accompanying the ambassadors and leading the talks, but now that the negotiations were taking place on English soil, Henry himself sought to set the tone. He was determined that the negotiations would be different from those that had gone before, that no misunderstandings or diplomatic coldness should undermine the genuine desire for reconciliation. It had already been agreed that talks would proceed in French, with friendly language and reverence shown on both sides. To prevent drunken brawls from erupting into diplomatic incidents, the French delegates forbade their servants to go out at night or to pick quarrels with the English.

The morning after the French embassy entered London, Henry greeted the diplomats personally at Westminster Palace. The now twenty-three-year-old king met them in a magnificently decorated chamber within the palace, surrounded by his advisers and sumptuous blue and gold wall hangings. One tapestry must have been chosen for its relevance to this debate about the dual monarchy: prominently positioned behind the king's throne, it showed a group of ladies presenting the arms of France to their lord. Charles VI's motto, *Jamais*, was embroidered all over the walls, alongside the broom plant that both Valois and Plantagenet had adopted, further emphasizing Henry's dual French and English royal heritage.* Many of the king's advisers were well known to the French from previous peace talks. There was Adam Moleyns, Henry's keeper of the privy seal, and Cardinal Kempe, his chancellor. The marquess of Suffolk was of course front and centre of proceedings. Perhaps less welcome to the French ambassadors was the sight of the duke of Gloucester, looming over Henry's left shoulder and eyeing this embassy with more suspicion than welcome.[4]

As soon as the French delegates entered the chamber, Henry got up from his throne and came down to stand 'exactly in front of' it. He looked as magnificent as the setting, his robe of red cloth of gold sweeping all the way to the floor, but he put aside all royal hauteur to greet the French, removing his hat and

---

* The 'Plantagenets' were said to have derived their name from their ancestor Geoffrey, count of Anjou, who wore a sprig of broom, *planta genista*, in his helmet.

taking them each by the hand. This was a remarkable reversal
of normal royal protocol. In any encounter between men of
different status, the lower ranked was expected to remove his
hat in greeting, physically abasing himself by bowing or even
kneeling. In the presence of kings, men might remain on their
knees throughout the entire encounter, as Hue de Lannoy had
seen the noblemen of England kneel around Henry as he read
a letter from Philippe of Burgundy in 1433. Touching the royal
person was usually strictly forbidden. In departing so markedly
from royal convention in his greeting to the French envoys,
Henry was giving visible expression to his oft-stated desire for
peace. Such behaviour was not, in fact, without precedent – his
father Henry V had similarly lowered himself before Charles
VI of France during their peace negotiations at Troyes – but it
made his message abundantly clear: these peace talks should be
different. They should be respectful and affectionate, not coolly
diplomatic and suspicious. Such intentions were admirable but
they were unfortunately counterproductive.

So committed was Henry to avoiding any hint of hostility
that he interrupted Cardinal Kempe during his address to the
ambassadors to chastise him in English for not being friendly
enough. 'He was not pleased,' he told his chancellor in an under-
tone, 'that he had not spoken words of greater friendship.' Kempe
was an experienced diplomat, whereas Henry was unused to the
formality of international negotiation, which demanded cool
heads and long-established ritual behaviours. Henry, however,
wished 'to proceed plainly and openly'.[5] Kempe had to bite his
tongue, and the English advisers must have wanted to roll their
eyes. Henry's fervent desire for peace threatened to undermine
the English position, and even inadvertently to reveal the
divisions in English politics. When the archbishop of Reims
presented letters from Charles assuring Henry of his 'cordial
love and affection', desiring 'above all things that there should
be between them good peace and reasonable', Henry darted
looks in the direction of the duke of Gloucester. He smiled

at Suffolk and said to Kempe in English, pressing his hand, 'I am very much rejoiced that some who are present should hear these words; they are not at their ease.' For the king to allude so clearly to discord with the current heir to the throne, and reveal the fracture between Gloucester's bellicose views and the 'peace party' led by Kempe and Suffolk was supremely impolitic.[6]

Henry's behaviour throughout his meeting with the French revealed his political naivety. He made asides to Suffolk and Kempe, joyfully doffing his hat and muttering his favourite oath, 'St Jehan, grant mercis' ('Thank you, St John'). He patted the French envoys on the back and shook their hands more than once, making 'many tokens of joy'. His motivation was commendable, but his behaviour came across as odd. This was, quite simply, not how things were done in international negotiations. Plain speech and honest behaviour might have been encouraged in Henry's educational texts, but so was circumspection and self-control. Henry's breezy optimism made a palpably poor impression. It was probably something of a relief when he left and the diplomats were able to proceed according to the usual script.

The reality of the talks with the French was that fundamentally little had changed. There was still a vast disconnect between what each side wanted and what they could get. Either Suffolk had oversold the French offers hinted at in Tours, or the French had exaggerated Charles's capacity for compromise. At Tours the English had offered what they considered to be the most generous terms yet: Henry would give up the French crown in return for the duchies of Normandy and Gascony, to be held in complete sovereignty. The French had countered by insisting that Gascony be held as a vassal state from Charles and that Normandy was excluded, substituting instead some territories around Calais. This was completely unacceptable to the English, who had hoped that in the time since the talks at Tours King Charles might have been persuaded to offer something better. But the archbishop of Reims offered the English identical terms in July 1445 as had been rejected in May 1444.

Unwilling to see the talks founder within days of their opening, Suffolk charmed and distracted everyone, convinced that
the French had a compromise held in reserve. After a week
of negotiations, however, even he was growing impatient. 'For
God's sake,' he cried, 'we should state all plainly.'[7] The French
finally revealed their last card: they would add the Limousin, in
the Massif Central, to their offer. The English were crestfallen.
No Normandy. No sovereignty for Gascony. Not even the buffer
lands of Poitou. Cardinal Kempe neatly expressed his colleagues'
frustration when he complained that these 'offers were the very
smallest that ever had been made to them, and yet they had
expected that they would have been greater than at any other
time'.[8] With little alternative now left to them, the crestfallen
English ambassadors said they would have to take this unhappy
news to King Henry.

At this critical moment the Angevin lord of Précigny added a
completely new dimension to negotiations. 'Would to God that
[the kings] would meet,' he said, then 'they would make peace
without any limitation whatever.' To this all parties said 'Amen'.[9]
This changed everything. A state meeting between Henry and
Charles could finally resolve these intractable issues. Of more
immediate value, it would require an extension of the truce to
make the necessary preparations. When the French embassy took
their leave of Henry at Fulham Palace on 30 July, the truce was
extended from 1 April 1446 to the feast of All Saints following it
(1 November). In the autumn, a second French embassy extended the deadline up until 1 April 1447. It was agreed that Henry
and Charles would meet by the end of November 1446.

For the French, a meeting between Charles and Henry had
advantages that had only become more apparent during their
negotiations that summer. Rumours of Henry's naivety, even
mental incapacity, must have reached France some time ago
and Henry's behaviour during the negotiations had done little
to counter French assumptions of his pliability. Even his own
subjects denounced him as a fool. In 1442 a Kentish yeoman had

been called before the court of King's Bench for calling Henry 'a lunatic', and this theme of royal folly peppered indictments throughout the 1440s. Reports of the king's child-like face seemed only to emphasize that he was 'not steadfast of wit as other kings have been before'.[10] Since Charles VII had a reputation for being wily it was not unreasonable to assume that a face-to-face encounter between the Valois king and the pliant Henry might play to French advantage. Unsurprisingly, English commitment to such a meeting was, from the first, wavering. Leaving aside Henry's inability to negotiate for English benefit, the conspicuous magnificence that a state meeting between kings would demand was beyond the means of Henry's treasury, especially as Charles insisted that Margaret must join her husband to act as mediator. Henry and his queen were probably alone in believing that the meeting would ever take place. In the interim, with the truce extended, peace talks could at least continue.

If any further evidence were needed that Henry was a poor champion of his own interests, it was provided when the French embassy returned to England to continue negotiations that autumn. At some point in July, Henry had given Lord de Précigny an oral promise that, to ease the peace process, he was willing to restore the county of Maine to the control of Margaret's family. This province between Normandy and Anjou had been won and occupied by the duke of Bedford in 1424, but Margaret's family continued to assert their rights there. Henry probably agreed to restore the territory on the understanding that the Angevins would use their influence over Charles VII to transform the short-term Anglo-French truce into a conclusive treaty that would end the war, but when the French envoys returned in November 1445 they revealed that René had given Charles the authority to oversee the cession of Maine – and Charles insisted that the return of Maine must take place before a permanent peace could be negotiated. What Henry had understood as a gesture of goodwill was now insisted upon by the French as the price of maintaining the truce.

Henry and Margaret were soon both anxiously composing letters of reassurance to Charles, insisting that their commitment to peace and to the surrender of Maine was unwavering. Days after Margaret had promised Charles that she would 'stretch forth the hand' to achieve his designs, on 22 December 1445, Henry wrote himself, assuring the king of France 'in good faith and on our kingly word to give and deliver really and actually... the comté of Maine, by the last day of April next coming'. He identified Margaret as the motivating force behind the cession of Maine: 'Our most dear and well-beloved companion the queen... has requested us to do this many times.'[11] However, the possibility of surrendering the county in return for concessions from France was not a wholly novel idea. In 1439, during the Anglo-French conference at Calais, England had failed to list Maine among its territorial demands and the grant of the governorship of Maine made to Edmund Beaufort in 1442 included a clause allowing for its future surrender to the French.[12] Suffolk may even have suggested English willingness to return the county to Angevin control during the negotiations at Tours in 1444, long before Margaret was in a position to influence Henry with heartfelt appeals. Margaret might well have believed that a territory which until very recently had been part of her family's patrimony *should* be returned to them, but if she encouraged Henry to commit to ceding Maine, she was pushing at an open door. They had been married only for a matter of months and she was unlikely to promote an agenda that would displease her new husband.[13]

Henry's promise to surrender Maine was neither completely unexpected, then, nor was it entirely foolish. The summer embassy had revealed the alarming possibility that Charles would reject any peace treaty allowing Henry to keep Normandy. The English knew they must concede some territories to win peace, and if the return of Maine allowed Henry to hold on to Normandy, it would be a sacrifice worth making. What was undeniably unwise, however, was Henry's offer to return Maine without any guarantee of reciprocation from Charles, which was born of naive faith that Charles's rhetoric about wanting peace was as genuine as his own. Henry failed to realize until it was too late that Charles was as ruthless and self-interested a political operator as Philippe of Burgundy.

The full extent of Henry's mistake became clear early in the new year as word of the imminent cession of Maine began to seep out. In letters to Charles explaining his reasons for choosing to surrender the territory, Henry's rhetoric uncannily mirrored the words he had used when justifying the release of the duke of Orléans five years earlier – he acted, he wrote, out of a sincere belief that ceding Maine 'was one of the best and aptest means to arrive at the blessing of a peace'. But the precedent of Orléans's release ought to have served as a warning to Henry. If the release of one man had inspired defiance from Gloucester and 'noise and grudging' from his subjects, Henry should have realized the level of resistance that would be unleashed at the cession of an entire county, won and held with the blood of his soldiers and kinsmen.[14]

Although Henry was blind to the dangers of popular discontent, his advisers were not. They foresaw an outcome in which the English lords who had negotiated with the French embassy were blamed for Henry's precipitate promises. In April 1446, the date by which Henry had initially promised to surrender Maine, the chancellor John Stafford, archbishop of Canterbury,* made a declaration on behalf of all the lords in parliament, publicly distancing them from any part in Henry's decisions regarding the terms for peace. 'It has pleased our Lord [God] to incline your highness', the parliament roll recorded Archbishop Stafford saying,

> to... [appoint] a day of convention for the matter of peace
> and for the good conclusion of the same to be had between

---

* John Stafford succeeded Henry Chichele as archbishop of Canterbury in 1443.

your most royal person and your uncle [Charles] of France...
To which said motions and promptings, as he knows, it has
pleased only our Lord to stir and move you; *none of the lords
or your other subjects of this your realm* have in any way stirred or
moved you to do so.

He reiterated the point by appealing to parliament – and by
extension Henry's subjects across the realm – 'to understand
that all the said lords have always done their duty... [and] to
hold them discharged and excused from anything which goes
beyond this'.[15] The next item on the parliament roll was an
annulment of the terms of the Treaty of Troyes, the necessary
first step towards an anticipated peace treaty with Charles VII.
Whether Henry's subjects wanted it or not, the cession of Maine
and the treaty with Charles was forging ahead.

It was already apparent that Henry's promise to transfer
Maine to French control within a matter of months was over-
ambitious, and to force through the surrender in anywhere close
to the timescale Henry had set, his government were forced to
negotiate serious compromises. Edmund Beaufort, since 1438
captain-general and governor of Maine, derived considerable
authority and wealth from the county, controlling all offices
there as well as maintaining his own treasury and government
independent of Normandy. To give all this up, Edmund insisted
on a suitable reward: a pension of 10,000 *livres tournois* and the
role of governor and lieutenant-general of Normandy. Unfortunately for Henry, that role was already filled by the duke of
York, who had served for the majority of the period since 1436
and expected to be re-appointed after his indenture expired in
September 1445. At the time, York's disgruntlement seemed a
small price to pay for placating Edmund Beaufort; in December 1446 Edmund was appointed the new lieutenant-general
of Normandy. To force York's compliance and legitimize
this change in personnel, Henry sought to discredit York as
lieutenant-general. When accusations of financial misconduct

were levelled at York's lieutenancy in autumn 1446, York believed Henry's keeper of the privy seal, Adam Moleyns, was responsible. York complained to the Lords that Moleyns was spreading false rumours, and Moleyns countered that such claims were general knowledge in France. After investigation by the council, York's financial dealings were vindicated but it did not regain him his lieutenancy, and it left York with a justified sense of bitterness towards Edmund Beaufort and Henry's regime.[16]

With York cowed, Edmund Beaufort compensated and Charles applying ever more pressure to peace negotiations, Henry summoned a parliament for February 1447 to make the final preparations for the surrender of Maine and his planned meeting with the French king. One last bastion stood in the way: Humphrey, duke of Gloucester. Suffolk had gone out of his way during the French embassy of July 1445 to suggest that Gloucester was a spent force in English politics. He mockingly repeated a rumour he had heard in France that 'monsieur of Gloucester was a hindrance to the king'. This was absurd, said Suffolk, as Gloucester 'had not the power' to hinder any-thing.[17] Yet despite Gloucester being sidelined by Henry and his court, he maintained a remarkable level of popularity among the people of England. To them he was still the 'good duke of Gloucester', hero of Henry V's wars and champion of the commonweal. Even Eleanor Cobham, a condemned traitor who had colluded with witches and necromancers, inspired surprising depths of sympathy. As such, Gloucester remained dangerous to Henry's regime. He would not quietly tolerate the loss of Maine, and if he addressed his complaints to the Commons in parliament he was likely to be supported. Adding a further layer of complexity, if Henry and Margaret left England for their state meeting with Charles, it would be necessary to appoint a keeper to protect England in their absence and the obvious candidate was Gloucester. He was the only person with the necessary experience and nobility, but could he be trusted with the governance of England when he so openly opposed

Henry's policies? Suffolk and his allies on the council – James Fiennes, Adam Moleyns, Bishop William Aiscough and perhaps also Margaret and Henry themselves – realized the potential threat that Gloucester represented. For twenty-five years he had been the eye of the storm in English politics, a focus for factionalism and discontent. In the coming parliament, for the good of Henry's peace policy, Gloucester would be silenced once and for all.

16

'The mutability of worldly changes'[1]

Bury St Edmunds
18 February 1447

E ighty riders surged towards Bury St Edmunds, their bodies hunched against the bitter winter chill. In their midst was the brooding form of the duke of Gloucester, arriving a week late to a parliament whose location had already changed three times: it was first summoned to the seat of Henry's education foundation in Cambridge, then to distant Winchester. Finally, it was meeting in the heartland of the marquess of Suffolk, in an atmosphere of anxious enmity. Gloucester had been ordered to bring a small escort, but every other lord had arrived armed and well attended. Gloucester could hardly fail to notice the pockets of armed locals dotting the landscape around the abbey town, watching him pass with raw, frozen faces.[2]

Half a mile outside the town, Gloucester's men halted. Two of the king's senior household officials – the controller of Henry's household, Sir Thomas Stanley and his treasurer Sir John Stourton – had been sent to meet the duke, with a message from his nephew. Given the long journey Gloucester had made and the unpleasantness of the season, Henry bade his uncle go straight to his lodgings and warm up with a meal. Today he could ignore the usual royal protocol of calling on the king first. Gloucester followed Henry's bidding, turning his horse towards the town, past the horse market and over a rutted lane. His lodgings were at the hospital of St Saviour outside the north gate of Bury. It was there, either while he was still at his dinner, or a little later in the afternoon, that another royal delegation burst in on the duke. It comprised the duke of Buckingham, Edmund Beaufort, Ralph Botiller, Viscount Beaumont and Richard Neville, earl of Salisbury. In his capacity as high constable of England, Beaumont promptly arrested Gloucester on suspicion of treason. He was confined to his room. Any attempts to reach or communicate with Henry were blocked. That night, and over the three days that followed, around forty of Gloucester's attendants were arrested, including his illegitimate son Arthur, and dispatched to prisons across the country, from the Tower of London to Nottingham Castle.

Five days later, on the morning of 23 February, Gloucester's servants entered his lodgings in St Saviour's to make a grim discovery: Gloucester's dead body. In all likelihood he had died of a heart attack or stroke brought on by the shock of his arrest, but to allay any rumours of assassination, Gloucester's body was publicly displayed the following day. The members of parliament filed past in respectful silence to acknowledge the duke's death and observe that there were no signs of violence on the body.

The duke of Gloucester's death under such ignoble circumstances sent shockwaves across England. 'He died for sorrow as some men said,' reported the anonymous author of the contemporary *English Chronicle*, 'because he might not come to his answer and excuse him of such things as were falsely put on him.' More lurid rumours were soon circulating. The *Brut* chronicle repeated whispers 'that he was murdered between two featherbeds [or] that a hot spit was put in his fundament'.[3] Popular opinion insisted that he had been killed at the behest of the clique surrounding Henry. They had turned the king against his uncle, brought down Eleanor Cobham and exiled Gloucester from royal favour. Now they had done what they must have been planning all along and destroyed the 'good duke of Gloucester' completely. The finger of blame pointed firmly at Suffolk, whose dominance at court was now infamous. But others were also implicated, chief among them James Fiennes, Lord Saye and Sele.* Even Queen Margaret was later suspected of complicity. These individuals had accused Gloucester of treason to prevent him bringing his influence to bear on Henry, and now his blood was on their hands.[4]

Gloucester's arrest was undoubtedly pre-planned and the measures taken to ensure his downfall must have had Henry's approval. On 30 January 1447 Henry had taken the unprecedented step of suspending the hearings of royal justices, presumably in order to summon them to parliament to preside over Gloucester's impending trial. The decision to hold that parliament outside London, where Gloucester enjoyed popular support, and to increase the guard around Henry ahead of the duke's arrival also suggest advance preparation to isolate Gloucester ahead of his arrest. For years Henry and his uncle had been drifting apart, until by 1447 they had little common interest except their lineage. Henry was a peacemaker by inclination and policy and Gloucester's noisy opposition to his means of securing peace had become a constant vexation. The treason of Eleanor Cobham had only fractured an existing fault line, but after her arrest Henry never fully trusted Gloucester again. It seemed in the months leading up to his downfall that the spectre of Gloucester's ex-wife had been ever-present. In July 1446, Henry had entrusted Sir Thomas Stanley with the task of transferring Eleanor to imprisonment on the Isle of Man, perhaps to preclude any attempts at rescue or escape, but Gloucester had not given up his wife's cause. Robert Bale's London chronicle reported that Gloucester came to Bury intent

---

* Fiennes was created Lord Saye and Sele shortly after Gloucester's death.

on pleading for Eleanor's release, a move that would have been as painful as it was politically disturbing to Henry.[5]

In these tense circumstances it would have been easy to play on Henry's anxieties and it may well be that Suffolk and Lord Saye and Sele did just that, interpreting Gloucester's opposition to royal policy as akin to treason. Henry probably did not want Gloucester dead, but he would not have been sorry to see him removed from politics, and his closest advisers would have helped provide the means to do it. That his resistance was seen as embarrassing to Henry's government and undermining of its policy is entirely believable. The reaction among Gloucester's colleagues in the council and Lords was so muted as to suggest that few disagreed with the disgrace that preceded his demise. If they did, their compliance was easily bought with generous grants from Gloucester's estate, which was parcelled out to new owners before his corpse was cold. On the very day he died a number of grants were made to Queen Margaret, members of Henry's household and Henry's cherished educational foundations. Even those whom Gloucester had regarded as his supporters swallowed any unease they may have felt on receipt of the late duke's estates. The duke of York readily accepted Gloucester's Suffolk estate of Great Wratting two days after his purported ally's death.[6]

As for Gloucester's unfortunate son and servants, the duke's death left them in limbo. No formal charges were laid against Gloucester, but it served the interests of Henry's regime to keep his alleged wrongdoing in the public consciousness, so his men were accused of conspiring to rebel against Henry with a Welsh army that would free Eleanor and bring down the king. In July 1447, five of the alleged plotters, including Gloucester's son Arthur, were condemned as traitors. Suffolk and Lord Saye and Sele were prominent on the commission of *oyer et terminer* that indicted them.*

---

* A criminal court held under a royal commission of *oyer et terminer* (literally, 'to hear and determine').

On 14 July 1447 the condemned men were led out of their prison cells, strapped to hurdles and dragged to Tyburn to be hanged, drawn and quartered. Their velvet doublets were dirtied as they jolted through the filthy streets, protesting their innocence. Gloucester's son Arthur clutched a gold cross between his manacled hands, and even as he mounted the scaffold he still pleaded for mercy. Despite their protests, coarse rope nooses were tightened around the men's necks, their ladders kicked away and they were left to hang until almost dead. The men knew what awaited them next: first they would have their bowels drawn out and displayed before their still-seeing eyes, then they would be castrated and finally their heads would be chopped off and their limbs severed. Their bloody quarters would be dispatched to the restive corners of Henry's realm as a grisly warning to potentially unruly subjects of the fate that befell traitors.

But suddenly the ropes from which the men were dangling were cut. Before the crowd, the marquess of Suffolk stepped forward to stay the executioner's hand, brandishing a charter of pardon. In honour of the Feast of the Assumption, Henry had decided to show mercy to the traitors. Shaking and confused, Arthur and his accomplices were hauled off the scaffold and allowed to go free. They returned through the city 'thanking God and the king of that grace'. Henry had given a last brutal reminder of his authority over Gloucester's men, and by extension over any who opposed his will. A fortnight later he appointed commissioners to complete the surrender of Maine. It was hoped that this pageant of torture and mercy would prevent others from resisting his plans in France.[7]

As for Gloucester himself, he had been quietly buried in his beloved St Albans Abbey. One of the few acts passed in the parliament that arrested him debarred Eleanor Cobham from inheriting his estate. She was left to grieve in prison without the comfort of dower. By coincidence, in April of the same year, Cardinal Beaufort also died, although in markedly different circumstances. Having largely retired from politics in the wake of John Beaufort's disastrous expedition in 1443, the cardinal passed away peacefully in his own bed at Wolvesey Palace in Winchester. The influence of the two uncles over the king had steadily diminished in recent years, eclipsed by the marquess of Suffolk and Queen Margaret. With the deaths of these two pillars of Henry VI's minority, the old regime of the king's youth was gone for good.

Le Mans, Maine
15 March 1448

The Cathedral of St Julien thrust its pinnacles into the sky above Le Mans, an architectural legacy of Henry's Plantagenet, Capetian and Valois ancestors. One of the immense rose windows within had been installed as an act of thanksgiving by Henry's grandfather Charles VI, following his recovery from his first episode of mental illness. On this early spring day the old town of the capital of Maine was encircled not only by brick-red Roman walls but by the threatening gaze of 6–7,000 French soldiers and an artillery force that drove fear into many an English soldier's heart. Nine miles (15 km) to the northwest, secure in the castle of Lavardin, Charles VII was ideally positioned to monitor his army's progress. After two years of obfuscation and delay, he had grown tired of Henry's broken promises. If need be, Charles was willing to pound the ancient walls of this majestic city on the River Sarthe into dust.

Henry received news of Charles's advance towards Le Mans with dismay. He immediately dispatched his herald and two of his most experienced negotiators – Sir Robert Roos and Adam Moleyns – to treat with Charles, hoping to avert the catastrophe of open warfare. For good measure, he and the council issued a flurry of commands to prepare for Edmund Beaufort's departure to France to take up his long overdue appointment as lieutenant, in the company of 200 spears and 3,000 archers.[8]

Henry was almost as frustrated as Charles at the endless delays in the promised surrender of Maine. Time and again he had issued orders for the county to be handed over, and time and again he had been defied. Not content with supplanting York as lieutenant-general and governor of Normandy, Edmund Beaufort had prevaricated until Henry was reduced to 'bitter displeasure', having to threaten and cajole his own lieutenant to force through the surrender without further 'pretenses, excuses or delays'.[9] Edmund Beaufort had succeeded in extracting considerable promises of remuneration for his compliance, and, perhaps inspired by his example, demands for compensation from the other office-holders in Maine had dragged out the surrender for months on end. Even Henry's own commissioners and captains had joined in, quibbling about legal points and technicalities to delay progress with both Henry and the French. A meeting of Anglo-French emissaries that crammed 500 attendants into the chapter house of St Julien in Le Mans had failed to bring about resolution.[10] Charles had grown increasingly impatient. By late 1447, with yet another deadline missed, he had written to Henry complaining of the 'subterfuges, pretenses and dissimulations' of Henry's subjects, which served 'rather to disturb and hinder the blessing of the peace' than to prolong it. By January 1448 he had taken matters into his own hands and his army had rumbled up to the gates of Le Mans to force the city's surrender.[11]

Fortunately, in the short term, diplomacy won out over militarism. On 15 March 1448 Adam Moleyns was able to extend the truce between England and France for another year. That very day, Henry's commissioners, a pair of Welsh veterans called Matthew Gough and Fulk Eyton, opened the gates of Le Mans to present the city keys to the French. But before they handed them over, they insisted on lodging a protest, demanding that if Charles failed to provide the promised compensation or otherwise failed to keep the peace, the English could retake the city.[12]

Two years later than planned, Maine had been restored to

the French. It seemed that a crisis had been narrowly averted. But the tensions revealed by the handover of Maine remained. Gough and Eyton's protest was only the latest show of discontent among Henry's subjects at the unequal bargain into which the king had entered with Charles VII. Maine had been lost for little more than a two-year extension of the truce (which would now run until 1 April 1450) and a commitment that at some point Charles would hand over letters allowing René and Charles of Anjou to make an alliance. There was no peace treaty.[13] And perhaps more immediately concerning, the speed with which Charles had been able to mount the siege of Le Mans raised questions about French activities during the last three years of truce. How had Charles been able to mobilize so large a force in so little time? While England had used the peace to justify stepping back from costly warfare, Charles had taken the opportunity to reform his armed forces under the supervision of his Breton constable, Arthur de Richemont, establishing the first standing army in France. In 1448 military service was established under a system of *francs archers*. Every community of fifty to eighty house-holds provided a soldier – usually a crossbowman – for royal service in return for certain tax exemptions.[14]

Meanwhile, the English had ignored their commanders' advice to reform and restore their defences. As long ago as June 1445 Suffolk had advised parliament to improve the defences in Normandy during the truce, to ensure that the English could negotiate with the French from a position of strength.[15] His advice had been ignored. Since September 1445 there had not even been a lieutenant present in Normandy, never mind any attempts to repair and reorganize. When Edmund Beaufort finally landed in Normandy in May 1448 – now bearing his late brother's title of duke of Somerset – he found the duchy in a state of 'profound anarchy'.[16] Before the 1444 Truce of Tours there had been 3,500 of Henry's men stationed in Norman garrisons but when Somerset arrived desertions fuelled by unpaid wages had seen this figure fall to only 2,100. The frontier territory between Normandy and Brittany had suffered serious unrest as a result. English outlaw bands seized the fortresses of Pontorson and Saint-James de Beuvron to use as bases for local raids and the French garrison of Mont St Michel was 'daily committing infinite mischief, murders, robberies [and] seizures... just as if it were time of war'.[17]

In February 1449 Edmund Beaufort sent an embassy from the council in Normandy to the English parliament in the hope of enlisting some much-needed support for the duchy.[18] At Henry's command, Somerset's concerns were presented by the chancellor of Normandy, Thomas Hoo, and his fellow councillor Reginald Boulers, abbot of Gloucester, before both houses of parliament. Boulers repeated alarming tales of Charles VII's remilitarization – as many as 60,000 soldiers were 'ready, mounted, armed and in ways prepared [to attack] … within fifteen days warning' while the defences of Normandy lay in ruins, even in the few places where they were properly manned, and the Estates General of Normandy so impoverished that they threatened to abandon the duchy to the enemy rather than pay another tax. With the truce due to run for another fourteen months only, Abbot Boulers pleaded that the English must help restock, rebuild and re-man the Norman forts. 'The shameful loss of [Normandy],' he declared, 'which God forever forbid, would... [be] an everlasting slur, and permanent denigration of the fame and renown of this noble realm.'[19] Yet the government was still debating how to respond to the Norman councillors' urgent request four months later.[20]

The difficulty, as always, was money. Henry could not support Somerset from his own revenues – royal debts now stood at £372,000 – and appeals for loans to support the war in France were yielding less than ever. Personal appeals to lords in 1449 yielded little more than £3,000, mostly from Suffolk and Moleyns, who had a vested interest in maintaining the territories that had been endangered by their foreign policy. The Commons had always been reluctant to grant taxation and the appeals of

Boulers and Hoo did not change that. It took Henry six months to extract any tax in the 1449 parliament and its real value was minimal as its collection was based on an outdated assessment made before the Black Death which bore no real resemblance to the distribution of wealth in fifteenth-century England.[21]

Unfortunately for Somerset, his demands for military aid in Normandy arrived at a time when Henry's realms seemed to be menaced on every front. Throughout summer and autumn 1448 England's northern borders were threatened by King James II of Scotland.* Henry had to progress as far north as Durham in late 1448 to discourage border raiding. On 23 October Scottish forces defeated and captured English soldiers in 'mire ground' on the River Sark, in the western part of the Anglo-Scottish borderlands. So great were the fears of a possible Scottish invasion that a number of northern lords, including representatives of the houses of Neville and Percy, were told to remain in the north rather than attending parliament in spring 1449. Embassies were dispatched north to treat for the renewal of truce with the Scots and various marcher castles were repaired and reinforced, all of which needed tax money to support it. Most of the rest of the money raised in 1449 went towards the defence of Calais and safeguarding the sea from the depredations of pirates. In February 1449, with fourteen months of the French truce left to run, trading interests and anxiety over immediate threats to England's northern border won out over longer-term fears about France. Henry and his government failed to consider the likelihood that Charles would break the truce before its term was complete.[22]

The most significant challenge facing Henry's French crown was that England was weary of war, and as a result interest in the dual monarchy had waned. Parliament believed Abbot Boulers' prediction that the war would end in disaster for England to be

---

* James II succeeded to the Scottish throne after the murder of his father, James I, in 1437.

exaggerated. English armies had bested the French at Crécy, Agincourt and Verneuil – and, if need be, they would defeat them again. For now, their support was needed elsewhere.[23]

The unhappy relations between England and France were not helped by Henry's appointment of Edmund Beaufort as lieutenant-general of Normandy. In his relations with Charles VII, the proud and assertive duke of Somerset proved overly combative, addressing the French king in a manner that Charles found 'derogatory to the honour of the king, and different from what had been used in time past by the duke of York and the other lords of the blood'. Charles complained to Henry that Somerset's style of address was 'framed either by too great arrogance or ignorance', but the duke resisted Henry's appeals to moderate his tone. The activities of lawless bands of English soldiers on the Norman frontier were also attributed to Somerset's malign influence and, when summoned to account for attacks on neutral garrisons, Somerset angrily threatened to arrest Charles's ambassadors.[24]

With lawlessness and violence spilling into the border territories of Normandy, garrisons depleted, the duchy's finances drained and Somerset and the king of France so clearly at odds, it would take only a little spark for the entire, unhappy peace to explode. And, early in spring of the following year, Henry would provide it.

17

'Great and grievous reverses and fortunes of war'[1]

Fougères, Brittany
24 March 1449

It was two o'clock in the morning, and the wealthy market town of Fougères slumbered. Neutrality in the endless wars between England and France had seen its many residents grow fat and rich, its warehouses overflowing. Now, under cover of darkness, a force of 600 or 700 men crept towards its walls. Leading them was a soldier they called *L'Aragonnais*, François de Surienne, a Spanish soldier of fortune who had fought for the English time and again in the wars. Proudly displayed on his calf was the blue and gold belt loop that signalled he was a knight of Henry's Order of the Garter. At Surienne's command, his men laid their scaling ladders softly against the walls. They were over the defences and in control of the town before anyone could raise the alarm. As panic roused the citizens of Fougères from their beds, the streets filled with fleeing families, some trying to carry their riches with them, scrambling over the ramparts and sliding down the outer walls in their desperation to escape. Surienne's men plundered the town, confiscating booty worth 3 million *livres tournois*.[2]

The sack of Fougères caused an outcry at the Breton court. François, duke of Brittany, appealed to Charles VII to help him retake the town and gain reparation for the damage inflicted. Although Brittany was traditionally an ally of England, François had done homage to Charles VII in 1446 and Charles now took up François's cause with alacrity, claiming that the attack contravened the Anglo-French truce. Henry publicly disowned Surienne's actions but both Duke François and Charles believed that the English government was responsible. And they were right.

The seizure of Fougères was the result of years of secret talks between Surienne and senior members of Henry's government, chief among them the dukes of Suffolk* and Somerset, and the news of Surienne's success was read aloud by Suffolk to parliament in June 1449, to general approval.[3] As long ago as December 1447 Surienne had been in England to be invested as Knight of the Garter – a singular honour for a foreign-born captain of mercenaries. The investiture had provided the necessary smokescreen for him and Henry's government to discuss a daring plan that would apply pressure to both François and Charles in the vital border territories where English and French soldiers were scrambling for control while talks for an extension to the truce continued their uneasy course. By tasking a mercenary with this mission, Henry's government could disavow any knowledge if things went awry. If Surienne was successful, however, he would be supported by Henry's troops and press on against Charles and his Francophile Breton allies.

For Henry, this plan was not just political, it was personal. The origins of the English seizure of Fougères lay almost twenty years earlier, in the visit of the eight-year-old Gilles of Brittany to King Henry's court in 1432. Gilles was the younger son of Jean V, duke of Brittany, a man so determined to protect his duchy from the ravages of the Hundred Years War that he had even

---

* Suffolk had been elevated from marquess to duke of Suffolk on 2 June 1448.

brought up his family to please both sides of the divide. His eldest son and heir, François, was given a French bride,* while his youngest son Gilles was sent to the English court to be raised in the household of the earl of Warwick with Henry VI between 1432 and 1434. The boys developed a close bond and Henry took 'very great and very singular pleasure' in the company of his cousin.† They remained devoted to each other even after Gilles returned to his father's court in the summer of 1434. Nine years later, when Gilles visited England as an ambassador in 1443, Henry loaded him with gifts: fine song books for his chapel bound in white leather, a 1,000-mark pension, a gold cup filled with £100. Henry's indulgence was amply rewarded. In the finest tradition of chivalric knighthood, Gilles swore himself to Henry's service 'to serve him in all the ways that it would please the king to command'.[4]

Unfortunately the divided political loyalties inculcated in Gilles and his brother made for an uneasy relationship in later life. François resented Gilles for being their father's favourite and Gilles envied his older brother for his superior inheritance. When François succeeded to the dukedom of Brittany in 1442, the rift between them deepened. François grew suspicious of Gilles's close friendship with Henry VI, especially when Gilles rejected the inheritance their father had granted him. As the estates lay in Anjou, and therefore under the power of Charles VII,‡ Gilles claimed that taking possession of them would contravene his sworn oath to Henry VI. He could not hold lands as a vassal of Henry's enemy.[5]

There was something of the Jekyll and Hyde to Gilles's character. To Henry he was always a faithful, if occasionally avaricious,

---

* This was Yolande of Anjou, younger sister of René of Anjou.
† Gilles's and Henry's mothers were sisters, Catherine and Jeanne Valois. POPC, IV, p. 278.
‡ Gilles was granted the captaincy of the port of Saint-Malo in Brittany and the estates of Champtocé-sur-Loire and Ingrandes in Anjou.

subject. Towards his brother, he demonstrated nothing but jealousy, arrogance and fits of temper. To acquire a better landed estate for himself, in 1444 Gilles kidnapped and married an eight-year-old heiress, Françoise de Dinan, thereby seizing control of her barony of Châteaubriant and the magnificent coastal castle of Le Guildo. Unfortunately, despite her youth, Françoise was already betrothed to the heir of another prominent Breton family and the resulting feud had to be mediated by an increasingly frustrated Duke François. Still not content with his estate, Gilles threatened to take his complaints to King Henry – whom he regarded as his true liege lord – and have his inheritance settled more to his liking.

By 1445 it was becoming apparent to François that Gilles was being supported in his defiance – perhaps even incited to it – by members of Henry's administration. Gilles's valet was at the English court wearing a Lancastrian livery collar, while Gilles himself had started communicating with various high-placed Lancastrian administrators and captains in France: the Welsh captain Matthew Gough, the English chancellor of Normandy Thomas Hoo, and Henry's ambassador Robert Roos. In a letter to Gilles of August 1445, Gough referred obliquely to 'the thing that you and I spoke of' which he claimed 'was going well'. The following October he referred again to certain secret matters, of which he said he would 'speak by mouth' when they were next together, 'but which I cannot write to you of'. Henry was almost certainly assisting Gilles in a plot to depose François and take the duchy for himself. Unfortunately, Henry's loyalty to his cousin blinded him to Gilles's failings as a conspirator. Gilles lacked the necessary circumspection to carry out a coup and by summer 1446 he was loudly proclaiming even in front of his brother's messengers his intention to raise an army in Normandy and win Brittany by force of arms. 'When I have five or six thousand English at my back,' he told François's astonished servant, 'I shall be able to ride as far as St Mathieu de Fine-Terre [at the very tip of the Breton peninsula]. He who holds the field has won the advantage.' Gilles's supporters struggled in vain to check his behaviour, or encourage him to flee to Normandy before his brother took reprisals, but Gilles stubbornly refused, believing his high standing with Henry would keep him safe.[6]

On Sunday 26 June 1446, an embassy from Charles VII arrived at the gates of Le Guildo. Gilles, who was playing a game of tennis, paused and wondered whether to allow admittance to Henry's enemy. Since he was confident that he had not personally offended Charles, he decided that it would be a worse breach of protocol to turn the embassy away than to allow them entry. But as soon as the Frenchmen were inside the walls of Le Guildo they arrested Gilles, imprisoned him and turned him over to François. Despite the mediation of their uncle, Charles's constable Arthur de Richemont, François showed no intention whatsoever of freeing his brother, or even – after one attempted reconciliation – of putting him on trial.[7]

Charles's seizure of Gilles – Henry's vassal – was technically a breach of the Anglo-French truce but unfortunately for Gilles, his arrest coincided with the most sensitive period of Henry's negotiations for peace, as he struggled to appease Charles over his unfulfilled promise to cede Maine. Moreover, as Henry must have realized, English complicity in Gilles's attempted coup had driven François into the arms of the French. Henry could not risk alienating his purported ally further by interfering in the family feud.

Breton loyalty remained a diplomatic battleground for the next three years. As the surrender of Maine and financial disorder in Normandy drove disgruntled English soldiers into the frontier territory on the Breton–Norman border, the question of Breton allegiance became crucial. Frontier territories were not allowed to be occupied during a truce, and Charles insisted that English occupation of border forts like Saint-James de Beuvron, Pontorson and Mortain was a breach of the peace. Urged on by Somerset's complaints, Henry countered that Charles's men had similarly contravened the truce with attacks in the equally disputed territories of Caux and Maine.[8] As the uneasy Anglo-French truce neared its end, Henry insisted that in all negotiations Brittany must be treated as his vassal, which legitimized the border activities of his men. The fact that François had done homage to Charles was studiously ignored.[9]

As diplomacy continued to yield little result and Gilles languished in a dungeon, starved and maltreated, Henry and his advisers hatched the scheme for Surienne to seize Fougères and hold it to ransom until François released his brother – and ideally until he admitted that Brittany *was* an English vassal. Surienne carried out the plan masterfully, refusing to surrender the town even when offered a Breton bribe of 50,000 crowns. Pointing to the blue and gold symbol on his calf, he rejected the money, saying, 'do you not see that I am of the Order of the Garter? I have the power to take [this town], but not to return it'.[10]

However, as the months passed Surienne began to suspect that he had been misled. The promised English support never arrived. With Surienne's attack condemned by Charles and François as an act of war, Henry got cold feet about the whole stratagem. Surienne and his men were abandoned as Fougères was besieged by Duke François's forces. After seven months Surienne was forced to surrender.*

The attack on Fougères had failed to achieve any of its aims. By the time of its conclusion Gilles was still imprisoned, François was more closely allied with Charles VII than ever before and Charles had gained an important moral victory. He now had more than sufficient cause to breach the truce himself. The farce of Fougères was to prove the undoing of Henry's peace.[11]

The first fort to fall was Pont-de-l'Arche, the fortress town controlling the riverway to Rouen. On Thursday 9 May 1449 a merchant

---

* Surienne survived to 1462, dying a respected retainer of the King of France.

of Louviers murdered the guard and blocked the bridge with his cart, allowing a Franco-Breton force to surge through the gates at dawn, slaughtering the English porters in their nightshirts and seizing and seriously wounding the unfortunate Englishman Lord Fauconberg, who had stopped off that night to break his journey.[12]

At Rouen, the duke of Somerset received word of the fall of Pont-de-l'Arche barely two hours after it was taken, woken early in the morning by breathless fugitives from the town. He ran around the castle of Rouen 'like a crazy person', rousing its inhabitants from their beds.[13] He ordered forces to stand ready to retake the town, for boats to be prepared in the port. The fugitives had seen Englishmen fighting in the towers of Pont-de-l'Arche as they fled. But barely had the forces mustered to take the fight to the attackers than they learnt it was too late. The town had already fallen. Two heralds arrived to inform Somerset that the attack was revenge for Fougères.[14]

In a last-ditch attempt to resolve their issues, English and French ambassadors met at Louviers in Normandy in June. The same worn-out arguments were rehearsed: the English insisted Brittany was their king's vassal, the French said Brittany was theirs; the English claimed the French had been the first to break the peace with their attacks on Pont-de-l'Arche and Dieppe, the French that the English had been the first, by seizing Fougères; the duke of Somerset had done everything possible to prevent the attacks on French forces, the duke of Somerset had done nothing. In a remarkable piece of spin the French ambassadors even claimed that Gilles and François had enjoyed a happy relationship until the English took Fougères. The gulf between the two realms was now too wide, the disparity in their resources and morale all too clear.

Even as the peace talks were ongoing, Charles was readying his army for attack. Everything he had learnt in the last five years encouraged him to believe his forces could triumph. Henry was a weak king who could barely control his own subjects, let

1. Henry V's career as warrior prince began early. Here, his face is presented in profile, perhaps to conceal the disfiguring scar he received in his first battle, aged only sixteen. His martial legacy cast a long shadow over his son.

2. Throughout his childhood, Henry VI was protected and guided by adults, including his 'master', the earl of Warwick. But despite the council ruling on his behalf, Henry was considered king from the moment he acceded to the throne as a baby.

3. Catherine of Valois's funeral effigy does not capture the beauty that attracted Henry V. The 'carnal queen's' romantic affairs were a cause of scandal during the reign of her son, but Henry VI continued to send gifts to his mother until days before her death.

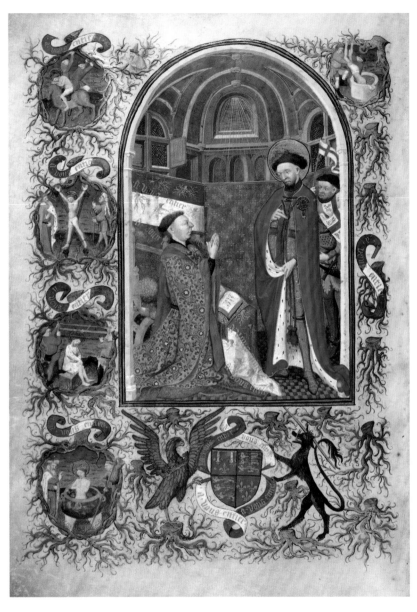

4. John, duke of Bedford, was the champion of Henry's Dual Monarchy, campaigning tirelessly as regent in France and attempting unsuccessfully to resolve political faction in England. Here he appears in a portrait from a Book of Hours he gave Henry.

5. Cardinal Beaufort's considerable wealth assured his primacy in politics. But despite his political astuteness, he could never overcome the animosity of his nephew Gloucester. This portrait by Jan van Eyck may have been painted during Beaufort's exile in Burgundian territory.

6. Henry's English coronation in July 1429, when he was eight years old, was a moment of profound personal and political importance. His coronation as king of France, following two years of intense struggle, took place in December 1431. Henry remains the only monarch to be crowned in both England and in France.

7. The Duke of Bedford found the perfect foil in his wife,
Anne of Burgundy – a shrewd diplomat and capable arbiter.
This image of her comes from the illuminated manuscript she
gifted to Henry during his coronation expedition.

▲ 8. Henry's dual heritage as king of England and of France was at the heart of his identity from childhood. This book of psalms featuring French saints was probably given to Henry by his mother Queen Catherine.

◄ 9. Ambitious and self-aggrandising, Humphrey, duke of Gloucester, was the first royal counsellor to attempt to mould Henry to his will. His wife's treason and his own opposition to Henry's peace policy were to prove his undoing.

10. Henry kneels at the shrine of St Edmund in a book presented to him by the Abbot of Bury St Edmunds. His time at the abbey was a brief period of serenity in an otherwise troubled childhood.

11. 'What he lacked in courage... he made up for in sense.' Henry's rival Charles VII was afraid of everything from wooden bridges to eating in front of strangers, but his relentless defence of his right to succeed won him the French crown.

12. The only man Henry ever said he wanted to wage war against, Philippe, duke of Burgundy, betrayed his English allies by making a treaty with Charles VII of France in September 1435. His defection was a turning point in the fortunes of the dual monarchy.

alone mount an effective resistance. He had ignored his senior advisers' counsel to repair his crippled continental defences. His commanders were unpopular and ineffective. His treasury was empty. Charles, on the other hand, was at the height of his powers, his army restored, his relations with his fellow French princes strong, his own rule almost absolute. With all these advantages, he prepared a three-pronged attack on Normandy with the active assistance, or passive submission, of most of the senior princes of France. On 27 June Charles and François confirmed an alliance to drive the English from Normandy. Charles VII declared himself absolved of the truce. England was at war once more.[15]

It is not clear how, or when, Henry received the news that his peace policy had failed. What cannot be in doubt is the bitter disappointment he must have felt. His entire adult life had been built around the pillar of peace: Gloucester had been sacrificed to his vision; the county of Maine lost; and his beloved cousin Gilles left to rot in a Breton dungeon. All of this had been done to ensure the hard-won truce with Charles VII was maintained. It had all been for nothing.

Perhaps if Henry had now given up his pacific intentions and donned a suit of armour he might have been able to check Charles's advance. A shocked and demoralized nation might have rallied behind their king and the miserly Commons in parliament might have been persuaded to fund one last great war effort under Henry's leadership. But there never seems to have been any suggestion – from Suffolk, from Margaret, from Somerset, from their councillors or ambassadors, least of all from Henry himself – that he would suddenly turn warrior and lead the charge against the French king. Instead, Henry and his government prevaricated while fortress after fortress fell to the advancing French army throughout the summer of 1449.

Names that had resonated as famous English victories were transformed into auguries of doom. Verneuil fell on 20 July,

Charles VII's herald Gilles le Bouvier attributing French victory
to a turncoat miller who helped the French soldiers scale the city
walls.[16] Harcourt surrendered in early September after the first
French bombardment took out an entire wall of the lower court.
The mighty fortress of Château Gaillard, which had stood since
the days of Richard the Lionheart, was forced into submission
after five weeks. In many cases, there was no resistance at all. At
Pont-l'Évêque the garrison fled and at the impregnable fortress
of Roche-Guyon, the Welsh captain gave up his station, it was
said, on the 'advice, procurement and direction' of his French
wife.[17] The bishop of Lisieux, Thomas Basin – who kept a chronicle of this time – surrendered not only his own city to the French
but seven of its dependent fortresses, gifting an entire district
to the enemy without a single blow being exchanged. Charles
was diplomatic in the extreme. He allowed surrendering towns
to continue their own way of life, to keep their goods and livelihoods, for many office-holders to retain their posts. Only when
he encountered resistance did he use violence to force the issue.
Little wonder that so many towns and castles were willing to bend
the knee to him with barely a sword drawn in defiance. By early
October 30,000 French soldiers under the command of Jean de
Dunois, 'the bastard of Orléans',* were nearing the walls of the
Norman capital of Rouen. As if to further underline the futility
of Henry's peace process, at Charles's right hand in the army
was Henry's own father-in-law, René of Anjou.[18]

Throughout this miserable period, the duke of Somerset had
stayed hidden away inside Rouen with his wife, children and
fellow captains. A commander of considerable experience, not
known for cowardice, he seems to have frozen in the face of
the enormous French forces bearing down on him. Perhaps
he realized how pointless resistance was. His appeal for aid to

---

* 'The bastard of Orléans' was the illegitimate half-brother of Charles of
Orléans (who had been imprisoned by the English). He had been one of
the most prominent French commanders fighting with Joan of Arc.

defend Normandy had been ignored. He knew how limited the financial and military resources were in England and how little commitment there was to defending Normandy. No relief force would save Rouen from its besiegers. But as the bastard of Orléans's men set up camp in the driving rain before the city walls, Somerset still refused to surrender.[19]

By the time the French forces arrived at the gates of Rouen, the city was already in a desperate state. Supplies had been cut off for six weeks and the citizens' morale was at rock bottom. They feared the town would be sacked if it resisted. So uncertain were the English commanders of the citizens' loyalties that they twice chased away French heralds bringing terms from King Charles. In their desperation, a pocket of Rouennais turned traitor and sent a message to the bastard of Orléans to tell him that if he attacked a specific wall, they would allow him to scale the ramparts and enter the town unopposed. Unfortunately for them, when the offensive was launched on 16 October the doughty veteran Lord Talbot was close enough at hand to lead a counter-attack that killed fifty or sixty Frenchmen and repulsed the bastard's forces. Some of the traitorous citizens were forced over the walls at swordpoint.[20]

Divisions were widening between the citizens of Rouen and Somerset's English garrison. When rumours started circulating that the English would kill any citizens who opposed them, panic set in. One of the Rouennais ran to the local clock tower, the *Tour d'Horloge*, and rang the bell as if the city were on fire. Makeshift barricades were set up in the streets – tables, chests, baskets, anything made of wood or iron was dragged into the street to prevent English soldiers and horsemen getting through. The citizens armed themselves. Amid the chaos, the garrison struggled to retreat to the outer fortifications of the town, meeting barricades at every turn, sometimes being pelted with stones. A handful of soldiers did not make it through at all.

With Somerset, his duchess, his children and others who remained loyal to Henry now confined to the castle in the northern part of Rouen, and the palace and bridge to the south, the citizens gave up their city to the French. The keys were handed over, the gates thrown open and the streets filled with French soldiers. Earthworks were built for machines of war and bombards, to pound Somerset's men into submission. With few provisions inside their fortifications, Somerset knew his forces could not long withstand a siege. He finally bowed to the inevitable.

On 29 October 1449, the city of Rouen was surrendered to the French without a single cannon being fired. In a magnificent figured robe of blue velvet, furred with sable, Somerset submitted to King Charles.[21] The pair had never got on, even during the period of peace, and Charles demanded harsher terms of Somerset than he had offered the citizens of Rouen. Not only must Somerset hand over Rouen but also the fortresses of Harfleur, Honfleur, Tancarville, Caudebec, Arques and Montvilliers. Hostages, including the renowned captain Lord Talbot, must be left as surety for the castles' deliverance. Moreover, within a year Somerset must pay more than 50,000 gold *saluts.**

On 5 November 1449 Somerset, his family and his garrison left Rouen, headed for Caen. On 10 November Charles entered Rouen in state. At his right-hand side was René of Anjou, his horse covered in the white crosses of France. Thirty years of English rule was at end.[22] Charles's herald Gilles le Bouvier marvelled at the speed and thoroughness with which his king had dismantled Henry's authority: 'And thus the whole duchy of Normandy was conquered, and all the cities, towns, and castles thereof brought in subjection to the king of France within one year and six days; which is a very wonderful thing.'[23]

In England, the loss of Normandy was viewed with very different emotions. Henry's subjects had watched their international reputation destroyed by one humiliating defeat after another

---

* 50,000 *saluts* was around £8,000. LP, II (2), pp. 607–19.

while their government seemed incapable of funding, never mind fighting, a defence and their king proved increasingly impotent and incapable. The Commons felt that they had ploughed endless loans and subsidies into Henry's campaigns while his courtiers grew fat and did nothing. It was little wonder that the English grew indignant. Perhaps if English affairs had seemed stable, Henry's regime would not have been so resented. But there, too, lawlessness and unrest seemed to be at their worst since Henry had come to the throne.

18

'O king, if king you are, rule yourself'[1]

Westminster
8 November 1449

In a star-spangled chamber within Westminster Palace, a council of Henry's senior lords was concluding. It was around four o'clock and the sun was low in the sky outside the glazed windows, casting long shadows across the tiled floors. Amid the members of the great council was Ralph, Lord Cromwell, once the unfortunate treasurer who had striven to curb royal household spending, now pushing sixty and still serving Henry as faithfully as he could. As Cromwell left the Star Chamber men surged towards him from the doorway with murderous intent, the swords and glaives in their hands glinting. At their head was a Lincolnshire squire called William Tailboys, a notorious 'murderer, manslayer, rioter, and continual breaker of [the] peace', and a man with a personal vendetta against Cromwell. This was only the most recent of Tailboys's attempts to kill him. It would not be the last. The quick response of Cromwell's servants saved him on this occasion, dragging him from the assassins' blades before they could pierce even the fine fabric of his clothing, but Tailboys's assault on Cromwell within the very precinct of government was representative of the general turmoil in English affairs as 1449 drew to a close. Tailboys had repeatedly escaped justice thanks to his position in the royal household and a long-standing association with Viscount Beaumont and the duke of Suffolk.* He had committed three murders and a number of assaults in the past two years, and Cromwell was one of the few lords who had made efforts to bring him to justice. For that, he had almost lost his life. Tailboys's murderous assault on Cromwell was just one example of a rash of disorder and violence that was afflicting the country. Across the realm, law had been abused, justice perverted, 'slaughterlads' allowed to roam free. And now England was losing the French territories where violence might legitimately be unleashed.[2]

The impression of England among Henry's subjects in 1449 was of a country dragged to the brink of lawlessness by royal indulgence and misplaced mercy. Pardons for wrongdoers and patronage of royal favourites were both expected of a king, but only in moderation and with due discretion. It was also the responsibility of a king to resolve the disputes of his most powerful lords before they turned violent, and yet personal feuds were erupting into bloodshed across the kingdom. As early as the mid-1440s the peace of the Midlands had been shattered by the jealous rivalry of Henry Beauchamp, earl of Warwick, and Humphrey Stafford, duke of Buckingham. Beauchamp was the son of Henry's old master, the earl of Warwick, and the boys had grown up together. With characteristic generosity, Henry had rewarded his friend with high office from an early age and among his many grants was the reversion of the stewardship of Tutbury in Staffordshire, an act that enraged Buckingham, who

---

* Tailboys had been a squire of Henry's household since 1441.

had already been granted the stewardship for life and expected it to remain in his family. To try to appease the choleric Buckingham, Henry made him a duke in September 1444 – only to then elevate Beauchamp to a dukedom in April 1445, with precedence over everyone except the duke of Norfolk. In a compromise that pleased no one, Henry decreed that the two dukes must take it in turns to have precedence over one another.

The lack of clear lordship in Buckingham and Warwick's territories across the Midlands led to splintering alliances, attacks on defenceless estates, housebreaking and violence. In the end the region was only pacified when the duke of Warwick died suddenly in June 1446, removing the chief cause of the conflict. Similar outrages had been seen in East Anglia, where the rivalry between the dukes of Suffolk and Norfolk, and their considerable number of gentry clients, smouldered throughout the 1440s. One local gentlewoman noted that 'ye can never live in peace without ye have [Suffolk's] good lordship'.[3]

Corruption and lawlessness followed inevitably in the wake of Henry's liberal and partisan patronage. The worst example of Henry's inattention ignited a spark that set most of the West Country ablaze. The cause of this conflagration was Henry's granting of the same stewardship – of the duchy of Cornwall – to two different men: William, first Baron Bonville, and Thomas Courtenay, earl of Devon. The tensions between this pair had been growing for years. The thirteenth earl of Devon was a preening young man obsessed with the past glories of his noble ancestors. A long minority and longer widowhood of his mother, the dowager countess, had kept real power out of his hands while parvenu families like Bonville's climbed the social ladder around him. Courtenay could not even live in the family seat of Tiverton Castle until his mother died in 1441. Bonville's riches were almost equivalent to Courtenay's own, and by marrying Courtenay's aunt he advanced another rung in Devonshire politics. All this was humiliating enough for Courtenay, but when

Henry appointed Bonville steward of the duchy of Cornwall in 1437, it gave the upstart Bonville authority in areas of traditional Courtenay influence.[4]

In summer 1439 the uneasy peace came to a violent end with a series of attacks on Bonville's estates and servants. Government reacted by imposing a potentially crippling recognizance* of 2,000 marks on Courtenay to 'keep the peace towards William Bonville... all his men and them of his household'.[5] In 1441, to try to tilt the balance of power back in his favour, Courtenay petitioned Henry for Bonville's stewardship. Even though Bonville had been appointed for life, Henry agreed to grant it. It took a week for his advisers to realize the mistake, and a hopelessly optimistic command was issued to Courtenay not to exercise his post until the issue had been resolved.[6]

Within months 'divers companies of men... arrayed in guise of war' were stalking the roads and byways of the West Country, attacking those of suspect loyalty. In a desperate bid to put a stop to the 'great riots, disorders, dissensions and debates... which hath caused manslaughter', Henry summoned Courtenay and Bonville to appear before the council in November 1441. There, the embittered rivals were ordered to swear that they would not sanction any further acts of aggression. At Henry's command the chancellor took each of the men by the hand as they made their oath. 'It fitteth to none', warned the chancellor, 'to take at his own hand to avenge his own quarrel.'[7]

The stewardship of Cornwall was put to arbitration, but in the meantime Henry tried to settle the issue by sending both men overseas to sate their bloodlust on the French. Bonville dutifully set sail for Gascony in spring 1443, but Courtenay refused. Even a reminder of his father's noble service in Normandy could not compel him. Instead, he remained on his estates, building his power base and trusting to an alliance with the Beauforts

---

* A recognizance was a bond of money that would be forfeit if someone failed to observe a set condition (in this case, to keep the peace).

to protect him. The Bonville–Courtenay feud was to blight the West Country for the next decade and more.[8]

It was not merely noble violence that was a cause for concern. For years, repeated appeals for justice had been put before parliament in the cases of women who had been abducted and forced into marriage, by which means unscrupulous men could acquire their estates. In 1437 the widowed Isabel Butler of Bewsey in Lancashire was abducted from her home at five in the morning by William Pulle of Cheshire. Pulle 'feloniously and most horribly raped the said petitioner, and took her naked, except for her kirtle and her smock, with him into the wild and desolate areas of Wales', where Isabel was forced 'against her will' to marry him under threat of murder. Legal loopholes had prevented him being brought to justice. A similar fate befell Margaret Malefaut of Pembrokeshire, who was pregnant and only recently widowed in 1439 when Lewis Leyson, from the marches of Wales, abducted, forcibly married and raped her. In 1444 Isabelle Forde and her twelve-year-old daughter Johane were both kidnapped from Parkham parish church in Hartland, Devon, by a 'multitude of people unknown, arrayed in manner of war'. The Fordes tried to hide in the vestry but were seized, beaten and carried off after the door was broken down. In 1453 a statute was finally put in place to try to curb the problem but such abductions and rapes continued.[9]

A further problem was the unpredictable nature of royal justice, exemplified by the case of Thomas Kerver, the abbot of Reading's bailiff. In 1444 he was overheard telling a colleague that it would have been better if Henry had never been born, and comparing him unfavourably with Dauphin Louis of France. 'If the king were of like stuff as he was of the like age as the dauphin,' mocked Kerver, 'he would be holding [France] peacefully and quietly.'[10] For his unwise words Kerver was condemned to be hanged, drawn and quartered as a traitor. However, at the very moment of his execution, he was cut down from the scaffold and whisked away by royal officers, to the bewilderment of the assembled crowd. Henry had chosen to pardon him, but to avoid muddying the message that treason would be punished to the fullest extent of the law, the pardon was ordered to be 'kept as secret as ye may'. Kerver was imprisoned under Suffolk's watch at Wallingford Castle. Kerver's fate was similar to that endured by Gloucester's son Arthur and the duke's servants in 1447. Henry wished it to 'be openly known to all our subjects... [that] though they were next of our blood, if they fall in case similar... we shall not show them neither favour nor grace'.[11] Yet he had baulked at punishing men condemned for treason through legal process. Henry was capable of ruthlessness, as his treatment of the mad woman who railed at him about Eleanor Cobham demonstrated, but he was not consistent.* 'Justice without mercy is cruelty,' as a contemporary proverb went, but 'mercy without justice, folly.'[12]

Folly and negligence were becoming the recognized charac-teristics of Henry's regime. Even in areas of his policy where he applied himself fully to the task, his interference could be a malign force. There is no doubting Henry's devotion to his educational projects at Eton and Cambridge, but his ambition and interest proved to be actively damaging to the colleges. As the years passed, Henry's ambition for his foundations grew, until the building works he had started no longer matched his aspirations. In 1443, King's College had proved so popular that Henry decided to expand it to support seventy, rather than the originally envisaged twelve, fellows and scholars. The college was extended south into a bustling thoroughfare of lanes and tenements, increasing the site's footprint sevenfold. Even more radical alterations were planned for Eton, six years into the building work, in 1448.[13] Henry's changes demanded the complete demolition of part of the chapel, which had already been roofed and fitted with stalls. Now Henry envisaged something far grander, and to realize his vision he sent his

---

* See above, p. 179.

surveyors to Salisbury and Winchester cathedrals in early 1449 to take measurements. Henry wanted not merely to emulate these magnificent gothic structures, but to exceed them, imagining a college chapel that would stand above even the greatest cathedrals of his age. His ambition and personal interest is clear in the surviving plans for the extensions at Eton from late 1448. A nine-page document laying out the dimensions of the choir that Henry intended to build is a case in point: almost every page is signed with Henry's own signature or initials next to alterations in the text. In places words or even entire sections were crossed out, with annotations, explanations and the exact type of stone to be used specified.[14]

But such finicky and vacillating interventions meant that two decades after he laid the foundation stone at King's, the chapel was still unfinished and only the east range of the domestic buildings had been started. By then Henry had spent almost £16,000 on his projects, but the scholars at Eton had to lodge in half-constructed buildings or in neighbouring houses and barns. It was 1450 before Eton Great Hall – which was already in use – was fitted with three large stone fireplaces and windows of 'storied glass'. Eton College chapel was intended to rival York Minster in size, but only Henry's planned choir was ever finished. By contrast, the college Queen Margaret founded at Cambridge in emulation of Henry's educational endeavours was completed within two years.* In his educational foundations, as in other areas of his governance, Henry's good intentions were undermined by his inconsistency.[15]

It was little surprise if Henry could not control his subjects or run his architectural projects, however, since he was incapable even of controlling his own household. The costs of maintaining Henry and Margaret's households had been mounting for

---

* Work on the central court of what is now known as Queens' College, Cambridge was completed by 1450. Some additional building work was undertaken in 1460.

years, despite ordinances put in place by parliament in 1445 to
control their spending. According to these regulations Henry
was allowed only 53 knights and esquires of the hall and chamber, but in 1446 he had 254 and by 1451 this figure had risen
to over 300. Margaret proved similarly incapable of controlling
her ballooning service wing. She was supposed to be served by
a household staff of 66, but in 1454 her household was *reduced*
to 120 servants and in 1452–3 she was being served by a staff of
151.[16] Even this was not the full story, for there were some who
were not even part of the royal household but who infiltrated
the king's hall to eat and drink at royal expense. With so many
interlopers, illegal activity was rife. The servants of Henry's
retainers were stealing food out of his kitchens, pocketing
expensive vessels, pots and cups from the scullery or torches
and logs from the porter, and smuggling them out of the gates
without even being queried. Henry's stables overflowed with
strangers' horses and his court with children, dogs and ferrets.[17]
In recent years 'rude husbandmen and artificers' had even
started masquerading as royal minstrels in fake livery to 'collect
in certain parts of the realm great exactions of money' with their
performances. In a bold bit of problem-solving that skirted the
wider issue, Henry appointed his real minstrels to examine and
punish the artificers accused of such deception.[18]

All these provisions had to be paid for and the system of purveyance, which fuelled and fed the royal household, had become
bitterly resented by Henry's subjects. Purveyance forced traders
in the locality where the king was staying to sell goods to royal
purveyors at knock-down prices with no right of refusal. Among
the items covered by purveyance were 'corn, hay, horses, oxen,
sheep, cows, pigs, piglets, poultry, fish or other victuals whatsoever; carts, wagons, boats, carriages, bedding straw or any goods',
even in seasons when such items were in short supply.[19] The
system was widely abused and despite a decade of parliamentary
complaint, purveyance continued to be an issue. Since Henry
seemed incapable of curbing the size of his household or

controlling purveyance, the Commons demanded in 1449 that Henry's household be supported with a parliamentary act of resumption, cancelling royal grants of office and land, which would then revert to the crown. This resumption would undo more than a decade of Henry's patronage. He successfully resisted the attempt the first time it was raised, but the question of resumption would be as persistent and divisive as purveyance in the years to come.

The cost of the royal household was particularly troublesome during a time of war, but it might have seemed worthwhile if the future of the dynasty was assured. However, the continued lack of an heir made the succession a source of serious concern. Henry and Margaret had now been married for four years, without even the hint of a pregnancy. As the first duty of a queen was to bear children, this had a serious impact on Margaret's popularity. The same voices that had shouted words of peace and welcome for Margaret in 1445 now muttered grimly that she had brought England nothing but trouble. A Canterbury man complained that 'our queen was none able to be queen of England... because that she beareth no child, and because that we have no prince in this land'. In 1447 another of Henry's subjects said he wanted to see Margaret drowned because no good had come from her arrival in England.[20]

In contemporary thought, infertility was usually blamed on women, but complaints about royal sterility undermined Henry's masculinity and even his authority. One rumour had it that the reason Henry and Margaret had produced no child was because the king was kept from 'his sport with his sovereign lady' by Bishop William Aiscough and the duke of Suffolk.[21] As Suffolk and Aiscough were closely associated with Henry's regime it is more likely that they would have wanted Henry and Margaret to have a child as soon as possible, but the accusation was meant to smear Henry's advisers as much as mock his weakness. However, there is a kernel of truth in the rumour. A text on royal ceremonial called the *Ryalle Boke* included provision for occasions when 'the king and the queen lie together'. After 'a traverse [was] drawn, the bed made, the cupboard served… as it requireth the king in his bed, the king's chamberlain or a squire for the body [should] come for the queen, and with her two gentlewomen and an usher'. Henry's chamberlain during his marriage was one of his closest attendants and both were associates of Suffolk and Aiscough: first Ralph Botiller, and from 1447 James Fiennes, Lord Saye and Sele. It was noted in the *Ryalle Boke* that while Margaret's servants waited outside the bedchamber, Botiller and Lord Saye and Sele sometimes followed her within. The *Ryalle Boke* does not make it clear at what point they left, leaving open the intriguing suggestion that they remained to make sure the marriage bed was being properly used. Was the king perhaps not performing his conjugal duties? [22]

Although the lack of an heir was a concern, Margaret may have been comforted somewhat by the example of the courtiers around her. The duke and duchess of Suffolk had only one living child in their twenty-year union, but as it was a healthy boy the continuance of their line was assured. Similarly, the duke and duchess of York had been married for at least ten years before Cecily Neville gave birth to their first child, and after that she had eight more in quick succession. Regardless of what was happening in the royal bedchamber, Margaret was certainly making every spiritual effort to ensure pregnancy. Several times she went on pilgrimage, both with Henry and alone, often to the shrine of Thomas Becket in Canterbury, a place associated with fertility. She also visited the shrine to the Virgin Mary at Walsingham in Norfolk. Later in life, Margaret explained that in times of trouble she had 'made divers and almost innumerable vows… for example many fastings, the observance of which vows very often involve fasting four or five times a week and several pilgrimages to divers places'. If she was fasting earlier in her marriage as a pious act to encourage divine intercession for a child, she may have adversely affected her fertility with poor nutrition, exacerbating any difficulties she and Henry were already having.[23] Despite Margaret's efforts, however, there was still no child, and with Gloucester dead the next in line to the throne was Henry's distant cousin the duke of York, who was away serving as lieutenant of Ireland.

In November 1449, the deteriorating situation in both England and France forced Henry to call a second parliament in the same year. The session opened to the news that Rouen had been lost. Henry's two kingdoms seemed to be teetering on the brink of collapse. His subjects on both sides of the Channel were enraged. Something, they felt, had to be done. Someone had to answer for these disasters. It could not be Henry – the concept of kingship at the time would not allow for that – but there were a number of leading figures surrounding him whose malign influence had been suspected for years. The new year would bring Henry face to face with the greatest crisis of his reign to date.

19

'Beware, King Henry, how thou do, let no longer thy traitors go loose'[1]

Portsmouth
9 January 1450

In the closing months of 1449, Henry's keeper of the privy seal, Adam Moleyns, had been kept busy. He attended the opening of parliament in Westminster before serving as a member of an embassy with Scotland that agreed a four-year truce on 15 November. Such incessant travel and toil had long been a feature of Moleyns's service to King Henry, and the ageing bishop of Chichester was now partially blind. Wishing to retire to his diocese and devote himself to religious matters, on 9 December Moleyns secured a royal licence releasing him from secular office, in the light of his failing health. Before he retired, he agreed to undertake one last office on behalf of Henry, delivering wages to the troops mustering in Portsmouth for a planned embarkation to France. As he arrived in the port town in January 1450 the atmosphere was uneasy. Troops had been assembling there since October, and after months of inactivity discipline had crumbled. When the soldiers and sailors learnt that the man tasked with paying their wages was the same Moleyns blamed for surrendering Maine and arranging the king's marriage to a barren Angevin pauper, they ambushed him. Words were exchanged, voices raised and the situation swiftly escalated to violence. Moleyns tried to save himself by blaming the duke of Suffolk for the loss of Normandy. It made no difference. By the day's end, Moleyns was dead, butchered in the streets for his service to King Henry.[2]

Moleyns had been in Henry's service for fifteen years and was closely associated with his regime and policies. Both the fact and the manner of his death must have been a profound shock to Henry. It was a grim augury of what was to come. As Henry made his way to the second session of parliament on 22 January the streets of London pulsed with rumour, 'odious and horrible words... in the mouth of almost every commoner'.[3] Word of Moleyns's dying accusation had quickly spread. Henry's subjects muttered of treason, of his crowns being bought and sold, of English law perverted. Their target now had become clear: it was the duke of Suffolk.

On 22 January 1450, Suffolk went before the king, Lords and Commons in Westminster and appealed 'that he might make his declaration concerning the great infamy and defamation that is said about him by many of the people of this land that he is other than a true man to the king and to his realm'. 'If any man would speak of it,' he said, 'then he might make his answer in person before the king, his lords and all his Commons in this present parliament.' This was a tactic that had been used by lords in the past to stall the progress of dangerous and disparaging rumour – Bedford, Cardinal Beaufort and most recently the duke of York had all successfully quashed whispers against them in this way. Since Suffolk enjoyed such a high place in Henry and Margaret's affections, he must have expected that royal influence would protect him even if he was accused, but he had made a terrible miscalculation. By 1450 the humiliating losses in France and the deteriorating state of law and order in England had reached such a pitch that the lords perceived as carrying responsibility for this state of affairs would not be allowed to quietly walk free. This time the Commons were out for blood.

Suffolk tried to win over his detractors by reminding parliament of his and his family's long record of military service. His father had died at Harfleur and his eldest brother at Agincourt in 1415, two more brothers at Jargeau in 1429 and a fourth in France as a hostage of the enemy. 'Myself,' he declared, addressing Henry,

> I have borne arms for thirty-four winters in the time of the king your father and your own time, and have been a member of the fellowship of the Garter for thirty, and during the aforesaid period I have remained continuously in the war [in France] for seventeen years without coming home or seeing this land.

Since returning to England he had 'continually served about [Henry's] most noble person for fifteen years'.

> If it shall ever please Our Lord that I die other than in my bed, my blood unshamed, I beseech Him for the well-being of my soul that I may die protesting that I have always been true to you, sovereign lord, and to your land, and to your prosperity and welfare.[4]

These were heartfelt protestations of innocence, but the Commons were unmoved. Four days later, on Monday 26 January, they queried why, since Suffolk himself had declared the 'grievous rumour and common talk of slander and infamy against him' he had not been committed to custody 'according to the course of the law'. In other words, why was Henry doing nothing? Henry consulted with the lords and chief justice of the King's Bench, who concluded that since no specific charge had been laid against Suffolk, there was no cause to imprison him.

Two days later, the Commons tried again, this time providing parliament with the specific charges demanded. 'From every part of England there has come to them a great rumour [...] that the realm of England is about to be sold to the king's enemy of France'. They accused Suffolk of fortifying and stockpiling his castle at Wallingford in Oxfordshire to serve as 'a place of refuge' when the French invaded. Although Suffolk insisted that as an English-born servant of the king it was absurd to suggest that he should seek enrichment through 'a Frenchman's promise', Henry had little choice but to commit his adviser into the custody of the Tower.

A week later the Commons presented more charges to Henry in parliament. It was asserted that Suffolk's plan was not merely to assist the French invasion but to take the crown for himself. After Charles VII had overthrown Henry, Suffolk would replace him as king with his own son, John de la Pole, who had recently married the child heiress Margaret Beaufort.* The surrender of Maine and the release of the duke of Orléans had been first steps in this nefarious scheme, forced on Henry by his wicked councillor. To further his sinister agenda, Suffolk had murdered the duke of Gloucester. Even the French negotiations that followed Queen Margaret's arrival were now interpreted as theatres of treachery, during which Suffolk had handed over state secrets and military intelligence to the French. Hyperbolic as such charges were, there was an unsettling kernel of truth at the heart of them. Suffolk could not deny that he had listed the duke of Brittany as an ally of France in his negotiations at Tours in 1444, and although he insisted that it was a deeply regrettable oversight rather than part of a conspiracy, his error had benefited Charles in the furore that resulted from the sack of Fougères.

Henry must have been painfully aware that his own inadequacies and policies were being laid at the feet of his chief minister. If Suffolk was attainted as a traitor, as the Commons wished,

---

* Margaret was the only child of John Beaufort, duke of Somerset, who had died in 1444 after returning from his disastrous French expedition.

he would be beheaded and his family destroyed, for attainder held a traitor's estate forfeit, effectively disinheriting Suffolk's son John and depriving his wife Alice of her dower lands.[5] Even setting aside the uncomfortable truth that the wrongdoings of which Suffolk was accused by the Commons were Henry's fault, the king was determined to protect his right-hand man from the charges laid against him and the violent vengefulness of the mob gathering in London. When the list of Suffolk's alleged crimes was presented to Henry and the Lords on 12 February, the king insisted that instead of referring the case to royal judges, it should 'be put in respite until he shall be advised otherwise'.[6] He was playing for time, but he could not crush the accusations completely.

By 7 March a majority of lords believed Suffolk should 'come to his answer' for his crimes; to avoid the duke wriggling free of his hook, on 9 March the Commons produced a further bill of eighteen charges of 'misprisions and dreadful offences' committed by Suffolk.* All the financial misconduct and judicial corruption of the past decade was now ascribed to Suffolk alone. It was he, the Commons asserted, who had encouraged Henry to alienate his wealth and impoverish his finances, forcing the Commons to be 'unbearably charged' with taxes. He had protected perverters of the law like William Tailboys and forced Henry to agree to meet Charles VII, 'to the likely destruction of your most royal person'. He had embezzled parliamentary grants and Orléans's ransom, and even supplied the French with secret intelligence to prevent Henry marrying a wealthy Armagnac princess instead of the impoverished Margaret of Anjou.[7]

Faced with such a litany of accusations, Henry had to bring Suffolk to answer the charges, but that did not mean he had to proceed as the Commons wished with a trial by his peers. On 13 March, under cover of bringing Suffolk from the Tower to

* Misprision was a lesser offence than treason: to conceal or to abet a felony or treasonable act.

the parliament chamber to hear the bill of accusations against him, Henry removed the duke to Westminster Palace within the same precinct in which Henry himself was staying. Then, by prior arrangement with Henry, Suffolk threw himself on the king's mercy.[8]

On 17 March, Henry summoned his lords into an inner chamber above a cloister within Westminster Palace.[9] The fifty-four-year-old Suffolk 'knelt continuously' before Henry and the lords as he protested his innocence of every crime alleged against him. He 'denied the days, the years, the places, and the conversations had' point by point and 'took his soul to everlasting damnation if he ever knew more of those matters than the child in the mother's womb'. Submitting himself 'completely to the king's rule and governance', Suffolk was declared by Henry to be 'neither declared nor charged' of treason.[10]

The charges of misprision, however, were more difficult for Henry to put aside. In an attempt to placate the Commons without sacrificing his chief minister to their vengeance, Henry sentenced Suffolk 'by his own advice and not resorting to the advice of his lords' to five years' banishment outside his territories. The lords witnessing this act of royal mercy were deeply uneasy. Many of them were Suffolk's long-term colleagues and some his allies, but Moleyns's murder at the hands of disgruntled soldiers must have loomed large in their memories, and none wanted to be accused by the Commons of helping Suffolk to escape justice. Their apprehension is palpable in the parliament roll that recorded the aftermath of Henry's judgement:

> Immediately Viscount Beaumont, on the behalf of the said Lords... declared to the king's highness that what was thus decreed and effected by his excellence concerning the person of the said duke did not proceed by their advice and counsel, but was done by the king's own direction and rule; whereupon they beseeched the king that this their speech might be enacted on the parliament roll.[11]

Under cover of darkness that night, before word of Henry's decision could spread, Suffolk was secretly escorted out of Westminster Palace. However, a mob had already assembled and pursued the duke around the walls of London as far as the church of St Giles without Holborn. Suffolk narrowly made his escape but one of his horses and a number of servants were seized and 'cruelly treated' by the Londoners.[12] Such was the anger in the city at news of Suffolk's release that on 21 March there was an abortive rising led by a vintner's servant called John Frammesley. Suffolk's freedom would be the end of Henry's regime, Frammesley insisted, repeating a vicious rhyme that resounded in the citizens' ears:

By this town by this town,
For this array the king shall lose his crown.[13]

The mood in the capital had grown sufficiently threatening for Henry to prorogue parliament on 30 March and announce that it would reconvene on 29 April in Leicester, safe in the heartland of Lancastrian loyalty. Henry's protection of Suffolk cost him in the next session of parliament, for to placate the Commons he was forced to agree to the act of resumption that they had been demanding for months. However, with a staggering 186 exemptions – characteristically, Queen Margaret and Henry's educational foundations were at the top of the list – Henry was able to circumvent some of the more radical demands. The price must have seemed worth it, in any case, to save the life of the man who had guided his household and transformed his policy into action for almost twenty years.

It was evident that even in exile, Suffolk's influence might still be felt on Henry. His wife, Alice, would remain in England close to the king and queen, to protect their son and the family estates until the duke could return. As Suffolk prepared for his exile, he stayed in contact with Henry and Margaret through their servants, including the yeoman of the crown Henry

Spenser. On 6 April Henry appointed his serjeant-at-arms, John Houghton, to commandeer ships in East Anglia to provide for Suffolk's departure and on 10 April Margaret's avener,* Jacques Blondell, requested a licence to attend on Suffolk after he left England. By 30 April Suffolk's fugitive household and fleet were assembled at Ipswich. To guard against possible reprisals, Henry had provided Suffolk with a military escort, armed and armoured, as well as the usual domestic staff.[14]

The night before he left England, Suffolk wrote with his own hand a last letter to his 'dear and only well-beloved son' John, urging him above all else to remain loyal to King Henry 'in heart, in will, in thought, in deed'. Suffolk advised John, who was not yet eight years old, to 'love, to worship [... and] obey' Alice, whose advice 'shall be best and truest to you'. With a final blessing 'as heartily and as lovingly as ever father blessed his child in earth', Suffolk dispatched his letter and boarded ship. His destination was the Low Countries, where Philippe of Burgundy had provided him with a safe conduct to reside. In the end, he never got beyond sight of the English coast.[15]

As Suffolk's small flotilla sailed south towards Calais it was intercepted by a ship of war called the *Nicholas of the Tower*. On learning that the despised duke of Suffolk was in their midst, the master of the vessel insisted that Suffolk come aboard, and reluctantly he complied. As Suffolk stepped on deck he was greeted with the words, 'Welcome, Traitor.' His safe conduct was torn to pieces, Henry's protection ripped from him at last. Years earlier, it was said, Suffolk had consulted an astrologer who told him 'to beware the Tower'. Thanks to Henry's help he had escaped the Tower of London, but he would not escape the *Nicholas of the Tower*. He was given a brief trial for treason, condemned and ordered into a little boat to be executed. His fine robes were stripped from him and on the bobbing waves,

---

* An avener was a chief officer of the stable.

a lowly member of the ship's crew clumsily hacked off his head with a rusty sword. It took half a dozen blows. On 2 May, the duke's severed head and body were rowed ashore and thrown on the pebbles beneath the white cliffs of Dover. His head was skewered, as befitted a traitor, on a pole. Suffolk's influence on Henry had been overcome at last.[16]

In her garden sanctuary at Greenwich Palace, Margaret must have heard of Suffolk's murder before Henry, for the news reached London two days before it arrived in Leicester.[17] The horror and indignation that both must have felt is easy to imagine, but the loss of Suffolk was soon overtaken by crisis. Henry ordered Suffolk's remains to be conveyed to his home in Wingfield for honourable burial, but as his body processed through Kent and Sussex it stirred ripples of righteous anger. Another threatening rhyme was circulating, a vicious satire of the office of the dead:

> Pray for this duke's soul that it might come to bliss,
> and let never such another come after this.[18]

The ballad called on Suffolk's friends to join the prayers, naming one royal officer after another associated with Henry's policies and blamed for his poverty and failure: Adam Moleyns, Lord Saye and Sele, Cardinal Kempe. With two royal advisers murdered, the rhyme started to resemble a hit list. Suffolk's death seemed to vindicate the outrage of Henry's subjects. The king had tried to deny them justice, but justice had come for Suffolk all the same. What else could the commons now achieve? As May progressed, armed bands were seen moving through the Kentish countryside. On 7 June the fields outside Canterbury were thronged with them. Clutching billhooks and knives, the Kentishmen glared across at the cathedral city, waiting to face resistance or welcome. Receiving neither, they eventually moved on, marching up the roads leading west. They were heading for London. While Henry was 100 miles (160 km) away in Leicester, they were going to take the justice that he had denied them.

20

'The harvest of heads'[1]

London
18 June 1450

The citizens of London woke to a remarkable sight. Through the city streets came a royal force that numbered into the thousands.[2] At its head rode the earl of Northumberland, and Lords Rivers, Scales and Grey, all arrayed for battle. Behind them marched their armed retinues, wearing their lords' heraldry over their armour to distinguish their allegiances, and at the rear rumbled a fearsome artillery train, its carts loaded with more than 200 cannon balls and lead darts.[3]

London had grown accustomed to such military processions. Six years ago the duke of Suffolk had trooped in just such a fashion with a military accompaniment en route to collect Margaret of Anjou for King Henry. What made this procession exceptional was that in the midst of this warrior band rode Henry, 'armed at all places', in gleaming plate armour. Henry processed through Cheapside and over London Bridge, making for the wide plains of Blackheath. The royal force looked ready to face an invading French army. Instead it went to confront a host of Kentish labourers. For the first time in Henry's reign, he rode to war. And it was against his own countrymen.

★

Henry had still been wrangling with parliament in Leicester when he received news of the 'great multitude of people' marching out of Kent in the direction of London. They were reported to number into the tens of thousands, arrayed like soldiers, bearing spears and bows, but also armed with bills of complaint against Henry's government. The realm of England, they said, was 'ruled by untrue counsel', causing the king's 'poor commons' 'injuries and oppressions', excessive taxation and injustice. Their captain, 'a subtle man' from Sussex who had complete authority over this vast army, went by a number of names. He called himself 'John Amende-alle'. Others knew him as Jack Cade. Most alarmingly to Henry and his councillors, he was reported to be an Irishman called John Mortimer. This name carried memories of previous Mortimer rebellions – traitor lords who had come out of Ireland or the Welsh marches with popular support and threatened the Lancastrian regime. Was this rebel horde part of a wider noble conspiracy? Was it connected to the duke of York, heir to the Mortimer inheritance and even now serving as Henry's lieutenant in Ireland?[4]

Henry and his advisers took no chances. On 6 June 1450 a commission of senior noblemen was appointed to go 'against the traitors and rebels in Kent and to punish and arrest the same'. Humphrey, duke of Buckingham, and the earls of Devon, Arundel and Oxford rode south as parliament dissolved and Henry prepared to return to London. Pausing en route at Newport Pagnell in Buckinghamshire on 10 June, Henry dispatched another commission against the rebels. This time experienced veterans of the French wars were included: Viscount Beaumont, the constable of England; Richard Woodville, Lord Rivers; and Lords Dudley, Scales and Lovell.[5] The next day the rebels reached the wide plains of Blackheath.[6] Five years earlier, almost exactly, this heathland with its majestic views over the capital had been the venue for Queen Margaret's state reception by the citizenry of London. Now it was dyked, ditched and bristled with stakes under Jack Cade's watchful eye. Queen Margaret was only a mile away, in Greenwich Palace, where she had moved after a freak fire at Eltham burnt down most of the service wing.[7]

When he reached London, Henry paused to hold council with his advisers at St John's Priory in Clerkenwell, just northwest of the city. The king was eager to meet the rebels himself, in the hope of resolving the situation without further bloodshed, but his more militarily experienced councillors advised against him going in person until they had reconnoitred the rebel forces to get an accurate sense of their numbers. Instead, on 16 June an embassy of lords went to meet Cade in Blackheath. The delegation included a number of figures who would have been well known to the Kentish rebels. John Stafford, archbishop of Canterbury, was the largest landowner in Kent. He was accompanied by the Kent-born Cardinal Kempe (formerly bishop of Rochester). The duke of Buckingham, who held Kentish property including the magnificent park of Penshurst, represented the senior temporal nobility with Viscount Beaumont, constable of England, at his side.[8]

Undaunted by this high-ranking delegation, Cade and his rebels presented their demands. For the first time in English history, a popular rebellion had a coherent written manifesto of grievances with proposed solutions. The Kentishmen insisted that they were not rebels but 'petitioners' to the king. They rejected any implication that they were involved with treasonable plots to overthrow Henry, maintaining that their demand was for government abuses to be reformed and for Henry's bad advisers to be removed and punished: men like Henry's treasurer James Fiennes, Lord Saye and Sele, and William Aiscough, bishop of Salisbury. Cade's followers insisted they did not want radical social change – 'we blame not all the lords, nor all those that is about the king's person, nor all gentlemen nor yeomen, nor all men of law, nor all bishops, nor all priests'. They simply wanted punishment for 'all such as may be found guilty by just and true inquiry and by the law'.[9] Henry's decision to contravene the will of the people and lawful judicial process in his treatment of Suffolk had come back to haunt him.

The lords offered the rebels a pardon in the hope that it would encourage them to disperse, but Cade's supporters were resolute. They insisted that Henry himself must respond to their petitions. The lords left Blackheath to return to Clerkenwell, taking little joy in revealing the size and preparedness of the rebel horde. Whatever the rebels may have hoped, Henry's desire to protect his councillors from the anger of the commons was undiminished and Cade's refusal to depart left Henry with little choice. Since the rebels insisted that they were not traitors, Henry would call their bluff and proceed against them in full military array, with banners raised. If the rebels maintained their defiance in the face of the royal army, they would be guilty of treason.

The following morning, Henry and his royal entourage marched forth from Clerkenwell. At most there were 20,000 men in Henry's army, meaning they were outnumbered around three to one by Cade's supporters. However, the royal army was made up of a large number of noblemen experienced in warfare, with their own retainers. Command and experience should win out over Kentish labourers. As it transpired, the difference in numbers was immaterial. When Henry reached Blackheath he found it deserted. Forewarned of the king's advance, Cade and his followers had drifted away in the night.[10]

Staking a physical claim to this vital territory on the route between Kent and London, Henry took up residence with Margaret at Greenwich Palace, leaving the lords' retainers to be quartered on Blackheath, guarding against the rebels' return. A force of loyal captains and retainers including Sir Thomas Stanley and two kinsmen of the duke of Buckingham, Sir Humphrey and William Stafford, were sent on southeast to chase down rebels and bring the county to order.[11] But then disaster struck. The

Staffords were ambushed by a party of Kentish men in a narrow lane near Sevenoaks. Both were slain with a large number of their men, and Sir Humphrey's fine armour presented to Jack Cade as a war trophy. For Henry, the rebel triumph over his forces spelled catastrophe. Word of the Stafford party's destruction soon reached the noble retainers stationed outside London, inspiring mutiny. 'Divers lords' men drew them together on the Blackheath,' a London chronicler reported, 'and said that they saw their friends slain and that they were like to be slain also if they followed the king and his traitors.'[12] Shouts of defiance echoed around the heath. The duke of Buckingham rode to Greenwich in a panic to warn Henry that he must answer the retainers' demands: 'His people would forsake him [unless] he would do execution on his traitors.'[13] Reluctantly, Henry agreed to place his chamberlain, James Fiennes, Lord Saye and Sele, in the Tower of London. His intention was probably to repeat the tactic that had enabled him to free the duke of Suffolk, covertly releasing Lord Saye and Sele into his own custody as he retreated from Greenwich to Westminster. However, when Henry tried to remove Lord Saye and Sele from his imprisonment, the constable of the Tower, Henry Holland, duke of Exeter, refused. Defiance seemed to greet the king at every turn.[14]

By now urgent discussions were being held between Henry and his council about whether they ought to remain in the vicinity of London at all. Unrest had infected the royal household, the lords could no longer trust their own servants and it was rumoured that Cade and his followers were regrouping ready to march on London once again. Now more than ever Henry missed the firm guidance of the duke of Suffolk. With so much uncertainty and violence swirling around the capital, Henry chose to flee. He would leave London until order could be restored. The mayor and aldermen were horrified: without the king's restraining presence it seemed certain the rebels would return. They pleaded with the king not to abandon them and even offered to pay the costs of his household for half a year if he stayed. But Henry's resolution was set. He had never fully trusted the Londoners, and with rebellion spreading he was not willing to trust his life to them. The day after midsummer, he was gone, headed for the refuge of Kenilworth Castle in the unquestionably reliable Midlands, 100 miles (160 km) from the suspect loyalties of the southeast.[15]

Although Henry took most of his lords with him, some representatives of royal government stayed close to the city to monitor the situation and to be on hand to react quickly if need arose. One of them was Queen Margaret, who was probably still at Greenwich. In 1465 one John Payne claimed that he had been consigned to the Marshalsea prison during Cade's rebellion 'at the queen's commandment'.[16] This suggests that Margaret was both close at hand and actively involved in suppressing the rebels. Queens traditionally played a mediatory role in such intractable situations and since none of the rebels' rhetoric was directed against Margaret it must have been assumed that she would be safe. From Greenwich, she could easily communicate with the few other representatives of Henry's government who stayed behind, including high-ranking bishops like Cardinal Kempe and Archbishop John Stafford of Canterbury. Like the queen, churchmen were expected to help restore harmony, but events in the West Country suggested that the archbishops' religion might not save them from rebel violence.[17]

As Henry fled north, one of the despised traitors of his inner circle was riding west. On 29 June William Aiscough, bishop of Salisbury, was making for the safety of Sherborne Castle in Dorset when he paused in his parish of Edington in Wiltshire to celebrate the feast of Saints Peter and Paul. No doubt he was feeling anxious. His name had featured in the sinister rhyme reciting the office of the dead for Suffolk as it echoed through Kent and Sussex, and in the manifestos issued by Cade. The day before the feast his baggage train had been robbed by locals, who seized 10,000 marks' worth of goods. Perhaps when his parishioners broke into his church at Edington, interrupting him at Mass,

Aiscough thought they were just after more of his possessions. In fact, they had bloodier vengeance in mind. Dragging him from the altar still wearing his vestments, Aiscough's parishioners led him up a hill a mile above the town and 'slew him horribly'. They tore the clothes from his body 'unto the naked skin, and rent his bloody shirt into pieces'. The rest of the bishop's moveable goods were ransacked – everything from books and chalices to oxen, sheep and swine were pillaged. Even the lead on his roofs was filed down and divided up among the locals. It was said that Aiscough's goods were scattered among every man and woman in Sherborne over the age of twelve so that Henry would have to either forgive or kill them all for the crime. If this was their plan, it seems to have worked. In the event, they were all pardoned.[18]

With parishioners killing their bishop, retainers attacking their masters and constables defying their king, it is little wonder Henry was mistrustful and feared for his safety. When he reached Berkhamsted Castle on 1 July he learnt from one of his yeomen, John Hillesdon, that the rebels in Kent had now been joined by forces from Essex. They were marching for Mile End and the northeastern gates of London even as Jack Cade's company returned to Blackheath. By the time Henry arrived at Kenilworth a day or two later, Cade had led his Kentish forces into the inns of Southwark. This area on the south bank of the Thames, only separated from the city of London by the gates and drawbridge of London Bridge, was renowned for its loose living: its prostitutes and bath houses, taverns and inns. Cade established it as the base from which to launch an assault on London.

On 3 July Cade forced his way on to London Bridge and cut the ropes of the drawbridge so that it could no longer be raised against him. Threatening to fire the entire structure unless he was allowed entry, he demanded and was given the keys of the city. He rode through London in triumph, wearing the blue velvet cloak and expensive armour that had been stripped from the body of the murdered Humphrey Stafford. In his brigandines, gilt spurs and sallet, a naked sword borne before him, he looked like a conquering knight. 'And yet,' as the anonymous author of the *English Chronicle* put it, 'was he but a knave'.[19] Although Cade insisted there must be no pillaging, he soon lost control of the rebels, who surged over London Bridge to despoil the houses of resented aldermen. The house of Philip Malpas in Lime Street was stripped of everything from its feather beds and jewels to the supplies of dyestuff and woollen cloth he kept there for his trade.

On 4 July, Cade took over the Guildhall and had Lord Saye and Sele removed from the Tower and dragged before its judges to face justice for his alleged crimes. Lord Saye and Sele reminded the judges that according to the law he should be tried by a jury of his peers, but his appeal was mocked and ignored by the commons gathered there, some of whom argued for killing him where he stood. A form of trial took place, although its outcome was never really in doubt. Having been condemned as a traitor, Lord Saye and Sele was dragged to the Standard in Cheapside. There, to the delight of the jeering crowd, he was beheaded. Cade had Lord Saye and Sele's body hitched by the feet to the tail of his horse and dragged naked through the streets 'so that the flesh cleaved to the stones' from Cheap, over London Bridge, all the way to St Thomas's hospital in Southwark. In the afternoon, for good measure, Cade had Saye's son-in-law, the unpopular sheriff of Kent William Crowmer, brought out of imprisonment in the Fleet and delivered up to the judgement of the Essex men at Mile End. Crowmer was also beheaded as a traitor, and then his and Saye's heads were placed on long poles and paraded through the streets, kissing each other. When this grisly pageant was finally over, their heads were skewered on London Bridge alongside others unfortunate enough to have provoked the ire of the rebels.[20]

By Sunday 5 July, the Londoners had had enough. Their city had been pillaged, their aldermen robbed, and twenty men condemned as traitors or extortioners at the sham trial in Guildhall. A host of leading citizens joined forces with Lord Scales, whom Henry had appointed to defend the Tower, and the veteran captain Matthew Gough, who happened to be in the city at the time. At nightfall, Gough and Scales led the citizens of London against the rebels in a ferocious battle across London Bridge. Driving back a number of Cade's men posted on the bridge, the gate was bolted against the rebels and a heavy chain drawn across. Cade called his men to arms and, to swell their numbers, threw open the south-bank prisons of Marshalsea and King's Bench to free those within. The battle that ensued was bloody and long, lasting throughout the night until morning. In the course of it, Cade set fire to the drawbridge, sending many of the soldiers plunging into the river 'harness, body and all'.[21]

Monday dawned to a scene of devastation. The bridge smouldered, smeared with blood. Bodies studded with arrows and lacerated with sword wounds were scattered across the street and bridgeworks, or bobbed in the river below. The Londoners won the battle, but in the course of it forty citizens were killed, as well as their commander, Matthew Gough. It was a cruel irony that the captain who had so persistently resisted the French by both military and diplomatic means should have met his end at the hands of his own countrymen. The London-based cleric who wrote *John Benet's Chronicle* placed the rebel dead at 200.*

Capitalizing on Cade's defeat, Margaret and Archbishops Stafford and Kempe hurried to announce a general pardon, restoring peace to the beleaguered city. The rebels steadily dispersed.[22] Although Cade was included in the pardon, under his assumed name of 'John Mortimer', he did not trust to it and fled for the safety of various Kentish castles, his booty loaded on to a boat bound for Rochester. When he was refused admittance to Queenborough Castle on the Isle of Sheppey he took to the woods, perhaps making for his native Sussex. On 10 July 'John Cade' was proclaimed a traitor and a 1,000-mark bounty promised to whoever could 'bring him to the king

---

* John Benet of Harlington in Bedfordshire copied the anonymous cleric's chronicle into his commonplace book, so it is known by his name.

quick or dead'.[23] It took only two days for Cade to be run to ground. Alexander Iden, appointed sheriff of Kent in place of the murdered William Crowmer, cornered Cade in a garden in Sussex on 12 July. As he attempted to fight his way out, Cade was mortally wounded. He died on the road back to London.[24]

To demonstrate that 'this captain of mischief' was dead, Cade's naked body was transported to Southwark in an open car 'that men might see him' and left on display overnight at the court of King's Bench. The wife of the innkeeper of the White Hart in Southwark, where Cade had based himself during the rebellion, was summoned to confirm that the body was indeed Cade's. The next day, he was beheaded and quartered and then drawn through the city of London on a hurdle, 'in pieces with the head between his breast'.[25] Saye and Crowmer's heads now made way for their killer's on London Bridge. Cade's dismembered body was dispersed throughout Kent.[26]

The city of London had been regained, but it was no thanks to Henry. Throughout the rebel occupation of the capital, and for some days after Cade's dismembered corpse had processed through the streets, Henry remained firmly ensconced within the red sandstone walls of Kenilworth Castle. There was a certain pragmatism to his decision, since in the absence of an heir the entire Lancastrian dynasty rested on Henry's shoulders: risking his life by staying in the vicinity of London as it collapsed into chaos and bloodshed would have been potentially dangerous not only to him but to national interests. Yet would Cade have been so bold as to cut the ropes of London Bridge and force an entry into the capital if the king had been within the city walls? Henry's continued presence would have acted as a deterrent, and if he had been close at hand he could have played the prominent role that Margaret and the archbishops did, reacting decisively to end the violence at the most opportune moment. From a distance of 100 miles (160 km), it was impossible for Henry to interact with a rapidly evolving situation in this way. His escape to Kenilworth resembles a frightened flight more than a tactical retreat. By contrast, Queen Margaret had stood firm. Her life was, practically speaking, less valuable to the nation than Henry's, but she still took a risk by remaining in the area of danger. Seventy years earlier, during the Peasants' Revolt, when the rebels had broken into the Tower of London, the queen mother had been caught in her bed by the ringleaders and sexually harassed.* This may be the first moment when the different personalities of Henry and Margaret emerged in public life. Margaret was still playing the expected queenly role of mediator and peacemaker in 1450, but she was, for the first time, demonstrating that she was made of sterner stuff than her husband.

London continued to be unsettled. On 21 July a group of soldiers who had been 'driven out of Normandy' broke into the church of Greyfriars where Lord Saye and Sele's corpse had been laid to rest, and tore his coat of arms from the pillars. In a final assertion of his treason the lord's arms were reversed. Such scenes were repeated throughout the southeast over the course of the summer. Three days after the attack at Greyfriars Henry had advanced as far as St Albans, where he met his council to determine if it was safe to proceed into the capital. Despite the ongoing unrest, it was decided that it was more important for Henry to be present to prevent further violence than that he should stay distant for fear of danger. On 28 July he entered London and held a service of thanksgiving for the suppression of the rebellion at St Paul's Cathedral. He then went to stay in Westminster.[27]

In the wake of such a rebellion, it might be expected that the

---

* According to the chronicler Thomas Walsingham the peasants 'dared with their worthless staves to force a way into the bedroom of the king [Richard II] [and] of his mother... even asking the king's mother for a kiss.' Preest, David, trans. and Clark, James G., ed. *The Chronica Maiora of Thomas Walsingham 1376–1422* (Woodbridge, 2005), p. 125.

streets of the capital would be hung with the corpses of executed insurgents and the city gates topped with their dismembered quarters. But even though the city was far from peaceful – when he attempted to leave London in August to celebrate the feast of the Assumption at Eton College Henry was prevented by angry veterans from Normandy – Henry was resolved to reconcile and placate rather than punish the rebels. Perhaps he believed that overly firm justice would only inspire further vengeful violence, or maybe Henry's natural instinct for mercy was uppermost in his mind. The rebels had called for justice, and now he gave it to them. From August until the end of October 1450 Henry sent out a commission to tour Kent and listen to locals' complaints about extortion and malpractice. Heading up these commissions were men of unquestioned loyalty to the crown, but who were not associated with Suffolk's inner circle. They were led by the prelates who had mediated the rebels' pardon, Archbishop John Stafford and Cardinal Kempe, and assisted by the duke of Buckingham, who was coming increasingly to represent a middle way in the faction-ridden politics of Henry's court. Even the fact that Buckingham's kinsmen had been ambushed and murdered by the rebels did not incline him, it seems, to harsh reprisals.[28]

Henry's decision to be merciful should not make us under-estimate the psychological impact of what had been, by any standards, a horrifying series of events. He had lost, in Suffolk, a faithful servant of his regime who had been in some ways a father figure and was unquestionably a constant, trusted presence in Henry's household from his childhood. Henry could comfort himself with the fact that he had done everything possible to save Suffolk, but Lord Saye and Sele's blood was on his hands, for he had been the one who committed the treasurer into the Tower then abandoned him to the rebels' vengeance. Adam Moleyns's murder in the course of his duty deprived Henry of another faithful adviser who had been a vital ambassador for his peace policy. Perhaps most disturbing of all for someone of Henry's profound piety, Bishop William Aiscough had been murdered by his own parishioners, the words of the holy Mass newly spoken on his lips. Even as he processed these losses, Henry received word of yet another personal tragedy. His childhood friend, Gilles of Brittany, who had been miserably imprisoned as punishment for his loyalty to Henry, had been found dead in his prison cell. His murder was a long time coming – his captors had been trying unsuccessfully to starve or poison him for months, before finally smothering him to death in his cell with such violence that he bled from every orifice.[29]

Over and above these personal losses, Henry had witnessed a wave of resentment and frustration against his rule such as he had never before encountered. Little wonder that he fled in the face of it. Since before he could walk or talk Henry VI had been cosseted from the harsh realities of kingship. He had faced resistance, certainly, and complaints, from his English subjects, but never outright rebellion. His earnest faith in peace and the goodwill of his fellow man had been sorely tested in the last year.

Just as he regained a little control over the southeast, he received alarming reports from the furthest reaches of his kingdom. Without permission, and with questionable intent, Henry's closest blood relative had left his post and was sailing for England. Whether he came to restore order or to cause further dissension – perhaps even to press his own right to the crown – was unclear. Whatever his reason, the duke of York was coming to England.

21

'The true blood of the realm'[1]

Beaumaris Castle, North Wales
September 1450

From the many towers of Beaumaris Castle a ship could be seen making for port. Nestled within that ring of stone on the southeastern tip of the island of Anglesey, the unfortunate Eleanor Cobham still languished. Almost a decade had passed since she had been condemned as a traitor and exiled to the furthest reaches of her nephew's realm.[2] The ship that passed beneath her windows carried a distant relation of Eleanor's late husband: a man whose taste for luxury and magnificence had already far outstripped his considerable wealth, and whose paranoid pride brought him unbidden to a land riven by unrest.

News of the return of Richard, duke of York, from Ireland reached Henry at Westminster before his cousin had even touched land. With memories of the last Mortimer captain who had demanded his attention still raw, Henry immediately dispatched panicked orders to his officers across north Wales to impede York's progress until his intentions could be discerned. When York tried to enter the port at Beaumaris, he was denied lodging or landing, and forced to sail another 30 miles (48 km) east to lands under his personal lordship, where he would face no resistance. By 7 September he was at his fortress of Denbigh, and within a week he had continued south to the marcher town of Shrewsbury. Despite his unexpected return, York insisted that he was in England solely to protest his loyalty to Henry in the wake of Cade's rebellion. He had a lot to lose if he was not believed.[3]

At the time of his return from Ireland, Richard, duke of York, was in the prime of his life. At almost forty years old, he had enjoyed a distinguished career as royal lieutenant in Normandy, France and Ireland. His marriage to Cecily Neville connected him to one of the leading magnate families of northern England, and the duke and duchess of York had followed the Neville tradition of siring an enormous nursery of offspring. Their eldest sons, Edward and Edmund, had been shown 'exceptional marks of royal favour' by Henry in the past, being allowed to enter the earldoms of March and Rutland as infants and encouraged towards marriage with French princesses.[4] York and Cecily's eldest daughter, Anne, was already married to another branch of the nobility with royal blood: the quarrelsome Henry Holland, twenty-year-old duke of Exeter. With Gloucester's death in 1447 York had become heir presumptive and the downfall of so many pillars of Henry's regime in 1450 offered him the enticing possibility of replacing Suffolk as chief councillor.

The deaths of Suffolk and his allies had left a void at the heart of government. Henry needed a chief adviser who could transform his vacillating policy into concerted action. Unfortunately for York, during the crucial summer of 1450 he was hundreds of miles away in Ireland. Events in England escalated far more quickly than communications could keep up with and York would have learnt of the opportunity opened to him by Suffolk's death only shortly before he discovered that his name had been invoked in open rebellion against Henry's regime. For many of Henry's subjects, York's status as heir to Gloucester's legacy was an advantage. It was widely perceived that he would take up where Gloucester had left off, holding Henry's government to account for its military and fiscal failings. But for Henry, this prevailing attitude was precisely the reason he did not welcome York back with open arms. Despite their close kinship, York and Henry were virtual strangers – the duke was more than a decade Henry's senior and had spent most of the past fifteen years outside England. Moreover, all Henry's most recent reminders of his cousin were associated with defiance and rebellion. In April 1450, as Henry headed to parliament in Leicester, he had been confronted by a sailor called John Harris, who thrashed the earth in front of him with a flail, loudly proclaiming that this was how York would deal with the traitors in parliament. For his unwise words, Harris was hanged, drawn and quartered, but his presentation of York as champion against government corruption had been a running theme throughout the months of turmoil and murder that engulfed Henry in 1450. As early as March a plot by two northern yeomen to depose Henry and raise an army to replace him with York had been uncovered in Ipswich.[5] The very real army raised by Jack Cade's rebels had insisted that they had no treasonable intentions regarding the duke of York, but Cade himself had played on the popular asso-ciation between York's Mortimer bloodline and reform when he called himself 'John Mortimer' and asserted his Irish heritage. One of the rebel demands had been for York, 'the true blood of the realm', to be installed as Henry's adviser. Little wonder that by the close of that bloody summer of 1450, members of Henry's household were encouraging the king to have York indicted for treason.[6]

York's actions as summer gave way to autumn did little to allay Henry's fears. The duke's precipitate abandonment of his post in Ireland without royal leave, and his determination to enter Henry's realm via the fortress where the duchess of Gloucester was imprisoned gave rise to all manner of suspicion. Did York intend to free Eleanor Cobham? Was he championing her cause? Even if all York sought was a public association with the late duke of Gloucester, Henry could hardly be expected to welcome the reminder of an uncle who had been defiant and possibly treasonous.

When he finally made landfall, York attempted to dispel Henry's anxieties without alienating those among his subjects who sought a champion of the commonweal. He met Lancastrian envoys including the duke of Buckingham and convinced them of his good faith. He also issued a range of public bills, asserting his loyalty as Henry's 'humble subject and true liegeman', and appealing to be allowed to come 'before your high presence, and I will declare me... as a true knight ought to do'.[7] But as he processed towards London, York's bills grew more explicitly critical of Henry's government. Certain royal officers had been over-zealous as they tried to bar York's entry into the realm, beating some of his servants and threatening the duke himself with arrest. At least one of York's bills dwelt, unwisely, on the injustice of such high-handed royal behaviour to one who had done no wrong.[8]

Henry received these bills at Westminster as he awaited York's arrival. Reports reached him, too, of the ever-increasing entourage of men flocking to York's side. The duke entered Stony Stratford in Buckinghamshire swathed in red velvet, riding a black horse at the head of a force 300–400 strong. By the time he neared London, his retinue had swollen into the thousands. Among those rushing to greet York and receive his patronage were a number of noblemen who shared the misconception that the duke would soon be at Henry's right hand in government. Lords Scales and Dudley and even Thomas Hoo, Henry's former chancellor of Normandy, all sought York's protection. Inevitably, this large assembly trailed disorder in its wake. Among the men who sought a meeting with York was William Tresham, a past speaker of the Commons and official of the royal household. He, too, may have been seeking to swear his allegiance to York's service but before he could make his intentions plain he was ambushed as he made his way along a Northamptonshire highway. A band of more than 100 men killed Tresham, pillaged his corpse and wounded his son. Tresham's murder seems to have been inspired by local rivalries rather than his intention to meet York, but the violent death of yet another government official as he rode towards the duke emphasized the unrest that seemed to swirl around Henry's kinsman.[9] When York finally arrived in London at the end of September, news of his coming precipitated a riot in Newgate prison at the edge of the city. As stones rained down from Newgate tower and smoke crackled, York and Henry met in Westminster Palace.[10]

It was a chilly encounter. 'The king did not show [York] heart-felt greeting.'[11] By now it was clear that York did not merely want Henry to affirm his loyalty, but also to welcome him as a royal adviser. His progress through England and Wales had evinced ample evidence of his popularity, and the bills he had sent to Henry had been copied and circulated widely. By the time Henry received the last bill, York's censure of his regime had become explicit. He dwelt on the 'inestimable extortions' and oppressions Englishmen were enduring, and offered his services to put down traitors 'about the king's person' and reform English government. This was going too far. By asserting his own suita-bility to reform government, he was implying Henry's inability to do so. Even worse, York's resolution to proceed against Henry's traitorous advisers unnervingly recalled the manifesto of Jack Cade. The losses of the past year had made Henry sensitive to affronts to his authority and determined to protect his remaining advisers from harm.

Playing York at his own game, Henry responded by publicly disseminating the entirety of their correspondence with an additional bill of his own, in which he explained why the duke had been debarred entry into the realm and defended himself and his officers against York's accusations of misconduct. In recent months, Henry reminded York and the realm at large, Henry's crown had been repeatedly threatened by people 'making menace unto our person by *your* saying', not merely in private but to Henry's face. If his officers had mistreated York or his men, it was York's 'sudden coming without certain warning' that was the cause. Henry was prepared to meet York as 'our true faithful subject and as our well-beloved cousin' but he was not willing to accept his criticism, and he would not let York incite a witch-hunt against his advisers. 'When the work requires it, or it is necessary,' he told York at Westminster, 'I will call upon your assistance.'[12] Otherwise, Henry had his own plans to deal with recent criticisms of his advisers, which he made explicit in his final bill. He intended to establish a 'sad and a substantial council' to deal with questions of justice and 'other our great matters'. York was invited to join this council but told he would have no superior authority in it to any other member.[13]

With this polite but firm rejection, Henry had checked York's ambitions. He asserted his own position as reformer, and York was left with no special role in Henry's regime at all. York retired to East Anglia to brood on his failure throughout the autumn and plan his ascendancy by other means. The manner of York's return set a pattern of mutual suspicion between the cousins that was never fully resolved, but the reality in 1450 was that even if York had arrived at a more auspicious time and been less heavy-handed in his demands for a position of influence, he would not have got want he wanted. The position of Henry's chief councillor had already been filled.

In August 1450, Edmund Beaufort, duke of Somerset, had limped back across the Channel as the final fortress in Normandy fell to the French. Somehow, despite the military disasters that had befallen him as lieutenant-general and governor of Normandy, Somerset talked his way back into Henry's favour almost immediately. The duke of Somerset had not always had the easiest relationship with his superiors. Charles VII had been grossly offended by his imperious manner during his lieutenancy, and the duke had almost ruined his career before it started by having an ill-advised affair with Henry's mother, Queen Catherine, in the mid-1420s. Yet he evidently had the ability to charm when he wished, and his long military record showed he did not lack courage or resolution. His chief vice was avarice. He 'could never have enough wealth', noted his Norman contemporary Thomas Basin, bishop of Lisieux.[14] Perhaps he had inherited this failing from his uncle, Cardinal Beaufort, who had been a crucial patron in the early years of his career. For Henry's subjects, memories of Somerset's heroic deeds of the 1420s and 1430s had been erased by the indignity of his losses in Normandy, but Henry seemed to overlook his kinsman's military failures. Perhaps the memory of his beloved uncle, Cardinal Beaufort, endeared Somerset to Henry. And perhaps, with Suffolk dead, he sought another quasi-father figure of high birth who was willing to guide his hand unobtrusively in government. Whatever the reason, by the time York reached Henry in late September, Somerset's ascendancy was a *fait accompli*. On 11 September 1450 Somerset had replaced another Lancastrian stalwart, Viscount John Beaumont, as constable of England.[15]

However, for York and the majority of Henry's other subjects, Somerset's elevation was unacceptable. That a man who had overseen the destruction of English rule in Normandy had stepped directly into Suffolk's position at the heart of government was deplorable. All the condemnations of Suffolk's regime were now refocused on Somerset: financial malpractice, military failure, corrupt government. Once again Henry had chosen a chief councillor whose reputation was tarnished. For York the matter was more personal. Somerset had replaced him as lieutenant-general and governor of Normandy and many of York's men had still been in office when the duchy fell to the French. York had still been nominal captain of Rouen when Somerset surrendered the city in November 1449. Somerset's failure therefore reflected directly on York's honour as a military commander. This was only the latest in a progression of indignities that had been imposed on York by the king for the benefit of the Beaufort family. Somerset's elder brother, John, had similarly usurped York's authority with his disastrous French campaign in 1443, and the accusations of financial misconduct laid against York in 1446 had been engineered to oust him from the lieutenancy in favour of Somerset. Until 1450, York had done little to right these collective wrongs but when he realized that his disgruntlement chimed with popular feeling it became clear there was valuable political capital to be gained from joining the ranks of Somerset's critics. With the public so desirous of a new champion of the commonweal, York cast himself as the anti-Somerset, the leader of a movement to reform corrupt government around Henry and place himself in a position of authority instead.[16]

From his East Anglian exile, York set about harnessing local support with his nephew, John Mowbray, duke of Norfolk. Only four years York's junior, Norfolk had a history of troublemaking. In his youth he had been forced to abide by council-appointed regulations to try and cure him of disordered living, with even the hours at which he should get up in the morning and go to bed prescribed by his fellow lords. The dominance of the duke of Suffolk in government had been an ongoing challenge to Norfolk's local authority, as the pair vied for control of the same area, and Norfolk had twice been imprisoned for clashes with Suffolk's retainers. For all that, Norfolk was a formidable ally for York, with a large swathe of territories under his control and a well-fortified base at Framlingham Castle in Suffolk.[17] As autumn progressed, the pair of them dispatched men to pack the coming parliament with their own supporters and weaken the influence of the royal household. Their activities were soon known in London, where Henry's household was said to be 'afeared right sore'.[18] The problems that had begun a year ago with Henry's stubborn refusal to try Suffolk for treason had never been resolved and, after a summer of bloodshed and turmoil, the parliament that opened in London on 6 November 1450 was the scene for a fierce contest between Henry and his regime – represented now by Somerset – and the Commons, coalescing around York. Henry would have to choose whether to continue to resist the drive for reform, which implicitly and sometimes explicitly threatened his friends and advisers, or to bend to the will of his subjects and risk further incidents of violent reprisal.

London
November 1450

The city crackled with tension as parliament opened. Henry and his lords arrived with vast entourages of armed men, their masters' livery and badges a visible statement of their divided loyalties. Waves of embittered soldiers and dispossessed refugees had started to stream back from Normandy. Any minor offence – a jostled arm or wrong look – could escalate to words and blows in a matter of moments. The mayor of London was forced to ride through the city streets with armed attendants, and issue a proclamation that any man who took up 'axe, glaive, sword or bill' within the walls would be imprisoned. Although bloodshed was averted, minor acts of rebellion persisted. One night the duke of York's badge, a fetterlock,* was torn down and replaced by the royal arms, only to be defiantly restored by his supporters the next morning. 'Strange bills' started to circulate, calling for revenge on the traitors and reform of government. They were pinned to the doors of Westminster Hall and St Paul's Cathedral. Most alarmingly of all, some made it all the way to the door of Henry's chambers. Tensions were only heightened by the late arrival of the dukes of Norfolk and York on 23 November, accompanied by a 'great multitude' of supporters, a naked sword borne before them through the city streets.[19]

If Henry had hoped his promise to create a 'sad and substantial council' would lay his critics' opposition to rest, the parliament soon disabused him of the notion. One petition after another

---

* A heraldic device representing the D-shaped fetter used to tether a horse by its leg.

attacked his closest friends, servants and advisers. The most extensive accused no fewer than thirty of Henry and Margaret's allies of 'behaving improperly around your royal person'. By their means, it was asserted, Henry's 'possessions have been greatly diminished, your laws not executed, and the peace of this your realm not observed nor kept'.[20] The Commons demanded that given the 'universal rumour and clamour' against these men and women, they must be removed from the royal presence 'for the term of their lives', and if they came within 12 miles (20 km) of the court they should face forfeiture of all their goods and lands. This demand offended both Henry's authority – the power to appoint one's own servants was an essential royal prerogative – and his sense of loyalty. Among the listed 'improper persons' were Edmund Hampden, who had served both Henry and Margaret for more than a decade; Henry's physician and old tutor, John Somerset, who was closely involved in his beloved educational establishments; and Alice Chaucer, dowager duchess of Suffolk, who had accompanied Margaret to England in 1445 and probably remained a close friend. As the duke of Suffolk's widow, Alice Chaucer bore the brunt of the Commons' anger. In this session of parliament they sought not only to try her for treason but also posthumously to attaint the duke of Suffolk, which would have deprived Alice of her dower and effectively disinherited her only child. In a final condemnation of Henry's regime, the Commons called for the duke of Gloucester to be 'proclaimed a true knight', a demand that explicitly defied Henry's own political decisions.[21]

The most personally distasteful Commons petition came from a Bristol lawyer called Thomas Young, who demanded that for the security of the realm Henry should name his heir and nominated the duke of York for the role. There was such general support for this petition among the Commons that they refused to deal with any further business until the lords in parliament supported York's nomination. For Henry, Young's proposal was an insult both to his own masculinity and his wife's reputation.

It suggested that the royal couple – still both in their twenties, Margaret barely out of her teens – were incapable of producing an heir for themselves.[22]

With such divisive efforts at reform in already volatile conditions, it did not take long for parliament to dissolve into scenes of chaos. On 30 November 1450 Westminster Hall was stormed by armed men: citizens, soldiers and even the retainers of the lords attending parliament. With a 'marvellous and dreadful storming and noise' they cried out, three times, for 'justice upon the false traitors'.[23] A triple shout such as this had profound symbolism for those in attendance. It recalled the similar shouts of acclamation made for kings at their coronation – a promise by the people to obey their monarch. Now it was invoked in defiance of King Henry.

The next day, as the duke of Somerset sat down to his dinner in his lodgings at Blackfriars, overlooking the River Thames, the same retainers who had invaded Westminster Hall broke into his house and attempted to haul him away to face justice. If Henry had not dispatched a rescue party under Thomas Courtenay, earl of Devon, to smuggle Somerset out on to the river to make his escape by boat, Somerset might have met the same end as Suffolk and Lord Saye and Sele. For his own safety, Henry brought Somerset downriver to the Tower of London, trusting to the fortress's many walls to protect him. Robbed of their vengeance on Somerset's person, the rioters ransacked his lodgings and made off with his jewels. On 10 December Somerset's chief residence, Corfe Castle in Dorset, was similarly pillaged and a number of Somerset's retainers seriously injured.[24]

Like Duchess Alice, Somerset had been prominent on the list of 'improper persons' the Commons wanted removed from Henry's presence. Two others on that list, Sir Thomas Hoo, the chancellor of Normandy, and Alice's henchman Thomas Tuddenham had their London homes looted in the unrest after the triple shout in Westminster Hall.[25] The situation in the capital was getting out of hand. On 2 December the dukes of

York and Norfolk decided to take matters into their own hands and assembled their armed entourages to march through the city streets rounding up looters. They issued proclamations against robbery and beheaded one thief on the Strand as an example to others. While their actions may have prevented further outrages, to Henry the dukes' march was an insulting usurpation of royal authority. While he was in the city, it fell to him and the civic authorities to restore order, not to York. For the second time in as many months, York's clumsy attempt to prove publicly his commitment to good governance had offended and roused the suspicions of his king. He received no thanks from Henry for his actions, and York's sensitive pride doubtless smarted from yet another royal snub.[26]

What made York and Norfolk's offence particularly brazen was that they were almost certainly responsible for the unrest in the first place. Norfolk's men had been among the mob who stormed Somerset's home, and York's complicity must also have been suspected.[27] His influence had certainly made itself felt in this unusually combative parliament. The speaker of the Commons was William Oldhall, a veteran of the French wars from as far back as 1416 and the duke of York's chamberlain. Oldhall had been among the duke's servants threatened by royal household officials when they landed in Wales and had accompanied York to put forward his complaints to Henry at Westminster in September.[28] Even more damningly, among York's other retainers was Thomas Young, the apprentice at law who had nominated the duke as Henry's heir. While York presented his actions as being for the common good, it was difficult for Henry and his allies in government to interpret them as anything other than aggressively self-serving.

In the face of such opposition and violent unrest, Henry could have faltered and fled as he did in the summer. Instead, he stood firm. He rejected the petitions for Gloucester's restoration and Suffolk's attainder, and he quashed attempts to put Duchess Alice on trial. He met demands for the removal of his courtiers

with a reminder that he had always tried to 'be accompanied
by virtuous persons and no others' and he saw no reason based
on the Commons' petition why any of his attendants should be
removed from his presence. He agreed, 'by his own volition and
by no other authority' to remove a few offensive individuals for
a year but hedged his agreement about with excuses that completely negated its efficacy.*

To reassert his control over London Henry made his own procession through the city on 3 December, this time pressing York
and Norfolk into his entourage with 10,000 armed attendants.
The citizens of London, many similarly garbed in armour, stood
on every side of the streets to watch as King Henry rode at the
heart of an impressive show of military force – a reminder that
he, not any over-mighty duke, was the ultimate authority in
the land. By Christmas, it was safe to bring Somerset out of the
Tower, and he was once more ensconced as Henry's chief councillor, inspiring a new, more vigorous royal response to lingering national unrest. To underline York's sidelining in Henry's
regime, in the new year Henry cancelled his plans for a 'sad
and substantial council' including the duke. Instead, he personally oversaw a range of judicial commissions to investigate
rebellious outbreaks in the southeast in the past year, sending
a new harvest of heads to leer over London Bridge. Although
half a dozen noblemen, including Somerset, accompanied
Henry on his commission, the dukes of York and Norfolk were
noticeably absent. Demonstrating that the dominance of the
royal household remained undiminished, an investigation into
accusations of wrongdoing by Henry's household men acquitted
every one of them.

Henry was swift to clip the wings of York's parliamentary champion Thomas Young: for suggesting York be confirmed as heir

---

* He exempted all lords and 'certain persons... who have been accustomed to wait continually upon his person' – in other words, all his usual
attendants.

to the throne, Henry had him arrested and sent to the Tower. Since the Commons refused to proceed with business until Young's suggestion was addressed, Henry arbitrarily dissolved parliament. In an attempt to remove the root of the problem, Henry confirmed York as lieutenant of Ireland for the remaining seven years of his term on 11 February 1451. He must have hoped that York would return to Irish exile as soon as possible. His wish was to be frustrated. The following months saw ripples of unrest spread widely throughout Henry's realm, and York was resolutely at the heart of them.

22

'My most dread sovereign lord'[1]

Taunton
27 September 1451

A cross Somerset, 5,000 men were on the march, an army supported by five cartloads of guns and weapons. They came at the bidding of Thomas Courtenay, 13th earl of Devon, to unleash vengeance on his enemies in the west, the latest violent outburst in a decade-long vendetta. As Devon's men passed the cathedral city of Wells, Henry's councillor, Bishop Thomas Beckington, made a desperate attempt to stall them before blood ran in torrents through the West Country clay. But the earl of Devon would not be dissuaded. He continued his march, indulging his men in an orgy of pillage and ransack through the manors of the earl of Wiltshire. By the end of the month they were nearing Taunton, where Devon's old enemy, Lord William Bonville, had taken refuge within the castle. On 27 September Devon drew up his men and prepared to lay siege. The Bonville–Courtenay feud that had riven the West Country since Henry's adolescence had now assumed the aspect of a civil war.[2]

Reports of the siege engines being readied around Taunton reached Henry as he prepared to hold council in Coventry. He had had a long, trying year, touring ceaselessly through the southern counties to preside over judicial commissions to try to bring peace to his troubled realm.[3] In Sussex and Kent, order had never been fully restored after Cade's rebellion. In late January 1451 a man called Stephen Christmas tried to raise Kent, and even after his quarters had been dispersed throughout the county his cause was taken up by Henry Hasildene and Henry Wilkhouse, Jack Cade's secretary, who assembled followers in Sussex and Kent by decrying Somerset's failings and bewailing the disappointed hopes of the recent parliament. The duke of Buckingham's deer park at Penshurst was attacked by 100 men armed with lances, bows and arrows. Their faces were blackened with charcoal and they wore long beards, disguising their identities further by calling themselves the servants of the queen of the fairies. Despite the head rotting on London Bridge there were persistent rumours that Cade himself was still alive.[4]

By the summer of 1451 the unrest had spread to the already troubled western counties, where there were fears of French invasion. Charles VII's military reconquest of Henry's continental territories continued unchecked and Gascon cities were now falling to his advancing forces. It was no great leap of the imagination to suspect that Charles might soon turn his attention north to Henry's English realm. A fleet raised by Richard Woodville, Lord Rivers, to defend Gascony was urgently diverted to southwestern England, where his men burdened the locals with their demands for supplies and lodgings, while their excessive numbers of camp followers fomented further disorder. The government found it impossible to pay the wages of this army and the duke of Somerset had to resort to sending Lord Rivers a silver and gold statue of St George in place of ready cash.[5] Eventually Rivers's fleet became so frustrated with the delays and excuses that they refused to wait any longer for pay and simply went back to their own homes.

Lord Rivers's fleet had been badly needed in Gascony; without it, the English campaign there collapsed. By August 1451, both the capital city of Bordeaux and the vital trading port of Bayonne had fallen to Charles's forces. With Normandy and northern France already in Valois hands, the English hold on what had once been an extensive continental empire was growing ever weaker.[6]

As bad blood among his nobility reached critical levels Henry had summoned his lords to a great council in his Midlands sanctuary at Coventry, away from the febrile atmosphere of a parliament in London. It was there that news of the earl of Devon's campaign arrived in the panicked form of James Butler, earl of Wiltshire. His manor at Lackham had been ransacked by Devon's men and he had only just escaped ahead of them. The conflict engulfing the West Country had been brewing for years, exacerbated by Henry's careless granting of the stewardship of the duchy of Cornwall to both Thomas Courtenay, earl of Devon, and his local rival William Bonville.* In the past decade, Bonville's star had risen thanks to faithful military service in Gascony and the patronage of the duke of Suffolk, while Devon's fortunes had waned. In 1449, the parvenu Bonville had been made a baron, whereas Devon suffered the indignity of having his status downgraded so that his earldom was rendered inferior to that of the earl of Arundel. In the honour culture of Henry's court such matters of precedence were of material importance to local honour. By 1451 the Bonville–Courtenay feud had escalated to a full-scale vendetta, involving a significant number of the neighbouring nobility and cleaving the western counties of Henry's realm into two clear factions. In the wake of Suffolk's fall Bonville had moved into the clientage of James Butler, earl of Wiltshire, who was himself the enemy of Edward Brook, Lord Cobham. As Bonville and Wiltshire moved into the inner circle of Henry's court faction, Devon and Cobham had found common cause with the duke of York.[7]

As soon as he learnt of the violence being unleashed in Somerset

---

*   See above, p. 236.

in September 1451, Henry dispatched the duke of Buckingham, John Talbot and the earl of Salisbury to restore order with a royal army, but they arrived too late. The duke of York had already intervened, assembling a force of 2,000 men and marching on Taunton. In Coventry, the suspicious ease with which York had mustered so large a force only served to confirm Henry's doubts about his kinsman, and it was unclear if York intended to raise the siege or help his ally Devon to win it. Before Henry's royal forces could arrive at Taunton to provide an answer, the siege had been abandoned. Bonville appealed successfully for York's protection and Devon agreed to disperse his forces peacefully.

Outwardly, it appeared York had restored order to a febrile situation. To Henry and his allies, however, York's interference was yet another unwelcome usurpation of royal authority. York's precipitate intervention had kept Devon from being taken into royal custody for his actions, which presumably was his intention – the earl was one of very few noble allies that York possessed, and he could not afford to lose him to royal imprisonment. For Henry's new chief adviser, the duke of Somerset, York's intrusion was a rebuke to his own influence in the county from which he took his title. York may not have expected royal thanks for his efforts but he must have at least anticipated royal approval. Instead, Henry angrily summoned all of the lords involved at Taunton to present themselves before his council, casting York not as a peacemaker but an aggressor. If he had come to Coventry he would almost certainly have been imprisoned, as the other lords involved were.* However, both Devon and York refused to obey their summons. Under the circumstances, their defiance did little to mend relations between Henry and his ambitious kinsman. It would not be long before their relationship reached a crisis.[8]

---

* Lord Bonville and the earl of Wiltshire were imprisoned in Berkhamsted Castle, Devon's allies Lords Cobham and Moleyns in Wallingford Castle. Benet, p. 205.

★

In the winter of 1451, as he made his way south for his traditional Thameside Christmas season with Queen Margaret, Henry doubled his bodyguard. The defiance of York and Devon was a worrying demonstration of dissatisfaction with Henry's judgement, but more alarming still were the whispers arriving from Northamptonshire, Lincolnshire and Hertfordshire that members of York's retinue were planning armed risings against the government.[9] The ringleader of this rebel band appeared to be Sir William Oldhall, the duke's chamberlain and the man who had presided over the unrest in the last parliament as speaker of the Commons. In November, Henry and his council ordered Oldhall to remain in London to face questioning about his activities. Instead, he made a pre-dawn flit into sanctuary at St Martin-le-Grand near Westminster.[10]

The duke of York insisted that he and Oldhall had done nothing wrong. In early January 1452 York sent a letter to Henry from his family stronghold at Ludlow Castle, appealing for the king not to believe the 'sinister information of [his] enemies'. He was no traitor, he insisted, as he had declared 'divers times, as well by mouth as by writing'. It grieved him that Henry still behaved as his 'heavy lord, greatly displeased'.[11] York offered to swear an oath of loyalty on the holy sacrament, if only Henry would send two lords to him to hear it. He suggested that two of his most distinguished neighbours, Reginald Boulers, bishop of Hereford, and John Talbot, earl of Shrewsbury, take up the task. To Henry, York's unwillingness to come to the royal presence to make his excuses in person undermined his sincerity, but there was some legitimacy to York's concerns about Henry's courtiers.

On 28 January, between eleven and twelve at night, a large body of armed men led by Devon's enemy the earl of Wiltshire*

---

* With the earl of Wiltshire on 28 January were the earls of Salisbury and Worcester, and Lords Lisle and Moleyns.

broke open the sanctuary gates at St Martin-le-Grand and stormed inside to seize Oldhall. They had had enough of his privileged protection by the church and were resolved to get to the bottom of his conspiracy for the duke of York. Smashing doors and chests in their fury, they eventually found Oldhall hiding in a turret behind a secret door. He was thrown on to horseback and dragged to Westminster Palace for questioning. There Oldhall may have remained were it not for the return two days later of the dean of St Martin's, who protested at this illegal infringement of his sanctuary. It became clear that Wiltshire and his men were acting not on Henry's orders, but on Somerset's. When Henry learnt what had happened, he immediately ordered Oldhall to be released back to sanctuary. However, probably on Somerset's advice, he appointed a royal guard to keep watch lest Oldhall try to escape.[12]

Oldhall's mistreatment tipped York from surreptitious conspiracy to outright rebellion. On 3 February he wrote from Ludlow to the citizens of Shrewsbury, calling for them to join him in a rising against the duke of Somerset:

> It is well known unto you... what laud, what worship... was ascribed of all nations unto the people of this realm, whilst the kingdom's sovereign lord stood possessed of his lordship in the realm of France and duchy of Normandy; and what derogation, loss of merchandise, lesion of honour and villainy, is... reported generally unto the English nation, for loss of the same... through the envy, malice and untruth of the Duke of Somerset... [who] ever prevails and rules about the king's person.[13]

Similar calls to arms went out across the country, from Somerset to Essex and Kent to Norfolk. In Fotheringhay on 8 February, one of York's men, Thomas Mulso, was assembling supporters; while two days later Mulso's brother Sir Edmund did the same in Ludlow.[14] In the southwest, York's allies Lord Cobham and the earl of Devon were soon on the march, and the duke of York left Ludlow at the head of a force several thousand strong, headed for London. But York had overestimated the support his calls would receive. After two years of lawlessness, many of the cities that he called to his banner were reluctant to foment further unrest. Instead, they forwarded York's letters to the king with protestations of loyalty.[15]

After a brief attempt to negotiate with York in early February, Henry was convinced by his advisers that the only way to stop him was with military might. Chief among the voices encouraging Henry to take up arms was, of course, the duke of Somerset, who had a great deal to lose if York's campaign was successful. On 16 February Somerset and Henry left London to block York's path southeast from Ludlow. They were accompanied by fifteen other noblemen, including the premier lords of England: the dukes of Buckingham, Exeter and even York's old ally Norfolk. To counter York's summons, Henry sent letters under the privy seal to his 'true subjects' instructing them to resist the duke's forces.[16]

By 22 February, close to Northampton, Henry and York's forces were near enough to negotiate, but York refused to disband his army. He was not rebelling, he insisted; he was trying to save Henry from the traitors surrounding him and he would not submit until Somerset had been brought to answer for his wrongdoing. A day later, York moved southeast. His intention was to rouse the same Kentish rebels who had opposed Henry's regime in 1450 with his populist calls for justice against the traitors. To reach Kent and join up with these rebels, however, he needed to cross the Thames at London Bridge. When he realized York's intention, Henry hurriedly dispatched orders to London that York was not to be admitted. In light of events there in 1450 he must have been uncertain that his command would be obeyed. Fortunately for him, the city stood firm. York was forced to double back and cross the Thames at Kingston, 20 miles (32 km) upriver, before continuing his steady progress towards Kent.

Henry pursued his kinsman south, entering London on 27 February. He had assembled forces from Surrey, Sussex, Derbyshire and Nottinghamshire, making a royal army at least 20,000 strong. After a display of military power, parading his forces through the city streets and over London Bridge, Henry paused at the bishop of Winchester's palace in Southwark, waiting to see if the Kentishmen would join York's cause or not. But it was now becoming clear that York's hopes of a Kentish rising had been misplaced. Henry's bloody commissions had crushed the rebel spirit of Kent. What was supposed to be a popular rising to rid the government of Somerset's influence was starting to resemble nothing more than a disgruntled lord's revolt. At Dartford York, the earl of Devon and Lord Cobham prepared to make their stand.[17]

On 1 March, Henry's army rode out to face them. They found York, Devon and Cobham encamped outside Dartford in a defensive position on the heath, their location securely ringed with pits, pavises* and guns. Half a dozen ships gently rocked on the River Darent behind them, loaded with supplies. York dominated the middle of the field with his large artillery train, but it was clear that Henry's army considerably outnumbered their combined forces.[18]

Neither side attacked. York and his allies would lose any right to call themselves Henry's faithful liegemen if they moved against the royal army now. So long as Henry did not unfurl his banners, they could continue to stand in defiance of him without being called traitors. Henry thus had a considerable advantage over his kinsman, but rather than call York's bluff he once again tried to pull the lords back from the brink with negotiation. He sent a delegation riding across the heath to discuss York's complaints, hoping that some resolution could be

---

* A pavise was a shield, originally produced in Pavia, in northern Italy, generally large enough to be propped up to serve as a protective screen for artillerymen.

found that would avoid bloodshed. Among the envoys of peace were a number of York's relatives: his nephews, Viscount Henry Bourchier and Bishop Thomas Bourchier of Ely, his brother-in-law Richard Neville, earl of Salisbury, and Salisbury's son and namesake, the twenty-three-year-old Richard, earl of Warwick.[19] The men had a vested interest in restoring peace between Henry and their kinsman, but it was no easy task. York, Devon and Cobham insisted that they would not stand down until Somerset was arrested. Somerset, who was at Henry's side in the royal camp, was hardly likely to allow Henry to agree to such a condition. The most that York was permitted was to present his grievances against Somerset to the king. These were the same accusations that Henry had been unconvinced by two years earlier: that Somerset had traitorously surrendered France, that his ineptitude had encouraged Charles VII to attack Gascony and Calais, that he had made a profit from the surrender of Maine and encouraged the disastrous attack on Fougères. Henry was unprepared to arrest Somerset on these charges. He insisted that Somerset and York's dispute be treated as a personal matter, not a political one, and that it be resolved through the arbitration of their peers. With little option but to agree, York, Devon and Cobham rode across the heath and knelt in Henry's presence, publicly submitting themselves to his grace. Their rebel host was pardoned and allowed to disperse.[20]

That was not the end of York's submission, however. He was escorted back to London in the midst of the royal party, treated honourably, but no less obviously under restraint. To some of the citizens of London he appeared to be Henry's prisoner, riding between two of the men who had negotiated his surrender, not permitted to wear a sword. On 10 March, York stood at the altar of St Paul's Cathedral, and holding the gospels in one hand, his other outstretched to touch a cross, he solemnly swore his loyalty to King Henry. He promised not to assemble men unless at royal command and to come to the king when summoned barring 'sickness or impotency of my person'. Nor – with Somerset clearly in mind – would he 'anything attempt... against any of [Henry's] subjects'. In short, he humbly sued Henry for remedy and forgiveness and swore to be his 'humble subject and liege-man' from that day forward.[21] Among the many attendants at this ceremony of public submission and reconciliation, Henry would have hoped more than anyone that York would keep that promise.

Even once York had been restored to royal grace and retired quietly to his own estates, Henry could not relax. In the new year of 1452 alarming reports reached England that Charles VII was planning to besiege Calais, and if that vital port fell not only would it seriously harm English trade but it might also serve as a launch pad for an invasion of England itself. Within days of hearing York's submission at St Paul's, Henry was sending out orders for a fleet to assemble under Lord Clifford, to enable Henry to 'go over in our own person' as soon as possible to defend Calais. As early as 26 January 1452 Henry had appointed a commission to gather loans for the defence of Calais and its marches so that 'the king, in person' could lead an army 'across the sea' and throughout March Henry discussed the plans with Clifford in detail.[22]

However, it proved impossible for Henry to leave England while disturbance was still rife. In May, 300 Kentishmen joined the rising of a pedlar-captain called John Wilkins, who claimed that Jack Cade was still alive and that York's ten-year-old son Edward, earl of March, would join them to depose the king and remove his councillors. Violent lawlessness affected even Henry's household officers and his beloved educational institu-tions. Shortly after Henry had heard Vespers at Eton the Sunday after Easter, the college was robbed of its jewels and goods. On 20 April near Ludlow, one of Henry's yeomen of the chamber, Richard Fazakerley, was set upon by a jealous love rival while bearing letters to the duke of York. Only the concerted exercise of clear and unambiguous royal authority could restore harmony to the kingdom, and from the summer of 1452 Henry applied unprecedented reserves of energy – and brutality – to the task of imposing order on his divided realm.[23]

To crush festering discontent once and for all, on 23 June 1452 Henry set out from Eltham Palace to preside over a judicial tour that would last almost six months. From Eltham Henry rode to Exeter, Somerset, Wiltshire and Gloucester, where there had been such trouble between the earl of Devon, Lord Cobham and Lord Bonville. The priority placed on restoring order to these counties suggests that the critical factor in Henry's reinvigoration was probably the duke of Somerset. In a show of royal favour, Henry paused at Bonville's home at Shute in Devon. From the southwest, Henry made his way through the marches of Wales to Ludlow, where he pointedly stayed with the Carmelite friars rather than accepting any hospitality from the duke of York. After a brief return home to see Margaret at Eltham and Greenwich, he set off again to assert his control over York's strongholds of Hertfordshire, Cambridgeshire and Northamptonshire.

Throughout this judicial tour, Henry not only presided over trials but also made public demonstrations of royal grace for condemned traitors. Despite the mercy eventually offered, the high-handed manner in which these pardons were bestowed left a bitter taste in some mouths. The pro-Yorkist chronicler whose work survives as 'Rawlinson B.355' described how

> by the advice of the duke of Somerset, the king rode to divers towns under the lordship of the duke of York where he forced the tenants to come before him naked with nooses around their necks, in great ice and snow, to submit themselves to the king's grace... and the king pardoned them of being hanged.[24]

The message was clear: whatever criticisms might be levelled at Henry, it must not be forgotten that he held the power of life and death over his subjects. Even this famously merciful king had his limits. Divisive though such tactics may have been, they were effective. Under Somerset's strong, if vindictive, influence Henry showed that his government would no longer be wavering and inclined to mercy. A new steel core lay at the heart of Henry's regime and a renewed vigour seemed to inspire him. Gradually, through such displays of authority, Henry's realm was quietening. And by the time he returned to Eltham Palace in November, it seemed that his efforts were being rewarded with victories overseas as well.[25]

23

'The most precious, most joyful and most comfortable earthly treasure that might come unto this land'[1]

Bordeaux
23 October 1452

D awn had not yet broken over the streets of the St Michel quarter. Yet through the narrow alleyways, where the smell of the river rose damp and cool, soldiers were moving stealthily. They were led by Pierre de Montferrand, who, like many Gascons, had both emotional and economic ties to England. Montferrand's wife was Mary of Bedford, an illegitimate cousin of King Henry.[2] The parish of St Michel was full of sailors, merchants and traders whose livelihoods depended on that English connection. Since their city had fallen to the French in July 1451, those ties had been sundered, and now they hoped to restore them. They flocked to the Beyssac gate, which opened on to the lapping waters of the river, and, pulling together as a single entity, they broke it down. It was through this breach, while most of the city still slept, that John Talbot, earl of Shrewsbury, and 5,000 Englishmen streamed into Bordeaux. Their surprise attack carried the city before the garrison awoke, and within a matter of hours Bordeaux was in English hands once more.[3]

This victory was the result of months of planning. Henry had appointed Talbot as his lieutenant in Gascony on 2 September 1452 and dispatched him south in a scheme whose foundations had been laid the previous June. Much of the duke of York's criticism of Somerset and Henry's government had focused on their losses in France, and now Henry could counter such accusations with clear evidence of his regime's military success. From Bordeaux Talbot proceeded to successfully besiege more than thirty further towns and castles in Gascony. It was a remarkable reversal of English fortunes.[4]

Recent developments in the war with France had turned Henry's mind towards his succession. If he was ever to lead an army overseas, it was essential for English unity that he provide for his lineage in the event that he died on campaign, but he and Margaret had now been married for seven years and there was still no sign of a child. Any chance of York being named as Henry's heir had been undermined by Thomas Young's insensitive petition to parliament in 1451, and now that he had reached the twentieth year of his reign Henry started to take steps to provide for an alternative line of succession. The first indication of his intentions was revealed at the vigils of Epiphany (5 January) 1453, with the knighting of his half-brothers, Edmund and Jasper Tudor.

After his mother's death in January 1437, Henry had taken care that his half-brothers, who were almost a decade his junior, should be brought up honourably and respectably. By July 1437 they were in the care of Katherine de la Pole, abbess of Barking Abbey in Essex, the younger sister of the duke of Suffolk. They remained at Barking until March 1442, with £50 a year granted from the royal purse for their upkeep.[5] Barking Abbey was only 10 miles (16 km) from London, and the third wealthiest abbey in the country.* When they reached adolescence, the Tudor brothers were taken from Katherine's care, and probably entered into a life at court. Henry's earliest biographer, the priest John Blacman, claimed that the king was concerned that the boys should not be corrupted by their exposure to the court, particularly by the sexual licence that sometimes prevailed there. He put 'them under the care of virtuous and worthy priests, both for teaching and for right living and conversation'.[6]

By 1452 both Jasper and Edmund had entered their twenties and proven 'their most noble character... [and] most refined nature'. Partly out of respect for his mother's memory Henry decided to elevate his half-brothers' status.[7] On 5 January 1453, Henry brought the Tudors to the Tower of London, where they were knighted in a heavily ritualized ceremony with a number of other young courtiers. The timing and circumstances of his brothers' knighthood suggests there was as much political as personal imperative to the occasion. Although two of the other youths to be spurred and presented with a sword on this occasion were loyal Lancastrians, a number of the Tudors' companions in knighthood were associated with the duke of York, perhaps singled out to restore their loyalty at York's expense. William Herbert was the heir of one of York's former councillors and he was joined by two of York's Neville nephews, John and Thomas, younger sons of the earl of Salisbury.[8] The date of the ceremony was also significant, for Epiphany was the feast of three kings, when English monarchs traditionally held a public crown-wearing. By holding a ceremony that forged binding ties of martial loyalty on the vigils of a feast exalting kingship, Henry

---

* As abbess, Katherine de la Pole held her estates by military service and was expected to provide soldiers for King Henry in wartime, as well as maintaining a prison and law courts. Perhaps it was Katherine's independent authority as well as her de la Pole blood that merited her inclusion in the vicious rhyme celebrating her brother's murder that circulated in the southeast in 1450 (see p. 253).

was making a powerful association of his rule with military and chivalric values.

In honour of this occasion, Henry also endowed his brothers with estates, creating Edmund earl of Richmond and Jasper earl of Pembroke. These were royal demesnes that had previously been held by Henry's uncles, the dukes of Bedford and Gloucester.[9] Edmund was granted one more sign of royal affection: a bride. His chosen spouse at first sight does not seem ideally suited, since she was nine years old and already engaged to someone else. Edmund's intended was Margaret Beaufort, the sole heir to the unfortunate John Beaufort, duke of Somerset, who had died – possibly at his own hand – after commanding the disastrous expedition to France in 1443. On 12 May 1453 Henry authorized the payment of 100 marks for Margaret's 'arrayment' so she could have the necessary fine clothing to attend court with her mother. By then Margaret's previous union, to the son of the late duke of Suffolk, had been dissolved, and her wardship granted to the Tudors instead. In 1455, when Margaret was barely of legal age, at twelve years old, she and Edmund married.[10]

By uniting the lines of his half-brother and the Beaufort heiress, Henry established an alternative line of succession for the crown. Through his infant wife, Edmund Tudor gained a claim to the throne which his half-blood connection to Henry did not provide. The founding of this rival Beaufort dynasty must have had the approval of Margaret's uncle Somerset; as it ensured a family stake in a potential future queen of England, the appeal for him was obvious. For Henry, a Beaufort–Tudor line of succession was a source of considerably less unease than having York as heir.

Ironically, just as Henry was providing for a potential future without children, it became clear that his efforts were unnecessary. For the first time in their eight-year marriage, Queen Margaret was pregnant.

★

Walsingham
April 1453

In the bright freshness of a spring day in 1453, Queen Margaret of Anjou followed in the footsteps of her fellow pilgrims to walk the last mile of a journey that ended at the shrine of Our Lady at Walsingham. Also called 'the Nazareth of England', Margaret's destination was a full-scale replica of the house in Nazareth where the Angel Gabriel had appeared to the Virgin Mary and told her she would bear the son of God. It was a site particularly associated with fertility and motherhood. At new year Margaret had given a considerable gift to the shrine at Walsingham, 'with her own hands' presenting a gold tablet embellished with a treasury of pearls, sapphires and rubies, bearing an image of an angel holding a cross in its centre. Only Henry had received a more lavish gift that year. By the spring it was clear that her prayers had been answered and Margaret returned to give thanks.[11]

Henry had greeted the news of Margaret's pregnancy in characteristic fashion, with a burst of generosity. Richard Tunstall, the esquire of the body who brought the news to him, was rewarded with a lifetime annuity of £40, while Margaret herself – Henry's 'most dear and most entirely beloved wife the queen' – received a jewel called the demi-cent which was worth £200.[12]

After she had made her thanksgiving pilgrimage, Margaret travelled with Jasper and Edmund Tudor to meet Cecily, duchess of York. As news of the queen's pregnancy spread, Cecily had seized the opportunity to congratulate Margaret and use this happy news as an excuse to appeal for the queen's intercession on her husband's behalf. Despite the tensions in Henry and York's relationship, Margaret and Cecily seem to have remained on good terms. Cecily would have been able to provide the queen with some comfort during her long years of childlessness, for she too had taken many years to conceive her first child. In spring 1453, she was still recovering from her most recent birth, a boy named Richard in honour of his father. The pair met at Cecily's home in Hitchin, where Margaret listened 'full benignly' to Cecily's insistence that York was Henry's 'humble... obeisant liegeman', although if Margaret did attempt to intercede on the duke's behalf after this meeting she did not succeed in reconciling him with Henry.[13]

Cecily described Margaret's pregnancy as 'the most precious, most joyful and most comfortable earthly treasure that might come unto this land and to the people thereof'. Her sentiments were shared by many of Henry's subjects, who demonstrated their joy at the news with gifts of money and grants. The timing of Margaret's pregnancy was particularly useful to Henry, who had been forced to call a parliament for March 1453 to pay for the military efforts in Gascony and Calais. Most of the tax grants of previous parliaments had expired in 1452. After years of bitter and vituperative clashes with parliament, on this occasion Henry faced an unusually contented and compliant assembly. Margaret was rewarded by parliament with considerable concessions, including full judicial rights over her estates, an enhancement of her authority that she would have welcomed, for she was an attentive landlord.[14] Never before had Henry been able to extract promises of money from the Commons so easily, nor on such favourable terms. A grant of a tenth and fifteenth was given, as was customary, but the Commons also granted tunnage and poundage,* a subsidy on wool, woolfells† and hides, and a poll tax on 'aliens' (i.e. foreigners living or working in England), all for the remainder of Henry's life. Such unbounded generosity had not been seen since the glory days of Henry V. Henry was effusive in his gratitude. Breaking with the usual convention of addressing parliament through his chancellor, Henry personally thanked the Commons for their generosity. 'Do not doubt,' he promised them, 'that we shall be a gracious and benevolent lord to you' in return.[15]

---

*   Tunnage and poundage were duties and taxes levied on imported wine.

†   A woolfell was a sheepskin with the wool still attached.

Henry's stated intention to lead an army to France was probably behind a unique grant made on the last day of parliament, which provided for the raising of 20,000 archers for six months' service. This would have created a formidable force, particularly given the fame of English archers in the wars with France, but in the end the grant was reduced to 13,000 archers and postponed for two years in favour of an immediate grant to finance Talbot's reinforcements for Gascon service.[16]

The unexpected compliance of this parliament also gave Henry a welcome opportunity to reverse some of the concessions that had been forced on him in recent years. In 1451 he had granted an act of resumption, to which he now added a substantial list of exemptions, and two of the foremost targets of Commons aggression in the last parliament were actively rewarded in 1453. Alice Chaucer, the widowed duchess of Suffolk whom the Commons had tried to have removed from the king's presence, was awarded the wardship of her son, John, enabling her to retain control over the boy, his lands and his marriage. This was a personally and politically advantageous grant from the king, perhaps given as compensation for Henry having dissolved John's betrothal to Margaret Beaufort in favour of his half-brother Edmund Tudor.[17] Unsurprisingly, the duke of Somerset was also promoted, being granted precedence over the duke of Norfolk, and thereby providing restitution for Norfolk's part in the attacks on Somerset in 1450. Somerset was now second in importance only to the duke of York. Had it not been for the longer history of York's family title, Somerset might have leapfrogged him as well.[18]

York's political isolation was becoming ever more apparent. Little wonder that his wife had tried to intercede on his behalf with Margaret. York found himself unable even to protect his chamberlain Sir William Oldhall; in spring 1453 Oldhall still languished in sanctuary at St Martin-le-Grand. Somerset and his allies, including the earl of Wiltshire, finally got their wish in parliament and Oldhall was attainted as a traitor for his 'false, accursed and traitorous disposition'. Among the many instances of his wrongdoing, the parliamentary record showed that he had given 'false, unfaithful counsel and assistance' to York at the field of Dartford, and counselled the traitors John Wilkins and John Cade, among others. Just above Oldhall's attainder on the list of Commons' petitions came a bill requesting that Jack Cade, 'calling and naming himself sometimes Mortimer', also be condemned as a traitor. The reminder of Cade's association with York's Mortimer relatives, and the placing of this petition next to that condemning Oldhall, was a deliberate move to smear York by association.[19] Such distressing associations for York's honour were accompanied by other, more material losses. In September 1452 the lordship of the Isle of Wight had been taken from York and granted to the duke of Somerset, and among the grants given to the Tudor brothers had been York's lordships of Builth, Hadleigh and his London residence of Baynard's Castle. On 12 May 1453 York even lost his lieutenancy of Ireland, which was given to his rival, the earl of Wiltshire.[20]

When parliament was prorogued on 2 July 1453, to enable the lords to return to their estates to hunt and the Commons to attend to the harvest, Henry seemed at last to be a sovereign in command of his kingdom. He had cowed his adversaries in parliament, temporarily neutralized the duke of York as a political threat, finally enjoyed a little of the military success that had eluded him since coming into his majority and restored a measure of peace to his disordered realm. The child growing in Margaret's belly gave hope for the future security of his dynasty, so that he might finally be able to follow in his father's footsteps and unite his warrior lords in a campaign to regain their lost territory in France. In July, Henry set out west, where a local aristocratic feud demanded his attention.* As he rode out with

---

* The duke of Somerset and Richard Neville, earl of Warwick, had been in competition in the West Country and south Wales for some time. Their wives, Eleanor and Anne Beauchamp, held competing claims to local estates. The latest bone of contention was the lordship of Glamorgan and Morgannok.

his household, the indulgent king, the child ruler, seemed to have finally approached the power and respect of his father's kingship. He was a true king at last.[21]

PART III

'A Kingdom Divided Against Itself'[1]

24

'The beginning of sorrows'[1]

Castillon, Gascony
17 July 1453

Through the shimmering haze of summer heat, the soldiers marched towards the town of Castillon. At their head was the 'English Achilles' and 'terror of the French', John Talbot, earl of Shrewsbury, still in harness in his sixty-sixth year. With his son, Lord Lisle, Talbot had led a force of between 6,000 and 10,000 men on a triumphant march out of Bordeaux. His Gascon campaign had been a rousing success, but summer had brought Charles VII's army surging over the border to check Talbot's progress. For four days the French had been besieging the vital fortress town of Castillon on the River Dordogne* – long, anxious days in which a force of 700 French labourers had dug out a vast fortified ring around the town. Now between Castillon and relief was a deep trench, a wall of earth set with tree trunks and studded along the top with a deadly array of gleaming culverines, serpentines† and giant crossbows. But

---

* Now the small town of Castillon-la-Bataille in the département of Gironde.
† Culverines and serpentines were types of cannon.

the citizens of Castillon were not afraid. When they heard that Talbot was coming to their aid, they redoubled their defiance. The French would not withstand 'this famous and renowned English commander... the most formidable and committed enemy of France'. The siege would soon be at an end.[2]

Talbot spurred his men towards Castillon with such enthusiasm that soon his mounted cavalry had far outrun his infantry and the lumbering English artillery train. Talbot was not overly concerned. Even without the support of the footsoldiers who made up the vast majority of his forces, his knights managed to see off a company of *francs archers*, butchering them in a forest at the outskirts of Castillon.

A rising dust cloud on the other side of the town spurred Talbot still faster. It seemed that the French were retreating, chicken-hearted, in the face of the combined might of Castillon's citizens and Talbot's army. His spies confirmed his suspicion, and Talbot rushed on once again. However, as he surged out of the woods with his mounted soldiers, he discovered that the reports of French retreat were woefully inaccurate. In fact, the French encampment was fearsomely well defended. Undeterred, Talbot resolved to launch his attack immediately. Some of his captains were uneasy and believed the English ought to await the rest of their army. Both the Norman chronicler Thomas Basin and his Picard contemporary Matthieu Escouchy reported that one English veteran shared his fears with Talbot but was angrily repulsed. The grizzled lieutenant of Gascony would not be swayed. The English dismounted and readied themselves for battle. As was the custom of their country, they would fight on foot – all but the sexagenarian Talbot, who chose to remain on horseback for the coming battle.

The English standards were displayed – Henry's royal coat of arms showing the fleur-de-lys and lions of England; the red cross of St George, barely fluttering in the hot, heavy air. With a fearsome cry of 'St George!' and 'Talbot! Talbot!' the English attacked, marching with grim determination towards the French barricades and directly into the line of fire of 300 pieces of artillery. A frenzy of hand-to-hand combat ensued, sword and axe flashing in the piercing sunlight. But unlike most melees, this one was punctuated with ear-splitting, bowel-loosening booms as the French siege engines sent tongues of flame and deadly balls of lead and stone into the midst of the English forces. A single shot could send half a dozen soldiers sprawling to the earth. For an hour, the English battered at the French defences, struggling to force an entry. In the heart of the battle, Talbot was an easily recognizable figure – never retreating, never surrendering, his crimson velvet brigandine raised high above his fellow soldiers. He was still on horseback, roaring his forces on, even as the standard of St George tumbled into the ditch beneath him.

A tongue of flame fired from a culverine shot Talbot's horse dead, sending him crashing to the earth. As he struggled to free himself, trapped beneath his fallen mount, a group of French archers recognized the commander of the English forces and lunged at him. Under the usual rules of warfare, Talbot should have been taken prisoner and honourably ransomed. But the French archers had heard of the butchery Talbot had inflicted on their friends in the forest beyond the town. Intent only on revenge, they set on the English commander with their swords and daggers. One blow struck him in the neck. Another slashed across his face. A letter written the day after the battle claimed that 'Talbot was killed by an archer who stabbed him with a sword in the fundament so hard that the blade burst out of his throat.'[3] His legs and thighs had been lacerated as he fought on horseback and now his face was so cruelly mistreated that in order to identify his body later his herald had to root inside his mouth to check for a missing tooth.[4]

Seeing their commander fallen and their standards tattered, the English forces fled. Talbot's son was killed, either trying to defend his father or in the crush of flight. The retreat swiftly turned into a rout. The victorious French surged out from behind their palisades, pursuing the English as they scattered.

Some ran for the town of Castillon. Others struggled across the
fields, chased down by French cavalry. Many drowned as they
tried to escape across the Dordogne. English heralds would later
estimate their dead at 4,000. Now lacking any hope of relief,
the citizens of Castillon surrendered the next day. The Norman
chronicler Thomas Basin reported that, 'after this battle, hope
and courage were abandoned by the Bordelais, who had had
such great confidence in the bravery and ability of Lord Talbot'.[5]
With Castillon fallen and Talbot dead, Charles VII's forces
marched swiftly through demoralized Gascon territory, advancing all the way to the capital within a matter of weeks. Although
Bordeaux resisted until the autumn,* Talbot's death was the fatal
blow dealt to Henry's continental inheritance. Three hundred
years of English rule in Gascony were over.

Clarendon hunting lodge, Wiltshire
August 1453

Hot winds and taut sails bore the terrible news from one end
of Henry's dominions to the other. By the first week of August
word of the fall of Gascony had reached all the way to Wiltshire,
finding King Henry sheltering with a small riding household en
route to deal with yet another noble feud. At thirty-one, Henry's
years of toil were starting to show. He was tired, physically and
mentally. As the summer heat rose, he paused to refresh himself
in the woodland cool of Clarendon hunting lodge. It was there,
in the middle of the night, that he suddenly fell ill, 'smitten
with a frenzy and his wit and reason withdrawn'.[6] The symptoms
of this sudden mental breakdown were horrifying. If there was
indeed an initial frenzy, it swiftly passed, transformed into a
paralyzing physical and mental catatonia. Henry could not talk.

---

* Bordeaux surrendered on 20 October 1453.

He could not walk. He did not recognize his companions, nor respond to their concern. He was barely able to hold up his head, sitting slumped and silent in their presence like a rag doll. In every way possible Henry had retreated inward into a state from which no questions, entreaties or physical intervention could stir him. And most alarming of all, there was no telling when – if ever – he would recover.[7]

The cause of Henry's devastating episode of psychosis, as we would term it today, has inspired debate ever since it afflicted him. Henry was sparsely attended when he fell ill and the details of his condition were soon suppressed. There are very few eyewitness accounts of the illness and those that exist are frustratingly vague.[8] In the twentieth century it was suggested that Henry may have suffered from some form of schizophrenia, possibly inherited from his maternal grandfather Charles VI.[9] Like Henry, Charles first fell ill in the height of summer, but unlike Henry he initially recovered within days. Thereafter, for the rest of his life, Charles was afflicted with repeated episodes of mental illness interspersed with periods of apparent recovery. But both the pattern of Charles's illness and its symptoms were radically different from Henry's. When Charles was 'in his sickness' he refused to be washed or to change out of his soiled, vermin-infested clothes. He would run as hard as he could from one end of his palace to another, believing enemies pursued him, until the entrances to the palace of St Pol in Paris had to be bricked up to stop him running into the street, where his subjects might hear his cries. To their distress, Charles did not recognize his wife or children and tried to erase the coats of arms he saw in his stained glass windows and painted on the walls, claiming that he was really called George and that his coat of arms was an impaled lion. Even during the periods where his contemporary historian, a monk of St Denis, considered him 'calm' and apparently governing 'sensibly', Charles still suffered considerable distress at the thought of his illness, pleading with his advisers to remove their knives so he would not hurt them if his sickness came on suddenly.[10] He saw his illness as a form of torture or witchcraft, imposed on him by his enemies. He would rather die, he said once, than continue to suffer as he was.[11]

Almost none of Charles's medical history matches Henry's, beyond the sudden onset of their illnesses in their adulthood and their apparent inability to recognize those around them.[12] The two kings' different personalities could have affected the presentation of their conditions, but they may simply not have shared the same illness. Inherited schizophrenia is a satisfyingly neat explanation for Henry's illness from summer 1453, but history is seldom neat. It may be that Henry was suffering from a particularly severe episode of depression, exacerbated by the traumatic events of recent years and his continuous physical exertion, and that this led to a psychotic break in summer 1453 when he received the terrible news from Gascony. In the past three years Henry had been forced into an active form of kingship that was far from customary, or presumably comfortable, for him. By 1453 it finally seemed that his efforts were paying off, as parliament became more compliant, progress was made in Gascony and there was the prospect of an heir at last, but even amid this joy there was just cause for anxiety. Margaret's pregnancy might be a source of comfort to the nation but there was no certainty of the child's safe deliverance, nor of Margaret's survival (there was good reason for women in childbirth to call for precious relics and prayer to keep them safe in their labour). It is also worth noting, for a man whose father had died soon after the birth of his first child in his thirties, that Henry's breakdown coincided with his own approaching thirty-second birthday and imminent fatherhood. Such anxieties, and unaccustomed physical and mental effort, could be endured while they seemed to be yielding results, but the Battle of Castillon shattered Henry's sense of having any control over events – worse, it threatened to unleash yet more chaos and bloodshed on Henry's still fractured realm.

Henry may not have fully processed the trauma of 1450, so to receive news from France that recalled the military reverses of 1449–50 would have been deeply unsettling. The loss of Normandy had destabilized Henry's regime with murder and rebellion, and that was before there was a duke of York to rally the masses. How much worse might things be now that the last of Henry's French territories was gone and York stood ready as a champion for discontent? He had already fomented unrest with bills criticizing Henry's foreign policy. What horrors might befall Henry's realm as news of Castillon spread? If Henry had escaped the full appreciation of his own inadequacies as a man and as a king before, he was now brutally confronted with them. Under these circumstances, while definitive diagnosis is impossible, it may be wiser to identify not one single cause for Henry's breakdown, but a combination of the many stresses and strains that simply overwhelmed him in that summer of 1453.

If Henry's condition puzzles us today, it was no less confounding to his contemporaries. Until 1453 he seemed to enjoy good mental and physical health; confronted with his total collapse, even Henry's own doctors were uncertain how best to proceed. A commission provided by the royal council to Henry's medical team contains a list of treatments they could attempt, which is extensive to the point of scattershot, including everything from baths and gargles to bloodletting and head purges.[13] Medieval medicine was still heavily dependent on classical theories that derived from the works of the ancient Greek physicians Hippocrates and Galen,* according to which human beings were made up of four humours – blood, phlegm, choler (or yellow bile) and black bile – which mixed together in the veins. When these humours were out of balance it caused illness. According to humoral theory, Henry's initial frenzy would have been caused by an excess of choler, destabilizing his naturally cold and moist brain. Treatment demanded cooling the fevered brow with shaving, drenching with water or even bloodletting

---

* Hippocrates of Kos (460 BC–370 BC), Galen of Pergamon (AD 129–216).

from the scalp, to draw hot blood away from the brain and restore it to its normal state.[14]

The extreme lethargy that was the most prominent feature of Henry's illness, however, required completely different care. Stupor was associated with an excess of cold, wet phlegm, a humour that Henry already possessed in abundance, for he had been born in the depths of winter, 'a phlegmatic time of year'.[15] Excess phlegm could affect the brain's memory faculty, since it was believed that memories were stored as imprints on the wet matter at the back of the brain. This explained why Henry could not recognize or respond to those around him. Treating this superfluity required heating and drying, and among the remedies that 'relieveth and repaireth wits enfeebled' in this way was *theriac* or treacle, a hot medicine derived from snake flesh, matured for twelve years. Such was the potency of *theriac* that royally appointed alchemists inspected its quality on import. Alchemy itself – the attempt to turn base metals into gold – could be a possible curative for phlegmatic conditions as gold was a hot, dry metal. Royal commissions to practise alchemy had been established since 1436, initially to replenish the royal treasury, but among the licensed alchemists of the 1450s were a number of royal physicians and chaplains.[16]

Henry's medical team probably began treating their royal patient cautiously with holistic therapies: a change of diet, herbal baths, specially brewed syrups and measures to envelop the king in a pleasant and soothing environment. Music was probably provided for him, as it had been for Charles VI. The medical care of a king was a risky business. Charles VI grew to despise his doctor, Regnault Freron, and eventually banished him. Even worse fates awaited two friars called Pierre and Lancelot who treated Charles with a medicine distilled from powdered pearls. When they fell from grace they were beheaded, and their quarters displayed across Paris.[17] As time passed and the efforts of Henry's doctors yielded no result, some of the more invasive treatments listed on the council commission may have been deemed necessary, administered by two royal surgeons. It is doubtful how much improvement in Henry's condition could have been wrought by head shaving, enemas or incisions on the body.

Despite the medical attention lavished on him, however, Henry showed no signs of recovery. His incapacity was an unprecedented challenge for the government of England. There had been child rulers, even baby rulers, and in the later years of Edward III's reign the aged king had drifted into sickness until he was little more than a cipher, but never in English history had there been an adult king so wholly incapable of ruling. For the duke of Somerset, who had gained his ascendant position in Henry's regime purely through royal patronage, concern for the king was mingled with pressing anxiety about his own fate. Henry's protection had been all that stood between Somerset and the mob who besieged his home in 1450 and it had saved him from York's wrath at Dartford in 1452. With the king unable to defend him, Somerset was in real danger of losing his position at the heart of government – and if the malcontents in England got their way, also perhaps his life. There was still widespread discontent that he had not been called to account for his military failures. However, Somerset was not wholly unsupported. He had his allies on the royal council, and crucially he had the favour of Queen Margaret. In November 1451 Somerset had been granted a 100-mark annuity as the queen's 'very dear cousin... for the good counsel and praiseworthy service that [he] has given and will give [her] in the future'.[18] The Burgundian chronicler Jean de Waurin believed Somerset's ascendancy was due to the queen's influence and Margaret, no less than Henry, was concerned to protect Somerset. She must have been as disturbed as her husband by the fate of their advisers three years earlier and she was unlikely to agree to any course of action now that might put Somerset into the same danger that had destroyed Suffolk.

The key advantage Margaret and Somerset had was their knowledge of Henry's condition. They resolved to suppress the full details of Henry's illness, maintaining the illusion of minor indisposition and hoping for a swift recovery. By mid-August 1453 no more royal orders were being issued from Clarendon, and real authority was transferred to Westminster, where the council attempted to rule in Henry's absence, issuing commands 'by order of the king with the advice of his council', the same fiction of royal rule that had been used in Henry's minority.[19] In maintaining this subterfuge, Somerset and Margaret had the crucial support of the chancellor, Cardinal Kempe, who had control of the great seal that validated royal orders. Margaret and the septuagenarian Kempe had worked together in 1450 to restore order in the wake of Cade's rebellion. Another pillar of this interim government was Humphrey Stafford, duke of Buckingham. Now in his fifties, Buckingham had proven his loyalty to Henry by arresting the duke of Gloucester in 1447 and – like many royal officers – allowing himself to be driven into severe debt through service as captain of Calais (until 1451) and warden of the Cinque Ports. His wife, Anne Neville, was one of the myriad nieces of Cardinal Beaufort and in recent years Buckingham had taken on the traditional Beaufort mantle of conciliation and peacemaking.

But time was not on Margaret and Somerset's side. Parliament was supposed to resume in November, when Henry would be expected to appear publicly. Even before then, Margaret's immediate influence on proceedings would be removed. By September she was in her eighth month of pregnancy and had to enter her 'confinement' to prepare for birth. From the moment she took to her chambers in Westminster Palace until a month after her child was born, the queen would be cloistered from the affairs of state. She could not receive male visitors nor leave her rooms, making it difficult for her to actively participate in events. At least she was physically close to the seat of government, and the wives of Buckingham and Somerset may have been among her attendants in the dark, warm royal apartments. In a parting demonstration of where royal loyalties lay, as Margaret processed in formal state to her confinement, she was accompanied by the dukes of Buckingham and Somerset. By then, Henry had been ill for almost two months. In autumn he was moved to Windsor Castle, where he could be attended by a larger household. But despite the attentions of his attendants and medical staff, and the fervent hopes of his wife and closest advisers, there was no sign of improvement. It was now a matter of waiting – for Henry's recovery, or the birth of his heir.[20]

25

'Misrule doth rise'[1]

Yorkshire
24 August 1453

Across the open pastureland north of York, a magnificent wedding party was making its way home after a long and tiring journey. They had come all the way from the brickwork splendour of Tattershall Castle in the Fens and now they were barely half a day's ride from the forbidding towers of Sheriff Hutton Castle which would mark their journey's end. The Nevilles were returning to the seat of their power with a new member, and they came with all possible pomp. Amid the gleaming red- and black-liveried attendants rode the head of the family, Richard Neville, earl of Salisbury, and his formidable wife Alice Montagu. Two of their younger sons, John and Thomas, had been among the youths elevated to knighthood alongside Henry's half-brothers at Epiphany, and now Thomas had gained a wife to match his new-found status. Maud Stanhope was not only a wealthy young widow with no children – a desirable prospect for any nobleman's son – but also the niece and heiress of Ralph, Lord Cromwell. Lord Cromwell and the earl of Salisbury had served together on the royal council for decades and they were so eager for this marriage that Maud's first husband had only been dead a matter of months when they finalized the agreement for her wedding to Thomas. Maud and Thomas's union thus marked an alliance between two of the leading courtier families, redrawing old allegiances. It was inevitable that some would find this new alliance a threat.

Barely a mile from the city walls of York, on Heworth Moor, the Nevilles were halted by the sight of a large army. These were not well-wishing locals curious to see the new Lady Neville, but tenants and retainers of the mightiest rival family in the north. The Neville wedding party had ridden straight into a Percy ambush.[2]

For many years the chief rivals of the earl of Salisbury's family had been their own kinsmen. Salisbury's father Ralph, earl of Westmorland, had sired an impressive twenty-three children during his two marriages, and there was persistent grudging between the senior and junior branches of the family. In recent months, however, tensions had developed with the Nevilles' fellow wardens of the northern marches of England, the Percys. Like the Nevilles, the Percy family was headed by a war veteran in his fifties – Henry, earl of Northumberland – and contained an unfortunate number of unruly, hot-headed adult sons. The Nevilles and Percys divided the borderlands of England between them, with the Percys serving as wardens of the eastern march and the Nevilles defending the west. The nobility always jealously guarded their estates, often lashing out violently when they felt their honour was impugned, and the persistent threat of Scottish border raids meant that the castles and armies of the marcher lords were more vigorously stocked than many southern noblemen's homes. This ready supply of men and weaponry meant feuds could quickly escalate to bloodshed, and so it had proven for the Nevilles and Percys. In the summer of 1453 the Percys had embarked on a rampage of violence and false imprisonment across Neville territory.

The marriage of Sir Thomas Neville and Maud Stanhope poured oil on these already flickering flames. The earl of

Northumberland had his own grievance against Lord Cromwell –
a matter of two Percy manors currently in Cromwell's possession
– and his family was determined to stamp its authority on the
north before the Cromwell–Neville alliance could challenge
their interests still further. The ambush at Heworth Moor was
an assassination attempt on the whole wedding party.

As hundreds of Percy tenants swarmed from the Yorkshire
fields, and citizens laid down their tools in the workshops of York
to join the fight, the Percy brothers rallied their forces. Among
the yeomen and leatherworkers in their army were local knights,
militarily experienced and striking with deadly intent. In the
ensuing confusion of shouts and shying horses, of billhooks and
drawn swords, 'many men of both parties were beaten, slain
and hurt'.[3] Somehow, amid the chaos on the moor, the earl of
Salisbury, his wife, sons and new daughter-in-law managed to
escape, spurring their horses to Sheriff Hutton and thoughts
of vengeance. Such a vindictively personal attack demanded an
answer. That autumn the north of England roiled with unrest.

As King Henry stared, uncomprehending, at the walls of
Windsor, violence rippled across his realm. In south Wales the
Neville heir, Richard, earl of Warwick, was in violent contest with
the duke of Somerset, while in Bedfordshire Lord Cromwell had
for months been in dispute with the ambitious young duke of
Exeter over properties including the 'fair castle' of Ampthill. In
Westminster, the council struggled in vain to regain control of
these escalating noble feuds. Commissions were established and
letters of condemnation sent, but neither threats of imprisonment nor seizure of estates restored order. Without the authority
of a king to back up their threats, the council could achieve little.
To make matters worse, as autumn wore on attendance at the
council in Westminster dwindled to unprecedentedly low levels.
In early October only three men came to the Star Chamber:
Henry's confessor, John Stanbury, bishop of Hereford; the
chancellor, Cardinal Kempe; and the duke of Buckingham. The
need to 'set rest and union betwix the lords', to unite them in

restoring order to the country rather than fostering bitter feuds that bred violent disorder, was becoming desperate.[4]

Westminster
13 October 1453

Bells rang out in celebration in London and prayers were heard issuing from every church in the city, as thanks was given for a lone bright spark amid this turmoil. At Westminster Palace, Queen Margaret had given birth to a son. Mother and child were both healthy, and in honour of the English saint and monarch on whose feast day he was born, St Edward the Confessor, the boy was called Edward.

Henry, however, did not even realize that his long-awaited son had been born. What should have been the highpoint of Margaret's career as queen was tinged with anxiety. With the king's health still so uncertain, she over-compensated with a lavish display of court ceremonial for the rituals surrounding the prince's birth. His baptism – which, as was traditional, Margaret did not attend – was held in the magnificent surroundings of Westminster Abbey, the wriggling little figure of the prince swaddled in embroidered cloth of gold and furs. He was carried to the font by godparents carefully chosen for their importance to both Margaret and Henry: Cardinal Kempe, the duke of Somerset and Anne, duchess of Buckingham. The child's baptism was entrusted to Henry's confessor and one of the key architects of his educational foundations, William Waynflete, bishop of Winchester. More than £550 was spent on the lavish chrism robe Prince Edward wore to his baptism and the gown Margaret had for the 'churching' that marked her re-entry into the world beyond the birthing chamber. For that occasion, two duchesses were appointed to draw back the curtains around the queen's bed, revealing her once more to the male gaze of her court after weeks in exclusively female company. One of the women playing this vital ceremonial role was almost certainly Cecily, duchess of York, whose name headed the list of invitees in the record of the exchequer.[5] Cecily was the premiere duchess in the country and it would have been an affront not to invite her to Margaret's churching, but the queen may also have been genuinely concerned to placate the duke of York at a time of heightened anxiety. With Prince Edward's birth, York's dynastic threat to the royal family had diminished, and after months of unrest in the country it was in Margaret's interests to appear the peacemaker. She need not necessarily feel any less mistrustful of York to publicly demonstrate her own magnanimity.[6] Although the exchequer record only lists the noblewomen invited to Margaret's churching, York was in London six days before the ritual took place and Margaret may have thought it politic to include him in the next phase of her churching ceremony. After the royal bedcurtains had been drawn back, two dukes 'gently and humbly' took her arms, weighted down by heavy cloth of gold, and helped her rise from the bed to process to chapel. Whether York was afforded this position of honour or not, Margaret would almost certainly have appointed the duke of Somerset to perform the other role.[7]

The birth of Prince Edward assured the future of Henry's dynasty but the form that future might take was no less worrying. For if Henry never recovered from his illness and if Edward survived – which could not be taken for granted – there was the very real prospect of another child king, another long minority. Plans needed to be made to prepare for such an eventuality, to unite the lords of England in a common purpose. With that aim in mind, in October a great council of lords had been summoned to London. Initially, York was not invited. Somerset's hand must have been behind this pointed exclusion, probably with Cardinal Kempe's support. York trailed division and disorder in his wake and it is easy to see why Somerset would wish to keep him from any role in government. Twice in the past three years York had tried to bring down Somerset by force of arms.

However, more moderate voices were concerned that excluding York would cause more damage than inviting him. The duke of Buckingham was brother-in-law to Cecily, duchess of York and generally inclined to mediation. Queen Margaret, too, may have argued for allowing York a seat at the table. In early autumn 1453 Cecily appealed to Margaret in writing, begging her to believe York's protestations of loyalty and to intercede for his restoration to favour.[8] With the desperate need to unite the realm, and the unfortunate necessity that York would have to attend the parliament due to take place in November in any case, nine members of the council in Westminster took matters into their own hands. On 23 October, when both Somerset and Kempe were absent, York was sent an apologetic letter by these nine councillors, assuring him that his exclusion was an oversight and that they had always hoped he would join the great council to 'set rest and union betwixt the lords of this land'. Of these councillors, three had received patronage or gifts from Margaret in recent years and one was her confessor, Walter Lyhert, bishop of Norwich, which suggests that she may have been involved in the decision to summon York.[9]

Somerset and Kempe, who had been absent when this fateful invitation was extended, may have continued to oppose York's involvement. Kempe did what he could to undermine York's influence in the Commons, which had always been strong, by using his powers as chancellor to prorogue parliament until February. The excuse given was 'the great plague now prevailing in the said town' and Henry's inability to attend for, as Kempe put it euphemistically, 'other reasons'.[10] But Kempe and Somerset could not keep York from the great council. On 12 November the duke of York rode into London 'peaceably and measurably accompanied', as the council had requested. At his side, in a disquieting echo of the parliament of 1450, was his ally the duke of Norfolk. Despite the hopes of Margaret and the councillors, they did not come to be reconciled with Somerset, but to bring down their hated rival and take power for themselves.

On 23 November Norfolk launched a blistering attack on the
duke of Somerset in council, calling for him to be punished for
his military failures in France and Normandy. 'For the loss of
towns or castles without siege,' Norfolk reminded the lords, 'the
captains that have lost them [in the past] have been beheaded,
and their goods lost.' He insinuated that the only reason Somerset's failings had not been thoroughly investigated was because
some members of the council had been paid 'great bribes' to
turn 'their hearts from the way of truth and of justice'.[11] His
chief target was Cardinal Kempe, who, steadfastly – if ultimately
futilely – resisted Norfolk's attempts to arrest Somerset.

Two days later Norfolk's will prevailed and Somerset was committed to the Tower. There was no sign that Somerset would
be charged, tried, released or – despite Norfolk's blustering –
beheaded. York seemed content to let him languish out of the
way. In the Tower, his influence had at last been removed from
government.

On 4 December Henry's incapacity was, for the first time,
officially acknowledged. With the king incapable of ruling and
Somerset in prison, the question now was how the vacuum at
the heart of government should be filled? York asserted his own
right to govern, using the great council as the means to legitimize
his authority, but despite Somerset's absence he was not without
challenge. Margaret had been observing events in the great
council with mounting concern. Although she could not attend,
her allies, including Viscount Beaumont and Cardinal Kempe,
could keep her informed. Perhaps through them she learnt that
a clique associated with York had started to dominate conciliar
business, while more moderate lords nervously stayed away or
refused to commit themselves to opinions. This 'Yorkist' faction
was dominated by Norfolk and other kinsmen of the duke of
York, most notably his Neville in-laws the earls of Salisbury and
Warwick, and the brothers from the Bourchier family.

As Christmas 1453 approached, Margaret made a desperate
attempt to rouse Henry from his stupor. Accompanied by the

duke of Buckingham, she carried Prince Edward into Henry's chambers at Windsor Castle and begged her husband to give the baby his blessing. When Buckingham's efforts failed Margaret dropped to her knees in front of Henry and pleaded with him, but this too was in vain. Henry gave no sign of understanding or recognition. Once he raised his gaze and looked at Prince Edward. Then he cast down his eyes again.[12]

With hopes of Henry's recovery failing, Margaret took an unprecedented step. The council was divided between York's partisans, Henry's courtiers and anxious moderates. Someone needed to represent the centre, and to ensure that Henry's will was still maintained in his absence. Margaret saw that it fell to her to protect the interests of her four-month-old son and powerless husband. For the first time she stepped firmly out of Henry's shadow and asserted herself as a political agent in her own right. In January 1454 she presented the council with a bill calling for a regent to be appointed until Henry recovered, with the power to appoint the chief officers and take on the 'whole rule of this land'. That regent, she said, should be her.[13]

Queens regent were not unknown in England. The twelfth-century kings Henry I, Stephen and Henry II had all appointed their wives as regent during their absences from the realm and when Henry III left the country to wage war in 1253–4 his queen, Eleanor of Provence, ruled in his place. The French royal family had an even more illustrious history of female regency, exemplified by the celebrated Blanche of Castile, who became regent of France after her husband Louis VIII's early death on crusade. She survived armed rebellions, ruling on behalf of her son, Louis IX, until he was old enough to govern for himself. When Louis led a crusade to the Holy Land, he called on Blanche to serve as regent again from 1248 to 1252. The early fifteenth century had seen a number of French princesses step into their husband or son's empty throne, and their example must have been foremost in Margaret's mind. During the anarchic days of Charles VI's recurrent sickness and the resulting civil war, Henry VI's grandmother

Isabeau of Bavaria had been appointed regent with guardianship of their children. Even when not officially regent, Isabeau had been at the forefront of much political decision-making, forging the Treaty of Troyes that granted Henry V the French crown in 1420. Margaret had personally witnessed successful female rule during her childhood, when her father's prolonged absences demanded that both her grandmother, Yolande of Aragon, and mother, Isabella of Lorraine, governed in his place. Between them, Margaret's kinswomen governed Provence, Naples, Lorraine and Anjou intermittently for two decades and Yolande had been a trusted adviser of King Charles VII.[14]

These were all worthy precedents, but they could not resolve a fundamental weakness in Margaret's appeal: each of these queens had been appointed regent by her king, and as such acted as his representative, embodying his rule and will. This was perfectly in keeping with general understandings of government and female subordination, which denied women an independent public role in politics. The same subservience applied to marriages, where women were expected to be ruled by their husbands. For Margaret it was impossible to be appointed regent by a husband who could not communicate, and she could hardly represent the will of a man whose own willpower was currently non-existent.[15]

Despite these challenges Margaret's appeal was taken seriously by Henry's councillors and the question of how best to rule, whether through female regency or a protectorate under York, was debated in council for almost four months. It might have been debated longer still, but on 22 March 1454 Cardinal Kempe died. Without a king, government could just about continue. Without a king and a chancellor, it ground to a halt. The appointment of a chancellor was the prerogative of a king alone. One of Henry's earliest royal acts, at ten months old, had been handing the great seal of office from one chancellor to another. Although Henry had now been ill for seven months, it was vital to follow protocol and seek his opinion on who should replace Kempe for this vital office.

On Saturday 23 March Henry's quiet chambers at Windsor Castle were invaded by a delegation of twelve lords of church and state. The delegation had been carefully balanced to represent the interests of York, Margaret and the court with royal favourites like Viscount Beaumont and Bishop Waynflete of Winchester offset by York's allies the earl of Warwick and the Bourchier brothers. Three times the lords appealed 'skillfully, solemnly and respectfully' for Henry's opinion and three times they could get no 'answer or sign, to their great sorrow and distress'. 'They moved and roused [Henry] by all the ways and means that they could think of', pursuing him from dinner table to privy chamber, 'but they could obtain no answer'. Even when the king was led wearily to his bedchamber by two of his attendants, the lords continued to try and elicit a response. Eventually, when even their query if 'they should wait on him any longer, and to have answer at his leisure' yielded not the slightest response, they left.[16]

This visit brought the lords to a swift and firm decision. Government must be settled, and in the end it was settled as it had been the last time the monarchy had been vested in someone incapable of ruling, during Henry's minority. On 27 March 1454 the duke of York was elected chief councillor and protector and defender of the realm. The terms of his appointment were the same as those agreed with the duke of Gloucester in 1422. To allay Margaret's anxieties, and perhaps to encourage her quiet acquiescence, it was agreed that York's protectorate would only last until Henry recovered or Prince Edward was old enough to rule in his place. On 15 March, as a further assurance that Edward's rights would not be infringed, he was invested as prince of Wales.[17] This arrangement seems to have been carefully negotiated between Margaret and senior figures close to the duke of York and may be hinted at in a letter sent by the earl of Salisbury in March, which refers to Margaret sending messages to the council 'that might serve to rest and unity'.[18]

For the next two months Margaret stayed close to London,

but no longer pressed her case to be regent.[19] Yorkist chroniclers later reported of the duke's protectorate that he had 'honourably ruled and governed', 'miraculously pacifying all rebels and malefactors'.[20] The reality was more complicated. It would not have surprised contemporaries that on attaining this quasi-royal power York swiftly rewarded his key supporters, elevating them to high office to assist his government. His brother-in-law the earl of Salisbury was made chancellor, the first lay occupant of the title in more than forty years, while York's kinsman Thomas Bourchier, bishop of Ely, replaced Kempe as archbishop of Canterbury.[21] Nor was it surprising that York left Somerset languishing in the Tower in spite of queries about the legality of holding an untried and unconvicted prisoner indefinitely.[22] But York was barely appointed protector before resistance to his rule erupted. His own son-in-law, Henry Holland, duke of Exeter, raised a force of 200 in North Yorkshire and handed out Lancastrian livery, asserting his right to be protector in York's place. He found common cause with the Percy Lord Egremont, who was alarmed at the ascendancy of his Neville rivals under York's protectorate. York wasted no time crushing this rebellion, personally marching north and dragging Exeter from sanctuary to be safely imprisoned in Pontefract Castle, but the rising was clear evidence of division in the north between Yorkist and Lancastrian loyalties.[23]

More passive forms of resistance hamstrung York's attempts to rule with the council. His appointment as protector coincided with an apparent rash of sickness that kept many lords away from Westminster that spring. Clearly they felt considerable anxiety about publicly associating themselves with such a divisive new regime, especially one known to have been opposed by the queen. Lord Cromwell had perhaps the best justification to complain of 'his infirmity and feebleness', since he was sixty, but the duke of Norfolk, who similarly protested his 'infirmity', was only thirty-eight and had been closely associated with York until now. Cromwell's real anxieties were shown when he appealed for guaranteed safety in coming and going to the council. Having been attacked at the doors to the council chamber barely four years earlier, his unease was understandable. A number of bishops protested that they could not serve York since they were too busy in their parishes, and Pey Tastar, dean of St Seurin,* came up with the novel excuse that since he was poor he lacked the necessary wisdom. The most honest reason stated for reluctance to counsel York was given by Viscount Beaumont: 'He was with the Queen,' he said, so he would not leave her to take this charge. However, he did insist that any who served York must have their freedom of speech guaranteed, as per the articles of the council, 'without any displeasure, indignation or wroth' being visited on them as a result.[24]

Everywhere York faced opposition and disorder. In the north the Neville–Percy feud erupted once more, in south Wales and the West Country disorder was on the rise and the Calais garrison mutinied, for York was no more able to pay their wages on time than Henry had been. It did not help that the commanders in Calais were both Somerset's men, Lord Lionel Welles and Richard Woodville, Lord Rivers.[25]

While the seasons turned and York struggled to assert his authority, there was little sign of Henry's recovery. By the autumn of 1454, however, there was at last indication that the king was starting to emerge from his stupor, more than a year after his collapse. On 6 September 1454 an East Anglian gentleman wrote from plague-stricken London that he had witnessed Archbishop Thomas Bourchier make formal submission to Henry in his chambers, receiving his cross of office in return.[26] This was as nothing, however, to what happened as the new year approached. At Christmastide Henry roused himself completely. He spoke. He recognized his wife and councillors. The last council document signed by York instead of the king appeared

---

* Pey was a Gascon refugee who had fled Bordeaux to appeal for greater English support in his homeland.

on the penultimate day of 1454.[27] Soon, Henry was able to take up the reins of government again. York's protectorate was over.

When Henry emerged from his stupor at Christmas, he may have been slowly recovering for some months. To his subjects, however, his revival seemed to come as a miracle, overnight. One day he could neither communicate nor understand, and then on St John's Day (27 December) he was commanding one servant to ride to Canterbury to make an offering at the altar of St Thomas and another to visit St Edward's shrine at Westminster to do the same. The citizens of London took to the streets in thanks, their processions winding through the city in a mist of incense to the low rumble of prayer. Most thankful of all must have been Queen Margaret, who brought Prince Edward to belatedly meet his father. Henry remembered nothing of his period of his sickness, but on being presented with his fourteen-month-old son he 'held up his hands and thanked God'. All the decisions Margaret had made for the child pleased him, from Edward's name to the choice of godparents. By 7 January 1455 Henry was well enough to be visited by his councillors, cautiously assessing his recovery. When he 'spoke to them as well as ever he did... they wept for joy'. The only legacy of Henry's prolonged illness seemed to be a resurgent religious fervour, as one of Margaret's servants, Edmund Clere,* reported: 'Now he says Matins of Our Lady and evensong, and hears his Mass devoutly.'[28]

The birth of a healthy son, and survival of the queen, were the only glad tidings Henry had to enjoy in these early days of recovery. He had awoken to a radically different political reality. Margaret broke the sensitive news of Cardinal Kempe's death, probably with considerable trepidation given the terrible outcome of the

---

* Edmund Clere was Margaret's squire and one of the many servants on whose behalf the queen interceded for political benefit. Monro, *Letters of Margaret of Anjou*, pp. 119–20.

last shocking news Henry had received, but although Henry grieved to learn 'that one of the wisest lords in this land was dead' he suffered no relapse. Perhaps it was also Margaret who told him that York held political dominance with a coterie of noble supporters, and that through the duke's auspices two of Henry's senior kinsmen of the blood royal, Somerset and Exeter, were currently imprisoned without charge. The fractures that Henry had been struggling to mend before he fell ill were now deep rifts in the body politic. A 'Yorkist' clique had developed within government and with their grip on the key offices of protector, chancellor and archbishop of Canterbury they held a position of considerable power, while their opposition had steadily come to coalesce around the queen. If Margaret had previously shared Henry's propensity to reconcile and forgive, her mistrust of York and his allies had intensified markedly in the past eighteen months. She had appealed for York to join the great council and in return he had colluded at Somerset's illegal imprisonment. She may also have felt lingering resentment at his successful attainment of the protectorate when she had been denied the regency. Margaret was no longer willing to intercede for him or offer the benefit of the doubt. York had shown himself untrustworthy and self-promoting – he was, in short, dangerous to the Lancastrian regime.

Henry's feelings towards the duke of York were somewhat different when he emerged from his illness. Edmund Clere reported that the king was 'in charity with all the world and wished that all the lords were so'. However, Henry's actions suggested that his loyalties were fundamentally no different from what they had been before he fell ill: he still favoured Somerset over York, and he was still guided by his wife. His recovering strength was accompanied by a steady reversal of York's policies over the past year and a half. As soon as he was well enough to move, Henry went with Margaret to her garden palace at Greenwich and on 26 January the duke of Somerset was 'strangely conveyed' out of the Tower of London by the duke of Buckingham with the aid of Somerset's stepson Lord Roos and their old ally the earl of Wiltshire.[29] On 4 February these lords stood bail for Somerset, suggesting the duke might still answer for the crimes Norfolk had accused him of. However, within a month Henry had discharged the bail and before a council of lords summoned to Greenwich he 'openly declared the said duke of Somerset his faithful and true liegeman... willing it were [generally] known and understood'.[30] Somerset was thus free to reign supreme as Henry's right-hand man. Once again Henry insisted that the division between Somerset and York must be treated as a personal matter, not a political one, and put their dispute to arbitration on a 20,000-mark obligation of good behaviour. The accusations against Somerset of treason or military incompetence were ignored, and as a sign of his restoration he replaced York as captain of Calais. Even officers appointed by York were now turned out of office. York's treasurer, his ally the earl of Worcester, was replaced by Somerset's partisan the earl of Wiltshire; the duke of Exeter was released from imprisonment and honourably escorted back to court. In a futile act of protest the earl of Salisbury resigned as chancellor.* Perhaps he jumped before he was pushed, for nine days later he was relieved of the custody of Portchester Castle and town in Hampshire, both grants he had received during the protectorate. Thus, with Somerset and Margaret at the king's right hand once more, York's protectorate was swept away as if it had never existed.[31]

But for all Henry might wish that the world had frozen in place, as he had, in the summer of 1453, York was not the man he had been then: politically isolated, lacking noble support and frustrated in his attempts to gain power. He had now enjoyed a taste of real authority and in the Nevilles and Bourchiers he had gained important noble allies whose personal interests, as much

---

* On 7 March the office of chancellor was transferred to Thomas Bourchier, archbishop of Canterbury.

as their family loyalty, bound them to his cause. They would not just quietly accept the disintegration of their authority and retreat into rural obscurity. The triumvirate of York, Warwick and Salisbury had become tightly bound by bonds of kinship and vested interest over the past two years and their sense of injustice at Henry's actions early in 1455 united them in opposition to the current regime. In 1455, aged twenty-nine, Warwick shared his uncle York's suspicions of the government and had perhaps equal motivation to remove Somerset from political influence. For years he had contested estates connected to his wife's inheritance with Somerset and as long as Somerset held sway over Henry, Warwick knew that he would come out of the contest the loser. In the years ahead, Warwick would prove himself a ruthless politician, all too happy to settle disputes with brute force. Assassination was as much a part of his arsenal as his undoubted powers of rhetoric and charm. Warwick's father Salisbury was a more moderate man. Like his sister Cecily, duchess of York, the earl of Salisbury had carefully cultivated a relationship with Queen Margaret, endeavouring to keep her 'good ladyship' by offering his parklands for her hunts and acting as mediator in the dispute over York's protectorate in early 1454. It may have been Salisbury who negotiated the deal that made Margaret step back from the regency, saving Prince Edward's status at the expense of Margaret's personal ambition. But even for the placatory Salisbury Henry's decision to free Exeter was deeply troubling, for the duke was allied with the Percys, and any royal patronage of the duke or Percys was likely to damage Neville interests in the north.[32]

The first sign of trouble came when the Yorkist lords left court without permission. York and Warwick were gone by early March 1455 and Salisbury soon followed his kinsmen north. In April both sides of this political rift were moving to neutralize their rivals. Somerset had always known he was dependent on royal patronage but the past year had painfully brought home to him how fragile were the foundations of his authority. If Henry fell ill again, Margaret would not be able to protect him. She, likewise, had learnt the limits of her political influence in the face of York's protectorate. Both queen and chief counsellor were determined to remove the Yorkist threat. In April the Yorkist lords were excluded from an assembly of lords in Westminster, and shortly thereafter they were summoned to a great council that would meet on 25 May in Leicester. There, in the queen's castle and within the heartland of Lancastrian loyalty, York and his allies would be forced to submit to the king. Probably there would be a repetition of the mortifying public debasement that York had endured in the wake of Dartford: he, Salisbury and Warwick must kneel before the king and their rival, swearing their loyalty and accepting whatever settlement with Somerset Henry commanded. Under the circumstances it would, of course, be more favourable to Somerset than to them. It would in all probability be the end of their political influence. For the Yorkist lords, the summons to Leicester had alarming echoes of the command that had spelled Gloucester's downfall in 1447: he, too, had received a royal command to a meeting outside London when the king was under the power of his enemies. For Gloucester it had ended in dishonour and death. York, Warwick and Salisbury had no intention of surrendering themselves to that fate.

The first news that reached Henry's court as he prepared to leave London for Leicester was of an assembling army in the north. The Yorkists had failed to impose their will on government by peaceful means; they would now do so by force of arms. Still inclined to peace and mercy before conflict, Henry dispatched emissaries to try to talk the Yorkists back from the brink. Among the mediators was Salisbury's son-in-law (and York's late treasurer) the earl of Worcester, but their presence made no difference. On 18 May Henry's government sent a panicked letter to the city of Coventry, demanding the citizens send armed men 'to be with us wheresoever we be in all haste possible'.[33] It was still hoped that Henry's mediators could bring the Yorkists to Leicester, where royal military strength could overawe them and force them into compliance, but soon it became clear that even that level of persuasion was beyond Henry's power. On 20 May the Yorkist army had reached Royston, only 40 miles (65 km) north of London. Henry had been deceived. York and his allies had not been negotiating with his mediators; they had held them in the north to cover their southward march and to conceal the full extent of the force that they had assembled. Now an army 3,000 strong was surging down the Great North Road towards London. They intended to block Henry's route to Leicester and perhaps even to lay a trap and seize the king himself. Battle now seemed inevitable.

26

'The sword of vengeance'[1]

St Albans
22 May 1455

In the half-light of morning the early sun glistened on the spire of St Albans Abbey like a beacon, calling travellers out of London and south from the northern counties. Within those sacred stones lay the relics of the British martyr St Alban and the mortal remains, too, of the late duke of Gloucester. Henry awoke on the morning of 22 May ready to ride the familiar route towards the abbey, perhaps to offer his prayers there if there was time before continuing along the ancient road north. He had bidden farewell to Margaret at Westminster the previous morning, setting out for the great council at Leicester accompanied by the lion's share of the English nobility: the dukes of Somerset and Buckingham, of course, and their sons the earls of Stafford and Dorset, but also Henry's half-brother, Jasper Tudor, earl of Pembroke and the Percy earl of Northumberland, Thomas Courtenay, earl of Devon, Somerset's old ally the earl of Wiltshire and Lords Clifford, Roos, Sudeley, Dudley and Berners. Even Salisbury's brother Lord Fauconberg had joined the king's forces. The combined retinues of such a swathe of the nobility made a royal force 2,000 strong, with even more expected to join them as they made their way north. Such a large party moved slowly and they had paused at Watford, 8 miles (13 km) south of St Albans to reassemble. It was there, early on the morning of 22 May, that Henry awoke to the news that York's forces were 'hard by'. Although York's army was poorer in noble support – his thirteen-year-old son Edward, earl of March, and their kinsmen Viscount Bourchier and the earls of Warwick and Salisbury made up the bulk of their aristocratic supporters – his soldiers outnumbered Henry's by three to two.[2]

An urgent council of war was called in Henry's camp. It would make little sense to turn back to London, whose citizens were known to hate Somerset and favour the duke of York. Indeed, it was to escape York's partisans that they had left the capital in the first place. Should Henry and his men continue onwards to St Albans and put their faith in York's protestations of loyalty? This was the duke of Buckingham's advice. Somerset, however, disagreed. Until they had a better idea of York's intentions they ought to stay where they were. Henry made the final decision. He believed that York would prefer to negotiate rather than raise arms against his king. It had proven so at Dartford, and since then York had taken an oath of loyalty. He then replaced Somerset as constable of England with Buckingham, who would lead the negotiations to avoid antagonizing the Yorkist men with the sight of Henry's hated chief counsellor. Henry's faith in York was to prove woefully misplaced.

By the time Henry's forces reached St Albans, a little before the dinner hour of ten, York's army was already encamped east of the town centre, outside the city ditches and gardens. Henry's army hastily took control of the city, dispatching the northern Lord John Clifford to man the barricades of the unwalled settlement. Buckingham advanced to negotiate with the Yorkists.

In the centre of the town, Henry and his attendants waited anxiously beneath the royal standard. Henry had been provided with a new brigandine and gauntlets for his journey out of London, but his hope for peaceful resolution was strong enough that neither he nor the household members defending him donned their armour. The clock tower tolled the passing hour and as the bells faded they were replaced by distant shouts. Henry's men in the marketplace shifted. As far as they knew, the negotiations for peace were still ongoing but unmistakably, on the morning air, sounds of violence carried from the houses on the other side of the street. The barricades at the edge of town were being torn down. The earl of Warwick had grown tired of the pointless back and forth of negotiations. His men forced an entry into the town through the gardens and backs of houses.

Feathers flashed in the marketplace, and around Henry his men shrieked as they fell. Shapes glimpsed in the distance resolved themselves into soldiers, faces shadowed by helms, swords slashing, pouring into the marketplace. Six hundred battle-hardened marcher men invaded the town as Henry's men ran to ring the town alarm bell, calling soldiers back from the barricades towards the king's unfurled banner. They struggled into armour but many were still only half-armed as they fought.

Enclosed within a protective circle of servants, Henry looked on as his men were slaughtered in front of him. Unprotected by helmets or armour, many of them suffered deep slash wounds to their faces, while their limbs were hacked by swords and impaled with arrows.[3] This was Henry's first experience of battle, and it was one of utter chaos. An arrow glinted and there was a spurt of blood. Henry had been wounded – his neck? His shoulder? In the confusion it was unclear.[4] He was bundled from the marketplace as it fell to the enemy, away from the fallen bodies of the dying and dead, into the reek and darkness of a tanner's cottage. The royal standard that should have rallied Henry's forces was left leaning against a wall and was overturned, its bearer struggling to arm himself, to get into armour, and eventually just to run.[5]

From the moment the Yorkist forces battered down the barricades of St Albans it took only half an hour for them to wrest control of the town from Henry. Any semblance of order turned to rout as Henry's men shed what little armour they had been able to don and fled. As Warwick's men struck from the east, York and Salisbury advanced from the north. They cut down their noble enemies with deadly precision as the common soldiers scattered. The lords either fled in hope of saving their lives or made a last, desperate stand. The duke of Buckingham, wounded in three places by enemy arrows, ran for the sanctuary of the abbey, where the earl of Wiltshire had already fled. Warwick's men cut down the Nevilles' northern rival Lord Clifford as he defended the barricades. The despised head of the Percy family, the earl of Northumberland, was another easy target for vengeful Neville retainers. The true focus of the Yorkist forces' vitriol, the duke of Somerset, retreated into the Castle tavern with his nineteen-year-old son and their men. Their hiding place was soon discovered, and the Yorkists broke down the tavern doors. The *English Chronicle** claimed that Somerset had once heard a prophecy that he would die beneath a castle, and now beneath the painted sign of the tavern he came out fighting, perhaps determined to take as many enemy soldiers as he could with him. After killing four men he was felled with an axe and hacked to death in the street. His son, Henry Beaufort, was wounded so badly that his bloody body was carried from the battlefield on a cart.[6]

Within the walls of the tanner's cottage, Henry waited for the butchery to end. The sounds of battle must have reached him through the walls, mingling horribly with the stink of curing leather and iron tang of his wound. Even his unerring certainty in the mercy of others must by now have been wavering. He had faced down an army once before, but he had never been in the midst of battle. No one had ever dared injure him. Now that he had been wounded by his Yorkist enemies could he really be certain they would not kill him too?

The doorway opened to reveal the duke of York. Though the

---

* A *Brut* continuation, written early in the reign of Edward IV.

day was undeniably his, he was probably as horrified to see the king injured as Henry was himself. With incongruous reverence York escorted Henry out of the tanner's cottage and towards the safety of the abbey. Pillaging had already started in the streets. As he went, Henry passed bodies left lying in pools of blood in the filthy streets while their horses and harness were plundered. Among the scattered corpses were men Henry might have recognized, although their bodies were disfigured by dirt and gore.[7]

Even when he reached the sanctuary of the abbey, Henry's ordeal was not over. Some of York's men were still chasing down the fleeing Buckingham and Wiltshire within the abbey precinct. York ordered his men to stop their hunt but did not let the lords go free. He insisted that Henry order them to surrender themselves as prisoners, or 'see them killed in front of him'.[8] Henry had little option but to comply, and the badly wounded Buckingham was brought before York. The earl of Wiltshire had already escaped, disguised as a monk.* Finally, Henry was faced with the triumvirate of Yorkist lords. Their clothing still probably smeared with the filth of battle, they knelt before him in the abbey and asked to be acknowledged as his true liegemen. They had never intended any harm to the king, they said, only to remove the traitors who surrounded him. If Henry had not known before, he must by now have realized that Somerset and the other enemies of York and the Nevilles were dead. Under these circumstances, Henry could hardly refuse his grace to his captors. Only after their allegiance had been accepted did York call a halt to the pillaging and allow the butchered bodies in the streets to be honourably buried within the abbey church.

The impact on Henry of this morning's events, as he sat in the abbey, watching bodies being carried in, one after the other, for burial, can hardly be exaggerated. Although only sixty men had been killed, a number of them were known to Henry and some

---

* Escaping battle, in disguise or otherwise, came to be the earl of Wiltshire's calling card.

were his closest advisers, men who had served him his entire life. For the past five years Somerset had been his guiding hand. More immediately traumatic even than the grief of these losses was the fact that, at the age of thirty-three, Henry had finally had his first experience of the brutality of battle. By the standards of his time, Henry's first taste of warfare came very late in life. York's thirteen-year-old son Edward, earl of March, was at St Albans and although he was probably kept out of the serious fighting the presence of a teenage soldier on the battlefield was far from unusual. Henry VI's father had been half his age when he first fought – and was wounded – in battle. Henry's unfamiliarity with bloodshed, the visceral reality of slaughter, the chaos of battle, the sensory overload of the experience, must have made it all the more disturbing. And once again, Henry had been reduced to a state of almost infantile impotency. Medieval kings were trained for combat from childhood, and Henry had not lacked for such schooling, yet he had watched his servants die and been wounded himself, whilst apparently playing no active part in the battle at all. Now, as the adrenaline surge and immediate threat receded, Henry found himself bloodied, aching, and faced with the reality of his own powerlessness: the prisoner, to all intents and purposes, of his chief counsellor's killer.

In the days after the battle Henry seemed to retreat into a state of complete passivity. The following morning, Friday 23 May, he was escorted back to London encircled by the three Yorkist lords, a public assertion of their new place as the ruling regime around the king. York took the place of honour on Henry's right hand, Salisbury rode to his left and Warwick proudly bore the king's sword before them. After being paraded through the streets like a trophy, on Whitsunday (25 May) Henry was brought to his traditional crown-wearing ceremony at St Paul's. At the high point of this ritual of kingship, the glistening crown on Henry's head was placed there by the hands of the duke of York.

★

In less than three hours of battle, York had achieved more than he had managed in five years of politics. The first business of the Yorkists now that they had taken control of government and eliminated their rivals was to legitimize their actions with a parliament. To have raised arms against the king was a serious enough infraction under normal circumstances, never mind actually fighting his army, killing several leading noblemen and wounding the royal person. It was vital that York, Warwick and Salisbury protect themselves from accusations of impropriety and in this Henry would play a leading role. He was to be used, much as he had been in the aftermath of the battle, to publicly vindicate the Yorkist regime.

Only four days after the Battle of St Albans, a parliament was called for Henry to open on 9 July, and in the interim the king was kept under the watchful supervision of his captors. At Windsor and Hertford, back in the company of Margaret and Prince Edward, Henry was only a matter of miles from York's household at Ware and Warwick's at Hunsdon. Meanwhile, York and his allies set about reasserting their control over key offices of government. Wiltshire was replaced as treasurer by Viscount Bourchier and the long-contested captaincy of Calais (most recently held by the late duke of Somerset) was bestowed on the earl of Warwick.[9]

The trauma of the battle compromised the recovery Henry had made since Christmas. A fortnight after St Albans the physician and alchemist Gilbert Kymer was summoned to Windsor to treat Henry's 'sickness and infirmities'.[10] Perhaps the wound he received in battle weakened him, but it is also likely that Henry was suffering from problems with his mental health again. He slept more often after the battle, which can be a sign of depression,[11] and while he was not in the paralyzing stupor that had afflicted him through 1453–4 he was lethargic and passive, seeming to lose interest even in his beloved educational foundations. In July he handed control of his two colleges at Eton and Cambridge to Bishop William Waynflete and John Chedworth, bishop of Lincoln.[12]

Yet Henry was well enough to fulfil the public functions of king. He opened parliament on 9 July and a week later he was in attendance when a violent quarrel broke out at Westminster between Warwick and Lord Cromwell over responsibility for the Battle of St Albans. One noble retainer in London noted that the king seemed healthy in body, if perhaps not at ease in his heart.[13] Ongoing Lancastrian resistance made it essential for the king to visibly preside over this parliament and a degree of compulsion may have been brought to bear on Henry. The chambers of Westminster were far from soothing to a man still recovering from serious illness and recent trauma. So tense was the atmosphere in the city that York and his allies travelled along the river each day surrounded by armed men, their barges loaded with weapons.

While Henry fell into line, his chief supporters were not all so quick to accept the new regime. The duke of Buckingham attended parliament grudgingly, bound over by substantial bonds of good behaviour, while the earl of Wiltshire refused to come at all. The Yorkists imprisoned both the duke of Exeter and Henry's ex-treasurer Lord Dudley, rather than risk them causing the sort of ugly scene that Cromwell had with Warwick. The day after that altercation, on 19 July, an emphatic statement was enrolled in parliament that Henry had 'declared his beloved kinsmen' Warwick, Salisbury and York 'to be his faithful lieges'.[14] The Battle of St Albans was recast as an attempt to kill the Yorkist lords masterminded by the wicked duke of Somerset and two other royal servants who had displeased York in the past.[15] To further emphasize the Yorkists' loyalty and try to reconcile the fractured nobility in the wake of battle, on 24 July all the lords in Westminster assembled before Henry in the great council chamber and swore 'to show the truth, faith and love which they have and bear to his highness'. Every bishop placed his hand on his breast and every lay lord took the king by the hand as he made his oath.[16] The Yorkist message was clear: 'All things done [at St Albans had been] well done, and nothing done there... after this time [was] to be spoken of.'[17]

In August parliament paused for the summer and Henry retired to Hertford Castle. York's efforts in parliament had failed to restore peace to the realm. When James II of Scotland laid siege to Berwick in early July, the task of repulsing him fell to the new earl of Northumberland, Henry Percy.* At the other end of the kingdom, as autumn lengthened shadows and brought chill winds, the West Country once again dissolved into chaos. The authoritative presence of a king had never been needed more. If Henry was unwilling, or unable, to rule himself, it might be necessary to force an alternative solution.[18]

Devon
23 October 1455

A little before midnight, on the southern fringes of Exmoor, Nicholas Radford and the other inhabitants of Upcott Manor were roused from sleep by the crackle of flame and smell of smoke. Radford was the recorder of Exeter,† a respected man whose long life of tireless civic endeavour had seen him skilfully navigate the endless feud between Lord William Bonville and the earl of Devon: Bonville was one of his oldest clients, but Radford was also the godfather of the earl of Devon's younger son Henry. As Radford struggled to the window in the darkness, he saw that a gate in the wall encircling his manor had been set alight. In the leaping shadows cast by the fire Radford could make out a posse of around 100 men beneath his window. Radford called down to them: who were they? Was there a gentleman among them? One of the men made himself visible and called for Radford to come down so they could talk. He was the earl of Devon's eldest son, Sir Thomas Courtenay. The sight of the arms and light armour

---

*   Son and namesake of the earl killed at St Albans.
†   A recorder was a legally trained civic record keeper and judge, appointed by the local mayor and aldermen.

of Courtenay's men gave Radford pause. Only when Courtenay swore on his honour as a 'true knight and gentleman' that Radford would come to no harm did the aged lawyer agree to meet them.[19]

But Radford had been deceived. When he opened his doors to Courtenay, his posse surged in. A petition to parliament for justice against the thieves recorded how 'Sir Thomas Courtenay's men broke open the chamber doors and coffers', seizing everything from jewels and gowns to chapel ornaments and books. 'And among other riflings then and there, they found the said Nicholas Radford's wife in her bed, sore sick as she has been these two years and more and rolled her out of bed and took away the sheets that she lay in.'[20] With their booty trussed up in Mrs Radford's still-warm sheets and loaded on to the backs of Radford's horses, Courtenay's men set off into the night.

Courtenay now insisted that Radford accompany him to meet the earl of Devon. 'Sir,' pleaded Radford, 'I am aged and may not well go upon my feet.' But Courtenay insisted, drawing Radford out into the darkness outside the house. Barely a stone's throw from the manor walls, Courtenay's men attacked. 'With a glaive [one] smote the said Nicholas Radford a hideous deadly stroke across the face, and felled him to the ground, and then... gave him another stroke behind his head so that his brains fell out.' Finally, 'with a long dagger [they] feloniously cut the throat of the said Nicolas Radford'.

Still Courtenay had not finished with him. The following week, as Radford's mutilated body lay in his local chapel, Courtenay's men forced their way in and held a mocking 'inquest' in which they brought a verdict of suicide. The chapel stones echoed with lewd ballads as the men

rolled the body of Nicholas Radford out of the chest he was lying in, and rolled him out of his winding sheet, and cast the body all naked into a pit and threw on it to the stones that he had bought to make his tomb, and broke and crushed his head and body.[21]

Radford's brutal murder was the most notorious event in an escalating crisis in the West Country. The contest for local dominance between Bonville and Courtenay had been waged, intermittently, for nearly thirty years. The Courtenays felt that they had been excluded from power, a process little helped by the earl of Devon's involvement at Dartford. In 1452 Henry had sealed Bonville's primacy in the southwest when he did him the honour of visiting his manor at Shute. By 1455 the Courtenays had had enough. In a concerted campaign of violence and terror throughout the autumn they took back control, occupying the city of Exeter and pillaging or besieging the manors and castles of Bonville's affinity with no respect for status or for the law. Legal sessions were interrupted by Courtenay bully boys and religious clerks held to ransom. Even the dean of Exeter Cathedral was taken hostage.

These events were reported in London as members of parliament returned after the summer recess. As if near anarchy in the west was not enough cause for alarm, the day before parliament opened, on 11 November, York was given a commission to hold parliament in Henry's place, since the king was 'not able to be present in person at our said parliament for certain just and reasonable causes'.[22] Rumours were rife that the king was ill again.[23] If he could not attend parliament, how could he possibly suppress the unrest in Devon? Every day messengers seemed to bring news of fresh atrocities. A decisive response was needed. The day after parliament opened, a representative of the commons, William Burley, appealed on behalf of all his colleagues that if Henry was incapacitated, someone else should be appointed to see to the 'defence and protection' of the realm so that 'such riots and injuries would the sooner be punished, justice fully administered, and the law proceed more properly'.[24] Two days later he suggested York for the job.

Although the Lords of parliament attempted to prevaricate, the Commons pushed relentlessly for a protector to be named, demanding an answer three times in five days. On the fifth day they threatened to go on strike. The tactic worked. By 19 November York was appointed protector, with powers expanded from those he had possessed in his protectorate of 1454–5. Now he could appoint councillors and only be relieved of his position by the king in parliament with the support of the Lords. Henry's will alone would not remove him from power.[25] Much about York's appointment is suspect. The concerted pressure applied to the Lords and the speed with which the Commons achieved their aim was highly unusual, as was the fact that the Commons were led not by their speaker but by Burley, who was a councillor and feoffee of York. In other words, York's appointment was a put-up job on the part of a Commons packed with his supporters.

Exactly how unwell Henry really was is unclear. Unlike in 1454 no delegation was sent to visit the king and report back to parliament. When the Commons appealed for a protector they did so not because Henry was known to be ill but because there were fears that he might become so. The parliamentary record referred with frustrating vagueness to 'the present infirmity which it has pleased Our Most High Saviour to visit on [Henry's] person' and acknowledged that the strain of government business might 'be an obstacle to the swift recovery of his health'. However, there is no suggestion that Henry had suffered another episode of psychosis, or even whether his current 'infirmity' was more mental or physical. What seems clear is that Henry himself was content to submit to the will of parliament, and of the duke of York. He had always shied away from confrontation and in the wake of the Battle of St Albans he was more inclined to passivity than ever. He may also have felt a profound sense of impotent fatigue. He had struggled with considerable effort to protect Suffolk and Somerset from the vitriol of his subjects, and in both cases he had failed spectacularly. The futility of defying the will of his people had been brought violently home to him in recent years. Even if he wished to resist the pressure for York to be made protector, he may not have been able to summon the resources to do so. As it was, he stayed away from Westminster for the duration of the winter session, finally returning only because parliamentary favour had swung against York.

York's second protectorate was to prove even shorter and unhappier than his first. He had never enjoyed widespread noble support, so to provide the necessary popular foundation for his regime he carefully cultivated the favour of the Commons, championing policies in parliament that matched their anticourt sympathies. It was probably York who finally enabled the enrolment of a bill that had been presented, unsuccessfully, by the Commons in every parliament since 1447: the rehabilitation of the duke of Gloucester. It served York's interest to continue to identify himself in the popular imagination with the 'good duke of Gloucester' and especially to exonerate an accused traitor and heir to the throne who had, he claimed, been brought down by wicked counsellors around King Henry. Gloucester's exemplary royal service was recited on the parliament roll during the first session of parliament and then writs were sent out to sheriffs and bailiffs in every county instructing them to make public proclamation that the duke had died a loyal man.[26]

Equally popular with the Commons were York's attempts to regulate royal finances. In his last protectorate, in November 1454, York had attempted to reform household finance, introducing such radical measures that the treasurer of the household, Lord Dudley, resigned in protest.[27] Henry's recovery at Christmas 1454 meant that York's reforms were never implemented, but in his second protectorate the duke tried again. The insufficiency of Henry's household to support itself was associated in the popular imagination with his liberal generosity and right from the beginning of parliament in 1455, there were appeals in the Commons for a resumption of royal grants to finance the household. Such appeals had been lodged repeatedly in past years, but although attempts had been made to implement reform in 1450 and 1452, on each occasion Henry had limited the efficacy of the act by protecting his chosen individuals and projects. In July 1455 the Commons petitioned for a resumption once more, this time attempting to remove the loopholes that Henry had left open. They wanted duchy of Lancaster lands to be under crown control, which threatened the financial under-pinnings of Henry's cherished educational projects, and they also sought to limit Queen Margaret's dower to 10,000 marks. But the most radical Commons' demand was couched in the most cautious and humble language:

> Given that the said resumption before this has not been effectively carried out: we, your humble, true, obedient and faithful people… most humbly pray you to consider most nobly, graciously and sympathetically… that it may please your highness that if you choose… to make any provisos or exceptions other than those contained in this our petition, that the said provisos and exceptions may be sent down to us, so that we may give our assent to them, if it seems to us expedient and necessary.[28]

In other words, the Commons sought the power to veto Henry's exemptions if they thought them unwise. This was an extra-ordinary profession of collective mistrust in royal judgement; a control over royal grace such as had not been inflicted on Henry for twenty years. The petition went on to request that if Henry made any further unilateral grants after the act of resumption had come into effect then the recipient should be fined 1,000 marks, effectively limiting Henry's royal powers of prerogative in the future.

Radical as such demands were, they were widely supported in the Commons and by the time parliament was prorogued for Christmas York felt sufficiently confident to add his own support

to the petition. With the protector on board, it seemed that the
Commons would finally succeed in enforcing an act of resumption that controlled Henry's unbound liberality. However, they
had reckoned without the Lords. *John Benet's Chronicle* reported
that 'almost all the lords resisted' the bill that the Commons had
drawn up, since it threatened their own royal grants.[29]

By early February 1456, with parliament ready to resume its
business, York's protectorate was in jeopardy. If the duke stayed
in power, reported John Bocking (a servant writing a letter
home to his master), the bill of resumption would be forced
through, so in order for the Lords to prevent the full rigours of
resumption from being enacted, York must be removed.[30] But
the Lords alone could not end York's protectorate. That power
lay with the king.

Reluctantly, Henry was roused from his sanctuary in Hertford
Castle by the complaints of his nobility. Presumably emissaries
were sent as representatives of the Lords, perhaps the duke of
Buckingham or Bishop Waynflete of Winchester, to appeal against
the unreasonableness of the Commons' demands. No medieval
king could accept such stringent controls on his prerogative, and
although Henry would have preferred to absent himself from
parliament he could not allow the act of resumption to pass as the
Commons wished. On 25 February he returned to Westminster
Palace and in York's presence, with the encouragement of the
Lords, discharged the duke from his protectorate. For the second
time in a year, York's pretensions to office had been dismissed
by the king. York left parliament before the end of the session.

Although the resumption bill passed, it was considerably rewritten: the Commons' desire for a veto was rejected outright,
as was any punishment for those receiving future royal grants.
Henry reserved his right to make exemptions, ultimately listing
143 exempted grants which would not be resumed. Chief among
those protected were Queen Margaret, his educational foundations and the noblemen who had blocked the bill's passage.
Two of Henry's physicians, William Hatcliffe and John Faceby,

made good use of their access to the monarch and secured exemptions of their own.* The most outspoken rejection of a petition for resumption recorded that it 'is thought to the king and to all the lords that this bill is unreasonable and therefore the king wills that it be laid apart'.[31]

Although he may not have been fully restored to health, Henry had proven that with noble support he was still capable of asserting himself. Political assassination had deprived Henry of two chief counsellors in five years, but his need for a motivating force to rouse him from passivity was undiminished. Despite York's best efforts neither warfare nor politics had enabled him to succeed Somerset as the leading force in government. John Bocking reported in his letter that Henry himself might have been willing to allow York to continue to rule on his behalf as a chief counsellor appointed during royal pleasure, but that he was overruled by his wife: 'The queen,' wrote Bocking, 'is a great and strong laboured woman, for she spareth no pain to sue her things to an intent and conclusion to her power.'[32] Bocking's letter indicates a shift in the dynamic between Henry and Margaret. Before Henry's first illness Margaret had played the traditional queenly role – intercessor, peacemaker and intermediary – but the anxieties of the past three years, Henry's continued incapacity and Margaret's new status as a mother had driven the queen into new territory. Now, at the age of twenty-six, Margaret stepped into the space left vacant since Somerset's death. She took Henry and the government firmly in hand. For the next decade the force transforming Henry's weak will into action, the true head of the Lancastrian dynasty, would be Queen Margaret.

---

* Royal grants to Henry's childhood wetnurse, Joan Asteley, were also safeguarded.

27

'Of queens that be crowned, so high none know I'[1]

Coventry
Feast for the Exaltation of the Holy Cross
(14 September) 1456

The wealthy cloth town of Coventry was rightly proud of its pageants. Every midsummer its streets crowded with sweet-smelling angels and leaping demons, waving their pitchforks from vast set-piece hell mouths, while everyone from lowly citizen to mayor and noblewoman looked on. One day in early autumn 1456 all of the town's considerable dramatic resources were directed towards welcoming Queen Margaret and her infant son as they came home. For Coventry was the 'queen's secret harbour', in the heart of Margaret's Midlands dower estates and close to the duchy of Lancaster.[2] Mother and son had spent the summer touring their estates together and now Margaret brought little Prince Edward, just shy of his third birthday, to enjoy the comforts of the town. They were greeted with fourteen pageants in which prophets and patron saints, cardinal virtues and conquering kings vied to provide the most obsequious praise for the royal pair. At one gateway

St Edward the Confessor and his 'brother in virginity' St John the Evangelist promised to pray for the well-being of this 'mother of meekness' and 'his ghostly child', while around the marketplace nine heroes, from Julius Caesar to Charlemagne, pronounced their welcome in rhyming verse. A local man richly costumed as the prophet Isaiah compared Margaret to the Virgin Mary:

As Mankind was gladdened by the birth of Jesus
So shall this empire [of England] joy the birth of your body.

At the climax of the piece, by the conduit in the centre of town (arrayed 'with as many virgins as might be') the queen's namesake St Margaret slayed a dragon before delivering her own welcoming rhyme.[3]

King Henry was in Coventry that day too, but from the scant attention paid to him in this procession of praise you would hardly know it. He had arrived in the city some weeks earlier and was probably watching the pageants as his wife and son entered the city, but he was a shadowy presence, only mentioned four times in the fourteen pageants that were staged. He may have been ill again, for twice the actors expressed their concern for his good health. These pageants represented a new political reality: royal authority was no longer represented solely by the ailing king. Trinitarian imagery echoed throughout the display, reflecting how Henry, Margaret and little Prince Edward were a united focus of loyalty and authority. They were the father, the son and the holy spirit of the realm. Henry might technically remain the head of that trinity, and Edward was its hope for the future, but in autumn 1456 it was Margaret who was really in control: as the Coventry pageants described her, 'empress, queen, princess excellent in one person all three'.[4]

The pageants to welcome Margaret and Prince Edward marked a reunion of the royal family, as for much of the spring and summer of 1456 Henry had been forced to remain around London to deal with a wave of xenophobic violence surging through the city streets. Riots broke out after a young London apprentice attacked one of the many Italian residents of the city, breaking the man's dagger over his head. Henry was rowed upriver to personally preside over a commission in the Guildhall to try and restore order, but it took over a week to calm the capital and the hanging of three rioters at Tyburn brought noisy protests from the citizens.[5]

Meanwhile, the king of Scots, twenty-three-year-old James II, made the most of English disarray to indulge in border raids into Northumberland throughout the summer. The fiery red birthmark that covered half of James's face was seen as an outward manifestation of his hot temper. He was constantly plotting military efforts against the English and had assembled a large collection of cannon, some of which he had used to pound Berwick Castle in June 1455.[6] Clearly it was no longer enough to rely on the Nevilles and Percys to resist James's efforts – a royal army was needed to drive him back. But the army that marched north to deal with the Scottish threat in summer 1456 was not led by Henry. Instead, he gave that role to the duke of York. York wrote to James in fighting spirit from Durham on 26 August, threatening to confront him in open battle unless he retreated, and chastising the young Scot for attacking defenceless homes rather than legitimate military targets. Although York probably acted under a royal commission, his military activities in the north further underlined Henry's weakness. It was a king's job to defend the realm. If Henry could not do this, it was bad enough – if he would not, even worse.[7]

The immediate reason for Henry's retreat into the Midlands was an outbreak of violence in the marches and further reaches of Wales. For months Henry's half-brother Edmund Tudor had been attempting to assert royal authority at the expense of the duke of York's men but by summer 1456 the situation had deteriorated into open warfare. To Henry's considerable alarm the ringleaders of the trouble were York's two close associates, Sir Walter Devereux of Weobley and his son-in-law Sir

William Herbert of Raglan. Although York himself was absent in northern England and the rising was presented as a local feud, his involvement in this Welsh unrest must have been suspected. In August Herbert and Devereux raised 2,000 men and laid siege to Carmarthen Castle, where the unfortunate Edmund was captured and imprisoned. Henry's presence in the Midlands, close to north Wales, might have been intended to cow the rebellious Welshmen with his royal authority but it had little immediate effect.[8] Peace was only restored when Margaret travelled through the border counties of Wales in October, offering pardons to the chief troublemakers.[9]

For both Henry and Margaret, the Midlands represented a safe refuge from these troubles. With Margaret's castles of Tutbury, Leicester and Kenilworth close by, Coventry became a new royal capital. As the third city of the realm, close to the duchy of Lancaster and with good communication links in all directions, the city had long held Lancastrian loyalties. In 1451 Henry had declared the citizens of Coventry 'the best ruled people then within my realm'.[10] As well as being able to offer four religious houses within the city to accommodate the court – always a boon to the cash-strapped royals – Margaret and Henry could also benefit from the close proximity of a number of their key allies. The duke of Buckingham's residence of Maxstoke Castle was only 11 miles (18 km) away, while Lord Sudeley and the earls of Wiltshire and Shrewsbury all had estates close by.[11]

This retreat into the Lancastrian heartland highlighted the growing rift in the political realm. That summer one contemporary correspondent described York lurking in his Yorkshire fortress of Sandal while Margaret sat in Tutbury Castle, each brooding suspiciously on their rival's movements.[12] The events of the past three years had transformed what had once been an apparently functional relationship between queen and premier lord into one of intense mistrust and hostility. Margaret may already have suspected York of angling for the throne, directly threatening the rights of her husband and son. At the very least she knew that, if he could, York would happily use the pliant Henry as his puppet to rule in his own interest. She also now knew that he was willing to resort to violence to get what he wanted. York, meanwhile, could hardly regard Margaret's ascendancy as anything but threatening. To him, her removal to the Midlands with Henry and Prince Edward and the steadfast refusal of the royal regime to hold a parliament were intended to deny him access to power.

Both York and Margaret knew the fundamental fact of Henry's rule, which was that whoever controlled the king controlled the kingdom. York, denied access to the monarch, had no direct influence but he could at least exercise his military rights as a nobleman. Margaret could not even do that. Her only routes to political influence lay through Henry and her son. Since contemporary opinion rejected independent female authority she had to couch her actions in terms that were more acceptable: she was a devoted mother and wife, and any decisions that appeared to be hers were really those of her infant son and incapacitated husband. It was a fiction of masculine rule disguised behind female subservience – the very ideals of maternal activity that had been repeated over and over in the Coventry pageants.

Yet this representation of Margaret's idealized submissiveness – her 'mellifluous meekness' as the pageants put it – was far from the reality, for in autumn 1456, in the security of their Coventry court, Margaret set about asserting her control over Henry's government. In early October a great council was called to the city, confirming the transfer of government offices to trusted Lancastrian servants. The Bourchier brothers, who had been appointed to key positions by York in the wake of the Battle of St Albans, were both supplanted by men of less suspect allegiance. Thomas Bourchier's replacement as chancellor was Bishop Waynflete of Winchester, Henry's confessor and the man he trusted to oversee his educational foundations. Meanwhile Viscount Bourchier was replaced as treasurer by John Talbot, earl of Shrewsbury, the son of the 'English Achilles' who had been killed fighting Henry's cause in Gascony. Margaret's most partisan appointment was the choice of her own chancellor, Laurence Boothe, as keeper of the privy seal.

With the most important governmental roles now firmly in Lancastrian hands, Margaret moved to establish a similarly loyal council for Prince Edward. The council of the prince of Wales was responsible for managing his estates, particularly overseeing its finances: collecting revenue and authorizing its expenditure. Chief stewardship of the council was put in the capable hands of Margaret and Henry's old ally Viscount Beaumont, who already served as chief steward for the queen's Midlands estate. The duke of Buckingham had been displeased at the ousting of his half-brothers the Bourchiers from office, so it may have been to placate him that Margaret appointed his son and heir Humphrey, earl of Stafford, to oversee the prince's interests in the Welsh marches. Many familiar court figures, like Buckingham, were rewarded for their service: Prince Edward's council also held the earl of Wiltshire (who had finally emerged from hiding after his flight from the Battle of St Albans); Lord Dudley, who had pursued Jack Cade's rebels for the king in 1450; Lord Stanley, Henry's chamberlain; Laurence Boothe; and the ubiquitous Bishop Waynflete of Winchester. One of the earliest appointments was Robert Whittingham as receiver-general. As an usher of Henry's chamber married to Katherine Gatewyne, one of Margaret's ladies, Whittingham represented the tenacious hold of the royal household over political affairs. He was to prove staunchly loyal in the troubled years ahead.[13] The work of the council was to be undertaken 'with the approval and agreement of... the queen', so not only was the council dominated by Margaret's trusted allies but it also had to answer to her in its decision-making.[14]

Bonds of kinship and marriage already connected many of these Lancastrian courtiers. Buckingham's son, for instance, was married to Viscount Beaumont's daughter Joan. A good marriage was one of the key forms of patronage available to the royal family, and the next two years saw a flurry of royally approved or arranged marital alliances being forged among Margaret's courtiers. The earl of Shrewsbury's sister married Lord Sudeley's heir; Edmund, Lord Grey of Ruthin, married the earl of Northumberland's daughter. Buckingham's children were particularly fortunate, with marriages to the earl of Shrewsbury's heir, a wealthy Midlands landowner and – most desirable of all – in March 1458 the duke's second son Henry married Margaret Beaufort, the teenage heiress to the vast Beaufort fortune. Although Margaret was still only fourteen, this was her third marriage. Her last husband, Henry's half-brother Edmund Tudor, had contracted sickness during his imprisonment in Carmarthen Castle and died in November 1456, leaving his widow six months pregnant. His posthumous son was named Henry Tudor in honour of the king.[15]

The marriage which most clearly owed its existence to Margaret's influence was that between her cousin Marie, the bastard daughter of Charles of Maine, and Thomas Courtenay, the twenty-five-year-old heir of the earl of Devon. Given that Courtenay was last encountered murdering a lawyer in cold blood while his father waged a civil war in Devon, this comes as something of a surprise. However, the Courtenay influence in the West Country was vitally important to maintain royal control there, particularly if it could be divorced from any connection with the earl's old ally, the duke of York. By 1457 Devon and York had become estranged as the earl's enemy Lord Bonville, an associate of the Nevilles, rose in Yorkist favour.[16] Margaret leapt at the opportunity to detach a prominent nobleman in the localities from her rival. Thus, Courtenay and his brother were pardoned for their involvement in Nicholas Radford's murder and he was married off to a woman of French royal blood, whose wedding gowns were provided at Henry's expense. This velvet-glove treatment of York's old ally worked well. The earl of Devon continued to publicly serve the Lancastrian court and died in January 1458 at Abingdon Abbey still attendant on Queen Margaret.[17]

It was now tacitly understood that those associated with York would have no place in Margaret's regime and Yorkist allies must either join Margaret's court or lose out in key areas of royal patronage. In early 1456 York's pugnacious son-in-law Henry Holland, duke of Exeter, was released from the Yorkist imprisonment inflicted on him in the wake of St Albans; his allies the Percys steadily gained ground over their Neville rivals in the north. The new earl of Northumberland, Henry Percy, had inherited his title after his father died fighting for Henry at St Albans and the family's loyalty to the crown was not forgotten. Northumberland was granted a new, unusually long, contract as warden of Berwick and the east march and his brother Sir Ralph Percy was appointed to the key Northumbrian fortress of Dunstanburgh. Even more important for their dominance of the north, when the bishopric of Durham fell vacant it was bestowed not on a Neville – the earl of Salisbury's brother had held it last – but on Margaret's chancellor Laurence Boothe. Durham was a prince-bishopric with substantial independent authority, including the power to raise its own armies, so it was deemed wise to entrust it to loyal hands.[18]

The new earl of Northumberland was one of a number of young lords who had lost their fathers at St Albans and now flocked to the queen's court, where their personal grievances against York, Warwick and Salisbury were allowed to fester, occasionally spilling over into violence. The most persistent disturber of the peace was Henry Beaufort, the new duke of Somerset. Still only just in his twenties, Henry Beaufort had been gravely injured fighting alongside his father at St Albans and may well have witnessed Somerset's final desperate moments. The loss of his parent was bad enough but Henry Beaufort had been forced to endure the dishonour heaped on his father's memory in the Yorkist parliament of summer 1455, when the late duke of Somerset was cast as a traitor and the chief agitator of the conflict. This affront could not be endured. At Margaret's court Henry Beaufort associated with his fellow St Albans orphans, Northumberland and John, Lord Clifford.

These young lords were all of an age, united in their righteous rage against the Yorkists and determined to seek vengeance.
Their bitter hatred infected their retainers and seeped out
across the realm. In September 1456, when York was in London
ahead of an autumn great council, a grisly spectacle appeared
outside his lodgings: five severed dogs' heads, speared to the
standard in Fleet Street. In each bloody maw was a verse laden
with meaning. One bemoaned how the decisions of despised
political leaders were leading innocent servants to their deaths.
It wished that their commander's head was on the spike instead:

> What planet compelled me, or what sign,
> To serve that man that all men hate?
> I would his head were here for mine,
> For he hath caused all the debate.[19]

This foreboding public display may have lingered in York's mind
as he rode north to join Henry, Margaret and the other lords at
a great council summoned to Coventry on 7 October 1456. The
earl of Warwick joined him but the earl of Salisbury chose to
absent himself, perhaps fearing the reception they would receive.
His misgivings were understandable. Having strengthened her
hold over Henry, Margaret used this council to emphasize Yorkist
political isolation by confirming her appointments to office, and
may even have sought a more permanent victory over York. The
lawyer James Gresham wrote to a correspondent on 16 October
that the duke was 'in right good conceit with the king, but not
in great conceit with the queen; and some men say... had my
Lord of Buckingham not have letted it, my Lord of York had be
distressed.'[20]

Whether Margaret and her allies sought York's arrest or more
violent retribution for the events of the past eighteen months
was unclear, for the decision was taken from their hands. When
York and Warwick were called before the great council and
King Henry to answer for their actions, Henry once again chose

the path of mercy. He announced that he was willing to accept York and Warwick back into royal grace, as long as they swore their loyalty to him. To many of those in attendance at the great council this seemed excessively charitable, not to say guilelessly optimistic, given the recent history of such sworn promises. Since York's first public oath of loyalty to Henry in 1452 he had raised arms against him, held him captive, used him as a puppet and then disregarded his rule in favour of a protectorate. Yet still Henry believed that the route to unity and peace was forgiveness.

Here, in essence, was the weakness of Margaret's position – the same fundamental flaw that had beset every one of Henry's chief counsellors. Regardless of which adviser was uppermost in the king's confidence, delicately guiding his policy and applying firm will to his vacillating or disinterested rule, Henry would occasionally assert his royal will in a way that demonstrated invariably poor judgement and which almost always faced opposition. He had pressed for Orléans's release despite protests from Gloucester, he had ceded Maine in the face of widespread popular discontent, he had tried to protect Suffolk and Somerset even when their presence was political poison, and now he was willing to freely pardon the men who had killed his loyal attendants and usurped his royal authority. But despite the political folly of these actions, on the rare occasions that Henry chose to assert himself, it was impossible to naysay him. He was a weak king, but he was still king.

Whatever private frustration Margaret may have felt at Henry's actions, public expression of disagreement was left to the lords. The duke of Buckingham was once again called on to act as mediator between the forces of discord and harmony. Addressing King Henry before his council and the Yorkist lords, he

gave [York] to understand that he had nothing on which to rely, save only your [i.e. Henry's] grace... And then and there the said duke of Buckingham and all the other lords, kneeling, prayed you that because of the great danger to your most

noble person, and the frequent burden on the lords, and the
frequent disturbance of a great part of your realm, it might
please you not to show grace to the said duke of York, or anyone else hereafter, if they should again attempt to act against
your royal estate... but that they be punished as they deserve.[21]

Henry promised that he would heed Buckingham's words. York
and Warwick then swore on the gospels and signed a declaration
promising their good behaviour. This was their last chance.

Had certain of the lords present at the council had their way,
it would also have been York's last act. Royal mercy had done
nothing to cool the ire of the young Lancastrians. Henry Beaufort
had to be restrained by the lords from attacking York, and during the council Buckingham was once again called upon to
restore order after a violent affray broke out between Beaufort's
men and the watchmen of Coventry. When the lords returned
to London in November, Henry Beaufort turned his violent
attentions towards York's Neville allies. Beaufort's half-brother
Lord Roos, the duke of Exeter and the earl of Shrewsbury
banded together, intending to 'ride against' Warwick with 400
men but Warwick was warned in time and managed to evade his
enemies' ambush. At Cheapside in December, Beaufort tried to
attack Warwick's younger brother Sir John Neville. This time he
was frustrated by the timely arrival of the mayor and his watchmen. The escape of the Nevilles' enemy, Thomas Percy, Lord
Egremont, from Newgate Prison in November did little to calm
an already volatile situation.[22]

None of this would have pleased Henry. His capacity to forgive
and forget was as unimpeachable as ever, but the Battle of St
Albans had established blood feuds that would not be resolved
by a single great council. Something considerably more all-
encompassing than a public act of royal grace was needed if he
was to restore peace among his fractured nobility. He needed to
reconcile his lords and his queen. Ironically, it was an act of war
that gave him the opportunity to do so.

28

'Rejoice, England, in concord and unity'[1]

Sandwich
28 August 1457

Early morning broke over the small Kentish port of Sandwich in a welter of clanging alarm bells, screams and
dancing flames. Before dawn had roused the citizens
from their beds, 3,000 Frenchmen had poured into the town,
from land and sea. They had sailed from Honfleur, under the
command of Pierre de Brézé, Charles VII's trusted seneschal
of Normandy, and anchored overnight in the Downs, ready to
launch their attack at first light. Facing no effective resistance,
the French ransacked the port, pillaging the wealthy merchants'
homes, seizing Englishmen as prisoners and then torching the
town. *John Benet's Chronicle* reported that as a mocking show of
defiance the triumphant French spent the rest of the day playing tennis.[2] It was evening before an English defence could be
mounted and the French driven back into the sea, over 100 of
them drowning as they attempted to board their ships.[3]

The attack may have been little more than a harrying expedition, but it left a deep impact on the English. For the first time
in generations their shores had been invaded. It was yet another

demonstration of how English fortunes had deteriorated since the glorious 1420s, when their soldiers had occupied most of northern France and their allies had lined the continental shoreline. It was widely believed that the attack on Sandwich was the precursor to a full-scale French invasion, perhaps even an attack on two fronts. For years, James II of Scotland had been trying to persuade Charles VII to join him in a combined assault on Henry's realm.[4]

With such threats looming, it was vital that the English put aside their differences. Henry called on all his noblemen to unite against their common enemy and protect England's borders. To defend the marches towards the Scottish border he needed the support of York, the Nevilles and their Percy rivals. The south coast, meanwhile, was put in the control of Lancastrian loyalists. In November Richard Woodville, Lord Rivers, a long-term Lancastrian servant married to Henry's aunt Jaquetta, was made constable of Rochester Castle. Henry Beaufort, the young duke of Somerset, was given his first military command, inheriting his father's role as custodian of Carisbrooke Castle and lieutenant of the Isle of Wight.[5] If it seemed that the enemies of the House of York were being given too much authority, the role Henry accorded the earl of Warwick countered accusations of favouritism. During the second protectorate Warwick had been appointed captain of Calais and Henry had not overturned his appointment. By May 1457 Warwick and his countess, Anne Beauchamp,* were living in the last outpost of English rule in France, so it was a logical extension of his maritime authority to make him keeper of the seas in December 1457.[6] Unfortunately this appointment offended Henry's erstwhile supporter, the thin-skinned duke of Exeter, who viewed the extension of Warwick's powers to the seas as a diminishment of his own position as lord admiral.[7]

---

* Anne Beauchamp was the daughter of Henry's old master, the earl of Warwick. Richard Neville held the earldom by right of his wife.

The spectre of foreign invasion, rendered a visceral reality by the attack on Sandwich, offered Henry the opportunity finally to heal the rift that had been torn in the English body politic by the Battle of St Albans. Determined 'to set apart such variances as be betwixt divers lords of this our realm',[8] and resolve his noblemen's issues once and for all, Henry left the sanctuary of his Midlands base in October 1457. A great council was summoned to Westminster, relatively neutral ground for all parties concerned. As a demonstration of good faith and to keep the bristling noble retinues in check, shire levies were summoned and paraded through the city.[9] The last thing Henry wanted was for another attempted attack like those Henry Beaufort had inflicted on the Yorkists a year earlier. To allay the fears of the earl of Salisbury, Henry sent Viscount Beaumont – firmly a 'queen's man' but also Salisbury's brother-in-law – to Doncaster to escort Salisbury south through what might otherwise be regarded as 'enemy territory'. The council continued into 1458, with Henry insisting that he would accept no excuses for absence.[10]

In spite of Henry's good intentions, the new year brought the citizens of London a vast flock of lordly entourages and considerable anxiety. The lords descending on the city did not seem ready to put aside their grievances. Instead, they came – from the north, from the Welsh marches, from Calais, from the West Country – accompanied by forces of armed retainers numbering into the thousands. The mayor and aldermen of London did everything possible to avert unrest but by mid-February the city resembled an armed encampment. Inside the walls, the Yorkist lords held sway. York and his 400 men lodged at the waterside residence of Baynard's Castle; Salisbury in the *Arbour*, accompanied by 500 retainers. Delayed by adverse winds in the English Channel, Warwick arrived late to proceedings, encircled by a vast force of 600 men in vivid red livery, the Warwick ragged staff glaring white on their chests and backs. Meanwhile, outside the city walls, the opposing faction of lords lodged at Temple Bar and in the houses of bishops. The dukes of Exeter and

Somerset had come with 800 men, while the northern royalist lords – Northumberland, Egremont, Clifford – had a collective force of 1,500. Little wonder that the mayor and sheriffs of London had strengthened the watches, nightly checking the city gates were locked and personally leading armed forces to patrol the streets in an attempt to keep the peace. These civic patrols prevented at least one violent attack, for partway through Lent the dukes of Somerset and Exeter plotted with their allies Lords Egremont and Clifford to ambush Warwick as he travelled upriver to Westminster. Although the heirs of the men killed at St Albans lurked with 'their men harnessed and arrayed in form of war', Warwick was warned as he boarded his barge and safely diverted.[11]

Oblivious to the unease, or optimistic beyond reasonable measure, Henry met his lords on the first day of the council to deliver a speech designed to promote friendship and peace over rancorous vengeance. He reminded the lords present that discord was a corrosive force that 'rusts steel, rends cloth, is a cancer in the limbs, a brute in the herd, a contagious boil, an infectious virus' whereas concord was a virtue that enabled them to live justly. Private vengeance must be laid aside, he argued, for the public good. Having set the tone for the talks, Henry retired to Berkhamsted while the lords thrashed out a settlement at Westminster.[12]

Given Henry's sincere desire to foster peace, his absence from the negotiations between the warring parties is striking. Was his intention to publicly demonstrate royal impartiality by absenting himself, doubly important in light of Margaret's known antipathy towards York? If so, it was unwise for him to privately receive Henry Beaufort, Exeter, Clifford and Egremont at Berkhamsted on 1 March.[13] Perhaps the reality was that Henry was simply unable to maintain the energy and focus required for the daily grind of politics. The task of resolving the issues between the lords proved to be an exhausting one.

By mid-March, the bishops Henry had appointed to lead the

process of arbitration were having to hold separate meetings with each faction: in the morning visiting the Yorkists at Blackfriars, and in the afternoon journeying to the White Friars in Fleet Street to treat with Somerset and his allies. Reluctantly, Henry realized that it was not going to be possible to bring this dispute to an accord without his presence. He might be a flawed king, but he was still monarch and the authority of his crown – the threat of royal displeasure – was the trump card the arbitrators were able to play. And they needed to do so, for by 16 March nothing had yet been agreed. Henry returned to the capital to assume leadership of the negotiations. The following morning he rode to pray for divine intercession at St Paul's Cathedral. Within a week, his prayers were to be answered.[14]

London
25 March 1458

The streets of London, cramped with goldworkers' stalls and traders' guild chapels, had been the scene for many royal processions during Henry's reign, but they had never witnessed anything quite like the 'Love Day' of 1458.* Winding through the streets came the highest nobility of the land, not gleaming in armour and marching to war, but expensively robed for peace, filing hand in hand towards St Paul's Cathedral to give thanks for concord and unity. 'Love hath underlaid wrathful vengeance', a contemporary ballad proclaimed. 'Rejoice, England, our lords accorded to be.'[15] In the heart of this ritual of reconciliation was King Henry, crowned, robed and surely beaming with the beatific contentment of a peacemaker triumphing over the forces of hatred. It had taken a month of hard negotiation but finally Henry had succeeded.

---

* A 'Love Day' was a medieval term for a peacefully mediated arbitration ending a feud.

Ahead of Henry, pressed between the curious, bobbing heads of his subjects, he could see two pairs of adversaries, walking side by side in brotherhood: the vengeful young duke of Somerset with the proud earl of Salisbury, the arrogant duke of Exeter paired with a defiant earl of Warwick. The victims and the victors of the Battle of St Albans, in harmony at last. Behind Henry, the duke of York led Queen Margaret by the hand, the twin pillars of the rival factions united in this display of magnanimity. Only Henry walked alone, a king who promoted no faction and had no enemies, and yet for all that, the monarch whose fallible rule had enabled his kingdom to fracture like glass under pressure.[16]

The date of this procession was accidental, but significant, for in the Christian calendar it was known as Lady Day or the feast of the Conception – the date when the Virgin Mary had miraculously conceived Jesus Christ. The Lancastrians had long fostered their devotion to the Virgin Mary, and it must have seemed a good omen to Henry as he progressed through his capital, surrounded by warring lords now apparently loving friends once more. This public demonstration 'that love was in heart and thought' marked the conclusion of the fiercely contested arbitration.[17] The day before, 24 March, Henry had announced the settlement that underpinned this truce. £78,000-worth of bonds bound the rival lords and their servants to the terms of the settlement, condemning any who broke it to financial ruin. Henry had publicly declared the Yorkist lords his faithful lieges, but York's justifications for the Battle of St Albans, which had been enrolled in parliament in summer 1455, were ignored. York, Warwick and Salisbury were cast as the aggressors in the conflict, and as such they suffered the heaviest penalties. The duke of York agreed to pay £2,000 in tallies to the widowed duchess of Somerset, and the same amount again to her bellicose son, the current duke Henry Beaufort. The earl of Warwick was to compensate the new Lord Clifford to the tune of 1,000 marks, implying his culpability in the late lord's death. Most importantly for lasting peace, the Neville–Percy feud was put into abeyance – at least in theory – as

Salisbury and his sons agreed to forego the fines they were owed by Lord Egremont, while Egremont himself promised to keep the peace towards the Nevilles for ten years, and to go on pilgrimage, presumably to keep him distracted and out of the way. As an enduring legacy of the reconciliation between the warring lords, York, Salisbury and Warwick undertook to found a chantry chapel at St Albans Abbey, where alms and prayers would be given for the souls of all those who had been killed in battle nearby.[18]

The one feud that received no restitution in this arbitration was the one that was perhaps most dangerous to future peace: that between Margaret and York. In the theory and rhetoric of government, there was no place for a queen who was herself part of the political problem. Thus, in the text of the 1458 settlement recorded at the Abbey of St Albans (whose inhabitants had an understandable interest in the resolution to the violence that had unfolded in their streets), Margaret was presented in the traditional queenly role of pacificator.[19] It was reported that Henry had restored harmony, 'at the great instance, heartfelt desire and prayers made to [him] by [his] dearest and best-beloved wife, the queen, who was and is as desirous of the said unity, love and friendship, as it is possible to be'.[20]

But the rhetoric of Henry's regime did not match its actions. Throughout the vexed process set in motion in autumn 1457, Henry had clearly been the chief intercessor for peace, and when he finally returned to London on 16 March to apply pressure to proceedings, he arrived in the guise of a mediator, not an authoritative monarch. According to John Bocking and a London chronicler, Henry processed to St Paul's to pray for peace the morning after his return, and it was Margaret who assumed the more kingly role, arriving into the city later with a noble escort including the duke of Buckingham.[21] The inversion of Henry and Margaret's roles was so complete that during the Love Day procession, it was he who stood apart from the feuding lords, crowned and benevolent, while Margaret was placed among the agitators, reluctantly taking the hand of her chief rival in the cause of friendship.[22]

By now the inverted roles of the royal couple were the topic of open censure among their subjects. In November 1457 one Robert Burnet was indicted for blaming the loss of Henry's French realm on the king's lethargy (he said he slept too much) and for claiming that Queen Margaret was preparing to lead an army overseas.[23] The same autumn a commission in Norfolk inquired into treasonable words spoken against Margaret and Prince Edward, and these were not the first aspersions cast against the queen as a mother. In February 1456 a man had been hanged, drawn and quartered for producing bills that insisted the prince was not Queen Margaret's son but a change-ling placed in the royal bed.[24] Such scurrilous attacks portrayed Henry as inept and easily deceived, and Margaret as manipu-lative and belligerent. As political circumstances encouraged such criticisms, the characterization of Margaret as an overween-ing wife and Henry as a hen-pecked simpleton gained greater currency, and most of the accounts in chronicles produced under Yorkist rule or influenced by their propaganda present the couple in this light. The *Brut* chronicle (written some years after 1461*) noted that around the time of the Love Day the lords in England 'dared not disobey the queen, for she ruled peaceably all that was done about the king, who was a good, simple and innocent man'.[25] Betraying its Yorkist influence more overtly, the *English Chronicle* described how 'the realm of England was out of all good governance... for the king was simple and... the queen with such as were of her affinity ruled the realm as her liked'.[26]

The insinuations against Margaret undermined her carefully fostered self-image as a submissive wife and mother, but were also a tacit criticism of Henry's authority, since the first duty of an adult male was to rule his household. If the king could

---

* As we will see in Chapter 33 (see p. 439), 1461 was to be a significant year for Henry's regime.

not control his wife, he could scarcely be considered a man at all. However, although some of Henry's subjects interpreted Margaret's increasing political dominance as a usurpation of her husband's natural authority, there were others who believed she was forced into this unusual role by Henry's inadequacies as a ruler. The theologian Thomas Gascoigne, who was no supporter of Queen Margaret, admitted that she took on 'many things in England' only after Henry had fallen ill and proven himself incapable.[27]

The image of Margaret walking hand in hand with York revealed the fundamental weakness of Love Day and at the heart of government: Henry himself. Both queen and duke sought to dominate Henry and only he could resolve this conflict, for it was up to him to either promote York or proceed against him as a traitor; to distance himself from Margaret or continue to allow her political dominance. Since satisfying either Margaret or York meant that one would be left aggrieved, Henry instead fell back on the solution he had imposed on his warring uncles as a child: he made them hold hands and promise to be friends. But, just as with Bedford and Gloucester, Margaret and York could not be so easily reconciled to one another. Each knew that the other's ascendancy would entail their own exclusion. As Henry walked slowly ahead of them towards the looming spire of St Paul's, did he feel the jealous eyes of the duke and queen on his robed back?

For all Henry's good intentions the Love Day of 1458 fundamentally changed nothing. The duke of Exeter still resented Warwick's powers on the sea. The duke of Somerset still harboured hatred for his father's killers. York was free but still politically excluded. In the jousts to celebrate the Love Day Margaret sat at Henry's left hand* and as if to demonstrate her

---

* A king traditionally took the right, dominant, side whenever he sat next to his queen. Occasionally his throne might be placed higher than hers.

influence one of the three tournaments was hosted in her palace, at Greenwich.* In the jousts the names that predominated were Margaret's supporters: the duke of Somerset and Anthony Woodville, eldest son of Henry's aunt Jaquetta and Richard Woodville, Lord Rivers.[28]

Immediately after the Love Day celebrations, Henry and Margaret rode to St Albans to spend Easter together – a pointed choice of location given recent events. While there Henry dwelt on his mortality, asking the prior to ensure that after his death, the monks of St Albans would pray for him.[29] It was not unusual for fifteenth-century princes to make preparations for their death far in advance of the event – tombs would be planned, charitable works undertaken, wills written and rewritten – and Henry had already given some consideration to his legacy in his foundations at Eton and Cambridge. But the timing of this discussion is revealing. After five years of ill health, mentally and physically, did Henry contemplate his mortality with more equanimity? After all, he had been king for thirty-six years and he may have felt he was moving towards the end of his mortal achievements. He had – he hoped – resolved the divisions within his kingdom. He had provided the realm with an heir. Unlike most medieval kings, he had no ambition to expand his territories or claim ancient rights by going to war. Instead, his chief policy remained his commitment to peace. Before his life ended, he wanted to spread the harmony and accord of the Love Day to his adversaries overseas. Yet even here the factions still gnawing at the heart of the English body politic would frustrate Henry's good intentions.

In 1458 the time seemed ripe for reconciliation between the Christian kingdoms of western Europe. It was five years since the last bastion of the Christian Byzantine (or Eastern Roman)

---

* The others took place at the Tower of London and what is now Lincoln's Inn Fields.

empire, Constantinople, had fallen to the Ottoman sultan Mehmet II and in August 1458 a new pope, Pius II, was elected with a zealous crusading agenda. He was soon dispatching legates across the continent appealing for Christian princes to put aside their differences and unite to combat the 'unbelievers'.[30] Nine years since the last Anglo-French peace talks, circumstances were also propitious to treat with Charles VII, who had endured sufficient personal and political trouble in recent years to incline him more genuinely towards a lasting peace. In the summer of 1458, Charles was enduring the latest outbreak of a long-running feud between himself and the princes of the royal blood. John, duke of Alençon, had never been fully reconciled to Charles's kingship since becoming embroiled in the *Praguerie* revolt in 1440. As recently as 1456 he had attempted to entice the English government to join him in a conspiracy against Charles that demanded an English invasion of Normandy. Although the bellicose duke of York had been eager to consider Alençon's plot, Henry had rejected it, going so far as to rebuke Alençon's emissaries. 'I am amazed how the princes of France can have such a great desire to displease [their king],' he said. 'But then, I have the same problem in my own country.'[31]

By the summer of 1458, Alençon was on trial for treason but the French king had not been able to bring his unruly son, Dauphin Louis, to heel. Louis and Charles had not seen each other since 1447, although with a certain dysfunctional familiarity they continued to exchange new year gifts until 1451.* In August 1456, fearful that his father might have him arrested or assassinated at any moment, Louis had fled to the rival court of Burgundy, which did little to allay Charles's suspicions.[32] From autumn 1455, political anxieties were exacerbated by Charles's persistent ill health. In 1457 one of his courtiers, the Burgundian chronicler Georges Chastellain, described him as

---

* In January 1449 Louis sent Charles a leopard.

suffering from an 'incurable disease in one leg… that constantly discharged pus',[33] necessitating specially designed stockings and long gowns to conceal his sore and swollen limb.

Henry's eagerness to make peace with his uncle Charles to prevent future invasion was understandable; surprisingly, given Charles's recent naval assault on Sandwich, the concern was entirely mutual. As a king in the twilight of his reign, the possibility of an English invasion gave Charles considerable – albeit undue – anxiety. As he explained in a letter to James II of Scotland in January 1457, Charles was all too aware that 'only six hours of a favourable wind suffice to pass from England into the said country of Normandy'. His resources were stretched thin and the borders he must defend vast:

> At present [he] must daily and continually watch all the sea-coast, on both sides, from Spain to Picardy, which amounts to more than four hundred and fifty leagues of country… The more especially as the English, having held the said country for the space of twenty-two years, or more, know the landing places and all the condition of the country quite as well as those persons do who reside therein… [among whom] they still have some adherents.[34]

In autumn 1458 an embassy was dispatched to Charles's court to negotiate a potential peace, with royal marriages at its heart: Henry offered Prince Edward or kinsmen of the dukes of York and Somerset as potential bridegrooms. Economic imperative dictated that Henry approach Burgundy, one of England's major trading partners, with similar overtures of peace and marriage, so from May 1458 he opened talks with Philippe and Isabella of Burgundy as well. It is hard to imagine that Henry's attitude to this embassy was anything other than half-hearted. He had told Alençon's emissaries in 1456 that

the duke of Burgundy is the man in the world with whom I

would most like to make war, because he abandoned me in my youth, even though he had sworn me an oath, and even though I had done nothing against him. If I live long enough, I will make war against him.[35]

Despite apparently genuine expressions of interest from the courts of both Burgundy and France, nothing came of Henry's peace talks. This was partly the fault of continuing uncertainty surrounding the political situation in England. Foreign princes did not know how much store to set by Henry's overtures for alliance when it was unclear who was really running the country. It seemed all too likely that any treaty agreed with Henry's current regime might be overthrown by another in the near future. During the last serious talks with France, in the mid-1440s, the duke of Suffolk had steered Henry's nebulous peace policy in a clear direction to produce the Treaty of Tours in spite of some opposition. Now Isabella of Burgundy found the political future of England so opaque that she insisted that she would proceed no further 'until she should be certified of the pleasure of the said king *and* duke of York'.[36] Charles, similarly, refused to commit himself until he had gained a more accurate sense of the situation in England, and sent a herald to observe 'the king, the queen and their council'. Regrettably for Henry's ambitions, these continental observers were greeted with a court in chaos: one diplomat observed 'how very few of the lords were at the court of the said king', that there was division between the earl of Warwick and Henry, and that the duke of Exeter was holding the law to ransom after illegally arresting a judge in Westminster.[37] All this was bad enough but, unbeknown to Henry, there was another, more nefarious reason for the failure of the peace negotiations with Burgundy and France in 1458–9: the king of England's ambassador was acting as a double agent.

The divisions in English politics, so deep-rooted in the domestic realm, extended even to foreign policy. Although Henry's preference for a French alliance was well known, the Yorkist lords, and particularly the earl of Warwick, favoured an alliance with Burgundy. Not only was Burgundian territory geographically close to Warwick's base in Calais, but the economic interests of Warwick's chief supporters in Calais and in the southeast of England were deeply enmeshed with Burgundy. Warwick may also have feared that an Anglo-French alliance would diminish the importance of his role as captain of Calais and keeper of the seas, dangerously undercutting his authority. The earl was determined to maintain ties with Philippe of Burgundy, even if it meant defying Henry's interests. By late 1458 he had acquired a secret ally: John Wenlock, Henry's ambassador to Europe and a one-time servant of Margaret of Anjou.

Wenlock's loyalties had been suspect for some time. Although he had once served as Margaret's chamberlain and had been wounded fighting for Henry at St Albans, he had been removed from the queen's household and reprimanded for his partiality towards York as early as 1453. During Wenlock's embassies to France and Burgundy he deliberately obfuscated and deceived in order to prevent a French alliance, as a newsletter sent to Charles VII by an anonymous informant at the Burgundian court reveals.[38] Wenlock informed the Burgundian court of the French terms for peace and promised to reveal to them any discoveries made by Charles's herald during his visit to England. 'Boldly and personally' he assured Isabella and Philippe that 'those of the party of France desired much more to have a truce... than those of the party of England do', and yet when he returned to England he incited panic with misleading reports of imminent French invasion. Little wonder that the French 'much suspected' Wenlock of double-dealing.[39]

And this was not the only arena in which Warwick had stirred up international tension in direct opposition to Henry and Margaret's interests. Since taking up his post at Calais in 1457 he had caused a number of diplomatic incidents. The first took place at four o'clock on the morning of 28 May 1458, when, having been alerted to the presence of a Spanish fleet near Calais, Warwick set out before dawn with a dozen of his own ships to assault the vessels and seize their cargo. After six long hours of hand-to-hand combat, Warwick had seized six Spanish ships, sunk a further half dozen and lost more than 200 of his own men, either captured or killed. It was little enough reward for the effort, but Warwick was determined to repeat the attempt.[40] Within weeks he had attacked a Hanseatic fleet travelling from La Rochelle and seized its cargo of salt. Later that same summer he took on a combined flotilla of Genoese and Spanish ships, capturing all but one of them.[41]

Warwick claimed that such activities were necessary to cover the considerable wages owing to the Calais garrison – which were, as ever, in arrears – but in reality, they amounted to little less than piracy. Warwick seemed to care little that his attacks seriously damaged international relations or that his ambush of the Hanseatic fleet was a flagrant violation of a truce. Following appeals for compensation and restitution from the owners of the vessels involved, Henry was faced with the embarrassing prospect of having to investigate for piracy the very man he had appointed to protect the seas. It was an unnecessary diplomatic mortification at a time when Henry was striving for international cooperation.

Warwick's piracy not only threatened international trade but also raised the spectre of retaliatory attacks on the English coast, and yet his deeds were met with nationalistic delight by the English. A public starved of military success leapt on Warwick's meagre victories and reported them as glorious endeavours such as had not been seen in decades. Patriotic feeling had been offended by government policy towards immigrants, which was consistently deemed overly sympathetic, and Warwick's piracy seemed to offer the necessary corrective.[42]

As Warwick was cast as an English hero, 'as famous a knight as was living', Margaret's reputation was once again under attack.[43] Rumours circulated that she had intrigued with Pierre de Brézé to attack Sandwich. Margaret's French birth could always be invoked as a means to question her patriotism and the fact that Brézé was both Angevin and an old servant of Margaret's father René made their association even more suspect.[44] But it would hardly have served Margaret's purposes in 1457 to collude with Brézé, let alone to plot an attack on her own subjects. The likely origin of such stories was Warwick and his supporters, which would explain how they came to be repeated and reported at the Burgundian court, where the Yorkists had allies. By autumn 1458 it was in Warwick's interest to undermine the credibility of Margaret's regime, for she had started manoeuvring with Henry to remove him from the captaincy of Calais, depriving him of his most important powerbase.[45]

Initially Margaret and Henry probably hoped that by allowing Warwick to serve as a semi-independent prince in Calais, they would distract him from his intriguing with York, and thereby divide the leaders of the Yorkist regime. It had now become evident, however, that giving the earl authority over a vital trading port with easy access to key international courts and a large body of professional soldiers funded at crown expense was deeply unwise. Warwick's piracy provided the necessary excuse to remove him from office and in autumn 1458 he was summoned before a great council in Westminster to answer for his actions.

On Warwick's return to England it became clear how little Henry's Love Day had achieved. The earl arrived a month late to the council, reaching London in early November. He vehemently protested Henry's attempt to remove him from office, claiming that he could not be replaced as captain of Calais by any authority other than parliament's. Since Henry and Margaret had no desire to call a parliament, which would in all likelihood side with York and his allies, the matter was dropped.[46] However, the hot tempers of the royal household and the paranoid suspicions of Warwick's attendants combined to unleash chaos in the court. In the service quarters of the palace, a royal servant stood on the foot of one of Warwick's men, triggering an angry protest. Shouts turned to violence, weapons were drawn and a riot broke out in the corridors of Westminster. Warwick was jostled towards his barge on the Thames as cooks and scullions ran from the kitchens brandishing pestles and spits to strike him and his men down. He departed London with some dispatch, and was soon back behind the sheltering walls and ditches of Calais, from which sanctuary he refused to emerge, claiming that the attack had been premeditated, and that his Lancastrian enemies were behind it. Margaret was sufficiently alarmed by the outbreak of such violent disorder so close to the king that she called for Warwick's arrest but it was too late. Warwick was gone – and he was certainly not in a mood to obey any further royal summons.[47]

The fracas of November 1458 marked a turning point in relations between the Yorkists and Henry's court. While the riot was not a sign of a conspiracy against Warwick, it was evidence of how little authority Henry exhibited. If he could not maintain order within his own palace when he was a matter of feet away, how could he possibly hope to keep the peace of the realm? He might personally have no desire to punish the Yorkists but the atmosphere of his court was toxic to them. When Buckingham and the lords of the great council at Coventry in 1456 had argued that Henry should have punished York rather than pardoned him, they had been right. Henry's indulgence and careless clemency meant violent reprisals went unchecked and any assurances he might give of protection for his nobility, on either side of the political divide, could no longer be trusted.

Even worse, the attack on Warwick hardened the hearts of the Yorkists, finally dispelling any thoughts they might have had of a peaceful negotiation for their political misfortunes. Inside the mighty stone walls of Middleham Castle in November, the earl of Salisbury met with his wife and council and committed himself, once and for all, to York's cause. His days of attempting to court both sides of the political rift were over. It was clear now that Margaret was the dominant force in politics, and as long as she held sway over Henry there was no place for York, Salisbury or Warwick in government. Salisbury's compact with York marked the end of the potential concord Henry had striven for in March 1458. Now it was not a matter of if civil war would break out, but when.[48]

29

'Our mortal and extreme enemies'[1]

Coventry
late June 1459

B y the summer of 1459 the shadow of imminent catastrophe loomed so dark over Henry's kingdom that even the heavens wept blood. According to one chronicle of the time, when a woman in a little town in Bedfordshire hung out her sheets to dry, a shower of blood-red rain stained them, a disturbing reflection of the turbulence of Henry's kingdom.[2] At Coventry, citadel of Lancastrian loyalty, in a stark break with tradition Henry appeared before his great council accompanied by Margaret and their five-year-old son Prince Edward. If any noblemen needed reminding of where their loyalties ought to lie, it was made clear to them: for here was the Holy Trinity of the Lancastrian dynasty, the father, son and matriarch of the line, at the front and centre of political life. It was only eighteen months since Henry's Love Day but the Coventry council had been called with a very different aim in mind. Instead of reconciling the realm, this assembly of noblemen would excise the canker at England's heart.

There were some notable absences: York, Warwick and Salisbury were nowhere to be seen, and neither were their erstwhile allies Viscount Bourchier and his brother Thomas, archbishop of Canterbury. Other men of suspect loyalty were also absent: Warwick's brother George Neville, bishop of Exeter, and William Grey, bishop of Ely, who had negotiated with the Yorkists before the Battle of St Albans.[3] The absence of these lords was no coincidence. The general council had been summoned with the express purpose of proceeding against them for their fomenting of disorder and resistance to Henry's regime.

For months, ever since Warwick's flight from court, tensions had been mounting between the two factions. Both parties had watched each other suspiciously, hesitating to make the first move but nonetheless arming themselves against a coming conflict. In December 1458, 500 pikes and over 500 leaden clubs were ordered for the royal household to protect Henry from 'certain misruled and seditious persons'.[4] By spring 1459 whispers of a Yorkist conspiracy had reached Margaret's ears and she reacted immediately. Weapons were stockpiled at Kenilworth: 3,000 bows and sheaves of arrows and three serpentines powerful enough to turn castle walls to rubble. In April 1459 Henry put his signature to writs summoning men to gather, 'defensibly arrayed' in Leicester on 10 May. After yet another bout of violent unrest in London had been suppressed, Henry and his court withdrew once again to the sanctuary of the Midlands. Margaret, meanwhile, gathered her own forces in her son's name, handing out livery with the prince's swan symbol emblazoned on it.[5]

Against such a background, it is little wonder that the Yorkists refused to attend the general council at Coventry in June. This may have been Margaret's intention all along. Although the presence of the Yorkists at Coventry would have made it easier to detain and perhaps arrest them, there was the potential danger that Henry would again be moved to mercy by their personal appeals. He had promised in the great council of 1456 that he would no longer allow York and other lawbreakers to go unpunished, but in June 1459 there was considerable rumour and anxiety with little concrete evidence of Yorkist treason. By defying Henry's summons, York and his allies legitimized the court's suspicions of treason and enabled their Lancastrian enemies to move against them. If this was the outcome that Margaret intended to bring about, however, she would soon have cause to regret it.

Messages were soon flying between the heartlands of Yorkist influence. In London in July, York's untiring supporter Sir William Oldhall illicitly dispatched warnings to Warwick about the proceedings of the great council. By August the marcher town of Shrewsbury had received a mysterious message from its lord, the duke of York, hinting at a plot. In the sand dunes and ditches of Calais, 600 garrison soldiers were readied to cross the Channel in the ships of Warwick's mighty navy. At Middleham Castle, the Yorkshire monument to Neville authority, preparations were directed by Alice Montague, countess of Salisbury, herself. Alice was an heiress in her own right with considerable estates under her command, and she risked them all now to preserve her family's honour. In September the countess waved farewell to her husband and 5,000 of their tenants and retainers, while another armed host set out from Ludlow Castle. The mistress of Ludlow, Cecily Neville, duchess of York, held tightly to her younger children as she watched her two eldest sons, the earls of March and Rutland, ride out with their father. As these three armies marched north, south and east across England it soon became clear that their target was the Midlands. They were moving to 'surprise' Henry at Kenilworth Castle, though whether their purpose was to capture and rule through him or to usurp him entirely was unclear.[6]

It was vital that Henry and Margaret prevent these three forces from converging. Panicked orders were sent out to trusted commanders to shadow the Yorkist armies and block their paths. Henry Beaufort, duke of Somerset, was dispatched to tail Warwick's small mobile army as he travelled from the south coast, via London and Warwick Castle. While Margaret guarded Prince Edward at Eccleshall in Staffordshire, Henry personally led a sizeable force north from Kenilworth, intending to bar the progress of Salisbury's enormous Yorkshire host. By taking possession of Nottingham Castle, Henry seized control of the crossing of the River Trent, forcing Salisbury to divert west towards the marches and the security of York's heartland.[7]

But Salisbury's westward progress would lead him directly into the path of another royal army, close to Staffordshire's border with Shropshire. This army was under the direction of the Midlands nobleman James, Lord Audley, a veteran of the French wars, now in his sixty-first year. He had not seen combat since 1431 but he had the benefit of having a substantial local force to call upon, among whom some had received the swan livery of Prince Edward from Margaret that summer. Audley also had a personal motive for seizing Salisbury, since the pair of them had clashed in a property dispute.

On the morning of 23 September 1459, Audley's army of around 10,000 men were marching east along the road from Market Drayton when their scouts encountered the earl of Salisbury's advance guard. Lord Audley swiftly prepared for battle, lining his force of mounted cavalry and foot soldiers along a mile (1.6 km) of barren heath on a shallow ridge, a stream called Hempmill Brook protecting their front line. Having been dammed at the mill, in places this stream was deceptively deep.[8]

By the time Salisbury emerged from a wood straddling the road from Newcastle-under-Lyme, it was clear that the odds were against him. Not only were his forces outnumbered at least two to one by Audley's, but there was another Lancastrian army only 10 miles (16 km) away at Eccleshall. If he were to stand any chance of victory, he needed to force Audley to attack before the second Lancastrian army arrived. Taking advantage of the woodland to protect his left flank, Salisbury used some old English tricks learnt in the wars with France to create a strong defensive position. The right flank of his army was protected by a horse-wall such as John of Bedford had used at Verneuil, with wagons and horses tied together. Archers' stakes were driven hastily into the earth in front of the men, where the ground sloped down towards the road and brook below. To the rear, a trench was dug. Having made what preparations he could in the time available, Salisbury then feigned a retreat, harnessing the draught-horses to his wagons as if turning back from the fight.

With the command to prevent Salisbury's flight ringing in his ears, Audley ordered his men to mount their horses and pursue the fleeing enemy. As the Lancastrians forded Hempmill Brook their forces were strung out, some in the water, some already climbing the lower reaches of the slopes beneath Salisbury's army, others still preparing to cross. It was then that Salisbury's forces attacked. A storm of arrows fell on Audley's men. The Lancastrians fell back in confusion, horses stumbling and throwing their heavily armoured riders into the deep water. Audley pulled his men back, out of bowshot, to regroup. After a second concerted cavalry assault ended in failure he sent forward his infantry and desperate hand-to-hand fighting ensued on the barren slopes of Blore Heath. It was in this murderous melee that Lord Audley fell, hacked down by Salisbury's men.

Seeing their commander dead and the battle turning against them, the Lancastrian cavalry took flight. Panic set in among the infantry. As they too fled back across the brook and on to the heath beyond, Salisbury's men fell upon on them. On the banks of the River Tern, the Lancastrians were cut down in such large numbers that the area became known as 'Deadman's Den'. As many as 2,000 men lost their lives in the Battle of Blore Heath, a death toll that appalled the Lancastrians as much as it raised Yorkist morale. Salisbury rode away in triumph, bearing the heartening news of their victory to York and Warwick.

★

Despite Audley's attempted interception and a near-miss between Warwick's forces and Somerset's at Coleshill, near Coventry, all three of the Yorkist lords made it safely to their rendezvous in the marches at Worcester. Some of the other Neville offspring were not so fortunate: John and Thomas, Warwick's younger brothers, overreached themselves riding down fleeing Lancastrians at Blore Heath and were taken prisoner. They now languished in Chester Castle. For the Yorkists, these events hardened their resolve. They had been disappointed in their attempt to take Henry by surprise at Kenilworth and they now used their customary strategy of sending out bills, publicly presenting their grievances as faithful lords denied access to their sovereign. Beneath the ancient arches of Worcester Cathedral, the three kinsmen swore a compact, binding it with a solemn oath, signatures and by sharing holy communion. This oath was sent to Henry and disseminated 'at large' as 'proof of the truth and duty that, God knoweth, we bear to your said estate'. In reality, however, this ritual forged a brotherhood of arms. Whatever the Yorkist lords faced next, they would endure it together.[9]

Their loyalty to each other was immediately tested. To try to bring the rebel armies to heel without further bloodshed, Henry offered a pardon for all those in arms against him, except those who had fought at Blore Heath. In other words, Warwick and York could save themselves if they gave up Salisbury. Henry's offer of a pardon broke the promise he had made at the Coventry council in 1456 (that he would properly punish York for raising arms against him in the future), but if it had succeeded in ending the Yorkist rising, his lords would doubtless have overlooked such leniency. Unfortunately York and Warwick could not be turned. Henry's pardon went ignored. Instead, the Yorkists sent Henry a copy of their Worcester oath and an appeal to come before him to put their side of events. The Yorkists claimed they had assembled armies only to protect themselves and that although they were being 'proclaimed and defamed in our name unrightfully, unlawfully, and... untruly' they had 'forborne and avoided all things that might serve to the effusion of Christian blood' – a claim that in the wake of the 2,000 dead at Blore Heath seems disingenuous.[10] They insisted that they were still the king's loyal subjects and would remain so unto death, but their expressions of fidelity rang false when they refused a royal pardon.[11]

The royal faction now began to demonstrate its frustration with the Yorkists. On 9 October Warwick was finally dismissed as captain of Calais and replaced by Henry Beaufort, duke of Somerset. The following day, King Henry sent out summonses for his first parliament in four years. The Yorkist lords were not among those summoned, a clear indication that the proceedings begun in the summer great council would now be completed. The policy of reconciliation was abandoned: the Yorkists would henceforth be treated as traitors. As Henry's royal army circled around towards Worcester, chasing the Yorkist lords back towards Ludlow Castle, York's principal seat, it harried the local area. The violent alternative to submission was plain.

In the second week of October 1459 the Yorkists assembled their armies at Ludford Bridge to make their stand. This stone bridge was the southern entrance point into the town of Ludlow. Above it, the town climbed steadily up the hillside, the sky-line dominated by the vast complex of buildings that made up Ludlow Castle. Cecily, duchess of York, and her younger sons and daughters were inside the keep at the heart of the fortress, while her two eldest sons, the teenaged earls of March and Rutland, stood at their father's side in the encampment below.[12] On the south side of Ludford Bridge, the Yorkist lords took up their positions, protecting their front ranks with a ditch and sharpened stakes driven into the earth. York's cannons were set up on carts in front of the troops.[13]

Henry and his men advanced towards this strongly defended position through a landscape of swollen rivers. Royal heralds still loudly pronounced the promise of pardon, even as the royal banners fluttered above Henry's men, reminding the rebel soldiers that any subject who remained in armed defiance against him would be considered a traitor. Although Henry must have been weary after a month on campaign, he could take heart from the strength of the royal forces. The combined Yorkist armies – Welshmen, northern retainers and Calais soldiers – were heavily outnumbered, perhaps by as much as three to one. Yet York, Warwick and Salisbury continued to hold their ground.[14]

By the time Henry's forces had picked their way through the narrow roads and boggy fields to reach Ludford Bridge, the sun was dipping behind the crenellated shadows of Ludlow Castle. It was Friday 12 October, the vigil of St Edward the Confessor and the eve of Prince Edward's sixth birthday. As Henry's men pitched their tents and placed their divisions beneath the prominently displayed royal banners, there was a shocking barrage of sound: the Yorkist guns had fired on the royal encampment. The Yorkist lords had lied to their men, spreading the rumour that Henry was dead and that therefore their actions were not treasonable. The militarily experienced Buckingham, who was with Henry at Ludford Bridge, may have encouraged Henry to call their enemy's bluff, for the king appeared in front of his troops on horseback, the last rays of daylight glinting on his armour. This decisive action had an almost immediate effect.[15]

That night, under cover of darkness, the Calais garrison abandoned their commanders and defected to Henry's camp. The commander of the Calais regiment, Andrew Trollope, appealed for a pardon on the garrison's behalf, explaining that they had been deceived into their treasonable activity. Warwick had told them that they were crossing the Channel in the service of the king and they had been appalled to find themselves instead opposing Henry in open battle. Trollope had served in France in 1443 and, like many of the Calais garrison, he had a long history of loyalty to the Beaufort family, so Henry readily accepted his submission, pardoning the men in honour of St Edward the Confessor. It seemed Henry's favourite saint was smiling on his endeavours. That night, all was quiet.[16]

But the next morning, as Henry and his forces rose to prepare for battle, they heard confusion and dismay in the Yorkist ranks. During the night, pretending that they were seeking refreshment in the town, the Yorkist lords had fled, leaving their soldiers to cover their departure. By the time Henry's men realized the deception, it was too late. The royal forces never caught up with the Yorkists, who had divided into two fleeing parties: York and his second son, Edmund, earl of Rutland, tore west across Wales, destroying bridges as they went, and eventually reaching the safety of Ireland; while Warwick, Salisbury and York's heir, the seventeen-year-old Edward, earl of March, made for Devon. They had a harder time of it, relying on the support of a local knight called John Dynham, and his mother, to shelter them and provide them with the ship necessary to ferry them across the Channel. They did not reach Calais until 2 November.[17]

With no Yorkist traitors to fight, Henry's royal forces vented their frustrated bloodlust in an orgy of drunken pillaging in the town. The soldiers rampaged through the streets, smashing open barrels of wine until they were wading through it, up to their ankles, to rob the local residents. Rich furnishings, clothes and precious plate were torn from the citizens' anxious hands and the pillage that ensued was such that one chronicler claimed the town was 'robbed to the bare walls'. Perhaps some of the royal soldiers remembered, or had even witnessed, the devastation wrought by York's men after the Battle of St Albans. Now they took their revenge on the Yorkist town of Ludlow.

Henry would hardly have tolerated such scenes of violence and theft, and it is likely that he was steered away from them. The loyal lords in attendance upon him were more experienced in the ways of warfare and could turn a blind eye to the destruction wrought by their disappointed troops. Perhaps Henry was escorted to Ludlow Castle, or perhaps he remained encamped by Ludford Bridge, but what *is* known for certain is that, as the pillaging of the town played out, Cecily was brought through the wine-drenched streets to kneel before her king and crave pardon. The scene in which the duchess of York holds her children's hands as she bravely faces down the drunken Lancastrians in Ludlow marketplace – beloved of popular folklore and later writers – does not appear in contemporary sources. Only the *English Chronicle* (written under Yorkist rule and heavily influenced by their propaganda) suggests that Cecily was 'unmanly and cruelly... treated and spoiled'.[18] A more even-handed chronicler, whose work survives as *Gregory's Chronicle*, admits the sack of Cecily's home town but goes on to relate how Henry 'full humbly granted her grace', showing his customary capacity for compassion and forgiveness. Had Henry's commanders allowed their men to inflict violence on a woman of Cecily's station, regardless of her husband's political choices, it would have been an outrage that neither Henry nor his lords could permit. But it does not follow that Cecily and her children did not feel threatened, nor that they were unaware of the very real danger they could fall into if Henry had been a less merciful monarch.

Having accepted Cecily's appeal for royal grace, Henry sent her into the keeping of her sister Anne, duchess of Buckingham, a woman of unquestioned loyalty to the royal family but apparently one who was not very sympathetic to her sister's situation. Cecily 'was kept full straight and [suffered] many a great rebuke' under Anne's acerbic hospitality.[19] But probably, under the circumstances, Cecily realized she had escaped lightly. Her husband's flight from the field had, in all likelihood, saved him and his sons from a brutal settling of scores by the Lancastrians; and Henry's kind-heartedness meant her life and livelihood – and those of her youngest children – were safeguarded.[20]

This royal policy of mercy was not extended to Cecily's rebellious kin. In the parliament that Henry summoned to Coventry in November 1459 the leading Yorkists were summarily punished. By raising arms against their king for the third time in four years, they had proven themselves incorrigible. Margaret, the duke of Somerset, the earls of Wiltshire and Shrewsbury, and even the once-moderate Bishop Waynflete and duke of Buckingham all agreed that it was time to take serious action against the rebels. They must not only be condemned, but attainted of treason.

The penalty of attainder had not been used on the scale it was in 1459 since the closing years of Richard II's reign in the last century. It was the most serious penalty in common law for it not only forfeited the traitor's possessions to the crown, it also tainted their entire bloodline, preventing any future generation from inheriting their title or estate.[21] The sole proviso was that a wife or widow's personal inheritance and jointure (the estate she held jointly with her husband) would be safeguarded, to ensure that she was not adversely affected by her husband's treason. Attainder was an extreme penalty, but given the consistency of Yorkist rebellion and defiance, the Lords in parliament in 1459 felt it was justified.[22]

Henry himself, despite everything, took some convincing to follow the path of attainder. There is a hint of the frustration Margaret and her supporters must have felt at Henry's limitless magnanimity in the parliamentary roll, which recites York's wickedness, ending with a note that 'even though your grace chooses not to take displeasure in this; yet your liege people are well aware of his devious... false and traitorous schemes'.[23]

The struggle to persuade Henry to attaint York and his allies, and to ensure that this unpopular punishment was seen to be justified by his English subjects at large, is preserved in two long texts that survive describing the debates about how to treat the Yorkists. One, known as *Somnium Vigilantis*, was produced hastily before parliament met, perhaps by Margaret's trusted chancellor Laurence Boothe. Structured as a debate between two opposing voices – one arguing for attainder of the Yorkists and the other for their pardon – it bears considerable similarity to a work copied in the chronicle of the abbot of St Albans. There, the argument takes place between Justice and Mercy – a representation in literary Latin of the competing forces in Henry's mind. Justice demands the Yorkists be punished, since they have proven themselves incorrigible and to let them go free would undermine security and set a dangerous precedent. It might seem harsh, Justice admits, but such treatment could be justified by ample examples from ancient classical and Christian precedent. Mercy, however, advises that rulers are more likely to win the loyalty of their enemies by kindness than hostility, again giving examples from biblical and classical works. Henry was inclined to side with Mercy, but eventually at the fervent desire of the Lords and Commons he allowed Justice to hold sway, and for the Yorkists to be attainted. However, he insisted that he be allowed the leeway to offer pardons to the attainted in the future if they demonstrated sincere remorse for their actions. A proviso was inserted into the bill to this effect, a testament to Henry's almost unshakeable belief in redemption.[24]

In all, twenty-six men were attainted of treason, including, of course, York, Salisbury and Warwick. The attainder extended also to York's sons the earls of March and Rutland, and the noblemen who had supported them in the field, including two more of Salisbury's sons, the unfortunate Sir John and Sir Thomas Neville captured after Blore Heath. John de la Pole, the only child of the late duke of Suffolk and now married to York's daughter Elizabeth, had his title degraded from duke to earl. As his father had won his high rank by loyal service to Henry and Margaret, the royal family probably wanted to remind the young Suffolk that he should not take his status for granted.

In a break from convention, one woman was also attainted: Alice, countess of Salisbury. It seems that, unlike her sister-in-law Cecily, Alice was not inclined to submit to Henry's grace. She may already have fled to Ireland, as she was certainly hiding out with York in spring 1460.[25] The fact that Alice was, unlike Cecily, a considerable heiress in her own right is likely also to have been a factor in the government's decision to attaint her. Cecily was the eighteenth child in a brood of more than twenty, whereas Alice was the sole heir to the vast Montagu fortune. Between them, she and Salisbury could count on £3,000 of annual income from their estates. To allow an unrepentant plotter access to such vast resources – with every likelihood that she would spend them on aiding and abetting her rebellious family in exile – was deemed unacceptable. With such widespread punishment meted out it is little wonder the Coventry parliament of November 1459 became known as the 'Parliament of Devils'.[26]

The impoverished government was no doubt delighted at the prospect of the vast sums forfeited by the Yorkists being funnelled into the exchequer. Everything possible was done to ensure royal control over the resources generated. Only a few of the estates forfeited by the Yorkists were regranted to royal supporters – the arch-loyalists Eleanor, duchess of Somerset, and John, Lord Dudley were among these favoured individuals – and a few life annuities went as rewards to others. Henry's old nurses and his stepfather, Owen Tudor, received such grants. However, the vast majority of the estates were assigned to royally appointed stewards – faithful courtiers and members of the royal household – who were appointed for life. On 1 December 1459, the master of the king's ordnance was ordered to survey the Neville and York castles and towns, ensuring that their forts were kept in good repair for royal use.[27]

On the last day of the parliament, 11 December, every lord and bishop in attendance took an oath of loyalty not only to Henry, but to Margaret and Prince Edward as well, swearing on the gospels and both signing and sealing the promise that 'if God in his infinite power takes [Henry] from this transitory life while I am still living, then I shall take and accept my said dread lord Prince Edward, your said first-born son, for my sovereign lord'.[28]

Insinuations about Edward's parentage and criticism of Margaret's actions had clearly grown loud enough that a public display of fealty to the whole family was felt necessary to bolster the dynasty's security. Perhaps it was also in Margaret's mind to reassure the body politic that although Henry was forgiving to the point of political folly, he would one day be succeeded by a

boy growing up in a different mould. Prince Edward was almost
seven, old enough to leave the care of nurses and governesses
and 'be committed to the rules and teachings of men wise and
strenuous'.[29] He must have been demonstrating the first sparks
of personality, one that promised to be as different from his
father's as Henry VI was from Henry V.

Despite this public assertion of commitment to the Lancastrian
regime, Henry and especially Margaret could not rest easy. As
long as York and his allies were alive and in exile, rather than
crushed in battle and dead, the threat of their return was ever-
present. The royal family had only delayed the inevitable.

30

'The test of the sword'[1]

Sandwich
26 June 1460

The party that disembarked at Sandwich just after midsummer had all the appearance of a crusader force. It came with the pope's representative in its midst, a papal banner as its battle standard and was welcomed into port by the head of the English church, Thomas Bourchier, archbishop of Canterbury. Its army – a force of 20,000, carried in ships that had been liberated from royal control only months earlier – was met with zealous acclaim by the people of Kent. Off these ships, in the bright midsummer sunshine, stepped three men whom locals greeted as homecoming heroes: the aged earl of Salisbury; his tall, handsome young nephew Edward, earl of March; and the people's champion, the earl of Warwick. Behind the archbishop's cross, the three men were cheered all the way from Calais, through Kent and on to London. A stream of propagandist bills and manifestos had preceded them, so the English commons knew very well what the trio stood for. They came, they insisted, for the good of king and country: 'For the tender love that we [have] unto the commonweal and prosperity of this realm and... to the king's estate.' Henry was surrounded, claimed the earls, by deceivers and traitors who kept him from his true advisers, who impoverished him and his realm, had cost him his territories in France and threatened now to bring down the whole government with their excessive taxation and tyranny. 'Murders, robberies, perjuries and extortions' were rife, and the law bought and sold. Now the king's self-proclaimed most loyal and worthy lords were returning to reform these wrongs once and for all. It was a far from novel rallying cry – indeed, one of the Yorkist bills was simply a reissue of the Kentishmen's demands from Cade's revolt a decade earlier – but its familiarity had cost it none of its popularity.[2]

Alarmingly for the royal family, as Salisbury, March, Warwick and their retinue swept from the narrow streets of Sandwich towards London, they trailed in their wake one or two more scurrilous rumours. Whispers were now widely circulating about Prince Edward's parentage. Since Margaret of Anjou was known to transgress acceptable female behaviour as a wife, usurping the natural authority of her cowed husband, it was an easy leap to claim that she asserted her dominance by cuckolding Henry also. The earl of Warwick had told the papal legate Francesco Coppini that 'the royal power is in the hands of [Henry's] wife and those who defile the King's chamber'[3] and Warwick may also have been the source for the rumours repeated on both sides of the Channel that Prince Edward was not the king's true child but 'a bastard got in adultery'.[4] It was even reported by newsletters and ambassadors in territory belonging to Warwick's ally Philippe of Burgundy that in order to maintain her grip on power Margaret planned to force Henry to abdicate and install her changeling son as king in his place.[5] It is little surprise that alongside the public ballads proclaiming Yorkist loyalty and concern for the commonweal, more slanderous works were secretly disseminated, including one tacked to the gates of Canterbury that likened contemporary England to the realm of Satan, where 'false heirs [were] fostered'.[6]

Who was taking the king's place in the queen's bed, according to this smear campaign? Likely the same men now lambasted in Yorkist manifestos for embezzling hard-working commoners' coin, overseeing a reign of tyranny and for turning the king's heart against York 'to the intent of our destruction... and that they might have our livelihood and goods'.[7] Chief among these alleged tyrants was the handsome young James Butler, earl of Wiltshire, a committed Lancastrian who distinguished himself by fleeing (often disguised) from every single battle in which he fought, allegedly because he feared marring his good looks with scars.[8] More pertinently, Wiltshire was treasurer in 1460 and therefore closely associated with the government's financial misconduct. Two other noble counsellors were singled out by the Yorkist bills as their 'mortal and extreme enemies':[9] the ex-treasurer, John Talbot, earl of Shrewsbury,* and Henry and Margaret's faithful councillor Viscount John Beaumont.

Rumours of Margaret's infidelity are not corroborated by any contemporary source, but through repetition they took on something of the veneer of truth, dangerously undermining the image that Margaret had carefully cultivated for the past four years: that the trinity of the royal family must be the focus of English loyalty; that all three of them were the hope of the nation. Yorkist rumour-mongering was attacking not merely the present basis of Lancastrian power, but – by asserting Edward's illegitimacy and Margaret's self-interested conspiracy – its future too. This was an altogether murkier allegation; if Prince Edward was not the future of the crown, the clear implication was that someone else might rightfully take his place. In the wake of the last decade of increasingly bloody campaigning, there was only one dynastically legitimate alternative: the duke of York. A newsletter circulating in Bruges in July 1460 suggested that the English would soon 'pass over the king's son, as they are beginning already to say that he is not the king's son'.[10] It was

---

* Namesake son of the hero of the French wars who had died at Castillon.

becoming clear that for all their customary bluster about being true liegemen of the king, this feted Yorkist trio had not come from Calais to save Henry and the commonweal. They had come to seize the throne.

In the seven months since the 'Parliament of Devils', the royal family had singularly failed to bring the Yorkist lords to heel. Henry and Margaret did not even know where the anticipated Yorkist invasion would come from: would York sail from Ireland to Wales or to northwestern England? Would Warwick land his Calais garrison on the south coast, or sail to the northeast to link up with Salisbury's following there? A flurry of commissions went out to lords and sheriffs across the country to root out insurrection. At Newbury, the duke of York's tenants made the mistake of inciting resistance to the earl of Wiltshire's tax collector and for their rabble-rousing the protesters were subjected to stringent proceedings under Wiltshire and Lords Scales and Hungerford and Moleyns: a number of those involved were hanged and seventy-five others imprisoned in Wallingford Castle. Meanwhile, the royal family pursued its customary strategy and retreated to the safety of the Midlands. A long caravan of wagons loaded with armaments and guns wound its way from the stores of the Tower of London to Kenilworth Castle, where Henry was now based.[11]

In Ireland, York rested on his laurels, trusting to more than a decade of carefully fostered loyalties and national self-interest to protect him. A royal attempt to appoint the earl of Wiltshire as lieutenant of Ireland in his place failed almost as soon as it was conceived. When the earl's agent arrived to deliver an order for York's arrest he was seized and executed by locals. York purchased military and financial support by allowing the Irish parliament concessions that undermined the control of the English crown.[12]

Deprived of control in Ireland, Henry's government had to be content with stamping their authority on Wales instead. It was suspected that York's invasion would make landfall at his castle of Denbigh, which had easy access to the sea, so the attainted duke's fortress was transferred to the control of Henry's half-brother Jasper Tudor, earl of Pembroke.[13]

An attempt to forcibly remove Warwick from Calais by appointing Henry Beaufort, duke of Somerset, as captain was similarly doomed, although Somerset showed characteristic pugnacity in the attempt. Having been appointed on 9 October 1459, Somerset crossed the Channel with 1,000 men and the support of such experienced Calais commanders as Andrew Trollope (who had defected from Warwick's Calais garrison to Henry's forces at Ludlow), the treasurer of Calais Sir Gervase Clifton, and Richard Woodville, Lord Rivers. They enjoyed initial success when the neighbouring fortresses of Guisnes and Hammes came over to the Lancastrian cause, and there were also desertions to their armies from Calais and Rysbank Tower. However, attempts to starve Warwick into submission by blockading Calais only served to make the government unpopular with the merchants of the Staple on both sides of the Channel, and a steady drift of money and men from Kent bolstered Warwick's cause.[14]

Somerset's early successes were soon reversed, and the dawn of 1460 heralded a wave of humiliating defeats for the Lancastrian cause at the hands of Warwick's navy. A Lancastrian relief force under Lord Rivers and his son, Anthony Woodville, docked at Sandwich en route to Guisnes. While Rivers and Woodville slept, Warwick's ally John Dynham attacked with 800 men and seized the port, making off with the Lancastrian ships and taking Rivers, Woodville and Rivers's wife Jaquetta of Luxembourg captive. When Rivers and his family docked at Calais they were treated to a display of scornful mockery from the Yorkist lords, as a London-based correspondent reported in a letter to his brother:

My Lord of Salisbury berated [Rivers], calling him knave's son, that he should be so rude to call him and these other lords

traitors... And my Lord of Warwick berated him, and said that
his father was but a squire, and brought up with King Henry
V, and himself made by marriage... And my Lord of March
berated him and... Sir Antony... in like wise.[15]

This public humiliation of Henry's commanders was bad enough,
but worse was to come. With the captured ships Warwick assembled a war fleet, sailing in complete safety from Calais to Ireland
for a meeting with York and back again. On his return he brought
his mother, Alice, countess of Salisbury, to Calais for her security.
All this despite the fact that the same seas were being patrolled
by a force of more than 3,000 men under the command of the
duke of Exeter. Disturbed by the size of Warwick's navy and by
the questionable loyalties of his own men, Exeter chose to put
into port at Dartmouth rather than fight the traitors.

Meanwhile, an army under the command of Warwick's deputy and uncle Lord Fauconberg defeated Somerset's forces in
a decisive battle at Newnham Bridge,* near Guisnes. In June,
Fauconberg led another armed raid to finally wrest control of
Sandwich from the crown, again making off with a Lancastrian
commander, Osbert Mundeford, who was dragged to the sands
beneath Rysbank Tower and beheaded. With ports on both sides
of the Channel now firmly under Yorkist control, Salisbury, March
and Warwick crossed the Channel without any impediment on
26 June 1460.[16]

On learning that the Yorkists had finally returned and had
taken the most direct route from Sandwich to London, Henry
sent orders to the governing body of the capital not to admit
them. In the past, such orders had been decisive – in 1452 the
closed gates of London had thwarted York's schemes and forced
him to take a circuitous route to eventual defeat at Dartford.
However, Henry had reckoned without the Londoners' impulse

---

* This coastal defence, called Fort Nieulay by the French, was rebuilt in
the seventeenth century.

for self-preservation. The Yorkists arrived with substantial artillery support, which played on the fears of the nervous freemen of London. Moreover, the presence of the papal legate Coppini and Archbishop Thomas Bourchier lent the Yorkist cause credibility. Coppini and Bourchier appealed to the citizens to let the lords in, insisting that they intended no harm to the city and just wanted to pass through. If these representatives of the churches of Rome and England could not be trusted, then who could be? The Londoners opened their gates, but there was a price. The mayor and aldermen of London insisted that the Yorkist earls make a public declaration of their loyalty to Henry at St Paul's, which they duly did on 2 July. Word of this declaration reached Henry's court in the Midlands only shortly before a missive arrived from the papal legate himself.[17]

Francesco Coppini was well known to Henry, as he was to the citizens of London, since he had spent a considerable proportion of the past eighteen months in England, trying to negotiate English aid for Pope Pius II's planned crusade to reconquer Constantinople. That last bastion of the Christian Roman empire had fallen to the Muslim Ottoman empire in 1453. Coppini recognized that in order to gain English support in the crusade, he had first to mediate peace between Henry's court and the Yorkists: 'A kingdom divided against itself,' he wrote to Henry, quoting the gospel of St Matthew, 'cannot stand.'[18] However, Coppini revealed himself not to be the most impartial of mediators. According to the *Register* of John Whethamstede, abbot of St Albans, what Coppini lacked in stature – he was 'very little' – he more than made up for in loquacity and verve for self-promotion. 'Eloquence flowed from his lips like drops of dew.'[19] Perhaps recognizing a kindred spirit in the earl of Warwick, Coppini had swallowed whole the Yorkist tales of mistreatment at the hands of traitorous royal advisers. Following the attainder of the Yorkist lords, he had fled to the continent in Warwick's wake, protesting that the royal court had spurned his efforts at peacemaking.[20]

When Coppini returned to England, it was in the heart of the Yorkist army, having raised the papal standard for their cause and proclaimed that their opponents were 'enemies of the Faith' – in short, that Henry's supporters were little less than heretics. For good measure, he also excommunicated the lords who opposed the Yorkist cause: the earls of Wiltshire and Shrewsbury and Viscount Beaumont. This, along with other religious sanctions he imposed in Warwick's favour, went far beyond his remit as papal legate.[21]

Coppini wrote to Henry from within the Yorkist army on 4 July, apologizing for sending a letter rather than appealing to him in person, but he feared that his life was in danger because his loyalties were considered 'suspect' – as well they might be. However, whatever Coppini's failings as a mediator, there was no criticizing his rhetoric. His letter to Henry played on the king's long-held anxiety to avoid war. It was down to Henry alone, Coppini claimed, 'to prevent so much bloodshed, now so imminent. You can prevent this if you will and if you do not you will be guilty in the sight of God in that awful day of judgement.'[22] To further drum home his message, Coppini's letter was sent in copy to the pope and to Queen Margaret and was read publicly at St Paul's Cross in London.

Despite Coppini's professed intentions, and despite Henry's reluctance, battle was inevitable. The Yorkists could repeat all they wanted that they had brought their armies for their own protection and their only wish was to gain access to Henry's presence unimpeded, but the speed and decisiveness of their march belied any pacific intention. The earl of Warwick had already explained his purposes to Coppini while they sheltered together in Calais. 'Our king is a dolt and a fool,' he said, 'who is ruled instead of ruling. The royal power is in the hands of his wife and those who defile the king's chamber.' This situation had gone on long enough. Warwick and his allies intended to 'put our fortunes to the test of the sword. If God gives us the victory, we shall drive our foes from the king's side and ourselves govern the kingdom. The king will retain only the bare name of sovereign.'[23]

In other words, a test of strength in battle was always part of the Yorkist plan. And this time the intention was not merely to drive out their enemies from the royal chamber, but to use Henry as a puppet for a new Yorkist regime.

On 5 July the Yorkist army left London in two columns: a smaller force under Lord Fauconberg, and a larger one under the earls of March and Warwick. The earl of Salisbury remained behind to deal with lingering Lancastrian resistance. A few Lancastrian lords had retreated into the Tower, from which they bombarded the city. The report ran in London that the royal court intended to escape east to the Isle of Ely, and perhaps thence through the Fenlands to the coast. The Yorkist forces divided to block that path. In fact Henry and his family still lingered in the Midlands, for by early July it was still unclear if the Yorkist army advancing from London was the only one they would have to face. York himself had not made an appearance, and his approach was still watched for anxiously in Wales. There were rumours that the duke had allied with James II of Scotland. Since the Nevilles were unlikely to welcome Scottish incursions into their border territories, such fears were probably misplaced but in his north Midlands heartland, Henry and his army were well positioned to respond to military threats from any corner of the realm.[24]

When news arrived of the rapid advance of the two columns moving out of London Henry prepared to lead his own army out to face them. At Coventry, he bade farewell to Margaret and their son, uncertain if they would be reunited. 'He kissed her and blessed the prince and commanded [Margaret] that she should not come unto him until he sent a special token unto her that no man knew but the king and she.'[25] This secret token suggests that royal suspicion about the Yorkists' true intentions was very much alive. It seems unlikely that such a stratagem was dreamed up by the guileless Henry – it is far more probable that Margaret already foresaw an outcome in which Henry fell into Yorkist hands once more and was ruled by Warwick rather than his queen. Warwick had assured Coppini that he intended to treat Henry as a loyal liegeman should – essentially, that he would not kill or mistreat him – but considering the ruthlessness with which the earl had assassinated his enemies at St Albans, Margaret was understandably suspicious. Who was to say Warwick did not already have a scheme to usurp the throne for his master, the duke of York? The best insurance policy for the Lancastrian dynasty in that event was to keep the family apart. Thus, if Henry was captured but Prince Edward was not, the Lancastrian dynasty would still have a male figurehead to lead, and legitimize, their resistance to the Yorkists.[26]

Henry thus rode out of Coventry at the head of his forces, surrounded by old allies, including his faithful duke of Buckingham and Viscount Beaumont, while Margaret, Prince Edward and a diminished royal household remained in Coventry to await the outcome of the battle.

Northampton
10 July 1460

Driving rain lashed the guylines and finials of the royal encampment, a tented fortress that had been established in a loop of the River Nene outside Northampton. It was not far from the old medieval convent of Delapré Abbey, but the walk between there and the camp was a boggy and waterlogged one. Unseasonably foul weather had swollen the riverbanks and turned the open fields into a quagmire. From inside the royal camp Henry could see the hill where the Yorkists had drawn up their forces – and perhaps, through the torrential rain, even the shadowy figures of Warwick, March and Fauconberg looking down on their enemies. The royal camp was strongly defended and armed, with a ditch and maze of stakes encircling it. In the artillery park cannon had been set up, although the heavy rain was doing its best to render them useless.[27]

For all the apparent strength of the royal position, Henry's army was outnumbered and had already been weakened by some notable desertions. The earl of Wiltshire had departed some weeks beforehand and it was unclear whether the Genoese ships in which he left England were carrying him into another cowardly flight from battle or if he intended to gather reinforcements overseas. Henry's trusted chancellor, Bishop Waynflete of Winchester, resigned his office three days before battle and thus saved himself from any involvement in the fray. Others had followed: Margaret's chancellor and the keeper of the privy seal, Bishop Laurence Boothe of Durham, and even Henry's confessor John Stanbury, bishop of Hereford, abandoned their royal master in the face of the Yorkist horde.[28]

The first emissaries from the Yorkist army to pick their way through the hazardous quagmire surrounding the Lancastrian camp were a suitably pacific collection of clergymen, including probably Thomas Bourchier, archbishop of Canterbury, and the papal legate Coppini, who had ridden with the forces all the way from Kent and beyond. Warwick's younger brother George Neville, bishop of Exeter, was probably also among their number. They found Henry in his royal tent at the heart of the compound, the duke of Buckingham standing grim-faced at his side. When he saw the sizeable military escort that accompanied the ecclesiastical emissaries, Buckingham lost his temper: 'Ye come not as bishops for to treat for peace,' he accused them, 'but as men of arms.'[29] Like Queen Margaret, the duke must have been seriously displeased to read Coppini's letter – threatening and cajoling by turns – excusing the Yorkist lords of all wrongdoing and casting Henry as the aggressor in the conflict. The bishops explained that they had come with an armed escort because 'they that are about the king are not our friends'. Henry sat passively while

Buckingham dismissed the bishops' appeal. 'Forsooth,' said the duke, using one of the few mild oaths that Henry allowed, 'the earl of Warwick shall not come to the king's presence, and if he come he shall die.'[30]

By two o'clock in the afternoon two more emissaries had arrived at the royal camp. In the Yorkist encampment, Warwick was starting to match Buckingham's belligerence threat for threat: he demanded that either he would speak with Henry in person, or he would die in the field. Once again, his demand was refused. And so, trumpets blared and the Yorkist forces advanced down the hill towards the royal camp.

In marked contrast with his position in the battles of St Albans and Ludlow, Henry stationed himself inside his royal tent at Northampton. He does not seem even to have addressed his troops, nor did he appear beneath his standard as he had at St Albans. Presumably the duke of Buckingham, who was in command of the royal forces at Northampton, felt it was too dangerous for the king to appear out in the open by his standard. The potentially deadly risk of such a prominent position had been demonstrated at St Albans when Henry was wounded in the fray. However, it was clearly deemed important for Lancastrian morale that Henry remain in the royal camp rather than seeking the security of the nearby abbey or town to await news of the battle.

Within his tent, Henry was close enough to the action to hear the shouts of the advancing Yorkists through the driving rain, the blast of their trumpets, the triumphant cries and panicked calls of the soldiers. Through the canvas Henry could not tell which army was in the ascendant. While his life was in less immediate danger, the sense memory of the events at St Albans, the trauma and anxiety he may have felt, must have been disturbing. Once again he was reduced to a state of impotency, observing the horrors of warfare without playing an active part.

Outside, the battle was over almost as soon as it began. Lord Grey of Ruthin, in command of the Lancastrian vanguard, submitted without a fight, perhaps by prior collusion with the Yorkists.* As the Yorkist soldiers approached, Ruthin's men, recognizable in their livery of the black ragged staff, seized them by the hand and hauled them over the defences, allowing them to completely outflank the ditches, stakes and guns that had been so carefully prepared to hold them back. The royal guns that had looked so imposing were rendered waterlogged and unusable.[31]

The Yorkists poured through the gap Lord Grey had opened. Soon, moving with deadly efficiency, they were close to the royal tents. Warwick and March had ordered their troops not to kill the common soldiers, but no such mercy was showed to the noblemen, knights and squires. The Battle of Northampton was a mass political assassination that liquidated Henry's most trusted counsellors, the men the Yorkists had condemned as their enemies for no more reason than that they stood in their path to power. Did Henry hear their cries as they fell to their enemies' blades? The maligned earl of Shrewsbury and the Neville family's long-time enemy, Thomas Percy, Lord Egremont, received no quarter from Warwick's men. Viscount Beaumont, who had grown up with Henry and who had faithfully served the king his entire life, was slaughtered in the mud. Finally, the duke of Buckingham, standing close to Henry's tent, acting as the king's bodyguard to the last, succumbed to the slashing swords of his enemies. Many Lancastrians drowned trying to flee across the river at a mill, unable to escape from the carefully defended compound they had created. Surprisingly, despite the aristocratic slaughter unleashed on those close to Henry, the casualties of the battle were relatively few: perhaps 300–400 dead, with one source suggesting as few as fifty men were killed.[32]

When the entrance of his royal tent was opened to reveal the victorious Yorkist lords Henry must have realized, even without

---

* Waurin suggested this defection was premeditated and that Warwick had ordered his soldiers not to attack men wearing the black ragged staff badge. Waurin, V, p. 323.

the grisly sight of his advisers' bodies lying in the churned mud beyond, what it meant. Here, too, was a disturbing echo of St Albans – Warwick advancing towards him in his hiding place, ready to take control of the king's person and, by so doing, seize the reins of government. Henry surrendered himself meekly into the lords' keeping. Perhaps the trauma of the battlefield triggered a bout of illness that hindered his ability to resist, or perhaps he had been unwell throughout, and that was the reason he had played no role in the battle. It is hard to understand why the Yorkists lingered with Henry at Northampton for three days rather than marching straight back to London unless it was because Henry was unwell.

There was at least one cause for Lancastrian gratitude. As Henry was paraded back towards the capital, a Yorkist captive once again, it was known that Margaret and Prince Edward had escaped. Whether they could stay ahead of the men pursuing them from Coventry was a different matter. For now, Warwick and his allies could celebrate. Just as the Yorkists had wished, Henry had been separated – permanently, in some cases – from his advisers, and the king, as their captive, would 'retain only the bare name of sovereign'.[33] Exactly what that would mean for Henry's future and for the security of his family would be revealed when they reached London.

31

'Enemies on every side'[1]

Harlech Castle, Wales
September 1460

Perched on a cliff face above the Irish Sea, the gun-grey walls of Harlech Castle loured over the landscape. Beneath the castle rock, the sea pounded and churned, while beyond the cluster of buildings nestling in the fortress's shadow, the mountains of Snowdonia were visible in the distance. It was a bleak prospect, but to the exhausted, travel-soiled party who approached it that autumn day, Harlech Castle represented sanctuary at last. They were a small group: a mother riding pillion behind a trusted servant, her young son riding alongside, and a small bodyguard of eight other servants clustered around them. They had endured much on their journey. At Malpas in Cheshire they had been ambushed and their baggage plundered, thieves making off with the few valuables they carried. It had been a stark reminder of how uncertain the loyalties of those they met on the road could be. But now comfort was in sight. Harlech Castle was held by King Henry's half-brother, Jasper Tudor, and it was to him that Queen Margaret and Prince Edward now turned for support.[2]

With the disastrous outcome of the Battle of Northampton

forcing them to flee west into Wales, their trusted allies butchered and Henry a Yorkist prisoner, Margaret must have been grateful simply to stay ahead of the Yorkist scouts who were hunting them. As she dismounted wearily within the encircling walls of Harlech, she could briefly feel a sense of relief. She had kept herself and her son safe. Now she must regroup while awaiting word of the Yorkists' treatment of her husband. The news that reached them in this distant corner of northwest Wales was far from encouraging.

As Margaret and Edward had navigated the tortuous 145-mile (233 km) journey from Coventry to Harlech, the duke of York had finally landed in England. His progress through the country, from the marches of Wales to London, where parliament had been summoned, was the polar opposite of Margaret's experience. He travelled in state, like a king, surrounded by soldiers wearing his white and blue livery, his fetterlock badge proudly displayed. Trumpets sounded to announce his arrival, and the banners borne before him showed the arms of England, and of his forebear Lionel of Clarence – both indications of royal lineage that suggested regal status.* There were other indications that he was moving to establish his own authority in opposition to Henry's: indentures drawn up to retain marcher supporters to York's cause left out the usual clause demanding loyalty to the king and failed to use Henry's regnal year in their dating. As York neared London, his wife Cecily rode out to meet him seated in a blue velvet chair like a queen.[3]

Just as he had done after the Battle of St Albans five years earlier, York rode towards a parliament that had been summoned to legitimize the actions of the Yorkist lords and reverse the moves made against them by their enemies. Until he arrived, Henry and the government of England were both in the hands of the earl of Warwick. To all outward appearances the king was treated

---

* Lionel, duke of Clarence was the second surviving son of Edward III and provided York with his claim to the throne (see family tree, p. xvii).

with respect, lodged in the royal palace at Westminster, but there was no avoiding the fact he was a Yorkist prisoner.[4] Henry may have sought solace, as he had many times before, in the hushed sanctuary of Westminster Abbey a short walk away. Over the years he had often been found kneeling in silence or pacing the mosaic floor close to the tomb of Edward the Confessor – the king of England who had become patron saint of the realm, for whom Henry's son was named. It was here that Henry had decided to be buried, in the inner sanctum of the abbey, where his ancestors lay in an encircling ring around St Edward, under the shadow of the vast tomb of his father Henry V. Henry had been seen marking with his feet – and later, watching a mason carve out with an iron pick – the exact dimensions of the spot where his mortal remains would one day rest. Perhaps that event did not seem so far distant; perhaps Henry even contemplated it with equanimity. As a deeply devout Christian, he hoped for redemption after death. There must have seemed little to be redeemed while he lived.[5]

Henry's sojourn in the southeast of England was far from easy. The earls of Warwick and March escorted him to London, the traitorous Lord Grey of Ruthin in their entourage.[6] Arriving on 16 July, the lords proceeded to a public display of thanksgiving, progressing through the streets of the city on horseback to make an offering to the altar of St Paul's Cathedral. The spectacle must have been distasteful to Henry – praising God for the murder of his friends and servants – but he submitted to it with as little outward protest as he submitted to all of the Yorkists' demands.

Some of his noble allies were less obliging. While the Mass of thanks was intoned within the lofty stonework of St Paul's, a distant rumble could be heard, and the occasional deep boom reverberated around the stones. The Lancastrian Lords Scales, and Hungerford and Moleyns had opposed the Yorkists' entrance into London before the Battle of Northampton, retreating to the Tower of London, where they continued to put up a defiant bombardment. The citizens of London and the earl of Salisbury

– who had stayed behind while his kin marched for Northampton
in order to marshal the siege – had set up guns on the south
bank of the Thames. They monitored the land and river routes
to prevent any supplies getting into the Tower, in the hope of
starving the Lancastrians into submission. Already a number of
Londoners had been injured and even killed in the streets as a
result of the wildfire* and shot the Lancastrians loosed on the
city. It did little to engender warm feelings towards the men who
claimed to be Henry's loyal supporters in the Tower. If anything,
it seemed to corroborate the Yorkist propaganda that the king
was surrounded by self-preserving traitors.

On Saturday 19 July the Tower garrison was finally starved
into surrender. While Lord Hungerford and Moleyns managed
to escape unscathed, his unpopular colleague Lord Scales was
recognized by a woman of London while attempting to sneak
upriver to the sanctuary at Westminster. He was promptly seized
and butchered. Before the month was out more blood had been
shed on the streets as other Lancastrians trying to escape the
city were caught and slaughtered at Holborn. Lower-ranking
defenders were executed at Tyburn in a public assertion of Yorkist control.[7]

To quash the last vestiges of resistance and tighten their
control over Henry and the government, the Yorkist lords also
used less sanguinary methods, making sweeping changes to the
personnel of government and the royal household. The most
important offices went to members of the Neville family. The
earl of Salisbury was made chamberlain of Henry's household, a
position that controlled access to the king, and which had previously been held by Lancastrian stalwarts like Ralph Botiller,
Lord Ralph Cromwell and James Fiennes, Lord Saye and Sele
(who had paid for his loyalty with his life in 1450). Perhaps to
take revenge for his encroachment on their territory, Margaret's

---

*   A highly flammable mixture of substances, used in liquid form, that
was very difficult to extinguish. Essentially, medieval napalm.

supporter Laurence Boothe, bishop of Durham, was removed as keeper of the privy seal. Salisbury's younger son, George Neville, bishop of Exeter, was given the prime official position: on 25 July he was appointed chancellor and handed his three great seals in Henry's presence. York's brother-in-law Viscount Henry Bourchier was also rewarded for his loyalty, taking the place of the late earl of Shrewsbury as treasurer.[8]

Having cowed London and ensured Henry was firmly under their control, the Yorkist lords and the now-ubiquitous legate Coppini escorted Henry on a pilgrimage of thanksgiving to Canterbury while they awaited York's return and the assembly of a parliament that would enshrine their regime in law.

Westminster
10 October 1460

York's triumphal progress only intensified in bombast as he neared London. Trumpet blasts heralded his approach to Westminster, where parliament had opened on 7 October. At ten o'clock in the morning of 10 October York's armed escort of 800 mounted soldiers halted at the entrance to Westminster Palace and he dismounted as a sword was drawn and held aloft before him in regal fashion. York followed this naked blade, buoyed on a wave of confidence, the cheers that had accompanied him from Ireland still ringing in his ears as he crossed the vast expanse of the great hall. Onwards he strode, into the heart of Westminster Palace, up to the long, narrow Painted Chamber where the Lords and Commons met. There, a royal throne was raised, resplendent beneath a luxurious canopy of estate. Today it was empty, Henry quietly distracting himself in his chambers nearby or perhaps deep in prayer before St Edward's tomb. It was towards this throne that York now stalked, along the length of the chamber, its famous wall paintings of biblical rulers and ancient battles providing a magnificent backdrop for the moment that York expected to be the apogee of his ambition. He did not bow before the dais on which the throne was mounted, but strode up to it as if intending to take possession of the empty seat – as if he were already a crowned and anointed king. He stood boldly beneath the canopy of estate – a place permitted only to the king himself – and as he rested his hand in a proprietary manner upon the throne he turned to face the assembled crowd, as if 'awaiting their applause'.[9] Instead, he was met by a stupefied, even embarrassed, silence.

Thomas Bourchier, archbishop of Canterbury, was the first man to interrupt this awkward scene. He approached the duke and asked whether York wished to see the king? No, York declared, irritated by the question. Henry ought rather to visit him. For – gesturing perhaps to the raised sword beside him – 'he purposed not to lay down his sword but to challenge his right' to the throne.[10] Next should have come acclamation, applause, a collective bending of the knee before their true king, but instead York was met with consternation. The lords of parliament had no desire to depose an anointed king and replace him with a man who had repeatedly sworn to be Henry's faithful servant – especially on little more than York's say-so. It was suddenly apparent that York had made a disastrous miscalculation.

York's resolution to take the throne from Henry had been made months before. He and Warwick had almost certainly discussed how best to achieve this end when they met in Ireland the previous spring. Warwick and March's much-vaunted professions of loyalty to Henry since landing in June had been so much hot air. This had always been their real endgame. Part of the reason that York remained in Ireland so long after his allies had returned to England was to allow the forcefully eloquent Warwick to pave the way for a Yorkist accession. But for all Warwick's rhetorical powers, for all Henry's state of depressed submission, for all Coppini's persuasion, Henry's subjects had remained stubbornly loyal. Henry was a failure as king, that was painfully apparent, but he was no tyrant. And to justify usurpation he would have needed to be. His coronation had proceeded with the acclaim of his subjects and the sacred anointing that gave him a semi-divine position in his people's understanding. Moreover, to force his deposition and replace him with York while Margaret was still at large and while her supporters, powerful lords like Somerset, Exeter and Jasper Tudor were still fiercely loyal to Henry, would only be to invite more conflict, not unite the people in peace. Unity of purpose was what was required now. York might be a strong leader – he was certainly far more strong-willed than Henry had ever been – but he was tainted by years of rebellion and factionalism. He was, in short, not going to get what he wanted.[11]

All of this was explained to York in heated exchanges between the Yorkist lords and bishops at Blackfriars over the course of the next week. Well might York feel frustrated when he discovered that Warwick – who as recently as September had seemed completely committed to the plan – was now appealing for compromise. But Warwick was a political animal and he recognized regrettable realities. He had failed to get the requisite support York needed from the Lords and Commons so he knew the plan must evolve. York was ambitious to a fault. He had already planned the coronation ceremony that would take place on 1 November, and giving up his cherished ambition was mortifying. Eventually, however, he was persuaded to proceed in a more conciliatory fashion and present his claim to parliament for the Lords to settle the issue.

In the interim, York expressed his irritation by asserting his dominance over the royal palace at Westminster. Henry had not been in the Painted Chamber when the duke made his grand entrance, although he had attended the opening of parliament.[12] Now Henry found that his peaceful sanctuary close to St Edward's shrine at Westminster Abbey had become a Yorkist encampment. Six of York's guards were posted on Henry's door and to gain access to the royal apartments the duke's men broke open the locks and the bars sealing them shut. This use of brute force disturbed Henry's peace to such an extent that he gave way to York, allowing him the king's apartments while Henry took refuge in the queen's. It was in these chambers almost exactly seven years earlier that Prince Edward had been born, and perhaps that thought afforded Henry a little comfort.[13]

There was little else to soothe him at this troubled time. His advisers were scattered or dead, his wife and child God knew where – reports placed them variously in Scotland, Wales, northern England or France – and even the household men whose constant presence should have been a source of comfort had been replaced. The earl of Salisbury, his new chamberlain, was sympathetic to Henry's plight but he was still one of York's foremost kinsmen and supporters.

Already bowed under the stress of these changes and possibly still reeling from the psychological impact of Northampton, Henry was disturbed once more on 17 October when 'all the lords spiritual and temporal' then in parliament called on him. At a minimum, nineteen men surged into his chambers and, through the chancellor George Neville, bishop of Exeter, informed him that the duke of York had presented his claim to the throne of England. The lords said they felt the decision whether or not to counter this claim must fall to the king alone. Henry made his opinion known, in the best manner he could, as was recorded in the parliament roll: 'It pleased him to pray and order all the said lords to search as best they could for anything which might be objected and laid against the claim and title of the said duke.'[14]

In other words, he offered his opposition. Henry could quite legitimately be accused of generally giving in to York's demands, but on this occasion he expressed his desire for York's claim to be opposed, by whatever means it could be. Unfortunately, this was not enough for the lords. York had drawn up documents containing elaborate explanations of genealogical claims and moral arguments, and presented them before parliament. He was pressing for an answer to his claim, and he wanted it quickly.

The lords appealed to Henry, who 'had seen and understood [so] many different writings and chronicles' if he could not think of some objections for himself? Presumably he could not, for the next day the lords presented the case to the king's justices without his help.

Confronted with such a large body of men demanding certainty from him, Henry was probably overwhelmed. He had rarely been able to resist the opinions of others, and was seldom able to assert himself at their expense. When he had promoted his own policies, his will was accomplished with the guiding hand and through the means of more forceful individuals: his uncles Bedford and Gloucester, Cardinal Beaufort, Suffolk, Somerset, Margaret. All those guiding influences were now gone. Without them, Henry faded away to virtual insignificance. He was like a ghost, roaming the corridors of his wife's chambers, trying not to see York occupying the apartments nearby.[15]

Meanwhile, as the parliament roll goes on to record, others in Westminster feverishly applied themselves to finding some resolution to this debacle. The king's justices failed to provide a solution and when the Lords referred York's claim to the serjeants-at-law and the king's attorney, they simply referred it back. For nine days this process continued, with the Lords manfully fielding objections that York (or 'Richard Plantagenet' as he now called himself) batted away as of no concern. He insisted that Henry VI's grandfather Henry IV had 'unrightfully entered upon' the crown that ought to have descended to York's ancestors 'by law and custom'.[16] When the Lords objected that both they and York had sworn to be liegemen of Henry VI, York insisted that they 'should be guided by truth, right and justice in this matter in accordance with the will of the law of God, rather than by any promise or oath made by him to the contrary'. Objections based on Henry IV's inheritance of the throne, precedent through earlier acts of parliament, entails of the crown made by previous monarchs – all were swiftly dispensed with by York.[17] As if to prove Henry's situation hopeless, while the

Commons were debating York's claim in the refectory of Westminster Abbey, a crown hanging in the middle of the house
suddenly crashed to the floor.[18]

At last, the lords produced a solution that mirrored the Treaty
of Troyes, which had been signed almost exactly forty years
earlier. As if any better illustration were needed of the medieval
concept of Fortune's Wheel turning kings from their thrones
and elevating the lowly to greatness, four decades after the treaty
that gave Henry his dual crowns, he lost them in the same manner. The Act of Accord, as this agreement was known, allowed
Henry to reign until he died, or when it pleased him to 'lay down
or yield the crown', but his throne would then be inherited not
by Henry's son, but instead by York or one of his line. In other
words, Henry disinherited his own dynasty in favour of York's. It
was a remarkable concession and one it is impossible to imagine
Margaret assenting to – or allowing Henry to agree to – had she
been present. It starkly demonstrates how lost Henry was without her guiding influence, and how damningly successful the
Yorkist slurs against Prince Edward must have been that the lords
in parliament would agree to deprive him of his inheritance.

As a final affront to the prince, York was granted an annual
10,000 marks to be divided between himself and his two eldest sons, and the sum was to be drawn from Prince Edward's
inheritance of the principality of Wales and the earldom of
Chester. There is a suggestion that Henry attempted to preserve
something for his son in the fact that the title of Henry and his
heirs to the duchy of Lancaster was protected in the agreement
– presumably in the hope that Edward would eventually enjoy
it. There, at least, his minimal resistance yielded some benefit
for his disinherited son, but it was a miniscule victory compared
to York's.

To ensure that the terms of the agreement were maintained,
the latest in a seemingly endless round of collective oath-
swearings took place on 31 October. Henry promised to abide
by the Act of Accord, and all the attendant lords swore to accept

Henry as king and York as heir to the kingdom. York and his eldest sons, the earls of March and Rutland, took an oath that they would not do anything to 'cause or lead to the shortening of the natural life of King Henry VI'.[19] To protect York from Lancastrian resistance, it was declared that he and his kin would be covered by the same treason laws that protected the royal family. He was also given the material aid of a commission to 'repress, subdue and pacify' the realm, acting in Henry's place as head of an armed force to proceed against the king's enemies. For taking on this role – which, effectively, enabled him to lead an army against Henry's wife and loyal supporters – he was to receive wages, assistance from royally appointed sheriffs and obedience as if he were the king himself.[20]

Why did Henry agree to an act that was so patently against his and his family's interests? Some of his contemporaries claimed it was out of mental deficiency. 'Our king is a dolt and a fool,' Warwick told Coppini. Pope Pius II – relying largely on Coppini's not unbiased reports – tended to agree, condemning Henry as 'a man more timorous than a woman, utterly devoid of wit or spirit'.[21] A London chronicler similarly attributed witlessness to Henry but went on to suggest that 'the king for fear of death granted [York] the crown' because he was kept at Westminster 'by force and strength'.[22] The truth probably lay more in Henry's anxieties than in his alleged imbecility. Clearly Henry was not witless. The Lords consulted him for his opinion in October and he offered his opposition to York's accession, but what he was not capable of doing – what he had almost never been capable of doing – was providing the iron will necessary to oppose York personally. Without his queen or principal advisers he was isolated and impotent. That does not mean, however, that he was a willing puppet of the Yorkist regime. Arguably, the resistance he offered was all he could muster in a situation that was purposefully designed to intimidate him. He had been kept a virtual prisoner in Westminster for two weeks with his rival, his rival's substantial bodyguard and supporters ever-present.

While Henry does not seem to have been physically threatened, he certainly endured mental pressures from the Yorkist camp. On the very night that York swore not to interfere with Henry, 31 October (the vigils of All Hallows), the duke had Henry removed from Westminster Palace against his will and lodged in the bishop of London's palace, where he had spent most of July. There, according to *Gregory's Chronicle*, York finally held a private meeting with Henry, arriving by torchlight and behaving as if he were already king. He repeatedly insisted that the throne was his by right but if he hoped that Henry would immediately abdicate in York's favour, the duke was to be disappointed.[23] Although this is the only recorded visit made to intimidate Henry, there may well have been others, applying pressure to an already stressed and anxious king. Certainly, the earl of Salisbury was uneasy at York's displacement of Henry from the king's apartments, and if the duke's most consistent ally was disturbed by his behaviour it seems likely that Henry would have been.

The day after Henry was removed to the bishop's palace was the feast of All Saints, a holy day when the king traditionally processed through London, crowned and surrounded by the nobility. In 1460, more than ever, it was essential for the Yorkist lords to present a united front to the subjects who watched Henry progress through the streets of London in royal splendour. The citizens needed to be convinced that Henry had agreed to the Act of Accord without mistreatment and that the political realm was united in support of York's new status as heir. The fact that the queen, the dukes of Somerset and Exeter, Henry's half-brother and half a dozen northern lords were absent meant that the spectacle rang somewhat hollow.

As autumn gave way to winter York prepared to ride north to deal with the mounting challenge of the Lancastrian loyalists. More blood would be shed. The prospect would have been as sickening to Henry as it had ever been. He paraded through London, crowned, robed, tall and pale, looking every inch the king. He had, after all, been exhibiting himself in these regal parades since he was a baby on his mother's lap. Yet to all intents and purposes he was a Yorkist prisoner, the puppet of their regime. And so he would remain until Margaret wrested him from York's control.[24]

32

'Out of the north an evil shall break'[1]

Margaret and Henry must have contemplated the approaching Christmas festivities of 1460 with little enthusiasm or optimism. In London, Henry was costumed for more ritual processions from the bishop of London's palace to St Paul's Cathedral – Christmas Day, New Year's Day, both had to be endured – while at the opposite end of the British Isles, Margaret was embroiled in desperate political machinations at a court that was still technically that of their enemy. Lincluden Priory, in the south of Scotland, was where Margaret spent her Christmastide, as a guest of another royal matriarch. Queen Mary of Scotland – Mary of Guelders, a niece of Duke Philippe of Burgundy – was not the most obvious ally for Queen Margaret. Duke Philippe was the one man Henry VI said he wanted to make war upon,[2] and Mary's husband James II had expended most of his efforts in the last five years attacking English border fortresses and attempting to unite Henry's enemies in a combined invasion – most recently, he had schemed with York to assist his usurpation of the throne. However, James's military ambitions had been his undoing.

On 3 August 1460, while leading the siege of Roxburgh Castle on the River Tweed, James had been killed when one of his own cannons exploded next to him. Within days, Queen Mary had escorted their eldest son – the eight-year-old boy now acclaimed as King James III – to command the siege, and sure enough the castle fell. To ensure their English enemies could not reap the benefit of this vital border fortress, Mary of Guelders ordered Roxburgh Castle to be destroyed.[3]

Now, by playing host to the refugee English queen and Prince Edward, Mary saw an opportunity to pursue her late husband's ambitions by subtler means. Although she had spent the vast majority of her queenship pregnant and therefore isolated from the political realm, giving birth to seven children in ten years of marriage, Mary had proven herself a wily political operator. During the twelve days of Christmas 1460 she and Margaret thrashed out an agreement to secure a truce between England and Scotland, guaranteeing Scottish neutrality while Margaret went south at the head of a Lancastrian army to liberate Henry from Yorkist control.

Margaret needed Scottish assistance because the European situation was otherwise not inclined towards the Lancastrian cause. By mid-1460, out of a tangle of international disputes and divided loyalties, a bloc of allies had formed that was opposed to Henry's interests. Among them were the papacy, Francesco Sforza, duke of Milan, Philippe, duke of Burgundy, King Ferrante of Aragon and the Yorkists. Pope Pius II's chief concern after ascending the papal throne in 1458 was to mount a crusade against the Ottoman empire in the east, and his international policy was almost entirely determined by who would help him achieve that end. One of the few completely committed crusaders was Duke Philippe of Burgundy, who had raised an army and even been prepared to lead it personally to fight the Ottoman threat. Philippe had developed a good relationship with the earl of Warwick during Warwick's captaincy of Calais, and tended to favour the Yorkist cause. Moreover it was in Burgundian

interests to keep England divided and inward-looking, to prevent it offering any support to Philippe's long-term adversary
King Charles VII of France. For similar reasons, Philippe had
welcomed Charles's rebellious son, Dauphin Louis, into his court
and much to the pope's delight the dauphin was making all the
right noises about allowing papal authority to increase in France
once he inherited his father's throne. Charles VII had seriously
displeased Pope Pius by sending a belligerent embassy to a papal
council, insisting that France could not offer support for the
crusade until he had made a permanent peace with England.
Peace between England and France was all well and good but
the pope, Burgundy and Warwick had no interest in promoting
such a treaty as long as it would bind Henry VI closer to Charles
and his Angevin counsellors – the latter being all too likely to
support Margaret and Prince Edward's cause rather than the
Yorkist regime. To round out papal hostility towards Margaret's
cause, there was a long-standing rivalry over the kingdom of Sicily
between Margaret's father, René of Anjou, and King Ferrante of
Aragon. Pope Pius firmly took Ferrante's side, which goes some
way to explain his readiness to believe Yorkist slanders against
the Angevin Queen Margaret.[4]

Throughout summer and autumn 1460, the papal legate
Francesco Coppini had been pushing for an alliance that would
assist papal plans for a crusade, boost Yorkist authority inter-
nationally and – since even the legate could be self-interested
– also earn Coppini promotion to cardinal as reward for his success. This compact would include a marriage alliance between
Burgundy and the House of York.[5]

Thus it seemed in winter 1460 that, for their own reasons,
every house in Europe was opposed to Margaret's efforts to
regain control of Henry and restore Prince Edward to the line of
succession. Under these circumstances, Margaret was forced to
rely on England's traditional enemies in France and Scotland to
achieve her ends. Earlier in the year she had – via secret channels
– negotiated with Pierre de Brézé, seneschal of French-controlled

Normandy, a scheme to use his navy to bring down Warwick. This was a remarkable decision given that Brézé was the despised French captain who had infamously burnt Sandwich in 1457. However, before his ascendancy in the service of Charles VII, Brézé had been a prominent figure at the Angevin court, and this long-term familial connection probably inspired Margaret to trust him in her time of need. Certainly, he proved an astute and – crucially – discreet ally to Margaret. He recognized all too well the danger that Margaret faced if her dealings with England's old adversary became public knowledge. It was neither possible nor sensible, Brézé warned Charles VII, for the king to communicate directly with Margaret about this assistance, since if the letters fell into English hands even her own allies would turn on her: 'If those on her side knew her plan and what she had done, they would join her enemies and kill her.'[6]

The stakes were similarly high in Margaret's dealings with the Scots. Henry and James II shared a distant relationship through James's Beaufort mother but that had not stopped the Scottish king from colluding with Henry's enemies and raiding his borders. Margaret's negotiations with Queen Mary could therefore be interpreted in England as a conspiracy with the enemy.

However, not all Englishmen viewed Margaret's activities with suspicion, and she still had supporters among the nobility. Many lords had not attended the parliament where the Act of Accord was proclaimed and shared Margaret's unease at Henry being under Yorkist control. Unsurprisingly, most of them were long-term Lancastrian servants or those who had personal vendettas against the Yorkist lords. They now gathered to Margaret's banner to affirm an alliance with the Scots and muster an army to take back the throne. Henry Beaufort, duke of Somerset, had been released from his futile resistance at Guisnes by a treaty with Warwick, and now assembled a large force in his West Country estates and marched it north with the earl of Devon. Meanwhile, their neighbour the earl of Wiltshire led an army west to support Jasper Tudor, who was almost single-handedly asserting Lancastrian authority in Wales. Among the northern lords flocking to Margaret's cause there were many with personal grudges against the Nevilles: the earl of Northumberland and his Percy brothers; the earl of Westmorland and his kinsmen; Lord Dacre; Lord Clifford. That winter these lords mustered their armies in the port town of Hull, moving with such speed and precision that the Yorkist government in London scarcely believed the reports of their progress.

York had known that he would have to test his supremacy on the field of battle. This was why he had ensured that parliament granted him the necessary powers to lead an army against his enemies. Early in December, he left London at the head of an armed force to crush the assembled 'evildoers' in the north. He was accompanied by his teenage son Edmund, earl of Rutland, the earl of Salisbury and Salisbury's son Sir Thomas Neville and son-in-law Sir Thomas Harrington. At the same time, York's eldest son, the eighteen-year-old Edward, earl of March, headed west on his first solo military campaign, his task being to halt the eastward advance of Wiltshire's and Tudor's forces and prevent them from joining the northern assembly. The earl of Warwick remained in London to keep a watchful eye on King Henry – and to remind the populace at large of the threat to their well-being that Margaret's activities represented. The Yorkist cause had legitimacy only as long as Henry was alive and under their control. The stage was set for the issue of just rule to be decided on the field of battle.

Sandal Castle, Yorkshire
30 December 1460

Sandal Castle, a majestic Norman motte and bailey positioned a mile or so from Wakefield across ditched and hedged fields, was a suitably grand location for the duke of York to celebrate the Christmas season. Conditions inside the fortress, however, were bleak. York and his kinsmen had marched north in a spirit of undue optimism about their prospects, but either York had not taken the Lancastrian threat seriously or he was receiving outdated information. It was only as he neared the Lancastrian stronghold of Pontefract Castle that he realized he had made a serious miscalculation. The 'queen's army' – as the Lancastrian lords and their supporters were known, although Margaret was still in Scotland – outnumbered the Yorkist forces by a considerable margin. York had expected to gather recruits on the journey north but he seems to have encountered little enthusiasm for his cause. Perhaps the miserable winter conditions made men loath to leave their firesides and turn out in what was still a questionable cause.[7]

Having traipsed his way along waterlogged roads and flooded fields, when York reached Sandal Castle – an oasis of Yorkist authority in hostile territory – on 21 December he found it poorly provisioned. A meagre £4 6s 7d was expended on the household during the traditional feasting period between Christmas and New Year's Day.[8] By 30 December, supplies were running alarmingly low. Perhaps it was the temptation of the well-stocked parkland, rich with venison, on the north bank of the River Calder that enticed York out of the security of the castle on the afternoon of 30 December for a foraging expedition. Contemporaries eager to ascribe York's error of judgement to Lancastrian treachery insisted that he was tricked into leaving his fortress during a period when a truce was in place. Either way, York, Salisbury, Rutland and their men were some way beyond the protective walls of their castle when they were surprised by a vastly superior Lancastrian force under the dukes of Somerset and Exeter and including Lords Clifford and Roos.[9]

As the afternoon light dwindled, York and his men found themselves trapped in the narrow fields north of the castle, their escape blocked by the river behind them and relief from the castle cut off by the enemy. They suffered a brutal defeat. York's son, the seventeen-year-old Edmund, earl of Rutland, was cut down by Lord Clifford as he fled the field, a bloody vengeance for the death of Clifford's father at Yorkist hands during the Battle of St Albans.[10] The earl of Salisbury survived the battlefield and was escorted back to Pontefract Castle to be ransomed by the duke of Somerset. Perhaps Salisbury's unease at Henry's mistreatment won him some leniency from the Lancastrian commander, but he received little mercy from the locals. The day after the battle Salisbury was dragged from the castle by a mob and beheaded.[11]

According to the pro-Yorkist *Register* maintained at St Albans Abbey, York was captured alive and humiliated by the Lancastrians in Christ-like fashion:

They stood him [York] on a little anthill and placed on his head, as if a crown, a vile garland made of reeds... and bent the knee to him, saying in jest, 'Hail King, without rule. Hail King, without ancestry. Hail leader and prince, with almost no subjects or possessions.' And having said this and various other shameful and dishonourable things to him, at last they cut off his head.[12]

In all likelihood, York was killed during the battle, 'manfully fighting' among his soldiers.[13] After their deaths, York and Rutland were beheaded and their heads sent with Salisbury's to rot on Micklegate Bar, the ceremonial entrance to the city of York, mounted on spikes like common traitors. York's head was topped with a paper crown, a final mocking rejection of his royal pretensions.[14]

When Henry received word of York's death he was said to be 'much moved', as ever showing a capacity for compassion that far exceeded political reason.[15] While she played no part in the Battle of Wakefield, it is hard to imagine Margaret being anything but pleased with its outcome. For the Lancastrian cause in general, the victory was a morale boost, strengthening Margaret's position in her negotiations with Scotland. By

5 January 1461 she had finally reached an agreement with Queen Mary – a marriage between Prince Edward and one of Mary's two daughters at its heart. Now that York and his army had been swept from the north of England, Margaret and Prince Edward could travel south from Scotland to join the assembly of Lancastrian loyalists. At York, on 20 January 1461, the Anglo-Scottish agreement was formally recognized by a council of Lancastrian lords, including a number of the commanders who had fought at Wakefield: Somerset, Northumberland, and the earl of Westmorland's brother Lord John Neville. The lords made a pact to 'labour by all means reasonable' to bring Margaret's Anglo-Scottish truce to a 'good and effectual conclusion' and to wrest Henry from Yorkist control.[16]

As a depleted parliament reassembled in London late in January 1461, this northern band of lords rode out with Margaret and Prince Edward through the gates of York to retake the kingdom. The prince was placed at the forefront of the Lancastrian army, the soldiers' livery emblazoned with his ostrich-feather badge. Although he was still only seven years old, it was vital for Edward to be seen as a symbol of royal authority, the future of the Lancastrian dynasty.

One hundred and fifty miles (240 km) to the southwest, in the marcher town of Shrewsbury, the prince's namesake and rival, Edward, earl of March, was preparing to take revenge for the events at Wakefield.[17] March was eighteen, unusually tall, strongly built and already a veteran of battlefields and political intrigue. Yet, notwithstanding the recent tragedies that had befallen his family, Edward, earl of March, had been born under a lucky star. Unlike Henry VI, whose astrological and biological make-up suggested to contemporaries an unstable, lethargic and uncertain future, the earl of March was a spring baby, born early on the morning of 28 April 1442. His horoscope predicted that he would grow up to be a sanguine, lusty and vigorous young man, well mannered, cheerful and popular.[18] A leader more unlike Henry VI it is hard to imagine: the Burgundian diplomat

Philippe de Commines, who met March on the continent, considered Edward 'the most handsome man of his time', an inspiring military commander and also a libidinous pleasure-seeker.[19] By the terms of the Act of Accord it was March, and not Prince Edward, who was now Henry's heir. It remained to be seen which Edward could secure his right to the crown.

Crowland Abbey, Lincolnshire
February 1461

The first news that arrived at the abbey doors was of 'a whirl-wind from the north', an army storming down the Great North Road, trailing thieves and beggars in its wake 'like so many locusts'. Through every county the Lancastrian army passed, it was said, the surrounding area was denuded of its treasures and given over to spoil and rapine. Nothing was sacred. Chalices and sacrament boxes were ripped from the hands of priests and churchyards desecrated with the blood of those who attempted to defend themselves. Crowland Abbey was only 13 miles (21 km) from Stamford, a major town on the road south, and the monks listened to the horrifying rumours wide-eyed, reporting what they heard in their chronicle.* Precious vestments were bundled into coffers and silver vessels and charters concealed in the walls to preserve them. Their neighbours flocked to the abbey for sanctuary through gates continually guarded, their few personal treasures clasped anxiously in their arms. 'But blessed be God!' wrote one anonymous monk in the abbey chronicle, although the army passed within 6 miles (10 km) of its boundaries, the monks and their neighbours escaped unharmed.[20]

---

* Two overlapping 'continuations' of this fifteenth-century *Crowland Chronicle* survive, the first written by the prior of the abbey and the second by a well-informed cleric based there in 1486.

The dark legend of Margaret's army from the north had developed quickly. As early as November 1460 the queen had written to the Common Council in London to assure them that although she had heard the rumours 'that we... draw towards you with an uncounted power of strangers, disposed to rob and to despoil you... we will that ye know for certain that... none of ye shall be robbed, despoiled or wronged [by us]'.[21]

Similar assurances followed from Prince Edward and the earl of Northumberland, but with London under the control of the earl of Warwick they may never have been disseminated.[22] Certainly, the capital was as gripped by terror as the monks of Crowland at news of Margaret's advance. A ballad circulating that spring suggested that 'all the lords of the north' had gathered 'for to destroy the south country'. 'We will dwell in the south country and take all that we need,' the ballad imagined the northmen cackling, 'these [southern] wives and their daughters our purpose shall they speed.'[23] The official Yorkist record, enshrined in parliament before the year's end, earnestly reported 'the seduction and ravishing of religious women, widows and maidens, the inhuman and abominable treatment of women then in labour and struggling to give birth... [who were thrown] naked from their beds and [robbed] of all their goods'.[24]

Warwick, the arch-propagandist, was once again harnessing public anxiety to his own cause, stoking the increasingly hysterical rumour mill of the southeast with appeals for military assistance against 'those misruled and outrageous people in the north parties of this realm... coming towards these parts to the destruction thereof'.[25] Southern fears of northern invaders were a 'race memory' extending back to the time of the Vikings and beyond.[26] Many would have known the words of the Old Testament, which now seemed horrifyingly prophetic: 'Out of the north an evil shall break forth upon all the inhabitants of the land.'[27] An East Anglian gentleman probably expressed general prejudice when he fretted in a letter of 23 January 1461

that 'the people in the north rob and steal and be appointed
to pillage all this [south] country'.[28] By then the arrival of the
northern horde was expected any day.

But the reality of Margaret's 'northern' army as it marched
south was somewhat different. It was inevitable that an army
marching hundreds of miles in the depths of winter would
denude the territory through which it passed of provisions that
were in short supply. Even in summer, illicit foraging and petty
theft followed in the footsteps of the retainers, recruits and
mercenaries who served in fifteenth-century armies. But while
alarming to contemporaries, the long-term impact of Margaret's
march was more imagined than real. The northeastern towns
allegedly devastated in its wake showed remarkable signs of
peaceful prosperity in the years that followed. Regrettably for
the southern doom-merchants, the fearsome army from the
north cannot even be claimed to have been entirely 'northern'.
The duke of Somerset and earl of Devon had brought substantial forces from their West Country estates, and Margaret had
called up a number of her officers based in the Midlands to
boost her forces. Even the northern lords had mustered levies
from their southern lands. The most inaccurate report, made in
the Latin *Brief Notes* compiled at a monastery in Ely, was that the
queen's army was stuffed with foreign mercenaries. Margaret
had been painfully unsuccessful in recruiting King Charles and
Queen Mary to support her militarily, and any Scottish or French
troops were considerably outnumbered by the English, wearing
the red and black ostrich-feather livery of Prince Edward.[29]

There was, however, enough fire to fuel the smoke of rumour.
The earl of Northumberland had attacked the northern territories that once belonged to the duke of York and across the
north violence and unrest had been widespread through the
later months of 1460. As is often the case in politics, the truth
was less important than public perception, and in the early days
of 1461 the whole of the southeast seemed convinced that the
apocalypse was swooping down on them. The conclusion to

the ballad threatening northern destruction cast one man as southern England's salvation: Edward, earl of March, 'the rose of Rouen'.* 'Had not the rose of Rouen been, all England had been destroyed... Blessed be the time that ever God spread that flower!'[30] But before he was in a position to impede the Lancastrian progress south, March had first to face Henry and Margaret's supporters in the Welsh marches.

Far to the west, more armies were on the move. Jasper Tudor and the earl of Wiltshire had assembled a considerable force of Welsh, French, Breton and Irish soldiers. By February 1461 they had marched at speed along the ice-covered roads of south Wales and the marches to reach Herefordshire. Their plan was, ultimately, to rendezvous with Margaret and the main body of Lancastrian forces. The earl of March had spent the winter close to the Welsh border, preparing to halt Jasper Tudor's eastward progress. On 2 February 1461, he assembled his men outside the walls of Hereford and led them to Mortimer's Cross, where ancient roads intersected near the River Lugg. On the way, the intense cold created a meteorological phenomenon that appeared to March and his men to be a portent of either doom or divinity: three suns seemed to stand in the sky at once.[†] Many of March's soldiers were disturbed and disheartened by the sight, but displaying a charismatic leadership that perhaps owed something to years in Warwick's company, March 'comforted' his men, telling them to 'be of good cheer and dread not; this is a good sign, for these three suns betoken the Father, the Son and the Holy Ghost, and therefore let us have a good heart and in the name of Almighty God, we go against our enemies'.[31]

And indeed, Fortune favoured him that day. Tudor and

---

* Edward was so called because he had been born in Rouen while his father was serving in Normandy.
† Caused by the refraction of ice crystals in the atmosphere, this phenomenon is known today as a 'parhelion' or 'sun dog'.

Wiltshire's polyglot army was crushed, and the two Lancastrian earls put to flight. Cheated of vengeance on these commanders, March insisted on taking it instead on ten lesser captains, including Jasper's father – and Henry's loyal stepfather – Owen Tudor. They were marched to Hereford and condemned to be beheaded in the marketplace. Until the last, Owen trusted in a pardon. Even as he was stripped down to his fine red velvet doublet in the market, he held out hope. But when he saw the axe and block prepared for him he realized death was imminent. According to *Gregory's Chronicle*, Owen's last thoughts were of his wife, Henry's mother Catherine. 'That head shall lie on the stock,' he said, 'that was wont to lie on Queen Catherine's lap.'[32] Then 'he put his heart and mind wholly to God and full meekly took his death'. His severed head was mounted on the highest point of the market cross. One story tells that 'a mad woman combed his hair and washed away the blood of his face, and she got candles and set them about him burning, more than a hundred', as a votive offering.[33]

Henry would have received news of his stepfather's death and his supporters' defeat at the Battle of Mortimer's Cross against a rumbling backdrop of military preparations in London. This pattern of loss must by now have been becoming painfully familiar – another loyal servant from his infancy cut down violently. Henry was now approaching forty, advanced middle age in the fifteenth century, and grief was an expected part of life, but the loss of so many of his friends and servants by sudden violence must nonetheless have been disturbing. And now there came the prospect of losing more.

On 12 February 1461, Henry was bundled on to horseback in the ranks of a Yorkist army as it rolled north out of London towards St Albans. This, too, was a familiar sensation, although the faces at Henry's heels were men who had been his opponents on the battlefield more often than they had been his supporters: the rebellious Kentishmen and southeastern citizens who had defied him so consistently in the past decade; the duke of

Norfolk; Henry Bourchier; Warwick's brother John Neville;* and, leading the army, the steel core of the Yorkist cause, the earl of Warwick. Warwick had assembled a formidable arsenal of weaponry to block the route of Margaret's 'northern' army before it could reach the capital. Stored in the baggage train were all the horrors that medieval warfare could devise: bombs that loosed 'wildfire'; vast nets studded with iron nails to rip at horses' hooves and men's feet; and large spiked shields called pavises.

When he reached St Albans, Warwick's scouts informed him that he had plenty of time to prepare a strong defensive line. It was believed that Margaret's army had not yet passed Northampton, 45 miles (72 km) away. Warwick dispatched a force to Dunstable to block the route to the west, placed archers in the centre of St Albans and established a fortified camp to the northeast of the town. It seemed impossible for Margaret's army to pass unopposed.[34]

However, there were indications that not all was well in Warwick's camp. A lack of provisions – the same problem that had dogged Margaret's forces as they marched south – spread disgruntlement in the rank and file. Even before the preparations for battle were completed, there had already been a considerable number of desertions, and mutterings of betrayal inevitably followed. Hearing nothing from the scouts he had dispatched towards the Lancastrian forces, Warwick decided to change the location of his forces, moving the army further from the town.

Henry was escorted to the outer edges of the battlefield, his royal tent pitched beneath a large tree a mile away across the heath. He was appointed a guard including two Lancastrian servants who had defected to the Yorkist cause, Lord William Bonville and Sir Thomas Kyriell. There was no question of him fighting: even leaving aside his distaste for violence, Henry was

---

* Bourchier and Neville had recently been elevated to the peerage as Lords Berners and Montagu respectively.

hardly going to raise arms against an army that proudly bore his son's livery and was led, to all intents and purposes, by his wife. Warwick had brought Henry to St Albans solely to act as a figurehead to legitimize his army's cause. Fighting beneath the royal standard of the king, Warwick could condemn any who stood against him as rebels and traitors, to be suppressed with brutal violence. Warwick had probably also been disinclined to leave the king alone in London. It was possible that Margaret's army could skirt around the Yorkists and take the capital, which would be disastrous if Henry was within it. Bringing Henry to the battlefield was not, however, without its dangers, hence the king's exile to the outer limits of the heath.

But was there another reason for Warwick's decision to isolate Henry from his forces? Did he fear that hints of royal resistance might undermine his troops' morale? It must have been suspected by some of Warwick's soldiers that the king would rather be in the queen's army than theirs, and Henry's refusal to endorse the Yorkist cause with the public appearances he had made before his troops at Ludlow and the first Battle of St Albans may have started to undermine Yorkist morale. Even at Northampton he had remained inside the encampment close to his men. The *Register* maintained by John Whethamstede, abbot of St Albans, who may have witnessed the events of 1461, reported that Henry could not conceal that 'in his heart he inclined' to the army led by his wife and that this led to desertions among Warwick's men. Such passive resistance was hardly substantial, but under the circumstances it was probably all that Henry could manage. Warwick's habit of ruthlessly assassinating his enemies gave Henry little confidence that he could openly defy the earl without suffering the consequences.[35]

Henry's muted opposition was soon the least of Warwick's concerns. When the attack came, it took his forces completely by surprise. His scouts had been misled, reporting that Margaret's army was still 9 miles (14 km) away, when in fact the Yorkist outpost in Dunstable had already fallen. Under cover of darkness, the

Lancastrian army approached St Albans not from the northeast, as Warwick had expected, but from the northwest, bypassing Warwick's carefully prepared encampment to march straight into the town. They went unopposed as far as the market square, where, under the shadow of the clock tower and Eleanor Cross, they were driven back by a hail of arrows loosed from Yorkist bows. It was only a temporary impediment. The Lancastrians poured through an undefended gateway and up a lane that entered the major thoroughfare of St Peter's Street. It had been near here that Henry had been captured in 1455. Fierce fighting broke out, but soon the Lancastrians were surging forward to meet the bewildered rearguard of Warwick's army, under the command of his brother John Neville, Lord Montagu. Somerset's cavalry smashed into Montagu's forces before Warwick and the rest of his army could organize themselves. His men scattered in disarray, chased down by Somerset's horsemen. Lances flew on the open heathland and many of Montagu's soldiers were skewered into the earth. Montagu himself was captured.

When he had finally marshalled his men, Warwick attempted to fight his way through his fleeing forces and resurgent Lancastrians to control the town, but St Albans had already fallen. He retreated towards his encampment, trusting to the gunners, ordnance and Burgundian mercenaries he had assembled, but already the artillerists were abandoning their long-range firepower to take up axes and swords instead. Shouts from the camp made Warwick fear that he had been betrayed and, spurring his heels to his horse's flank, he fled the battlefield. Many of his men did the same, the early winter darkness covering their retreat. The mighty arsenal Warwick had assembled went largely unused, scattered across the heath in the soldiers' haste to flee. Most of Warwick's commanders escaped with their lives – the duke of Norfolk and earl of Arundel rode hot on his heels – but 3,000 men were left dead on the field.

Henry was discovered by Lord Clifford, safe beneath his tree at the edge of the battlefield, where Kyriell and Bonville still guarded him, two of the only Yorkist commanders to stand their ground. According to two sources – Waurin and a Milanese ambassador – Henry may have distracted himself as the battle raged by chanting prayers for the safe deliverance of his family.[36] After being escorted to the Lancastrian camp he was reunited with Margaret and Prince Edward, embracing them and thanking God for their victory.[37] Margaret may have had more mixed feelings about their reunion. In the seven months in which they had been apart Henry had showed himself to be hopelessly incapable of resisting Yorkist pressure, even to the extent of disinheriting his only child. His failings as both a husband and a king when deprived of her guidance had become painfully apparent.

It was almost certainly Margaret who guided Henry and their son to perform two rituals of kingship in the immediate aftermath of this second Battle of St Albans. To remind their subjects of Prince Edward's status as Lancastrian heir to the throne, in defiance of the Act of Accord, on the very evening of the battle Henry dubbed the boy a knight. This sacred ritual of masculine honour and loyalty had been performed for Henry by his uncle Bedford and, just as Henry had done as a child, after Edward had been knighted, the seven-year-old prince, gleaming in his gilded purple velvet brigandine, knighted a number of the men who had fought for his family's cause that day. Among them was Andrew Trollope, the captain of the Calais garrison, who had been injured by standing on one of the murderous spikes that studded the field. He made light of the wound before the prince, protesting that he had hardly earned the right of knighthood, 'for I only killed fifteen men. I stood still in one place and they came to me – but they bode still with me.'[38]

The next morning, Prince Edward participated in a darker ritual of masculine royal authority when he witnessed the summary execution of Henry's guards, Bonville and Kyriell. Some pro-Yorkist sources even claimed that the seven-year-old Edward condemned the men himself.[39] Margaret's influence must have lain behind such a decision, for it asserted the prince's status as arbiter of royal justice and ultimate authority over his subjects' lives. Partly of necessity and partly from policy, it seems to have been decided that Edward would be exposed to the harsh realities of kingship far earlier than Henry had been. Henry's rule, after all, was hardly a shining example of the merits of kingship based on theory and delegation rather than direct experience.

The decision to kill Bonville and Kyriell, however, was to prove a costly mistake. It was soon reported that Henry had assured the men that they would be pardoned; allowing them to be executed suggested weakness and a lack of good faith. It is as easy to believe that Henry might make such a promise as it is understandable that Margaret and the Lancastrian commanders saw no injustice in breaking it. Kyriell and Bonville, after all, owed their careers to the Lancastrian dynasty: Kyriell had served both Henry V and VI as a captain in Normandy, and Bonville had been created a peer by Henry VI as a reward for his service in Gascony. Yet both men had gone over to the Yorkist cause after Northampton and in February 1461 both had been elected as Knights of the Garter alongside the earl of Warwick and the turncoat Lord John Wenlock, who had once been Margaret's chamberlain. The Order of the Garter demanded loyalty to the king and fellow knights unto death, but Bonville and Kyriell had abandoned their true king to serve the House of York. According to their own professed code of chivalry such a breach of allegiance deserved death.

That their execution was more politically than maliciously motivated is suggested by the identity of those whom Margaret and her commanders allowed to walk free. Had the Lancastrians been concerned only with taking vengeance on the Yorkists, they could have tried to equal March's toll of executions after Mortimer's Cross* or struck at the Neville and Bourchier families by killing Lords Montagu and Berners, who had both been taken captive. But these Yorkist commanders were spared. Unlike

---

* Ten captains were killed by March after the Battle of Mortimer's Cross. See above, p. 432.

Bonville and Kyriell, Berners and Montagu had not changed their allegiance – both had fought for their own kin at St Albans. By the standards of their time, both deserved honourable imprisonment and that is what they got.[40]

With Warwick having departed the scene and March's army still in the west, London now lay open before the Lancastrian army. It would surely be a simple matter to advance on the capital, restore Henry to his throne and Edward to the succession. The Yorkist cause would be quashed once and for all.

33

'Lost irretrievably'[1]

London
20 February 1461

Ever since Henry had marched out of London with Warwick's army, the city had lingered in a purgatory of anxious waiting that left the streets eerily quiet. Shops were kept shut, trading effectively ceased. On street corners the usual dawdlers and wanderers had been replaced by an unfamiliar emptiness, punctuated only by the clatter of hooves as the mayor and sheriffs policed the streets. The city gates were carefully guarded and watches permanently mounted. From beneath the shadows of these gates, three well-dressed noblewomen emerged, riding up the road north towards St Albans. They had been trusted by the city council with a particularly delicate mission, to negotiate with Henry and Margaret over the terms by which the king and queen could enter the city. These ladies had been chosen for their unimpeachable loyalty to the Lancastrian regime, for all had received reward for their service and suffered for the cause. Despite being a Neville at birth – sister to both Cecily, duchess of York, and the earl of Salisbury – Anne, duchess of Buckingham, had been as stalwart a defender of the Lancastrian cause as her late husband. As

Prince Edward's godmother, she was trusted to act as Cecily's gaoler after the Battle of Ludford Bridge and had been widowed at the Battle of Northampton. With her was another Lancastrian widow, Lady Ismania Scales, whose husband had been butchered by sailors as he fled the siege of the Tower of London in July 1460. The last member of this trio was Jaquetta of Luxembourg, who at seventeen had married Henry's uncle Bedford and was now the wife of the faithful Richard Woodville, Lord Rivers.[2]

The arrival of this noble delegation at St Albans was the first indication to Henry and Margaret that their plan to re-enter London would not proceed as smoothly as they hoped. They pleaded on behalf of the city of London for grace, asking that no army should come within the gated walls of the capital and begging the king and – most importantly – the queen for mercy. The fact that the leading citizens sent an all-female embassy to St Albans, and one composed of women so closely connected to Margaret, demonstrates that although Henry had been restored to Lancastrian control it was still generally believed that it was the queen who commanded strategy. More worrying for Henry and Margaret, it suggested that the Londoners had not been convinced by the queen and Prince Edward's earlier assurances that no one would be 'robbed, despoiled or wronged' by their forces. On meeting the embassy in St Albans, Henry and Margaret repeated their earlier reassurances that they 'had no mind to pillage the chief city and chamber of their realm... but at the same time they did not mean that they would not punish the evildoers'.[3] When the ladies returned, the Lancastrian response was proclaimed throughout London.[4]

Within an hour of the royal proclamation, however, the city erupted into chaos, as a rumour spread like wildfire through the cramped and anxious streets. It was said that the earl of March was on his way back to the capital with 100,000 Welsh and Irish soldiers. A mob led by a local brewer demanded that the city council hand over the keys to the gates so that they could control which army would enter. With considerable effort, calm was restored, but the next week passed in a confused ferment.[5]

For Henry and Margaret the anxiety of the Londoners was a serious problem. Hungry and footsore from the long march south – and having been in the field for more than a month – Margaret's army badly needed fresh provisions. Its soldiers were growing restive, and the last thing the Lancastrians needed was for further reports of pillaging and plunder to reach London. To prevent unrest and lighten the provisioning load on St Albans, a portion of the Lancastrian army was marched to Dunstable. But without prompt revictualling Margaret and Henry would soon face the same desertions and desperate foraging that Warwick and York had endured in their recent campaigns, potentially with the same disastrous results. In return for the promise that no pillaging would take place, the mayor of London arranged for provisions to be sent out to the Lancastrians. But as the carts of 'bread and victuals' trundled towards the city gates another wave of anxiety sent a force of Londoners spilling through the streets to seize the carts. The provisions never made it beyond the walls. This mob was led by John Bishop, chief cook to Warwick's associate Lord Wenlock, and his Yorkist sympathies were shared by many in the city. The stories of northern hordes rampaging their way towards London had undermined the promises Margaret had made to treat the citizens fairly.[6]

Little by little, events were turning against Margaret and Henry. No provisions ever reached St Albans. A delegation of Lancastrian knights attempting to reach Westminster was driven back and skirmishes broke out at the gates of the city. An advance party of Yorkists lurking at Aldgate was unable to enter the city but perfectly able to disrupt the Lancastrian embassy. Initial rumours that Warwick and Norfolk had been captured proved to be false – the earl had, in fact, rendezvoused with the triumphant young March in the Cotswolds and was advancing on London with a sizeable combined force.[7]

The royal party was faced with a decision: should it remain at St Albans and await the arrival of a Yorkist army that its own dissatisfied and hungry force was unlikely to defeat? Or should it move south and try to take London by force before March and Warwick arrived, breaking the covenant it had made to keep the peace and potentially becoming stuck between an angry city and the Yorkists? Even if the Lancastrians entered the capital, could they rely on the citizens to keep them safe, or would they end up with the whole royal family and its leading commanders captive in the city? The only alternative was for the Lancastrian force to cut its losses and retreat north, where loyalty and provisions were assured. Under the circumstances, the choice was obvious.

Long before March and Warwick reached the capital, Margaret, Henry and their army had turned north, back towards the loyal city of York. They had failed to take the capital, but by regaining control of Henry they had achieved their main objective nonetheless. The royal couple had never been confident of the loyalty of London, but they hoped that by keeping their promise to the city they had given its citizens a reason to remember their allegiance to Henry. They had disproved the swirling rumours about unruly, plundering Lancastrian forces and shown they could be trusted. Once Henry and Margaret's army had been replenished they could return to the capital and restore Prince Edward's rights. Or so they hoped.

But unbeknown to Margaret and Henry, the Yorkists had changed their plans. Having lost control of Henry, they no longer had a royal puppet to legitimize their rebellion. March and Warwick had instead come up with a new way to justify their ambitions, a call to arms that swiftly won over the divided Londoners. Before February was out, Warwick and March had retaken London. It would have been little surprise to Margaret and Henry to learn that the Yorkist leaders had been welcomed into the city of London, but nothing would have prepared them for the next news they received from the south: March had not only taken the capital, he had accused Henry of breaking the

Act of Accord by defecting to Margaret's army, claiming that by this faithlessness Henry had forfeited his right to the throne. In a set-piece ritual in the fields of Clerkenwell, north of the city, on 1 March and then again in the packed halls of Westminster on 4 March, the earl of Warwick and his allies staged what was nothing less than a Yorkist *coup d'état*. The people were asked if Henry was still worthy to reign. The assembled crowd cried 'Nay!' Then, when asked whether they would have March as king in Henry's place they replied, as at the acclamation ritual of a coronation: 'Yea!'[8]

Thus was March acclaimed King Edward IV. Henry and Margaret faced not merely a resurgent Yorkist cause with a considerable army, but one with a rival king at its head. And the army of the new King Edward IV was marching north to bring his enemies to bay.

Towton, Yorkshire
Palm Sunday (29 March) 1461

The open plain between Towton and Saxton, which in early spring was usually alive with the noisy toil of ploughmen, presented a scene of horror. As night descended, hail and snow froze the furrowed soil, but amid the grey-brown patchwork of ice and earth, streaks of blood were still clearly visible. Everywhere the eye fell, it gazed on death. Maimed and battered bodies lay, unburied, their bloodied faces turned unseeing to the darkening sky. As many as 28,000 men had fallen here, and more beyond – at Ferrybridge to the south, and at Dintingdale where yesterday Lord Clifford had met his end by an arrow to the throat in the first phase of this two-day orgy of violence. The Lancastrians had been driven back from the river crossing over the Aire at Ferrybridge, back beyond the village of Saxton to this high plateau, near to Towton. On the northern fringe of this plain, the main Lancastrian force had assembled, flanked by thick woodland on the slopes above Cock Beck. The churned landscape of blood and snow, stretching as far as the eye could see, told the story of how this day had unfolded, and of a battle that had lasted longer than any in living memory.[9]

On the morning of Palm Sunday, the Yorkist force had assembled on the southern edge of this network of fields, stamping their feet up the slight incline from Saxton to ward off the biting cold. A mile or so from the town, a mass of footprints and hoof marks showed where an army numbering into the tens of thousands had drawn up. They cheered as one when the newly proclaimed King Edward IV – the one-time earl of March – addressed them in the gloomy morning light, their shouts seeming to rouse the skies, sending flurries of snow into the faces of their enemies. The royal standard could just be made out in the heart of the Lancastrian host facing them, whipping above the left battle in the command of the earl of Northumberland.

King Henry, Queen Margaret and Prince Edward were nowhere to be seen. They were 14 miles (22 km) north, inside the protective walls of the city of York, waiting anxiously for word of the battle's outcome. That news would be many hours in coming. In their place, Henry and Margaret's captains took their positions on the battlefield: the vanguard was commanded by Sir Andrew Trollope, hero of St Albans, and alongside him ranged the vast majority of the chief lords of England – the dukes of Somerset and Exeter, the earls of Northumberland, Wiltshire and Devon, Lord Rivers. By contrast the Yorkist cause was, as ever, a family affair: Edward IV was joined in command by his uncle, Warwick – limping from an arrow wound to the leg sustained at Ferrybridge the day before; by Warwick's uncle Lord Fauconberg, a veteran of the battlefield; and Edward's brother-in-law the duke of Suffolk. Edward's cousin the duke of Norfolk had fallen ill and his forces were still some distance away, but the fight would not wait for him.[10]

Battle opened in a hail of arrows, Yorkist steel puncturing the Lancastrian front line. The Lancastrian return volley fell short, leaving a bristling carpet of feathers and sticks in the snow between the two armies. With the weather turning against them, Sir Andrew Trollope, Somerset and Rivers spurred their horses in the vanguard into action, making the ground tremble with their advance. The Yorkist cavalry shuddered and then collapsed. The puncturing force of the Lancastrian right wing drove through the southern horsemen and on, chasing them miles away from the battlefield. Panic followed hot on the fleeing horsemen's heels, threatening to destabilize Edward's army before it had even joined battle. But although 'the Rose of Rouen' was only eighteen years old, he had calm and strength of purpose far beyond his years. He rode the entire length of his battlelines, rallying his soldiers. These men had marched all this way to support his right to the throne, he reminded them. He had been proclaimed king by the people and they stood beside him to oppose the Lancastrian usurpers. Then, in a flourish as dramatic as it was inspiring, he dismounted his horse, standing before his standard, sword in hand. He intended that day to fight beside his men and he announced that he would live with these men, or he would die with them. The contrast between the vibrant young Edward IV and the absent, pacific Henry VI had never been clearer, or more damning. Virtually by force of will alone, Edward IV rallied his panicking forces, a sea of tens of thousands turned to his command. Inspired by his example, they set to battle with grim purpose and advanced across the plain.[11]

On the bleak plateau above Towton Dale, blade hacked into undefended flesh, blows raining down as men fell, insensible, into the bloodstained earth, their broken bodies impeding the progress of their comrades. The slaughter was immense, a mutually incompatible desire to live pitching one desperate hand against another. For hours it went on like this, in a slugging match of sword and axe, halberd and mace. At last, as the noonday sun – if it showed at all – was high above their heads, a shout of triumph from the Yorkist men. A relief force had arrived under the duke of Norfolk, finally turning the odds in their favour. Whether the men themselves, or just the hope they offered, was the deciding factor was not clear. It hardly mattered. The Lancastrian line began to falter, to fall back, and at last to flee. Back, towards the road to York; away, to the wooded sanctuary to their west where they might ford the brook in safety; to the pinch point at Tadcaster to the north, where desperate men converged. As their opponents fled, the Yorkist forces, exhausted and enraged in equal measure, chased them down. What had started as a battle became a massacre. Those men who escaped the blade fell into the treacherous depths of the Cock Beck, turning its waters blood-red and creating a grim raft of bobbing corpses. In total, an area 6 miles (10 km) wide was covered with the mangled remains of the dead and dying.[12]

When word reached Henry and Margaret at York it was of a decimation. Heralds later said that 'besides the wounded and those who drowned', 28,000 men lost their lives at Towton.[13] What despairing thoughts must have assailed Henry, to see all his peaceful intentions twisted into slaughter on a scale unknown in English history? His own subjects, cutting one another to pieces on his account. Among the 28,000 corpses were men who had been vital to his resistance over the last two years: the earls of Northumberland, Devon and Westmorland; Lord John Neville; Lord Welles; the recently knighted Sir Andrew Trollope. And the final bitter conclusion was that God was against him. Battle-fields were a form of divine decision-making writ large, and whoever won the field enjoyed God's blessing. It was clear to all observers that Henry had lost it. The true king now was Edward IV, the white rose of the House of York. The Battle of Towton offered a final judgement. Henry VI was king no more. Now he and his family were fugitive traitors, rebels against the new, Yorkist regime.

Before darkness fell on the devastated field at Towton, Henry had fled the city of York. Margaret, their son and the few faithful surviving commanders were at his side, spurring northeast towards Newcastle. And above the fleeing Lancastrian family, leering from the gates of the city, the head of the duke of York was still grimly silhouetted against the sky – a warning, as if it were needed, of where Henry himself might end, if he did not stay ahead of his enemies.

PART IV

'The Great Rebellious Henry'[1]

34

'Perverse and variable fortune'[1]

Westminster and Carlisle
28 June 1461

Westminster Abbey was a riot of colour and celebration. The customary raised platform had been set in the centre of the nave, and in the very midst of it, the coronation throne. A dull-looking chunk of Scottish stone was encased within an elaborately carved and gilded chair of state. On this throne, which had accommodated more than one usurper and conqueror, now sat the nineteen-year-old Edward, earl of March. He was surrounded by his family and the senior lords of England. To bolster the ranks of honourable attendants thirty-two new Knights of the Bath, created the previous night as tradition dictated in the Tower of London, stood resplendent in their robes. Among them were Edward's two younger brothers, George and Richard. The elder, eleven-year-old George, had just been created duke of Clarence, and eight-year-old Richard would be raised to similar status as duke of Gloucester in November. They had enjoyed a remarkable six months. In the wake of the Battle of St Albans their panicked mother Cecily had sent them into exile in Burgundy, but Edward's improved fortunes meant the pair were shown 'great reverence' by the duke of Burgundy himself.² Now they enjoyed further elevations as a result of their brother's success. The future was bright for the House of York.

As Edward stepped out of the shadows of the abbey into the brightness of the churchyard, heading for Westminster Palace, a clamour of excited cheers greeted him. He had the impressive height, strength and auburn hair of his royal ancestors and the people of London already seemed to have taken him to their hearts. 'Words fail me to relate how well the commons love and adore him', wrote a Milanese correspondent from London. Edward's new subjects in the south treated him 'as if he were their God'.³

But even as adoring cheers echoed in the ears of the new King Edward IV outside London, at the northern tip of the realm, artillery wagons trundled as an army of rebels and Scots surged across the border, massing ominously before Carlisle. These forces did not recognize a Yorkist king. To them, he was merely the 'earl of March'. This army bore the standard of the man they still believed was the true king of England. They fought for Henry of Lancaster.

It had been a desperate royal family who had staggered across the Scottish border early in April 1461. Some divine good fortune had kept them ahead of the Yorkist soldiers at their back, but only just. The city of York – where they had awaited the outcome of the Battle of Towton – had promptly submitted to King Edward when he arrived at its gates, and their next refuge at Newcastle soon fell in its wake. At Edinburgh the dowager Queen Mary of Scotland had come to meet Henry, Margaret and Prince Edward in state. She offered them sanctuary again on behalf of her son, King James III, but the price for such assistance was going up. With his kingdom in the hands of another and his supporters depleted by death and imprisonment, Henry's negotiating hand was weak. In return for a renewal of the promise of a marriage alliance and some military assistance, in April he ceded the

13. Isabella, duchess of Burgundy, was an important mediator in the diplomatic negotiations between England, Burgundy and France. Despite her purported impartiality, she was as shrewd and self-serving as her husband Philippe.

14. After being pulled from a pile of corpses on Agincourt battlefield, Charles, duke of Orléans, endured twenty-five years of imprisonment, including a spell in the Tower of London. Henry's decision to release Orléans defied his father's will – and proved a costly mistake.

15. Eleanor Cobham was said to have lured the duke of Gloucester into marriage with her wiles. Her attempts to take Henry's throne through necromancy and prognostication led to her disgrace – and almost to her death.

16. An image from a book presented to Margaret of Anjou on her marriage to Henry presents them as an idealised royal couple: the queen submissive, the king regal. But as Henry faltered, Margaret became the steel core of the Lancastrian regime.

17. The claim of Richard, duke of York to the throne was arguably superior to Henry's, but his overly assertive attempts to press his rights aroused Lancastrian suspicions. A pattern of mutual mistrust was established that he and Henry never resolved.

18. Libidinous, charismatic and martial, Edward IV of York was everything Henry VI was not, as both a man and a king. But his romantic intrigues would almost cost him his throne.

19. The Wars of the Roses rent the northern Neville family in two: Richard, earl of Salisbury, and Cecily, duchess of York, became leading Yorkists, but their sister Anne, duchess of Buckingham, remained a fervent Lancastrian.

20. Silver-tongued and ruthless, Richard Neville, earl of Warwick, impressed international onlookers with his charm and Englishmen with his naval exploits. 'The Kingmaker' was the source of many of the scurrilous rumours that undermined the Lancastrian regime.

21. In the aftermath of the Battle of Tewkesbury, Edward IV swept away the last vestiges of Lancastrian resistance, dragging Henry's supporters from sanctuary and summarily executing them. This illuminated miniature shows Edward watching the decapitation of Edmund Beaufort, 4th duke of Somerset. Such brutal efficiency assured the restoration of Yorkist rule – and cost Henry his life.

22. After his death, the protracted suffering and quiet forbearance of 'holy King Henry' won him the affection of his former subjects. His tomb at Windsor became a shrine, and many miracles were attributed to his intercession.

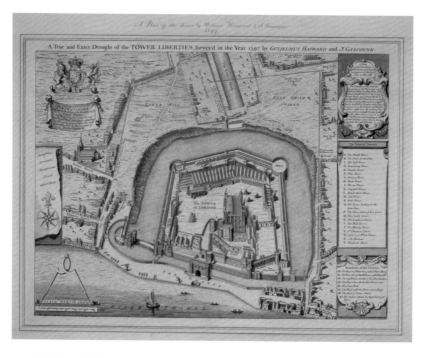

23. Site of Henry's triumphs and tragedies, the Tower of London served as his palace, fortress and prison. On the night of 21 May 1471 Henry died here. Despite Yorkist claims that he expired of melancholy, he was almost certainly murdered.

24. In a manuscript that was probably intended as a gift for Henry, Fortune's Wheel spins inexorably. Few kings have so amply fulfilled this image of the monarch laid low by fate, only to rise again, as Henry VI.

border fortress of Berwick to the Scots. This was a heavy loss, for it had been in English hands for over a century and many men had lost their lives contesting it. Henry's subjects were likely to resist its surrender. But then again, currently Henry's subjects seemed to consist of little more than his wife, his son and the thirty or so faithful servants who had followed them north. Under the circumstances, the loss of Berwick was a necessary evil.[4]

The Lancastrian court in exile that established itself at Edinburgh contained a number of supporters who had served the House of Lancaster for many years and were determined to see it restored. Henry Beaufort, duke of Somerset, was unsurprisingly prominent, as was his half-brother Thomas, Lord Roos, a powerful northern lord who had consistently worked alongside his Beaufort relatives and Percy neighbours. Roos had been as active a Lancastrian captain in recent years as Somerset himself, fighting at Guisnes, Wakefield, St Albans, Ferrybridge and Towton, and he now brought his six-year-old son Edmund to Scotland to join Henry and Margaret.[5] Presumably there were suspicions about further family assistance on Roos's behalf as King Edward ordered Roos's wife, Philippa, to be arrested in June 1461. Philippa had been one of the ladies invited to participate in the ceremonies to celebrate Prince Edward's birth, and she and her husband were not the only couple to share a family loyalty to Henry and Margaret.[6]

A number of the men attendant on them in Scotland at this time had met their wives while in royal service: Giles St Lowe, Sir Robert Whittingham and Sir William Vaux were all married to women who had long served Margaret. Whittingham's wife Katherine had been one of Margaret's 'damsels' in 1452, and he himself had served every member of the family, working as one of Henry's ushers before becoming keeper of the queen's great wardrobe and receiver-general for Prince Edward. Giles St Lowe, who was married to another 'damsel', Edith, had been a squire in Margaret's household and an esquire of the king. Sir Edmund Hampden, another stalwart in Edinburgh, had served

Margaret since she arrived in England in 1445 and in 1458 was made Prince Edward's chamberlain.[7]

With such dedicated followers, it is little wonder that this group showed no intention of living out its days in quiet obscurity in exile. From the beginning, the intention was to restore the Lancastrian dynasty to the throne. This project would be dependent not merely on the Englishmen and women still loyal to Henry, but on the fostering of relations with international powers. With foreign aid – and, crucially, with foreign money – there was hope of recovering Henry's crown. They placed their first hope on the family connections of Margaret and Henry. The House of Anjou was still high in the favour of Charles VII of France, and the 'auld alliance' that bound the interests of Scotland and France made the fugitive Lancastrians hope that those nations would now combine their efforts to help Henry. By May 1460, Charles's chief councillor (and old Angevin servant) Pierre de Brézé had been enlisted to launch an attack on the Channel Islands, which ended with a successful invasion of Jersey.* This was the prelude to a summer of concerted troublemaking by Henry's supporters across England and Wales.[8]

In the first weeks after Towton, Edward IV had attempted to cow the areas of his new realm with particularly strong Lancastrian sympathies. In the north, which clung tenaciously to Henry's cause, Edward oversaw the capture of key rebel leaders including Lord Rivers and his son Anthony Woodville, and he had personally attended the execution of his old enemy the earl of Wiltshire in Newcastle. Showing a capacity for reconciliation that could occasionally rival even Henry's, Edward also worked to win over key Lancastrians. Bishop Laurence Boothe of Durham, who enjoyed near-independence in the vast prince-bishopric over which he presided, had once been Queen Margaret's chancellor. Having abandoned Henry before the Battle of Northampton,

---

* Although mainland Normandy was lost by King John in 1204, Jersey and the other Channel Islands remained attached to the English crown.

Boothe was perhaps more malleable than some of his colleagues, and he became pliant as a lamb when Edward appointed him his personal confessor. It was the bishop's armed host that helped drive back a Lancastrian force that raised its standard over Brancepeth and Ryton in Northumberland that June.[9] 'Edward has not yet made himself supreme over the whole kingdom', Coppini informed the pope in June, nor had he 'reduced it to peace'.[10]

There was sufficient residual sympathy for the Lancastrian cause for Edward to turn to the tried and tested weapon of character assassination to undermine it, his regime churning out ballads in praise of the 'rose of Rouen' while condemning the foolish and cuckolded Henry. Officially, these sentiments were expressed in the first parliament of Edward's reign, summoned in November 1461, which attainted Henry, Margaret and '*her* son' Prince Edward of treason. Henry was condemned for his 'great, heinous and detestable malice' and Margaret for intending 'the complete destruction of the said realm, namely of its southern regions'.[11]

The subtle reference to Edward's illegitimacy was repeated in broader brushstrokes abroad. From Burgundian territory, the Milanese ambassador Prospero di Camulio reported rumours of Margaret's plans to 'unite with the duke of Somerset', poison Henry and force her son on to the throne. Henry was said to be so confused about the child's paternity that he believed Prince Edward was 'the son of the Holy Spirit'. Juicy though such gossip was, Prospero did not entirely believe it: 'These may only be the words of common fanatics, such as they have at present in that island.'[12] However, sexual slander of this sort reflected a wider representation of Margaret and Henry's relationship. If she was unruly and disordered, he was 'unwise or innocent'. One contemporary ballad imagined Henry lamenting:

I wedded a wife at my device
That was the cause of all my moan.[13]

Another ballad decried both Henry's naivety and Margaret's unnatural female authority:

> Scripture sayeth, 'Woe be to that region
> Where is a king unwise or innocent.'
> Moreover it is right a great abusion,
> A woman of a land to be a regent –
> Queen Margaret I mean, that ever hath meant
> To govern all England with might and power.[14]

In rumour, as in reality, the true motivating force behind Lancastrian resistance was Margaret. Although Henry was accused
by Edward IV's parliament of participating in the rebel attack
on Ryton and Brancepeth in summer 1461, he was playing little
more than a puppet role, acting as figurehead while the real
effort of promoting and sustaining the Lancastrian cause was
Margaret's. By August Margaret was at the heart of the resistance
court in Edinburgh with their seven-year-old son, directing their
faithful Lancastrian commanders to resist sieges, lead armies
and set off on daring diplomatic missions, while Henry took
a small travelling household to the coastal priory of Kirkcud-
bright in the southwest of Scotland to seek solace in the ritual
and quiet of monastic life.[15]

It is hard to escape the impression that Henry's desire for
his own restoration was distinctly ambivalent. His experience of
kingship had been one of intense stress, external pressure and
an increasing awareness of his own deficiencies. For almost a
decade he had presided over a fracturing government, a disappointed populace and a bleeding realm. The motivation to maintain the mental and physical exertions of not only ruling, but
now regaining, a kingdom must have been difficult to summon.

But what was the alternative? Perhaps Henry, Margaret and
Edward could retreat into quiet obscurity, living off whatever
meagre support their continental relatives were willing to
spare for their survival. But as Edward of Lancaster grew into

manhood, he would represent a threat to the Yorkist regime. A rival prince returning to claim the inheritance of which he had been dispossessed, and thereby ousting the present king, was fast becoming a cliché of English politics. Thus had Henry IV usurped Richard II in 1399, and Edward IV had repeated the tactic with Henry VI in 1461. It seemed extremely unlikely that the proactive and occasionally ruthless Edward IV would let the Lancastrian prince survive if he showed any indication of becoming such a threat. It would be a far from tranquil exile under those circumstances, as Henry himself must have realized. Even if Henry had been willing to risk the life of his son – and there is nothing to suggest he had anything but natural paternal feeling for Prince Edward – there was no way Margaret would do so. Already, like a lioness, she held her cub close, keeping a watchful eye on any potential threat.

Then there was the question of duty. A king had a personal and dynastic duty to defend his realm and that did not end simply because he had been temporarily deprived of his throne. The very nature of fifteenth-century kingship was that it did not involve choice – you were born to be king, anointed in a sacred ceremony and acclaimed by your people, then ruled until you died. A king's exalted status came not merely with superior power and wealth, it also came with a heavy sense of responsibility. 'The king... is given for the kingdom,' as Henry's chancellor Sir John Fortescue wrote, quoting St Thomas Aquinas, 'and not the kingdom for him.'[16] If kings who inherited the throne as adults understood the basic principle that their unique position entailed lifelong responsibility to their subjects, how much more aware must Henry have been, who had never known any other existence – and certainly no other career – than as king? It might suit him far more to retire to a Scottish monastery with a handful of servants and pray his days away. But his son's future, his family honour and his responsibility to the crown demanded that he regain his throne. If he was ever uncertain of this responsibility, it is hard to believe that his companions in exile would have been slow to remind him of the fact.

As the year wore on, it became clear that regaining the throne would be no easy task. Summer gave way to autumn and resistance to Edward's regime steadily crumbled. In September, the Northumbrian strongholds of Alnwick and Dunstanburgh fell to King Edward's northern supporters while Pembroke Castle – Jasper Tudor's Welsh seat – submitted to Yorkist forces. In October Jasper himself, with the duke of Exeter and their allies, was defeated in battle at Twt Hill outside Caernarvon; Jasper and Exeter fled into exile in Brittany. By October Hammes Castle in the pale of Calais had also submitted to Edward's rule and even the duke of Somerset, briefly imprisoned by Louis XI, had settled into temporary exile in the Burgundian territories. In the West Country, a resistance led by William, 'bastard of Exeter', and Sir Baldwin Fulford, with French naval support, was crushed and the leaders executed in Edward's presence. Fulford's head was impaled in the marketplace of Exeter for eighteen months, only eventually being removed in March 1463 because 'it daily falleth down'.[17]

With crushing punishment for rebels, and open-armed forgiveness offered to those who bent the knee to Edward, it is little wonder that many Lancastrians now chose to make peace with the new regime. Sir Ralph Percy, the acting head of the powerful northern family, was allowed to remain constable of Dunstanburgh Castle after surrendering the fortress to Edward in September 1461. Lord Rivers and his son, Anthony Woodville, who had faced personal humiliation and military defeat at the hands of Edward and the Nevilles, nonetheless submitted to him. In August Lord Rivers spoke to a Milanese ambassador about the hopelessness of Henry's restoration. The Lancastrian cause, he believed, 'was lost irretrievably'.[18]

The heavens themselves seemed to have turned against the House of Lancaster, expressing celestial displeasure with supernatural signs. In Hertfordshire in July, it rained blood.

In November, a strange star was seen in the sky over southern England, its rays extending 'marvellously' like swords.[19] That summer there was an eclipse, and Francesco Coppini was reliably informed by 'some astrologers, and, in particular... a worthy man who is a member of a religious order and a prelate' that the event would spell death for a European prince.[20]

Yet as desperate as the situation seemed in England, there was still hope of support for Henry's cause from abroad. His island nation had strong international connections, and it was to those that Henry and Margaret turned for support. If they could win foreign assistance for their cause, they could hope to raise sufficient money and manpower to launch an effective invasion and could also apply serious diplomatic pressure to Edward's regime. Henry and Margaret were related to the ruling families not only of France but also of Sicily, Castile and Portugal, even to their old adversary Burgundy. But to forge international alliances demanded risking the lives of their supporters, perhaps even of themselves, to the treacherous seas that divided them from Europe. And almost before their mission had begun the international situation conspired against them.

Dieppe, Normandy
August 1461

The ship that put into Dieppe bore a small party of men, but a considerable burden of hope. The group had set out from Edinburgh with a commission from Henry and Margaret to forge an alliance with King Charles of France, strengthening the union that they had recently made with Queen Mary of Scotland. As a sign of its seriousness the embassy was headed by Henry Beaufort, duke of Somerset, and supported by Sir Robert Whittingham, a long-term servant of the House of Lancaster, and Robert, Lord Hungerford and Moleyns, who had been one of the last commanders to attempt to hold London against the Yorkists in

1460. Margaret and Henry trusted that appeals to their uncle, Charles VII, for military and financial aid would be able to achieve a combined assault on the Yorkists in England, with Scottish, French and loyal English soldiers in their ranks. Since Charles's chief counsellors included Margaret's Angevin relatives and the old Angevin servant, Pierre de Brézé, there seemed every reason to hope. Every reason, that is, until the embassy reached port.

On 30 August Whittingham and Lord Hungerford and Moleyns wrote to Margaret in a panic. Three times before they had attempted to convey a message to the king and queen across the sea. One letter they sent via Bruges, to be carried on the first ship bound for Scotland. Another was dispatched in the same caravel* that brought them to France, and the last in another vessel that happened to be in port at Dieppe. 'But madam,' wrote the pair, 'all was one thing in substance': King Charles VII was dead, and the Lancastrian ambassadors under arrest. Their letters and writings – instructions from Henry and Margaret, and their safe conducts, rendered useless by the death of the king – had all been seized on arrival. Whittingham and Lord Hungerford and Moleyns were in Dieppe. Somerset had been carted off to imprisonment at the more secure fortress in Arques. All the optimistic diplomacy that the Lancastrian ambassadors had planned was swept away in an instant.[21]

Charles's death was not unforeseen; there had been rumours of ill health and astronomical predictions of his imminent demise for almost a decade. By 1457 he was suffering from an incurable disease in his leg – perhaps a varicose ulcer – which suppurated with pus. But this was not what killed him. His death was heralded by an apparently innocuous toothache. When a rotten tooth was removed, an abscess formed that led to an infection in his jaw so serious that he could neither eat nor drink without pain. In an age before antibiotics, the infection

---

* A caravel was a small, swift ship.

was incurable and he died early in the afternoon of Wednesday 22 July 1461.[22]

The new king of France was no friend to the House of Lancaster. At thirty-eight, Charles's son Louis XI already had a reputation for double-dealing. There was little to recommend him as an ally beyond his new title and the fact he was first cousin to both Henry and Margaret. Louis had inherited his father's ruthlessness. He had also inherited Charles's bad legs, walking with an awkwardness exacerbated by an old war wound: while campaigning in Alsace twenty years earlier he had been pinned to his saddle when an arrow pierced his knee. His ungainliness infected his speech too – he had a slight impediment – and his manners were far from impressive. He ate and drank to excess, made crude remarks and dressed so shabbily that more than once he was mistaken for a servant. For over a decade Louis and his father had been estranged as a result of the dauphin's treasonable plotting and since 1456 Louis had lived at the Burgundian court, taking a morbid interest in astrological prognostications of his father's death. Despite Charles's attempts at reconciliation, when the king died Louis was still 300 miles (480 km) away.

Henry and Margaret were concerned that after so many years in the court of their enemy, Louis would have grown to share Philippe of Burgundy's Yorkist sympathies. Initial signs were not encouraging. One of Louis's earliest acts as king was to imprison Margaret and Henry's new French ally, Pierre de Brézé. No longer would Margaret's Angevin relatives and friends be at the heart of royal affairs. Charles VII had been subtle and self-serving, but he had occasionally demonstrated some familial feeling for Henry and Margaret. Louis's arrest of the Lancastrian embassy suggested that the new king would not let kinship cloud his judgement.[23]

Even worse, that summer both Louis and Philippe of Burgundy applied pressure to Mary of Guelders to give up her Lancastrian refugees. After a Scottish–Lancastrian attempt to take Carlisle ended in humiliating retreat, Mary's commitment to Henry's cause cooled considerably. Fortunately for the Lancastrians, just at the point it seemed they might lose their Scottish sanctuary, consensus around Mary's rule fell apart.

As Henry would have been all too aware, a child king encouraged factionalism: the adult politicians around him struggled to gain control of the monarch and, through him, the realm. Within months of Henry and Margaret's arrival in Scotland a rift had opened up around James III between a young party associated with Queen Mary and a faction of 'old lords' led by James Kennedy, bishop of St Andrews. Kennedy had been absent on diplomatic missions during the crucial period of 1460–1 in which James II died and Mary was granted guardianship of James III, but as soon as he returned he challenged the queen's authority. Kennedy's ascension was vital to Henry's cause, for, unlike the Burgundian Mary, he was firmly pro-French and pro-Lancastrian. He had even promised the late Charles VII to aid Henry to the best of his powers.[24] With Kennedy assuming dominance in Scottish politics, there was hope that Margaret and Henry could persuade Louis to join them and offer support. Where the king of France led, it was fervently hoped that others would soon follow, and by early 1462 the full scale of Lancastrian ambition in Europe was revealed.

Hertford
February 1462

Although his coronation had been greeted with acclaim, as the first anniversary of Edward IV's accession approached the Yorkist regime could still not consider itself securely established. Edward struggled with many of the same anxieties, both domestic and international, as his predecessor. Throughout the winter, the earl of Warwick's fleet patrolled the seas and beacons lined the south coast, prepared at any moment for an anticipated invasion. The new year brought reports from the Low Countries that Philippe of Burgundy was seriously ill, prompting Edward to hold processions and religious services to pray for his recovery. If Philippe died, the next duke of Burgundy would be his handsome young son Charles of Burgundy who, unlike his father, was a firm supporter of the Lancastrian cause. Charles had recently had Henry Beaufort, duke of Somerset, freed from French imprisonment and brought to his court in Bruges. Soon after, the other members of the Lancastrian mission to France, Robert, Lord Hungerford and Moleyns, and Sir Robert Whittingham, were also at liberty and on their way back to Henry in Scotland.

In England there were fears of imminent rebellion. The West Country saw 'suspicious congregations' assembling and in the abbey of Bury St Edmunds three monks and the abbot were arrested for pinning notices to local church doors proclaiming that the pope had given absolution to all of Henry's followers and excommunicated those taking the side of King Edward. Edward IV was forced to appoint commissions of *oyer et terminer* to investigate treason in eight major English cities and towns, and in counties across the realm. This unrest all stemmed from the same source: from the small collection of Lancastrian partisans at Margaret and Henry's court in Scotland. For months Margaret's agents had been active, striving to unite Lancastrian loyalists, disgruntled Yorkists and foreign princes in a concerted attack on Edward's rule.[25]

The full extent of their ambition became clear when a number of arrests were made early in 1462. First, a Lancastrian spy called John Worby was seized in Hertford. The international conspiracy to which he confessed was staggering in its scope and ambition, involving the rulers of Denmark, Aragon, Navarre, Castile, Portugal and even Burgundy and a force numbering into the hundreds of thousands. The plan, Worby confessed, was for foreign troops to land in concert with Lancastrian commanders while Edward was distracted by rebellion in the north of England: Exeter and Jasper Tudor would lead Breton soldiers to Beaumaris in Anglesey, Margaret's brother Jean of Calabria would join Lord Hungerford and Moleyns and the duke of Somerset to land 60,000 Spanish troops on the coast of East Anglia. Sandwich would be the launching point for an invasion by Louis's French forces, while at the opposite end of the kingdom Henry would command a Scottish army over the border.

Details of how the invasion would commence were only discovered when Edward's men intercepted messengers riding between the Lancastrian court in Scotland and East Anglia. Secret letters revealed plans for a royal assassination to be carried out as the king rode towards Northumberland. The murderer would not be a Lancastrian soldier but one of Edward's own noble attendants: John de Vere, earl of Oxford.[26] Oxford had long been a servant of Lancaster. His eldest son, Aubrey de Vere, was married to the late duke of Buckingham's daughter and was known to be 'great with the queen'.[27]

On 13 February 1462 Oxford, Aubrey and their co-conspirator Sir Thomas Tuddenham (Henry's old keeper of the wardrobe) were suddenly arrested. Within a fortnight all three were attainted as traitors and condemned to death. For good measure, the fifty-year-old countess of Oxford was also imprisoned.[28] The citizens of London were said to pity Aubrey, whose 'goodly personage and youth' made them hope for a royal pardon, but Edward IV showed no such mercy. Six days after Aubrey was beheaded his father the earl of Oxford walked barefoot through the city streets to Tower Hill, where a 2.5-metre (8 ft) scaffold awaited him. The Burgundian chronicler Jean de Waurin claimed that Oxford was hanged and eviscerated, his entrails being thrown on a fire, before he was quartered and beheaded. However, Waurin was not an eyewitness to these events; it is more likely that Oxford was given the relative mercy of a swift beheading.[29]

The discovery of the Oxford conspiracy not only deprived Henry and Margaret of three useful and prominent supporters, it also spoiled their scheme for an invasion on several fronts

– if not, indeed, for Edward's final removal from politics. It was now more important than ever for the Lancastrian leaders to gain international support for their cause, to ensure that they could go ahead with some form of assault on England. With the stakes so high, it was no longer enough to rely on their noble supporters to act as ambassadors. In August 1461 Whittingham and Lord Hungerford and Moleyns had sent a stark warning to Margaret from Dieppe: she must not follow them across the Channel. 'Adventure not your person, nor my lord the prince, by the sea,' they wrote. 'And for God's sake,' they added, almost as an afterthought, 'the king's highness [should] be advised the same.'[30] But by spring 1462, Margaret had no choice. Carefully laid Lancastrian plans were in disarray and vital allies lost. They must gamble the queen's safety in the hope that direct appeal to their kin in Europe would yield the assistance they needed to regain the throne. The queen would take Prince Edward and a small, trusted coterie of servants with her to France, while Henry would remain in Scotland. Deficient as Henry's kingship was, he was still a vital figurehead for the Lancastrian cause and if he fled overseas it would appear alarmingly like an abandonment of his realm. Moreover, given Henry's known inadequacies as a diplomat, it must have seemed unwise to entrust complex and potentially dangerous international negotiations to him. The pliant Henry was not the man to treat with Louis XI, a prince so infamously subtle that he later earned the nickname 'the universal spider'.

Thus, with £290 of Mary of Guelders's money in her purse, a commission from Henry to act as his envoy, and their son at her side, Margaret set sail from Scotland in April 1462, headed for France.

35

'Outwards enemies'[1]

Tours, France

28 June 1462

Inside the armour-producing city of Tours, among the steeply pitched roofs and brick-and-timber staircases that wound up the outside of its buildings, Margaret had gathered a party of defiant Lancastrians. Their journey from Scotland had been a circuitous one, allowing for disembarkation in Brittany – where they had been royally received by Duke François and laden with gifts – and a brief family visit to Angers, for Margaret's father René to finally meet his grandchild, Prince Edward. To Margaret it was a strange sort of homecoming. She had not seen her family, or the land in which she grew up, for seventeen years. The heavy-jowelled features of her father may have sunk a little with age but the undulating, vineyard-rippled landscape of Anjou and the distinctive tufa buildings bordering the Loire were little changed. It was just outside her father's territory, in the city of Tours, where she had celebrated her proxy marriage to King Henry in 1444. Now, in very different circumstances, the fugitive queen finally secured the aid that her ambassadors had been unable to prise out of the French king. On 28 June 1462, Margaret sealed and proclaimed an alliance with the 'most illustrious and serene prince, our cousin' King Louis of France.[2]

The hundred-year truce between Louis and Henry was to commence immediately. Even more significantly for the Lancastrian cause, Louis promised that henceforth any Englishmen entering his realm must show a certificate from Henry or Margaret proving that they were loyal – i.e. Lancastrian – subjects. No safe conducts would be permitted to Edward's subjects and trade of victuals and merchandise between Edward's followers and Louis's domains was forbidden. To show the strength of Louis's adherence to Henry's cause, he ordered proclamations to be made throughout his lands announcing their treaty and he swore not to enter into any alliance with Henry's 'rebellious subjects'. Despite Louis's antipathy towards him, Pierre de Brézé was released from prison to lead an army of Frenchmen to assist Margaret's planned invasion of England. By 16 August Louis was ordering the impressment of ships and sailors to transport Margaret and her invading army across the Channel to England. Duke François of Brittany had also promised to send his own soldiers to join her.[3]

However, the compact publicly agreed at Tours was not the full story. Five days earlier, in the castle of Chinon, high above the River Vienne, 28 miles (46 km) to the southwest, Margaret and Louis had privately negotiated a very different agreement. This undertaking was so potentially damaging to the Lancastrian cause that it did not feature in the terms of the public accord at Tours. Just as Margaret and Henry had surrendered Berwick Castle to the Scots as payment for their alliance, now they handed Calais to the French to secure Louis's support. This was a monumental concession to Louis's ambition. Calais had been in English hands since 1347 and had remained so throughout the Hundred Years War despite multiple French attempts to seize it. It was also a crucial economic centre for English trading interests. Ballads had been written in praise of the English defence of Calais in 1436. It was the last vestige of Henry's dual monarchy to survive on the continent and now it had been promised to Louis for a mere 20,000 *livres tournois*. When their subjects learnt of the heavy price the Lancastrians were paying for their restoration to the throne, would they still be willing to support them?[4]

Evidently, Henry and Margaret believed so. And for the rest of the summer, Margaret enjoyed being feted by Louis's subjects as she made her way, in leisurely fashion, north to the Channel coast. When she entered Rouen, Louis ordered that she be treated as if she were the queen of France herself.[5] She was also given the honour of being named godparent, with Louis, of a royal baby that was born to the duchess of Orléans in June. The baby's father was the same Charles, duke of Orléans, who owed his freedom to Henry's fervent attempts to make peace with France in 1440. For a little while it must have felt to Margaret like the years of warfare and exile could be forgotten and that she was queen of England once more. When she returned to her kingdom with the army that Brittany, Scotland and France had promised to raise for her, she would enforce her right to be queen once more.[6]

Bamburgh, Northumberland
25 October 1462

Bamburgh Castle was an imposing spectacle from sea and land, dominating the skyline with its jagged range of sandstone walls and towers. From the powder-soft dunes below the fortress, the sea stretched away to a horizon that, on rainy days, was often obscured by eerie mist. When bright, the sea and sky seemed to mingle at the edges of vision. Now shimmering into view on that distant horizon, the sky was punctured by the bristling masts of a French flotilla, cloud and sail indistinguishable. Henry and Margaret's invasion fleet had come at last. Onto the dunes and sharp, rustling grasses surged a force of men from France, Scotland and England. They disembarked from forty-three ships, commanded by Pierre de Brézé, who had laid Sandwich to waste in 1457. But for all the alarm that news of this invasion sparked, it was a pale shadow of the vast forces that had been rumoured earlier in the year. The ships carried at most 2,000 – and perhaps as few as 800 – men. The hundreds of thousands of foreign troops that the Yorkists had feared in the spring had not materialized.[7]

Margaret's grand invasion had been undermined by the self-interest of her supposed allies. Even as Margaret and her supporters toiled to conclude their treaty with Louis, their Scottish confederates played them false. After secret negotiations with the earl of Warwick, in June 1462 Mary of Guelders concluded a peace treaty with the Yorkist government. It was only to last until 24 August, but it meant that Margaret could not count on Scottish military aid for their cause at the crucial moment.[8] Henry and Margaret now relied more than ever on the tempering force of the Francophile Bishop Kennedy, but it took him months to usurp Mary as effective ruler in Scotland. The revelation that the Scottish queen's new Yorkist allies had secretly colluded with rebel Scots to pillage the western marches of Scotland seriously undermined Mary's hold on government, and Kennedy was happy to spread further scurrilous rumours about the queen's love life. Through these means Kennedy steadily gained mastery in government and by autumn 1462 he secured the guardianship of King James. With Kennedy in control of policy, the likelihood of further Yorkist alliances diminished and the Lancastrian court was guaranteed a refuge for a little longer, but it was too late to provide much material support for the Northumbrian invasion.[9]

Unfortunately, in France Louis proved no more steadfast. Barely was the ink dry on the Treaty of Tours than he started to change his mind about it. His chief concern when he concluded the agreement was not really Margaret's invasion force – or even a Lancastrian victory, necessarily – but the opportunity it had afforded him to regain Calais. However, in order to assume control of the city Louis needed military assistance from his ally

Charles of Burgundy and the permission of Charles's father, Philippe of Burgundy, to march an army through Burgundian territories. Philippe firmly denied his acquiescence to a venture that undermined his own interests and ran counter to his York-ist sympathies.[10]

Even worse for Louis, Edward IV proved to be a very different king from Henry VI, reacting swiftly and aggressively to the Lancastrian–French alliance. On 30 July Edward appointed his uncle, Lord Fauconberg (now earl of Kent) lord admiral and gave him a fleet to harry the coasts of France and Brittany. Through-out the summer of 1462, Fauconberg's fleet pillaged and burnt its way along the shores of Brittany, and down the French littoral as far south as the Île de Ré. While its military gains were few, this coastal rampage had the desired effect: François II of Brittany offered Margaret no further assistance and the support Louis was willing to give his cousin also dried up.[11]

As a result, instead of the overwhelming invasion on multiple fronts that had been envisaged, Margaret and Henry had to be content to take a handful of fortresses in the northeast in the hope of using them as a rallying point to assemble loyal supporters for a southward thrust to regain the rest of their realm. They were, at least, successful in the first stage of their plan. After collecting Henry in Scotland, Margaret and Pierre de Brézé seized Bamburgh Castle. The fortress was being held for King Edward by William Tunstall, brother of Henry's supporter Sir Richard Tunstall. Within a short time, the Lancastrians had also regained control of the royal coastal fort at Dunstanburgh and the Percy stronghold of Alnwick Castle. Now all Henry had to do was wait for the neighbouring gentry to flock to his cause and they could march south against the usurping Edward of York.

But as time passed, Henry's subjects did not gather. It was a bitterly cold winter and, ensconced high above the North Sea in their chambers at Bamburgh Castle, the royal family looked out on a landscape lashed by rain and snow, obliterating the view and transforming the landscape. Any loyal souls who might have gathered would have to trudge along icy roads to reach them. As the short November days trickled by, it became clear that Edward IV was all too aware of their weakness. With characteristic energy and decisiveness, when Edward heard of the Lancastrian invasion he immediately assembled an army and marched out of London. He appointed the earl of Warwick, who was already in the north, to besiege the Northumbrian fortresses until Edward could arrive with ordnance. But having reached Durham, Edward suffered an unusual stroke of bad luck. He fell ill with measles and the entire direction of the northern campaign had to be entrusted to Warwick. The earl was left to command the three sieges, travelling daily the 27 miles (43 km) between the Lancastrian-held fortresses and his base at Warkworth to the south. More guns were sent under the duke of Norfolk from Newcastle, but Warwick had orders not to bombard the castles unless absolutely necessary. There was little need. With provisions in short supply and the Lancastrian fortresses poorly stocked, Warwick could simply starve out Henry and Margaret's forces. By Christmas the garrisons were already eating their horses to survive.[12]

It swiftly became clear to the Lancastrian leadership that they could not overcome the odds in these circumstances. On 13 November, Margaret, Henry, Pierre de Brézé and 400 French soldiers sailed from Bamburgh. The king and queen's purported intention was to gather Scottish reinforcements, but with so little support for their cause in the northern counties, they probably also feared becoming trapped between an advancing army and the sea. However, more misfortune befell them as they fled.

A violent storm struck as their ships plunged and rolled on the churning waters of the North Sea, splitting their fleet. The French forces struggled to Holy Island, where in order to prevent their ships falling into enemy hands they burnt the vessels and sought sanctuary in a church. They were soon surrounded and either captured or killed by Edward's supporters, the survivors dispatched to imprisonment in the south. The Lancastrian

royal party may well have been travelling in different ships –
it would be a sensible precaution to keep Henry and his son
and heir Prince Edward apart when one jagged rock or surging
wave could utterly destroy a ship. Henry's vessel reached port at
Berwick safely, but Margaret's ship was overtaken by the storm.
It was so badly damaged that the queen had to be bundled into
a little boat and rowed ashore. As she reached safety, her ship
broke up behind her. All of her possessions still on board – and
any crew members valiantly fighting to stay afloat – were lost.[13]

Their commanders may have fled, but the Lancastrian garrisons of the northern fortresses stood firm in the face of Warwick's
forces. At Alnwick the 300-strong Lancastrian and French army
was under the command of Lord Hungerford and Moleyns
and Sir Robert Whittingham. Somerset, Jasper Tudor and Sir
Ralph Percy defended Bamburgh with another 300, while
Dunstanburgh held out with a much smaller, largely English garrison. They were not only outgunned but also out-provisioned
and outnumbered. John Paston,* who served in the Yorkist army,
estimated their forces at 20,000 men.[14] The only parity between
the armies was that Yorkist and Lancastrian soldiers both were
suffering from the incessant cold and damp.[15]

It now became a race against time for Henry and Margaret.
They must send a strong Scottish force south before their garrisons were ground into submission by hunger and misery. In
order to win Scottish support, Henry and Margaret blithely
made bargains they might not be able to keep, promising that
when Henry was restored to his throne Kennedy would be made
archbishop of Canterbury, and that his ally the earl of Angus
could have an English dukedom. Their northern forces held
out throughout the long, lean weeks of Advent but as Christmas approached, morale was low. On Christmas Eve, Bamburgh
and Dunstanburgh surrendered. With his scouts warning that a

---

* This was the younger of two John Pastons whose correspondence
forms part of the invaluable fifteenth-century source, the *Paston Letters*.

Scottish army was already massing on the border with England, Edward was prepared to be merciful to his vanquished foes. Pardons were freely given, even to his old enemy Henry Beaufort, duke of Somerset. Sir Ralph Percy was permitted to stay on as commander of Bamburgh and Dunstanburgh, perhaps because the northern garrison refused to accept an outsider. When Jasper Tudor and Lord Roos refused to be received into Edward's grace they were both allowed to return to Scotland with safe conducts. The Scottish force under the command of Pierre de Brézé and the earl of Angus was left with only one fortress to relieve: Alnwick Castle. In the hope of defeating the garrison before the Franco-Scottish army could reach it, all of Warwick's considerable strength was now brought to bear on Lord Hungerford and Moleyns and his 300 soldiers.[16]

On the morning of 5 January 1463, from his position in the fortress above a loop in the River Aln, Lord Hungerford and Moleyns saw the Scottish army emerge from the winter gloom. At the sight of this large host, Warwick's miserable soldiers panicked and retreated away from the castle. To Hungerford and Moleyns's surprise, even though the way was now clear, the Scottish army did not approach. They suspected that Warwick's move was a feint, intended to lure them closer and then trap them in the open. Within the walls of Alnwick Castle, Lord Hungerford and Moleyns looked between these hesitant forces and refused to wait any longer. He broke out with most of his men, leaving a skeleton force behind to defend the castle. Perhaps if now the reunited Scots, French and Lancastrian forces had fallen on Warwick's men they could have defeated them, but believing their odds too uneven they chose caution and retreated. Abandoned by their own relief force, the next day those left inside Alnwick surrendered to the earl of Warwick. The Scottish force that Henry and Margaret had struggled desperately to send south returned to them without exchanging a blow with the enemy.[17]

Thus by Epiphany 1463, all that Margaret had achieved in two months of armed defiance and nearly two years of diplomatic effort had been overturned. Hard-won northern fortresses were again in Edward's hands, and the army for which the Lancastrians had sacrificed Berwick and Calais had achieved nothing. The French had failed them. The Scots had lost their patience. Even their own noblemen were abandoning their cause. Edward IV seemed more firmly established on Henry's throne than ever. Henry and Margaret were forced to consider an alliance that they had refused to countenance for decades. They had to trust their lives to their enemy.

Sluys, Flanders
3 August 1463

Accompanied by an impoverished coterie of faithful followers, Margaret stepped ashore into uncertain territory. A century ago, one of the most famous sea battles of the Hundred Years War had been fought in the waters off the Flemish port of Sluys, destroying the French navy and bringing the English king dominance of the Channel. It was fair to say that English fortunes had declined since then. Now the queen and prince of England came not as conquering heroes, but as penniless fugitives begging for aid from an enemy. For this was the domain of Philippe, duke of Burgundy. Circumstances were desperate indeed, for Margaret and Henry to be seeking the support of a man who had consistently disappointed, betrayed and attacked them for the past thirty years.[18]

Since their flight from Bamburgh Castle in November 1462, Henry and Margaret's fortunes had gone from bad to worse. At first it had seemed that 1463 might bring a flicker of hope. In the spring the Northumbrian commanders who had surrendered to Edward reverted to their Lancastrian allegiance, and by May Alnwick, Bamburgh and Dunstanburgh were once again loyal to Henry. In June, Henry and Margaret felt confident enough to embark on another invasion, laying siege to Norham Castle, which controlled a vital ford over the River Tweed. For the first time in almost two years, James III and his mother Queen Mary had joined forces with the Lancastrian army, presumably on the condition that this border fortress would be restored to Scottish control if it was won. However, the campaign proved to be the death knell of James's support for the Lancastrian cause.

After eighteen fruitless days of siege, Henry and James's army was attacked by a relief force under the command of the earl of Warwick and his brother John Neville, Lord Montagu. Not only did Warwick raise the siege, he also scattered the Lancastrian forces. The Yorkists pursued the retreating soldiers 63 miles (100 km) into Scottish territory, pillaging and burning as they went. They inflicted such extensive damage that its effects were felt for years. Meanwhile, under orders from Edward IV, the rebellious Scottish earl of Douglas had been harrying the western marches of Scotland. This damaging attack on two fronts persuaded the Scottish government to abandon their support for Henry. By the year's end, they would be in alliance with the Yorkist regime.[19]

It seems that in the disordered flight from Norham Margaret and Prince Edward became separated from Henry's army. Margaret later told Anne, duchess of Bourbon (sister of Philippe of Burgundy) a hair-raising tale of her desperate flight across northern England to reach safety, with nothing but her own wits to keep her and Prince Edward from mortal danger. The story evidently circulated at the Burgundian court, for both Jean de Waurin and Georges Chastellain related Margaret's plight, with suitably romanticized flourishes. According to Chastellain and Waurin, as Margaret and Prince Edward travelled through a thick forest, they were set upon by thieves. The robbers were brutally efficient, tearing the jewels from Margaret's clothing before resolving to cut the throats of their victims. But as the thieves were distracted, arguing over the division of their spoils, Margaret was able to seize her son and escape into the forest.

Their headlong flight through the trees, however, eventually brought them face to face with yet another thief. Margaret threw herself on her knees before him and begged for mercy, for the prince if not herself. 'Save the son of your king,' she pleaded, and, remarkably, the man did just that. He helped Margaret and Edward escape the forest and reunite with Henry.[20]

By July 1463 Edward IV seemed to have established enough control over England that foreign powers were willing to treat him seriously as king, and he in turn resolved to use all diplomatic means at his disposal to deprive Henry and Margaret of international aid. He was determined to make an alliance with both France *and* Burgundy. At St Omer in Artois, within Duke Philippe's territory, a French embassy from King Louis agreed to meet Edward's envoys, led by Warwick's brother, George Neville, bishop of Exeter. The very real danger existed that Louis would renege on Margaret's hard-won Treaty of Tours and instead ally with the Yorkists. It was vital for the Lancastrian cause that the talks at St Omer were disrupted. Thus, late in July, Henry bade farewell to his wife and son for what would turn out to be the last time. Their intention was that while Henry remained in Scotland, Margaret and Prince Edward would lead a delegation to Philippe of Burgundy and attempt to detach him from his allegiance to Edward IV, or at the very least to sufficiently obstruct proceedings at St Omer that the Yorkists were prevented from allying with both Philippe and Louis.

When Margaret finally reached Sluys, accompanied by her chief commander Pierre de Brézé, she was met not by the duke but by his chamberlain, Philippe Pot. Pot warned the queen that it would be impossible for the duke to receive her while he was negotiating at St Omer and that she would be well advised to return to England, for the area was crawling with Yorkists. But Margaret was undeterred. She had promised Henry that she would meet Philippe, she told Pot: 'I will go and search him out, whether it be dangerous to me or not.'[21] Leaving Prince Edward with allies in Bruges, Margaret, Brézé and three trusted ladies rode almost 60 miles (95 km) through uncertain territory west to St Pol, near Dunkirk, to find Philippe and force him to meet with her. According to Georges Chastellain, to evade capture on the journey Margaret disguised herself as a 'poor woman', travelling in a rustic carriage.[22]

Margaret's courage did not go unrewarded. When he learnt that the one-time queen of England was close at hand, Philippe – who prided himself on his chivalry – could not defy the code of civility, and begrudgingly agreed to a private interview to hear Margaret's concerns. Unfortunately, the duke was full of flattery and hospitality but noticeably short on concrete assistance. He stayed only one night in St Pol, he and Margaret steadfastly maintaining the diplomatic pretence that neither of them had ever really disliked the other, but although Margaret appealed to him as strongly as she could that the negotiations at St Omer should not prejudice the Lancastrians, Philippe refused to give firm assurances of his support. The following morning, he mounted his horse and left, granting Margaret a parting gift of a 'diamond of great cost' and 2,000 gold crowns. In diplomatic terms, however, Margaret was little better off as she left Philippe's territory than she had been when she entered it a month earlier. In September, Margaret, Edward and the skeleton court they had brought with them threw themselves on her father's mercy and took up residence in René's castle of Koeur in the duchy of Bar.[23]

Philippe of Burgundy's rejection marked the turning of the tide against the Lancastrian cause in Europe. On 8 October 1463 Louis XI made an alliance with Edward IV, promising to give no further aid to King Henry. Two months later, the Scottish government announced its own treaty with Edward. Most damningly of all, the decision to make this alliance was taken not by Mary of Guelders, who died on 3 December 1463, but Henry's old ally Bishop Kennedy. It was no longer safe for Henry to remain in Scotland. He retreated first from Edinburgh to Bishop Kennedy's residence at St Andrews, then to a palace by the sea and finally he left Scotland altogether, making for the Lancastrian bastion of Bamburgh.[24]

1463 was a year of disappointment and frustration for Henry's cause, but Margaret remained defiant. Her good faith was to be rewarded, for even now, as Henry was abandoned by old friends, left seeking sanctuary in a realm in the control of his enemy, in a castle that had changed hands three times in the past two years, hundreds of miles from his wife and son, with the major powers of Europe united against him, there was a small glimmer of hope. It arrived in the dishevelled form of the man who had defected from the House of Lancaster almost exactly a year before.

36

'False imaginations'[1]

'Beside Durham'
December 1463

The party that paused outside Durham to rest had endured a long and anxious journey. They had ridden all the way from northeast Wales, without royal licence and with Yorkist anger growing as it pursued them. At last, their destination was in sight. Henry Beaufort, duke of Somerset, retired that night knowing he only had a day's ride ahead of him. He and his men were making for Newcastle, and the armour stored with their baggage was ample testimony to their hostile intentions once they reached it. But as he travelled north the unpopular duke had been recognized. That night he was roused suddenly from his bed. There was an attempt to seize him – a struggle – and two of his men were captured. Somerset had to abandon his helmet, harness and most of his clothes, fleeing barefoot into the night in only his shift. But when Somerset finally reached a safe haven – not Newcastle, but Bamburgh, 50 miles (80 km) to the north – he brought renewed hope and purpose to Henry's cause.[2]

It was eleven months since Henry Beaufort, duke of Somerset, had apparently abandoned the Lancastrian dynasty. His submission to Edward IV had been a propaganda coup for the

Yorkists and Edward had done everything he could to vaunt his victory in winning such a hardened Lancastrian to his regime. Somerset was pardoned, restored to his estates and feted around the country by Edward as if he was his brother-in-arms. They went hunting together, jousted for each other's amusement and even shared a bed.* So marked was Edward's trust in Henry Beaufort that he allowed him to provide his royal bodyguard and garrison Newcastle on his behalf. Edward's subjects, however, did not share the royal willingness to forgive and forget. They complained that Edward pardoned those who ought to be punished.³ In July 1463 Edward had to save Somerset from a riot when the townspeople of Northampton became enraged at the sight of this Lancastrian enemy standing guard over their king. For his own safety, Somerset was dispatched 'full secretly' to his castle of Chirk in northeast Wales, close to the border with England.⁴

In November 1463 it became clear that Edward's trust was indeed misplaced. Without royal permission, Somerset fled Chirk, intending to raise Newcastle, where his men made up the bulk of the garrison, in Henry's name. The nocturnal attack near Durham had taken place when he was recognized as he was making for the city. In its aftermath, his supporters in Newcastle were rounded up and imprisoned. Some were beheaded. Despite his failure to rouse the town, when Somerset reached Bamburgh he was welcomed back into the Lancastrian fold with open arms. Henry, as always, found it easy to forgive, but the fact that the comrades whom Somerset had abandoned apparently accepted his change of heart suggests it was motivated by genuine feeling. Perhaps Somerset had been offended by the violent rejection of Edward's supporters or he found that he could not, after all,

---

* To modern eyes, bed-sharing has homoerotic overtones but for Edward and Somerset, used to a total lack of privacy and room-sharing in many different permutations, it would have been understood in a fraternal rather than sexual context. Gregory, p. 219.

stomach association with men who, for so many years, had been his enemies. By December 1462 it was clear that Somerset still believed in Henry's restoration, and he was far from alone.

Despite his apparently strong grip on power, Edward IV's popularity was in free fall. Even Louis XI had heard tales of Englishmen who sighed nostalgically for Henry's reign, saying that their taxes had been lighter and their quality of life better. Edward IV's subjects had grown frustrated with his tendency to make financial demands of the Commons for the defence of the realm, and then withdraw from fighting at the last moment. In summer 1463 Edward had put a navy to sea and assembled a formidable army against the Scots and Lancastrians, yet as *Gregory's Chronicle* expressed it, 'all was lost and in vain and came to no purpose by water nor by land'.[5] By 1464 Edward was planning a substantial recoinage, which left his subjects with unfamiliar – and poorer quality – coins in their purses. All this at a time when epidemic and economic disruption were causing a recession across Europe. It is hardly surprising that disgruntlement was rife.[6]

As he travelled north, Somerset had left behind him the flickering embers of rebellion, which erupted into roaring flames of resistance as the New Year of 1464 dawned. In January, the duke of Norfolk was dispatched to deal with treasonable disturbances on the Welsh border, and Edward IV was forced to personally oversee commissions to suppress disorder in Gloucestershire and Cambridgeshire throughout February. The traditionally Lancastrian counties of Cheshire and Lancashire rose up, with one report placing the rebel numbers at 10,000. In Northumberland, a handful of Lancastrian fortresses served as launching points for incursions into Yorkshire, the Tyne Valley and the marches. One mighty stone keep after another fell to Henry's supporters: Norham, Langley, Bywell, Prudhoe, Hexham and Skipton-in-Craven were taken and held. With most of the border region in Lancastrian hands, the vital Yorkist supply base at Newcastle was under threat. The risings stretched far beyond these troublesome shires: Edward was forced to appoint

commissions of *oyer et terminer* for fifteen counties, 'from Cornwall to Kent and Warwick to Leicester'. Every day, it seemed,
reports reached Henry at Bamburgh of how his subjects longed
for his restoration.[7]

Somerset's return reinvigorated the Lancastrian cause in England and Wales, while on the continent Margaret's diplomatic
efforts were finally yielding some fruit. Bamburgh became a hive
of rebel activity, the coastal stronghold abuzz with international
visitors and messages. News arrived from Margaret (care of the
duke of Exeter's servant) that Duke François of Brittany and
Charles of Burgundy had allied with one another and were both
now willing to offer Henry their support. Louis XI's chamberlain, Guillaume Cousinot, was also in Bamburgh early in 1464,
suggesting that the French king was no more committed to the
Yorkist cause than he had been to the Lancastrian. Cousinot was
an experienced diplomat who had featured prominently in the
peace talks with England in 1445. When he returned to France
in February 1464, he took with him messages signed by Henry
himself with instructions to Louis, Margaret, her father René,
Duke François of Brittany and probably Charles of Burgundy.[8]
Henry reassured his neighbouring princes that the country was
now so determined for his restoration that if he was 'given a little
assistance in men and money' he could regain his throne. From
René he requested artillery, crossbowmen and gunners, 'all
according to the advice and discretion of the queen'. If the duke
of Brittany could send some men-at-arms to enter the realm
with Jasper Tudor through Wales, 'at the pleasure of God all
the country will rise and the king will... receive his realm swiftly
thereafter'.[9] Henry's reliance on Margaret's political and military
wisdom is clear from his instructions to Cousinot. Not only was
she to advise on the provision of artillery and troops, but she was
also to guide Cousinot if he felt any uncertainty about the best
course of action.

By spring 1464 the activities of Henry's supporters in Northumberland even managed to disrupt Edward's ongoing peace

talks with Scotland, forcing him to transfer negotiations from Newcastle to the city of York, 80 miles (130 km) to the south. It seemed the time was ripe for the Lancastrians to strike a definitive blow against the Yorkist regime. In April Henry's northern supporters learnt that Warwick's brother John Neville, Lord Montagu, was traversing Northumberland in order to escort the Scottish ambassadors south. The opportunity for an ambush was too good to miss. Sir Humphrey Neville of Brancepeth* concealed eighty men-at-arms and archers in the woods south of Newcastle through which Montagu would pass. Unfortunately for the Lancastrians, Montagu's scouts warned him of Neville's forces and he took a different route, reaching Newcastle and gathering 'a great fellowship' of soldiers to continue north.

Montagu may have escaped this first attempt on his life, but he still had to take his men past the bulk of the Lancastrian army, which had now moved south from Bamburgh towards Alnwick Castle. On 25 April the Lancastrian forces blocked Montagu's path in the hilly moorland of Hedgeley Moor, 9 miles (14 km) northwest of Alnwick. Henry was kept away from the battlefield, presumably at Bamburgh, so Somerset took co-command with his half-brother Lord Roos, Sir Ralph Percy and Alnwick's one-time commander Lord Hungerford and Moleyns. In a chaotic clash of steel Percy was killed, demoralizing the Lancastrian forces to such an extent that they simply fled. The Lancastrian commanders seem to have been first to horseback. The loss of Sir Ralph Percy was a serious blow to Henry's cause in the north, since he was the acting head of this influential Northumbrian family. Worse still, Lancastrian failure at Hedgeley Moor enabled Montagu to slip, unscathed, through their territory to Norham, where he collected the Scots and escorted them safely back to York. Edward's treaty with the Scots was confirmed for fifteen years.[10]

---

* Sir Humphrey Neville was a cousin of Warwick's who remained loyal to the Lancastrian cause.

By May news reached Henry's fellowship that Edward was making substantial military preparations in the south. Unable to escape to Scotland, their best hope was to win a decisive victory over the Yorkists before the full might of Edward's royal artillery could be turned against them. In mid-May Somerset, Hungerford and Moleyns, Roos and Sir Ralph Grey moved their army south into the Tyne Valley. This time, Henry came with them, riding through the hedgerows and moorland bearing his sword and double-crowned helmet, reminding his subjects of his status as anointed king of England and of France. With the royal banner flaring in the wind above him, Henry could act as a rallying point for subjects to return to the Lancastrian fold. At the very least, his presence might make some northerners think twice about fighting for Lord Montagu.[11]

On 15 May 1464, the Lancastrian army was encamped in a meadow 2 or 3 miles (3–5 km) from the market town of Hexham. Henry lodged 9 miles (14 km) east, nestled in a loop of the River Tyne inside the sandstone keep of Bywell Castle. Safely removed from imminent danger, Henry and a handful of blue-liveried servants anxiously awaited news of the Battle of Hexham. When it arrived, it was devastating. Four thousand Yorkist soldiers routed Henry's forces on the hillside above the town, scattering the Lancastrian commanders across the surrounding countryside. In a desperate game of chase, Henry's men sought places to hide in local forests and coalpits. As condemned rebels, in some cases twice over, they knew they had forfeited any entitlement to mercy. If they fell into Yorkist hands, they would not be honourably ransomed, they would be killed. And so it transpired.

Somerset was captured as he fled the battlefield. His previous attacks on Lord Montagu may have been as important a motivation for Neville retribution as his betrayal of Edward IV and on 15 May he was marched to Hexham marketplace and summarily beheaded with four of his comrades. Lords Roos and Hungerford and Moleyns were found hiding in woodland on 17 May and beheaded in Newcastle. The next day, at Middleham, another seven men lost their lives. Fourteen Lancastrians were executed in York. Sir William Tailboys ran the Yorkists a merry dance, eventually being discovered in a coalpit loaded down with money that had been gathered for Henry's cause. Now the booty was divided up among Montagu's men and Tailboys joined the long list of loyalists to meet his end by the axe's blade. In the days after the Battle of Hexham no fewer than thirty of Henry's supporters were executed in the towns of Northumberland, a warning to any with lingering loyalty to the Lancastrian cause that resistance would no longer be tolerated.[12]

In the face of such mass slaughter, defiance seemed futile. By midsummer, Alnwick and Dunstanburgh Castles had submitted to Montagu's men. One fortress, however, held out: Bamburgh. Sir Ralph Grey, who had stumbled from Hexham all the way back to the castle, stubbornly refused to submit, bolstered by his fellow rebel, Sir Humphrey Neville. On 25 June, when Yorkist heralds arrived to demand Bamburgh's surrender, Sir Ralph Grey told them that he was determined 'to live or to die within the said place'.[13] By now Lord Montagu had been joined by his brother, the earl of Warwick, and an extensive artillery train. The heralds warned Grey that the Neville brothers would maintain this siege for seven years if necessary. King Edward had ordered that the fortress should be taken with as little damage as possible, so if Grey forced Warwick and Montagu to unleash their guns on it, a heavy punishment would be inflicted when the castle eventually fell: for every gunshot, a defender within would lose his head.

Grey and Neville stood firm, so the walls of Bamburgh were pounded by Warwick's cannon, sending stones flying into the sea. A Burgundian gun called Dijon 'smote through Sir Ralph Grey's chamber often times'. In one such assault Grey was knocked unconscious by a fall of masonry and lay concussed for so long that his life was despaired of. Finally, Humphrey Neville surrendered, on condition that everyone within the fortress could leave with their life, except the injured Grey. Unfortunately for

Sir Ralph, he recovered sufficiently to be brought before King Edward at Pontefract and condemned to execution. On 10 July, he was beheaded at Doncaster and his head dispatched south to London Bridge.[14]

With the fall of Bamburgh, the whole of Northumberland was finally in Edward's hands. After four years, Henry had lost his last foothold in England.* He had lost, too, the entirety of his command network in the country. The leading men who had championed his cause were gone, along with servants who had long sustained him. Among those who fell to the axeman's blade that terrible summer were Henry's purser and usher, his footman, warden, gentlemen and knights. For a man whose distaste for war was so well known – who had decried the shedding of Christian men's blood for decades – the knowledge that so much had been sacrificed in his name must have weighed heavily indeed.[15]

The only high-ranking survivor of this slaughter was Henry himself, although he only just escaped Bywell Castle in time. When Montagu's victorious forces marched on the castle, they found three of Henry's henchmen in their blue velvet gowns still there, along with the discarded trappings of Henry's kingship: his sword, crowned helmet and other accoutrements of war had all been abandoned. Henry himself had disappeared into thin air.[16]

---

* Harlech Castle in north Wales fought on until August 1468.

37

'I am the rock
of the English kingdom'[1]

Koeur Castle, duchy of Bar,
René of Anjou's territories
Christmas 1464

Margaret and Prince Edward celebrated their second Christmas as exiles in the place that they had called home since September 1463: one of the many manors of her father René. Koeur Castle was a moderately sized noble residence on the right bank of the River Meuse in the duchy of Bar near Lorraine; just the sort of place Margaret might have visited briefly as queen but below the standard of the castles and palaces in which she had resided with Henry. She, Edward and their court had to squeeze into the twenty-four principal chambers of the castle, the queen or prince probably occupying the 'king's chamber' while their attendants ate in the great hall with its sixteen fine windows. Margaret, who appreciated gardens, could at least seek solace in the pleasant grounds that stretched along one side of the towers and galleries of the castle down to a canal. At the entrance to Koeur, a dovecot with four pillars greeted guests, most of whom were either related to Margaret or returning from diplomatic missions on her behalf.[2]

René was a frequent visitor and he may have spent some of the festive season with his daughter and grandson. His own residence, the *Maison du Roi*, was less than 4 miles (6 km) away in the town of St Mihiel and both he and his second wife, Jeanne Laval, offered what support they could to the impoverished Margaret. As well as providing his daughter with this residence, René also gave her an annuity of 6,000 crowns a year, and where Margaret lacked attendants or transportation, he and his family provided it. Margaret's brother, Jean of Calabria, was probably another visitor at her table over Christmas 1464, as he was a number of times over the years of her exile.[3] Both Margaret's nephew the marquis of Pont and her brother-in-law, the count of Vaudemont, also visited her court in exile.[4]

Such family support was essential, as out of Margaret's annuity she had to provide lodgings and 'meat and drink' for her entire household, a court of fifty middle-ranking, long-term loyalists. These men and women had served the royal family for decades and followed their mistress from Scottish exile to French. Chief among these loyalists were Sir Robert Whittingham and his wife, Catherine, *née* Gatewyne. Catherine was an Angevin who had served her mistress for twenty years and named her only surviving child in the queen's honour. A number of ecclesiastics had joined this near-permanent court too, from Thomas Bird, bishop of St Asaph (who had been invested archbishop-of-Canterbury-in-exile by the Lancastrians) to a chaplain who simply appears in records as 'David'.[5] Bird had accompanied the duke of Suffolk to France to fetch Margaret in 1445 and still loyally served as her confessor twenty years later, despite being deprived of his living by Edward IV.

That Christmas Margaret also welcomed many of her aristocratic supporters to Koeur – the last vestiges of noble families clinging to Lancastrian loyalty. The latest 'duke of Somerset', Henry Beaufort's younger brother Edmund Beaufort, and his brother John; John Courtenay, who called himself the earl of Devon, even though the title had been declared forfeit by Edward IV in 1461;* Courtenay's brother Henry, a servant of Robert Whittingham and the duke of Exeter; and possibly their widowed sister-in-law, Margaret's cousin Marie of Maine. Despite being brother-in-law to Edward IV, Henry Holland, duke of Exeter, also proved an unrepentant Lancastrian.[6]

Many of those at Koeur had lost their livings, even their loved ones, for their cause. The current duke of Somerset was one of many whose father and brothers had been killed fighting for Henry's kingship. A Northamptonshire landowner called Sir William Vaux had lost his father at Northampton, and William Grimsby's Lancastrian loyalty cost him his wife – she divorced him during his exile at Margaret's court. Perhaps she might have been happier to have handed him over to Edward IV, as Grimsby – like Whittingham – had a £100 bounty on his head.[7] The duke of Exeter was also divorced by his wife, Edward IV's sister Anne, who deprived him of most of his estate for good measure.

To avoid stretching Margaret's resources to breaking point and to maintain a Lancastrian presence at a number of international courts, some of Margaret's high-ranking supporters dispersed across Europe. In December 1463 Prince Edward's tutor Sir John Fortescue wrote to John Butler, earl of Ormond[†] (then in Portugal) about the 'great poverty' of the court in Koeur, sustained only by Margaret's provision of 'meat and drink, so as we be not in extreme necessity'.[8] Henry's half-brother Jasper Tudor, earl of Pembroke, travelled between Wales, Brittany and the French court of King Louis. Where Louis proved reluctant to assist the free movement of Margaret's supporters, Charles of Burgundy often filled the gap, providing the necessary letters of

---

* John was the son of the earl of Devon, whose feud with William Bonville had rent the West Country.
† John was the younger brother of James Butler, earl of Wiltshire and Ormond, who had died at Towton.

safe conduct for the Lancastrians.[9] By 1466 he had also provided
the dukes of Somerset and Exeter with pensions and lodgings
in his territory and the earl of Devon probably joined them
there.[10] Since 1465, the increasing ill health of Charles's father,
Duke Philippe, had forced Charles to assume the governance of
his territories, offering hope that the Lancastrian cause might
finally be advanced in the Low Countries.[11]

Even after the crushing defeat at Hexham, Margaret refused
to concede that the Lancastrian cause was lost. From Koeur
she dispatched trusted emissaries to European powers whose
'nighness to their blood' might make them look favourably on
their plight.[12] After raising rebellion in Ireland John Butler,
earl of Ormond, was sent to the court of Alfonso V, king of
Portugal, to entreat Alfonso to donate 3,000 men for their
cause and to encourage the other princes of Europe to do likewise. Among the relatives Margaret hoped to win over through
Alfonso's intercession were Alfonso's sister, Eleanora; her husband, Emperor Frederick III of Germany; and Alfonso's brother-
in-law, King Henry of Castile. The marriages of two of Henry
VI's great-aunts to the rulers of Portugal and Castile had given
Henry a blood tie to most of the ruling dynasties of Europe.*
Yet it was hard for Margaret's court to capitalize on this kinship
when they seemed so woefully ill-informed: in 1464 they did not
even know the name of the king of Portugal to whom they were
appealing.[13]

---

* Henry's great-grandfather John of Gaunt had married three times:
among the offspring of his first marriage to Blanche of Lancaster were
Henry IV of England (Henry VI's grandfather) and Philippa of Lancaster.
Philippa's grandchildren included Alfonso, king of Portugal; Eleanor,
empress of Germany; and Charles of Burgundy. John of Gaunt's second
marriage, to Constance of Castile, had led to grandchildren ruling Castile
and Aragon; and his third, to his long-term mistress Katherine Swynford,
led to the Beaufort line, of which the dukes of Somerset and Margaret
Beaufort (wife of Henry's Tudor half-brother) were the most politically
important descendants by the 1460s.

In 1465 an opportunity seemed to present itself when a number of potential Lancastrian allies united against King Louis of France in a rebellion called 'the League of the Public Weal'. Among the opponents of Louis were Margaret's father René and brother Jean of Calabria, and their old allies the duke of Brittany and Charles of Burgundy. To show his dedication to the cause, the duke of Somerset actually fought alongside Charles at the Battle of Montlhéry in July. However, despite Margaret's personal intervention in attempts to reconcile the factions – and, of course, encourage them to unite their efforts instead in restoring Henry VI to the English throne – the League helped the Lancastrian cause as little as did their appeal to blood ties. It neither put sufficient pressure on Louis to force him to maintain his support of their cause nor succeeded in overthrowing him and replacing him with a prince more Lancastrian in sympathy.[14]

From here on, Lancastrian policy was to be determined by two assumptions: firstly, that Louis could not be relied upon to keep his word; and, secondly, that the best hope for the dynasty's restoration lay not with the cowed King Henry but with the young Prince Edward. Growing up under his mother's tutelage, the prince was revealing himself to be a very different personality from Henry. By the time he entered his teens in 1466 a Milanese ambassador could report that Prince Edward talked 'of nothing but cutting off heads or making war', and that he revelled in military pursuits, neglecting his more academic lessons. His tutor, Sir John Fortescue, reported that the prince 'gave himself over entirely to martial exercises', sitting 'on fierce and half-tamed steeds' to practise his skills at arms. 'He often delighted in striking and assailing the young companions attending him, sometimes with a lance, sometimes with a sword, sometimes with other weapons, in a warlike manner.' Yet, 'a certain aged knight' was heard to sigh that he wished 'he observed [the prince] to be devoted to the study of laws with the same zeal as [he was] to that of arms'.[15] Still, Prince Edward was clearly a bright boy and in December 1464 he wrote to the earl of Ormond and to the king of Portugal himself, one letter in Latin and one in English, 'with my own hand', as he proudly and perhaps jocularly put it to Ormond, 'that you may see how good [a] writer I am'.[16]

Yet Prince Edward was a fragile thread on which to hang all of Lancaster's hopes. At least twice during their stay at Koeur he fell ill, once so seriously that René's physician had to be called to attend him. The prince's illness in 1464 was sufficiently alarming that on his recovery Margaret made a thanksgiving pilgrimage to the shrine of St Nicholas at Saint-Nicolas-de-Port, around 46 miles (74 km) to the east.* Edward's second serious illness, in 1467, seems to have been measles or smallpox. Money was dispensed for a carpenter to fit planks 'under, over and around' the prince's bed to keep out light and any unnecessary draughts.[17]

For now, although Prince Edward was the hope of the future of the dynasty, Henry's restoration remained the purported aim of the Lancastrian cause. From hiding, Henry was still in communication with Margaret. In December 1464 she was able to inform King Alfonso of Portugal that the king was 'in good health, out of the hands of his rebels, and in surety of his person' thanks to a sealed and personally signed letter she had recently received from him.[18] But by then Henry had been on the run for seven months and Edward IV was determined to capture his adversary. Henry's good fortune could only hold for so long.

Waddington Old Hall, Lancashire
13 July 1465

Sir Richard Tempest and his household were just sitting down to dinner in their ancestral great hall at Waddington when

---

* One wonders if St Nicholas was chosen as the patron saint of children or if, like Henry, Margaret felt a strong attachment to that particular holy man.

their meal was noisily and unexpectedly interrupted. Like all gentlemen, Sir Richard expected to provide hospitality to well-born visitors as they passed through his land and recently he had been playing host to a party whose true identity was shrouded in mystery. These guests were sitting alongside Sir Richard in the hall now. Their master was a tall man in his mid-forties, his hair still auburn despite his middle age. It was clear that he was a person of some importance since he enjoyed a seat at Sir Richard's table, and he travelled with a household of at least four servants: two chaplains, a chamberlain, and a groom called Ellerton kept him company. The intruders who disturbed Sir Richard's dinner were led by his brother John and brother-in-law Sir Thomas Talbot. Outside, a large party of armed men who had accompanied them remained hidden beyond the thick grey-stone walls of the manor, waiting for a summons to charge in. Their purpose was to arrest and take into their custody the quiet gentleman eating at Sir Richard's table. For they had at last discovered the true identity of this unassuming stranger: he was none other than the country's most wanted fugitive, Henry of Lancaster.[19]

For more than a year Henry had eluded the clutches of the men Edward IV dispatched through the northern counties of England. His survival in the wilderness for so long was later interpreted as miraculous. Edward had begun to believe that his rival must have escaped into Scotland, so complete was his disappearance. In reality, Henry owed his survival to lingering Lancastrian loyalty and a capacity for uncomplaining discomfort. As he moved from one safe house to another, across Lancashire and Westmorland, he was accompanied by a small coterie of devoted attendants. Chief among them was Sir Richard Tunstall, who had served as Henry's chamberlain since he went into exile with him in 1461.

In the centuries after his death, stories grew up about where Henry spent this wilderness year and miraculous occurrences were connected with sites he was said to have visited: everywhere from Eskdale in the western Lake District down to the Ribble Valley in Lancashire claimed to have offered him sanctuary. More than once Sir John Maychell of Crackenthorpe in Westmorland offered Henry hospitality, whereas at Irton Hall in Eskdale he was said to have been turned away by a Yorkist sympathizer and forced to spend the night sleeping under an oak tree.[20] Having made his way across Muncaster Fell he was hosted by Sir John Pennington of Muncaster Castle, leaving him a glass drinking bowl that is known today as the Muncaster Luck. Tradition dictated that as long as the glass remained unbroken the luck of Muncaster and the Penningtons would hold. Relics of Henry's visits proliferated in later centuries and at Bolton Hall in Bolton-by-Bowland he was said to have left his spoon, glove and boots. At Bolton, 7 miles (11 km) from Waddington, Henry was hosted by Sir Ralph Pudsey, proud father of twenty-five children, and was said to have discovered a spring known today as King Henry's Well.[21]

According to Henry's later biographer, the priest John Blacman, Henry experienced a premonition of his imminent capture a fortnight before the fateful events at Waddington Hall. 'An audible voice' chimed in his ears as his pursuers closed in, which Blacman claimed was a 'revelation from the Blessed Virgin Mary and Saints John the Baptist, Dunstan and Anselm'.[22] Perhaps Henry realized he had been recognized. Contemporary chroniclers claimed that a perfidious 'black monk' of Abingdon identified him and betrayed his presence to the authorities, but given the identity of Henry's attempted captors it is equally likely that his host, Sir Richard Tempest, was the traitor in his midst. However they came to know of Henry's location, John Tempest and his party were determined to take Henry captive and claim their reward before he could escape into the wilderness again.

Tempest's men timed their arrival to coincide with a moment when Henry's attendants would be distracted and hopefully have their guard down. They had reckoned without the Lancastrians' loyalty. When Tempest's men closed in to seize Henry in Waddington Great Hall, Henry's servants violently resisted. Henry's chamberlain Sir Richard Tunstall drew his sword to drive back his would-be captors as they struggled to seize the king, and as confusion broke out in the hall Henry fled down a narrow winding stairwell in the stone walls, escaping from Waddington towards Clitheroe. He was able to struggle on to horseback and gallop for Clitherwood where there was hope of losing his pursuers in the forest, perhaps even of evading them altogether by crossing the River Ribble.

But as Henry reached the stepping stones that crossed the River Ribble at Bungerley Hippingstones, his enemies caught up with him. He and his men were seized and possibly held overnight within the tiny keep of Clitheroe Castle. His journey south, under close escort, took ten days. Henry eventually reached Islington, to the north of London, on 24 July. There, his old adversary the earl of Warwick was waiting for him. He officially placed Henry under arrest and paraded the captive king through the city with his feet bound to his stirrups by leather straps as a sign to any Lancastrian sympathizers that their king was finally in Edward IV's power. Henry was imprisoned in the Tower of London.[23]

As a captive king – even one who, official documents insisted, had ruled in deed and not by right – Henry was treated 'with becoming respect'. The claim of one sympathetic chronicler that Edward IV 'ordered all possible humanity be shown towards him' seems to be true.[24] Five marks a week were allowed for Henry's expenses with a number of attendants to serve him. 'Clothes, beds and other necessary items' were provided, together with wine from the royal cellars, and, on one occasion, several yards of velvet and 'cloth of violet ingrain' were bought to make gowns and doublets for him. Henry was probably most grateful for the provision of a chaplain, William Kymberly, who performed daily divine service, being paid $7\frac{1}{2}d$ per day. In short, it is hard to believe the claims later made by Henry's first biographer, John Blacman, that during his imprisonment Henry endured 'hunger, thirst, mockings, derisions, abuse and many other hardships'.[25]

The *Warkworth Chronicle** claims that visitors were allowed 'to come and speak with him by licence of the keepers', but who such visitors might have been is unclear.[26] It is easier to imagine Henry retreating into a world of religious observance, resignation and regret. For the first time in his entire life, no one had anything to ask or demand of him. He had simply to eat, sleep and pray. While this lack of obligation may have been a relief after a lifetime of intensely stressful responsibility, there was little to divert Henry from the reality of where his actions had led. If he was no longer surrounded by counsellors attempting to direct his activities, he was also stripped of faithful servants, family members and friends. The Tower of London could offer little in the way of relief from dark trains of thought. We do not know exactly where Henry was kept but there is no suggestion that he was allowed the liberty to venture beyond the Tower walls as some previous royal captives had been, or even, despite the claims of the Warkworth Chronicle, that he received any visitors.

John Blacman claimed that Henry had visions in these years. He saw 'the glory of the Lord appearing in human form' and the Virgin Mary appearing to him 'both corporal and spiritual'. Henry was also reported to have had a vision of a woman trying to drown her child while he was locked in the Tower. Blacman described how Henry sent the woman a message about his premonition and, as a result, the child was saved.[27] These claims have to be taken with a pinch of salt however, since Blacman had a deliberate desire to cast Henry as a holy individual; if we unquestioningly accepted everything Blacman wrote we would have to believe that Henry also miraculously multiplied loaves of bread for his followers in the north. Literal-minded descriptions

---

* This chronicle (written *c.*1478–84) is attributed to John Warkworth, the Northumbrian master of Peterhouse, Cambridge.

the French monarch).[3] The fact that Edward did not take counsel from any of his lords on so important a political decision was alarming, for royal marriage was a political game, not a matter of the heart. In fact, although some mentioned love as the basis of his union with Elizabeth Woodville, many contemporaries assumed that what really lay behind his marriage was Edward's youthful horniness. Now twenty-two years old, Edward was already considered 'a lusty prince' who freely indulged his sexual appetites.[4] But despite the inadvisability of the king's secret wedding, it was impossible to annul it, for Edward and Elizabeth had slept together several times and been married by a priest in front of witnesses including the bride's mother. However much Warwick and Edward's other advisers might resent it, Elizabeth Woodville and her huge parvenu family had to be accepted.[5]

The entry of Elizabeth Woodville and her kin on to the English political scene spelled the end of Neville dominance in the Yorkist regime and, as the years passed, the resulting rift in the fabric of English political life grew wider. Warwick found himself ostracized from the king he had helped put on the throne as Elizabeth and her kin monopolized royal counsel and aggrandized themselves at Warwick's expense. The early Yorkist policy of reconciliation and generous endowments of forfeited traitors' estates had left Edward with little patronage available to reward his favourites later in his reign. Marriages in the king's gift, particularly of wealthy wards and widows, were one of the last sources of grace he had available and were therefore fiercely contested among his courtiers. Here, the sheer size of Queen Elizabeth's family represented a challenge to men like Warwick. As well as two sons from her first marriage, Elizabeth had five brothers and seven unmarried sisters, all eager for advantageous matches, and the queen was only too happy to promote their interests. The Milanese ambassador noted that Elizabeth 'always exerted herself to aggrandize her relations',[6] with the result that soon the best marriages had been snapped up by her family before the likes of Warwick – with his two unmarried adolescent daughters – could get a look-in. In 1466 Elizabeth's eldest son, Thomas Grey, was betrothed to Edward's niece Anne,* who had been intended for Warwick's nephew, George Neville; Queen Elizabeth's infant and undowered sister Katherine married the ten-year-old duke of Buckingham. Most infamously, in 1465 a 'diabolical marriage' was arranged between Elizabeth's twenty-year-old brother Sir John Woodville and Warwick's aunt, Catherine, dowager duchess of Norfolk, a woman reported by one scandalized chronicler to be almost eighty (in reality she was sixty-five).[7] The Woodvilles were not the only newcomers monopolizing royal rewards: Edward's faithful servant William Herbert secured similarly advantageous marriages and as the newly instated earl of Pembroke came to dominate south Wales, directly challenging Warwick's ambitions there.[8]

Yet in spite of Edward's apparent profligacy in marriage-brokering for his new favourites, he staunchly refused Warwick's appeals to arrange the marriage of his daughters to Edward's younger brothers. Since Warwick lacked a son, he needed his two daughters Isabel and Anne to make the best matches possible, and the teenaged dukes of Clarence and Gloucester were Warwick's ideal grooms. The vain and luxurious Clarence was particularly enticed by the prospect of marrying the wealthy Isabel, but Edward denied both his brother and his cousin their desired match. Undeterred, Warwick continued to plan the union and secretly appealed to the pope for a dispensation.[9]

As damaging as these jealous rivalries over patronage were, however, the final rupture between king and kingmaker arose from a dispute over foreign policy. After Henry's capture Edward's rule was at last accepted overseas as likely to endure, and the young king was courted with numerous international embassies bearing luxuries and exotic creatures. With the ambassadors of Castile came fine Spanish horses, and with the Aragonese

---

*   Only child of Anne of York and Henry Holland, duke of Exeter.

lions that were housed in the Tower of London. The Patriarch of Antioch escorted six camels from the Holy Roman Emperor Frederick to Edward's court, one of which later found its way to Ireland. Exactly who brought an elephant as a gift for Edward (and what befell it) is unclear.[10]

Flattering though such international attention was, the crucial diplomatic question of the day was how England ought to proceed in its relations with Burgundy and France, for it had become clear that Edward could not forge an alliance with both realms. Although the rebellion known as the League of the Public Weal had ended, formally reconciling Charles of Burgundy with Louis XI, the two princes remained bitter rivals. Both saw a defensive treaty with Edward as a means of deterring their adversary from further military intervention in their lands. The challenge for Edward's regime was deciding which alliance would support English interests better. On this his chief advisers were divided: Warwick shared Louis's distaste for Charles of Burgundy and was flattered by the French king in diplomatic communications, which inclined him in favour of an alliance with France, whereas Edward's Woodville in-laws believed an agreement with Burgundy would be more economically advantageous (although, since Edward's new mother-in-law was Jaquetta of Luxembourg, a relative of the Burgundian ruling family, their advice can hardly be considered disinterested).

Having played such a pivotal role in helping Edward achieve and maintain his crown, Warwick believed that his advice should prevail, but in a display of evenhandedness Edward insisted that ambassadors should be sent to both rulers before a decision was made. Warwick was granted the honour of leading these embassies. The French court particularly feted the earl and by the summer of 1467 Warwick had negotiated an agreement in principle with Louis: a brotherhood in arms between Kings Edward and Louis would bring perpetual peace to England and France, cemented by a suitable royal marriage and advantageous trade agreements. But the price of peace was a 'war of extermination' against Philippe of Burgundy and his son Charles, their territories being divided between the victorious kings in the aftermath. Edward found such terms hard to stomach.

Warwick returned to England at midsummer 1467 believing that he had secured an alliance with the king of France, only to discover that negotiations with Burgundy had continued in his absence. A French embassy that arrived to conclude the agreements Warwick himself had promised found itself ostracized and treated with disrespect by King Edward, and in September, against Warwick's wishes, Edward made a compact with Burgundy.[11] By then Charles of Burgundy had inherited the title of duke of Burgundy from his father Philippe, who had died on 15 June 1467. The alliance between the new duke and the king of England was sealed with Charles's marriage to Edward's younger sister Margaret of York. Louis took his revenge by casting aspersions about the bride's virginity to foreign ambassadors – the Milanese ambassador was told she already had a son.[12]

Warwick left court under a cloud, heading north to brood on these indignities in the solitude of his own estates. As a further indication of how far Neville influence had fallen at court, during Warwick's absence his brother George Neville, archbishop of York, had been dismissed as chancellor and it was later discovered that the position of cardinal promised to George would instead go to Thomas Bourchier, archbishop of Canterbury.[13]

Warwick's self-imposed exile lasted so long that it roused Edward's suspicions and necessitated mediation. At Nottingham at Epiphany 1469 Warwick and Edward were apparently reconciled through the efforts of George Neville. But as the Warkworth Chronicle succinctly observes, although Warwick and Edward 'were accorded diverse times... they never loved together after'.[14] By spring 1469 Warwick was taking steps to force his will on King Edward by military means.

If Henry heard of the trouble that his usurper's imprudent

marriage had set in motion, he might well have shaken his prudish head – lechery was a vice Henry had always warned would lead to ruin. Where Henry might see a morality tale, however, Margaret spied an opportunity. Rumours of Warwick's dissatisfaction with Edward's new bride reached her in Koeur as early as February 1465 and she immediately moved to capitalize on their estrangement. Here at last was a chink in the charismatic young king's armour that could be exploited in the Lancastrian cause. She appealed to Louis for aid to attack England while the Yorkist regime was divided. Louis responded only with disdain, mocking her efforts in front of the Milanese ambassador. 'Look how proudly she writes!' he said, denying her any further assistance.[15] But while Margaret's action may have been precipitate, her instincts were right. The breach between Edward and Warwick would prove terminal.

Over the next five years Margaret observed carefully the shifting dynamics of Edward and Warwick's relationship. Initially she and her allies intended only to exploit the breach between king and kingmaker in order to recover Henry's throne, but as time passed they began to consider the possibility of using Warwick himself in the Lancastrian restoration. The first ripples of such a confederacy were reported by the Milanese ambassador Giovanni Pietro Panicharola, who witnessed a heated argument between King Louis and Margaret's brother Jean, duke of Calabria, in February 1467. Perhaps testing Angevin sympathies, Louis praised Warwick as he and Duke Jean ate dinner together. Jean, however,

> angrily rejoined that [Warwick] was a traitor; he would not say or suffer any good to be said of him; he only studied to deceive, he was the enemy and the cause of the fall of King Henry and his sister the queen of England... As the king persisted in his praise of the earl of Warwick, the duke said that as he was so fond of him he ought to try and restore his sister in that kingdom.[16]

Hot though Angevin tempers were, the distasteful necessity of an alliance between Louis, Margaret and Warwick in the Lancastrian cause was clearly already under consideration. By May 1467 the possibility was openly discussed in the French court. Panicharola told the duke of Milan that if Edward IV came to an understanding with Charles of Burgundy, Louis intended to take his revenge by 'treating with the earl of Warwick to restore King Henry in England'. Margaret had already installed her ambassador at Louis's court in Chartres, to ensure that Louis's vengeful threats against King Edward could be directed in their interest.[17]

Margaret's efforts received their reward in June 1468, when Louis funded an invasion of Wales led by Jasper Tudor, which succeeded in raising an army of 2,000 men and burning the defiant Yorkist port of Denbigh. Alarming though this assault was, it had little long-term benefit. Tudor's men were swiftly hounded out of the realm, forcing the last Lancastrian-held fortress at Harlech into submission. But that summer, for the first time, the possible collusion of Warwick in Margaret's conspiracy to retake the English throne reached Edward's ears.[18]

In June 1468 a Lancastrian messenger called John Cornelius was captured carrying letters between the Lancastrian court in exile and the disaffected subjects of Edward IV in England and Wales.* After being tortured with hot irons, Cornelius revealed a network of dissidents that extended far beyond Harlech, to encompass London, the southeast, the West Country and Calais. Most alarmingly of all, among those implicated in the attempted rebellion were Warwick's brother-in-law, John de Vere, earl of Oxford, and a servant of Warwick's deputy in Calais, Lord Wenlock. Both Oxford and Wenlock had longer-term Lancastrian connections: Oxford's father and eldest brother had been executed as traitors for conspiring against Edward IV in 1462,

---

* Cornelius was a servant of Margaret's long-term servant and supporter Sir Robert Whittingham.

and Wenlock had been Margaret's chamberlain before defecting to the Yorkist cause. While Warwick's complicity in Margaret's network of spies and conspirators was suspected, there was no evidence yet that he was considering a Lancastrian restoration. His chief concern was his own hold on government, and for the time being it seemed that the best means of tightening his grip was by harnessing Yorkist disaffection and removing his rivals around King Edward, not by freeing Henry.[19]

As the support for the Cornelius conspiracy suggests, by 1469 disgruntlement with Edward's regime stretched far beyond Warwick's allies and unrepentant Lancastrian loyalists. A decade of Yorkist rule had achieved little but disillusionment, as the Warkworth Chronicle relates: while Edward's subjects had hoped that the new king would 'amend all manner of things that was amiss and bring the realm of England in great prosperity and rest', all he had achieved was 'one battle after another and much trouble and great loss of goods among the common people... and many men said that King Edward had much blame'.[20]

At first it seemed that the sputters of unrest that broke over northern England in spring and summer 1469 were motivated by these popular grievances. Risings under 'Robin of Redesdale' and 'Robin of Holderness' were easily quashed, so when trouble resurfaced in June 1469, Edward was not overly concerned. Dispatching an army north, he continued on a leisurely pilgrimage through East Anglia.[21] But he had been deceived. For this was no minor popular uprising, it was a Neville-promoted coup to seize control of government. The articles of complaint issued by the northern rebels had an eerie air of familiarity, recalling the 'great inconveniences and mischiefs' that had befallen the land under Edward II, Richard II, and Henry VI – kings who, it was surely not lost on Edward IV, had all been deposed by their enemies. The northern rebels complained of wicked counsellors usurping the rightful advisers of the king, subverting the law and forcing the commons to bear the brunt of royal impecunity. Save for a change of names, the articles could have

been issued by Jack Cade's followers in 1450 or by the Yorkist
lords in 1459. But the names of the wicked counsellors vilified
for their 'insatiate covetousness' in 1469 revealed who was really
behind this rebellion, for every one of them was a rival of the
earl of Warwick: Queen Elizabeth's parents Lord Rivers and
Lady Jaquetta; Edward IV's faithful servant William Herbert;
Humphrey Stafford, recently made earl of Devonshire; 'and
others of their mischievous assent'.[22]

Too late, Edward realized the true purpose of this rebellion.
By the time he urgently called up his levies to face the rebels their
numbers had swollen into the tens of thousands and Warwick
had fled the country.[23] He had slipped away to Calais with his
daughter Isabel, his brother George Neville, archbishop of York,
their brother-in-law the earl of Oxford and, most alarmingly of
all, Edward's younger brother George, duke of Clarence. On 11
July 1469 Archbishop George Neville presided over the wedding
of Clarence and Isabel in Calais and within days the Neville
faction were making for England once more, now reciting the
rebel manifesto as a call to arms.[24]

Warwick's rebellion was ruthlessly efficient. After his allies
had crushed Edward's forces in battle at Edgecote in Northamptonshire on 26 July, Warwick captured William Herbert and had
him summarily executed as a traitor. Herbert's co-commander
Humphrey Stafford was lynched as he attempted to escape
through Bridgwater, and the leader of the Woodville faction,
Elizabeth's father Lord Rivers, was hunted down in the Forest
of Dean and executed at Kenilworth with his son Sir John
Woodville. Unaware that the royal army was defeated and his
commanders dead, Edward was captured by Archbishop George
Neville attempting to rendezvous with them near Northampton.
The triumphant rebels imprisoned the king in the Neville strong-
hold at Warwick Castle before transferring him to their base at
Middleham in Yorkshire.[25]

With his rivals dead and the king in his power, Warwick intended to pursue the same tactics that had swept him to power

in 1460: he would summon a parliament to formalize his rule and reduce the king to little more than a cipher. It may even have been Warwick's intention to depose Edward in favour of the more biddable Clarence, by casting aspersions on Edward's legitimacy.*

But Warwick had unleashed forces he was unable to control. Raising the north of England meant fomenting unrest in counties that still clung to Henry's cause. Within weeks a Lancastrian army under the veteran Lancastrian Sir Humphrey Neville of Brancepeth threatened to unhinge Warwick's tenuous control of government. Warwick knew that to levy the necessary armies to put down this Lancastrian rising he needed royal authority, but Edward refused to assist him until he was granted his liberty. Perhaps for the first time Warwick considered how much easier it would be to assume power with a king as pliant as Henry VI, instead of the strong-willed Edward IV.

With no alternative to end the creeping chaos within the realm, Warwick was reluctantly forced to release Edward. At York and Pontefract Edward issued commands against the rebels in his own name and by the end of September the rebellion was crushed. As a sign of the king's renewed authority Sir Humphrey Neville was beheaded in Edward's presence at York. Warwick's bid for power had failed.[26]

An uneasy truce settled over English affairs that autumn: Edward publicly forgave Warwick and Clarence, and they submitted to his authority, but the murder of so many associates of Queen Elizabeth would not be forgotten. Sir John Paston reported to his mother from London in October 1469 that 'the king himself hath good language of the Lords of Clarence [and] of Warwick... saying they be his best friends'. 'But,' he

---

* Edward 'the rose of Rouen' and three of his siblings were born outside England, making them more vulnerable to accusations of illegitimacy. For the question of Edward's legitimacy see Jones, Michael K., *Psychology of a Battle: Bosworth 1485* (Stroud, 2003), pp. 75–87.

added, sounding a warning note, 'his household men have other language, so that what shall hastily fall I cannot say.'[27] Warwick feared that it was only a matter of time before his enemies would take their vengeance on him and Clarence. Rather than trusting to chance, Warwick resolved to strike first.

In spring 1470, a rising in Lincolnshire sent Edward riding north again. Lord Richard Welles and his son Sir Robert were blamed for the rebellion, but it soon became clear that they were acting at the instigation of Warwick and Clarence, whose livery some of the rebels were seen wearing. Warwick intended to lure Edward out into the open where he could be trapped between the Lincolnshire rebels and an advancing force of Warwick's Yorkshiremen. Instead Edward quashed the rebellion, executing both Lord Richard Welles and his son in spite of a promised pardon. This decisive royal action deprived Warwick and Clarence of support, sending them fleeing south, and eventually across the Channel to Warwick's sanctuary at Calais. But now even that safe harbour was closed to him. Charles of Burgundy sent his chamberlain Philippe de Commines to ensure the loyalty of the port at this critical moment. Even though Warwick's fleet bore his wife and heavily pregnant daughter Isabel, he was refused admittance. Warwick's ships lay at anchor as he hesitated between fighting his way into port or attempting to return to England. Isabel went into labour when the guns of Calais fired a warning shot at their fleet and her child, a son, was stillborn. Finally, around 1 May 1470, Warwick's fleet and grieving family limped into Honfleur, in Normandy, and threw themselves on the mercy of King Louis. At last, Warwick was ready to unite his interests with the exiled Lancastrians.[28]

The negotiations were not easy. With such a long history of mistrust and conflicted interests on all sides, it took nearly three months to finally bring about the alliance between Warwick, Louis and Margaret, with Louis acting as intermediary to 'shape matters a little'. On 29 June, six days after Margaret had arrived at Amboise in the Loire Valley to negotiate the alliance, the

Milanese ambassador Sforza de'Bettini reported that 'the queen has shown herself very hard and difficult'.[29] It was clear that while Margaret was willing to consider a deal with Warwick, she still did not trust him.

Margaret's reticence was understandable, however, given the diverse interests that she had to balance in the negotiations. A document that survives from this period, *The Maner and Guydyng bitwene the Quene Margarete and of here soone and therle of Warrewi[c]* hints at Margaret's struggle to avoid alienating her own supporters at the same time as ensuring that Warwick and Louis were held to the agreement. Although Margaret's court had been contemplating the possibility of an alliance with Warwick for years there were still many prominent Lancastrians in exile who bitterly opposed collusion with the man who was 'the great causer of the fall of King Henry'.[30] Others opposed alliance with the French, believing that a treaty with Charles of Burgundy was the best means of bringing about a Lancastrian restoration. Leading this opposition were the exiled dukes of Exeter and Somerset, who had suffered for their loyalty to the Lancastrian cause in the past decade and who each had good reason to despise Warwick: the father of Edmund Beaufort, fourth duke of Somerset, had been butchered at St Albans and his brother Henry had died at the command of Warwick's brother Lord Montagu after the Battle of Hexham. Exeter had been a zealous opponent of the Nevilles long before he was humiliated by Warwick while serving as lord admiral. Somerset in particular enjoyed a close relationship with Charles of Burgundy, even after Charles had married Margaret of York, and would not favour a French alliance that entailed combined military action against Charles.[31]

It was to persuade diehard Lancastrians like Exeter and Somerset that *The Maner and Guydyng* was written, to prove that the alliance with Warwick was a hard-won necessity, in Lancastrian interests, rather than a Yorkist or French ploy. The text presented Margaret carefully considering the 'parties and

friends which they might lightly lose by this mean, and that
should be a thing that greatly might grieve them and do them
more harm and hindrance than the said earl and his allies might
bring or bear unto them profit or advantage'.[32] *The Maner and
Guydyng* deliberately misrepresents the nature and duration
of Margaret's talks with her new allies, suggesting that she and
Warwick debated with one another from 15 July to 4 August.
The missives of the Milanese ambassador Sforza de'Bettini, who
was an eyewitness, show that in reality Margaret and Warwick
negotiated their agreements with King Louis separately and
were only brought together at Angers once the thorniest issues
had already been agreed. According to *The Maner and Guydyng*,
throughout the talks with Louis Margaret took on the traditional
role of a king, unyielding to the point of being 'right difficult',
at first insisting that she 'never of her own courage... might
be contented with [Warwick] nor pardon him'. Agreeing the
marriage settlement between Prince Edward and Anne Neville
alone took fifteen days, as Margaret at first 'saw neither honour
nor profit for her nor for her son' in it. Only 'after many treaties
and meetings' with her father's counsellors and the French, and
after strong assurances from Warwick himself, was she persuaded
into a more pliant position. It was 20 July, Bettini reported, when
Margaret was 'induced to consent to... the marriage alliance'.[33]

On one point, according to both Milanese and Lancastrian
sources, Margaret was immovable: Prince Edward's role in the
forthcoming invasion of England. Warwick insisted that Edward
should accompany him when he led the Lancastrian army to
retake Henry's throne, but Margaret was not prepared to trust
her precious son's life to the unreliable Warwick. Instead, Warwick would have to be content with the assistance of Henry's
half-brother Jasper Tudor. Prince Edward would follow once the
realm was secured, and act as regent and governor for his father
– the first public acknowledgement by the Lancastrian cause
that Henry was not personally capable of ruling.

Only once these agreements had been hammered out did

Margaret and Warwick finally come face to face. On the evening of 22 July 1470, they met for the first time in a decade. Warwick penitently knelt before her 'and asked her pardon for the injuries and wrongs done to her in the past. She graciously forgave him and he afterwards did homage and fealty.'[34] On 30 July, after Edward and Anne had been officially betrothed, Warwick, Margaret and Louis all swore to uphold the alliance with oaths in Angers Cathedral. The duke of Clarence, who was not present at the ceremonies in Angers, and seems barely to have featured in the negotiations, had to be content with his father's title of duke of York and the restoration of the estates he had lost while fighting his brother.[35]

For a man who had begun his conspiracy with Warwick on the promise of a crown, this was slight reward indeed. Margaret was probably not overly concerned with pandering to the ambitions of the brother of the man who had usurped her husband, but Warwick ought to have been more alive to the danger of side-lining his son-in-law. For by marrying into the Lancastrian dynasty, Warwick had effectively displaced Clarence and Isabel from any real interest in the removal of Edward IV.[36] The Burgundian chronicler Philippe de Commines, who observed these events at first hand, suspected that Warwick had 'deluded' Clarence and that he now had almost nothing to gain from the restoration of Lancaster.[37]

Clarence was not the only one with conflicted feelings about this alliance. Margaret had to hope that her alliance with Warwick would not cost her the support of such stalwarts as the dukes of Exeter and Somerset.[38] Thus, even before Warwick took ship for England, the Lancastrian restoration had a conflict of interests at its heart. These disappointed interests and festering resentments would not lessen as time passed, and they contained within them the seeds of the final doom of Margaret and Henry's cause.

39

'That puppet of a king'[1]

Tower of London
3 October 1470

T he atmosphere within the Tower of London was uneasy. After five years of imprisonment, the rhythm of the place, its sounds and moods, must have become familiar to Henry, perhaps reassuringly so after the long years of upheaval. Echoing up to his windows might come the tramp of guards and scurrying of servants, occasionally the lap of oars on the River Thames outside or the distant roar of the tower lions. But over the course of the past weeks, these familiar noises had started to be punctured by other, more disturbing sounds. Rebellion and riot had taken hold of the city streets, inciting a cacophony of noise. Had Henry heard the rumble of cannon at the city gates as London's defences were mounted? The clatter of hooves as leading citizens patrolled, trying to silence the hammering of bills on to church doors, spreading messages of defiance? Or the outraged shouts of Dutch brewers as their beer houses were smashed open by rioters capitalizing on the unrest to attack their neighbours with xenophobic zeal?

Perhaps these distant sounds could not penetrate the rings of stone encircling Henry, but he can hardly have failed to hear the panicked movements of young children as they and their possessions were bundled from the royal apartments; on 1 October Elizabeth Woodville fled the Tower. The latest woman to call herself queen of England was eight months pregnant and she did not trust the life of her unborn child, or the other children she had brought inside the Tower, to the mob seizing control of London – and especially not to the army advancing from the west. Under cover of darkness she had made for sanctuary at Westminster, leaving the long suite of royal apartments within the inner ward echoing and empty.[2]

Two days later, on 3 October, the outside world intruded into Henry's captivity for the first time in five years. The doors of his chamber opened to reveal the old, familiar face of the man who had once been his close friend and adviser, William Waynflete, bishop of Winchester. With him were the mayor and aldermen of London. They told Henry – who was neither so cleanly kept nor so well-dressed as they had expected – that he was no longer a prisoner. Edward IV had fled the realm. Henry was king once more.

How had this miracle been accomplished? As they moved Henry into the vacant royal apartments and fetched more suitable clothing for him from the Wardrobe Tower, Henry's liberators would have explained the astonishing circumstances of his release and restoration. Less than a month ago, after delays occasioned by Burgundian blockades, contrary winds and unpaid mariners, Warwick's fleet had finally set sail from France. Landing in the West Country on 13 September, Warwick, Clarence, the earl of Oxford and Jasper Tudor had advanced north and east, dispensing articles decrying the regime of the 'usurper, oppressor and destroyer' Edward IV and issuing proclamations in Henry's name.[3] Edward was hundreds of miles away in Yorkshire, lured there by a rising of Warwick's allies. Edward hurried south when he learnt of Warwick's arrival, pausing at Doncaster to be joined by promised reinforcements under Warwick's brother Montagu. But there he learnt that Montagu had defected to Warwick's cause, sick of too 'many fair words and no lordships'.[4] Abandoned by his key supporters, Edward fled towards King's Lynn, crossed the Wash by night and took ship to Holland with little more than the clothes he stood up in.[5]

When they heard that the king had abandoned them, the leading officers of government in the south had run for sanctuary and London had dissolved into chaos. Queen Elizabeth tried to fortify the Tower as Kentishmen attacked the gates and criminals broke out of sanctuary to open prisons. It was all the mayor could do to broker the peaceful capitulation of the Tower as the queen fled. All the while, Warwick and Clarence had been advancing on the capital. They reached London on 6 October and Warwick went straight to Henry, testing his knees with another display of fealty. Margaret might have been belligerent, but Henry was – as ever – entirely conciliatory. Any fight he might once have had in him was long gone.

As a symbol of Henry's restoration, on the feast day of St Edward the Confessor (13 October) Warwick escorted Henry on a procession through London.* Warwick bore the king's magnificent train and the earl of Oxford his sword as Henry, crowned once more, rode the old familiar route through the city. On this occasion, however, instead of going all the way to Westminster Abbey, where Edward the Confessor lay buried, they stopped at St Paul's, where Henry moved into the bishop of London's lodgings. Perhaps after the rigours of his years of confinement, Henry was too exhausted to travel any further.

On 15 October, parliament was summoned in Henry's name. This command, like all royal documents Henry issued in this period, now had an innovative royal dating: 'in the forty-ninth year from the beginning of our reign, and the first year of our readeption of our royal power'.[6] But while the document may have borne Henry's seal, the power behind it was Warwick's.[7]

---

*   By a strange piece of symmetry, it was ten years to the day since York had made the same journey through London as a sign of his royal rights.

Parliament met at Westminster on 26 November, with George Neville restored as chancellor, basing his opening sermon on Jeremiah 3.14: 'Return to me O backsliding children.'[8] Warwick was named Henry's lieutenant and Edward IV was proclaimed a traitor.[9] However, beyond the attainder of Edward and his brother Richard, duke of Gloucester, leniency and reconciliation were the order of the day in 1470. Of course, a few key offices of state changed hands: Warwick was re-appointed captain of Calais and chamberlain, and Clarence, after considerable delay, restored as lieutenant of Ireland. Lord Montagu, whose defection had been so important to Henry's readeption, was made warden of the east marches. Richard Tunstall, who had fought so strongly for Henry in Northumberland and Harlech, was made master and warden of the king's mints.* The office of treasurer went to Warwick's confidant John Langstrother, who was confirmed in his office of prior of St John of Jerusalem.[10] A government promise not to disturb those who had fled into sanctuary was particularly beneficial for the heavily pregnant Queen Elizabeth Woodville, who was still sheltering in Westminster Abbey with her family. Demonstrating characteristic sympathy for his opponents in their affliction, Henry's council sent Elizabeth's servant Elizabeth, Lady Scrope, to help her in her labour.[11]

With one eye firmly on the favour of the masses, Warwick chose the deeply unpopular John Tiptoft, earl of Worcester, as the sole Yorkist to suffer the executioner's axe. Worcester had earned himself the nickname 'the Butcher of England' for punishing Warwick's rebels in 1469 by impaling their executed corpses on spikes, 'contrary to the law of the land'.[12] Londoners were so eager to watch Worcester paraded to his execution that it took two days for him to make the 3-mile (5 km) journey from his trial in Whitehall to the scaffold at Tower Hill. One chronicler claimed that as a last pious act, Worcester asked for

---

* Tunstall had been pardoned and released from the Tower of London by Edward IV in December 1468.

his executioner to behead him with three blows, in honour of the Holy Trinity. This painful tribute was duly carried out.[13]

During the first weeks of Henry's readeption he stayed in Westminster Palace, where people flocked to receive an audience with the restored king. That Henry was not fully capable even of this aspect of kingship is suggested by a meeting that was later mythologized into a critical harbinger of the later course of fifteenth-century history. On 27 October, Henry met with his only nephew, thirteen-year-old Henry Tudor. The child had been named in Henry's honour and was the sole offspring of the marriage that King Henry had arranged between his half-brother Edmund Tudor and his cousin Margaret Beaufort. Margaret Beaufort seems never to have forgotten the king's kindness to her on that encounter in 1453 and came with her brother-in-law Jasper and now adolescent son to pay their respects to the man who had played such an important role in their lives. It was one of the few times that Margaret and her child had been together: since Edward IV's accession Henry Tudor's wardship had been transferred out of her control. The young Henry had grown up with Edward IV's chief supporter William Herbert and may even have accompanied him to the Battle of Edgecote where Herbert was seized and executed.[14]

The tall, slender adolescent who now stood before King Henry would go on to become Henry VII, the first Tudor king of England, and his entourage of historians and memoirists would later claim that sparks of greatness had been glimpsed by Henry VI on this, their only recorded meeting. Looking from Tudor to the others in the chamber, Henry was said to have remarked, 'This truly, this is he unto whom both we and our adversaries must yield and give over the dominion.' In other words, he prophesied the child's accession as king.[15] Leaving aside the convenience of a legend that first appeared in Henry VII's reign, when Henry VI was viewed as a holy man, what is revealing here is that although the Tudor party was permitted a meeting with the king, they soon left his company. They ate dinner only with Henry's chamberlain, Sir Richard Tunstall, suggesting that protracted social engagements were beyond Henry's capabilities.

With Henry perhaps too unwell to rule himself, it was vital that Margaret brought Prince Edward to England to act as regent on his father's behalf as quickly as possible. On 27 November 1470 Henry issued a command for the necessary funds for Warwick to assemble a fleet to bring 'our most dear and entirely beloved wife' Margaret and Prince Edward to England.[16] The reunion of the royal family could only strengthen their cause. Henry had never been especially inspiring as king and years of captivity had taken their toll. By contrast, the energetic young Prince Edward of Lancaster, just turned seventeen and with a suitable wife who might soon fall pregnant, was sure to rouse English support.[17] If a peaceful Lancastrian accession could be assured, it could swing the tide of popular opinion in their favour, since all Edward IV's restoration could offer at present was further bloodshed. However, despite the regime's urgent need for Margaret and Prince Edward to return to England, Louis stymied them. To him, the Lancastrian royal family were bargaining chips – an assurance that he would get what he wanted out of this alliance, which had always been English assistance in the war against Burgundy.

As early as 8 October, two days after reaching London, Warwick had written to Louis confirming the restoration of the Lancastrian dynasty. Not willing to trust the earl's rhetoric, in November Louis sent a French embassy to see for themselves. Until he had confirmation from his ambassadors that Henry's succession was assured and that Warwick would send men to support his war against Burgundy, Louis would not allow Margaret and Edward to leave France. The royal pair tried to play their part, agreeing a treaty on Henry's behalf, but the final declaration of war with Burgundy was delayed by Warwick, probably until it had been announced in parliament or until Prince Edward was present to make the announcement himself.[18]

By the new year of 1471, Louis had grown tired of waiting. In early January he invaded Charles's territories and made it clear that he expected Warwick to follow. Unable to prevaricate any further, on 13 February Warwick wrote to Louis assuring him that war would soon be underway and that he would personally lead the troops. On 16 February, the Anglo-French truce was announced in parliament. The same day, John Langstrother was granted a warrant to take Warwick's place and escort Margaret and Prince Edward back to England.[19]

Warwick's declaration of war freed Margaret and Prince Edward from Louis's control at last, but the Anglo-French treaty had a devastating impact on the Lancastrian cause. Since September 1470 the exiled Edward IV and his supporters had been sheltering in the territories of his brother-in-law, Charles of Burgundy. The Yorkists, including Edward's teenage brother Richard, duke of Gloucester, owed their refuge there far more to the abiding family loyalty of Charles's wife Margaret of York than to any sense of kinship on Charles's part, for despite the fugitive king's presence Charles remained an ally of the Lancastrian cause. As Charles's diplomat and chronicler Philippe de Commines reported, Charles was far from happy to welcome Edward into his territory and refused to meet him, publicly expressing his belief that the treaty of peace he had made with the king of England in 1468 still applied, regardless of the fact that the king himself had changed. This was good news for the Lancastrians, especially the dukes of Somerset and Exeter, who were maintained on the continent at Charles's expense. Through the diplomatic efforts of these English dukes, it had seemed possible that Henry VI's regime might yet win a treaty with Charles, which could expel Edward IV from his Burgundian sanctuary and assure the readeption of the Lancastrian dynasty once and for all.[20]

Louis and Warwick's actions had destroyed this possibility. In January 1471, with Margaret of York at his side, Charles finally met with Edward IV. Publicly, Charles maintained his refusal to aid the Yorkist cause. Privately, he furnished Edward with 50,000 florins* and three or four 'great ships' with which to return to England and contest his right to the throne.[21]

Edward IV knew that time was of the essence – he needed to reassert his claim in England before Prince Edward of Lancaster could return and lend further weight to the Lancastrian dynasty. By March, Margaret of Anjou, Prince Edward and Edward IV had all reached the Channel ports facing England: the Yorkist force at Veere in Burgundian territory, Margaret's supporters further south, in the Norman port of Honfleur. But storms raged in the Channel and when both Yorkist and Lancastrian attempted to sail for England they were driven back into port again and again. Across the Channel, Warwick set out from London to meet Margaret at Dover, at last reuniting Henry's hard-won forces. He waited in vain. When news finally reached Henry of a fleet landing on English shores it heralded the arrival not of his wife, but of his enemy. The wind had changed; Edward IV had won the race.[22]

The first information that reached Henry in London early in March 1471 was of Edward's defeat. The Yorkist fleet had cautiously put ashore at Cromer in Norfolk and been driven back to sea by the earl of Oxford. Storm-tossed, Edward and his 1,000 men eventually struggled ashore at Ravenspur† in East Yorkshire. The name was ominously familiar to Henry, for it was here that his grandfather Henry IV had made landfall when he invaded to take the throne from Richard II in 1399. Still, there was initially cause for hope as Edward announced that he came only to claim his birthright, the duchy of York. The people of Yorkshire he met as he marched south were largely sympathetic to this

---

* A florin was a Florentine gold coin worth about half an English noble. 50,000 florins equated to over £8,000.
† This town used to stand on Spurn Head at the mouth of the River Humber, but has since been lost to coastal erosion.

intention, and on the understanding that he did not intend to steal the crown, the city of York allowed Edward to enter. The Warkworth Chronicle claimed that Edward even led a chorus of cheers for King Henry, swearing oaths of loyalty and donning the ostrich-feather livery of Prince Edward of Lancaster.[23]

Henry might have been willing to accept Edward's assertion of the limited nature of his aims, but it is hard to believe that Warwick was. When Edward IV's landing was confirmed, Warwick left London with his brother-in-law the earl of Oxford and the duke of Exeter to meet Edward's army as it travelled south. They established a base at Coventry in the Midlands, using the traditional Lancastrian loyalties of the area to assemble a force that was said to be 30,000 strong.[24] Henry stayed behind in London with Edmund Beaufort, duke of Somerset, the earl of Devon and Warwick's brother George Neville, archbishop of York, to watch over him. The changeable loyalties of the citizens of London were a concern, but Warwick seems to have trusted to their dissatisfaction with Edward and his own popularity among the commons to hold the city.

The first warning sign came when Edward IV was allowed to pass through the northern counties without any obstruction. Even Warwick's brother Montagu 'suffered him to pass'.[25] Worse, when Edward reached Doncaster, he revealed his true intentions and reasserted his claim to the throne. Edward offered battle to the Lancastrian forces in Coventry but Warwick, waiting on the arrival of the duke of Clarence with his several thousand West Country followers, steadfastly refused. Unlike Edward, who was all too willing to risk his life to the fortunes of the battlefield, Warwick preferred to fight only when the odds were firmly in his favour.

On 3 April, Clarence finally approached. But as he neared Banbury one observer claimed that Clarence's soldiers wore the Lancastrian livery with a pointed addition – the white rose of York.[26] Clarence had defected to his brother's cause. Realizing that Warwick's plans would be of no material advantage to him,

Clarence had been won back to Edward IV by the unfailing efforts of his sisters and mother. His elder sister Margaret, duchess of Burgundy, had been instrumental in this reconciliation, reminding him of how little he had to gain from a Lancastrian restoration and of how bitter the hatred of some Lancastrians was for their family. Philippe de Commines even claimed that Clarence's family had dispatched a lady through Calais to suborn him and his wife Isabel.[27]

Bolstered by Clarence's reinforcements and with little indication that Warwick would ever leave Coventry to face him in open battle, Edward turned his army towards London. Although he had no certainty that the city would return to its old allegiance, the opportunity to seize Henry and thus deprive Warwick of his most important pawn was too good to miss.

On 10 April two messages reached the citizens of London, commanding the city to defend itself against the enemy – one came from Warwick and the other from Edward. In an effort to inspire the Londoners in Warwick's cause, his brother George Neville, archbishop of York, brought Henry out of the bishop's palace at St Paul's to parade through the streets the next day. As it was Maundy Thursday, Henry wore the traditional royal mourning robes, a long blue velvet gown, and his lowly appearance had the opposite effect from the one desired. A city accustomed to the still youthful and vigorous Edward IV was confronted instead with a greying and dishevelled figure. All Henry inspired was pity. One London chronicler wrote that as Henry rode through the city streets surrounded by hastily assembled soldiers he was led by the hand by George Neville. Henry's choice of sword bearer did little to elevate the scene: the septuagenarian Ralph Botiller, Lord Sudeley, had served Henry since he was a baby and his presence was a reminder of how far Henry had fallen since the hopes of the nation were invested in their infant king.[28]

By the time Henry returned to the bishop's palace, he had lost the little support he still enjoyed. George Neville realized

Henry's cause was lost and wrote to Edward IV, appealing for royal grace. Edmund Beaufort, duke of Somerset, and the earl of Devon had already left the city and marched west. They claimed to be going to muster forces for Margaret and Prince Edward, but it is hard to see their departure as anything other than an abandonment of Henry. The remaining Lancastrians were now more concerned about the future of the Lancastrian dynasty, represented by Prince Edward, than they were about preserving the liberty – even perhaps the life – of King Henry.[29]

When Edward arrived at the gates of London he was welcomed into the city unopposed. After a celebratory Mass in St Paul's Cathedral, Edward ordered George Neville to bring Henry to him in the bishop's palace. It was probably the first time the two men had seen each other in eleven years. Edward held out his hand to greet Henry, but Henry instead embraced the man who had deposed him, saying, 'My cousin of York, you are very welcome. I know that my life will not be in danger in your hands.' Edward replied that Henry had nothing to fear and should be of good cheer.[30] Then Henry, Ralph Botiller and George Neville were all escorted to the Tower of London. Henry's readeption had lasted barely six months. He was a Yorkist prisoner once more.

Barnet
Easter Day (14 April) 1471

Henry awoke to a dawn obscured by mist. It was not yet fully light, but even if it had been there was little Henry would have cared to see. Easter was the most important day in the religious calendar, the day according to Christian belief when Jesus had risen from the dead. But Henry was not greeted that morning by the customary Mass and celebration. Instead, it was by the blast of trumpets and firing of guns, by men rattling into their armour and readying their weapons. Even the night had brought little relief. His sleep had been broken by the pounding of cannon shot, shaking the marshy ground beneath him but always, mercifully, overshooting. From the enemy camp, all night long, could be heard the anxious voices of men and restless movements of their horses. In Henry's own army, silence had reigned. And thus, on the holiest day of the year, this pious king found himself yet again in a battle that was none of his choosing. This time, he was in the army of King Edward IV.[31]

With his keen ability to bend ill omens into signs of divine favour, Edward might well have considered this the ideal date for a battle. Religious devotion should have taken precedence over political necessity, but Edward was determined not to lose the upper hand he had gained in seizing London and Henry in one fell swoop. Warwick had banked on the city denying Edward entry, planning to catch his nephew in the open outside the city walls, penned between the citizens' guns and his own army where he could have annihilated them. Instead, Warwick was now at the disadvantage. He had raced south to try and catch up with Edward, but by the vigil of Easter he was still on the Great North Road near Barnet.

It was there that Edward had found Warwick on the evening of 13 April, his army stretched across the road with a protective hedgerow at its back. Edward was not going to make Warwick's mistake and entrust Henry to the questionable loyalties of London, so Henry was dragged from his religious devotions in the Tower to join Edward's army. There was no question of him fighting, but Edward would perhaps not have been overly concerned if his rival met with misfortune in the coming battle. His only concern was to prevent Henry falling into Warwick's clutches again. If Henry had an opinion about which side he wished to be held captive by, no one bothered to record it. His brief readeption had proved that any will the king once possessed was now eradicated. Years of exile, fugitive existence and imprisonment had worn him to intangibility. As his contemporary Georges Chastellain wrote of him at this time, '[Henry is] a stuffed wool sack lifted by its ears, a shadow on the wall, bandied about as in a game of blindman's buff.'[32] In the battle at Barnet he would be an onlooker, nothing more.

They had arrived after darkness had already fallen across the plain north of Barnet and Edward had misjudged the battlefield. He arranged his men at an odd angle, slightly off-centre against the enemy forces. During the night, this misalignment had been obscured and Edward's chief concern had been to silence his men so that Warwick's cannons overshot them. With no noise echoing back to guide him, Warwick did not realize that he was causing little damage to anything but the ground beyond. On Easter morning, Edward's mistaken orientation was still not apparent as mist shrouded the heathland. The fog lay so thick that Edward's three forces could barely see each other. Edward had Clarence under his watchful eye in the centre while their brother Richard, duke of Gloucester, commanded the right battle on the east and Edward's trusted friend Lord William Hastings took the west.

The course of the battle long remained uncertain, as the mist clung heavy in the air. Shouts echoed across the plain and trumpets blasted but the soldiers fighting desperately in the melee could not tell whether their forces were winning or being driven into retreat. Commanding Warwick's right battle, the earl of Oxford won an early victory, driving almost into the flank of Hastings's men owing to the strange orientation of the battlefield. Hastings's line collapsed and Oxford's men surged through, chasing their enemy all the way to Barnet, almost a mile away. Thinking the day was won, Oxford's men fell to looting and it took considerable effort on the earl's part to regroup his forces and drag them back to the battlefield, where – unaware of Hastings's collapse – Edward's men fought on undaunted.

But as Oxford marched back through the fog, he lost his way. Unbeknown to him the armies had swivelled around, and when he came across a battle line at last it was not the enemy but his ally Lord Montagu's men. Montagu's soldiers looked up at the press of returning soldiers, their banners swirling in the mist.

Through the half-light it seemed that the star crest they wore was Edward's badge, the sun with streamers. They attacked Oxford's troops. Shouts of 'treason!' echoed across the battlefield. Vision might be obscured, but sound carried. The Lancastrian army degenerated into chaos and soon broke completely. Warwick's forces fled the field. The Warkworth Chronicle claimed that in an attempt to save his life, Montagu donned Edward's livery and attempted a final defection but the turncoat was cut down where he stood.[33]

Warwick had been persuaded by his brother to fight on foot that day, instead of pursuing his usual tactic and watching the battle from horseback, waiting until victory was assured to charge into the thick of the fighting.[34] Now he struggled back to the rear of his forces, and tried to escape into woodland. As he fled, Edward's men fell on him. Warwick was struck down and killed. The earl of Oxford managed to escape,[35] but the duke of Exeter was so badly wounded in the fray that his life was despaired of. He was stripped naked and left on the battlefield for nine hours until he was eventually recognized by a servant and dragged into sanctuary at Westminster.[36]

A German merchant in London heard that in the midst of this chaos Henry had slipped Edward's leash, and been carried halfway to St Albans by his allies. If this was true, that was as far as Henry got. By the close of the battle he was back in Edward's clutches, and that afternoon Edward marched his army back to London in triumph, with Henry his prisoner once more. In this sorry company of bandaged men, their legs battered and their faces in some cases missing noses, Henry was paraded through the streets of London that Easter afternoon. At St Paul's Cathedral, Edward paused to lay his banners, badly torn and shot through by Warwick's guns, at the rood screen of the north door in thanks. The next morning St Paul's received two more mementos of the Battle of Barnet: the bodies of Warwick and Montagu, stripped naked except for cloths over their private parts, laid out in the body of the church for everyone to see that they were finally dead. Thousands of curious Londoners came to peer at the faces of the kingmaker and his brother.[37]

Henry, meanwhile, had been escorted, still wearing the blue velvet gown in which Edward had found him five days earlier, to the Tower of London. Fortune's Wheel had now twice turned him from his throne. As a Norfolk gentleman wrote to his mother in the wake of the battle: 'God hath showed himself marvellously like Him that made all – and can undo again when he wants.'[38]

In a cruel irony, that very day, far to the west, Margaret and Prince Edward finally reached England. Fortune was not done with Henry yet. It had one more cruel twist in store for the House of Lancaster.

40

'The shadow on the wall'[1]

Weymouth
14 April 1471

After almost three weeks of attempting to cross the Channel, Margaret, Prince Edward and their faithful supporters finally stepped ashore at Weymouth.[2] Pausing only to send out proclamations calling the men of the West Country to gather to their banner, they rode straight for the Beaufort stronghold of Cerne Abbey in Dorset, where Edmund Beaufort, duke of Somerset, and the earl of Devon awaited them. It was there that Margaret learnt that after eight years in exile and eleven months of planning, she had returned to England at the most dangerous moment possible. Her husband was a prisoner once more, her chief ally's corpse lay cold on the stones of St Paul's Cathedral and her enemy possessed a large army ready to advance upon her at the earliest opportunity. Margaret's first impulse was simply to board ship with Prince Edward and set sail back to France. Further along the coast, the countess of Warwick's ship had put in at Portsmouth and when she learnt of her husband's death at Barnet she immediately fled into sanctuary at Beaulieu Abbey.[3]

Somerset, however, insisted that the misfortune of Barnet

could be a blessing in disguise. He, Devon and Exeter had never fully trusted Warwick and now that the kingmaker was dead, the Lancastrian cause was unquestionably loyal. Somerset and Devon had forces at their disposal in the West Country and Jasper Tudor was mustering men in Wales. The Lancastrian heartland of Lancashire and Cheshire could provide considerable firepower and would surely respond to their call. If they could defeat Edward IV in a decisive battle there was every possibility that they could regain the kingdom. Somerset was an experienced soldier, having served in the campaigns of Charles of Burgundy in 1465, and his reassurance mattered to Margaret. Prince Edward, with his keen interest in martial matters, was probably also eager to blood himself in battle. The fateful decision was made. Margaret and Prince Edward would stay in England. They would put their fortunes to the test of war.[4]

At present, their forces were scattered so it was vital to unite them before engaging the Yorkists. For that, Margaret's army needed to join up with Jasper Tudor's in Wales and thence proceed to rally the loyal Lancastrians of the northwest. To rendezvous with Tudor they had to cross the River Severn. The closest crossing was at Gloucester, so, pausing to gather more men in Exeter and artillery in Bristol, they set off north.[5]

Within days, Edward IV had learnt of Margaret's landing and marched his army out of the capital to pursue her. In an attempt to mislead the Yorkists, Margaret's men played a game of cat and mouse with the Yorkist scouts, misleading Edward with feints in the wrong direction. By May Day, however, it was clear that the Yorkists had discerned the Lancastrian course and were moving to block Margaret's path across the Severn. The early spring heat was oppressive and Margaret's forces had to struggle at speed through rough and unpleasant terrain in the hope of reaching Gloucester before Edward IV caught up with them. On 2 May they were almost overtaken by Edward at Sodbury Hill, northeast of Bristol, and when Lancastrian outriders finally made it to Gloucester they found that Yorkist messengers had got there first and the town refused to admit them.[6]

Their passage over the Severn impeded at Gloucester, Margaret and her increasingly weary men had to trudge onwards, through 'foul country' to the next river crossing at Tewkesbury. By four o'clock in the afternoon on Friday 3 May they were finally approaching the town, the spire of its abbey visible for miles around, a lone highpoint in an expanse of low-lying water meadow, river bends and fields. Margaret's forces had marched almost 50 miles (80 km) in thirty-six hours. They were exhausted. The footmen could barely stand and even the soldiers on horseback were too tired to go on. The choice before them now was stark. Edward IV 'ever approached towards them, nearer and nearer, ever ready', and was within a few miles of their location.[7]

Once again, the Lancastrian camp was divided on the best course of action. Somerset argued that they must stand and fight – the men, after all, could scarcely go any further – but the other commanders insisted it was vital to combine their forces with Jasper Tudor's before they risked open battle. Among those who opposed Somerset's scheme was Lord Wenlock, who had travelled from Calais to join his old ally Warwick in the Lancastrian cause.[8] Somerset and Wenlock were uneasy allies and this division over their strategy did nothing to resolve their grievances.

Margaret allowed Somerset's will to prevail. It was decided, too, that Prince Edward would fight and he was appointed a sword bearer, John Gower, to accompany him on the battlefield.[9] Dangerous as it was to risk the prince's life in battle, Margaret and her advisers knew that there were advantages to doing so. Edward IV had won his crown by personally taking the field for his cause. The promise of a prince to stand and die with his men was a compelling boost to the morale of his army. It was something that Henry had always been extremely loath to do – he had not experienced his first taste of battle until he was more than thirty – and with his unfortunate example in Lancastrian minds it must have seemed sensible to give Prince Edward command as early as possible. The prince was now seventeen, not an unusual age to experience warfare. Accompanying Edward IV to Tewkesbury was his eighteen-year-old brother Richard, duke of Gloucester, already a veteran of Barnet. If the Lancastrian army won the day at Tewkesbury, Prince Edward's cause would be strengthened by his presence on the field. If it looked like they would lose, provision must have been made for his flight. It was decided that he would stand beside the experienced Wenlock in the main battle, at the heart of the army.

That night the Lancastrian forces took up a defensive position in grazing land to the south of the abbey, with a maze of dykes, hedges and ditches defending them from Edward IV's encroaching forces. By nightfall Edward was within 3 miles (5 km) of the town, encamped in the open fields nearby. The Lancastrians had the upper hand in numbers, but Edward's men were probably better equipped and armed, and their artillery was stronger. Richard, duke of Gloucester, would command the vanguard, and Edward's close friend Lord William Hastings was to lead the rearguard. Edward IV himself would be positioned in the main battle. That night the armies watched each other, 'determined to abide there the adventure that God would send them'.[10]

The following morning the battle opened with the thunder of ordnance. Edward IV's guns and arrows 'sore oppressed' Somerset's forces in the vanguard. Eventually the fire became too heavy and to try and escape the rain of missiles Somerset led his men in a feint away from the main battle, towards the northern slopes of a local park. Hoping to outflank Edward's forces, Somerset instead found himself trapped on the hillside between the bulk of the Yorkist forces in the field and a company of 200 mounted spearmen who had been hidden in the park woodland. The spearmen swooped down on Somerset's soldiers, striking their flank and putting them to flight. When Somerset eventually struggled back to the main battle he found that Wenlock had done little but 'stood looking on'. Enraged, Somerset accused Wenlock of being a traitor and in the heat of the moment struck Wenlock in the head with his axe, spilling his brains on the ground.[11]

Seeing disorder seize the Lancastrian ranks, Edward IV advanced his men towards them. The fiercest combat now set in, men fighting hand to hand. The Lancastrian line trembled and then collapsed. Soldiers ran in all directions, making for the lanes and dykes or fleeing into the meadow and park, and many of the men who had been in the centre struggled north towards the town and abbey, hoping to find sanctuary within its walls. Around 2,000 Lancastrians fell during the battle and its bloody rout, a death toll that earned a local field the name of 'Bloody Meadow'. Among those killed in the field were the earl of Devon and Somerset's brother John Beaufort. But, most damaging of all, Henry's teenage son Prince Edward, the hope and pride of the Lancastrian cause, was cut down as he fled towards the town, crying out for help from his brother-in-law the duke of Clarence.[12]

A group of desperate Lancastrians, including the duke of Somerset, made it to the sanctuary of Tewkesbury Abbey. With the battle won, Edward IV pursued them, so intent on snaring his quarry that he marched his mud-stained boots on to the very tiles of this sanctuary, still bearing his naked sword. A priest ran from Mass with the holy eucharist still in his hands, appealing to the king not to pollute the abbey with bloodshed.

For two days, Edward allowed the Lancastrians to remain within the abbey walls, but on 6 May they were dragged out to the market square and condemned to immediate execution by Edward's brother Richard, duke of Gloucester, in his capacity as constable of England. As many as nineteen men fell to the headsman's axe in the shadow of Tewkesbury market cross, including Edmund Beaufort, duke of Somerset, John Langstrother and Hugh Courtenay. The one mercy shown to them was that their corpses were not quartered and displayed. Their bodies, like Prince Edward's, were buried within the abbey precincts according to their status, the lowliest in the churchyard and the loftiest close to the high altar. Meticulous notes were kept of where their bodies were interred, recording a patchwork of graves that radiated out from the central sepulchre in the choir where Prince Edward's mangled body lay. The violence inflicted on the abbey by the Lancastrians' forced removal was deemed so polluting that no services could be held there for a month.[13]

Queen Margaret was found days after the battle, hiding in 'a poor religious place'[14] where she had fled with her daughterin-law, Anne Neville, and her faithful lady-in-waiting, Katherine Vaux. Anne and Katherine had both been widowed by the slaughter of Tewkesbury. Margaret seems to have been paralyzed by the outcome of the battle. In a single day she had lost not only her most important commanders, Somerset and Devon, but also attendants who had loyally supported her for decades. Sir Robert Whittingham, Sir William Vaux and Sir Edmund Hampden were among such stalwarts, men who had shared her sufferings in exile and must have become friends as much as servants. None of these losses however, none of them, could equal the pain of losing her son. Everything Margaret had done for seventeen years had been for him. And in one terrible gamble she had, by losing him, lost everything.[15]

Any instinct Margaret had to resist seems to have been crushed irrevocably. She submitted to captivity and was marched north to face Edward IV. By a savage irony, when Margaret was brought to the king, he was breaking his journey in Coventry. It was thus in the 'queen's secret harbour' where pageants had praised Prince Edward of Lancaster as the future of England that his mother submitted to his killer. There was one more humiliation for Margaret to endure. On 21 May, Edward IV entered London in triumph, surrounded by the whole host of his army. Trundling on a cart in front of this victorious band of men was Queen Margaret. Twenty-six years had passed since she first entered London as a queen on a litter, her long hair loose over her white cloth-of-gold gown. Now, defeated and grieving, she returned as a captive.

At the Tower of London she was let down from her transport and escorted into her cell. She and Henry were probably imprisoned separately. Their lives were now in Edward's hands.[16]

The Tower of London
21 May 1471

The Tower of London had held a complex place in the hearts of its owners ever since William the Conqueror first laid its foundations in the wake of his Norman Conquest. It had never really been a home and yet here princes were born, kings and queens took shelter, Christmases were celebrated, knights created and prisoners housed. Royal wardrobe towers stocked with lustrous robes and the crown jewels nestled alongside cannon stores and stockpiles of armour. It was an uneasy combination and even warrior kings did not feel comfortable within the Tower's grim stone embrace. During Henry VI's reign the Tower had been the setting for some of the most important moments of his life, some perhaps the happiest and others undoubtedly the worst.

From here, Henry had set out as a boy of seven to ride to his coronation at Westminster Abbey. On the eve of Margaret's coronation sixteen years later, it had been within the chapel of St John in the White Tower that Knights of the Bath had been created in her honour. Here they had celebrated Epiphany, the feast of kings, together with his half-brothers, Edmund and Jasper, shortly before Margaret fell pregnant. Yet here also were stored the arms and artillery that had been rumbled out, time and again, during Henry's lifetime, intending both to aid and to destroy him. In 'Mint Street', the long road in the outer walls, the air was alive with the hammering of dies and blanks, spewing foul-smelling clouds as new coins were minted for the king, the changing names struck there revealing the fall from grace of Henry's regime and the rise of his Yorkist usurper. Into the Tower had gone one after another of Henry's chief counsellors:

Suffolk, Lord Saye and Sele, Somerset. Some Henry had saved, others had only emerged to be butchered by his subjects. Eventually the Tower's jagged portcullis mouth had swallowed up Henry and his queen too.

In the early weeks of May 1471, as Henry retreated into his last imprisonment, the Tower fulfilled what was always its first purpose. It was a fortress again. One of Warwick's supporters had refused to bow to the harsh reality that the Lancastrian regime was defeated: Thomas Neville, the illegitimate son of Warwick's uncle Lord Fauconberg. 'The bastard of Fauconberg,' as he was known, rallied the Calais garrison, his own privateering sailors and a formidable force of Kentish rebels to free Henry from the Tower and attempt to force him back on to the throne. All he succeeded in doing was signing Henry's death warrant.

Fauconberg's rebellion collapsed, although not before burning down the houses closest to London Bridge and loosing guns on Bishopsgate and Aldgate. To the east of the Tower a wall in St Katherine's dock was levelled, to prevent Fauconberg from setting up his own battery there; on the Tower riverbank, bulwarks were dug and casks filled with sand to take the pounding blows from his artillery. As Henry heard the whip-like crack of guns and perhaps even felt the reverberations of Fauconberg's artillery, he might have been able to look out on to the river to see his supporter's fleet unleashing its men on the capital. All this Henry might have observed, but whether he actually knew that this fleet fought for him is another matter. Within days of Fauconberg's arrival, the rebellion was over. Fauconberg was seized by King Edward and, in spite of a charter of pardon, executed at Middleham Castle. The last flames of rebellion had been doused. Edward IV was unchallenged ruler of England once more.[17]

For Henry, this last sputter of resistance sealed his doom. On the same night that Edward returned to London, driving Margaret before him as a triumphal offering, Henry died in the Tower. His body was found the next morning, and it was believed that he had expired as the hour approached midnight.

Edward IV's official line on his death, presented in a Yorkist-disseminated document called *Historie of the Arrivall of Edward IV in England and the Finall Recouerye of His Kingdomes from Henry VI*, was that Henry had been overcome with melancholy after learning of recent events.[18] *The Arrivall* asserted that when 'the certainty of all which [had happened] came to the knowledge of the said Henry... of pure displeasure, and melancholy, he died'.[19] This account of Henry's last hours was so feeble that it was not even believed at the time. The author of the Warkworth Chronicle was clear that Henry had been 'put to death'.[20] The Croyland Chronicle condemned the 'tyrant' who 'dared to lay sacrilegious hands on the Lord's Anointed' and by June word had reached France that Edward had 'caused King Henry to be secretly assassinated in the Tower... He has, in short, chosen to crush the seed.'[21]

The Warkworth Chronicle, written no later than 1484,* noted suggestively that when Henry died he was kept company in the Tower by 'the duke of Gloucester', Edward's youngest brother and the man who had only a few weeks before condemned most of Henry's surviving commanders to execution in Tewkesbury. But Gloucester was certainly not alone in the Tower. At one point during Fauconberg's rebellion, the lieutenant of the Tower, the septuagenarian Lord Dudley, was commanding a hundred soldiers there and thirty-six men are named as being in attendance on Henry during his last imprisonment. Any one of these men might have been Henry's murderer. Even the exact cause of Henry's death was unclear. A legend soon arose that Henry had been stabbed. However, when his body was exhumed in 1910, the skull was found to be 'apparently matted with blood' and broken in several places. He may therefore have died from a blow to the head.[22] What is certain is that in spite of the legends that later wove themselves around Richard, duke of Gloucester, connecting

---

* The chronicle was completed early in the reign of Richard III (formerly Richard, duke of Gloucester), although its narrative only extends to 1471.

his hand with Henry's death, the ultimate responsibility for it lay with Edward IV. As constable of England, Gloucester was responsible for imparting royal justice and may have carried a royal command for Henry's death. But that order had to come from Edward.[23]

Whatever befell Henry the night before, on the morning of 22 May 1471 his body was embalmed with wax and spices, then wrapped in linen for burial. But before he could be laid to rest there was one last forced procession he had to make. To prove, once and for all, that the House of Lancaster was defeated, Henry's corpse was loaded on to a wagon to wind its way through London's streets to St Paul's Cathedral, surrounded by torch-bearers and soldiers. For a few days he was left on display in the cathedral, his unseeing face open to public scrutiny. As his body lay on the pavement of the church it was seen to bleed, a sign that was generally understood to indicate that Henry had been murdered.*

Finally, Henry's body was loaded on to an illuminated barge decked in black and rowed 15 miles (24 km) upriver to Chertsey Abbey, where it was laid to rest in the Lady Chapel. Edward IV paid the four orders of friars in London more than £8 to say funeral Masses for the dead king.[24] So ended Henry's life, but his involvement in the political realm was not quite over. Even in death, Henry VI was still used to further the agendas and ambitions of others.

---

* It has been suggested that it was physically impossible for a corpse to bleed hours after death, but consultation with a forensic archaeologist and pathologist confirms that the claims made by the Warkworth Chronicle could be correct. If the body was turned when it was moved, any blood that had pooled might have seeped out through injury holes or orifices. My thanks to Abi Carter and Dr David Rouse at Forensic Resources Ltd for discussing this with me.

PART V

Afterlife

41

'Very dolorous and discomforted queen of England'[1]

Anjou
24 August 1482

From the fairytale turrets of Saumur Castle, atop which golden fleur-de-lys glistened in the summer light, to the bulbous towers of Angers, where the château loomed on a cliff edge above the River Loire, the funeral cortege of Margaret of Anjou carried the queen on her last journey. For six years she had been exiled back to the lands in which she grew up, a half-welcome guest of her father and King Louis, with little more than hunting dogs, books and a casket of relics to remind her of past glories. She was going now to rejoin her ancestors. Her last request to King Louis was that he would allow her to be buried with her parents* in their sepulchre at Angers Cathedral.[2]

Since her capture at Tewkesbury in 1471 Margaret's life had become one of solitary retirement. She had not stayed long in the Tower of London, although she must have been there when

---

* René of Anjou had died in 1480.

Henry was killed. For a time she was kept at Windsor Castle, and by January 1472 she had moved to Wallingford in Oxfordshire, where her keeper was her old friend, Alice Chaucer, dowager duchess of Suffolk.[3] The women had once been close, Alice perhaps even having something of a maternal place in Margaret's heart. Since Suffolk's murder their lives had taken very different courses, and their enforced time together during Margaret's imprisonment cannot have been entirely happy. Where Margaret had resisted the Yorkist regime with all her strength, Alice had come to terms with it even before Henry VI was first deposed. In 1458 Alice had overseen the marriage of her only child, John, to York's daughter Elizabeth. At the time this must have seemed a dangerous move, but her gamble had paid off. Her son still lived, a prominent member of the court of King Edward IV, and a king's brother-in-law. Margaret, by contrast, had lost her family to the wars. Under house arrest, she was reliant on Edward to provide her with enough money to cover the expenses of herself and her servants.[4]

One of those servants was Lady Katherine Vaux. Katherine had lost her husband, Margaret's old servant Sir William, at Tewkesbury and the pair were bound so tightly together, whether through shared grief or the loyalty of many years' service, that Katherine stayed with Margaret until the end. The pair of them probably appear in an image in the Guild Book of the London Skinners' Fraternity in 1475. Margaret wears an ermine-lined dark gown, her head covered like a nun, kneeling forward to read a religious text from her prayer book while a discarded crown and sceptre lie beside her. Behind Margaret is a more fashionably dressed woman, evidently in attendance on the queen, with her prayer book in her hands, her eyes more on her mistress than her prayers. Both Katherine and Margaret were members of this fraternity in honour of the Assumption of the Virgin Mary – who Margaret, like Henry, always particularly revered.

As this image in the Skinners' record suggests, Margaret's imprisonment under Edward IV was not especially stringent.

Other members of the Skinners' Guild Fraternity included Queen Elizabeth Woodville and her ladies, so the fraternity would not have risked their ire by welcoming Margaret without their consent. Margaret was provided with clothing, mostly black, at royal expense and had enough freedom not only to join this guild but also to enjoy the services of the dean of Edward's chapel in 1474. Having moved from Wallingford to London for most of the intervening years, in 1475 an international treaty between Edward and Louis XI was finalized that ransomed Margaret to Louis for £50,000.[5]

In return for being able to return to her father's territories with a small pension from Louis, Margaret was forced to renounce all of her claims not only in England, but also in France. The woman who had clung so tenaciously to her family's right to the English crown was now willing to give up virtually everything she owned to go home. After all, there was no one to inherit her titles or lands after her death. Thus, in November 1475, she was transferred into the keeping of Sir Thomas Montgomery to be escorted to France.

For several years Margaret lived in her father's castle at Reculée, near Angers, but when René died in 1480 she had to rely on one of his servants to provide her with a manor. She spent the last two years of her life at Dampierre near Saumur, taking solace in her relics and her literary interests. Some years earlier she had commissioned the Burgundian memoirist Georges Chastellain to write *Le Temple de Bocace*, a consolation piece dwelling on the changing fortunes of the world and the unjust criticism that had been levelled at her. Presumably she also occasionally rode or hunted through the verdant rolling fields and woodland surrounding her, enjoying at least one pastime from her old life. Margaret may have ridden from her modest home at Dampierre to the more imposing Château Montsoreau on the banks of the River Loire, as over time she developed enough of a relationship with the castle's owner, Madame de Montsoreau, to gift her all of her hunting dogs shortly before her death – a high-status offering for a lady who had perhaps been a friend in the queen's last years.[6]

In the summer heat of 1482 Margaret fell ill and, with the faithful Katherine Vaux at her side, she made her last will and testament on 2 August. Louis XI, who had once mocked her proud writing style, would have found little to displease him in the humble petitions that filled this short document. 'Sound of mind, reason and thought, however weak and feeble of body', Margaret asked to be buried in the cathedral church of St Maurice in Angers beside her parents, 'in whatever manner it pleases the king to ordain, or in another place if he prefers'. She wrote that she did not have enough money to cover the cost of the funeral and suggested that Louis sold her remaining possessions to pay for her burial – as indeed he did. And perhaps thinking of Lady Katherine, she 'recommend[ed] very humbly and affectionately' her 'poor servants... to the good grace and charity of the said King'. She had evidently lived on the charity of others for some time, and implored Louis, as her sole heir, to cover any remaining debts she had incurred.[7]

Louis did as Margaret asked and had her honourably buried with her parents, but he insisted on reclaiming the hunting dogs that she had gifted to Madame de Montsoreau. 'You know [Margaret] has made me her heir,' the king reminded Montsoreau in a letter written days before the queen actually died, 'and that *this* is all I shall get; also it is what I love best. I pray you not to keep any back, [or] you would cause me a terribly great displeasure.'[8]

Even in death, Henry and Margaret were the pawns of others.

42

'Holy King Henry'[1]

Salisbury
23 February 1484

At the gallows, a crowd was assembling. This was no bustling holiday throng, come to see justice done. Many there muttered that this hanging was a mockery of justice. Their murmurs grew louder as the condemned man was called before them. Richard Beys was a young man, handsome and previously of unquestioned character. His only crime was having a master who had fallen foul of a powerful local lord. To punish him, that lord had had Beys arrested, imprisoned in a foul dungeon and condemned to death by a corrupt jury. Despite the injustice and horror of his position, Beys seemed oddly calm as he mounted the ladder on the gallows. At his last confession he said he believed he would escape death. The crowd watching him were less convinced. They groaned and lamented as Beys's neck was placed in the noose and the ladder jerked out from under his feet. Beys beat his chest four times with his fist as the rope swung him from west to east, writhing as he was slowly strangled. At last he hung still.

His executioner cut his corpse down to bury it as soon as possible. But as a cross was laid on his body to ready it for burial, Beys

was seen to revive. He breathed again. The executioner tried to
jostle him back into the gibbet to finish the job but the crowd
surged forward, angrily preventing him. A local churchman
insisted that since he had put the cross on Beys's chest the condemned man was now under his protection. To the cheers of a
rejoicing crowd, Beys was borne through the city to sanctuary to
await a royal pardon.

When asked how he had escaped death, Beys related that as
he beat his breast in the noose, a vision had appeared to him.
A tall figure, royally dressed in a blue velvet gown, accompanied
by the Virgin Mary. While Mary held up Beys's body with her
hands under his feet, the grey-haired royal figure had slipped
his hand between the noose and Beys's neck, thus preserving
him from strangulation. Beys's saviour was none other than King
Henry VI.[2]

This was only one of more than 300 miracles reported to the
monks who tended Henry's tomb, who faithfully recorded them
as proof of the king's sanctity. Richard Beys travelled to Henry's
tomb to report his miracle and give thanks, leaving there the
noose that had hanged him. It nestled alongside other proofs
of Henry's miraculous intervention, an array of items that shows
how staggeringly diverse the miracles connected to his agency
were. In one corner a wax effigy of a ship recalled the vessel
that had grounded on a Norfolk sandbank, ripping out fifteen
rivets, but which on prayer to Henry had been lifted and sailed
on to London without repair. Elsewhere lay a pilgrim's badge
swallowed by a nine-month-old, choking him until he coughed it
up at the invocation of Henry's name. Here, a silver ear given in
thanks by a Devonshire man who had lived for thirty-seven years
with a bean in his ear before prayer to Henry released it; there,
the crutches of a thirteen-year-old girl whose painful, swollen
leg had healed so well that she could walk to Henry's tomb to
give thanks on her own feet. The chains of freed prisoners hung
over wax candles left by plague victims and the insane, restored
to life and sense by Henry after all hope was gone. While some

miracles were minor examples of pastoral good fortune – horses cured of sickness and lost pigs that wandered home – others impressed with the grisly details of salvation. One wax figure had a round hole in its abdomen, an offering given by the sister of a soldier whose guts had been opened by cannon shot so damaging that his digesting food could be seen inside. A knife on the tomb was the very blade with which Helen Barker had attempted suicide, cutting 'her throat from ear to ear'. Both Barker and the soldier had survived.[3]

The cult of Henry VI developed shortly after his death. By unfortunate chance – to contemporaries, perhaps, by divine displeasure – within months of his death in the Tower there was an outbreak of plague so serious that the roads were thronged with pilgrims praying for salvation. Towns emptied and even the royal family went on bended knee to the shrine at Walsingham. If Edward IV was made uneasy by this coincidence he did not reveal it. But he was extremely displeased when he heard reports from his namesake city of York that his subjects had turned in their time of need to the man that he had deposed and killed. By 1473 an image of Henry VI had been set on the rood screen in York Minster. The devout were already treating it as a holy talisman. Within six years, the attentions being paid to this image were so intense that Edward commanded the archbishop of York to condemn it. The city of London was similarly chastised, with King Edward issuing proclamations that forbade pilgrimage without a letter of authority under his great seal detailing the reason for the pilgrimage and the pilgrim's destination. In spite of these strictures in 1480 the Mercers' Company had to remind its members that pilgrimage to Henry's tomb was forbidden.[4]

Henry's sufferings in life – his long illness, imprisonment, his deposition and exile, his unjust death – had made him seem a sympathetic ear for those enduring hardship in their own lives. In the years after his death in the Tower, they called on the blessed king to intercede with God to help them. And time and again, he did. The king who had been such an ineffective ruler in life was now recast as the most popular and obliging of saints. He was not remembered as the grey-haired and downtrodden prisoner who had ridden through the streets of London hand in hand with Archbishop George Neville, although the blue velvet gown he had worn on that occasion made repeat appearances in pilgrims' visions, but instead as the boy king in whom so much hope had been placed. He was remembered for his generosity and patronage of learning, his concern for the young and dedication to the Virgin Mary. His quiet, internal piety and naivety became a form of holy innocence. He had once been condemned as a fool – the hatted idiot who waved bladders on sticks – and perhaps representations of him now, crowned and holding a sceptre, owed a little to this popular image. Like fools, he had had an otherworldly simplicity – and simplicity then, as now, could have both a negative and positive connotation. It could mean folly, but it also meant being untainted by worldly matters. It was asserted that it was his advisers, not he himself, who had led the country into civil war.[5]

Although the House of York had triumphed in 1471, civil war did not cease in the years after Henry's death. In 1483, Edward IV died at forty, prematurely aged by 'libertinism and high living'.[6] It seemed at first that the succession would be straightforward: with the Lancastrian line apparently crushed, he had two young sons, the eldest now twelve years old, who could take the throne unchallenged. Instead, the two princes were detained in the Tower and their uncle, Edward's brother Richard, duke of Gloucester, took the crown himself in a ruthlessly efficient coup. A number of Queen Elizabeth's relatives and Edward's faithful adviser, Lord Hastings, were killed. Elizabeth fled into sanctuary with her daughters, just as she had done when the earl of Warwick returned in 1470. Within months, the princes in the Tower were rumoured to be dead and rebellion reared its head. For the first time, a new name in the House of Lancaster was whispered: Henry Tudor. The boy who had been the product of Henry VI's matchmaking – only child of Margaret Beaufort and Edmund Tudor – had grown into a cool-headed young man. Like a number of Lancastrians, he had spent the last twelve years in exile on the continent. Now he returned to claim the throne.

In 1485, in a field near Market Bosworth, Henry Tudor defeated Richard III and took his crown. 1485 saw the dawn of a new dynasty. Being an upstart who had spent half his life in Europe and the other half in Wales, the new King Henry VII needed to use every tool at his disposal to ingratiate himself with his subjects. Winning the throne in battle was a clear indication of divine sanction and marrying his enemy's niece Elizabeth of York to unite the warring bloodlines was a pleasing indication of peaceful intentions. But Henry VII needed not only to look to a united future, he also needed to assert his history. In this, the late Henry VI was singularly useful. This popular 'saint' was his half-uncle. If Henry's sanctity could be officially recognized by the pope it would be a major coup for the Tudor regime. A legend arose of how Henry VI had prophesied the accession of Henry VII,* and letters were soon dispatched to one pope after another, appealing for the old king's canonization. With characteristic forward planning, Henry VII planned to have his own tomb built, in the latest Italian gothic fashion, close to his blessed forebear.

By then Henry VI was no longer at Chertsey Abbey. He had been moved to his birthplace at Windsor Castle, into the newly erected chapel of St George. This was a site more suited to his royal lineage and increasing fame among pilgrims. Surprisingly, it was not his half-nephew who moved Henry VI to this more exalted location, but Richard III. By the time Richard had taken the throne, Henry VI's cult had grown enormously in popularity. It is possible that some sense of personal guilt – whether for his own role in Henry's death, or for his brother's – prompted Richard to have Henry exhumed from the isolation

---

* Henry VI had met the future Henry VII, and allegedly seen sparks of greatness in him, in 1470. See above, p. 518.

of Chertsey and brought to Windsor. But it is also possible that it represented the combination of piety and self-interest in which fifteenth-century minds saw no contradiction. From 1473, Windsor Chapel had been converted into a dynastic religious centre for the House of York, linking them inextricably to the royal and chivalric rituals of the place. Edward IV had been buried there, and in the future his queen would choose the same gravesite. Thus, by bringing a popular saint to the chapel at Windsor, Richard brought his family's favoured religious site a potential cash flow from pilgrims, and also won the gratitude of the religious within the chapter.

When Henry's body was exhumed from the quiet isolation of Chertsey and moved to Windsor in August 1484, his body was reported by the chronicler John Rous to be uncorrupted despite thirteen years in the grave. He smelt sweet and the only sign of mortality was that his bearded face was slightly leaner than it had been in life. Both smell and preservation were probably down to the swift embalming with spices that had taken place in the Tower, but to contemporaries they provided further proof of Henry's sanctity. His body was removed to Windsor and there reburied. To facilitate the burial Henry was dismembered and placed in a small lead chest – a not unusual practice, for John Talbot had been similarly buried after the Battle of Castillon – although as it transpired, not all of Henry made it to Windsor. At some point during the reburial someone stole Henry's right arm, presumably to keep as a relic, and replaced it in the coffin with the left humerus of a pig. The switch was not discovered until Henry's tomb was re-opened in 1910, and where exactly Henry's arm ended up remains a mystery.[7]

Other relics of Henry were now proliferating. At Bridgnorth in Shropshire Henry's coat was piously displayed and, more alarmingly for Richard III's subsequent reputation, the Lady Chapel on the bridge at Caversham near Reading had 'the holy dagger that killed King Henry'.[8] Rumour soon had it that Richard himself had wielded the blade. Not content with Henry's body, Windsor also boasted the late king's spurs, a chip from his bedstead and his red velvet hat, 'a sovereign medicine against headache'.[9] Pilgrim badges representing Henry and his antelope heraldry were soon doing a brisk trade, finding their way in pilgrims' pockets to Bristol, Kings Lynn and even Rouen, where they tumbled out and were lost for centuries. Images of Henry or his symbols, rendered in stone and painted screens, were to be found as far afield as Alnwick in Northumberland, Hereford Cathedral, East Anglia, Devon and Essex.[10]

Among those supporting Henry's pilgrim trade were members of the royal family. Henry VII's queen, Elizabeth of York, paid two men to undertake pilgrimages on her behalf when their son Arthur was terminally ill in March 1502. They visited both Caversham and Windsor.[11] When Prince Arthur died in April, he was buried in Worcester Cathedral and later a magnificent chantry chapel built as a tomb for him. Among the heraldic symbols carved on this monument are the orb and sceptre, symbols of the blessed King Henry VI.[12] The family loyalty to Henry probably stemmed from its matriarch, Margaret Beaufort, who never forgot the king's kindnesses to her as a child, nor that she owed her own son's existence to his matchmaking. She possessed a similarly zealous inward piety to Henry, still bending her knees in lengthy prayer long after arthritis had crippled her fingers. Margaret seems genuinely to have believed that Henry was a saint, and no doubt her influence was as important as Henry VII's in pushing forward the attempts to have their relative canonized.

Unfortunately, despite years of effort, the Tudors did not succeed in establishing their Lancastrian saint. In the sixteenth century the failure to gain papal recognition for Henry VI was blamed on Henry VII's legendary miserliness, but this seems unfair. In fact Henry was perfectly willing to fund English saints – he gave the necessary money for the eleventh-century archbishop of Canterbury, Anselm, to be canonized in 1494. The difficulty lay with the popes themselves, who were uneasy about canonizing murdered laymen. Between 1254 and 1481 no one who died a violent death was canonized, despite popular and sometimes royal support for their sanctity.[13]

This tussle over Henry VI's reputation was not the last disagreement he caused. Even the location of his grave was argued over in death. In 1498, with his cult bringing hundreds of pilgrims and their full purses to Windsor, Westminster Abbey complained that Henry ought to be moved into their church. Chertsey then took up the cause, protesting that the king should be put back where he had originally been buried. A legal case ensued, overseen by Henry VII's Star Chamber Court, with aged witnesses reeled out to recite how they had heard the young Henry declare his intention to be buried in Westminster. Finally, judgement was found in favour of Westminster. This was a double blow to Windsor, as Henry VII now declared his intention to move his own tomb to Westminster Abbey along with his saintly uncle.[14]

However, time and distraction won out. Although Henry VII's tomb was prepared at Westminster, and even in his will plans were still being made for Henry VI to be translated, he never left Windsor. The second Tudor king, Henry VIII, had other interests. Although he visited Henry's tomb in 1529, he never made good his father's promise to transfer it to Westminster. In the end, Henry VIII was to bring about the end of the cult of Henry VI, for his regime's religious changes saw the widespread destruction of pilgrims' shrines. Henry VI's relics were dispersed, along with the other items kept at Caversham, including the wing of an angel and the assorted bone shards of two dozen saints. Being so closely associated with the royal family, Windsor Chapel survived slightly better. Henry's grave was left where it was and the wrought-iron money box into which pilgrims had deposited their coins in thanksgiving for Henry VI's intervention is still beside his grave in Windsor to this day.[15]

For nearly 430 years, Henry lay undisturbed. Then, in 1910, his vault was opened and his remains inspected by a team including a professor of anatomy, Dr A. Macalister, and their findings were recorded in a journal article. Amid the adipocere* and rotten linens were found 'a decayed mass of human bones lying in no definite order'. 'The bones of the head were unfortunately much broken' but in some places brown hair could still be seen clinging to them. Although Professor Macalister found the state of the remains 'so unsatisfactory that I could not make any trustworthy measurements', his colleague from the Society of Antiquaries made much of the fact that in one part of the skull the hair looked 'much darker and apparently matted with blood'. Was it perhaps the case that Henry had not been stabbed, as legend told, but instead killed by a blow to the head? The evidence was too slight to make a definite diagnosis, and although forensic testing for human blood had been invented the dark matter on Henry's skull was not tested for it.[16]

Among the men standing around the vault of Henry as it was re-opened in 1910 were representatives of Eton College and King's College, Cambridge. Henry's most enduring legacies were to be these educational institutions, where his memory is still venerated to such a degree that he is almost unfailingly referred to simply as 'The Founder'.

---

* Literally, corpse wax.

Epilogue

The story of Henry's kingship is an unexpected one. That the son of Agincourt's victor should grow up never to raise a sword against an enemy is surprising. That he should posthumously become a popular 'saint' is unusual. That the baby who was king of England and of France before his first birthday should die a prisoner, shabbily dressed, retreating into melancholy visions and abandoned in the Tower of London is unique. His was an exceptional position and perhaps the reason he failed to live up to his early promise is that Henry was, ultimately, a far from exceptional man. He was kind-hearted, charitable, generous to a fault, but he was never strong-willed nor focused enough to fulfil the hopes invested in him. Henry knew off by heart the lessons he had learnt in his education about what a king *should* be, but he never witnessed what a king really was, the core of steel necessary at the heart of a medieval monarch.

Henry also, perhaps, took the wrong lessons from his education. He believed that peace was a cardinal virtue and chastity and self-denial crucial for a ruler: after all, if you could not rule yourself, how could you rule others? But the English, fundamentally, did not mind a king who drank and prostituted himself. Edward IV over-indulged in hunting, women and food but his subjects were, largely, contented as long as he won his battles, lived within his means and raised arms against the

French occasionally, as he did in 1475. What the English could not bear was a ruler who did not rule. They did not want the country in the hands of advisers, whether they were dukes or the queen. They did not want other men commanding armies in France while that realm was steadily lost and their king sat at home. They especially did not want to be charged excessive taxes for a royal household consistently living beyond its means while law and order crumbled. And due to Henry's inattention, disorder engulfed his realms. This gave Henry's rivals – from Cade to York to Warwick to Edward IV – clear opportunities to tap into popular dissatisfaction.

Yet it is worth remembering that for a remarkably long time even those of Henry's subjects who had seen, at first hand, that he was not up to the job refused to deprive him of his throne. In 1460, it was Henry's own inertia that saw York triumph and even then, he was allowed to retain his crown for as long as he lived or could endure York's intimidation. Exasperation with Henry's rule was consistently tempered by affection for Henry himself. It was his misfortune that he lacked the necessary guile to harness that ability to win hearts into the charismatic leadership displayed by his father and, occasionally, his uncles.

Was this sympathy for Henry, both during his lifetime and in his posthumous career as saintly intercessor, inspired by concern about his mental state? The fullest expression of the notion of Henry as 'holy innocent' is found in William Shakespeare's three eponymous plays. There, Henry VI is portrayed as an otherworldly pacifist, more suited to the realm of religion than the ruthless political sphere. However, despite the occasional angry railing of his subjects and the propaganda of his Yorkist enemies, Henry was not the holy fool of Shakespearean conception. He was well read and concerned for education. Even after his mental breakdown in 1453, he was far from the 'mad king' of popular memory. His recovery in 1454 may not have been complete, but nor was his mental illness all-encompassing and it is plausible that had it not been for the Battle of St Albans in 1455 Henry might have been fully restored to health. The trauma of that experience of battle was repeated during 1459–61 and exacerbated by the loss of his throne, the stress of years in exile and months on the run, and his eventual imprisonment from 1465. When his body was exhumed in 1910 Henry's teeth were found to be ground down, perhaps reflecting the anxiety of these troubled years. If he did retreat into trances and visions during his captivity it would be little wonder under the circumstances, but in an age of zealous and literal-minded piety we cannot take such assertions as indications of mental illness.

One root of exasperation with Henry was the disparity between him and his father. But the legacy of warfare Henry V left his son was acknowledged even by his most admiring contemporaries as problematic. In the *Gesta Henrici Quinti* (*Deeds of Henry V*), written in 1417, and which I quoted in the first chapter, it was acknowledged that the king's victory at Agincourt gave 'reason to rejoice in the victory gained and... reason to grieve for the suffering and destruction wrought in the deaths of Christians'.[1] The fundamental difference between father and son was that Henry VI could neither rejoice in, nor justify, a victory that entailed suffering as his father could. His inclination for mercy and peace put him out of step with many of his contemporaries, and it is a terrible irony that a man so devoted to peace was the trigger for the bloodiest battle in English history.*

Perhaps the most enduring image of Henry's kingship is provided in the pages of a manuscript commissioned by two of his leading opponents, the Yorkist Sir William Herbert and his wife Anne Devereux. Towards the close of Henry's first reign, the Herberts commissioned a new edition of the *Troy Book* by John Lydgate, the poet whose previous works included plays to amuse Henry as a child and encomia for Henry and

---

* At the Battle of Towton, more soldiers died in a single day than were killed in the first day of the Battle of the Somme in the First World War, 1 July 1916.

Margaret themselves. This mirror for princes had first been
written at the beginning of Henry VI's reign and opened with
a prologue praising Henry V. The Herberts probably intended
their manuscript to be presented to Henry VI as a gift, although
whether he ever saw it is unclear, since by the time of its com-
pletion he faced deposition.[2]

In the top left-hand corner of a folio of the manuscript is
an image of a king, his crown poking out of the square frame
struggling to contain it, its glister imitated in the golden stars that
stud the painted sky behind him. He bears the visual symbols of
his authority: the orb and sceptre in his hands, his body swathed
in crimson robes that reach all the way to the cushion at his
feet. His eye is cast down, god-like, since everyone is beneath
him. But his position is far from secure, because his throne is
perched on the top of a giant wheel, that is spun carelessly by a
woman at its centre. As she turns the wheel, the king slips and
falls, staring back in vain at what he has lost. The outward signs
of kingship are dragged into the spokes and torn away: first his
crown, then his ermine-lined crimson mantle, and finally his
rich coat until he is left, miserable and lowly, crushed beneath
the weight of the wheel, face pressed into the earth. But then he
rises once more, donning again these precious robes and jewels
as he claws his way back up the wheel, Dame Fortune smiling on
benignly as she spins, scarcely even noticing.

Henry VI's life seems a textbook example of the medieval
concept of Fortune's Wheel, but where for many the image
was a metaphorical expression of the fragility of human power,
in Henry's case he literally was toppled from his throne into
obscurity and then restored. However, Fortune's Wheel suggests
an implacable progress against which people struggle in vain,
whereas Henry's story is fundamentally one of human fallibility
and choice. Contrary to the theory of Fortune, the natural progression of Henry VI's kingship would have been for him to
maintain his throne – in 1421 it was relatively unusual for kings
of England to be toppled from power. Only two of Henry's royal

predecessors had been successfully deposed since 1066.* Henry's
fall from grace was, then, far from inevitable and it resulted not
from the benign – or malevolent – revolutions of a power beyond
his control, but from a complex array of competing forces in
which Henry's choices and character were crucial.

---

*   Three if we include Empress Matilda, who was heir to the throne in
1135 but usurped by her cousin Stephen before she could be crowned.

Appendix I: Where did Henry VI die?

In the heart of the Tower of London, overlooking Traitors' Gate and squeezed between the Bloody Tower and the battlements, lies the Wakefield Tower.* In the floor of what used to be a small chapel within this medieval tower there is a white marble slab that reads:

> By tradition, Henry VI died here 21 May 1471.

Here, on 21 May of every year for almost a century 'the ceremony of the lilies and roses' has been performed, with representatives of King's College Cambridge and Eton College attending to commemorate Henry's murder in the Tower. But the equivocal wording of the memorial in the Wakefield Tower testifies to lingering uncertainty about its veracity, for there is no evidence to suggest that this is, in fact, where Henry died or even where he was kept prisoner in the Tower. But if Henry did not die in the chapel of the Wakefield, where did he die? And how did the Wakefield Tower come to be considered 'the precise spot' where he was murdered?[1]

The building we now call the 'Wakefield' was built by Henry's

---

* The name of the Wakefield Tower has varied throughout its history. For simplicity I have used the modern title throughout.

ancestor, King Henry III, from the 1220s onwards. At that time, it was part of the outer wall of the Tower, leading directly on to the River Thames. The Wakefield Tower was sandwiched between, on one side, a water gateway now called the Bloody Tower, and on the other a great hall and suite of royal lodgings that hugged the south wall all the way to another mural tower called the 'Lanthorn'. This last building was at that time the queen's lodgings, magnificently painted with flowers and externally whitewashed. The Wakefield served for a time as the king's bedroom and later probably as a council chamber. By 1238 it contained one of the six small chapels that dotted the Tower complex. Fifty years later, extensions to the Tower of London added an additional outer wall and the Wakefield became something of a through route from the outer to inner wards. By the fourteenth century it seems it was no longer used as a private space for the king and instead clothes, furnishings and records started to be stored within its octagonal walls. The Lanthorn Tower to the east now became the centre of the king's apartments, and the queen's lodgings were removed into a new complex that stretched north towards the White Tower. This entire vast suite of palace buildings was left to deteriorate throughout the Tudor period and by the seventeenth century was in such a state of decay that it had to be pulled down, leaving a gaping hole in the inner ward of the Tower that now houses the ravens, the south lawn and a giftshop.[2]

As the functions of the Wakefield Tower changed, so did its name. It was sometimes known as the 'Hall Tower' in memory of the lost palace beside it or the 'Records Tower', for records were still stored there in the nineteenth century. From 1856 to 1939 this octagonal, vaulted room housed the crown jewels and was known as the Jewel House. The name 'Wakefield' derived from a fourteenth-century clerk of that name, although Victorian authors claimed completely erroneously that it was because prisoners of the Battle of Wakefield (1460) had been kept there.[3]

Would Henry VI have been imprisoned in this tower? Almost certainly not, since to move him in, a large quantity of records would have had to be moved out. As Henry was attended by a considerable number of guards and servants, accommodating them all within the space would also have been a challenge. Moreover, there was a slight security risk in using the Wakefield, since it was so close to the gateway into the inner ward. It would have been more secure to keep Henry in one of the other mural towers, perhaps the Salt Tower, at the furthest reach of the inner walls. It was there, in the thirteenth century, that the ex-king of Scotland, John Balliol, lived very comfortably as a captive for three years.

The sole near-contemporary source that provides a clue to Henry's location within the Tower is the *Great Chronicle of London*,* which states that when Henry was restored to the throne in October 1470 he was 'fetched out of the place he was long before imprisoned, and then lodged in the *king's lodgings* where the queen before lay'.[4] The king's lodgings would have been close to, or within, the Lanthorn Tower so Henry was presumably *not* imprisoned within the royal apartments. This makes sense, since Edward IV consistently referred to his adversary as king 'in deed, and not by right' and would have avoided allowing him any of the trappings of royalty.[5] Even while refusing Henry the title of king, though, Edward would probably still have imprisoned Henry in a high-status apartment, not a dank and grim dungeon as we might imagine. King Jean II of France had been imprisoned in the White Tower in the fourteenth century and a fifteenth-century manuscript showing the prisoner of war Charles, duke of Orléans, also locates him within the White Tower.[6]

Unfortunately, no sources reveal exactly where Henry was imprisoned once he returned to the Tower in May 1471. At that

---

* The *Great Chronicle* was not written until the first decade of the sixteenth century but its London-based author (possibly the alderman Robert Fabyan, d. 1513) was a close contemporary to events.

time, space was at a premium. Edward IV's issue roll shows that from 21 April to 14 May 100 soldiers were lodged within the Tower with the constable, John, Lord Dudley.[7] Queen Elizabeth, her children, her brother Anthony Woodville and his soldiers were also staying in the Tower during the period when it was under attack by the Bastard of Fauconberg in early May.[8] And, if the Warkworth Chronicle is to be believed, Richard, duke of Gloucester, was also staying there on 21 May with 'many other'.[9] With so many high-status residents, their servants and guards to accommodate, Henry would probably have been moved down the pecking order and consigned to a space customarily used for keeping prisoners, rather than one of the chambers in or close to the palace apartments. Again, the sheer proximity of the Wakefield Tower to the royal apartments and great hall might have precluded its being used by Henry.

If Henry was not kept in the Wakefield, might he have gone there to make his devotions in the chapel? Possibly, but as mentioned there were a number of other chapels he could use, probably more easily. It is also not certain that when Henry died, he was even in a chapel. No contemporary record provides this degree of detail on the location of his death, or his activity at the time. He was simply 'inward in prison in the Tower'. Even in the sixteenth century, chroniclers and playwrights who blithely asserted that Richard III killed Henry with a dagger gave no location for his murder.[10]

With so little to support the association of the Wakefield Tower and Henry's death, how then did it come to be considered the traditional location for his murder? For centuries, it didn't. Having combed reference works and guidebooks connected to the Tower, the earliest reference I have found stating that Henry was killed in the Wakefield is the 1830 work *Memoirs of the Tower of London*, by John Britton and E. W. Brayley. Although earlier guides do not locate Henry's death anywhere specific within the Tower, Britton and Brayley claim the association is based on 'vulgar tradition' and by 1867 Baron de Ros could claim in his

Memorials of the Tower of London that the Wakefield 'has been *always traditionally* pointed out as the scene of Henry VI's murder'.[11] Even then the association was with the Wakefield in general and not specifically with the chapel. It was another six years before John Wesley Thomas's work identified that Henry had been 'bent in prayer' in the private chapel of that tower when Richard, duke of Gloucester killed him.[12]

It was only in 1923, after an appeal to the office of works, that it was decided to memorialize the site as the definitive location for Henry's murder. By then, the vogue for allocating specific locations to historical events in the Tower had created an execution memorial for Anne Boleyn in a place she probably did not die, created the legend of 'Traitors' Gate' being the entrance point for the future Elizabeth I when she in fact entered the Tower via a postern gate (now the Byward Tower), and attributed the fate of the 'Princes in the Tower' to the Bloody Tower, a building substantially rebuilt more than a century after their disappearance.[13] As Sir Charles Peers of the office of works wrote in frustration in 1923: 'The desire to earmark a definitive site for a historical event is common and seldom resisted. The country bristles with bogus attributions of this nature... [But] *if people want to be deceived, let them be!*'[14]

The driving forces behind the Wakefield memorial were an old Etonian and graduate of King's College Cambridge, the Reverend Thomas Carter, and the keeper of the crown jewels, Sir George Younghusband. Having attended the two educational establishments that owed their existence to Henry VI, Carter wanted a memorial to the late king and initially sought the support of the lord chamberlain simply to place a bunch of lilies in the chapel annually on the anniversary of Henry's death. Younghusband had lived in the Tower for six years and become convinced that the Wakefield chapel was where Henry had died, although when Sir Charles Peers queried why he was so certain, Younghusband could not produce any new evidence. 'There is circumstantial evidence of a very interesting and convincing nature,' he insisted, without providing further details. Younghusband's chief motivation seems to have been dogged traditionalism in the face of a rapidly changing world: 'It is rather a nice idea (especially in these Bolshevich days) keeping thus in touch with the old England of five hundred years ago.'[15]

Forced against his will to accept 'one more lucrative fake in the Tower', Peers insisted that the memorial 'should bear a qualified inscription – "by tradition", or something of that sort'. And thus, by tradition, Henry's death in the Wakefield Tower came to be an established part of the fabric of the Tower of London in a place where he almost certainly did not die.

The association of Henry's death with the Wakefield is, then, misleading. But given the desire for a memorial for Henry, was there any other realistic alternative? We do not know exactly where he was imprisoned, and even the buildings he almost certainly inhabited as king during his readeption are now gone. While the Salt Tower has survived intact, the current Lanthorn Tower is a nineteenth-century building recreated by Anthony Salvin. At the very least, the Wakefield Tower has the virtue of having existed in Henry's time and is a survival of the medieval palace in the Tower of London which would still be recognizable to Henry VI today.

Appendix II: Key characters

William AISCOUGH, bishop of Salisbury (d. 1450): Henry VI's confessor, associated with the duke of Suffolk.

ANNE of Burgundy (1404–32) a.k.a. **Anne, duchess of Bedford:** Philippe of Burgundy's sister, married to John, duke of Bedford. A mediatory, pacific force in the uneasy Anglo-Burgundian alliance.

Henry BEAUFORT, bishop of Winchester a.k.a. **Cardinal Beaufort (c.1375–1447):** The richest bishop in England, Beaufort was uncle to Henry V, Gloucester and Bedford and great-uncle to Henry. His many international relatives and vast treasury gave him primacy in English politics but he vied for authority with Bedford and Gloucester.

Margaret BEAUFORT (1443–1509): heiress of John Beaufort, 1st duke of Somerset; mother of Henry VII.

John, Viscount BEAUMONT (c.1409–60): Faithful companion to Henry VI from youth and key ally for Margaret, serving as councillor to her and Prince Edward. Lancastrian to the core.

John, duke of BEDFORD (1389–1435): Eldest surviving uncle of Henry VI, he became regent of France. A cultured, artistic and dependable nobleman.

Ralph BOTILLER, Lord Sudeley (c.1394–1473): The son of Henry VI's governess, he was a faithful Lancastrian councillor and chamberlain of Henry's household.

Henry, Viscount BOURCHIER (c.1408–83): The brother-in-law and councillor of the duke of York became one of his stalwart supporters, for which he was rewarded handsomely under Edward IV.

Thomas BOURCHIER, archbishop of Canterbury (c.1411–86): Despite his family connection to the duke of York, he was a trusted conciliator of noble quarrels, including that between York and Somerset. However, by 1460 his increasing alienation from power pushed him into support for the Yorkist cause.

Humphrey Stafford, duke of BUCKINGHAM (1402–60): An experienced soldier of the wars in France and mediator in the early years of the conflict with York. Eventually became one of the key Lancastrian commanders.

Anne Neville, duchess of BUCKINGHAM (d.1480): Sister of Cecily Neville and the earl of Salisbury, but nonetheless remained a faithful ally of Queen Margaret. Prince Edward's godmother.

CATHERINE Valois, queen of England (1401–37): Daughter of Charles VI and Isabeau of Bavaria, she married Henry V as part of the Treaty of Troyes. She lived in Henry VI's household until he was crowned, then retreated from court and married her servant Owen Tudor, with whom she had Edmund and Jasper Tudor.

CECILY Neville, duchess of York (1415–95): One of the twenty-three children of Ralph, earl of Westmorland; wife of Richard, duke of York. Cecily shared her husband's taste for the expensive and magnificent, but had a greater ability to conciliate. Like her old mistress Queen Margaret, her chief aim was to protect her family from the vagaries of civil war.

CHARLES VI, king of France (1368–1422): a.k.a. 'Charles the well-beloved' or 'Charles the mad'; Henry VI's maternal grandfather, whose episodes of mental illness drove France into civil war. Ruled France 1380–1422.

CHARLES VII, king of France (1403–61): a.k.a. 'Charles the victorious' or **Dauphin Charles**. Charles VI's only surviving son and Henry's rival for the French throne. A paranoid and ruthless man who steadily won back all that his forebears had lost to the English.

CHARLES 'the bold', duke of Burgundy (1433–77): a.k.a. Charles, count of Charolais. The son and heir of Philippe of Burgundy, who had an uneasy relationship with his father. For many years a supporter of the Lancastrians, his marriage to Edward IV's sister Margaret eventually changed his allegiance.

Henry CHICHELE, archbishop of Canterbury (*c.*1362–1443): Served as archbishop and royal councillor from 1414 to 1443. His chief aim was to keep the English church independent of papal interference.

George, duke of CLARENCE (1449–78): Younger brother of Edward IV, who married Isabel Neville, daughter of Warwick the kingmaker. His changing allegiances in 1469–71 proved crucial.

Thomas, duke of CLARENCE (1387–1421): Younger brother of Henry V and stepfather of the Beaufort dukes of Somerset. Killed fighting at the Battle of Baugé in 1421.

Ralph, Lord CROMWELL (*c.*1393–1456): A royal councillor and veteran of the French wars, he served as Henry VI's chamberlain and lord treasurer. The rise of the duke of Suffolk meant Cromwell was increasingly sidelined and he became a natural ally of the Nevilles and duke of York.

EDWARD, earl of March a.k.a. Edward IV (1442–83): a.k.a. the 'rose of Rouen'. The charismatic teenage earl was reported to be the 'most handsome man of his time'.[1] Courageous and charismatic, he deposed and eventually killed Henry VI.

EDWARD of Westminster, prince of Wales (1453–71): Henry and Margaret's only child.

ELEANOR Cobham, duchess of Gloucester (*c.*1400–52): Gloucester's second wife, who yearned for a crown. Her intriguing with necromancers landed her in prison.

Henry Holland, duke of EXETER (1430–73): Married York's daughter Anne but remained a fervent Lancastrian and ally of the Percys in the north. The belligerent young Exeter was repeatedly imprisoned and went into Lancastrian exile after 1461.

Thomas Beaufort, duke of EXETER (*c.*1377–1426): Soldier and elder brother of Henry Beaufort, bishop of Winchester. Named by Henry V as one of Henry VI's guardians.

GEORGE Neville, bishop of Exeter/archbishop of York (1432–76): Younger son of the earl of Salisbury and brother of Warwick the kingmaker. A Yorkist keenly protective of his family's interest. Briefly chancellor during Henry's readeption.

Humphrey, duke of GLOUCESTER (1390–1447): The youngest of Henry VI's uncles, he was named protector and defender of the realm during Henry's minority (although only when his brother the duke of Bedford was not in England). An ambitious, proud and factionalizing force in politics.

Richard, duke of GLOUCESTER (1452–85): Youngest brother of Edward IV. The future King Richard III.

HENRY IV, king of England (1367–1413): a.k.a. Henry Bolingbroke, a.k.a. Henry of Lancaster, earl of Derby. Henry VI's grandfather. Usurped the throne from his cousin Richard II after being briefly exiled, ruling from 1399 to 1413.

HENRY V, king of England (1386–1422): Henry VI's father, ruled 1413–22. According to the terms of the Treaty of Troyes, also heir to the French throne. A warrior king and victor of Agincourt, he died after the siege of Meaux and never met his only child.

HENRY VI, king of England (1421–71): Youngest ever king of England and only monarch to be crowned king of France and England.

HENRY VII (1457–1509): a.k.a. Henry Tudor, earl of Richmond. Product of Henry VI's matchmaking, the only child of heiress Margaret Beaufort and Edmund Tudor. Grew up in Wales and on the continent, before returning to England in 1485 and becoming King Henry VII, first of the Tudor dynasty. He and his mother tried unsuccessfully to canonize Henry.

ISABEAU of Bavaria, queen of France (1370–1435): Wife of Charles VI and mother of Catherine Valois and Charles VII. A woman with a taste for the luxurious, she was one of the three architects of the Treaty of Troyes.

ISABELLA of Portugal, duchess of Burgundy (1397–1471): Niece of Cardinal Beaufort, she was trusted by the English more than her husband Philippe of Burgundy but proved to be just as diplomatically shrewd and self-serving as he was.

JACQUELINE of Hainault (1401–36): The brave and spirited countess of Holland, Hainault and Zealand was Henry VI's godmother. Humphrey, duke of Gloucester married her to help win back her territories but soon abandoned her. She continued her war against Philippe of Burgundy alone.

JAQUETTA of Luxembourg (c.1416–1472): Second wife of the duke of Bedford. After his death she married the Lancastrian commander Richard Woodville, Lord Rivers. Their daughter Elizabeth Woodville went on to marry Edward IV.

JAMES I, king of Scotland (1394–1437): A prisoner of war in England 1406–24, he married Joan Beaufort (niece of Cardinal Beaufort). Murdered on the orders of his uncle in 1437.

JAMES II, king of Scotland (1430–60): A bellicose young king eager to retake northern English territory for Scotland, he was killed by one of his own cannon at the siege of Roxburgh in 1460.

JAMES III, king of Scotland (1452–88): Child king whose regime offered the Lancastrians sanctuary in 1461.

JEAN 'the fearless', duke of Burgundy (1371–1419): The father of Philippe of Burgundy, he was murdered in 1419 by Charles VII's men.

JOAN of Navarre, queen of England (1368–1437): Princess of Navarre and second wife of King Henry IV of England. Henry V imprisoned her on charges of witchcraft in 1419. She retained a close relationship with the duke of Gloucester until her death in 1437.

Cardinal John KEMPE, archbishop of York (1380/1–1454): Henry Beaufort's ally and Henry VI's adviser. Closely associated with Henry's diplomatic efforts with France.

LOUIS XI, king of France (1423–83): a.k.a. 'the universal spider', **Dauphin Louis.** Charles VII's son. Rebelled against his father in the *Praguerie* revolt of 1440 and lived for many years in Philippe of Burgundy's court. An uncouth and duplicitous prince who tried to play the Yorkists and Lancastrians against each other.

Edmund Mortimer, earl of MARCH (1391–1425): Uncle of Richard, duke of York. Although he represented a rival blood claimant to the English throne, March was a trusted Lancastrian commander for Henry V.

MARGARET of Anjou, queen of England (1430–82): French princess who married Henry at fifteen. The effective leader of the Lancastrian regime from 1453 onwards.

Queen MARY of Scotland (1434–63): a.k.a. **Mary of Guelders.** The niece of Philippe of Burgundy and wife of James II, on the death of her husband she assumed control of their infant son and thus the government of Scotland.

Adam MOLEYNS, bishop of Chichester (d.1450): Associate of the duke of Suffolk and Henry VI's keeper of the privy seal. His death prompted a year of rebellion and murder.

John Neville, Lord MONTAGU (c.1431–71): Younger brother of Warwick the kingmaker and son of the earl of Salisbury. One of the leading figures in the Neville–Percy feud and one of Edward IV's chief commanders during the Lancastrian rebellion in Northumberland.

John Mowbray, duke of NORFOLK (1415–61): His rivalry with the dukes of Suffolk and Somerset drove him to support his uncle, the duke of York, in 1450–2.

Charles, duke of ORLÉANS (1394–1465): Senior member of the French royal family, he was captured at the Battle of Agincourt and Henry V insisted that he must remain a prisoner until Henry VI reached his majority. Henry VI's decision to free Orléans was to prove one of his costliest mistakes in the name of peace.

PHILIPPE 'the good', duke of Burgundy (1396–1467): With Queen Isabeau and Henry V, one of the chief architects of the Treaty of Troyes. Famed for his chivalric court, his first loyalty was always to his own ambition.

RENÉ of Anjou, king of Jerusalem and Sicily (1409–80): Margaret of Anjou's father, a man renowned for the fantastical pageantry of his court.

Edmund, earl of RUTLAND (1443–60): Second son of Richard, duke of York.

Alice Montagu, countess of SALISBURY (c.1406–62): A great heiress in her own right, Alice was married to Richard Neville, earl of Salisbury. She had the dubious distinction of being the only noblewoman to be attainted for treason during the Wars of the Roses, for inciting Yorkist rebellion in 1459.

Richard Neville, earl of SALISBURY (1400–60): Brother of Cecily Neville, duchess of York, and one of the chief protectors and power-holders of northern England. A long-time Lancastrian servant, his association with York forced him into the role of rebel leader.

Thomas Montagu, earl of SALISBURY (1388–1428): A hero of the French wars and ally of the duke of Gloucester, he died besieging Orléans. His widow, Alice Chaucer, remarried William de la Pole, earl of Suffolk.

James Fiennes, Lord SAYE AND SELE (c.1390–1450): A long-time servant in Henry VI's household and one of the many close attendants who benefited from royal generosity. His association with Suffolk's policies and Henry's disastrous finances spelled his doom.

John Talbot, second earl of SHREWSBURY (c.1413–1460): Son of the famed John Talbot and ally of Ralph, Lord Cromwell. From 1456 he was associated with Queen Margaret; his position as treasurer made him a focus of anti-court hostility that was to prove his undoing.

John Beaufort, 1st duke of SOMERSET (1404–44): Nephew of Cardinal Beaufort, he was a prisoner of war in France for seventeen years before returning to military service. His shambolic campaign in 1443 cost him his career and possibly his life.

Edmund Beaufort, 2nd duke of SOMERSET (c.1406–55): The nephew of Cardinal Beaufort and alleged lover of Queen Catherine. An experienced commander in France, Somerset grew to be a wily, if avaricious, politician. He eventually became Henry's chief adviser and Margaret's councillor but could never live down the loss of France.

Henry Beaufort, 3rd duke of SOMERSET (1436–64): Son of Edmund Beaufort, the angry young Henry Beaufort was seriously wounded fighting alongside his father at the first Battle of St Albans in 1455 and became an inveterate enemy of the Yorkists as a result. A (mostly) loyal supporter of the Lancastrian cause.

Edmund Beaufort, 4th duke of SOMERSET (*c.*1438–71): Younger son of the second duke of Somerset, he continued the family tradition of Lancastrianism and paid for it with his life.

William de la Pole, duke of SUFFOLK (1396–1450): a.k.a. earl and marquess of Suffolk. After years of fighting in France, Suffolk married Alice Chaucer and became steward of Henry's household in 1433. He and Alice were the dominant forces in Henry and Margaret's youth but his role in forging Henry's peace policy made him deeply unpopular.

Alice Chaucer, duchess of SUFFOLK (*c.*1404–75): The thrice-married Alice (also Lady Phelip/countess of Salisbury) was a cosmopolitan and intelligent noblewoman. As one of Margaret's earliest attendants she had a hold over Henry and his queen that led to her condemnation in parliament. After her husband's death she read the political situation shrewdly enough to transition to York's faction and survived until 1475.

John, Lord TALBOT (*c.*1387–1453): a.k.a. earl of Shrewsbury, a.k.a. 'the Terror of the French'. A career soldier with fifty years' military service, Talbot was a justly famed English captain. His chivalrous (if militarily futile) last charge at Castillon was the deathknell for Henry's rule in Gascony.

Edmund TUDOR, earl of Richmond (*c.*1430–56): Elder son of Catherine Valois and Owen Tudor. Married Margaret Beaufort when she was twelve. Died in 1456 as a result of a Yorkist siege, leaving his wife six months pregnant with the future Henry VII.

Jasper TUDOR, earl of Pembroke (*c.*1431–95): Younger son of Catherine of Valois and Owen Tudor, a committed Lancastrian and Henry's representative in Wales.

Owen TUDOR (*c.*1400–61): Second husband of Queen Catherine, the father of Edmund and Jasper Tudor. Killed fighting for Henry at the Battle of Mortimer's Cross.

Richard Beauchamp, earl of WARWICK (1382–1439): One of Henry V's companions in war; famed for his chivalry and military skill, he was Henry VI's 'master', 1428–37.

Richard Neville, earl of WARWICK (1428–71): a.k.a. the 'king-maker'. Son of the earl of Salisbury, he was a charismatic but ruthless political force. With control of the port of Calais and the ability to manipulate popular opinion, Warwick was the steel core of the Yorkist resistance. His dissatisfaction with Edward IV drove him into an unlikely alliance.

John, Lord WENLOCK (d.1471): After serving as a diplomat and Queen Margaret's chamberlain, he supported the Yorkist cause by 1458. A close associate of Warwick the kingmaker.

James Butler, earl of WILTSHIRE (1420–61): a.k.a. earl of Ormond. Allegedly so handsome he feared marring his good lucks with war wounds, Wiltshire fled from every battle he attended. Nonetheless, as Treasurer in the 1450s he was a staunch Lancastrian and paid the price at Yorkist hands.

Richard, duke of YORK (1411–60): The proud and ambitious York was highly conscious of his status as Henry's heir after 1447. His determination to vigorously oppose threats to his authority and his desire to dominate political life brought him into conflict with Somerset, Margaret and eventually Henry VI.

Acknowledgements

My debts are growing as my books get fatter, and this one falls down firmly on the side of voluptuous. Thank you, first and foremost, to Anthony Cheetham and Georgina Capel, who guided me towards Henry. Enormous thanks also to Richard Milbank and the whole brilliant team at Head of Zeus for all their hard work and trust in this book. As always, it was a joy to work with them. I have to express my gratitude for the work of Henry and Margaret's biographers who have gone before, particularly Ralph Griffiths, Bertram Wolffe, John Watts, Helen Maurer, Helen Castor, Joanna Laynesmith and Katherine Lewis.

While writing *Shadow King* I have been repeatedly surprised by, and grateful for, the willingness of others to help with my weird queries, from the size of warhorses and medieval theories of mental illness to the gory details of adipocere. I particularly wish to thank Jeremy Ashbee, whose research into the history of the Tower of London and Henry's imprisonment was invaluable; Abi Carter of Forensic Resources Ltd; the staff of Eton College, especially Philippa Martin, Eleanor Hoare and William Waldegrave; Malcolm Mercer of the Royal Armouries; Daniel F. Gosling; Sophia Tobin of the Goldsmiths Company; Nathen Armin, Helen Castor, Michael K. Jones and Ralph Griffiths, for responding so readily to my queries; Amy Rhodes and Alex Rowe-Mayer of Past Pleasures Ltd and Historic Royal

Palaces, who supported my research into Margaret of Anjou's coronation; Chris Gidlow, George Roberts and Cate Milton of Historic Royal Palaces; Will Ewart and Matthew Payne of Westminster Abbey; Philip Morgan and his colleagues at Keele University for digging up a half-lost thesis; Mark Griffin; Judith Ridley; my old supervisor Rowena E. Archer and my college mate Antonia Fitzpatrick, for sharing their considerable fifteenth-century knowledge; Rosanna Heverin-West, for ploughing through the early draft of the book and both encouraging and questioning in exactly the right quantity; Drs Jessica Meyer, Joanna Phillips and Claire Trenery at Leeds University, who discussed their research into medical history with me – and additional thanks to Joanna and Claire for reading an early draft of my chapter on Henry's mental breakdown and providing their feedback. Adela Baker and Jessica Green also lent me much-appreciated insight into mental health in the modern world. Thank you to John Gregor, Fiona Ashley, Emma Hatton and Lucy Moore for directing me towards them. As ever, the staff of the National Archives, London Library, Bodleian Library and British Library were a fount of assistance and support.

Both my previous books benefited from the 'editorial' attentions of my dear friend Claire Chate-Fawcett. She was one of the first people I discussed this book with and her death during the course of writing it was incredibly hard for all of us who loved her. It meant a huge amount that her dad, Robert Chate, took up where Claire left off and cast his critical eye over my first draft, providing the same insightful guidance and encouragement that Claire so often had in the past. A firm self-admonition to 'be more Claire' kept me going when weariness and word fatigue set in. Thanks, CCF.

In general, for helping to maintain my equilibrium when writing about a long-dead king got too much, I thank my colleagues, friends, sprats, family and everyone who was on the other end of a phone call, cup of coffee, glass of wine or WhatsApp message.

As always, my last thanks have to go to the people who have been first on hand throughout this process, chivvying, cheerleading (and occasionally chauffeuring): my parents, Anne and Keith Johnson, and Joe, without whom none of this would be possible.

Bibliography

Archives

Bodleian Library:
  MS Film 428.
Eton College Archives:
  ECR 39: Royal Patents.
National Archives:
  E 101: Exchequer, King's Remembrancer, wardrobe and
    household accounts.
  E 403: Issue rolls and registers.
  KB 9: King's Bench, ancient indictments.
  KB 27: King's Bench, coram rege rolls.
  Work 14: Office of works, ancient monuments and historic
    buildings.

Online sources

Archer, Rowena E., 'Chaucer [*married names* Phelip, Montagu, de la
  Pole], Alice, duchess of Suffolk (*c.* 1404–1475)', *ODNB*. Oxford
  University Press: 2011, https://doi.org/10.1093/ref:odnb/54434.
Bodleian Library, MS. Bodl. 277: http://bodley30.bodley.ox.ac.uk:
  8180/luna/servlet/detail/ODLodl~14~14~76776~135161:
  Henry-VI,-King-of-England,-invoked-?sort=Shelfmark&qvq=w4s:/
  what/MS.%20Bodl.%20277;sort:Shelfmark;lc:ODLodl~29~29,O
  DLodl~7~7,ODLodl~6~6,ODLodl~14~14,ODLodl~8~8,ODLo.

'Bolingbroke–Bonby', in Lewis, Samuel, ed. *A Topographical Dictionary of England.* London: 1848, British History Online, http://www. british-history.ac.uk/topographical-dict/england/pp295-302.

British Library:

Cotton MS Domitian, A. XVII: http://www.bl.uk/manuscripts/Full-Display.aspx?ref=Cotton_MS_domitian_a_xvii.

Add MS 18850: http://www.bl.uk/catalogues/illuminatedmanu-scripts/record.asp?MSID=6474andCollID=27andNStart=18850.

Royal MS 15 E VI: http://www.bl.uk/manuscripts/FullDisplay. aspx?ref=Royal_MS_15_E_VI.

Royal MS 16 F II: https://www.bl.uk/catalogues/illuminatedmanu-scripts/record.asp?MSID=7982&CollID=16&NStart=160602.

Royal 18 D II: http://www.bl.uk/catalogues/illuminatedmanuscripts/ record.asp?MSID=8704&CollID=16&NStart=180402&_ga= 2.64312687.1390438930.1529398102-157633210.149581 1005.

MS Harley 2278: http://www.bl.uk/catalogues/illuminatedmanu-scripts/record.asp?MSID=6643&CollID=8&NStart=2278.

Brown, Rawdon, ed. *Calendar of State Papers Relating To English Affairs in the Archives of Venice, Volume 1, 1202–1509.* London: 1864, British History Online, http://www.british-history.ac.uk/cal-state-papers/ venice/vol1.

Bush, Ruth, 'Pole, Katherine de la (1410/11–1473)', *ODNB.* Oxford University Press: 2012, http://www.oxforddnb.com/view/article/ 54452.

Hinds, Allen B., ed. *Calendar of State Papers and Manuscripts in the Archives and Collections of Milan 1385–1618.* 1912, British History Online, http://www.british-history.ac.uk/cal-state-papers/milan/ 1385-1618.

Curry, Anne, 'Fitzalan, John, seventh earl of Arundel (1408–1435)', *ODNB.* Oxford University Press: 2008, https://doi.org/10.1093/ ref:odnb/9532.

'English Heritage Battlefield Report: Barnet 1471': https://content. historicengland.org.uk/content/docs/battlefields/barnet.pdf.

'English Heritage Battlefield Report: Blore Heath 1459': https:// content.historicengland.org.uk/content/docs/battlefields/ blore.pdf.

'English Heritage Battlefield Report: Northampton 1460': https:// content.historicengland.org.uk/content/docs/battlefields/ northampton.pdf.

'English Heritage Battlefield Report: Tewkesbury 1471': https://content.historicengland.org.uk/content/docs/battlefields/tewkesbury.pdf.

'English Heritage Battlefield Report: Towton 1461': https://content.historicengland.org.uk/content/docs/battlefields/towton.pdf.

Given-Wilson, Chris, Brand, Paul, Phillips, Seymour, Ormrod, Mark, Martin, Geoffrey, Curry, Anne and Horrox, Rosemary, eds. *Parliament Rolls of Medieval England* Woodbridge: 2005, British History Online, http://www.british-history.ac.uk/no-series/parliament-rolls-medieval.

Harriss, G. L., 'Humphrey [Humfrey or Humphrey of Lancaster], duke of Gloucester [*called* Good Duke Humphrey] (1390–1447)'. *ODNB*. Oxford University Press: 2011, https://doi.org/10.1093/ref:odnb/14155.

Hinds, Allen B., ed. *Calendar of State Papers and Manuscripts in the Archives and Collections of Milan 1385–1618*. London: 1912. British History Online, http://www.british-history.ac.uk/cal-state-papers/milan/1385–1618.

Horrox, Rosemary, 'Grey, Edmund, first earl of Kent (1416–1490)', *ODNB*. Oxford University Press: 2004, http://www.oxforddnb.com/view/article/11529.

Lang, S. J., 'Bradmore, John (d.1412)', *ODNB*. Oxford University Press: 2008. https://doi.org/10.1093/ref:odnb/45759.

Linsley, Chris, 'Louis Robessart – a Border-Crossing Knight?': https://www.englandsimmigrants.com/page/individual-studies/louis-robessart-a-border-crossing-knight.

Lydgate, John and Claire Sponsler, ed. *Mummings and Entertainments*. Kalamazoo: Medieval Institute Publications, 2010, http://d.lib.rochester.edu/teams/publication/sponsler-lydgate-mummings-and-entertainments.

Richmond, Colin, 'Mowbray, John, third duke of Norfolk (1415–1461)', *ODNB*. Oxford University Press: 2012, https://doi.org/10.1093/ref:odnb/19454.

Rymer, Thomas, ed., *Rymer's Foedera*. Vols. 10–11. London: 1739–45, British History Online, http://www.british-history.ac.uk/rymer-foedera/vol11.

Smith, Bill, 'Moleyns, Adam (d.1450)', *ODNB*. Oxford University Press: 2004, http://www.oxforddnb.com/view/article/18918.

Stamp, A. E. and Flower, C. T., eds. *Calendar of Close Rolls, Henry VI*.

Vols. 1–6. London: 1933–47, British History Online, http://www.
british-history.ac.uk/cal-close-rolls/hen6/vol1/.
Stratford, Jenny, 'John [John of Lancaster], duke of Bedford (1389–
1435)', *ODNB*. Oxford University Press: 2011, https://doi.org/
10.1093/ref:odnb/14844.
'The parish of Pennington', Farrer, William and Brownbill, J., eds. *A
History of the County of Lancaster: Volume 8*. London: 1914, British
History Online, http://www.british-history.ac.uk/vch/lancs/vol8/
pp338-342.
Twemlow, J. A., ed. *Calendar of Papal Registers Relating to Great Britain
and Ireland: Volume 12, 1458–1471*. London: 1933, British History
Online, http://www.british-history.ac.uk/cal-papal-registers/brit-
ie/vol12/pp269-283.
Watts, John, 'Pole, William de la, first duke of Suffolk (1396–1450),'
ODNB. Oxford University Press: 2012, https://doi.org/10.1093/
ref:odnb/22461.
——, 'Beaumont, John, first Viscount Beaumont (1409?–1460)',
ODNB. Oxford University Press: 2009, https://doi.org/10.1093/
ref:odnb/50239.

Printed primary sources

Asloan, John and Craigie, W. A., ed. *The Asloan Manuscript: A Mis-
cellany in Prose & Verse*, Vol. 1. Scottish Text Society. Edinburgh:
William Blackwood & Sons, 1923.
Bain, Joseph, ed. *Calendar of documents relating to Scotland preserved in
Her Majesty's Public Record Office*, Vol. 4. Edinburgh: H. M. General
Register House, 1881.
Basin, Thomas and Samaran, Charles, eds. and trans. *Histoire de
Charles VII*, Vols. 1–2. Paris: Les Classiques de l'Histoire de France
Au Moyen Age, 1933, 1944.
Bellaguet, M. L., trans. *Chronique du Religieux de Saint-Denis, contenant
le Règne de Charles VI, de 1380 à 1422*. Paris: L'Imprimerie de
Crapelet, 1840.
Bentley, Samuel, ed. *Excerpta Historica or Illustrations of English History*.
London: Samuel Bentley, 1831.
Blacman, John and James, M. R., trans. *Henry the Sixth: a reprint of John
Blacman's memoir*. Cambridge: Cambridge University Press, 1919.
Bordeaut, A. 'Gilles de Bretagne – Entre la France et l'Angleterre
– Les causes et les Auteurs du drame', in *Mémoires de la Société*

d'Histoire et d'Archéologie de Bretagne, Vol. 1. Rennes: Société d'histoire et d'archéologie de Bretagne, 1920.

Bouchard, A. *Les Grandes Croniques de Bretaigne, noubellement imprisonées à Paris, tant de la Grande Bretaigne de puis le roy Brutus qui la conduist et Les Grandes Annalles ou Cronicques parlans tant de la grant bretaigne a present nōmee Angleterre que de nostre petite Bretaigne de present erigee en duché.* Paris: J. de la Roche pour Galliot du Pre, 1514.

Brie, Friedrich W. D., ed. *The Brut, or The Chronicles of England.* London: Kegan Paul, Trench, Trübner & Co., 1906, 1908.

Bruce, John, ed. *Historie of the Arrivall of Edward IV in England and the finall recouerye of his kingdomes from Henry VI A.D. M.CCCC-LXXI.* London: J. B. Nichols and son, 1838.

Burnett, George, ed. *The Exchequer Rolls of Scotland, Vol. III: AD 1460–1469.* Edinburgh: General Register House, 1884.

Calendar of the Patent Rolls, preserved in the Public Record Office: Henry VI, 1422–1461, Vols. 1–6. Norwich and London: H. M. Stationery Office, 1901–10.

Calmette, J. and Périnelle, G. *Louis XI et L'Angleterre (1461–1483).* Paris: Mémoires et Documents Publiés par la Société de l'Ecole des Chartres, 1930.

Capgrave, John and Hingeston, Francis Charles, trans. *The Book of the Illustrious Henries.* London: Longmans & Co., 1858.

Clay, J. W., ed. *North Country Wills: Being Abstracts of Wills Relating to the Counties of York, Nottingham, Northumberland, Cumberland, and Westmorland at Somerset House and Lambeth Place, 1383–1558.* Surtees Society 116. Durham: Andrews & Co., 1908.

Chartier, Jean. *Chronique de Charles VII roi de France ... Nouvelle édition revue sur les manuscrits,* Vol. 2. Paris: P. Jannet, 1858.

Chastelain, George. *Le Temple de Bocace: édition commentée par Susanna Bliggenstorfer.* Berne, Editions Francke: 1988.

Chrimes, S. B. and Brown, A. L. *Select Documents of English Constitutional History, 1307–1485.* London: Adam & Charles Black, 1961.

Cunningham, W. R., Stamp, Alfred Edward, Trimmer, R. D., Crump, Charles G., and Lyte, H. C. Maxwell. *Calendar of the Charter Rolls preserved in the Public Record Office Prepared under the superintendence of the Deputy Keeper of the Records, Volume VI: 5 Henry VI - 8 Henry VIII. A.D. 1427–1516. With an Appendix, AD. 1215–1288.* London: His Majesty's Stationery Office, 1927.

De Beaucourt, G. Du Fresne, ed. *Chronique de Mathieu d'Escouchy: nouvelle édition,* Vols. 1–3. Paris: Mme Ve J. Renouard, 1863–64.

——, *Histoire de Charles VII*. Vols. 1–6. Paris: Librairie de la Société Bibliographique, 1881–91.

Devon, Frederick. *Issues of the Exchequer being a collection of payments made out of His Majesty's revenue, from King Henry III to King Henry VI inclusive*. London: J. Murray, 1837.

Dupont, L. M. E., ed. *Mémoires de Pierre de Fenin, comprenant le récit des événements qui sont passés en France et en Bourgogne, sous les règnes de Charles VI et Charles VII (1402–27)*. Paris: Jules Renouard, Société de l'Histoire de France, 1837.

——, ed. *Anchiennes Cronicques par Jehan de Wavrin: Choix de chapitres inédits annotés et publiés pour la Société de l'histoire de France par Mlle Dupont*, 3 volumes. Paris: Jules Renouard, 1858–63.

Davies, John Silvester, ed. *An English Chronicle of the Reigns of Richard II, Henry IV, Henry V and Henry VI, written before the year 1471*. Camden Society, Old Series 64. London: J. B. Nichols and Sons, 1856.

Ellis, Henry, ed. *The Chronicle of John Hardyng. Containing an account of public transactions from the earliest period of English history to the beginning of the reign of King Edward the Fourth. Together with the continuation by Richard Grafton, to the thirty-fourth year of King Henry the Eighth*. London: F. C. and J. Rivington etc., 1812.

——, ed. *Original letters, illustrative of English history; including numerous royal letters; from autographs in the British Museum, and one or two other collections*, Vol. 1. London: Harding & Lepard, 1827.

Fabyan, Robert and Ellis, Henry, eds. *The new chronicles of England and France, in two parts; by Robert Fabyan. Named by himself the concordance of histories. Reprinted from Pynson's edition of 1516. The first part collated with the editions of 1533, 1542, and 1559; and the second with a manuscript of the author's own time, as well as the subsequent editions: including the different continuations*. London: F. C. & J. Rivington, 1811.

Flenley, Ralph, ed. *Six town chronicles of England, 1399–1543*. Oxford: Clarendon Press, 1911.

Fortescue, Thomas, ed. *The Works of Sir John Fortescue, Knight, Chief Justice Of England And Lord Chancellor To King Henry The Sixth*. London: Whittingham and Wilkins, 1869.

Gairdner, James, ed. *The Historical Collections of A Citizen of London in the Fifteenth Century. Containing John Page's Poem on the Siege of Rouen, Lydgate's Verses on the Kings of England; William Gregory's Chronicle of London*. Camden Society, New Series 17. London: J. B. Nichols and Sons, 1876.

——, *Three Fifteenth-Century Chronicles with Historical Memoranda by John Stow, the antiquary and contemporary notes of occurrences written by him in the reign of Queen Elizabeth.* Camden Society, New Series 28. London: J. B. Nichols and Sons,1880.

——, *The Paston Letters 1422–1509 A.D. A Reprint of the Edition of 1872–5, which Contained upwards of Five Hundred Letters, etc., till then unpublished, to which are now added others in a Supplement after the Introduction.* 4 volumes. Edinburgh: John Grant, 1910.

Giles, Joannes Allen, ed. *Incerti scriptoris Chronicon Angliæ de regnis trium regum Lancastriensium, Henrici IV., Henrici V., et Henrici VI.* London: D. Nutt, 1848.

Giles, J. A., ed., *The Chronicles of the White Rose of York: A series of historical fragments, proclamations, letters, and other contemporary documents relating to the reign of King Edward the Fourth.* London: James Bohn, 1845.

Grafton, Richard. *Grafton's Chronicle; or, History of England.* Volume 2. London: J. Johnson etc., 1809.

Gragg, Florence Alden, trans., and Gabel, Leona C., ed. *The Commentaries of Pius II on the Memorable Events of His Times: Book I.* Smith College Studies in History 22. Northampton, MA: Department of History of Smith College, 1936–7.

——, *The Commentaries of Pius II on the Memorable Events of His Times: Books II and III.* Smith College Studies in History 25. Northampton, Massachusetts: Department of History of Smith College, 1939–40.

——, *The Commentaries of Pius II, Books VI–IX.* Smith College Studies in History 35. Northampton, Massachusetts: Department of History of Smith College,1951.

Grose, F., ed. *The Antiquarian Repertory: a miscellaneous assemblage of topography, history, biography, customs and manners. Intended to illustrate and preserve several valuable remains of old times.* Vol. 1. London: Edward Jeffery, 1807.

Hall, Edward and Grafton, Richard Ellis. *Hall's Chronicle; containing the history of England, during the reign of Henry the Fourth, and the succeeding monarchs, to the end of the reign of Henry the Eighth, in which are particularly described the manners and customs of those periods. Carefully collated with the editions of 1548 and 1550.* London: J. Johnson etc., 1809.

Halliwell, James Orchard, ed. *A Chronicle of The First Thirteen Years of The Reign of King Edward The Fourth, by John Warkworth.* Camden Society, Old Series 10. London: J. B. Nichols and Sons, 1839.

Hamblin, V. L., ed. *Le mistere du siege d'Orléans: edition critique.* Geneve: Droz, 2002.

Hardy, William, ed. and trans. *Recueil des croniques et anchiennes istories de la Grant Bretaigne, a present nomme Engleterre par Jehan de Waurin, seigneur du Forestel,* Vols. 1–4. London: Longman & Co., 1864–91.

——, *A Collection of the Chronicles and Ancient Histories of Great Britain, now called England by John de Wavrin, Lord of Forestel,* 3 volumes. London: Longman etc. 1864–91.

Harris, Mary Dormer, ed. *The Coventry Leet Book: or mayor's register, containing the records of the city Court leet or view of frankpledge, A.D. 1420–1555, with divers other matters.* London: Kegan Paul, Trench, Trübner, 1908.

Harriss, G. L. and Harriss, M. A., eds. *John Benet's Chronicle for the years 1400 to 1462.* Camden Miscellany 24. London: Royal Historical Society, 1972.

Hellot, A., ed. *Les Cronicques de Normandie (1223–1453): Réimprimées pour la première fois d'après l'édition de G. Le Talleur, mai 1487; avec variantes et additions tirées d'autres éditions et de divers manuscrits, et avec une introduction et des notes par A. Hellot.* Rouen: Ch. Métérie, 1881.

Hilton, Geoffrey, trans. *The Deeds of King Henry V, Told by John Strecche.* Kenilworth: G. M. Hilton, 2014.

Holinshed, Raphael. *Holinshed's Chronicles of England, Scotland and Ireland,* Volume 3. London: J. Johnson etc., 1808.

Hunter, Joseph. *Three Catalogues, Describing the Contents of the Red Book of the Exchequer of the Dodsworth Manuscripts in the Bodleian Library, and of the Manuscripts in the Library of the Honourable Society of Lincoln's Inn.* London: Pickering, 1838.

Kekewich, Margaret Lucille. *The Politics of Fifteenth Century England: John Vale's Book.* Stroud: Alan Sutton for Richard III & Yorkist History Trust, 1995.

Kempe, Alfred John, ed. *Historical Notices of the Collegiate Church, or Royal Free Chapel and Sanctuary of St. Martin-Le-Grand, London.* London: Longman, Hurst, Rees, Orme, Brown and Green, & John Nichols, 1825.

Kervyn de Lettenhove, Joseph, ed. *Œuvres de Georges Chastellain,* Vols. 1–8. Brussels: Académie Royale des Sciences, des Lettres et des Beaux-Arts de Belgique, 1863–6.

——, *Œuvres de Froissart.* Brussels: Comptoir Universel d'Imprimerie et de Librairie, 1871.

Kingsford, Charles Lethbridge, ed. *Chronicles of London*. Oxford: Clarendon Press, 1905.

———, *English Historical Literature in the Fifteenth Century*. Oxford: Clarendon Press, 1913.

Knox, Ronald and Leslie, Shane, eds. and trans. *The Miracles of King Henry VI: being an account and translation of twenty-three miracles taken from the Manuscript in the British Museum (Royal 13 c. viii)*. Cambridge: Cambridge University Press, 1923.

Leadam, I. S. and Baldwin, J. F., eds. *Select Cases before the King's Council 1243–1482*. Selden Society 35. Cambridge, MA: Harvard University Press, 1918.

Le Bouvier, Gilles. *Les Chroniques du Roi Charles VII Par Gilles le Bouvier dit Le Héraut Berry, publiées pour la société de l'histoire de France par Henri Courteault et Léonce Celier, avec la Collaboration de Marie-Henriette Jullien de Pommerol*. Paris: Librairie C. Klincksieck, 1979.

Leland, John. *Joannis Lelandi antiquarii De rebus Britannicis Collectanea cum Thomae Hearnii Praefatione Notis et Indice ad Editionem primam: Editio Alterta, Volume IV*. Farnborough: Gregg International, 1970.

Leland, John and Chandler, John, ed. *John Leland's Itinerary: Travels in Tudor England*. Stroud: Alan Sutton, 1993.

Legg, L. G. Wickham, ed. *English Coronation Records*. London: Archibald Constable & Co., 1901.

'Lettre sur la bataille de Castillon en Périgord, 19 juillet 1453'. *Bibliothèque de l'école des chartes* 8 (1847).

Lydgate, John and MacCracken, Henry Noble, ed. *The Serpent of Division by John Lydgate*. London: Henry Frowde, 1911.

Michaud, J. F., ed. and Poujoulat, J. J. F. 'Histoire de Charles VI, roy de France, par Jean Juvenal des Ursins', *Nouvelle Collection des Mémoires pour servir à l'histoire de France depuis le XIIIe siècle jusqu'à la fin du XVIIIe*. Paris: Chez l'Editeur du Commentaire Analytique du Code Civil, L'Imprimerie d'Edouard Proux, 1836.

Monstrelet, Enguerrand de, and Johnes, Thomas, trans. and ed. *The Chronicles of Enguerrand de Monstrelet: containing an account of the cruel civil wars between the houses of Orleans and Burgundy etc*, Vols. 1–2. London: William Smith, 1845.

Monro, Cecil, ed. *Letters of Queen Margaret of Anjou and Bishop Beckington and others. Written in the reigns of Henry V and Henry VI*. Camden Society, Old Series 86. London: J. B. Nichols and Sons, 1863.

Morice, Pierre Hyacinthe. *Mémoires Pour Servir de Preuves à l'Histoire Ecclesiastique et Civile de Bretagne*, 3 vols. Paris: Charles Osmont, 1742–6.

Myers, A. R. *The Household of Edward IV. The Black Book and the Ordinance of 1478.* Manchester: Manchester University Press, 1959.

Myers, A. R., ed. *English Historical Documents 1327–1485.* London: Eyre & Spottiswoode, 1969.

Nichols, John Gough, ed. *Chronicle of the Grey Friars of London.* Camden Society, Old Series 53. London: J. B. Nichols and Sons, 1852.

Nichols, John, ed. *A collection of all the wills, now known to be extant, of the kings and queens of England, princes and princesses of Wales, and every branch of the blood royal, from the reign of William the Conqueror, to that of Henry the Seventh exclusive.* London: John Nichols, 1780.

Nicolas, N. H. and Tyrrell, Edward, eds. *A Chronicle of London, from 1089 to 1483.* London: Longman, Rees, Orme, Brown and Green, 1827.

Nicolas, Nicholas Harris, ed. *Privy Purse Expenses of Elizabeth of York: Wardrobe Accounts of Edward IV with A Memoir of Elizabeth of York and Notes.* London, William Pickering, 1830.

——, *Proceedings and Ordinances of the Privy Council of England,* Vols. 1–7. London: G. Eyre and A. Spottiswoode, 1834–7.

Preest, David, trans. and Clark, James G., ed. *The Chronica Maiora of Thomas Walsingham 1376–1422.* Woodbridge: Boydell Press, 2005.

Pronay, Nicholas and Cox, John, eds. *The Crowland Chronicle Continuations, 1459–1486.* London: Richard III and Yorkist History Trust, 1986.

Quicherat, J., ed. *Histoire des règnes de Charles VII., et de Louis XI., par T. Basin, Évêque de Lisieux, jusqu'ici attribuée à Amelgard … publiée pour la première fois avec les autres ouvrages historiques du même écrivain,* Vol. 4. Paris: Société de l'Histoire de France, 1859.

Rickert, Edith, trans. and Naylor, L. J., rev. *The Babees' Book: Medieval Manners for the Young.* Cambridge, Ontario: In Parentheses Publications, Middle English Series, 2000.

Riley, Henry T., trans. *Ingulph's Chronicle of the Abbey of Croyland with the Continuations by Peter of Blois and Anonymous Writers.* London: Henry G. Bohn, 1854.

Riley, Henry Thomas, ed. *Annales monasterii S. Albani, 1421–30,* Vols. 1–2. London: Longman & Co., 1870–1.

Robbins, Rossell Hope, ed. *Historical Poems of the XIVth and XVth Centuries.* New York: Columbia University Press, 1959.

Scobie, Andrew R., ed. *The Memoirs of Philippe de Commines, Lord of Argenton: containing the histories of Louis XI and Charles VIII kings of France and of Charles the Bold, duke of Burgundy to which is added, The scandalous chronicle, or Secret history of Louis XI, by Jean deTroyes*, Vol. 1. London, Henry G. Bohn: 1855.

Shakespeare, William, and Bate, Jonathan and Rasmussen, Eric, eds. *Complete Works: The RSC Shakespeare*. Basingstoke: Macmillan, 2008.

Shirley, Janet, trans. *A Parisian Journal 1405–1449, translated from the Anonymous Journal d'un Bourgeois de Paris*. Oxford: Clarendon Press, 1968.

Skeat, Walter W., ed. *The kingis quair: together with a ballad of Good counsel: by King James I. of Scotland*. Edinburgh: W. Blackwood and sons, 1884.

Stevenson, Joseph, ed. *Letters & Papers Illustrative of the Wars of the English in France During the Reign of Henry the Sixth, King of England*, Vols. 1–2. London: Longman, Roberts and Green, 1861–4.

——, ed. *Narratives of the expulsion of the English from Normandy, M.CCCC.XLIX.-M.CCC.L, Rerum Britannicarum Medii Aevi Scriptores, or Chronicles and Memorials of Great Britain and Ireland during the Middle Ages*. London: Longman, 1863.

——, ed. *Letters & Papers Illustrative of the Wars of the English in France During the Reign of Henry the Sixth, King of England*, Vols. 1–2. London: Longman Green, Longman, Roberts and Green, 1861–4.

Searle, William George, ed. *Christ Church, Canterbury. I. The Chronicle of John Stone, Monk of Christ Church 1415–1471*. Cambridge: Cambridge Antiquarian Society, 1902.

Taylor, Craig, trans. *Joan of Arc: La Pucelle*. Manchester: Manchester University Press, 2006.

Taylor, Frank and Roskell, John S., trans. *Gesta Henrici Quinti: The Deeds of Henry the Fifth*. Oxford: Clarendon Press, 1975.

Thomas, A. H. and Thornley, I. D., eds. *The Great Chronicle of London*. London: George W. Jones, 1938.

Thornley, Isobel D., ed. *England Under the Yorkists 1460–1485*. London: Longmans, Green & Co., 1921.

Toulmin Smith, Lucy, ed. *The Itinerary of John Leland in or about the years 1535–1543 Parts VII and VIII with Appendices Including Extracts from Leland's Colleactanea*. London: George Bell & Sons, 1909.

Tuetey, Alexandre, ed. *Journal de Clément de Fauquembergue, greffier du Parlement de Paris, 1417–1435*, Vol 2. Paris, Société de l'Histoire de France, No. 6, 1909.

Vallet de Viriville, Auguste, ed. *Chronique de Charles VII Roi de France par Jean Chartier. nouvelle édition revue sur les manuscrit suivie de divers fragmens inédits*, Vol. 3. Paris: P. Jannet, 1858.

Vergil, Polydore and Ellis, Henry, ed. *Three books of Polydore Vergil's English history, comprising the reigns of Henry VI., Edward IV., and Richard III. from an early translation, preserved among the mss. of the old royal library in the British museum.* London: J. B. Nichols and Sons, 1844.

Wegemer, Gerard B. and Curtright, Travis, eds. *The History of King Richard the Third by Master Thomas More Undersheriff of London c. 1513.* Irving, Texas: Center for Thomas More Studies, 2013.

Williams, George, ed. *Memorials of the Reign of Henry VI. Official correspondence of Thomas Bekynton, secretary to King Henry VI, and bishop of Bath and Wells,* Vol. 2. London: Longman & Co., 1872; repr. Lessing-Druckerei Weisbaden, Germany: Kraus Reprint Ltd, 1964.

Wright, Thomas, ed. *Three Chapters of Letters Relating to the Suppression of the Monasteries.* London: J. B. Nichols and Sons, 1843.

——, *Political Poems and Songs Relating to English History Composed during the Period from the Accession of Edward III to that of Richard III,* Vol. 2. London: Longman & Brothers, 1861.

Secondary sources

Allmand, Christopher. *Lancastrian Normandy 1415–1450: The History of a Medieval Occupation.* Oxford: Clarendon Press, 1983.

——, *Henry V.* New Haven: Yale University Press, 1997.

Ancient Monuments and Historic Buildings: Ministry of Works. The Tower of London. London: HMSO, 1948.

Anglo, Sydney. *Images of Tudor Kingship.* London: Seaby, 1992.

Barron, Caroline M. 'London and the Crown, 1451–61', in Highfield, J. R. L. and Jeffs, Robin, eds., *The Crown and Local Communities in England and France in the Fifteenth Century.* Stroud: Sutton, 1981.

Barker, Juliet. *Conquest: The English Kingdom of France, 1417–1450.* London: Abacus, 2010.

Bean, J. M. W. 'The Financial Position of Richard, Duke of York', in Gillingham, John and Holt, J. C., eds. *War and Government in the Middle Ages: Essays in Honour of J. O. Prestwich.* Woodbridge: Boydell Press, 1984.

Bellamy, J. G. *The Law of Treason in England in the Later Middle Ages.* Cambridge: Cambridge University Press, 1970.

Briais, Bernard and Bullard-Axworthy, Marie, trans. *Tours Throughout History.* Monts, France: PBCO Editions, 2013.

Britton, John and Brayley, E. W. *Memoirs of the Tower of London: comprising historical and descriptive accounts of that national fortress and palace.* London: Hurst, Chance & Co., 1830.

Brown, Michael. *James I.* Edinburgh, John Donald: 2015.

Carey, Hilary M. *Courting Disaster: Astrology at the English court and University in the Later Middle Ages.* London: Macmillan, 1992.

Carpenter, Christine. *Locality and Polity: a study of Warwickshire landed society, 1401–1499.* Cambridge: Cambridge University Press, 1992.

Castor, Helen. *The King, the Crown, and the Duchy of Lancaster: Public Authority and Private Power, 1399–1461.* Oxford: Oxford University Press, 2000.

——,*She-Wolves: The Women Who Ruled England Before Elizabeth.* London: Faber and Faber, 2010.

——, *Joan of Arc: A History.* New York: Harper Collins, 2015.

Cherry, M. 'The struggle for power in mid-fifteenth-century Devonshire', in Griffiths, R. A., ed., *Patronage, the Crown and the Provinces.* Gloucester: Sutton, 1981.

Clarke, Basil. *Mental Disorder in Earlier Britain: Explanatory Studies.* Cardiff: University of Wales Press, 1975.

Colvin, H. M., ed., Brown, R. Allen and Taylor, A. J. *The History of the King's Works: Volume I: The Middle Ages.* London: Her Majesty's Stationery Office, 1963.

Curry, Anne. *The Battle of Agincourt: Sources and Interpretations.* Woodbridge: Boydell Press, 2000.

—— 'The "Coronation Expedition" and Henry VI's Court in France, 1430 to 1432', in Stratford, Jenny, ed., *The Lancastrian Court: Proceedings of the 2001 Harlaxton Symposium.* Donington: Shaun Tyas, 2003.

—— *Agincourt: A New History.* Stroud: Tempus, 2006.

De Ros, William Lennox Lascelles Fitzgerald. *Memorials of the Tower of London.* London: John Murray, 1867.

Dickinson, Joycelyne Gledhill. *The Congress of Arras, 1435: A Study in Medieval Diplomacy.* Oxford: Clarendon Press, 1955.

Doig, James A. 'Propaganda, Public Opinion and the Siege of Calais in 1436', in Archer, Rowena E., ed., *Crown, Government and People in the Fifteenth Century: Conference on Recent Research in Fifteenth-Century History.* Stroud: Alan Sutton, 1995.

Dumont, Charles Emmanuel. *Histoire de la ville de Saint-Mihiel.* Paris and Nancy: Reache Librarie and Imprimerie de Veuve A. Dard, 1860.

Dunn, Caroline. *Stolen Women in Medieval England: Rape, Abduction and Adultery, 1100–1500*. Cambridge: Cambridge University Press, 2013.

Dunn, Diana. 'Margaret of Anjou, Queen Consort of Henry VI: A Reassessment of Her Role, 1445–53', in Archer, Rowena E., ed., *Crown, Government and People in the Fifteenth Century*. New York: St. Martin's Press, 1995.

Famiglietti, R. C. *Royal Intrigue: Crisis at the Court of Charles VI, 1392–1420*. New York: AMS Press Inc., 1986.

Farcy, Louis de. *Monographie de la Cathédrale d'Angers. volume II: Les Immeubles par destination*. Angers: Chez l'Auteur, 1905.

Ferguson, John. *English Diplomacy, 1422–1461*. Oxford: Clarendon Press, 1972.

Fiorato, Veronica, Boylston, Anthea and Knüsel, Christopher, eds. *Blood red roses: the archaeology of a mass grave from the Battle of Towton AD 1461*. Oxford: Oxbow, 2007.

Gillingham, John. *The Wars of the Roses: Peace and Conflict in Fifteenth-Century England*. London: Weidenfeld and Nicolson, 1990.

Goodman, Anthony. *The Wars of the Roses: Military Activity and English Society, 1452–97*. London: Routledge & Kegan Paul, 1981.

——, *The Wars of the Roses: The Soldiers' Experience*. Stroud: Tempus, 2005.

Gransden, Antonia. *Historical Writing in England: Volume 2, c.1307 to the early sixteenth century*. London: Routledge & Kegan Paul, 1982.

Green, Vivian. *The Madness of Kings: Personal Trauma and the Fate of Nations*. Stroud: Alan Sutton, 1993.

Griffiths, R. A. 'The Sense of Dynasty in the Reign Of Henry VI', in Ross, Charles, ed., *Patronage, Pedigree and Power in Later Medieval England*. Gloucester: A. Sutton, 1979.

——, *The Reign of King Henry VI: The Exercise of Royal Authority, 1422–1461*. London: Benn, 1981.

——, ed. *Patronage, the Crown and the Provinces in Later Medieval England*. Stroud: Alan Sutton, 1981.

——, '"Ffor the myght off the lande, aftir the myght off thegrete lordes thereoff, stondith most in the kynges officers": the English crown, provinces and dominions in the fifteenth century', in Curry, Anne and Matthew, Elizabeth, eds., *Concepts and Patterns of Service in the Later Middle Ages*. Woodbridge: Boydell Press, 2000.

——, 'The Minority of Henry VI, King of England and of France', in Beem, Charles, ed., *The Royal Minorities of Medieval and Early Modern England*. New York: Palgrave Macmillan, 2008.

Griffiths, Ralph A. and Thomas, Roger S. *The Making of the Tudor Dynasty.* Gloucester: Alan Sutton, 1985.

Grummitt, David. *Henry VI.* London and New York: Routledge, 2015.

Hammond, P. W. *The Battles of Barnet and Tewkesbury.* Gloucester: Alan Sutton, 1990.

Harriss, G. L. 'Marmaduke Lumley and the Exchequer crisis of 1446–9' in Rowe, J. G. ed. *Aspects of Medieval Government and Society.* Toronto: University of Toronto Press, 1986.

——, *Cardinal Beaufort: A Study of Lancastrian Ascendancy and Decline.* Oxford: Clarendon Press, 1988.

——, *Shaping the Nation: England 1360–1461.* Oxford: Clarendon Press, 2005.

Harvey, I. M. W. *Jack Cade's Rebellion of 1450.* Oxford: Clarendon Press, 1991.

Hellinga, Lotte, Trapp, J. B., Barnard, John, McKenzie, Donald Francis and McKitterick, David, eds. *The Cambridge History of the Book in Britain,* Vol. 3. Cambridge: Cambridge University Press, 1999.

Hicks, Michael. *Warwick the Kingmaker.* Oxford: Blackwell, 1998.

——, *The Wars of the Roses.* New Haven: Yale University Press, 2012.

Hookham, Mary Ann. *The Life and Times of Margaret of Anjou, Queen of England and France.* London: Tinsley Brothers, 1872.

Hughes, Jonathan. *Arthurian Myth and Alchemy: The Kingship of Edward IV.* Stroud: Alan Sutton, 2002.

Jacob, E. F. *The Fifteenth Century: 1399–1485.* Oxford: Clarendon Press, 1976.

Johnson, P. A. *Duke Richard of York, 1411–1460.* Oxford: Clarendon Press, 1988.

Jones, Dan. *The Hollow Crown: The Wars of the Roses and the Rise of the Tudors.* London: Faber & Faber, 2014.

Jones, Michael. 'John Beaufort, duke of Somerset and the French Expedition of 1443', in Griffiths, Ralph A. ed., *Patronage, the Crown and the Provinces in Later Medieval England.* Stroud: Alan Sutton, 1981.

Jones, Michael K. *Psychology of a Battle: Bosworth 1485.* Stroud: Tempus, 2003.

Jones, Michael K. and Underwood, Malcolm G. *The King's Mother: Lady Margaret Beaufort countess of Richmond and Derby.* Cambridge: Cambridge University Press, 1999.

Keay, Anna. *The Elizabethan Tower: The Haiward and Gascoyne Plan of 1597.* London: London Topographical Society with Historic Royal Palaces and the Society of Antiquaries of London 2001.

Keen, Maurice. 'The End of the Hundred Years War: Lancastrian France and Lancastrian England', in Jones, Michael and Vale, M. G. A., eds., *England and her Neighbours, 1066–1453: Essays in honour of Pierre Chaplais.* London: Hambledon Press, 1989.

Kekewich, Margaret L. 'The Lancastrian Court in Exile', in Stratford, Jenny, ed., *Proceedings of the 2001 Harlaxton Symposium: The Lancastrian Court.* Donington: Shaun Tyas / Paul Watkins Publishing, 2003.

——, *The Good King: René of Anjou and Fifteenth Century Europe.* Basingstoke: Palgrave Macmillan, 2008.

Kingsford, Charles Lethbridge. *Prejudice and Promise in Fifteenth Century England.* Frank Cass & Co Ltd, 1962.

Laynesmith, J. L. 'Constructing Queenship at Coventry: Pageantry and Politics at Margaret of Anjou's Secret Harbor"', in Laynesmith, J. L. and Clark, Linda, eds., *Fifteenth Century 3: Authority and Subversion.* Woodbridge: Boydell Press, 2003.

——, *The Last Medieval Queens: English Queenship 1445–1503.* Oxford: Oxford University Press, 2004.

——, *Cecily Duchess of York.* London: Bloomsbury Academic, 2017.

Lewis, Katherine J. 'Edmund of East Anglia, Henry VI and Ideals of Kingly Masculinity', in Cullum, P. H. and Lewis, Katherine J. eds., *Holiness and Masculinity in the Middle Ages.* Toronto: University of Toronto Press, 2004.

——, *Kingship and Masculinity In Late Medieval England.* New York and Abingdon: Routledge, 2013.

——, '"Imitate, too, this king in virtue, who could have done ill and did it not": Lay Sanctity and the Rewriting Of Henry VI's Manliness', in Lewis, Katherine J., ed., *Religious Men and Masculine Identity in the Middle Ages.* Woodbridge: Boydell Press, 2013.

Lyte, H. C. Maxwell. *A History of Eton College, 1440–1884.* London: Macmillan & Co., 1889.

MacDougall, Norman. *James III.* Edinburgh: John Donald, 2009.

Mackenzie, James Dixon. *The castles of England, their story and structure.* New York: Macmillan, 1896.

Maurer, Helen E. *Margaret of Anjou: Queenship and Power in Late Medieval England.* Woodbridge: Boydell Press, 2003.

McKenna, John W. 'Piety and Propaganda: The Cult of King Henry VI', in Rowland, Beryl, ed., *Chaucer and Middle English Studies in Honour of Rossell Hope Robbins.* London: Allen & Unwin Ltd, 1974.

Marks, Richard. 'Images of Henry VI', in Stratford, J., ed., *The Lan-*

castrian Court: Harlaxton Medieval Studies, X. Donington: Shaun
Tyas, 2003.

Morgan, D. 'From a Death to a View: Louis Robessart, Johan Huizinga, and the Political Significance of Chivalry', in Anglo, S. ed.,
Chivalry in the Renaissance. Woodbridge: Boydell Press, 1990.

Parsons, John Carmi, ed. *Medieval Queenship*. Stroud: Alan Sutton,
1994.

Peters, Edward Murray. *The Shadow King. Rex inutilis in medieval law
and literature, 751–1327*. New Haven and London: Yale University
Press, 1970.

Piroyanski, Danna. *Martyrs in the Making: Political Martyrdom in Late
Mediaeval England*. Basingstoke: Palgrave Macmillan, 2008.

Pollard, A. J. *North-Eastern England During the Wars of the Roses: Lay
Society, War, and Politics 1450–1500*. Oxford: Clarendon Press, 1990.

——, *The Wars of the Roses*. Basingstoke: Palgrave Macmillan, 1995.

——, *Warwick the Kingmaker: politics, power and fame*. London: Hambledon Continuum, 2007.

Poulet, André. 'Capetian Women and the Regency: The Genesis of
a Vocation', in Parsons, J. C. ed., *Medieval Queenship*. Stroud: Alan
Sutton, 1994.

Powell, E. 'The strange death of Sir John Mortimer: politics and
the law of treason in Lancastrian England', in Archer, R. E. and
Walker, S., eds., *Rulers and Ruled in Late Medieval England*. London:
Hambledon Press, 1995.

Pugh, T. B. 'Richard Plantagenet (1411–60), Duke of York, as the
King's Lieutenant in France and Ireland', in Rowe, J. G., ed., *Aspects
of Late Medieval Government and Society: Essays Presented to J. R. Lander*.
Toronto: University of Toronto Press, 1986.

Radulescu, R. L. 'Preparing for her Mature Years: The Case of Margaret of Anjou and her books', in Niebrzydowski, Sue, ed., *Middle-
aged Women in the Middle Ages*. Cambridge: D. S. Brewer, 2011.

Rawcliffe, Carole. *The Staffords, Earls of Stafford and Dukes of Buckingham, 1394–1521*. Cambridge: Cambridge University Press, 1978.

——, 'Master Surgeons at the Lancastrian Court', in Stratford, Jenny,
ed., *The Lancastrian Court: Proceedings of the 2001 Harlaxton Symposium*. Donington: Shaun Tyas, 2003.

Rose, Susan. *Calais, An English Town in France 1347–1558*. Woodbridge: Boydell Press, 2008.

Rogers, Nicholas. 'Henry VI and the Proposed Canonisation of King
Alfred', in Cullum, P. H. and Lewis, Katherine J., eds., *Religious*

Men and Masculine Identity in the Middle Ages. Woodbridge: Boydell Press, 2013.

Roskell, J. S. *The Commons in the Parliament of 1422: English Society and Parliamentary Representation under the Lancastrians.* Manchester: Manchester University Press, 1954.

Ross, Charles. *Edward IV.* London: Book Club Associates, 1975.

Scattergood, V. J., *Politics and Poetry in the Fifteenth Century.* London: Blandford Press, 1971.

Scofield, Cora L. *The Life and Reign of Edward the Fourth King of England and of France and Lord of Ireland.* 2 vols. London: Fonthill Media, 2016.

Spencer, Brian. 'King Henry of Windsor and the London Pilgrim', in Bird, Joanna, Chapman, Hugh and Clark, John, eds., *Collectanea Londiniensia: Studies in London Archaeology and History Presented to Ralph Merrifield.* London: London & Middlesex Archaeological Society, 1978.

Stanley, Arthur Penrhyn. *Historical Memorials of Westminster Abbey*, Vol. 1. London: John Murray, 1876.

Steane, John. *The Archaeology of the Medieval English Monarchy.* London and New York: Routledge, 1999.

Steel, Anthony. *The Receipt of the Exchequer, 1377–1485.* Cambridge: Cambridge University Press, 1954.

Storey, R. L. *The End of the House of Lancaster.* London: Barrie and Rockliff, 1966.

Stratford, Jenny. 'John, duke of Bedford, as patron in Lancastrian Rouen', in Stratford, Jenny, ed., *Medieval Art, Architecture and Archaeology at Rouen. The British Archaeological Association Conference Transactions for the Year 1986.* Leeds: W. S. Maney and Son, 1993.

Taylor, Larissa Juliet. *The Virgin Warrior: The Life and Death of Joan of Arc.* New Haven: Yale University Press, 2010.

Thomas, John Wesley. *The Tower, The Temple and the Minster: Historical and Biographical Associations of the Tower of London, St Paul's Cathedral and Westminster Abbey.* London: Wesleyan Conference Office, 1873.

Thurley, Simon. *The Royal Palaces of Tudor England: Architecture and Court Life, 1460–1547.* New Haven: Yale University Press, 1993.

Trenery, Claire and Horden, Peregrine. 'Madness in the Middle Ages', in Eghigian, Greg, ed., *The Routledge History of Madness and Mental Health.* London: Routledge, 2017.

Vale, M. G. A. *English Gascony, 1399–1453: A Study of War, Government and Politics during the Later Stages of the Hundred Years War.* Oxford: Oxford University Press, 1970.

——, *Charles VII.* London: Eyre Methuen, 1974.

Vaughan, Richard. *Philip the Good: The Apogee of Burgundy.* London: Longmans, 1970.

——, *John the Fearless: The Growth of Burgundian Power.* Woodbridge: Boydell Press, 2002.

Vickers, K. H. *Humphrey Duke of Gloucester: A Biography.* London: Archibald Constable & Company Limited, 1907.

Virgoe, Roger. 'The Ravishment of Joan Boys', in Barron, Caroline, Rawcliffe, Carole and Rosenthal, Joel T., eds., *East Anglian Society and the Political Community of Late Medieval England: Selected Papers of Roger Virgoe.* Norwich: Centre of East Anglian Studies, University of East Anglia, 1997.

Watts, John. 'When Did Henry VI's Minority End?', in Clayton, Dorothy J., Davies, Richard G. and McNiven, Peter, eds., *Trade, Devotion and Governance: Papers in Later Medieval History.* Stroud: Alan Sutton, 1994.

——, *Henry VI and the Politics of Kingship.* Cambridge: Cambridge University Press, 1996.

Whitaker, Thomas Dunham. *The History and Antiquities of the Deanery of Craven, in the County of York.* London: Nichols & Sons, 1805.

Williams, E. Carleton. *My Lord of Bedford 1389–1435, Being a life of John of Lancaster first Duke of Bedford brother of Henry V and Regent of France.* London: Longmans, 1963.

Winstead, Karen A. *John Capgrave's Fifteenth Century.* Philadelphia: University of Pennsylvania Press, 2007.

Wolffe, Bertram. *Henry VI.* New Haven and London: Yale University Press, 2001.

Woosnam-Savage, Robert C. '"All kinds of weapons": The weapons of Agincourt' in Curry, Anne and Mercer, Malcolm, eds., *The Battle of Agincourt.* New Haven and London: Yale University Press in association with Royal Armouries, 2015.

Wylie, James Hamilton and Waugh, William Templeton. *The Reign of Henry the Fifth. Volume III (1415–1422).* Cambridge: Cambridge University Press, 1929.

Articles

Allmand, Christopher. 'La Normandie Devant l'Opinion Anglaise à la Fin de la Guerre de Cent Ans'. *Bibliothèque de l'École des Chartres* 128, no. 2 (1970).

Armstrong, C. A. J. 'Politics and the Battle of St Albans, 1455'. *Bulletin of the Institute of Historical Research* 33, no. 87 (1960).

Bark, N. 'Did schizophrenia change the course of English history? The mental illness of Henry VI'. *Medical Hypotheses* 59, no. 4 (2002).

Brown, A. L. 'The King's Councillors in Fifteenth-Century England'. *Transactions of the Royal Historical Society* 19 (1969).

Charlesworth, Dorothy. 'The Battle of Hexham, 1464'. *Archaeologia Aeliana*, fourth series, 30 (1952).

Cron, B. M. 'Margaret of Anjou and the Lancastrian March on London, 1461'. *The Ricardian* 11 (1999).

Dicks, Samuel E. 'Henry VI and the daughters of Armagnac: A Problem in Medieval Diplomacy'. *Emporia State Research Studies: Medieval Renaissance Studies* 15 (1967).

Dockray, Keith and Knowles, Richard. 'The Battle of Wakefield and the Wars of the Roses'. *The Ricardian* 9 (1992).

'Extrait d'un manuscrit de Megsire Guillaume Oudin, prêtre-sacriste de l'abbaye de Notre-Dame-du-Ronceray d'Angers (xve siècle). — Deuxième partie'. *Revue de l'Anjou et du Maine* 1, no. 3 (1857).

Freeman, Jessica. 'Sorcery at Court and Manor: Margery Jourde-mayne, the Witch of Eye next Westminster'. *Journal of Medieval History* 30, no. 4 (2004).

Gibbons, Rachel. 'Isabeau of Bavaria, Queen of France (1385–1422): The Creation of an Historical Villainess: The Alexander Prize Essay'. *Transactions of the Royal Historical Society* 6 (1996).

Gilson, J. P. 'A Defence of the Proscription of the Yorkists in 1459'. *English Historical Review* 26, no. 103 (1911).

Griffiths, Ralph A. 'Local Rivalries and National Politics: The Percies, the Nevilles, and the Duke of Exeter, 1452–1455'. *Speculum* 43, no. 4 (1968).

——, 'The trial of Eleanor Cobham: an episode in the fall of Duke Humphrey of Gloucester'. *Bulletin of the John Rylands Library* 51 (1968–9).

——, 'Richard of York and the Royal Household in Wales, 1449–50'. *The Welsh History Review* 8, no. 1 (1976).

——, 'Queen Katherine de Valois and a missing statue of the realm'. *Law Quarterly Review* 93 (1977).

——, 'The Winchester Session of the 1449 Parliament: a further comment'. *Huntingdon Library Quarterly*, 42 (1979).

——, 'The King's Council and the First Protectorate of the Duke of York'. *English Historical Review* 99, no. 390 (1984).

——, 'Richard, duke of York, and the crisis of Henry VI's household in 1450–1: some further evidence'. *Journal of Medieval History* 38, no. 2 (2012).

Hanham, Alison and Cron, B. M. 'Slain Dogs, The Dead Man and Editorial Constructs'. *The Ricardian* 17 (2007).

Harriss, G. L. 'The Struggle for Calais: An Aspect of the Rivalry between Lancaster and York'. *English Historical Review* 75, no. 294 (1960).

Head, Constance. 'Pope Pius II and the Wars of the Roses'. *Archivum Historiae Pontificiae* 8 (1970).

Hicks, M. A. 'The case of Sir Thomas Cook, 1468.' *English Historical Review* 193, no. 366 (1978).

——, 'Edward IV, the duke of Somerset and Lancastrian loyalism in the north'. *Northern History* 20 (1984).

——, 'The Last Days of Elizabeth, countess of Oxford'. *English Historical Review* 103, no. 406 (1988).

——, 'From megaphone to microscope: The correspondence of Richard duke of York with Henry VI in 1450 revisited'. *Journal of Medieval History* 25, no. 3 (1999).

——, 'Propaganda and the First Battle of St Albans, 1455'. *Nottingham Medieval Studies* 44 (2000).

Hodges, Geoffrey. 'The Civil War of 1459 to 1461 in the Welsh Marches: Part 2, The Campaign and Battle of Mortimer's Cross – St Blaise's Day, 3 February 1461'. *The Ricardian* 6 (1984).

Jones, Michael K. 'Somerset, York and the Wars of the Roses'. *English Historical Review* 104, no. 411 (1989).

——, 'Edward IV, the Earl of Warwick and the Yorkist Claim to the Throne'. *Historical Research* 70 (1997).

——, 'The Battle of Verneuil (17 August 1424): Towards a History of Courage'. *War in History* 9, no. 4 (2002).

Keen, M. H. and Daniel, M. J. 'English diplomacy and the sack of Fougères in 1449'. *History* 59 (1974).

Kekewich, Margaret. 'The Attainder of the Yorkists in 1459: Two Contemporary Accounts'. *Bulletin of the Institute of Historical Research* 55 (1982).

Kleineke, Hannes. 'The Commission De Mutuo Faciendo in the Reign of Henry VI'. *English Historical Review* 116, no. 465 (2001).

Knoop, Douglas and Jones, G. P. 'The Building of Eton College, 1442–1460'. *Ars Quatuor Coronatorum, being the Transactions of the Quatuor Coronati Lodge No. 2076 London 46.* London: Quatuor Coronati Lodge, 1933.

Lander, J. R. 'Henry VI and the Duke of York's Second Protectorate, 1455 to 1461'. *Bulletin of the John Rylands Library* 43, no. 1 (1960).

——, 'Attainder and Forfeiture, 1453 to 1509'. *The Historical Journal* 4 (1961).

Maurer, Helen. 'Bones in the Tower: A Discussion of Time, Place and Circumstance'. 2 parts. *The Ricardian* 8–9 (1990–1).

McKenna, J. W. 'Henry VI of England and the Dual Monarchy: Aspects of Royal Political Propaganda, 1422–1432'. *Journal of the Warburg and Courtauld Institutes* 28 (1965).

Meekings, C. A. F. 'Thomas Kerver's Case, 1444'. *English Historical Review* 90, no. 355 (1975).

Myers, A. R. 'Some Household Ordinances of Henry VI'. *Bulletin of the John Rylands Library* 36, no. 2 (1954).

——, 'The Household of Queen Margaret of Anjou, 1452–3'. *Bulletin of the John Rylands Library* 40, nos. 1–2 (1957–8).

——, 'The Jewels of Queen Margaret Of Anjou'. *Bulletin of the John Rylands Library* 42, no.1 (1959).

Parnell, Geoffrey. '1888: The Victorian Mutilation of the Tower Ends'. *Ripperologist* 123 (2011).

——, 'Riddle of the Tower Ravens Almost Resolved'. *Ripperologist* 124 (2012).

Payling, S. J. 'The Ampthill Dispute: A Study in Aristocratic Lawlessness and the Breakdown of Lancastrian Government'. *English Historical Review* 104, no. 413 (1989).

Pollard, A. J. 'Richard, duke of York, the King's "obeisant liegeman": A New Source for the Protectorates of 1454 and 1455'. *Historical Research* 60 (1987).

——, 'The Insanity of Henry VI'. *The Historian* 50 (1996).

——, 'Battle of St Albans, 1455'. *History Today* 55, no. 5 (2005).

Robbins, Rossell Hope. 'The Five Dogs of London'. *Publications of the Modern Language Association of America* 71, no. 1 (1956).

Roskell, J. S. 'The Office and Dignity of Protector of England, with Special Reference to Its Origins'. *English Historical Review* 68, no. 267 (1953).

Ross, C. D. 'Forfeiture for Treason in the Reign of Richard II'. *English Historical Review* 71, no. 281 (1956).

Scofield, Cora L. 'The Early Life of John de Vere, Thirteenth Earl of Oxford'. *English Historical Review* 29, no. 114 (1914).

Speak, Gill. 'An odd kind of melancholy: reflections on the glass delusion in Europe (1440–1680)'. *History of Psychiatry* 1 (1990).

Starkey, David, 'Henry VI's Old Blue Gown: The English Court under the Lancastrians and Yorkists'. *The Court Historian* 4, no. 1 (1999).

St John Hope, W. H. 'The Discovery of the Remains of King Henry VI in Saint George's Chapel, Windsor Castle'. *Archaeologia* 62, no. 2 (1911).

Strong, Patrick and Felicity. 'The Last Will and Codicils of Henry V'. *English Historical Review* 96, no. 378 (1981).

The Gentleman's Magazine 55 (June 1785).

Transactions of the Historic Society of Lancashire and Cheshire. New Series 12. Liverpool: Adam Holden, 1872.

Vale, M. G. A. 'The Last Years of English Gascony, 1451–1453: The Alexander Prize Essay'. *Transactions of the Royal Historical Society* 19 (1969).

Virgoe, Roger. 'The Death of William de la Pole, Duke of Suffolk'. *Bulletin of the John Rylands Library* 47 (1965).

Warner, Mark. 'Chivalry in Action: Thomas Montagu and the War in France, 1417–1428'. *Nottingham Medieval Studies* 42 (1998).

Warnicke, Retha M. 'Henry VIII's Greeting of Anne of Cleves and Early Modern Court Protocol'. *Albion: A Quarterly Journal Concerned with British Studies* 28, no. 4 (1996).

White, W. J. 'The Death and Burial of Henry VI, a review of the Facts and Theories'. *The Ricardian* 6 (1982).

Unpublished theses

Ashbee, Jeremy. 'The Tower of London as a royal residence: 1066–1400'. PhD diss., University of London, 2006.

Johnson, Lauren. 'The Impact of the Wars of the Roses on Noblewomen'. MSt diss., University of Oxford, 2007.

McGovern, C. J. M. 'Lancastrian diplomacy and Queen Margaret's Court in Exile, 1461–1471'. BA diss., Keele University, 1973.

Abbreviations

Amundesham: Riley, Henry Thomas, ed. *Annales monasterii S. Albani, 1421–30*, 2 vols. London: Longman & Co, 1870–1.

Annales: Stevenson, Joseph, ed. 'Wilhelmi Wyrcester Annales Rerum Anglicarum', *Letters & Papers Illustrative of the Wars of the English in France During the Reign of Henry the Sixth, King of England*. London: Longman Green, Longman, Roberts and Green, 1864. Vol. II (2), 743–93.

Arrivall: Bruce, John, ed. *Historie of the Arrivall of Edward IV in England and the finall recouerye of his kingdomes from Henry VI A.D. M.CCCC–LXXI.* London: J. B. Nichols and Sons, 1838.

Basin: Basin, Thomas and Samaran, Charles, ed. *Histoire de Charles VII: Tome Premier, 1407–1444.* Paris: Les Classiques de l'Histoire de France Au Moyen Age. Vol. 15, 1933.

Bekynton: Williams, George, ed. *Memorials of the Reign of Henry VI. Official correspondence of Thomas Bekynton, secretary to King Henry VI, and bishop of Bath and Wells.* Vol. 2. London: Longman & Co., 1872; repr. Lessing-Druckerei Wiesbaden, Germany: Kraus Reprint Ltd, 1964.

Benet: Harriss, G. L. and Harriss, M. A., eds. *John Benet's Chronicle for the years 1400 to 1462*, Camden Miscellany. Vol. 24. London: Royal Historical Society, 1972.

BL: British Library.

Blacman: Blacman, John and James, M. R., trans. *Henry the Sixth: a reprint of John Blacman's memoir.* Cambridge: Cambridge University Press, 1919.

Brut: Brie, Friedrich W. D., ed. *The Brut, or The Chronicles of England.* London: Kegan Paul, Trench, Trübner & Co., 1906, 1908.

CCC: Pronay, Nicholas and Cox, John, eds. *The Crowland Chronicle Continuations, 1459–1486.* London: Richard III and Yorkist History Trust, 1986.

CCR: Stamp, A. E. and Flower, C. T. eds. *Calendar of Close Rolls, Henry VI,* 6 vols. London: 1933–47, British History Online, http://www.british-history.ac.uk/cal-close-rolls/hen6/vol1/pp43-48.

Chastellain: Kervyn de Lettenhove, Joseph, ed. *Œuvres de Georges Chastellain,* 8 vols. Brussels: Académie Royale des Sciences, des Lettres et des Beaux-Arts de Belgique, 1863–6.

Chronicle of London: Nicolas, N. H. and Tyrrell, Edward, ed. *A Chronicle of London, from 1089 to 1483; written in the fifteenth century, and for the first time printed from mss. in the British Museum: to which are added numerous contemporary illustrations, consisting of royal letters, poems, and other articles descriptive of public events, or of the manners and customs of the metropolis.* London, 1827.

CPR: *Calendar of the Patent Rolls, preserved in the Public Record Office: Henry VI, 1422–1461,* 6 vols. Norwich and London: H. M. Stationery Office, 1901–10.

CSPM: Hinds, Allen B., ed. *Calendar of State Papers and Manuscripts in the Archives and Collections of Milan 1385–1618.* London, 1912, British History Online, http://www.british-history.ac.uk/cal-state-papers/milan/1385-1618.

CSPV: Brown, Rawdon, ed. *Calendar of State Papers Relating to English Affairs in the Archives of Venice, Volume 1, 1202–1509.* London, 1864, British History Online, http://www.british-history.ac.uk/cal-state-papers/venice/vol1.

Davies, *English Chronicle*: Davies, John Silvester, ed. *An English Chronicle of the Reigns of Richard II, Henry IV, Henry V and Henry VI, written before the year 1471.* Camden Society, Old Series 64. London: J. B. Nichols and Sons, 1856.

Dupont, *Waurin*: Dupont, L. M. E., ed. *Anchiennes Cronicques par Jehan de Wavrin: Choix de chapitres inédits annotés et publiés pour la Société de l'histoire de France par Mlle Dupont,* 3 vols. Paris: Jules Renouard, 1858–63.

EHD: Myers, A. R., ed. *English Historical Documents 1327–1485.* London: Eyre & Spottiswoode, 1969.

EHL: Kingsford, Charles Lethbridge, ed. *English Historical Literature in the Fifteenth Century.* Oxford: Clarendon Press, 1913.

Escouchy: Beaucourt, G. du Fresne de, ed. *Chronique de Mathieu d'Escouchy: nouvelle édition…* Paris: Société de l'Histoire de France, 1864.

Flenley: Flenley, Ralph, ed. *Six Town Chronicles of England.* Oxford: Clarendon Press, 1911.

Giles: Giles, Joannes Allen, *Incerti Scriptoris Chronicon Angliæ de regnis trium regum Lancastriensium, Henrici IV., Henrici V., et Henrici VI.* London: D. Nutt, 1848.

Gregory: Gairdner, James, ed. *The Historical Collections of a Citizen of London in the Fifteenth Century. Containing John Page's Poem on the Siege of Rouen, Lydgate's Verses on the Kings of England; William Gregory's Chronicle of London.* London, 1876.

Griffiths: Griffiths, Ralph A. *The Reign of King Henry VI: The Exercise of Royal Authority, 1422–1461.* London: Benn, 1981.

Hall: Hall, Edward and Grafton, Richard Ellis. *Hall's Chronicle; Containing the History of England, during the reign of Henry the Fourth, and the succeeding monarchs, to the end of the reign of Henry the Eighth, in which are particularly described the manners and customs of those periods. Carefully collated with the editions of 1548 and 1550.* London: J. Johnson etc., 1809.

Hardyng: Ellis, Henry, ed. *The Chronicle of John Hardyng. Containing an account of public transactions from the earliest period of English history to the beginning of the reign of King Edward the Fourth. Together with the continuation by Richard Grafton, to the thirty-fourth year of King Henry the Eighth.* London: F. C. and J. Rivington etc., 1812.

Harriss, Beaufort: Harriss, G. L. *Cardinal Beaufort: a study of Lancastrian ascendancy and decline.* Oxford: Clarendon Press, 1988.

Hellot: Hellot, A., ed. *Les Cronicques de Normandie (1223–1453): Réimprimées pour la première fois d'après l'édition de G. Le Talleur, mai 1487;*

avec variantes et additions tirées d'autres éditions et de divers manuscrits, et avec une introduction et des notes par A. Hellot. Rouen: Ch. Métérie, 1881.

Ingulph: Riley, Henry T., trans. *Ingulph's Chronicle of the Abbey of Croyland with the Continuations by Peter of Blois and Anonymous Writers.* London: Henry G. Bohn, 1854.

Johnson, *Richard of York*: Johnson, P. A. *Duke Richard of York, 1411–1460.* Oxford: Clarendon Press, 1988.

Kingsford, *Chronicles of London*: Kingsford, Charles Lethbridge, ed. *Chronicles of London.* Oxford: Clarendon Press, 1905.

LP: Stevenson, Joseph, ed. *Letters and Papers Illustrative of the Wars of the English in France During the Reign of Henry the Sixth, king of England,* 2 vols. London: Longman Green, Longman, Roberts and Green, 1861–4.

Maurer: Maurer, Helen E. *Margaret of Anjou: Queenship and Power in Late Medieval England.* Woodbridge: Boydell Press, 2003.

Monstrelet: Monstrelet, Enguerrand de, and Johnes, Thomas, trans. and ed. *The Chronicles of Enguerrand de Monstrelet.* Vols. 1–2. London: William Smith, 1845.

ODNB: *Oxford Dictionary of National Biography.* Oxford University Press: http://www.oxforddnb.com/.

Parisian Journal: Shirley, Janet, trans., *A Parisian Journal 1405–1449, translated from the Anonymous Journal d'un Bourgeois de Paris.* Oxford: Clarendon Press, 1968.

Scobie, *Philippe de Commines*: Scobie, Andrew R., ed. *The Memoirs of Philippe de Commines, Lord of Argenton: containing the histories of Louis XI and Charles VIII kings of France and of Charles the Bold, duke of Burgundy to which is added, The scandalous chronicle, or Secret history of Louis XI, by Jean deTroyes.* Vol. 1. London: Henry G. Bohn, 1855.

Polydore Vergil: Vergil, Polydore and Ellis, Henry, ed. *Three Books of Polydore Vergil's English History, comprising the reigns of Henry VI., Edward IV., and Richard III. from an early translation, preserved among the mss. of the old royal library in the British museum.* London: J. B. Nichols and Sons, 1844.

POPC: Nicolas, Harris, ed., *Proceedings and Ordinances of the Privy Council of England,* 7 vols. London: G. Eyre and A. Spottiswoode, 1834–7.

PL: Gairdner, James, ed. *The Paston Letters 1422–1509 A.D. A Reprint of the Edition of 1872–5, which Contained upwards of Five Hundred Letters, etc., till then unpublished, to which are now added others in a Supplement after the Introduction.* 4 vols. Edinburgh: John Grant, 1910.

PR: Given-Wilson, Chris, Brand, Paul, Phillips, Seymour, Ormrod, Mark, Martin, Geoffrey, Curry, Anne and Horrox, Rosemary, eds., *Parliament Rolls of Medieval England.* Woodbridge, 2005, British History Online, http://www.british-history.ac.uk/no-series/parliament-rolls-medieval.

***Ryalle Boke*:** Grose, F., ed., *The Antiquarian Repertory: a miscellaneous assemblage of topography, history, biography, customs and manners. Intended to illustrate and preserve several valuable remains of old times.* Vol. 1. London: Edward Jeffery, 1807.

Rymer: Rymer, Thomas, ed., *Rymer's Foedera.* Vols. 10–11. London, 1739–45, British History Online, http://www.british-history.ac.uk/rymer-foedera/vol11.

Scofield: Scofield, Cora L., *The Life and Reign of Edward the Fourth King of England and of France and Lord of Ireland,* 2 vols. London: Fonthill Media, 2016.

***Three Fifteenth-Century Chronicles*:** Gairdner, James, ed. *Three Fifteenth-Century Chronicles with Historical Memoranda by John Stow, the antiquary and contemporary notes of occurrences written by him in the reign of Queen Elizabeth.* Camden Society, New Series 28. London, 1880.

TNA: The National Archives.

Vale: Kekewich, Margaret Lucille, *The Politics of Fifteenth Century England: John Vale's Book.* Stroud: Alan Sutton for Richard III & Yorkist History Trust, 1995.

Warkworth: Halliwell, James Orchard, ed. *A Chronicle of The First Thirteen Years of The Reign of King Edward The Fourth, by John Warkworth.* Camden Society, Old Series 10. London: J. B. Nichols and Sons, 1839.

Waurin: Hardy, William, ed., *Recueil des croniques et anchiennes istories de la Grant Bretaigne, a present nomme Engleterre par Jehan de Waurin, seigneur du Forestel,* 4 vols. London: Longman, Green, Longman, Roberts, and Green, 1864–91.

Watts: Watts, John, *Henry VI and the Politics of Kingship.* Cambridge: Cambridge University Press, 1996.

Wolffe: Wolffe, Bertram, *Henry VI.* New Haven and London: Yale University Press, 2001.

Image credits

1   Royal Collection Trust / © Her Majesty Queen Elizabeth II 2019
2   Illustration from The Rous Roll, 1483–85 / © British Library Board / Bridgeman Images
3   Catherine de Valois / © Dean and Chapter of Westminster
4   f.256v Book of Hours (The Bedford Hours) c.1410-30 / © British Library Board / Bridgeman Images
5   Jan Van Eyck/ Public Domain
6   Cotton Julius E. IV, The Beauchamp Pageants, c.1483, Netherlandish School, (15th century) / © British Library Board / Bridgeman Images
7   f.257v Book of Hours (The Bedford Hours) c.1410-30 / © British Library Board / Bridgeman Images
8   Henry Psalter; Psalm 26: The young prince presented by St Louis to the Virgin / © British Library Board / Bridgeman Images
9   Hulton Archive / Getty Images / Contributor
10 King Henry VI visits the Shrine of St Edmund, illustration from the 'Lives of Saints Edmund and Fremund, 1434–44 / © British Library Board / Bridgeman Images
11 Jean Fouquet, Public domain
12 Rogier van der Weyden, Public domain
13 Rogier van der Weyden, Public domain
14 The Tower of London with London Bridge / © British Library Board / Bridgeman Images
15 Humphrey, Duke of Gloucester and his second wife, Eleanor Cobham / © Look and Learn / Bridgeman Images
16 f.2v Margaret of Anjou, seated with her husband King Henry VI, illustration from Shrewsbury Talbot Book of Romances, c.1445 / © British Library Board / Bridgeman Images

17 The genealogical table of descendants of Louis IX / © British Library Board / Bridgeman Images
18 National Portrait Gallery, Public domain
19 f.27v The Neville family at prayer, from the Neville Book of Hours, 1430–35/ Bibliothèque Nationale, Paris, France / Bridgeman Images
20 Universal History Archive / Contributor/ Getty Images
21 Ghent master, Public domain
22 Royal Collection Trust /© Her Majesty Queen Elizabeth II 2019
23 The Tower of London / © British Library Board / Bridgeman Images
24 f.30v Wheel of Fortune, illustration from the 'Troy Book', c.1455–62 / © British Library Board / Bridgeman Images

Notes

Prologue: 'Woe to thee, o land, whose king is a child'

1   Ecclesiastes 10:16.
2   For Henry V's funeral procession see Brut, p. 494; Monstrelet, I, p. 484; Preest, David (trans.) and Clark, James G. (ed.), *The Chronica Maiora of Thomas Walsingham 1376–1422* (Woodbridge, 2005), pp. 446–7; Wylie, James Hamilton and Waugh, William Templeton, *The Reign of Henry the Fifth. Volume III (1415–1422)* (Cambridge, 1929), pp. 420–1; Allmand, Christopher, *Henry V* (Yale, 1997), pp. 174–7.
3   '*Estoit une ombre en une paroit*' – Chastellain, V, p. 490.

PART I: CHILD KING
Chapter 1. 'That divine king your father'

1   'The Life of Henry V' by Titus Livius, quoted in Gransden, Antonia, *Historical Writing in England: c.1307 to the early sixteenth century* (London, 1982), p. 211.
2   The narrative of the Battle of Agincourt is based on Curry, Anne, *The Battle of Agincourt: Sources and Interpretations* (Woodbridge, 2000), pp. 164–268; idem, *Agincourt: A New History* (Stroud, 2006).
3   The surgeon John Bradmore recorded his efforts to remove the arrow in a Latin treatise called *Philomena*. Lang, S. J., 'Bradmore, John (d.1412)', *ODNB*, https://doi.org/10.1093/ref:odnb/45759 [accessed 1 May 2018].
4   Woosnam-Savage, Robert C., '"All kinds of weapons": The weapons of Agincourt', in Curry, Anne and Mercer, Malcolm (eds.), *The Battle of Agincourt* (New Haven and London, 2015), p. 147.
5   Hardy, William (trans.), *A Collection of the Chronicles and Ancient Histories of Great Britain, now called England by John de Wavrin, Lord of Forestel* (London, 1887) II, p. 203. Where Hardy's translation of Waurin is available (until 1431) I quote from his work. After that point, translations are my own, from Waurin's French texts.

6   This initial attack is described by Bellaguet, M. L. (trans.), *Chronique du Religieux de Saint-Denis, contenant le Règne de Charles VI, de 1380 à 1422* (Paris, 1840) II, pp. 19, 23; Kervyn de Lettenhove, Joseph (ed.), *Oeuvres de Froissart* (Brussels, 1871), pp. 26–41; Michaud, J. F. (ed.) and Poujoulat, J. J. F., 'Histoire de Charles VI, roy de France, par Jean Juvenal des Ursins', in *Nouvelle Collection des Mémoires pour servir à l'histoire de France depuis le XIIIe siècle jusqu'à la fin du XVIIIe* (Paris, 1836), II, pp. 388–90. For an overview of Charles's mental health see Famiglietti, R. C., *Royal Intrigue: Crisis at the Court of Charles VI, 1392–1420* (New York, 1986), pp. 1–19.

7   Gragg, Florence Alden (trans.) and Gabel, Leona C. (ed.), *The Commentaries of Pius II, Books VI–IX*, Smith College Studies in History 35 (Northampton, MA, 1951), VI, pp. 425–6; Bellaguet, II, pp. 26, 65–71, 85–91, 403–7, 543–7, 665–9; Michaud and Poujoulat, 'Histoire de Charles VI', II, pp. 394–5, 398, 437–8.

8   Estimates of both English and French numbers vary, but Anne Curry suggests that the English were outnumbered around 3 : 4 and that their force comprised around 9,000. Curry, *Agincourt: A New History*, p. 228; ibid., Appendix B for details.

9   Thomas Walsingham, quoted in Curry, *The Battle of Agincourt: Sources and Interpretations*, p. 52.

10   Quoted in ibid., p. 37.

11   The French soldier Ghillebert de Lannoy reported that he and a group of other prisoners were marched to a house, which was set on fire by the English in order to kill them. Curry, *Agincourt: A New History*, p. 263.

12   Contemporary sources placed the French dead anywhere between 3,000 and 12,000, while estimates of the English dead varied between 20 and 1,600. See Curry, *Agincourt: A New History*, Appendix C for details.

13   'Gesta Henrici Quinti,' quoted in Curry, *The Battle of Agincourt: Sources and Interpretations*, p. 39.

14   Gibbons, Rachel, 'Isabeau of Bavaria, Queen of France (1385–1422): The Creation of an Historical Villainess: The Alexander Prize Essay', *Transactions of the Royal Historical Society* 6 (1996), p. 64.

15   Chastellain, I, p. 132, n.1.

16   Chastellain, II, pp. 178–87.

17   Vale, M. G. A., *Charles VII* (London, 1976), pp. 3–4, 11, 229.

18   Castor, Helen, *Joan of Arc: A History* (New York, 2015), pp. 35–7; Vaughan, Richard, *John the Fearless: The Growth of Burgundian Power* (Woodbridge, 2002), pp. 274–86; Vale, *Charles VII*, pp. 28–31.

19   Parisian Journal, p. 150.

20   Preest and Clark, *The Chronica Maiora of Thomas Walsingham*, p. 436; Parisian Journal, p. 128; *EHD*, IV, pp. 225–6; Wylie, James Hamilton and Waugh, William Templeton (eds.), *The Reign of Henry the Fifth, Volume III (1415–1422)* (Cambridge, 1929), pp. 203–6; Monstrelet,

I, pp. 439–42; Chastellain, I, pp. 133–6; Barker, Juliet, *Conquest: The English Kingdom of France, 1417–1450* (London, 2010), pp. 28–9.

21 Parisian Journal, p. 151.

22 Chastellain, I, p. 133; Monstrelet, I, pp. 439, 442; Wylie and Waugh, *The Reign of Henry the Fifth*, pp. 205–6.

23 Preest and Clark, *The Chronica Maiora of Thomas Walsingham*, p. 437.

24 Parisian Journal, p. 156. He is also the source for the weather: ibid., p. 160.

25 Gregory, pp. 138–41; Nicolas, N. H. and Tyrrell, Edward (eds.), *A Chronicle of London, from 1089 to 1483; written in the fifteenth century, and for the first time printed from mss. in the British Museum: to which are added numerous contemporary illustrations, consisting of royal letters, poems, and other articles descriptive of public events, or of the manners and customs of the metropolis* (London, 1827), pp. 162–5.

26 Basin, II, p. 89.

27 Gragg, Florence Alden (trans.) and Gabel, Leona C. (ed.), *The Commentaries of Pius II on the Memorable Events of His Times: Book I*, Smith College Studies in History 22 (Northampton, MA: 1936–7), pp. 16–21.

28 'PR May 1421', Introduction, http://www.british-history.ac.uk/no-series/parliament-rolls-medieval/may-1421 [accessed 21 May 2016].

29 Hall, p. 108.

30 Wolffe, p. 27.

Chapter 2. 'In infant bands crowned king'

1 Shakespeare, William, *Henry V*, Epilogue, p. 9.

2 Parisian Journal, pp. 164–6. The description of Catherine's chamber and Henry's baptism is based on royal ordinances and records of the royal wardrobe. See PR 1423, item 31 (633), http://www.british-history.ac.uk/no-series/parliament-rolls-medieval/october-1423 [accessed 3 May 2018]; *Ryalle Boke*, pp. 304–6; Leland, John, *Joannis Lelandi antiquarii De rebus Britannicis Collectanea cum Thomae Hearnii Praefatione Notis et Indice ad Editionem primam: Editio Alterta, Volume IV* (Farnborough, 1970), pp. 179–82.

3 Wolffe, p. 28.

4 Parisian Journal, p. 176; Monstrelet, I, p. 478; Brut, p. 493.

5 Parisian Journal, pp. 161–2, 167, 172, 176; *EHD*, IV, p. 225.

6 Parisian Journal, p. 177; Wylie and Waugh, *The Reign of Henry the Fifth*, p. 409.

7 Preest and Clark, *The Chronica Maiora of Thomas Walsingham*, p. 445; *EHD*, IV, p. 230; Monstrelet, I, p. 482; Tuetey, Alexandre (ed.), *Journal de Clément de Fauquembergue, greffier du Parlement de Paris, 1417–1435* (Paris, 1909), II, pp. 52–3, 56; Wylie and Waugh, *The Reign of Henry the Fifth*, pp. 409–10, 414.

8 Monstrelet, I, p. 483.

9   *EHD*, IV, p. 231. For Henry's deathbed see ibid., pp. 230–1; Monstrelet, I, pp. 482–4; Chastellain, I, pp. 328–31; Preest and Clark, *The Chronica Maiora of Thomas Walsingham*, p. 445; Wylie and Waugh, *The Reign of Henry the Fifth*, pp. 414–15; Allmand, Christopher, *Henry V* (New Haven, 1997), pp. 170–2.

10 Strong, Patrick and Felicity, 'The Last Will and Codicils of Henry V', *English Historical Review* 96, no. 378 (1981).

11 Monstrelet, I, p. 483.

12 Ibid.

13 Ibid; Chastellain, I, pp. 328–31; *EHD*, IV, pp. 230–1; Preest and Clark, *The Chronica Maiora of Thomas Walsingham*, p. 445.

14 Monstrelet, I, p. 484; Wylie and Waugh, *The Reign of Henry the Fifth*, p. 414; Brut, p. 494; Tuetey, *Journal de Clément de Fauquembergue*, pp. 52–3, 56–7, 56; Chastellain, I, p. 328.

15 Preest and Clark, *The Chronica Maiora of Thomas Walsingham*, p. 445; Parisian Journal, p. 177; Monstrelet, p. 484; Hilton, Geoffrey (trans.), *The Deeds of King Henry V, Told by John Strecche* (Kenilworth, 2014) p. 56; Wylie and Waugh, *The Reign of Henry the Fifth*, pp. 416–18; Allmand, *Henry V*, p. 173.

16 Roskell, J. S., 'The Office and Dignity of Protector of England, with Special Reference to Its Origins', *English Historical Review* 68, no. 267 (1953), p. 195; PR 1422, item 13, http://www.british-history.ac.uk/no-series/parliament-rolls-medieval/november-1422 [accessed 17 May 2016]; CCR, 1422–9, http://www.british-history.ac.uk/cal-close-rolls/hen6/vol1/pp43–48 [accessed 17 May 2016].

17 Griffiths, R. A., 'The Minority of Henry VI, king of England and of France', in Beem, Charles (ed.), *The Royal Minorities of Medieval and Early Modern England* (New York, 2008).

18 Roskell, 'The Office and Dignity of Protector of England', pp. 193–233, and for the question of the *tutela* especially p. 206; Strong, 'The Last Will and Codicils of Henry V', pp. 84–5; Griffiths, 'The Minority of Henry VI, king of England and of France', pp. 169–70; Brown, A. L., 'The King's Councillors in Fifteenth-Century England', *Transactions of the Royal Historical Society* 19 (1969), pp. 107–9.

19 Williams, E. Carleton, *My Lord of Bedford 1389–1435, being a life of John of Lancaster first duke of Bedford brother of Henry V and Regent of France* (London, 1963), p. 81; Harriss, *Beaufort*, pp. 116–17.

20 CCR, 1422–9, http://www.british-history.ac.uk/cal-close-rolls/hen6/vol1/pp43–48 [accessed 18 May 2016].

21 *EHD*, IV, pp. 232–3.

22 Harriss, *Beaufort*, pp. 115–18; Harriss, Gerald, *Shaping the Nation: England 1360–1461* (Oxford, 2005), p. 596.

23 PR 1422: Introduction; items 27–32, http://www.british-history.ac.uk/no-series/parliament-rolls-medieval/november-1422 [accessed 17 May 2016].

Chapter 3. 'The universal joy and comfort of us all'

1   Address of the speaker of the commons to King Henry VI at the latter's
     visit to parliament on 17 November 1423. PR 1423, Appendix 1, http://
     www.british-history.ac.uk/no-series/parliament-rolls-medieval/
     october-1423 [accessed 6 June 2016].
2   'Julius B I', Kingsford, *Chronicles of London*, pp. 279–80.
3   Lydgate, John and Sponsler, Claire (ed.), *Mummings and Entertainments*
     (Kalamazoo, 2010), http://d.lib.rochester.edu/teams/publication/
     sponsler-lydgate-mummings-and-entertainments [accessed 17 November 2017].
4   Griffiths, pp. 51–7, 64, n.17; POPC, III, pp. 294–5.
5   Linsley, Chris, 'Louis Robessart – a Border-Crossing Knight?', https://
     www.englandsimmigrants.com/page/individual-studies/louis-
     robessart-a-border-crossing-knight [accessed 31 August 2016].
6   Rickert, Edith (trans.) and Naylor, L. J. (rev.), *The Babees' Book: Medi-
     eval Manners for the Young* (Cambridge, Ontario, 2000), p. 22.
7   POPC, III, p. 143.
8   CPR, 1437–41, pp. 46, 127, 367; Wolffe, p. 36; Griffiths, p. 55.
9   PR 1423, http://www.british-history.ac.uk/no-series/parliament-rolls-
     medieval/october-1423 [accessed 6 June 2016].
10   'Julius B I', Kingsford, *Chronicles of London*, p. 283.
11   Brut, p. 431; 'Julius B I', Kingsford, *Chronicles of London*, pp. 282–3;
     PR 1423, Introduction, http://www.british-history.ac.uk/no-series/
     parliament-rolls-medieval/october-1423 [accessed 6 June 2016];
     Powell, E., 'The strange death of Sir John Mortimer: politics and the
     law of treason in Lancastrian England', in Archer, R. E. and Walker,
     S. (eds.), *Rulers and Ruled in Late Medieval England* (London, 1995),
     pp. 83–97.
12   Mortimer had been indicted before the mayor of London at a trial in
     the Guildhall on 25 February. On 26 February parliament was acting
     in its capacity as the highest court in the realm. PR 1423, item 18,
     http://www.british-history.ac.uk/no-series/parliament-rolls-medieval/
     october-1423 [accessed 6 June 2016].
13   Skeat, Walter W. (ed.), *The Kingis Quair: together with a ballad of good
     counsel: by King James I of Scotland* (Edinburgh, 1884), p. 12; Rymer,
     X,   http://www.british-history.ac.uk/rymer-foedera/vol10/pp294-
     316 [accessed 2 May 2018]; http://www.british-history.ac.uk/rymer-
     foedera/vol10/pp316-335 [accessed 2 May 2018]; Brown, Michael,
     James I (Edinburgh, 2015), pp. 2–5, 20–5.
14   Monstrelet, I, p. 483. Also reported by Chastellain, I, p. 329.
15   Hardy, William (trans.), *A Collection of the Chronicles and Ancient Histo-
     ries of Great Britain, now called England by John de Wavrin, Lord of Forestel*
     (London, 1891), III, p. 17. For the treaty see ibid., pp. 16–19.
16   Parisian Journal, p. 282.
17   Gragg, Florence Alden (trans.) and Gabel, Leona C. (ed.), *The Com-

mentaries of Pius II, Books VI–IX, Smith College Studies in History, 35 (Northampton, MA, 1951), p. 585.

18 Barker, Juliet, *Conquest: The English Kingdom of France, 1417–1450* (London, 2010), p. 76.

19 For the battle and its context see Jones, Michael K., 'The Battle of Verneuil (17 August 1424): Towards a History of Courage', *War in History* 9, no. 4 (2002). See also Waurin, III, pp. 99–122.

20 Parisian Journal, p. 196; Brut, p. 564.

21 Hardy (trans.), *John de Wavrin*, III, p. 73.

22 Hardy (trans.), *John de Wavrin*, III, p. 75.

23 Jones, 'The Battle of Verneuil', p. 407.

24 Hardy (trans.), *John de Wavrin*, III, p. 75.

25 *Hardyng*, p. 393.

26 Parisian Journal, p. 201.

27 LP, II (2), p. 397.

28 Hardy (trans.), *John de Wavrin*, III, p. 90; Dupont, L. M. E. (ed.), *Mémoires de Pierre de Fenin, comprenant le récit des événements qui sont passés en France et en Bourgogne, sous les règnes de Charles VI et Charles VII (1402–27)* (Paris, 1837), p. 229.

29 Fenin, p. 229.

30 Hardy (trans.), *John de Wavrin*, III, p. 129. For Bedford and Burgundy's attempt at arbitration see Waurin, III, pp. 126–9.

31 Vaughan, Richard, *Philip the Good: The Apogee of Burgundy* (London, 1970), pp. 34–7; Vickers, K. H., *Humphrey duke of Gloucester: A Biography* (London, 1907), pp. 137, 140–9.

32 Hardy (trans.), *John de Wavrin*, III, p. 98. For the original correspondence in its entirety see Waurin, III, pp. 139–63.

33 Fenin, pp. 233–4; 'Julius B II', Kingsford, *Chronicles of London*, p. 75; Hardy (trans.), *John de Wavrin*, p. 38.

34 PR 1427 Appendix 1; PR 1427 item 13, http://www.british-history. ac.uk/no-series/parliament-rolls-medieval/october-1427 [accessed 19 June 2016].

Chapter 4. 'The serpent of division'

1 Lydgate, John and MacCracken, H. N. (ed.), *The Serpent of Division by John Lydgate* (London, 1911), p. 50.

2 'Julius B I', Kingsford, *Chronicles of London*, p. 285.

3 Harriss, *Beaufort*, p. 140.

4 PR 1426, item 33; Appendix 21, http://www.british-history.ac.uk/no-series/parliament-rolls-medieval/february-1426 [accessed 20 July 2016].

5 Giles, p. 7; Gregory, p. 158.

6 'Julius B II', Kingsford, *Chronicles of London*, pp. 76–88. Also provided in modern English in PR 1426, Appendix 1, http://www.british-history. ac.uk/no-series/parliament-rolls-medieval/february-1426 [accessed 20 July 2016].

7   'Julius B II', Kingsford, *Chronicles of London*, pp. 76, 81.
8   Harriss, *Beaufort*, p. 142.
9   Giles, p. 17; I follow Gerald Harriss's dating of the first rumours of Edmund and Catherine's relationship. Harriss, *Beaufort*, p. 144; Griffiths, pp. 60–1.
10 For the following see 'Julius B II', Kingsford, *Chronicles of London*, pp. 76–88. Also given in modern English in PR 1426, Appendix 1, http:// www.british-history.ac.uk/no-series/parliament-rolls-medieval/february-1426 [accessed 20 July 2016]; Davies, *English Chronicle*, pp. 53–4; Brut, pp. 432, 453, 567; Gregory, p. 159.
11 Brut, p. 432.
12 'Julius B II', Kingsford, *Chronicles of London*, p. 84.
13 Gregory, p. 160; Harriss, *Beaufort*, p. 144; Griffiths, p. 78.
14 Lydgate, John and Sponsler, Claire (ed.), 'Mumming at Eltham', *Mummings and Entertainments* (Kalamazoo, 2010), http://d.lib.rochester. edu/teams/text/sponsler-lydgate-mummings-and-entertainments-mumming-at-eltham [accessed 10 August 2016].
15 Gregory, p. 160; Brut, p. 433.
16 POPC, III, pp. 181–7.
17 Gregory, p. 160.
18 Ibid.
19 'Julius B II', Kingsford, *Chronicles of London*, p. 77. For the following see ibid., pp. 76–88.
20 Ibid., p. 78.
21 Ibid., pp. 83–4.
22 Ibid., pp. 89–96.
23 Twenty-four young men were summoned to receive the honour, but thirty-eight names appear on a list of those knighted. Wolffe, p. 38; Griffiths, p. 80; 'Julius B II', Kingsford, *Chronicles of London*, pp. 94–5; Giles, pp. 8–9; Amundesham, p. 10.

Chapter 5. 'Virtues and teachings convenient for the royal person'

1   POPC, III, p. 296.
2   Gregory, p. 162; Brut, p. 450; Amundesham, I, pp. 22, 27, 30.
3   Edward I's children had miniature wooden castles to play with as children, and a lead toy knight of *c.*1300 survives in the Tower of London collection. It is on display in the Lanthorn Tower. Griffiths, p. 53; CPR, 1452–61, pp. 247–8; Colvin, H. M. (ed.), Brown, R. Allen and Taylor, A. J., *The History of the King's Works: Volume I: The Middle Ages* (London, 1963), p. 202.
4   POPC, III, p. 170; Wolffe, pp. 36–7.
5   POPC, III, p. 297.
6   Ibid., pp. 296–300.

7   Hughes, Jonathan, *Arthurian Myth and Alchemy: The Kingship of Edward IV* (Stroud, 2002), p. viii.

8   BL, Cotton MS Domitian, A. XVII, f.50 r., http://www.bl.uk/manu-scripts/FullDisplay.aspx?ref=Cotton_MS_domitian_a_xvii   [accessed 30 October 2018].

9   Rogers, Nicholas, 'Henry the sixth and the proposed canonisation of King Alfred', in Lewis, Katherine J. (ed.), *Religious Men And Masculine Identity in the Middle Ages* (Woodbridge, 2013); Lewis, Katherine J., '"Imitate, too, this king in virtue, who could have done ill and did it not": Lay Sanctity and the Rewriting Of Henry VI's Manliness', in ibid; Lewis, Katherine J., 'Edmund of East Anglia, Henry VI and Ideals of Kingly Masculinity', in Cullum, P. H. and Lewis, Katherine J. (eds.), *Holiness and Masculinity in the Middle Ages* (Toronto, 2004).

10 POPC, III, p. 235. For events on 28 and 29 January see ibid., pp. 231–42.

11 Ibid., p. 241.

12 PR 1427–8, items 24–7, http://www.british-history.ac.uk/no-series/parliament-rolls-medieval/october-1427 [accessed 8 May 2018].

13 For Salisbury's quarrel with Philippe of Burgundy see Dupont, L. M. E. (ed.), *Mémoires de Pierre de Fenin, comprenant le récit des événements qui sont passés en France et en Bourgogne, sous les règnes de Charles VI et Charles VII (1402–27)* (Paris, 1837), p. 225. For the context to the military strategy of 1428, Harriss, *Shaping the Nation*, pp. 552–3, 598; Barker, Juliet, *Conquest: The English Kingdom of France, 1417–1450* (London, 2010), p. 96.

14 PR 1427, item 26.

15 Monstrelet, I, p. 544.

16 Barker, *Conquest*, p. 98.

17 Hamblin, V. L. (ed.), *Le mistere du siege d'Orléans: edition critique* (Geneva, 2002), pp. 166–7; Hellot, p. 76; Amundesham, I, p. 32; 'Cleopatra C IV', Kingsford, *Chronicles of London*, p. 132; Brut, pp. 434–5.

18 Taylor, Craig (trans.), *Joan of Arc: La Pucelle* (Manchester, 2006), pp. 84, 281, 314–15.

19 'Julius B II', Kingsford, *Chronicles of London*, p. 96; Taylor, *Joan of Arc*, pp. 280, 315.

20 Waurin, III, pp. 271–94, 300–5. See also Parisian Journal, p. 235.

21 Waurin, III, pp. 314–19.

22 POPC, III, pp. 332–3; Rymer, X, http://www.british-history.ac.uk/rymer-foedera/vol10/pp410–413 [accessed 29 July 2016].

23 Amundesham, I, p. 44; Gregory, p. 165.

24 Gregory, pp. 165–8; Amundesham, I, p. 44; Brut, p. 455; Legg, L. G. Wickham (ed.), *English Coronation Records* (London, 1901), pp. 182–3.

25 Gregory, p. 167.

26 McKenna, J. W., 'Henry VI of England and the Dual Monarchy: Aspects of Royal Political Propaganda, 1422–1432', *Journal of the Warburg and Courtauld Institutes* 28 (1965), pp. 145–62.

27 POPC, IV, pp. 10–1.

Chapter 6. 'The throne of his kingdom will be established'

1   PR 1431, item 1: http://www.british-history.ac.uk/no-series/parlia-
     ment-rolls-medieval/january-1431 [accessed 7 August 2016].
2   Curry, Anne, 'The "Coronation Expedition" and Henry VI's court
     in France, 1430 to 1432', in Stratford, Jenny (ed.), *The Lancastrian
     Court: Proceedings of the 2001 Harlaxton Symposium* (Donington, 2003),
     pp. 30–3; Griffiths, p. 190; 'Julius B II', Kingsford, *Chronicles of Lon-
     don*, p. 96; Parisian Journal, p. 250; Brut, p. 439; Monstrelet, I, p. 573.
3   Curry, 'Coronation Expedition', p. 30; Griffiths, p. 190; Parisian Jour-
     nal, p. 250.
4   ibid., p. 251.
5   LP, II (1), pp. 156–62; Curry, 'Coronation Expedition', p. 39.
6   Monstrelet, I, p. 567; Barker, Juliet, *Conquest: The English Kingdom of
     France, 1417–1450* (London, 2010), p. 209.
7   Basin, I, pp. 208–9.
8   Brut, p. 439; Monstrelet, I, p. 572; Parisian Journal, p. 248; Hellot,
     p. 77; Castor, Helen, *Joan of Arc: A History* (New York, 2015), p. 159;
     Barker, *Conquest*, pp. 146–7.
9   Taylor, *Joan of Arc*, pp. 176–7.
10   Parisian Journal, pp. 250, 252, 256.
11   For the 1430 campaigns see Barker, *Conquest*, pp. 149–52.
12   Taylor, Larissa Juliet, *The Virgin Warrior: The Life and Death of Joan of Arc*
     (New Haven, 2010), p. 125.
13   Taylor, *Joan of Arc*, p. 333.
14   For Henry's court in Rouen see Curry, 'Coronation Expedition', pp.
     34, 45; Rawcliffe, Carole, 'Master Surgeons at the Lancastrian court',
     in Stratford, Jenny (ed.), *The Lancastrian court: Proceedings of the 2001
     Harlaxton Symposium* (Donington, 2003), p. 205. Lady Talbot's role as
     hostess of the court in Rouen is attested by the Beauchamp House-
     hold Book: Bodleian Library, MS Film 428.
15   BL, Add MS 18850. The duke and duchess appear at f. 256v and
     f. 257v, http://www.bl.uk/manuscripts/FullDisplay.aspx?ref=Add_
     MS_18850 [accessed 30 October 2018].
16   Morgan, D., 'From a Death to a View: Louis Robessart, Johan Huizinga,
     and the Political Significance of Chivalry', in Anglo, S. (ed.) *Chivalry
     in the Renaissance* (Woodbridge, 1990), pp. 93–106; Linsley, Chris,
     'Louis Robessart: A Border-Crossing Knight', *England's Immigrants*,
     https://www.englandsimmigrants.com/page/individual-studies/louis-
     robessart-a-border-crossing-knight [accessed 31 August 2016]; Curry,
     'Coronation Expedition', pp. 46–7.
17   LP, II (1), pp. 156–62.
18   Taylor, *Joan of Arc*, p. 218.
19   Parisian Journal, p. 337.
20   See, for instance, a letter of 28 June 1431 to the prelates of France.
     Taylor, *Joan of Arc*, pp. 225–8.

21 Parisian Journal, p. 266; Taylor, *Joan of Arc*, pp. 225–8, 238.

22 Parisian Journal, p. 268.

23 Ibid., pp. 252–5, 267–8; Hellot, p. 78.

24 Monstrelet, I, p. 596. For the following see ibid., pp. 596–7; Parisian Journal, pp. 268–73; Brut, pp. 458–61.

25 English and French sources reverse the orientation of the lords, with the English putting the English lords on Henry's right (the place of honour) whereas the French claim their own lords were there. Since the Bourgeois of Paris actually saw these pageants, I have followed his description. Parisian Journal, p. 270; Monstrelet, I, p. 597; Brut, p. 460.

26 Parisian Journal, p. 271.

27 Monstrelet, I, p. 597.

28 Parisian Journal, pp. 271–2.

29 Curry, 'Coronation Expedition', p. 50; Tuetey, Alexandre (ed.), *Journal de Clément de Fauquembergue, greffier du Parlement de Paris, 1417–1435* (Paris, 1909), III, pp. 28–9.

30 LP, II (1), pp. 196–201.

31 Parisian Journal, p. 272.

32 Ibid., pp. 268, 273; Curry, 'Coronation Expedition', p. 51.

33 Hall, p. 162; *Hardyng*, p. 394; Harriss, *Beaufort*, pp. 207–9; Barker, *Conquest*, pp. 178–9.

Chapter 7. 'Earthly goods'

1 PR 1432, item 14, http://www.british-history.ac.uk/no-series/parliament-rolls-medieval/may-1432 [accessed 16 August 2016].

2 Harriss, *Beaufort*, p. 215.

3 POPC, IV, pp. 104–5; Wolffe, p. 66; Harriss, G. L., 'Humphrey [Humfrey or Humphrey of Lancaster], duke of Gloucester [*called* Good Duke Humphrey] (1390–1447)', *ODNB*, https://doi.org/10.1093/ref:odnb/14155 [accessed 20 November 2017].

4 Wolffe, p. 37.

5 POPC, IV, pp. 109–11; Grummitt, David, *Henry VI* (London and New York, 2015), pp. 89–90.

6 Brut, pp. 461–4; Gregory, pp. 173–5.

7 Thanks to Dr Daniel F. Gosling of Grays Inn for his assistance on this point. For context to the 1393 statute see PR 1393, introduction, http://www.british-history.ac.uk/no-series/parliament-rolls-medieval/january-1393 [accessed 19 June 2018].

8 Harriss, *Beaufort*, pp. 215–16.

9 Parliament had opened on 12 May but Beaufort arrived back in England only in June.

10 For the following see PR 1432, item 14, http://www.british-history.ac.uk/no-series/parliament-rolls-medieval/may-1432 [accessed 29 August 2016].

11 Ibid.
12 Ibid., item 17; Harriss, *Beaufort*, p. 219.
13 PR 1432, items 15–16. For context see Harriss, *Beaufort*, pp. 219–22.
14 POPC, IV, pp. 132–9.
15 The council's opinion of Henry's progress towards rule was given in a meeting with the king at Cirencester in November 1434. Ibid., pp. 287–9.
16 Ibid., p. 137.
17 Ibid., pp. 132–9.
18 Ibid., p. 287.
19 PR 1427, Appendix 2, http://www.british-history.ac.uk/no-series/parliament-rolls-medieval/october-1427 [accessed 19 June 2018].
20 Giles, p. 17; Basin, II, pp. 66–7.
21 The parentage of Catherine's eldest child, Edmund, has been the topic of some debate. The fact that the boy shared his name with Edmund Beaufort, Catherine's first lover, has led to the suggestion that Edmund 'Tudor' was really a Beaufort bastard. It seems unlikely, given the duke of Gloucester's desire to undermine Cardinal Beaufort – and the reputation blackening from later critics of Edmund Beaufort himself – that if there was any suggestion that Edmund Beaufort had got the dowager queen pregnant, it would have been kept secret. There was never any suggestion that Edmund was other than Owen Tudor's child. Most likely, the boy was named because he was born on the feast of St Edmund the Martyr (20 November), although since we do not know Edmund Tudor's birthdate it is not possible to be certain. Edmund was a popular English saint, and his example was cited to Henry as a king to imitate. Harriss, *Beaufort*, pp. 178–9, n.34; Griffiths, R.A., 'Queen Katherine de Valois and a missing statute of the realm', *Law Quarterly Review* 93 (1977), pp. 248–58.
22 Griffiths, Ralph A. and Thomas, Roger S., *The Making of the Tudor Dynasty* (Gloucester, 1985), pp. 25–31.

Chapter 8. 'Mother of mercy, save both realms'

1 Scattergood, V. J., *Politics and Poetry in the Fifteenth Century* (London, 1971), p. 148.
2 Parisian Journal, p. 281.
3 Ibid, pp. 281–3; Monstrelet, I, p. 610; Brut, p. 570; Stratford, Jenny, 'John [John of Lancaster], duke of Bedford (1389–1435)', ODNB, https://doi.org/10.1093/ref:odnb/14844 [accessed 12 July 2017].
4 Parisian Journal, pp. 275–6 (which misdates the fall of Rouen Castle to the first week of March); Monstrelet, I, pp. 599–600; Hellot, pp. 78–80; LP, II (1), pp. 202–4.
5 Parisian Journal, pp. 275, 278–81; Griffiths, p. 193.
6 Griffiths, pp. 195–6; Brut, pp. 570–1; 'Cleopatra C IV', Kingsford, *Chronicles of London*, p. 135.

7   Griffiths, pp. 192, 198; Barker, Juliet, *Conquest: The English Kingdom of France, 1417–1450* (London, 2010), p. 195; Wolffe, pp. 69–70; Brut, p. 466; Parisian Journal, p. 284.
8   Monstrelet, I, p. 614.
9   Barker, *Conquest*, pp. 189–90; Brut, p. 570; Parisian Journal, p. 284; Monstrelet, I, p. 614.
10 ibid., p. 615.
11 POPC, IV, pp. 128, 151, 181, 278; Bordeaut, A., 'Gilles de Bretagne – Entre la France et l'Angleterre – Les causes et les Autuers du drame', in *Mémoires de la Société d'Histoire et d'Archéologie de Bretagne* (Rennes, 1920), I, pp. 55–6. Lannoy's entire report is found in LP, II (1), pp. 218–48.
12 LP, II (1), p. 240.
13 Ibid, pp. 241–2.
14 Ibid., pp. 244–5.
15 Brut, pp. 466–7.
16 'Cleopatra C IV', Kingsford, *Chronicles of London*, p. 136; Parisian Journal, pp. 284, 286–7; Monstrelet, I, p. 623; PR 1433, item 13, http://www.british-history.ac.uk/no-series/parliament-rolls-medieval/july-1433 [accessed 30 August 2018].
17 Ibid., item 10.
18 Ibid.
19 Ibid., Introduction, items 24–5; Wolffe, pp. 73–4. For alterations to Henry's household see Griffiths, pp. 42–3.
20 Wolffe, pp. 74–5; BL, MS Harley 2278, f. 4v: http://www.bl.uk/manuscripts/FullDisplay.aspx?ref=Harley_MS_2278 [accessed 30 October 2018].
21 PR 1433, Introduction, items 18–19.
22 POPC, IV, pp. 210–13.
23 Ibid., pp. 222–32.
24 Ibid., pp. 287–9.

Chapter 9. 'Treason walking'

1   'Cleopatra C IV', Kingsford, *Chronicles of London*, p. 140.
2   Barker, Juliet, *Conquest: The English Kingdom of France, 1417–1450* (London, 2010), pp. 220–1; Wolffe, p. 82; Monstrelet, II, pp. 10–15.
3   Parisian Journal, pp. 294–5.
4   Monstrelet, II, pp. 1–4, 6; Griffiths, p. 198; Barker, pp. 224–5; Williams, E. Carleton, *My Lord of Bedford, 1389–1435, being a life of John Lancaster first Duke of Bedford brother of Henry V and Regent of France* (London, 1963), pp. 244–5; PR 1435, Introduction, http://www.british-history.ac.uk/no-series/parliament-rolls-medieval/october-1435 [accessed 19 June 2016]. For the siege of St Denis, see Parisian Journal, pp. 295–7; Monstrelet, I, p. 639; 'Cleopatra C IV', Kingsford, *Chronicles of London*, p. 138.

5 Dickinson, Joycelyne Gledhill, *The Congress of Arras, 1435: a study in medieval diplomacy* (Oxford, 1955), p. 155, n.2.
6 Ibid., pp. 145–6, 155–8; Basin, I, pp. 188–91.
7 LP, I, pp. 56–64 (where it is misdated to 8 September); Barker, *Conquest*, pp. 226–8; Harriss, *Beaufort*, pp. 250–1; Dickinson, *The Congress of Arras*, pp. 174–6.
8 Vaughan, Richard, *Philip the Good: The Apogee of Burgundy* (London, 1970), pp. 74–5, 98–101; Barker, *Conquest*, pp. 227–9; 'Cleopatra C IV', Kingsford, *Chronicles of London*, pp. 138–9; Parisian Journal, p. 299; Basin, pp. 188–95.
9 Monstrelet, II, pp. 20–1.
10 De Beaucourt, G. Du Fresne, *Histoire de Charles VII: Tome VI La Fin du Règne* (Paris, 1891), p. 137.
11 Monstrelet, II, p. 21.
12 PR 1435, items 1–3, http://www.british-history.ac.uk/no-series/parliament-rolls-medieval/october-1435 [accessed 17 August 2016].
13 Vaughan, *Philip the Good*, pp. 100–1.
14 Williams, p. 246; 'Cleopatra C IV', Kingsford, *Chronicles of London*, p. 139; Parisian Journal, p. 297.
15 ibid., pp. 298–9.
16 'Cleopatra C IV', Kingsford, *Chronicles of London*, pp. 137–9; Monstrelet, I, pp. 637–40; ibid., II, pp. 18–19; Basin, I, pp. 208–15; Parisian Journal, pp. 295, 299; Benet, p. 184; Allmand, C. T. *Lancastrian Normandy 1415–1450: The History of a Medieval Occupation* (Oxford, 1983), p. 40; Barker, pp. 231–2; Curry, Anne, 'Fitzalan, John, seventh earl of Arundel (1408–1435)', *ODNB*, https://doi.org/10.1093/ref:odnb/9532 [accessed 3 January 2018].

Chapter 10. 'The royal crown is in the hand of God'

1 PR 1437, item 1, http://www.british-history.ac.uk/no-series/parliament-rolls-medieval/january-1437 [accessed 29 August 2016].
2 POPC, IV, p. 352.
3 John Watts shows that Henry's first grant was to the duke of Gloucester on 26 July and not Cardinal Beaufort on 28 July, as suggested by Griffiths, pp. 231–2. Watts, John, 'When Did Henry VI's Minority End?', in Dorothy J. Clayton, Richard G. Davies and Peter McNiven (eds.), *Trade, devotion and governance: papers in later medieval history* (Stroud, 1994), pp. 125, 136, n.65, 68.
4 Winstead, Karen A., *John Capgrave's Fifteenth Century* (Philadelphia, 2007), p. 135.
5 Blacman, p. 28.
6 Ibid., pp. 26, 37–8.
7 Benet, p. 184. For other examples of Henry hunting, in contrast with Blacman's claims, see Griffiths, p. 250. Even if the plays put on in Henry's childhood were performed against his will, there is a record

of a disguising put on for his wife – at which Henry was almost certainly also present – in 1452–3. Blacman, p. 27; Winstead, *John Capgrave's Fifteenth Century*, p. 135; Myers, A. R., 'The Household of Queen Margaret of Anjou, 1452–3', *Bulletin of the John Rylands Library* 40 (1957–8), p. 88. For evidence of the plays staged in Henry's youth, see the records of John Lydgate's works, available online: Lydgate, John and Sponsler, Claire (ed.), *Mummings and Entertainments* http://d.lib.rochester.edu/teams/publication/sponsler-lydgate-mummings-and-entertainments [accessed 4 December 2017].

8   The translation of John Blacman's work by M. R. James in the early twentieth century obscures the fact that these women were prostitutes. Katherine Lewis's more recent translation of this section of Blacman makes the meaning clearer, so Henry appears less prudish. Lewis, Katherine J., '"Imitate, too, this king in virtue, who could have done ill and did it not": Lay Sanctity and the Rewriting of Henry VI's Manliness' in Lewis, Katherine J. (ed.), *Religious Men and Masculine Identity in the Middle Ages* (Woodbridge, 2013), p.138; Blacman, pp. 28, 30; Winstead, *John Capgrave's Fifteenth Century*, p. 135.

9   From the *Secreta Secretorum*. Lewis, Katherine J., 'Edmund of East Anglia, Henry VI and Ideals of Kingly Masculinity', in Cullum, P. H. and Lewis, Katherine J. (eds.), *Holiness and Masculinity in the Middle Ages* (Toronto, 2004), pp. 166–7.

10   Lewis, Katherine J., *Kingship and Masculinity in Late Medieval England* (New York and Abingdon, 2013), pp. 86–7, 96–7.

11   Rawcliffe, Carole, 'The Insanity of Henry VI', *The Historian* 50 (1996); Hughes, Jonathan, *Arthurian Myth and Alchemy: The Kingship of Edward IV* (Stroud, 2002), pp. 10–11, 47–8.

12   POPC, IV, pp. 287–9.

13   Wolffe, pp. 80–1, 87–9; Watts, p. 129; Harriss, *Beaufort*, p. 275. For Henry's transition from minority rule generally see Watts, pp. 129–38; Watts, 'When Did Henry VI's Minority End?', pp. 116–39; Wolffe, pp. 80–1, 87–92; Griffiths, pp. 231–6.

14   Goodman, Anthony, *The Wars of the Roses: The Soldiers' Experience* (Stroud, 2005), pp. 128, 137; Lewis, *Kingship and Masculinity*, pp. 170–1; CPR, 1452–61, pp. 247–8; Vale, M. G. A., *Charles VII* (London, 1974), p. 34.

15   'Cleopatra C IV', Kingsford, *Chronicles of London*, p. 140.

16   PR 1437, Introduction, http://www.british-history.ac.uk/no-series/parliament-rolls-medieval/january-1437 [accessed 29 August 2016]; 'Cleopatra C IV', Kingsford, *Chronicles of London*, p. 140; Parisian Journal, pp. 300–7.

17   Davies, *English Chronicle*, p. 56; Benet, p. 185; Brut, p. 505.

18   Doig, James A., 'Propaganda, Public Opinion and the Siege of Calais in 1436', in Archer, Rowena E. (ed.), *Crown, Government and People in the Fifteenth Century: Conference on Recent Research in Fifteenth-Century History* (Stroud, 1995), pp. 93–6. For Henry's addresses to Philippe's

subjects in the Low Countries see Monstrelet, II, pp. 26–7; POPC, IV, pp. 329–34; Griffiths, p. 203.

19 From Hue de Lannoy's report to Philippe of Burgundy in September 1436. Doig, 'Propaganda, Public Opinion and the Siege of Calais in 1436', pp. 79, 94–5.

20 Watts, 'When Did Henry VI's Minority End?', pp. 125, 136 n.65.

21 Griffiths, pp. 201, 203; Doig, 'Propaganda, Public Opinion and the Siege of Calais in 1436', p. 96; PR 1437, Introduction.

22 For the siege and English responses to it see Davies, *English Chronicle*, p. 54; Benet, p. 185; Monstrelet, II, pp. 26–8, 32–43; Brut, pp. 504–5, 572–84; Waurin, IV, pp. 157–205; Vaughan, *Philip the Good*, pp. 75–85; Griffiths, pp. 203–5; Doig, 'Propaganda, Public Opinion and the Siege of Calais in 1436', pp. 79–106.

23 PR 1437, items 1–4.

24 POPC, V, pp. 71–2; ibid., VI, pp. 213–15. For further context to the council appointments – with two very different conclusions – see Wolffe, pp. 91–2; Watts, 'When Did Henry VI's Minority End?', p. 127.

PART II: ADULT RULE
Chapter 11. 'A fixed purpose'

1 Griffiths, p. 243.

2 The works around Windsor were underway by October 1442. Knoop, Douglas and Jones, G. P., 'The Building of Eton College, 1442–1460', *Ars Quatuor Coronatorum, being the Transactions of the Quatuor Coronati Lodge No. 2076 London*, 46 (London, 1933), pp. 77–81.

3 Griffiths, p. 243.

4 Bekynton, pp. 270–1.

5 Colvin, H. M. (ed.), Brown, R. Allen and Taylor, A. J., *The History of the King's Works: Volume I: The Middle Ages* (London, 1963), I, pp. 245–8; Thurley, Simon, *The Royal Palaces of Tudor England: Architecture and Court Life, 1460–1547* (New Haven, 1993), pp. 8–10.

6 Hellinga, Lotte, Trapp, J. B., Barnard, John, McKenzie, Donald Francis and McKitterick, David (eds.), *The Cambridge History of the Book in Britain* (Cambridge, 1999), III, pp. 261–2; Grummitt, David, *Henry VI* (London and New York, 2015), p. 108; Steane, John, *The Archaeology of the Medieval English Monarchy* (London and New York, 1999), p. 200; Stratford, Jenny, 'John, duke of Bedford, as patron in Lancastrian Rouen' in Stratford, Jenny (ed.), *Medieval Art, Architecture and Archaeology at Rouen* (Leeds, 1993), p. 100; Williams, E. Carleton, *My Lord of Bedford 1389–1435, being a life of John of Lancaster first duke of Bedford brother of Henry V and Regent of France* (London, 1963), p. 272.

7 Grummitt, David, *Henry VI* (London, 2015), p. 111.

8 Griffiths, p. 70.

9 ECR 39 / 45; Bekynton, pp. 279–92, 297, 299, 306, 309; Wolffe,

p. 137; Lyte, *A History of Eton College, 1440–1884* (London, 1889), pp. 21–7; Grummitt, pp. 108–9.

10 Griffiths, pp. 296, 300.

11 Clay, J. W. (ed.), *North Country Wills: Being Abstracts of Wills Relating to the Counties of York, Nottingham, Northumberland, Cumberland, and Westmorland at Somerset House and Lambeth Place, 1383–1558* (Durham, 1908), p. 51; Watts, John, 'Pole, William de la, first duke of Suffolk (1396–1450),' *ODNB,* https://doi.org/10.1093/ref:odnb/22461 [accessed 19 January 2018]; Archer, Rowena E., 'Chaucer [*married names* Phelip, Montagu, de la Pole], Alice, duchess of Suffolk (*c.*1404–1475)', *ODNB,* https://doi.org/10.1093/ref:odnb/54434 [accessed 19 January 2018].

12 Wolffe, 'Appendix: The Itinerary of Henry VI, 1436–1461', p. 361. The description of the landscape is based on John Leland's early sixteenth-century journeys around England. Chandler, John, *John Leland's Itinerary: Travels in Tudor England* (Stroud, 1993).

13 Henry's New Year gift roll for 1436–7, transcribed in Bentley, Samuel (ed.), *Excerpta Historica or Illustrations of English History* (London, 1831), pp. 148–50.

14 Wolffe, p. 100; Harriss, *Shaping the Nation,* p. 606.

15 Ibid., p. 607.

16 Watts, John, 'Beaumont, John, first Viscount Beaumont (1409?–1460)', *ODNB,* https://doi.org/10.1093/ref:odnb/50239 [accessed 19 January 2018].

17 Griffiths, pp. 238, 353.

18 POPC, V, p. 3.

19 Granting away the constableship and stewardship of Chirk Castle lost him 1,000; pardoning a collector of customs cost the crown 2,000 marks. POPC, V, pp. 87–90.

20 POPC, V, pp. 144–5.

21 CPR, 1436–41, p. 255.

22 Ibid., pp. 46, 127, 367; CPR, 1441–6, p. 362.

23 PR 1439, items 16, 17, 19, 61, http://www.british-history.ac.uk/no-series/parliament-rolls-medieval/november-1439 [accessed 10 January 2017].

24 Griffiths, p. 297.

25 For the legend of Henry V's wild youth and transition to strong kingship on his accession to the throne, see Lewis, Katherine J. *Kingship and Masculinity in Late Medieval England* (New York and Abingdon, 2013), pp. 84–8.

Chapter 12. 'To the counsellors of peace is joy'

1 PR 1447, item 2, http://www.british-history.ac.uk/no-series/parliament-rolls-medieval/february-1447 [accessed 2 January 2018].

2 After providing a substantial loan for the army of his nephew, John

Beaufort, in December 1439, Beaufort only advanced £1,000 for the war in the following two years. Harriss, *Beaufort*, p. 325.

3 LP, II (2), pp. 451–60.
4 See also POPC, V, p. 356.
5 Rymer, X, http://www.british-history.ac.uk/rymer-foedera/vol10/ pp716–735 [accessed 16 January 2018]; POPC, V, pp. 354–62. For context to the talks of 1439 see Wolffe, pp. 146–8; Griffiths, pp. 443–54.
6 POPC, V, p. 356.
7 Ibid., p. 361.
8 Griffiths, p. 448.
9 'Protest of Humphrey duke of Gloucester'. This version in modern English is provided by PR 1439, Appendix 2: http://www.british-history.ac.uk/ no-series/parliament-rolls-medieval/november-1439 [accessed 10 January 2017]. A transcription in original language can be found at LP, II (2), pp. 440–51.
10 POPC, V, pp. 388–95.
11 'Protest of Humphrey duke of Gloucester'.
12 Rymer, X, http://www.british-history.ac.uk/rymer-foedera/vol10/ pp763–776 [accessed 16 January 2018].
13 LP, II (2), p. 452.
14 Isabella, duchess of Burgundy, helped Orléans raise the initial payment. Griffiths, pp. 453–4.
15 Wolffe, pp. 158–9.
16 For an alternative interpretation of Beaufort's position see Harriss, *Beaufort*, pp. 307–13.
17 PL, I, p. 40.

Chapter 13. 'Instruments of necromancy'

1 Davies, *English Chronicle*, p. 57.
2 Brut, p. 478.
3 'Brief notes for 1440–43', *EHL*, pp. 340–1; Giles, p. 30; 'Bale's Chronicle', Flenley, p. 115.
4 Davies, *English Chronicle*, p. 57.
5 Carey, Hilary M., *Courting Disaster: Astrology at the English Court and University in the Later Middle Ages* (London, 1992), p. 148.
6 The chronicles vary considerably in their dating of the events of 1441. I follow the chronology used by Griffiths, R. A., 'The trial of Eleanor Cobham: an episode in the fall of Duke Humphrey of Gloucester', *Bulletin of the John Rylands Library* 51 (1968–9).
7 Davies, *English Chronicle*, p. 57; Brut, p. 478.
8 Henry's grandfather, Henry IV, had been faced with a similar necromantic threat in 1401, revolving around a plot to kill him by poisoning his saddle. Carey, *Courting Disaster*, pp. 139–40; Freeman, Jessica, 'Sorcery at court and manor: Margery Jourdemayne, the witch of Eye next Westminster', *Journal of Medieval History* 30, no. 4 (2004), p. 347.

9 For Charles VII's interest in prognostication and astrology, see Vale, M. G. A., *Charles VII* (London, 1974), pp. 43–4.

10 Davies, *English Chronicle*, p. 59; Brut, p. 480; *Great Chronicle*, p. 176.

11 The *English Chronicle* similarly blamed Eleanor's 'pride, false covetousness and lechery' for her downfall. Davies, *English Chronicle*, p. 60.

12 'Julius B II', Kingsford, *Chronicles of London*, p. 73.

13 Davies, *English Chronicle*, p. 60; Nichols, John Gough (ed.), *Chronicle of the Grey Friars of London*, Camden Society 53 (London, 1852), p. 18; 'Bale's Chronicle', Flenley, p. 115; Brut, p. 481; Ellis, Henry (ed.), *Original Letters, illustrative of English History; including numerous royal letters; from autographs in the British Museum, and one or two other collections. With notes and illustrations by Henry Ellis, keeper of the manuscripts in the British Museum*, Second Series in Four Volumes (London, 1827), I, p. 107.

14 'MS Rawlinson B. 355', Flenley, p. 102; Brut, pp. 482, 508; 'Cleopatra C IV', Kingsford, *Chronicles of London*, p. 149; Griffiths, 'The Trial of Eleanor Cobham', p. 395.

15 Curiously, the last of the trio of priests who had carried out their unholy masses in 'hidden and inconvenient places' for Eleanor was completely pardoned. John Home survived to outlive even Henry VI himself. Perhaps his higher social status saved him. Brut, pp. 480–1, 508–9; Davies, *English Chronicle*, p. 60; *Great Chronicle*, p. 176; 'Bale's Chronicle,' Flenley, p. 115.

16 Brut, p. 483; 'Cleopatra C IV', Kingsford, *Chronicles of London*, p. 152.

17 Henry V married at thirty-three, decidedly late for a medieval king. The last English bachelor king had been Richard I, who married aged 31 in 1191. The next monarch to marry so late would be Mary I in 1554. Griffiths, R. A., 'The Sense of Dynasty in the Reign of Henry VI', in Ross, Charles (ed.), *Patronage, Pedigree and Power in Later Medieval England* (Gloucester, 1979), p. 32, n.8.

18 Johnson, *Richard of York*, Appendix II, pp. 226–7.

19 See Griffiths, 'Sense of Dynasty', p. 18.

20 Ferguson, John, *English Diplomacy, 1422–1461* (Oxford, 1972), pp. 48–51, 53–4, 114–15.

21 Also characteristically, Henry's new instructions invalidated his previous commission to the ambassadors, so even though they were 'ready to pass' over the seas they had to wait for a new royal commission before they could depart. Bekynton, pp. 181–4.

22 Ibid., pp. 186–93, 196. For the context of the invasion of Gascony and Armagnac marriage, see Dicks, Samuel E., 'Henry VI and the daughters of Armagnac: A Problem in Medieval Diplomacy', *Emporia State Research Studies: Medieval Renaissance Studies* 15 (1967).

23 Bekynton, p. 243.

24 The youngest of Henry's potential brides was Isabel, who went on to have an incestuous relationship and children with her brother, Jean V count of Armagnac. Dicks, 'Henry VI and the daughters of Armagnac', p. 12.

25 POPC, V, p. 229.
26 Jones, Michael, 'John Beaufort, duke of Somerset and the French Expedition of 1443', in Griffiths, Ralph A. (ed.), *Patronage, the Crown and the Provinces in Later Medieval England* (Stroud, 1981), p. 89.
27 POPC, V, pp. 251–4; Harriss, *Beaufort*, p. 338.
28 POPC, V, pp. 259–64.
29 Jones, 'John Beaufort, duke of Somerset and the French Expedition of 1443', p. 98, n.6.
30 POPC, V, pp. 409–14.
31 ibid., pp. 303, 411.
32 Jones, 'John Beaufort, duke of Somerset and the French Expedition of 1443', p. 95.
33 Ingulph, p. 399.
34 POPC, VI, pp. 20–1.

Chapter 14. 'Welcome... Princess, our lady sovereign'

1 Lydgate, John and Sponsler, Claire (ed.), 'Margaret of Anjou's Entry into London', http://d.lib.rochester.edu/teams/text/sponsler-lydgate-mummings-and-entertainments-appendix-margaret-of-anjous-entry-into-london-1445 [accessed 19 November 2016].
2 Briais, Bernard and Bullard-Axworthy, Marie (trans.), *Tours Throughout History* (Monts, France, 2013), pp. 32, 51.
3 POPC, VI, pp. 32–5.
4 Kekewich, Margaret Lucille, *The Good King: René of Anjou and Fifteenth Century Europe* (Basingstoke, 2008), pp. 7, 15–20, 26, 29, 32, 85–7, 112–13, 155.
5 CSPM, I, no. 26, http://www.british-history.ac.uk/cal-state-papers/milan/1385-1618/pp18-19 [accessed 8 December 2016]; BL, Royal MS. 15 E VI f.2v, http://www.bl.uk/manuscripts/FullDisplay.aspx?ref=Royal_MS_15_E_VI [accessed 30 October 2018]; Dunn, Diana, 'Margaret of Anjou, Queen Consort of Henry VI: A Reassessment of Her Role, 1445–53', in Archer, Rowena E. (ed.), *Crown, Government and People in the Fifteenth Century* (New York, 1995), pp. 110–11; Wolffe, p. 174.
6 Griffiths, p. 486; Wolffe, pp. 177–8.
7 Laynesmith, J. L., *Cecily Duchess of York* (London, 2017), p. 47; Dunn, 'Margaret of Anjou, Queen Consort', p. 131; LP, I, p. 452; Escouchy, pp. 89–90.
8 POPC, VI, p. xvi; LP, I, p. 452; Hookham, Mary Ann, *The Life and Times of Margaret of Anjou, Queen of England and France* (London, 1872), I, pp. 416–20; Rymer, XI, http://www.british-history.ac.uk/rymer-foedera/vol11/pp75-87 [accessed 25 November 2016].
9 'Margaret of Anjou's Entry into London'.
10 Margaret's entry into London is reported (with various confusions over the dating of the event) by Brut, p. 510; 'Bale's Chronicle,'

Flenley, pp. 119–20; Gregory, p. 186; *Great Chronicle*, p. 177; Hall, p. 205; 'Vitellius A XVI', Kingsford, *Chronicles of London*, p. 155. For preparations for Margaret's arrival, see Maurer, p. 19.

11 Rymer, XI, http://www.british-history.ac.uk/rymer-foedera/vol11/ pp75–87 [accessed 25 November 2016]; LP, I, pp. 450, 452; Myers, A. R., 'The Household of Queen Margaret of Anjou, 1452–3', *Bulletin of the John Rylands Library* 40 (1957–8), p. 86.

12 CSPM, I, no. 26, http://www.british-history.ac.uk/cal-state-papers/ milan/1385-1618/pp18-19 [accessed 8 December 2016]; Warnicke, Retha M., 'Henry VIII's Greeting of Anne of Cleves and Early Modern Court Protocol', *Albion: A Quarterly Journal Concerned with British Studies* 28, no. 4 (1996), pp. 577–82.

13 POPC, VI, p. xvi.

14 Rymer, XI, http://www.british-history.ac.uk/rymer-foedera/vol11/ pp75–87 [accessed 25 November 2016].

Chapter 15. 'Stretch forth the hand'

1   LP, I, pp. 164–7.

2   Ibid.

3   'A Relation of the Embassy' is given in LP, I, 88–159. The following is based on that account.

4   For Charles VI's use of 'Jamais' and other devices, including occasionally the broom plant, see Famiglietti, R. C., *Royal Intrigue: Crisis at the Court of Charles VI, 1392–1420* (New York, 1986), p. xv.

5   'A Relation of the Embassy', LP, I, p. 121.

6   Ibid., pp. 103–14, 157–9.

7   Ibid., p. 140.

8   Ibid., p. 141.

9   Ibid., p. 142.

10 KB 9/122/ 28; KB 9/262/1–2, 78; KB 9/260/85; KB 27/ 742/ rex 7.

11 LP, II (2), p. 640.

12 Watts, pp. 222, 223, n.75.

13 Diana Dunn and Helen Maurer both reject the notion that the return of Maine was down to Margaret's pressure on Henry. Dunn, Diana, 'Margaret of Anjou, Queen Consort of Henry VI: A Reassessment of Her Role, 1445–53', in Archer, Rowena E. (ed.), *Crown, Government and People in the Fifteenth Century* (New York, 1995), p. 142; Maurer, pp. 30–8.

14 LP, II (2), p. 451.

15 My italics. The terms of the Treaty of Troyes forbade an alliance with Charles without the assent of the Three Estates of England, i.e. the assent of parliament. PR 1445, items 23–4, http://www.british-history. ac.uk.ezproxy2.londonlibrary.co.uk/no-series/parliament-rolls-medieval/february-1445 [accessed 16 May 2018].

16 Ibid., Appendix 2–3; Pugh, T. B., 'Richard Plantagenet (1411–60),

Duke of York, as the King's Lieutenant in France and Ireland' in Rowe, J. G. (ed.), *Aspects of Late Medieval Government And Society: Essays Presented to J. R. Lander* (Toronto, 1986), pp. 124–5; Barker, Juliet, *Conquest: The English Kingdom of France, 1417–1450* (London, 2010), p. 243; Harriss, *Beaufort*, pp. 357–8.

17 LP, I, p. 123.

Chapter 16. 'The mutability of worldly changes'

1 'On the mutability of worldly changes,' *EHL*, p. 395.

2 For the events surrounding Gloucester's death and the 1447 parliament see Davies, *English Chronicle*, pp. 62–3, 116–8; 'MS Rawlinson B. 355', 'Bale's Chronicle', Flenley, pp. 104, 121; Ellis, Henry (ed.), *Original letters, illustrative of English history; including numerous royal letters; from autographs in the British Museum, and one or two other collections* (London, 1827), I, pp. 108–9; *Hardyng*, p. 400; Brut, pp. 512–13; 'Short English Chronicle,' 'Brief Notes', *Three Fifteenth-Century Chronicles*, pp. 65, 149–50; Waurin, IV, pp. 351–4; Basin, II, pp. 62–3. For the context see PR 1447, Introduction, http://www.british-history.ac.uk/no-series/parliament-rolls-medieval/february-1447 [accessed 2 January 2018].

3 Brut, pp. 512–3. This story is repeated in another London chronicle: 'Vitellius A XVI', Kingsford, p. 157. Closer contemporaries to the event ascribed Gloucester's death to his 'sadness' or 'heaviness' at losing the king's favour. Davies, *English Chronicle*, p. 63; 'Bale's Chronicle,' Flenley, p. 121; *Hardyng*, p. 400; Giles's Chronicle claims that he died of grief. Giles, pp. 33–4.

4 Suffolk and Lord Saye and Sele are held responsible by Basin, II, p. 63; Davies, *English Chronicle*, pp. 62–3; Brut , p. 513; 'Stowe's Memoranda,' *Three Fifteenth-Century Chronicles*, p. 97. Margaret's guilt in ostracizing Gloucester and failing to save him from a noble conspiracy is suggested by Polydore Vergil, pp. 71–2.

5 'Brief Notes,' *Three Fifteenth-Century Chronicles*, p. 149; POPC, VI, p. 51.

6 CPR 1446–52, p. 43; PR 1447, Introduction; Watts, p. 230, n.111; Pugh, T. B., 'Richard Plantagenet (1411–60), Duke of York, as the King's Lieutenant in France and Ireland', in Rowe, J. G. (ed.), *Aspects of Late Medieval Government and Society: Essays Presented to J. R. Lander* (Toronto, 1986), p. 127.

7 Davies, *English Chronicle*, p. 118; Gregory, p. 188; 'MS Rawlinson B. 355', 'Bale's Chronicle,' Flenley, pp. 104, 122; Brut, p. 513; 'Short English Chronicle,' *Three Fifteenth-Century Chronicles*, p. 65; CPR, 1446–52, pp. 74, 104, 110, 112; LP, II (2), pp. 698–702.

8 LP, I, pp. 198–201, 482–3.

9 LP, II (2), pp. 692–6.

10 Ibid., pp. 634–96, 704–10.

11 The letter is undated but internal evidence suggests it was written late in 1447. LP, II (1), pp. 361–8.

12 LP, I, pp. 207–8; Barker, Juliet, *Conquest: The English Kingdom of France, 1417–1450* (London, 2010), pp. 356–7; Griffiths, p. 503.

13 LP, I, p. 208.

14 Barker, *Conquest*, pp. 358–9.

15 PR 1445, item 19, http://www.british-history.ac.uk/no-series/parliament-rolls-medieval/february-1445 [accessed 31 January 2018].

16 Basin, II, pp. 53–7.

17 LP, I, pp. 223–32. For context see Barker, pp. 360–4.

18 For the dating of Somerset's embassy to the Winchester parliament of 1449 see PR early 1449, Introduction, http://www.british-history.ac.uk/no-series/parliament-rolls-medieval/february-1449 [accessed 1 February 2018].

19 PR early 1449, item 17.

20 Griffiths, R. A., 'The Winchester session of the 1449 parliament: a further comment', *Huntingdon Library Quarterly* 42 (1979); Myers, A. R., 'A parliamentary debate of the mid-fifteenth century', *Bulletin of the John Rylands Library* 22 (1938); PR early 1449, Appendices 2, 3.

21 Harriss, G. L., 'Marmaduke Lumley and the Exchequer crisis of 1446–9', in Rowe, J. G. (ed.), *Aspects of Medieval Government and Society* (Toronto, 1986), pp. 168–9. For the general fall in loans to government, see Steel, Anthony, *The Receipt of the Exchequer, 1377–1485* (Cambridge, 1954), pp. 259–64. For royal debts, see PR 1449–50, item 53, http://www.british-history.ac.uk/no-series/parliament-rolls-medieval/november-1449 [accessed 22 November 2016]. For parliamentary unwillingness to give subsidies in 1449, see 'Bale's Chronicle,' Flenley, p. 125; Kleineke, Hannes, 'The Commission De Mutuo Faciendo in the Reign of Henry VI', *English Historical Review* 116, no. 465 (2001), p. 4.

22 POPC, VI, pp. 65–6; LP, I, p. 491; Bain, Joseph (ed.), *Calendar of documents relating to Scotland preserved in Her Majesty's Public Record Office* (Edinburgh, 1881), IV, pp. 245–50; Griffiths, pp. 409–10; Griffiths, 'The Winchester session of the 1449 parliament', p. 188; PR early 1449, Appendix 1.

23 For the causes of waning English enthusiasm for the war see Jones, Michael and Vale, M. G. A. (eds.), *England and her Neighbours, 1066–1453: essays in honour of Pierre Chaplais* (London, 1989); Allmand, Christopher, 'La Normandie Devant l'Opinion Anglaise à la Fin de la Guerre de Cent Ans', *Bibliothèque de l'École des Chartes* 128, no. 2 (1970).

24 LP, I, pp. 213–17. The style of address in question was 'to the most high and powerful prince, the uncle in France of the king, my sovereign lord', which Charles – with some justification – claimed was too imprecise, since Henry had any number of 'uncles in France', including the princes of Orléans, Burgundy and Maine. York, by contrast,

had addressed Charles as 'very high, very excellent and very powerful prince and very formidable lord', at least while he was trying to marry his eldest son to one of the king's daughters. Barker, *Conquest*, p. 364.

Chapter 17. 'Great and grievous reverses and fortunes of war'

1   A minute of the king and his council. *EHD*, IV, p. 244.
2   Basin, II, p. 71; Stevenson, Joseph (ed.), *Narratives of the expulsion of the English from Normandy, M.CCCC.XLIX.-M.CCC.L, Rerum Britannicarum Medii Aevi Scriptores, or Chronicles and Memorials of Great Britain and Ireland during the Middle Ages* (London, 1863), p. 239; Escouchy, p. 154; Basin, II, pp. 69–75; Keen, M. H. and Daniel, M. J., 'English diplomacy and the sack of Fougères in 1449', *History* 59 (1974).
3   LP, I, pp. 278–98; Keen and Daniel, 'English diplomacy and the sack of Fougères in 1449', pp. 376–7, 381–2.
4   POPC, VI, p. 10. For Gilles and Henry's relationship see Morice, Pierre Hyacinthe, *Mémoires Pour Servir de Preuves à l'Histoire Ecclesiastique et Civile de Bretagne*, 3 volumes (Paris, 1742–6), II, pp. 1380–1; POPC, VI, pp. 9–11, 16–7; LP, II (1), pp. 439–41.
5   Bordeaut, A., 'Gilles de Bretagne – Entre la France et l'Angleterre – Les causes et les autuers du drame', in *Mémoires de la Société d'Histoire et d'Archéologie de Bretagne* (Rennes: 1920), I, pp. 54–6; Morice, II, pp. 1362, 1407–8.
6   Morice, II, pp. 1374, 1378–9, 1381–2.
7   Bordeaut, I, pp. 87–95.
8   LP, I, p. 218.
9   Wolffe, pp. 202–4; Morice, I, pp. 1430–7; POPC, VI, pp. 62–4.
10   The expression is stronger in French: '*J'ai le pouvoir de prendre et non de rendre.*' Keen and Daniel, 'English diplomacy and the sack of Fougères in 1449', p. 381.
11   Griffiths, pp. 509–13.
12   Basin, II, pp. 82–3; Stevenson, *Narratives of the Expulsion*, pp. 246–50; 'Bale's Chronicle,' Flenley, p. 125; Escouchy, I, pp. 163–6.
13   Basin, II, pp. 82–3.
14   Ibid., pp. 82–7.
15   Wolffe, p. 209.
16   Bouvier wrote a chronicle about Charles's recovery of Normandy as 'Berry, the King's Herald'. Stevenson, *Narratives of the Expulsion*, p. 258.
17   Ibid., p. 277.
18   Ibid., pp. 258–9; LP, II (2), pp. 619–34.
19   Chartier, Jean, *Chronique de Charles VII. roi de France ... Nouvelle édition* (Paris, 1858), pp. 138–9; Stevenson, *Narratives of the Expulsion*, p. 291; Basin, II, p. 155.
20   Ibid., pp. 115–19; Stevenson, *Narratives of the Expulsion*, pp. 291, 293–6; Chartier, pp. 138–42, 145.

21 Ibid., pp. 155–6.
22 Caen fell in June 1450 and the last city to hold out, Cherbourg, in August 1450. Stevenson, *Narratives of the Expulsion*, pp. 309–11.
23 Ibid., p. 368.

Chapter 18. 'O king, if king you are, rule yourself'

1 Wright, Thomas (ed.), *Political Poems and Songs Relating to English History Composed during the Period from the Accession of Edward III to that of Richard III* (London, 1861), II, p. 291.
2 For Tailboys's attack on Cromwell, see LP, II (2), p. 766; PR 1449–50, item 56, http://www.british-history.ac.uk/no-series/parliament-rolls-medieval/november-1449 [accessed 1 February 2018]. For more context to Tailboys's activities see Virgoe, Roger, 'William Tailboys and Lord Cromwell: Crime and Politics in Lancastrian England', in Barron, Caroline, Rawcliffe, Carole and Rosenthal, Joel T. (eds.), *East Anglian Society and the political community of late medieval England: selected papers of Roger Virgoe* (Norwich, 1997), pp. 287–307.
3 Rawcliffe, Carole, *The Staffords, Earls of Stafford and Dukes of Buckingham, 1394–1521* (Cambridge, 1978), p. 189; Watts, pp. 196–7; Carpenter, Christine, *Locality and Polity: a study of Warwickshire landed society, 1401–1499* (Cambridge, 1992), pp. 412–29; Castor, Helen, *The King, the Crown, and the Duchy of Lancaster: Public Authority and Private Power 1399–1461* (Oxford, 2000), p. 126. For wider context to the Suffolk/Norfolk rivalry see ibid., pp. 83–129.
4 CPR, 1436–41, pp. 133, 532. For an overview of the Bonville–Courtenay dispute see Cherry, M., 'The struggle for power in mid-fifteenth-century Devonshire', in Griffiths, R. A. (ed.), *Patronage, the Crown and the Provinces* (Gloucester, 1981), pp. 123–44; Storey, R. L., *The End of the House of Lancaster* (London, 1966), pp. 85–8.
5 CCR, 1435–41, p. 390, http://www.british-history.ac.uk/cal-close-rolls/hen6/vol3/pp394-400 [accessed 22 November 2016]. Instances of violence around Bonville's estate in 1439 can be found in CPR, 1436–61, pp. 370, 415, 448, 450.
6 Ibid., p. 532.
7 POPC, V, pp. 159–62, 173–5.
8 Bonville returned to England in 1447. POPC, V, pp. 203, 238–9. Griffiths, pp. 575–6.
9 Consent to abduction was a vexed question, and occasionally what at first appear to have been abductions may in fact have been elopements. See Virgoe, Roger, 'The Ravishment of Joan Boys', in Barron, Caroline, Rawcliffe, Carole and Rosenthal, Joel T. (eds.), *East Anglian Society and the Political Community of Late Medieval England: Selected Papers of Roger Virgoe* (Norwich, 1997) for an equivocal example from 1451. The cases cited are taken from PR 1437, items 14–15, http://www.british-history.ac.uk/no-series/parliament-rolls-medieval/january-1437 [accessed 29

August 2016]; PR 1439, item 28, http://www.british-history.ac.uk/no-series/parliament-rolls-medieval/november-1439 [accessed 10 January 2017]; Leadam, I. S. and Baldwin, J. F. (eds.), *Select Cases before the King's Council 1243–1482* (Cambridge, MA, 1918), pp. 106–7; Dunn, Caroline, *Stolen Women in Medieval England: Rape, Abduction and Adultery, 1100–1500* (Cambridge, 2013), pp. 48–9; text of statute given on pp. 200–2.

10 The following is drawn from Meekings, C. A. F., 'Thomas Kerver's Case, 1444', *English Historical Review* 90, no. 355 (1975). I disagree with Meekings's suggestion that Kerver's complaints were an expression more of frustration at English losses in the French war than of popular opinion about Henry's royal incapacity. Kerver was far from alone in suggesting Henry's inept rule in the 1440s. See above, pp. 204–5.

11 Bentley, Samuel (ed.), *Excerpta Historica or Illustrations of English History* (London, 1831), III, p. 281.

12 Capgrave, John and Hingeston, Francis Charles (trans.), *The Book of the Illustrious Henries* (London, 1858), p. 15. For context to this work see Winstead, Karen A., *John Capgrave's Fifteenth Century* (Philadelphia, 2007), p. 158.

13 Henry's planned alterations are revealed in his 'will and intent': Nichols, John, (ed.), *A collection of all the wills, now known to be extant, of the kings and queens of England, princes and princesses of Wales, and every branch of the blood royal, from the reign of William the Conqueror, to that of Henry the Seventh exclusive.* (London, 1780), pp. 295–302.

14 ECR 39 / 75.

15 Wolffe, p. 143; Knoop, Douglas and Jones, G. P., 'The Building of Eton College, 1442–1460', *Ars Quatuor Coronatorum, being the Transactions of the Quatuor Coronati Lodge No. 2076 London*, 46 (London, 1933), pp. 31, 34.

16 Wolffe, p. 98.

17 Myers, A. R., 'Some Household Ordinances of Henry VI', *Bulletin of the John Rylands Library* 36, no. 2 (1954); Myers, A. R., *The Household of Edward IV. The Black Book and the Ordinance of 1478* (Manchester, 1959), pp. 63–6. The ordinances of 1445 are given in full in ibid., pp. 63–75.

18 (1449) CPR 1446–52, p. 262.

19 PR 1445–6, item 21 (in which, ironically, Henry protected his foundation at Eton from any purveyance), http://www.british-history.ac.uk/no-series/parliament-rolls-medieval/february-1445 [accessed 31 January 2018].

20 TNA, KB 9/256/13; Dunn, Diana, 'Margaret of Anjou, Queen Consort of Henry VI: A Reassessment of Her Role, 1445–53', in Archer, Rowena E. (ed.), *Crown, Government and People in the Fifteenth Century* (New York, 1995), p. 107.

21 TNA, KB9/260/85.

22 *Ryalle Boke*, pp. 313–14.
23 The connection between Margaret's fasting and fertility is made by Maurer, pp. 42–3. The quote is from 'Vatican Regesta 527: 1467', in Twemlow, J. A. (ed.), *Calendar of Papal Registers Relating to Great Britain and Ireland: Volume 12, 1458–1471* (London: 1933), http://www.british-history.ac.uk/cal-papal-registers/brit-ie/vol12/pp269–283 [accessed 23 February 2017]. For examples of Henry and Margaret's pilgrimages to Canterbury see Searle, William George (ed.), *Christ Church, Canterbury. I. The Chronicle of John Stone, Monk of Christ Church 1415–1471* (Cambridge, 1902), pp. 39–43, 50–2, 56.

Chapter 19. 'Beware, King Henry, how thou do, let no longer thy traitors go loose'

1   Wright, Thomas (ed.), *Political Poems and Songs Relating to English History Composed during the Period from the Accession of Edward III to that of Richard III* (London, 1861), II, p. 230.
2   'MS Rawlinson B. 355', 'Bale's Chronicle,' Flenley, pp. 106, 127; Gregory, p. 189; Davies, *English Chronicle*, p. 64; Benet, p. 196; CPR, 1446–52, p. 297; Smith, Bill, 'Moleyns, Adam (d.1450)', *ODNB*, http://www.oxforddnb.com/view/article/18918 [accessed 6 Feb 2017].
3   The proceedings against Suffolk in parliament are provided by the parliament roll for 1449–50, http://www.british-history.ac.uk/no-series/parliament-rolls-medieval/november-1449 [accessed 22 November 2016].
4   Ibid., items 14–15.
5   Under attainder law, the wife of an attainted traitor could retain her own inheritance and jointure but not her dower or any lands held to the use of her husband. See Johnson, Lauren, 'The Impact of the Wars of the Roses on Noblewomen', MSt diss., University of Oxford, 2007, pp. 11–12.
6   PR 1449, item 27.
7   Ibid., items 29–46.
8   Ibid., item 48. Suffolk was 'guarded' by three royal servants: William Mynors, John Stanley and Thomas Staunton, esquires.
9   Ibid., item 50. The description in the parliament roll of the 'inner chamber which had a gable window over a cloister within his palace of Westminster' where this meeting took place is unusually precise.
10 Ibid., items 50–1.
11 The Lords were also concerned to retain their right to trial by their peers rather than by royal judgment. Ibid., item 52.
12 LP, II (2), p. 767.
13 Virgoe, Roger, 'The Death of William de la Pole, duke of Suffolk', *Bulletin of the John Rylands Library*, 47 (1965), p. 491. 'Bale's Chronicle,' Flenley, p. 128 says Suffolk 'privily got away' from Westminster on 25 March, which seems too late, given Frammesley's rising on 21 March;

LP, I, pp. 515–16 contains an order for Suffolk's dispatch dated 19 March.

14 CPR, 1446–52, pp. 380. Ironically, the entry just above this one in the Patent Rolls (dated 3 April) demands the arresting of a ship called the *Nicholas of the Tower*, to be armed 'to resist the king's enemies'. For Blondell and Spenser see Virgoe, 'The Death of William de la Pole, duke of Suffolk', p. 492, n.5–6.

15 PL, I, pp. 121–2.

16 In February 1453 an indictment was brought against two sailors for involvement in Suffolk's murder. The men said they did not recognize Henry as king, but only knew the crown of England to be embodied by the 'community of the realm' and they anticipated the return of Richard, duke of York (then in Ireland) to reform government once Suffolk was dead. Despite this tantalizing detail, York's complicity in Suffolk's death cannot be asserted with certainty. By 1450 the *Nicholas of the Tower* was to all intents and purposes a pirate ship, and its fateful interception of Suffolk's flotilla may have occurred entirely by chance. See Virgoe, 'The Death of William de la Pole, duke of Suffolk', pp. 495–502. PL, I, pp. 124–5; Davies, *English Chronicle*, p. 69; 'MS Rawlinson B. 355', 'Bale's Chronicle,' Flenley, pp. 105, 129; Benet, p. 198; Giles, p. 38; 'Short English Chronicle,' *Three Fifteenth-Century Chronicles*, p. 66; Brut, p. 516; Gregory, p. 190, which has Suffolk's body and head being thrown in the sea; *Great Chronicle*, p. 181.

17 'John Piggot's Memoranda,' *EHL*, p. 371; PL, I, pp. 124–6.

18 Wright, *Political Poems*, II, p. 232.

Chapter 20. 'The harvest of heads'

1   Gregory, p. 195.

2   *Gregory's Chronicle* says the king had 10,000 in his retinue; Benet says 20,000 and Davies 15,000. Gregory, p. 191; Benet, p. 199; Davies, *English Chronicle*, p. 66.

3   Harvey, I. M. W., *Jack Cade's Rebellion of 1450* (Oxford, 1991), p. 84; Devon, Frederick, *Issues of the Exchequer being a collection of payments made out of His Majesty's revenue, from King Henry III to King Henry VI inclusive* (London, 1837), p. 274.

4   Benet says 50,000 men from Kent; Flenley says 100,000; Gregory 46,000. Benet, p. 198; 'Bale's Chronicle,' Flenley, p. 129; Gregory, p. 190. Davies, *English Chronicle*, p. 64; Brut, p. 517.

5   CPR, 1446–52, p. 385.

6   'MS Gough London 10', Flenley, pp. 153–4; Benet, p. 198 gives 11 June as the date, which is supported by Griffiths, p. 611. 'Bale's Chronicle,' Flenley, p. 129 has the Kentish commons arriving on 12 June.

7   'Bale's Chronicle,' 'MS Gough London 10', Flenley, pp. 129, 153–4; Gregory, p. 195; Benet, p. 197.

NOTES TO PAGES 252–264

8   Benet, p. 198; 'Bale's Chronicle,' Flenley, pp. 129–30; Griffiths, p. 611.
9   'Stowe's Memoranda,' *Three Fifteenth-Century Chronicles*, p. 96.
10 Griffiths, pp. 619, 623.
11 The 'English Chronicle' mistakenly names them Sir *Edmund* and
    William Stafford. Davies, *An English Chronicle*, p. 131.
12 'MS Gough London 10', Flenley, p. 154.
13 Ibid.
14 'Bale's Chronicle,' Flenley, pp. 131–2; Benet, p. 199; 'Short English
    Chronicle,' *Three Fifteenth-Century Chronicles*, p. 67; 'Vitellius A XVI',
    Kingsford, *Chronicles of London*, p. 159; Davies, *An English Chronicle*,
    pp. 65–6; Giles, p. 40; Brut, p. 517. For the activities of Stanley and
    his fellow household officers in Kent see Virgoe, R., 'Some Ancient
    Indictments in the King's Bench referring to Kent, 1450–1452', in
    Du Boulay, F. R. H. (ed.), *Kent Records: Documents Illustrative of Medieval
    Kentish Society* (Ashford, 1964).
15 Giles, p. 40; 'Short English Chronicle,' *Three Fifteenth-Century Chroni-
    cles*, p. 67; 'Vitellius A XVI', Kingsford, *Chronicles of London*, p. 159;
    Brut, p. 518; *Great Chronicle*, p. 183; 'MS Gough London 10,' Flenley,
    p. 154; Harvey, p. 86.
16 PL, I, pp. 134–5.
17 When a pardon was offered to the rebels on 6 July, it was made 'at
    the request of the Queen'. Kempe and Stafford are mentioned by
    chroniclers as directly negotiating with the rebels. William Waynflete,
    bishop of Winchester, is also named by Gregory and Thomas Kempe,
    bishop of London, by Giles. CPR, 1446–52, p. 338; 'MS Gough
    London 10,' Flenley, p. 156; 'Short English Chronicle', p. 68; 'Vitellius
    A XVI', Kingsford, *Chronicles of London*, p. 161; Brut, p. 519; Benet,
    p. 201; Giles, p. 41. Wolffe suggests Margaret was still at Greenwich,
    and Griffiths that she stayed behind in London. Maurer, pp. 71–2;
    Griffiths, p. 662, n.215; Wolffe, p. 238. Dunn disagrees, interpreting
    the pardon as mere form. Dunn, Diana, 'Margaret of Anjou, Queen
    Consort of Henry VI: A Reassessment of Her Role, 1445–53', in
    Archer, Rowena E. (ed.), *Crown, Government and People in the Fifteenth
    Century* (New York, 1995), pp. 142–3.
18 Benet, p. 199; Davies, *English Chronicle*, p. 64.
19 Davies, *English Chronicle*, p. 66.
20 Brut, p. 519; 'Vitellius A XVI', Kingsford, *Chronicles of London*, p. 160;
    'MS Rawlinson B. 355', 'MS Gough London 10,' Flenley, pp. 105–6,
    155–6; 'Short English Chronicle,' *Three Fifteenth-Century Chronicles*,
    p. 67; Benet, p. 200.
21 Benet, p. 200; 'MS Rawlinson B. 355', 'MS Gough London 10,' Flenley,
    pp. 106, 133–4, 156; 'Vitellius A XVI', Kingsford, *Chronicles of London*,
    p. 161; Davies, *English Chronicle*, p. 67; 'Short English Chronicle,' *Three
    Fifteenth-Century Chronicles*, p. 68; Brut, p. 519.
22 CPR, 1446–52, p. 338.
23 'Short English Chronicle,' *Three Fifteenth-Century Chronicles*, p. 68.

24   A Sussex garden is mentioned by 'Short English Chronicle,' *Three Fifteenth-Century Chronicles*, p. 68; 'Vitellius A XVI', Kingsford, *Chronicles of London*, p. 162; Brut, p. 519. 'MS Gough London 10,' Flenley, p. 156, says Iden took Cade 'beside Maidstone'; Greyfriars, p. 19 says he was slain 'in Kent'; Gregory, p. 196 gives the Weald in Sussex. Nichols, John Gough (ed.), *Chronicle of the Grey Friars of London*, Camden Society 53 (London, 1852), p. 19; Benet, p. 201; Gregory, p. 196; Rymer, XI, http://www.british-history.ac.uk/rymer-foedera/vol11/pp273–279 [accessed 24 January 2017].

25   Gregory, p. 196.

26   'MS Gough London 10,' Flenley, pp. 156–7; 'Vitellius A XVI', Kingsford, *Chronicles of London*, p. 162; Davies, *English Chronicle*, p. 68.

27   'Bale's Chronicle', Flenley, p. 134; Benet, p. 202.

28   Griffiths, pp. 641–2.

29   Bouchard, A., *Les Grandes Croniques de Bretaigne, noubellement imprisonées à Paris, tant de la Grande Bretaigne de puis le roy Brutus qui la conduist et Les grandes Annalles ou Cronicques parlans tant de la grant bretaigne a present nōmee Angleterre que de nostre petite Bretaigne de present erigee en duché. Commencantz au Roy Brutus ... dan en an depuis ledict Brutus ... Iusques aux ans de present, etc.* (Paris, 1514), pp. ccxcvi–ccxcvii.

Chapter 21. 'The true blood of the realm'

1   'Stowe's Memoranda,' *Three Fifteenth-Century Chronicles*, p. 97.

2   Eleanor was transferred to Beaumaris on 10 March 1449 as a result of Scottish attacks on the Isle of Man, where she was formerly imprisoned. Griffiths, Ralph, 'Richard of York and the Royal Household in Wales, 1449–50' *The Welsh History Review* 8, No. 1 (1976), p. 24.

3   For York's failed landing at Beaumaris I follow Johnson, *Richard of York*, p. 78. Griffiths and Wolffe suggest that York *did* land at Beaumaris. Griffiths, p. 686; Wolffe, p. 241; Giles, p. 42; LP, II (2), p. 769. For Henry's response to York's return see Griffiths, 'Richard of York and the Royal Household in Wales', pp. 16–21.

4   Pugh, T. B., 'Richard Plantagenet (1411–60), Duke of York, as the King's Lieutenant in France and Ireland', in Rowe, J. G. (ed.), *Aspects of Late Medieval Government and Society: Essays Presented to J. R. Lander* (Toronto, 1986), p. 123.

5   The yeomen were Thomas Johnson of Driffield, Yorkshire and John Langley of Barton on Humber, Lincolnshire. Johnson, *Richard of York*, p. 79.

6   Griffiths, R. A., 'Duke Richard of York's Intentions in 1450 and the Origins of the Wars of the Roses', *Journal of Medieval History* 1, no. 2 (1975), pp. 191–2. For Buckingham's meeting with York see Griffiths, Ralph, 'Richard, duke of York and the crisis of Henry VI's household in 1450–1: some further evidence', *Journal of Medieval History* 38, no.2 (2012), p. 246.

7   Vale, p. 189.
8   For York's bills and their context see Hicks, Michael, 'From mega-phone to microscope: The correspondence of Richard duke of York with Henry VI in 1450 revisited', *Journal of Medieval History* 25, no. 3 (1999), pp. 243–56; Griffiths, 'Duke Richard of York's Intentions', pp. 187–209; Vale, pp. 185–90.
9   Tresham's 'grief-stricken widow' Isabella brought a petition for jus-tice against her husband's killers in the parliament of 1450–1. PR 1450–1, items 8–9, http://www.british-history.ac.uk/no-series/parlia-ment-rolls-medieval/november-1450 [accessed 22 May 2017]. See also 'Piggot's Memoranda,' *EHL*, p. 372.
10 'Bale's Chronicle', Flenley, p. 135; Johnson, *Richard of York*, p. 84, n.35; Griffiths, p. 646; Griffiths, 'Duke Richard of York's intentions', pp. 198–9.
11 Giles, p. 42.
12 Ibid.
13 Vale, p. 190; Griffiths, 'Duke Richard of York's Intentions', pp. 204–6; Hicks, 'From Megaphone to Microscope', p. 248.
14 Basin, II, p. 67.
15 Ibid., pp. 67–9; Annales, p. 770.
16 Jones, Michael K., 'Somerset, York and the Wars of the Roses', *English Historical Review* 104, no. 411 (1989), p. 304.
17 Storey, R. L., *The End of the House of Lancaster* (London, 1966), p. 79; Richmond, Colin, 'Mowbray, John, third duke of Norfolk (1415–1461)', *ODNB*, https://doi.org/10.1093/ref:odnb/19454 [accessed 20 May 2018]; Griffiths, p. 689.
18 Johnson, *Richard of York*, p. 86.
19 Gregory, p. 195; 'Bale's Chronicle,' Flenley, p. 137; Annales, p. 770.
20 PR 1450–1, item 16.
21 LP, II (2), p. 475; 'Bale's Chronicle,' Flenley, p. 136; PR 1450–1.
22 Young made his petition late in parliament's last session, in summer 1451. Nicolas, N. H. and Tyrrell, Edward (eds.), *A Chronicle of London, from 1089 to 1483* (London, 1827), p. 137; Annales, p. 770; Johnson, *Richard of York*, p. 98.
23 'Bale's Chronicle', Flenley, p. 137; Benet, p. 203.
24 Benet, p. 203; Annales, p. 769; 'John Piggot's Memoranda', *EHL*, p. 370; Giles, p. 42; 'MS Rawlinson B. 344', 'Bale's Chronicle', 'MS Gough London 10,' Flenley, pp. 106, 137, 157; 'Vitellius A XVI', Kingsford, *Chronicles of London*, p. 162; Gregory, p. 196; Waurin, V, pp. 264–5. For further attacks on Somerset's property see Jones, 'Somer-set, York and the Wars of the Roses', p. 288.
25 'Extract from London Chronicle,' *EHL*, p. 297; 'Vitellius A XVI', Kingsford, *Chronicles of London*, p. 162; Gregory, p. 196; Griffiths, p. 648; Johnson, *Richard of York*, p. 90.
26 Gregory, p. 196. This chronicle misdates most of the events surround-ing the ransacking of Somerset's house by a day.

27 One Yorkist London chronicle suggests York tried to save Somerset's life, but this partisan story is not corroborated by other sources. See Jones, 'Somerset, York and the Wars of the Roses', p. 287; Benet, p. 203; 'MS Rawlinson B. 355', Flenley, p. 106.
28 'Bale's Chronicle,' Flenley, p. 136; PR 1450–1, Introduction.

Chapter 22. 'My most dread sovereign lord'

1 PR 1453, item 49, http://www.british-history.ac.uk/no-series/parlia-ment-rolls-medieval/march-1453 [accessed 30 May 2017].
2 Storey, R. L., *The End of the House of Lancaster* (London, 1966), pp. 89–90.
3 Wolffe, p. 248.
4 Davies, *English Chronicle*, p. 68; Griffiths, p. 643.
5 'Piggot's Memoranda,' *EHL*, p. 372.
6 Griffiths, pp. 529–530.
7 Storey, p. 89.
8 Annales, p. 770; Benet, p. 204; Wolfe, p. 252.
9 Storey, pp. 94–5.
10 Kempe, Alfred John (ed.), *Historical Notices of the Collegiate Church, or Royal Free Chapel and Sanctuary of St. Martin-Le-Grand, London* (London, 1825), pp. 138–41.
11 PL, I, p. 96.
12 Kempe, *Historical Notices of the Collegiate Church*, p. 140.
13 *EHD*, IV, pp. 269–70.
14 Johnson, *Richard of York*, p.109.
15 Ibid., pp. 107–10; Storey, pp. 94–100.
16 POPC, VI, pp. 90–2.
17 Benet, p. 206; Davies, *English Chronicle*, p. 69.
18 Benet, pp. 206–7; 'Extract from London Chronicle,' 'Yorkist Partisan,' *EHL*, pp.297, 367. Davies, *English Chronicle*, p. 69, suggests the more conservative sum of 15,000 men being in the king's host. In general, sources agree that Henry's forces outnumbered York's.
19 Bishop William Waynflete of Winchester, Lord John Beauchamp of Powick and Ralph Botiller, Lord Sudeley, were also among the envoys. Benet, p. 207; 'Vitellius A XVI', Kingsford, *Chronicles of London*, p. 163; 'Yorkist Partisan,' 'Piggot's Memoranda,' *EHL*, pp. 367, 373; Waurin, V, pp. 265–6.
20 Later sources claimed that York was duped into his submission by false promises that Somerset would be tried for his crimes, but Henry's consistent protection of his chief minister belies such claims. That the painfully honest king would allow such a trick is in any case hard to believe, let alone the unlikelihood that his negotiators – most of them relatives or friends of York's – would enable it. Compare Benet, p. 207; 'MS Rawlinson B. 355', Flenley, p. 107; Davies, *English Chronicle*, p. 70; 'Piggot's Memoranda,' *EHL*, p. 373; Giles, p. 43 with the later

London chronicles, many of them sharing sources: *Great Chronicle*, p. 186; 'Short English Chronicle', *Three Fifteenth-Century Chronicles*, p. 69; Nicholas, *Chronicle of London*, p. 138; Fabyan, Robert and Ellis, Henry (ed.), *The new chronicles of England and France, in two parts; by Robert Fabyan. Named by himself the concordance of histories. Reprinted from Pynson's edition of 1516. The first part collated with the editions of 1533, 1542, and 1559; and the second with a manuscript of the author's own time, as well as the subsequent editions: including the different continuations* (London, 1811), p. 627.

21 PL, I, p. 101.
22 POPC, VI, pp. 119–21; CPR 1446–52, pp. 512–13, 537.
23 'Yorkist Partisan', *EHL*, p. 367; Benet, p. 207; Griffiths, p. 697; Wolffe, pp. 257–8.
24 'MS Rawlinson B. 355', Flenley, p. 107. Henry's general pardons and 'rigorous punishment' are mentioned, without the dramatic flourish of a snowscape, by Giles, pp. 43–4; Benet, p. 207. Henry had similarly stood in judgement over a group of Kentish rebels condemned in February 1451 for 'plotting the death of the king and the destruction of the realm': CPR 1446–52, p. 453.
25 For Henry's itinerary see Wolffe, pp. 259–61.

Chapter 23. 'The most precious, most joyful and most comfortable earthly treasure that might come unto this land'

1 A letter from Cecily, duchess of York to Margaret of Anjou in 1453. Rawcliffe, Carole, 'Richard, duke of York, the King's "obeisant liege-man": A New Source for the protectorates of 1454–1455', *Historical Research* 60 (1987), p. 241.
2 Mary was the illegitimate daughter of John, duke of Bedford. Pierre de Montferrand, often known by the title of Lord de la Sparre, was to remain a committed Anglophile and he eventually forfeited his goods and his life to the cause. On 12 July 1454 he was executed on the orders of Charles VII. In 1457 Mary was granted a 25-mark annual pension by King Henry. By that point, she claimed to have lost all her 'lands, possessions [...and] moveable goods, not having now anything to live on'. LP, II (2), pp. 508–9.
3 Vale, M. G. A., 'The Last Years of English Gascony, 1451–1453: The Alexander Prize Essay', *TRHS* 19 (1969), pp. 124–30, 137–8.
4 Benet, p. 207; Vale, M. G. A., *English Gascony, 1399–1453: A Study of War, Government and Politics during the Later Stages of the Hundred Years War* (Oxford, 1970), p. 141.
5 5 November 1442. Rymer, X, http://www.british-history.ac.uk/rymer-foedera/vol10/pp817–834 [accessed 24 February 2017]; Bush, Ruth, 'Pole, Katherine de la (1410/11–1473)', *ODNB*, http://www.oxforddnb.com/view/article/54452 [accessed 23 March 2017].
6 Blacman, pp. 30–1.

7   PR 1453, item 50, http://www.british-history.ac.uk/no-series/parliament-rolls-medieval/march-1453 [accessed 27 March 2017].

8   The other knights were Roger Lewkenor and William Catesby. Griffiths, p. 699.

9   Annales, p. 770; Benet, p. 208; PR 1453, items 50–3; Cunningham, W. R., Stamp, Alfred Edward, Trimmer, R. D., Crump, Charles G. and Lyte, H. C. Maxwell, *Calendar of the Charter Rolls preserved in the Public Record Office prepared under the superintendence of the deputy keeper of the records, Volume VI: 5 Henry VI- 8 Henry VIII. AD 1427–1516. With an appendix, AD. 1215–1288* (London, 1927), p. 122.

10 Benet, p. 209; CPR, 1452–61, pp. 78–9.

11 Myers, A. R., 'The Jewels of Queen Margaret Of Anjou', *Bulletin of the John Rylands Library* 42, no.1 (1959), p. 124.

12 PR 1455, item 47, http://www.british-history.ac.uk/no-series/parliament-rolls-medieval/july-1455 [accessed 10 May 2017]; LP, II (2), pp. 507–8.

13 Rawcliffe, 'Richard, duke of York, the King's "obeisant liegeman"', pp. 232–9; Maurer, p. 44.

14 For Margaret's personal attention to her own estates see Monro, Cecil (ed.), *Letters of Queen Margaret of Anjou and Bishop Beckington and others. Written in the reigns of Henry V and Henry VI* (London, 1863), pp. 98–9, 122–3, 126–8. For the other rights granted to Margaret see Maurer, p. 44.

15 Henry's reply was given at the end of the second session, 2 July, before parliament was prorogued for the summer. PR 1453, item 20, http://www.british-history.ac.uk/no-series/parliament-rolls-medieval/march-1453 [accessed 30 May 2017].

16 Ibid., item 15.

17 Ibid., Appendix 14.

18 Ibid., Appendix 36.

19 Ibid., items 63–4.

20 Johnson, *Richard of York*, p. 121.

21 The precise reason for Henry's journey west is unclear, but given his recent activities to restore order to the realm a judicial cause seems likely. Wolffe suggests the immediate impetus was the contest between Warwick and Somerset. See Wolffe, pp. 269–70; Griffiths, pp. 698, 715.

PART III: 'A KINGDOM DIVIDED AGAINST ITSELF'

1   CSPM, no. 37, http://www.british-history.ac.uk/cal-state-papers/milan/1385-1618/pp21-37 [accessed 20 June 2017].

Chapter 24. 'The beginning of sorrows'

1   Annales, p. 770.

2   Vallet de Viriville, Auguste (ed.), *Chronique de Charles VII Roi de France*

par Jean Chartier. Nouvelle édition revue sur les manuscrit suivie de divers fragmens inédits (Paris, 1858), III, p. 7. The following is based on reports of the siege and battle provided in ibid., pp. 1–7; Escouchy, II, pp. 35–43; Basin, II, pp. 189–201; 'Lettre sur la bataille de Castillon en Périgord, 19 Juillet 1453', *Bibliothèque de l'école des chartes* 8 (1847), pp. 245–7; Monstrelet, II, pp. 222–6.

3   'Lettre sur la bataille de Castillon', p. 247.

4   These grisly details are provided by Escouchy, II, pp. 41–3.

5   Basin, II, p. 201.

6   Bale's Chronicle suggests that Henry was already physically 'indisposed' before his mental collapse. 'Bale's Chronicle,' Flenley, p. 140.

7   Giles, p. 44; Whethamstede, p. 163. My thanks to Dr Joanna Phillips and Dr Claire Trenery, specialists in the history of medicine, for reading an early draft of this section and offering their feedback.

8   Henry's condition was reported to parliament by a delegation of lords who visited him in March 1454. See PR 1453, http://www.british-history.ac.uk/no-series/parliament-rolls-medieval/march-1453 [accessed 30 May 2017]. John Stodeley wrote of Margaret and Buckingham's visit to Henry in December 1453, PL, 1, p. 263. Abbot Whethamstede of St Albans may have been an eyewitness, and wrote a description of Henry's condition in his chronicle; Whethamstede, p. 163.

9   For the suggestion that Charles VI had schizophrenia see Famiglietti, R.C., *Royal Intrigue: Crisis at the Court of Charles VI, 1392–1420* (New York, 1986), pp. 7–10. The most definitive schizophrenia diagnosis for Henry is given by Bark, N., 'Did schizophrenia change the course of English history? The mental illness of Henry VI', *Medical Hypotheses* 59, no. 4 (2002). The likelihood of Henry suffering from a manic-depressive stupor is argued by Green, Vivian, *The Madness of Kings: Personal Trauma and the Fate of Nations* (Stroud, 1993), pp. 60–9.

10   The monk of St Denis functioned almost as an official royal historian and was well placed to observe Charles's changeable mental health. Bellaguet, M. L. (trans.), *Chronique du Religieux de Saint-Denis, contenant le Règne de Charles VI, de 1380 à 1422* (Paris, 1840), II, p. 405.

11   It is often said that Charles VI believed he was made of glass, but this seems to be a misunderstanding reported long after his death by Pope Pius II. French contemporaries do not record a glass delusion, but they do note that Charles wore a piece of iron under his clothes, probably to prevent assassination by the attackers he believed were lurking in his palace. Inspired no doubt by the glass delusions of others, Pius wrongly interpreted this iron as a rod that Charles believed was holding his glass form together. For Charles's symptoms see Bellaguet, II, pp. 405, 545; Michaud, J. F. (ed.) and Poujoulat, J. J. F., 'Histoire de Charles VI, roy de France, par Jean Juvenal des Ursins', *Nouvelle Collection des Mémoires pour servir à l'histoire de France depuis le XIIIe siècle jusqu'à la fin du XVIIIe* (Paris, 1836), II, pp. 394–5, 398, 437–8; Gragg, Florence Alden (trans.) and Gabel, Leona C. (ed.), *The Commentaries of*

Pius II: Books VI–IX, Smith College Studies in History 35 (Northampton, MA, 1951), VI, pp. 425–6. For context to the glass delusion, see Speak, Gill, 'An odd kind of melancholy: reflections on the glass delusion in Europe (1440–1680)', *History of Psychiatry* 1 (1990).

12 Even then, Charles occasionally did recognize his visitors, most notably the duchess of Orléans and certain members of his household. Michaud and Poujoulat, II, p. 394; Bellaguet, p. 405.

13 The commission to Henry's doctors was given in March 1454. POPC, VI, pp. 166–7.

14 Trenery, Claire and Horden, Peregrine, 'Madness in the Middle Ages', in Eghigian, Greg (ed.), *The Routledge History of Madness and Mental Health* (London, 2017), pp. 66–7. I am grateful to Dr Trenery for providing me with a copy of her article and for discussing Henry's mental health within the context of her research.

15 Rawcliffe, Carole, 'The Insanity of Henry VI', *The Historian* 50 (1996), p. 11.

16 Among the royally appointed alchemists were William Hatcliffe, Margaret's physician; Gilbert Kymer, a surgeon who attended Henry; John Faceby, Henry's physician; and John Kirkby, a royal chaplain. Hughes, Jonathan, *Arthurian Myth and Alchemy: The Kingship of Edward IV* (Stroud, 2002), pp. 49–53.

17 Bellaguet, pp. 405, 543, 669.

18 Myers, A. R., 'The household of Queen Margaret of Anjou, 1452–3', *Bulletin of the John Rylands Library* 40, no. 2 (1957–8), p. 418; Waurin, V, pp. 264–6; Watts, p. 294 n.144; Maurer, pp. 90–3 explores Somerset and Margaret's relationship.

19 POPC, VI, p. 164.

20 Maurer, p. 93.

Chapter 25. 'Misrule doth rise'

1 John Hardyng's Chronicle. Quoted in Scattergood, V. J., *Politics and Poetry in the Fifteenth Century* (London, 1971), p. 175.

2 For the context to the Neville–Percy feud see Griffiths, Ralph A., 'Local Rivalries and National Politics: The Percies, the Nevilles, and the duke of Exeter, 1452–1455', *Speculum* 43, no. 4 (1968); Storey, R. L., *The End of the House of Lancaster* (London, 1966), pp. 124–41.

3 Griffiths, 'Local Rivalries', p. 597, quoting a Whitby annalist.

4 POPC, VI, pp. 140–1, 147–9, 159–61.

5 Hunter, Joseph, *Three Catalogues, Describing the Contents of the Red Book of the Exchequer of the Dodsworth Manuscripts in the Bodleian Library, and of the Manuscripts in the Library of the Honourable Society of Lincoln's Inn* (London, 1838), pp. 277–8. For context to this ritual see Laynesmith, J. L., *Cecily Duchess of York* (London, 2017), pp. 62–3.

6 Helen Maurer has shown that Margaret was careful to maintain the appearance of even-handedness in her ritual acts, like gift giving,

even where tensions existed with the recipient; Maurer, pp. 85–90.

7 York arrived in London on 12 November and Margaret's churching took place on 18 November. 'Bale's Chronicle,' Flenley, p. 140; Benet, p. 210; Davies, *English Chronicle*, p. 70; Devon, *Exchequer*, p. 478; TNA E 101/410/12; *Ryalle Boke*, pp. 305–6; Leland, John, *Joannis Lelandi antiquarii De rebus Britannicis Collectanea cum Thomae Hearnii Praefatione Notis et Indice ad Editionem primam: Editio Alterta* (Farnborough, 1970), IV, pp. 179–82.

8 The letter is undated. Laynesmith suggests it was written before Henry's illness, but it is possible that if the duke and duchess of York did not know the seriousness of the king's condition the letter may have been sent later. Maurer suggests a date in late summer or early autumn. Laynesmith, *Cecily Duchess of York*, p. 203, n.66; Maurer, p. 90. For the text of the letter see Rawcliffe, Carole, 'Richard, duke of York, the King's "obeisant liegeman": A New Source for the protectorates of 1454–1455', *Historical Research* 60 (1987), pp. 237–8.

9 POPC, VI, pp. 163–4. Of the nine councillors responsible for the letter to York only one had obvious sympathy with his cause: Richard Beauchamp, bishop of Salisbury. The rest seem to have been inspired by the legitimacy of doing so. Johnson, *Richard Duke of York*, p. 125. For the councillors' connections to Margaret, see Maurer, p. 96.

10 PR 1453, item 22, http://www.british-history.ac.uk/no-series/parliament-rolls-medieval/march-1453 [accessed 30 May 2017].

11 PL, I, pp. 259–61. See also Giles, p. 68; Benet, p. 210.

12 PL, I, p. 263.

13 Ibid.

14 Laynesmith, J. L., *The Last Medieval Queens: English Queenship 1445–1503* (Oxford, 2004), pp. 157–9; Poulet, André, 'Capetian Women and the Regency: The Genesis of a Vocation', in Parsons, J. C. (ed.), *Medieval Queenship* (Stroud, 1994), pp. 114–15; Kekewich, Margaret Lucille, *The Good King: René of Anjou and Fifteenth Century Europe* (Basingstoke, 2008), pp. 7, 17–18, 29–32.

15 Maurer, pp. 108–10.

16 This is based on the report given by the lords in Parliament on 27 March 1454. PR 1453, items 31–2.

17 Rymer, XI, http://www.british-history.ac.uk/rymer-foedera/vol11/pp344–360 [accessed 10 February 2017].

18 For the possible dating of this letter, and its connection to Margaret's bid for the regency, see Maurer, pp. 106, 216–21.

19 Maurer, p. 115.

20 'Bale's Chronicle', Flenley, p. 141; Benet, p. 212.

21 Storey, *The End of the House of Lancaster*, p. 140; Griffiths, p. 727.

22 POPC, VI, pp. 206–7.

23 Wolffe, p. 282; POPC, VI, pp. 189–91, 217–18; 'Vitellius A XVI', Kingsford, *Chronicles of London*, p. 164; 'MS Gough London 10,' Flenley, p. 158; Giles, pp. 45–6; Benet, p. 211.

24 Beaumont was attending council meetings by July 1454. Griffiths, Ralph A., 'The King's Council and the first Protectorate of the duke of York, 1453–1454', *English Historical Review* 99, no. 390 (1984).

25 Wolffe, pp 284–5.

26 PL, I, p. 303.

27 From 3 February Henry's sign manual reappears. Wolffe, p. 285.

28 PL, I, pp. 315–16. Clere placed Henry's recovery on Christmas Day; Benet, p. 212 and 'MS Gough London 10,' Flenley, p. 158 say that Henry recovered on the last day of December.

29 'Bale's Chronicle,' Flenley, p. 141.

30 Lord Fitzwarin also gave surety for Somerset's bail. Rymer, XI http://www.british-history.ac.uk/rymer-foedera/vol11/pp360–370 [accessed 14 May 2017]; Benet, pp. 212–13; Giles, p. 47.

31 Giles, p. 47; 'MS Gough London 10,' Flenley, p. 158; Benet, p. 213.

32 Monro, Cecil (ed.), *Letters of Queen Margaret of Anjou and Bishop Beckington and others. Written in the reigns of Henry V and Henry VI* (London, 1863), pp. 90–1; Maurer, 'Appendix II', pp. 216–19.

33 Armstrong, C. A. J., 'Politics and the Battle of St Albans, 1455', *Bulletin of the Institute of Historical Research* 33, no. 87 (1960), p. 17.

Chapter 26. 'The sword of vengeance'

1   Whethamstede, p. 176.

2   Unless otherwise stated, the information about the Battle of St Albans is drawn from Armstrong, C. A. J., 'Politics and the Battle of St Albans, 1455', *Bulletin of the Institute of Historical Research* 33, no. 87 (1960).

3   Armstrong notes the number of Lancastrians injured on the face and arms, including Buckingham, Lord Dudley and the unfortunate Henry Filongley, who was 'shot through the arms in three or four places'. Armstrong, 'Politics and the Battle of St. Albans, 1445', p. 42. The Dijon Relation reports that a number of Henry's attendants were killed in front of him by arrow fire. *EHD*, IV, p. 277.

4   Henry is said to have been wounded in the neck by Benet, p. 214; Davies, *English Chronicle*, p. 72; Gregory, p. 202. The Dijon Relation reported that Henry had been grazed on the shoulder by the arrow. Benet, p. 214 is also the source for Henry's flight into the tanner's cottage, which is mentioned by Whethamstede, p. 169.

5   Henry's standard bearer is named in various sources as his lifelong servant Lord Sudeley, his carver Sir Philippe Wentworth or the earl of Wiltshire. Given Wiltshire's reputation for cowardice in battle, he seems the likeliest culprit.

6   Davies, *English Chronicle*, p. 72 is the source for the prophecy about the castle. The circumstances of Somerset's death are related in the Dijon Relation, transcribed in Armstrong, 'Appendix I', pp. 63–5 and translated in *EHD*, IV, p. 277.

7   The pillaging of the Lancastrian army and corpse-strewn streets were

witnessed by John Whethamstede, abbot of St Albans and author of the *Register*. Whethamstede, pp. 171–2.

8   'Dijon Relation', *EHD*, IV, p. 277.

9   Benet, p. 215.

10 Rymer, XI, http://www.british-history.ac.uk/rymer-foedera/vol11/pp360–370 [accessed 14 May 2017].

11 Maurer, p. 153.

12 Wolffe, p. 295.

13 PL, I, p. 345.

14 PR 1455, item 18: http://www.british-history.ac.uk/no-series/parliament-rolls-medieval/july-1455 [accessed 22 May 2017].

15 Somerset was accused of concealing letters from the Yorkists to the king, with the connivance of Thomas Thorpe and William Joseph, who had been among a number of household servants who tried to raise a garrison to protect Henry at Windsor during his illness in 1453–4. Thorpe was also speaker of the 1453 parliament and allegedly prepared articles against York. See PL, I, pp. 264–5; Johnson, *Richard of York*, pp. 130–1.

16 PR 1455, items 18–26.

17 PL, I, p. 346.

18 Benet, p. 142; POPC, VI, pp. 247–9; Griffiths, pp. 753–4.

19 The details of Radford's murder are provided by PL, I, pp. 350–1; *EHD*, IV, pp. 1230–3; PR 1455, Appendix 32, http://www.british-history.ac.uk/no-series/parliament-rolls-medieval/july-1455 [accessed 22 May 2017]. For the context to this West Country feud see Storey, R. L., *The End of the House of Lancaster* (London, 1966), chapters 5 and 13; Cherry, Martin, 'The Struggle for Power in Mid-fifteenth-century Devonshire', in Griffiths, Ralph A. (ed.), *Patronage, the Crown and the Provinces in Later Medieval England* (Stroud, 1981); Lander, J. R., 'Henry VI and the Duke of York's Second Protectorate, 1455 To 1456', *Bulletin of the John Rylands Library* 43, no. 1 (1960), pp. 60–4.

20 *EHD*, IV, p. 1232.

21 Ibid., pp. 1232–3.

22 PR 1455, item 30.

23 PL, I, p. 352.

24 PR 1455, item 31.

25 He received his patent as protector two days later, on 19 November. Parliament had only been sitting for a week. For York's reappointment as protector I follow Lander, 'York's Second Protectorate'.

26 'MS Rawlinson B. 355,' 'Bale's Chronicle,' Flenley, pp. 109, 142–3; PR 1455, Appendix 18, Introduction, items 18–26; Whethamstede, pp. 181–2.

27 Griffiths, p. 729.

28 PR 1455, item 47.

29 Benet, p. 216.

30 PL, I, pp. 377–8.

31 PR 1455, Appendix 3.
32 PL, I, p. 377.

Chapter 27. 'Of queens that be crowned, so high none know I'

1 'Julius Caesar' addressing Queen Margaret in a pageant at Coventry in 1456. Harris, Mary Dormer, (ed.), *The Coventry Leet Book: or mayor's register, containing the records of the city court leet or view of frankpledge, A.D. 1420–1555, with divers other matters* (London, 1908), p. 291.
2 Laynesmith, J. L., 'Constructing Queenship at Coventry: Pageantry and Politics at Margaret of Anjou's Secret Harbor', *Fifteenth Century* 3 (Woodbridge, 2003), p. 137.
3 *The Coventry Leet Book*, pp. 286–92.
4 Ibid., p. 287. For this trinitarian meaning behind the pageants see Laynesmith, 'Constructing Queenship at Coventry'.
5 'Bale's Chronicle,' Flenley, pp. 143–4; Griffiths, pp. 790–3.
6 'Short English Chronicle,' *Three Fifteenth-Century Chronicles*, p. 70; Benet, p. 217.
7 Bekynton, pp. 142–3.
8 Edmund Tudor was released in November 1456 but died of a sickness he had caught while imprisoned. Wolffe, p. 304; Griffiths, pp. 779–80; Storey, *The End of the House of Lancaster*, pp. 178–9.
9 CPR, 1452–61, pp. 360, 367; CCR, 1454–61, http://www.british-history.ac.uk/cal-close-rolls/hen6/vol6/pp158–161 [accessed 6 June 2018]; Griffiths, pp. 780–1; Storey, pp. 180–2.
10 *Coventry Leet Book*, p. 264.
11 Griffiths, pp. 777, 784.
12 PL, I, pp. 392–3.
13 Similarly, Prince Edward's keeper of the great wardrobe, Giles St Loo, had been Henry's esquire, was married to Margaret's attendant Edith Burgh and served as squire in Margaret's household. Maurer, p. 136; Myers, A. R. 'The Household of Queen Margaret of Anjou, 1452–3', *Bulletin of the John Rylands Library* part 2 (1957), p. 405.
14 Griffiths, p. 781.
15 Ibid., pp. 803–4.
16 Lord Bonville's grandson William married Salisbury's daughter Catherine Neville before the end of 1455. Cherry, Martin, 'The Struggle for Power in Mid-Fifteenth Century Devonshire', in Griffiths, R. A. (ed.), *Patronage, the Crown and the Provinces* (Gloucester, 1981), pp. 134–5.
17 Maurer, pp. 136–7; Griffiths, p. 802.
18 Storey, pp. 182–3.
19 'Bale's Chronicle,' Flenley, p. 144; Robbins, Rossell Hope (ed.), *Historical Poems of the XIVth and XVth Centuries* (New York, 1959), pp. 189–90. For a discussion of the poem's meaning see Robbins, Rossell Hope, 'The Five Dogs of London', *Publications of the Modern Language Association of America* 71, no. 1 (1956), pp. 264–8. An alternative trans-

lation, and the argument that the intended target of this poem was actually the duke of Somerset, is provided in Hanham, Alison and Cron, B. M., 'Slain Dogs, the Dead Man and Editorial Constructs', *The Ricardian* 17 (2007).

20 PL, I, pp. 407–8. Similarly, see Benet, p. 217.

21 PR 1459, items 11–12, http://www.british-history.ac.uk/no-series/parliament-rolls-medieval/november-1459 [accessed 7 July 2017].

22 Lord Egremont had been imprisoned for fighting the Nevilles at the Battle of Stamford Bridge in October 1454. PL, I, p. 408; 'Bale's Chronicle,' 'MS Gough London 10,' Flenley, pp. 144, 159; Brut, p. 523; 'Short English Chronicle,' *Three Fifteenth-Century Chronicles*, p. 70; Benet, p. 217; 'Vitellius A XVI', Kingsford, *Chronicles of London*, p. 167.

Chapter 28. 'Rejoice, England, in concord and unity'

1 'Reconciliation of Henry VI and the Yorkists (1458)', Robbins, Rossell Hope (ed.), *Historical Poems of the XIVth and XVth Centuries* (New York, 1959), p. 195.

2 Benet 218.

3 The figure of 3,000 is given in 'Short English Chronicle,' *Three Fifteenth-Century Chronicles*, pp. 70–1. See also Brut, pp. 524–5; Davies, *English Chronicle*, p. 74; 'MS Rawlinson B. 355,' 'MS Gough London 10,' Flenley, pp. 144–5, 110–11; Griffiths, p. 815.

4 In reality, Charles VII had no intention of joining James II in an invasion of England. He believed England might at any moment launch an attack on his own shores, perhaps in league with his rebellious son, or the old English allies in Burgundy. His anxieties are amply demonstrated in LP, I, pp. 340–4.

5 Griffiths, p. 815.

6 Hicks, Michael, *Warwick the Kingmaker* (Oxford, 1998), p. 13.

7 PL, I, pp. 424–5.

8 POPC, VI, p. 293.

9 This is the interpretation of these levies given by Johnson, *Richard of York*, p. 180. Griffiths believes they had a more threatening, proroyalist intention. Griffiths, p. 805.

10 As the earl of Arundel discovered when he tried to keep his distance from proceedings: POPC, VI, pp. 293–4. Ibid., pp. 290–3 for Henry's insistence that all lords attend when the council reconvened. Salisbury's escort is mentioned in 'MS Rawlinson B. 355', Flenley, p. 111.

11 'MS Gough London 10,' Flenley, p. 160. See also ibid., pp. 111, 159–60; Maurer, p. 150. For what follows see ibid., pp. 111–12, 145; Davies, *English Chronicle*, p. 77; Brut, p. 525; 'Short English Chronicle,' *Three Fifteenth-Century Chronicles*, p. 71; Benet, p. 221; PL, I, pp. 424–6.

12 Whethamstede, p. 295.

13 PL, I, pp. 425–6; Hicks, *Warwick the Kingmaker*, p. 132.

14 PL, I, pp. 426–7.

15 Robbins, *Historical Poems*, p. 195.
16 Benet, p. 221; 'MS Rawlinson B. 355,' 'Bale's Chronicle,' 'MS Gough London 10,' Flenley, pp. 112, 145, 160; Hall, p. 238.
17 Robbins, *Historical Poems*, p. 195.
18 Whethamstede, pp. 298–308.
19 This text may have been a copy or translation of the original document. Hicks, *Warwick*, p. 133.
20 Whethamstede, p. 301.
21 'MS Gough London 10,' Flenley, p. 160; PL, I, pp. 426–7.
22 For the inversion of Henry and Margaret's roles during the Love Day reconciliation see Maurer, pp. 156–7.
23 Maurer, pp. 45–7, 153–8; Lewis, Katherine J., *Kingship and Masculinity in Late Medieval England* (New York and Abingdon, 2013), pp. 233–5.
24 Maurer, p. 45.
25 Brut, p. 527.
26 Davies, *English Chronicle*, p. 78.
27 Unlike a number of contemporary chroniclers who wrote after Henry's usurpation and were influenced by Yorkist propaganda, Gascoigne died in 1458 while Henry was still king. Quoted in Lewis, *Kingship and Masculinity*, p. 238. For the construction of Margaret's reputation see Lee, Patricia-Ann, 'Reflections of Power: Margaret of Anjou and the Dark Side of Queenship', *Renaissance Quarterly* 39, no. 2 (1986); Dunn, Diana, 'Margaret of Anjou, Queen Consort of Henry VI: A Reassessment of Her Role, 1445–53', in Archer, Rowena E. (ed.), *Crown, Government and People in the Fifteenth Century* (New York, 1995).
28 *Great Chronicle*, p. 190; 'Bale's Chronicle,' 'MS Gough London 10,' Flenley, pp. 122, 160.
29 Whethamstede, p. 325.
30 LP, I, pp. 368, 371–5; 'Bale's Chronicle,' Flenley, p. 147.
31 As reported by Edmond Gallet, Alençon's emissary. Beaucourt, VI, p. 137. For an overview of Alençon's rebellion and trial see ibid., pp. 45–56, 137–8; Vale, M. G. A., *Charles VII* (London, 1974), pp. 76–82, 154–62.
32 Vale, *Charles VII*, pp. 163–77.
33 Chastellain, III, p. 444.
34 LP, I, pp. 340–2.
35 Beaucourt, VI, p. 137.
36 My italics. LP, I, p. 366.
37 Ibid., pp. 365–9.
38 Ibid., pp. 361–9.
39 Ibid., pp. 364–5, 367.
40 The attack was described by John Jernyngham (a correspondent of Margaret Paston's), who was captured during the battle and then exchanged for a Spanish prisoner. PL, I, pp. 428–9.
41 Rose, Susan, *Calais, An English Town in France 1347–1558* (Woodbridge, 2008), p. 81; Hicks, *Warwick*, pp. 146–7. Reports of Warwick's

naval endeavours appear in Whethamstede, pp. 330–1; 'Short English Chronicle,' *Three Fifteenth Chronicles*, p. 70; 'MS Rawlinson B. 355,' 'Bale's Chronicle,' 'MS Gough London 10,' Flenley, pp. 112, 147, 160–1; Davies, *English Chronicle*, p. 83–4; *Great Chronicle*, p. 190.

42 Hicks, *Wars of the Roses*, p. 150.

43 'Bale's Chronicle,' Flenley, p. 147. Warwick's exploits were also reported by ibid., pp. 112–13, 160–1; 'Short English Chronicle,' *Three Fifteenth-Century Chronicles*, p. 70; Davies, *English Chronicle*, pp. 83–4.

44 Escouchy, II, pp. 352–4; Chastellain, IV, p. 228. Margaret's 'Frenchness' was to become a recurrent stick used to beat her and her supporters in the years ahead.

45 LP, I, p. 369.

46 Davies, *English Chronicle*, pp. 78–9; LP, I, pp. 368–9; Whethamstede, I, p. 340.

47 'MS Rawlinson B. 355,' 'Bale's Chronicle,' Flenley, pp. 113, 146; Davies, *English Chronicle*, p. 78; Brut, p. 526; Waurin, V, pp. 271–2; *Great Chronicle*, p. 190, which differs in dating this event to February 1459 and claiming that the violence was started when one of Warwick's men 'smote' one of the king's servants in Westminster Hall – probably this is conflating the events involving Warwick and the duke of Exeter's illegal seizure of a lawyer from Westminster Hall. See above, pp. 373.

48 The countess of Salisbury's involvement in this decision is not recorded, but she was named as a motivator of Salisbury's treason in the parliament of 1459. It is unlikely that Salisbury would have committed himself to a course of action that would have material effects on his wife and children without consulting her. PR 1459, http://www.british-history.ac.uk/no-series/parliament-rolls-medieval/november-1459 [accessed 7 July 2017]; Pollard, A. J., *Warwick the Kingmaker: politics, power and fame* (London, 2007), pp. 38–9; Maurer, pp 161–4.

Chapter 29. 'Our mortal and extreme enemies'

1 Davies, *English Chronicle*, p. 88.

2 Ibid., p. 79.

3 The absence of the earl of Arundel seems more likely a matter of personal choice than political exclusion. Arundel had been chastised by Henry for non-attendance at the great council of early 1458 and preferred where possible to stay away from contentious gatherings of the nobility. The fact that he was Salisbury's son-in-law may, however, have made his loyalties suspect. This council is reported by Benet, p. 223.

4 Wolffe, p. 314.

5 LP, II (2), p. 511; 'MS Rawlinson B. 355,' 'Bale's Chronicle,' Flenley, pp. 113, 146; Davies, *English Chronicle*, p. 79; POPC, VI, pp. 298–9; Griffiths, pp. 808, 817.

6 Johnson, *Richard of York*, p. 186; PR 1459, items 14, 21.

7 Wolffe, p. 318.

8 'English Heritage Battlefield Report: Blore Heath 1459', https:// content.historicengland.org.uk/content/docs/battlefields/blore. pdf [accessed 28 July 2017]; Brut, p. 526; 'Bale's Chronicle,' Flenley, p. 148; Gregory, p. 204; Davies, *English Chronicle*, p.80; Benet, p. 224; 'Short English Chronicle,' *Three Fifteenth-Century Chronicles*, pp. 71–2; Whethamstede, p. 338; *Chronicle of London*, p. 140; Waurin, V, pp. 319–21.

9 Davies, *English Chronicle*, p. 81.

10 The majority of the dead were Lancastrian. Jean Waurin, the sole source to number the Yorkist soldiers slain at Blore Heath, reports that only fifty-six of their men were killed. Waurin, V, p. 321.

11 Davies, *English Chronicle*, pp. 81–3; Whethamstede, pp. 339–41.

12 Cecily's presence at Ludlow at this time is suggested by Davies, *English Chronicle*, p. 83; Brut, p. 528; Gregory, p. 203.

13 PR 1459, item 17: http://www.british-history.ac.uk/no-series/parliament-rolls-medieval/november-1459 [accessed 7 July 2017]; Gregory, p. 203.

14 'Bale's Chronicle,' Flenley, p. 148. According to contemporary reports, the Yorkist forces numbered between 20,000–25,000 while accounts of the royalist forces suggest a number anywhere between 30,000–60,000. Griffiths, p. 821.

15 PR 1459, items 16–17.

16 Brut, p. 527; CCC, p. 111.

17 Griffiths, pp. 822, 849 n.304; 'Bale's Chronicle,' Flenley, p. 148; Whethamstede, pp. 344–5; Benet, p. 224; Gregory, p. 205; PR 1459, item 19.

18 Davies, *English Chronicle*, p. 83.

19 Gregory, p. 205.

20 Brut, p. 528; Benet, p. 224; Whethamstede, p. 345.

21 Lander, J. R., 'Attainder and Forfeiture, 1453 to 1509', *The Historical Journal* 4 (1961), p. 119.

22 Ross, C. D., 'Forfeiture for Treason in the Reign of Richard II,' *English Historical Review* 71, no. 281 (1956).

23 PR 1459, item 7, http://www.british-history.ac.uk/no-series/parliament-rolls-medieval/november-1459 [accessed 7 July 2017].

24 Whethamstede, pp. 345–56; Kekewich, Margaret, 'The Attainder of the Yorkists in 1459: Two Contemporary Accounts', *Bulletin of the Institute of Historical Research* 55 (1982); Gilson, J. P., 'A Defence of the Proscription of the Yorkists in 1459', *English Historical Review* 26, no. 103 (1911).

25 Davies, *English Chronicle*, p. 85; Brut, p. 529.

26 Johnson, Lauren, 'The Impact of the Wars of the Roses on Noblewomen', unpublished MSt diss., University of Oxford, 2007, p. 29.

27 Griffiths, pp. 825–6. A financial motivation for the 1459 attainders is

suggested by Griffiths, pp. 824–5; Hicks, Michael, *The Wars of the Roses* (New Haven, 2012), p. 147.

28 PR 1459, item 26.

29 The changes to the prince's household were made in February and March 1460. Maurer, p. 177.

Chapter 30. 'The test of the sword'

1 Gragg, Florence Alden (trans.) and Gabel, Leona C. (ed.), *The Commentaries of Pius II on the Memorable Events of His Times: Books II–III*, Smith College Studies in History 25 (Northampton, MA, 1939–40), III, pp. 269–70.

2 For the popularity of the earls' arrival: Davies, *English Chronicle*, p. 94; Gregory, p. 206; Brut, p. 529; CSPV, no. 357, http://www.british-history.ac.uk/cal-state-papers/venice/vol1/pp74–92 [accessed 28 June 2018]; *Great Chronicle*, p. 191. On the role of the papal legate, see Gragg and Gabel, *The Commentaries of Pius II*, III, p. 270. The size of the force at the earls' disposal is given in CSPM, no. 38, http://www.british-history.ac.uk/cal-state-papers/milan/1385-1618/pp21-37 [accessed 20 June 2017]. 'Bale's Chronicle,' Flenley, p. 149 suggests the Yorkist force numbered 60,000; Benet, p. 226 believed Fauconberg left London with 10,000 men and March and Warwick with 60,000 – this may reflect the expansion of their forces once they reached England, rather than the number of soldiers they landed with. The Yorkist lords' complaints and demands were presented in a number of bills, some of which survive in copies that can be found in Vale, pp. 208–10; Davies, *English Chronicle*, pp. 86–90. They also recirculated the 'Articles of the Commons of Kent' from 1450. Vale, pp. 210–12; Gregory, p. 206.

3 Warwick's claims were reported by Pope Pius II, who probably heard them from Coppini. See Gragg and Gabel, *The Commentaries of Pius II*, III, p. 269.

4 Davies, *English Chronicle*, p. 79. See also CSPM, no. 38.

5 Rumours that Margaret was attempting to force Henry from the throne continued to surface in continental reports throughout 1460–1. CSPM, no. 38; ibid., nos. 71, 75, http://www.british-history.ac.uk/cal-state-papers/milan/1385-1618/pp37-106 [accessed 20 June 2017]. See also Davies, *English Chronicle*, p. 79.

6 Robbins, Rossell Hope (ed.), *Historical Poems of the XIVth and XVth Centuries* (New York, 1959), p. 208. For the context to this poem and its probable allusion to Prince Edward's legitimacy see Maurer, pp. 176–7.

7 The articles sent by the Yorkist lords to the Commons, copied in Davies, *English Chronicle*, p. 89.

8 As *Gregory's Chronicle* put it, Wiltshire 'fought mainly with the heels'. Gregory, p. 202.

SHADOW KING

9 *English Chronicle*, p. 88.

10 CSPM, no. 38.

11 Johnson, *Richard Duke of York*, p. 239 for the context to the Newbury revolt. Waurin mistakenly believed that Wiltshire imprisoned the men in the Tower of London. Waurin, V, p. 270. Davies, *English Chronicle*, p. 90; Benet, p. 225. For Lancastrian defensive actions and commissions see Griffiths, pp. 857–9.

12 Johnson, *Richard of York*, pp. 197–9; Griffiths, pp. 854–5.

13 Griffiths, p. 829.

14 Harriss, G. L., 'The Struggle for Calais: An Aspect of the Rivalry between Lancaster and York', *English Historical Review* 75, no. 294 (1960), pp. 48–9; Griffiths, p. 827.

15 William Paston to his brother John Paston. PL, I , p. 506.

16 PL, I, p. 506; Gregory, p. 206; Davies, *English Chronicle*, pp. 84–6; Benet, p. 225; 'Bale's Chronicle,' Flenley, p. 149; Brut, pp. 528–9; *Great Chronicle*, p. 192; Griffiths, p. 857.

17 For the complex loyalties of London in this period see Barron, Caroline M., 'London and the Crown, 1451–61', in Highfield, J. R. L. and Jeffs, Robin (eds.), *The Crown and Local Communities in England and France in the Fifteenth Century* (Stroud, 1981). Convocation was meeting in London at this time. Watts suggests that this may have played its part in encouraging Londoners to give the Yorkists access to the city. Watts, p. 355; *English Chronicle*, p. 95. Maurer suggests that the Londoners pressed for the public oath at St Paul's. Maurer, p. 179.

18 CSPM, no. 37, http://www.british-history.ac.uk/cal-state-papers/milan/1385-1618/pp21-37 [accessed 20 June 2017].

19 Whethamstede, p. 331.

20 For the context to Coppini's activities in this period see Head, Constance, 'Pope Pius II and the Wars of the Roses', *Archivum Historiae Pontificiae* 8 (1970).

21 Benet, p. 225; Davies, *English Chronicle*, p. 94; CSPM, no. 76, http://www.british-history.ac.uk/cal-state-papers/milan/1385-1618/pp37-106 [accessed 26 September 2017]; CSPV, no. 360, http://www.british-history.ac.uk/cal-state-papers/venice/vol1/pp92-126 [accessed 28 June 2018].

22 CSPM, no. 37; Head, 'Pope Pius II and the Wars of the Roses', p. 154.

23 Gragg and Gabel, *The Commentaries of Pius II*, III, pp. 269–70.

24 CSPM, I, no. 38.

25 Gregory, p. 208.

26 Davies, *English Chronicle*, p. 95.

27 'English Heritage Battlefield Report: Northampton 1460', https://content.historicengland.org.uk/content/docs/battlefields/northampton.pdf [accessed 21 June 2017]. The fullest chronicle description is provided by Davies, *English Chronicle*, pp. 96–8; Whethamstede, pp. 372–5; CSPM, no. 38.

28 Benet, p. 226; Griffiths, pp. 862, 877, n.41.

29 Davies, *English Chronicle*, p. 96.

30 Ibid.

31 The reason for Grey's defection is unclear, since until 1460 he seemed a loyal Lancastrian servant, regularly attending the royal council and trusted with royal judicial commissions. The likeliest motivation was Grey's anxiety to keep control of the manor of Ampthill, which had long been disputed between himself, Lord Cromwell (who died in 1456) and the duke of Exeter. Grey was in possession of the manor after Cromwell's death and feared for its future under a government dominated by Exeter. See Horrox, Rosemary, 'Grey, Edmund, first earl of Kent (1416–1490)', *ODNB*, http://www.oxforddnb.com/view/article/11529 [accessed 21 Aug 2017]; Leland, John, *John Leland's Itinerary: Travels in Tudor England*, ed. John Chandler (Stroud, 1993), p. 22; Payling, S. J., 'The Ampthill Dispute: A Study in Aristocratic Lawlessness and the Breakdown of Lancastrian Government', *English Historical Review* 104, no. 413 (1989).

32 Gregory is the source for Buckingham's death at 'his tent'. 'Bale's Chronicle' put the Lancastrian dead at fifty (in addition to the four key noblemen killed) and York's losses at eight. Benet believed about 400 were killed on Henry's side, a figure that roughly accords with the three hundred suggested by the Annales. Gregory, p. 207; 'Bale's Chronicle,' Flenley, p. 151; Benet, p. 226; Annales, p. 773.

33 Gragg and Gabel, *The Commentaries of Pius II*, III, pp. 269–70.

Chapter 31. 'Enemies on every side'

1 LP, II (2), p. 511.

2 Gregory, pp. 208–9 provides the fullest account of Margaret's trials after leaving Coventry. See also Annales, p. 773.

3 For York's journey across England see Johnson, *Richard of York*, p. 210. Griffiths, p. 867; Gregory, p. 208.

4 This was after his return from Canterbury. On first arriving in London he went to the bishop of London's palace. Davies, *English Chronicle*, p. 98; Benet, p. 226.

5 The question of where Henry wished to be buried was debated in 1498, and depositions taken from eyewitnesses who had seen him at various points before 1461, particularly c.1458–9, debating the location with his advisers and the abbot of Westminster. Stanley, Penrhyn, Arthur, *Historical Memorials of Westminster Abbey* (London, 1866), pp. 570–9.

6 He was among the small coterie who witnessed Warwick's brother George Neville being made chancellor in London on 25 July.

7 Davies, *English Chronicle*, pp. 95–6; Benet, p. 225; Vale, pp. 178–9; Griffiths, p. 863.

8 Pollard, A. J., *North-Eastern England During the Wars of the Roses: Lay Society, War, and Politics 1450–1500* (Oxford, 1990), p. 279; Griffiths, p. 864.

9 Whethamstede, pp. 376–7.
10 Ibid.; Tiptoft's letter, as reported in Johnson, *Richard of York*, pp. 213–4.
11 The idea that York's usurpation was planned in Dublin – and that Warwick and March were in on it – is outlined best in Jones, Michael K., 'Edward IV, the earl of Warwick and the Yorkist Claim to the Throne', *Historical Research* 70 (1997), pp. 342–52. See also Pollard, A. J., *Warwick the Kingmaker: politics, power and fame* (London, 2007), pp. 43–9; Johnson, *Richard of York*, pp. 205–6; Griffiths, p. 867. For an opposing opinion, see Wolffe, p. 321. The major contemporary source which presents an alternative version of events is Waurin, who casts Warwick as the hero of the piece and therefore shies away from acknowledging his implication in Henry's deposition. Waurin, V, pp. 313–15.
12 For his pains he was treated to an opening speech by the new chancellor, George Neville, about how badly governed the realm had been under his rule. Waurin, V, p. 313; PR 1460, Introduction, http://www.british-history.ac.uk/no-series/parliament-rolls-medieval/october-1460 [accessed 20 October 2017].
13 Exactly where York and Henry were, and how violently Henry was moved out, has been a vexed question. The closely contemporary 'Tiptoft letter' describes York as being in the queen's chambers but all other contemporaries who specify his location, including pro-Yorkist ones, place him in the king's apartments. Whethamstede suggests that Henry was already lodged in the queen's apartments, which is possible but would be somewhat curious. The queen's rooms would have been further from the business of parliament, so may have been preferable to Henry. The Tiptoft letter is transcribed in Johnson, *Richard of York*, pp. 213–14. Gregory, p. 208; Davies, *English Chronicle*, p. 99; *Great Chronicle*, p. 192; Whethamstede, p. 377; CCC, p. 112. The source for the guards placed on Henry's door is Waurin, V, p. 313.
14 PR 1460, item 12.
15 Benet, p. 227.
16 PR 1460, item 11. York's claim to the throne and the subsequent act of accord also survive in a collection of manuscripts collated by the contemporary Londoner John Vale. See Vale, pp. 195–202.
17 Gragg and Gabel, *The Commentaries of Pius II*, III, p. 271; PR 1460, items 13–17.
18 Brut, p. 530.
19 PR 1460, item 21.
20 The commission does not survive, but the reference in the patent roll suggests it. PR 1460, item 32.
21 Gragg and Gabel, *The Commentaries of Pius II*, III, pp. 268–9; Gregory, p. 208.
22 Gregory, p. 208.
23 Ibid.
24 *Great Chronicle*, p. 192; Benet, p. 227.

Chapter 32. 'Out of the north an evil shall break'

1   Jeremiah I:14, as given in Pollard, A. J., *North-eastern England during the Wars of the Roses: lay society, war and politics, 1450–1500* (Oxford, 1990), p. 26, n.66.

2   Beaucourt, VI, p. 137; Wolffe, p. 83.

3   Burnett, George (ed.), *The Exchequer Rolls of Scotland, Vol. III: AD 1460–1469* (Edinburgh, 1884), p. 8; Asloan, John and Craigie, W. A. (ed.), *The Asloan Manuscript: A Miscellany in Prose & Verse* (Edinburgh, 1923), p. 230.

4   Head, Constance, 'Pope Pius II and the Wars of the Roses', *Archivum Historiae Pontificiae* 8 (1970).

5   The interrelation of English affairs to those of Europe is clear in a letter of February 1461. The duke of Milan wrote to Coppini, alarmed at the reversals to the Yorkist cause in England, opining that 'every disaster to the cause there will tend to disaster to the cause here'. CSPM I, no. 67, http://www.british-history.ac.uk/cal-state-papers/milan/1385-1618/pp37-106 [accessed 20 July 2017].

6   Brézé, writing to Charles VII on 24 February 1460. Quicherat, J (ed.), *Histoire des règnes de Charles VII., et de Louis XI., par T. Basin, Évêque de Lisieux, jusqu'ici attribuée à Amelgard ... publiée pour la première fois avec les autres ouvrages historiques du même écrivain* (Paris, 1859), IV, pp. 358–60.

7   For the Battle of Wakefield and its context, Johnson, *Richard of York*, pp. 222–3; Griffiths, p. 870; Dockray, Keith and Knowles, Richard, 'The Battle of Wakefield and the Wars of the Roses', *The Ricardian* 9 (1992). Closer contemporary sources for this battle were Benet, p. 228; Gregory, pp. 209–10; Annales, p. 775; 'Short English Chronicle,' *Three Fifteenth-Century Chronicles*, p. 76; 'Vitellius A XVI', Kingsford, *Chronicles of London*, p. 172; Davies, *English Chronicle*, p. 106; Whethamstede, pp. 381–3; *Great Chronicle*, p. 193; Brut, p. 530–1.

8   Johnson, *Richard Duke of York*, p. 222, n.154.

9   Margaret was not at the Battle of Wakefield, although the rumour of her presence developed quickly, possibly from a misunderstanding of the Lancastrian army being under her personal command at this time. On 1 February 1461 the Milanese ambassador in the French court reported that 'the queen has recently fought with the duke of York'. CSPM, no. 62, http://www.british-history.ac.uk/cal-state-papers/milan/1385-1618/pp37-106 [accessed 2 July 2017]. Writing early in the sixteenth century, Edward Hall and Polydore Vergil both erroneously suggested Margaret was personally present. Hall, p. 250; Vergil, p. 108.

10 Annales, p. 775 claimed Clifford killed Rutland on Wakefield Bridge. This incident was vividly dramatized by Shakespeare, who presented Clifford butchering the 'innocent child' Rutland in his obsessive desire for vengeance on York's family. *Henry VI, Part 3*, Act 1, Scene 3.

11 Salisbury's widow, Countess Alice, later made a formal appeal of murder

against those she believed responsible for his death. The majority of the accused were connected with the earl of Northumberland. Storey, *The End of the House of Lancaster*, p. 194; Davies, *English Chronicle*, p. 107; Brut, p. 531; *Great Chronicle*, p. 193.

12 Whethamstede, p. 382. This translation comes from Dockray, 'The Battle of Wakefield', p. 248.

13 Hall, p. 250. The majority of contemporaries suggest York's death during battle. Davies, *English Chronicle*, pp. 106–7; Benet, p. 228; Annales, p. 775; Waurin, V, p. 326; Brut, p. 531; 'Bale's Chronicle,' Flenley, pp. 152, 167.

14 Annales, p. 775; *Great Chronicle*, p. 193; Brut, p. 531.

15 CSPM, nos. 62, 71: http://www.british-history.ac.uk/cal-state-papers/milan/1385-1618/pp37-106 [accessed 2 July 2017].

16 Quicherat, pp. 357–8; Waurin, V, pp. 454–5; Cron, B. M., 'Margaret of Anjou and the Lancastrian March on London, 1461', *The Ricardian* 11 (1999), p. 594.

17 March's desire for vengeance was attested by Brut, p. 531; *Great Chronicle*, p. 193.

18 Hughes, Jonathan, *Arthurian Myth and Alchemy: The Kingship of Edward IV* (Stroud, 2002), pp. 9–13.

19 Scobie, *Philippe de Commines*, p. 192.

20 Ingulph, pp. 422–3.

21 Vale, p. 142. There Margaret's letter is cited as postdating York's death but I follow B. M. Cron, who suggests York was still alive when the letter was written. See Cron, 'Margaret of Anjou and the Lancastrian March on London, 1461', pp. 593–4.

22 Edward's letter is reproduced in Vale, pp. 142–3. See Cron, 'Margaret of Anjou and the Lancastrian March on London, 1461', p. 593 for Northumberland's letter.

23 Robbins, Rossell Hope (ed.), *Historical Poems of the XIVth and XVth Centuries* (New York, 1959), pp. 216–17.

24 PR 1461, item 17, http://www.british-history.ac.uk/no-series/parliament-rolls-medieval/november-1461 [accessed 27 June 2017].

25 28 January 1461. POPC, VI, pp. 307–10. Although the commands are issued 'from the king', the witnesses are all Yorkist lords, including Warwick, his brothers John Neville, Lord Montagu, and George Neville, bishop of Exeter, and their ally Henry Bourchier, Lord Berners.

26 Cron, 'Margaret of Anjou and the Lancastrian March on London, 1461', p. 596. See Whethamstede, pp. 388–90, which considers the northerners worse than ancient pagans.

27 The quotation is from Jeremiah, I:14, as given in Pollard p. 26 and n.66. For contemporary antagonism between northerners and southerners see ibid., pp. 25–7.

28 PL, I, p. 541. Another Paston correspondent reported as early as October 1460 that it was rumoured the northerners would destroy all the friars minor in the south. See Cron, p. 596.

29 For a rejection of the mythology of Margaret's plundering march south, see Cron, 'Margaret of Anjou and the Lancastrian March on London, 1461', particularly pp. 596–601. The most hyperbolic descriptions of the 'northern' army can be found in CCC, pp. 422–3; Whethamstede, pp. 388–9.

30 Robbins, *Historical Poems*, p. 216.

31 Davies, *English Chronicle*, p. 110.

32 Gregory, p. 211.

33 The battle is variously dated 2 or 3 February. Davies, *English Chronicle*, p. 110; Waurin, V, pp. 327–8; Brut, p. 531; Annales, pp. 775–6; Gregory, p. 211; *Great Chronicle*, p. 193. Hodges, Geoffrey, 'The Civil War of 1459 to 1461 in the Welsh Marches: Part 2. The Campaign and Battle of Mortimer's Cross – St Blaise's Day, 3 February 1461', *The Ricardian* 6 (1984).

34 For the following see Gregory, pp. 211–14; Benet, p. 229; Annales, p. 776; Whethamstede, pp. 390–4; Waurin, V, pp. 328–30; Griffiths, p. 872; CSPM, nos. 64, 71, http://www.british-history.ac.uk/cal-state-papers/milan/1385-1618/pp37-106 [accessed 2 July 2017].

35 Whethamstede, p. 392. See also Maurer, p. 196; Wolffe, p. 328.

36 This is my interpretation of the continental report that Henry spent the battle singing or even laughing, since prayers at this time could be sung. Given the close diplomatic links between the Yorkists and the Burgundian and Milanese courts, it is possible Waurin and the ambassador were repeating rumours spread to undermine Henry's ability to rule. They recall Warwick's dismissive remarks about Henry being 'a dolt and a fool' to Coppini. No English sources record such behaviour. CSPM, no. 71; Waurin, V, p. 329.

37 Whethamstede, pp. 393–4.

38 Gregory, p. 214.

39 The sources suggesting Prince Edward's involvement in the men's death tend to be pro-Yorkist and suggest Henry had broken faith with Bonville and Kyriell by allowing their executions. Davies, *English Chronicle*, p. 108; Waurin, V, p. 330; CSPM, no. 63, http://www.british-history.ac.uk/cal-state-papers/milan/1385-1618/pp37-106 [accessed 2 July 2017]; Brut, p. 602. Bonville and Kyriell's death is associated with Henry's broken promise in 'Short English Chronicle,' 'Brief Latin Chronicle,' *Three Fifteenth-Century Chronicles*, pp. 76, 172. The deaths of Bonville and Kyriell do not feature in the accounts of battle given by Gregory, pp. 211–14; 'Vitellius A XVI', Kingsford, *Chronicles of London*, p. 173; Whethamstede, pp. 390–4.

40 Cron, B. M. 'Margaret of Anjou and the Lancastrian March on London, 1461', *The Ricardian* 11 (1999), pp. 602–3.

Chapter 33. 'Lost irretrievably'

1 CSPM, no. 120, http://www.british-history.ac.uk/cal-state-papers/milan/1385-1618/pp37-106 [accessed 20 June 2017].

2   *Great Chronicle*, p. 193; Annales, p. 776; CSPM, nos. 64–5, http://www.
     british-history.ac.uk/cal-state-papers/milan/1385-1618/pp37-106
     [accessed 2 July 2017].
3   CSPM, no. 65, http://www.british-history.ac.uk/cal-state-papers/
     milan/1385-1618/pp37-106 [accessed 2 July 2017].
4   Vale, p. 142.
5   CSPM, no. 65.
6   Ibid.; Gregory, pp. 214–15; Benet, p. 229; *Great Chronicle*, p. 193.
7   CSPM, nos. 65–6, http://www.british-history.ac.uk/cal-state-papers/
     milan/1385-1618/pp37-106 [accessed 2 July 2017]; Annales, pp. 776–
     7; *Great Chronicle*, p. 193; Waurin, V, pp. 330–1; Brut, p. 531.
8   'MS Gough London 10,' Flenley, p. 161; Annales, *EHD*, p. 287;
     CSPM, nos. 70, 76, http://www.british-history.ac.uk/cal-state-papers/
     milan/1385-1618/pp37-106 [accessed 2 July 2017]; Gregory, p. 215;
     CSPV, no. 370; *Great Chronicle*, pp. 195–6; Benet, p. 230; CCC, p. 113;
     Brut, pp. 531–2.
9   'English Heritage Battlefield Report: Towton 1461', https://content.
     historicengland.org.uk/content/docs/battlefields/towton.pdf [ac-
     cessed 31 July 2017].
10   Richard Beauchamp, bishop of Salisbury, and *Gregory's Chronicle*
     reported Edward's army as being close to 200,000 men, an inflated
     figure that nonetheless reveals how comparatively large the armies at
     Towton were. Benet believed there were 80,000 Yorkists and 40,000
     Lancastrian soldiers; Waurin reckoned Edward had 30,000 men and
     the Lancastrians 60,000; Hall's Chronicle agrees there were 60,000
     Lancastrians and a highly specific 48,600 Yorkists. Gregory, p. 216;
     CSPV, no. 370; Benet, p. 230; Waurin, V, pp. 336–7; Hall, pp. 255–6.
11   Edward's speech and the cavalry charge is reported by Waurin, V, pp.
     337–41.
12   CSPV, no. 370. A forensic report on a mass grave discovered at Towton
     reveals the types of wounds inflicted. See Fiorato, Veronica, Boylston,
     Anthea and Christopher Knüsel (eds.), *Blood Red Roses: The archaeology
     of a mass grave from the Battle of Towton AD 1461* (Oxford, 2007), espe-
     cially pp. 99–101.
13   This figure was repeated by the Yorkists George Neville and Richard
     Beauchamp, bishop of Salisbury; reported to Pigello Portinaro, a
     Milanese merchant in Bruges and the Milanese ambassador in the
     French Court; repeated by William Paston; and cited by the *Crowland
     Chronicle*. The bishop of Elphin was even more specific and said
     28,800 were killed. Chroniclers tended to cite 24,000–45,000 as the
     death toll. CSP, nos. 370, 372, 374, http://www.british-history.ac.uk/
     cal-state-papers/venice/vol1/pp92-126 [accessed 23 August 2017];
     CSPM, nos. 79, 81, 83, 94, http://www.british-history.ac.uk/cal-state-
     papers/milan/1385-1618/pp37-106 [accessed 20 June 2017]; PL, II,
     pp. 4–6; Ingulph, p. 425; Benet, pp. 230–1; Gregory, p. 217; Waurin,
     V, p. 341; 'The Rose of Rouen', Thornley, Isobel D. (ed.), *England*

Under the Yorkists 1460–1485 (London, 1921), p. 17; Brut, p. 533; Hall, p. 256; Hearne, *EHD*, IV, p. 290.

PART IV: 'THE GREAT REBELLIOUS HENRY'

1   Gregory, p. 221.

Chapter 34. 'Perverse and variable fortune'

1   Chastellain, IV, p. 291.
2   CSPM, no. 90, http://www.british-history.ac.uk/cal-state-papers/milan/1385-1618/pp37-106 [accessed 20 June 2017].
3   CSPM, no. 85, http://www.british-history.ac.uk/cal-state-papers/milan/1385-1618/pp.37-106 [accessed 20 June 2017].
4   PL, II, pp. 46–7 contains a list of twenty-four men in exile with Margaret and Henry in August 1461. By then Somerset, Lord Hungerford and Moleyns and Whittingham had all gone abroad on diplomatic missions, and it is possible others had done the same. The list does not name the ladies who almost certainly accompanied Margaret as attendants, some of whom were married to male Lancastrians.
5   PL, II, p. 46.
6   Philippa's arrest was mistakenly ordered by the name 'Elizabeth', CPR 1461–7, p. 33; Hunter, Joseph, *Three Catalogues, Describing the Contents of the Red Book of the Exchequer of the Dodsworth Manuscripts in the Bodleian Library, and of the Manuscripts in the Library of the Honourable Society of Lincoln's Inn* (London, 1838), p. 278.
7   McGovern, C. J. M., *Lancastrian Diplomacy and Queen Margaret's Court in Exile, 1461–1471*, unpublished BA diss., Keele University, 1973, pp. 21–30; Myers, A. R., 'The Household of Queen Margaret of Anjou, 1452–3', *Bulletin of the John Rylands Library* 40, no. 2 (1957), p. 405.
8   CSPM, no. 107, http://www.british-history.ac.uk/cal-state-papers/milan/1385-1618/pp.37-106 [accessed 20 June 2017]; Ross, Charles, *Edward IV* (London, 1975), p. 43.
9   Ibid., p. 43.
10   CSPM, no. 107, http://www.british-history.ac.uk/cal-state-papers/milan/1385-1618/pp.37-106 [accessed 20 June 2017].
11   PR items 17, 18, 26, http://www.british-history.ac.uk/no-series/parliament-rolls-medieval/november-1461 [accessed 26 February 2018].
12   CSPM, no. 107.
13   Robbins, Rossell Hope (ed.), *Historical Poems of the XIVth and XVth Centuries* (New York, 1959), p. 197.
14   Ibid., p. 224.
15   PL, II, p. 46.
16   Fortescue, Thomas (ed.), *The Works of Sir John Fortescue, Knight, Chief Justice Of England And Lord Chancellor To King Henry The Sixth* (London, 1869), p. 216.

17 Ross, p. 48; Goodman, Anthony, *The Wars of the Roses: Military Activity and English Society, 1452–97* (London, 1981), p. 56; PL, II, p. 416; CSPM, nos. 105, 110, 115, http://www.british-history.ac.uk/cal-state-papers/milan/1385-1618/pp.37-106 [accessed 20 June 2017].

18 CSPM, no. 120, http://www.british-history.ac.uk/cal-state-papers/milan/1385-1618/pp.37-106 [accessed 20 June 2017]; Goodman, *The Wars of the Roses*, p. 57; Waurin, V, p. 352.

19 'Brief notes', *Three Fifteenth-Century Chronicles*, p. 156.

20 CSPM, nos. 101, 107, http://www.british-history.ac.uk/cal-state-papers/milan/1385-1618/pp.37-106 [accessed 20 June 2017].

21 PL, II, pp. 45–7.

22 Vale, M. G. A., *Charles VII* (London, 1974), pp. 172–6, 182–90.

23 Ibid., pp. 95–6, 181–2, 190–3; Chastellain, IV, pp. 227–8.

24 For the pressure being mounted on Mary to give up the Lancastrian cause see CSPM, nos. 107, 109, 115; Waurin, V, pp. 355–6. For Kennedy's promise to Charles VII to help them, Dupont, *Waurin*, III, p. 166. For the context to the Scottish situation see MacDougall, Norman, *James III* (Edinburgh, 2009), pp. 44–8.

25 Ross, p. 43; Scofield, I, pp. 230–5; 'Brief Notes', *Three Fifteenth-Century Chronicles*, p. 158; CSPM, no. 125, http://www.british-history.ac.uk/cal-state-papers/milan/1385-1618/pp106-108 [accessed 2 August 2017]; CPR 1461–7, pp. 182–3.

26 The international conspiracy revealed by a spy is reported in 'Brief notes', *Three Fifteenth-Century Chronicles*, p. 158. That the earl of Oxford's plot was part of this wider scheme is suggested in a letter from a Yorkist envoy to Coppini in March 1462. CSPM, no. 125.

27 PL, I, pp. 516–7. Chastellain, IV, p. 207.

28 For more on the treatment of Elizabeth Howard, countess of Oxford, see Hicks, M. A., 'The Last Days of Elizabeth, countess of Oxford', *English Historical Review* 103, no. 406 (1988).

29 Waurin, V, p. 353; Warkworth, p. 5; *Great Chronicle*, p. 99; 'Hearne's Fragment' in Giles, J. A. (ed.), *The Chronicles of the White Rose of York: A series of historical fragments, proclamations, letters, and other contemporary documents relating to the reign of King Edward the Fourth* (London, 1845), pp. 11–12; CSPM, no. 125. The Oxford conspiracy is mentioned in a large number of chronicles: Gregory, p. 218; Benet, p. 220; 'Short Chronicle', Vale, p. 179; 'Short English Chronicle', 'Brief Notes', *Three Fifteenth-Century Chronicles*, pp. 78, 158.

30 PL, II, p. 46.

Chapter 35. 'Outwards enemies'

1 Ellis, Henry (ed.), *Original Letters, illustrative of English history; including numerous royal letters; from autographs in the British Museum, and one or two other collections. With notes and illustrations by Henry Ellis, keeper of the manuscripts in the British Museum* (London, 1827), I, p. 127.

2   Dupont, *Waurin*, III, pp. 176–7; Scofield, I, pp. 246, 250–1.

3   Waurin, V, p. 431; Chastellain, IV, pp. 227–8; Scofield, I, pp. 252–4.

4   Dupont, *Waurin*, III, pp. 176–7.

5   Scofield, I, p. 253.

6   Named for his godfather, this child would go on to become King Louis XII in 1498. Waurin, V, p. 415; Scofield, I, p. 253.

7   The number of troops reported varied considerably: Chastellain, IV, p. 250 (who puts the number at 800); Waurin, V, p. 431 (2,000); *Annales*, p. 780 (2,000); 'A Short English Chronicle,' *Three Fifteenth-Century Chronicles*, p. 77 (6,000).

8   Goodman, Anthony, *The Wars of the Roses: Military Activity and English Society, 1452–97* (London, 1981), p. 59; Scofield, I, pp. 247–8.

9   Dupont, *Waurin*, III, pp. 167–8; MacDougall, Norman, *James III* (Edinburgh, 2009), pp. 48–52.

10 Chastellain, IV, pp. 225–7.

11 *Great Chronicle*, p. 199; Scofield, pp. 255–9.

12 Waurin, V, p. 433.

13 Gregory, pp. 218–19; 'Vitellius A XVI', Kingsford, *Chronicles of London*, pp. 177–8; 'Brief notes', *Three Fifteenth-Century Chronicles*, p. 156; *Great Chronicle*, p. 199; Waurin, V, pp. 433–4; 'Hearne's Fragment' in Giles, J. A. (ed.), *The Chronicles of the White Rose of York: A series of historical fragments, proclamations, letters, and other contemporary documents relating to the reign of King Edward the Fourth* (London, 1845), p. 13.

14 PL, II, pp. 119–20.

15 'Brief notes', *Three Fifteenth-Century Chronicles*, p. 158–9; Gregory, p. 219; Warkworth, pp. 2–3.

16 *Annales*, p. 780; Gregory, p. 219; 'Short English Chronicle', *Three Fifteenth-Century Chronicles*, pp. 78–9; 'Vitellius A XVI', Kingsford, *Chronicles of London*, p. 178.

17 *Annales*, p. 780; Warkworth, pp. 2–3; Gregory, p. 220.

18 For Margaret's visit to Flanders: Waurin, V, pp. 435–7; Chastellain, IV, pp. 278–312; Gregory, p. 221; *Annales*, p. 781.

19 Gregory, p. 220; *Annales*, p. 781; Dupont, *Waurin*, III, pp. 159–63; Ross, pp. 53–5; Scofield, I, pp. 287–93, 300; MacDougall, pp. 54–5.

20 Waurin, V, pp. 434–5; Chastellain, IV, pp. 299–307 and Chastelain, George, *Le Temple de Bocace: édition commentée par Susanna Bliggenstorfer* (Berne, 1988), p. 95. In these works, Margaret's tale reads more like romance than reality, and undoubtedly at some point in the retelling it has been exaggerated. However, Margaret and Edward did flee for their lives in 1463 and it is entirely possible they were robbed or attacked, as they had been in 1460 as they rode from the disaster of Northampton to Harlech Castle.

21 Chastellain, IV, p. 282. For Margaret's time in Burgundian territory see ibid., pp. 277–314.

22 Chastellain, IV, p. 285.

23 Waurin, V, p. 437; *Annales*, p. 781; McGovern, C. J. M., *Lancastrian*

Diplomacy and Queen Margaret's Court in Exile, 1461–1471, unpublished
BA diss., Keele University, 1973, p. 13.
24 Dupont, *Waurin*, III, pp. 169–71; Annales, p. 781; Scofield, I, pp. 305–
12; MacDougall, pp. 55–6.

Chapter 36. 'False imaginations'

1   'Brief notes', *Three Fifteenth-Century Chronicles*, p. 158.
2   Gregory, p. 223.
3   PL, II, p. 30.
4   Gregory, p. 221. For context to Somerset's defection see Hicks, M. A.,
'Edward IV, the duke of Somerset and Lancastrian loyalism in the
north', *Northern History* 20 (1984).
5   Gregory, p. 221; Warkworth, p. 3; Scofield, I, p. 314.
6   'A Short English Chronicle,' *Three Fifteenth-Century Chronicles*, p. 80;
Gregory, p. 227; CSPM, no. 137, http://www.british-history.ac.uk/cal-
state-papers/milan/1385-1618/pp110-114 [accessed 14 June 2018];
Pollard, A. J. (ed.), *The Wars of the Roses* (Basingstoke, 1995), p. 44.
7   PL, II, pp. 151–3; 'Brief Latin Chronicle', *Three Fifteenth-Century Chronicles*, p. 179; Ross, p. 57; Scofield, I, pp. 318–19; Goodman, Anthony, *The
Wars of the Roses: Military Activity and English Society, 1452–97* (London,
1981), p. 63; Gillingham, John, *The Wars of the Roses: Peace and Conflict
in Fifteenth-Century England* (London, 1990), pp. 150–1.
8   Scofield, I, pp. 315–16.
9   Instructions to Sir Guillaume Cousinot, transcribed by Scofield, II,
pp. 463–5.
10   'A brief Latin chronicle', in *Three Fifteenth-Century Chronicles*, p. 179;
Gregory, p. 224.
11   Contemporary sources for Henry's movements in the north in this
period are extremely scanty, as most writers were based in the south,
and the royal documents that can be used to determine his itinerary
were either no longer being produced or preserved. The reference in
'Brief Latin Chronicle' to Henry leaving at Bywell his 'helmet... with
a crown and sword and trappings' (*le helmet regis Henrici cum corona
et gladio et faleris dicti Henrici*) suggests that Henry was armed and
armoured. Charlesworth, Dorothy, 'The Battle of Hexham, 1464,'
Archaeologia Aeliana, fourth series, 30 (1952), p. 60 suggests Henry
was being used as a rallying point ahead of the decisive final battle.
'Vitellius A XVI', Kingsford, *Chronicles of London*, p. 178; 'A brief Latin
chronicle', in *Three Fifteenth-Century Chronicles*, p. 179.
12   Gregory, pp. 223–6; 'Vitellius A XVI', Kingsford, *Chronicles of London*,
p. 178; Annales, p. 782; 'Brief Notes', 'Short English Chronicle', 'A
brief Latin chronicle', in *Three Fifteenth-Century Chronicles*, pp. 78, 179;
Charlesworth, 'The Battle of Hexham, 1464'.
13   Warkworth, p. 37.
14   Ibid., pp. 37–9; Gregory, p. 227.

15 Gregory, pp. 223–6; Short English Chronicle', 'Brief Latin Chronicle', *Three Fifteenth-Century Chronicles*, pp. 77, 178.

16 'Vitellius A XVI', Kingsford, *Chronicles of London*, p. 178; 'A brief Latin chronicle', in *Three Fifteenth-Century Chronicles*, p. 179; Charlesworth 'The Battle of Hexham, 1464', pp. 62–3 suggests Henry fled before the battle was over. This is possible, and we can reject the later suggestions by Hall and Grafton that Henry himself was at Hexham. Hall, p. 260.

Chapter 37. 'I am the rock of the English kingdom'

1 *'Je suis le perron du royame anglois'* – Margaret of Anjou addresses Georges Chastelain in his imaginary Temple of Bocaccio. Chastelain, Georges, *Le Temple de Bocace: édition commentée par Susanna Bliggenstorfer* (Berne, 1988), p. 91.

2 Dumont, Charles Emmanuel, *Histoire de la ville de Saint-Mihiel* (Paris and Nancy, 1860), I, p. 176; Kekewich, Margaret L., 'The Lancastrian Court in Exile', in Stratford, Jenny (ed.), *Proceedings of the 2001 Harlaxton Symposium: The Lancastrian Court* (Donington, 2003), pp. 97, 107.

3 Jean of Calabria and René were both in St Mihiel in January 1464. McGovern, C. J. M., *Lancastrian Diplomacy and Queen Margaret's Court in Exile, 1461–1471*, unpublished BA diss., Keele University, 1973, p. 13.

4 Vaudemont and Pont visited in May 1467. The count was married to Margaret's sister Yolande. René's support was supplemented by a pension of 4,000 or 5,000 francs from Louis in 1465. Kekewich, 'Lancastrian Court in Exile', pp. 97–8. Dumont, *Histoire de la ville de Saint-Mihiel*, p. 174; CSPM, no. 150, http://www.british-history.ac.uk/cal-state-papers/milan/1385-1618/pp117-122 [accessed 30 October 2017].

5 Dumont, *Histoire de la ville de Saint-Mihiel*, p. 173.

6 According to Warkworth, p. 19, 'the countess of Devonshire' was among Margaret's ladies captured after the Battle of Tewkesbury in 1471. Since John Courtenay is not known to have had a wife, and his mother the dowager countess was dead by 1471, it seems most likely this was Marie of Maine. Margaret had arranged Marie's marriage to the earl of Devon in 1457 and after her husband's death and attainder in 1461 Marie might have preferred exile with her kinswoman to an uncertain future in England. In a letter by Sir John Fortescue to the earl of Ormond dated 30 December 1464, he lists those present with the queen at the time. Fortescue, Thomas, (ed.), *The Works of Sir John Fortescue, Knight, Chief Justice of England And Lord Chancellor To King Henry The Sixth* (London, 1869), I, p. 24; McGovern, *Lancastrian Diplomacy and Queen Margaret's Court in Exile*, p. 13; Griffiths, R., '"Ffor the myght off the lande, aftir the myght off the grete lordes thereoff, stondith most in the kynges officers": the English crown, provinces and dominions in the fifteenth century', in Curry, Anne and Matthew,

Elizabeth, (eds.), *Concepts and Patterns of Service in the Later Middle Ages* (Woodbridge, 2000), pp. 86–8; PR 1461, item 27, http://www.british-history.ac.uk/no-series/parliament-rolls-medieval/november-1461 [accessed 27 June 2017].

7 McGovern, *Lancastrian Diplomacy and Queen Margaret's Court in Exile*, pp. 20–30.

8 Fortescue, *The Works of Sir John Fortescue*, I, p. 24.

9 As in 1465 for Pembroke and Fortescue: Ibid., p. 29.

10 McGovern, *Lancastrian Diplomacy and Queen Margaret's Court in Exile*, p. 39.

11 An overview of the movements of the Lancastrian courtiers is given in Kekewich, 'Lancastrian Court in Exile', Appendix 1, pp. 107–8.

12 Fortescue, *The Works of Sir John Fortescue*, I, p. 26.

13 Ibid., p. 25.

14 McGovern, *Lancastrian Diplomacy and Queen Margaret's Court in Exile*, pp. 37–9; Calmette, J. and Périnelle, G, *Louis XI et L'Angleterre (1461–1483)* (Paris, 1930), pp. 69–70; Kekewich, 'Lancastrian Court in Exile', pp. 101–2.

15 Quoted in Lewis, Katherine J., *Kingship and Masculinity In Late Medieval England* (New York and Abingdon, 2013), pp. 241–2.

16 CSPM, no. 146, http://www.british-history.ac.uk/cal-state-papers/milan/1385-1618/pp115-117 [accessed 26 February 2018]; Fortescue, *The Works of Sir John Fortescue*, I, p. 28.

17 Dumont, *Histoire de la ville de Saint-Mihiel*, pp. 175–7.

18 Fortescue, *The Works of Sir John Fortescue*, I, p. 26.

19 Waurin, V, p. 344; Warkworth, pp. 5, 41–2; Searle, William George (ed.), *Christ Church, Canterbury. I. The Chronicle of John Stone, Monk of Christ Church 1415–1471* (Cambridge, 1902), p. 93; Annales, p. 785; 'Short English Chronicle', *Three Fifteenth-Century Chronicles*, p. 80.

20 Rymer, XI, http://www.british-history.ac.uk/rymer-foedera/vol11/pp558-576 [accessed 26 February 2018].

21 'An oaken chest, containing the boots, gloves, and spoon of King Henry VI of England', which he had allegedly left at Bolton Hall, were exhibited in 1872 and were known of a century before that. *Transactions of the Historic Society of Lancashire and Cheshire* New Series 12 (Liverpool, 1872), pp. 197–8; *The Gentleman's Magazine* 55 (June 1785), p. 418. See also Mackenzie, James Dixon, *The Castles of England, their Story and Structure* (New York, 1896), p. 323; Whitaker, Thomas Dunham, *The History and Antiquities of the Deanery of Craven, in the County of York* (London, 1805), pp. 102–6; 'Bolingbroke – Bonby', in Lewis, Samuel (ed.), *A Topographical Dictionary of England* (London, 1848), http://www.british-history.ac.uk/topographical-dict/england/pp295-302 [accessed 26 February 2018]; 'The parish of Pennington', in Farrer, William and Brownbill, J. (eds.), *A History of the County of Lancaster: Volume 8* (London, 1914), http://www.british-history.ac.uk/vch/lancs/vol8/pp338-342 [accessed 26 February 2018].

22 Blacman, p. 43.

23 Warkworth, pp. 5, 41–2; Gregory, p. 228; Waurin, V, pp. 344–5; Searle, *The Chronicle of John Stone*, p. 93; Fabyan, Robert and Ellis, Henry (ed.), *The new chronicles of England and France, in two parts; by Robert Fabyan. Named by himself the concordance of histories. Reprinted from Pynson's edition of 1516. The first part collated with the editions of 1533, 1542, and 1559; and the second with a manuscript of the author's own time, as well as the subsequent editions: including the different continuations* (London, 1811), p. 654; 'Short Chronicle', Vale, p. 179; 'Short English Chronicle', *Three Fifteenth-Century Chronicles*, p. 80; 'Hearne's Fragment' in Giles, J. A. (ed.), *The Chronicles of the White Rose of York: A series of historical fragments, proclamations, letters, and other contemporary documents relating to the reign of King Edward the Fourth* (London, 1845), p. 14; Annales, p. 785.

24 Ingulph, p. 439.

25 Blacman, p. 43; Scofield, I, p. 383. Accounts for Henry's imprisonment appear on the Issue Roll of the Exchequer for Edward IV at E403/844. My thanks to Dr Jeremy Ashbee of English Heritage for providing me with a transcription of this document.

26 Warkworth, p. 5.

27 Blacman, pp. 42–4.

28 The fullest expression of this theory is provided by Bark, N., 'Did schizophrenia change the course of English history? The mental illness of Henry VI', *Medical Hypotheses* 59, no. 4 (2002).

29 Warkworth, p. 11.

Chapter 38. 'Have not the English always betrayed their kings?'

1 *N'ont pas des Anglois souvent leur rois trays?* A ballad written by the duke of Orléans in 1453, quoted in Scattergood, V. J., *Politics and Poetry in the Fifteenth Century* (London, 1971), p. 171.

2 'The Maner and Guyding bitwene the Quene Margarete and of here Soone and therle of Warrei[c] tyme of his being in France with the duc of Clarence', Vale, pp. 215–18.

3 CCC, p. 111; Fabyan, p. 654; Warkworth, p. 3; 'Hearne's Fragment' in Giles, J. A. (ed.), *The Chronicles of the White Rose of York: A series of historical fragments, proclamations, letters, and other contemporary documents relating to the reign of King Edward the Fourth* (London, 1845), p. 15.

4 'Hearne's Fragment', p. 15. The Croyland Chronicle charmingly says that Edward was 'prompted by the ardour of youth'. Ingulph, p. 439.

5 Gregory, pp. 226–7; CSPM, nos. 137, 138, 173, http://www.british-history.ac.uk/cal-state-papers/milan/1385-1618/pp110-114 [accessed 1 November 2017]; http://www.british-history.ac.uk/cal-state-papers/milan/1385-1618/pp128-134 [accessed 1 November 2017]; Fabyan, p. 654; 'Vitellius A XVI', Kingsford, *Chronicles of London*, p. 179.

6 CSPM, no. 173.

7   Annales, p. 783.
8   Ibid., p. 786; Ingulph, p. 445; Gillingham, John, *The Wars of the Roses: Peace and Conflict in Fifteenth-Century England* (London, 1990), p. 157.
9   Annales, p. 788; CSPM, no. 149, http://www.british-history.ac.uk/cal-state-papers/milan/1385-1618/pp117-122 [accessed 30 October 2017].
10 Gregory, p. 235; Scofield, I, pp. 400–1.
11 Whereas Warwick and his fellow ambassadors had received lavish gifts and hospitality from the French – including a gold cup costing over 2,000 *livres tournois* – Edward merely gave the French ambassadors some hunting horns, leather bottles and mastiff dogs. Scofield, I, pp. 424–9. See ibid., pp. 403–29 for the negotiations between England, France and Burgundy.
12 CSPM, nos. 148, 149, http://www.british-history.ac.uk/cal-state-papers/milan/1385-1618/pp117-122 [accessed 30 October 2017]; Annales, pp. 787–8, 790–1; Gregory, p. 237; CSPM, no. 162, http://www.british-history.ac.uk/cal-state-papers/milan/1385-1618/pp122-128 [accessed 26 February 2018].
13 *EHD*, IV, p. 296; Waurin, V, p. 543; Warkworth, p. 3; Annales, p. 786; Pollard, A. J., *Warwick the Kingmaker: Politics, Power and Fame* (London, 2007), pp. 59–61.
14 Warkworth, p. 4.
15 CSPM, no. 142, http://www.british-history.ac.uk/cal-state-papers/milan/1385-1618/pp115-117 [accessed 1 November 2017].
16 CSPM, no. 146, ibid.
17 CSPM, nos. 150–1, ibid.
18 Annales, p. 791; Gregory, p. 227; CSPM, nos. 165, 162, http://www.british-history.ac.uk/cal-state-papers/milan/1385-1618/pp122-128 [accessed 27 November 2017]; CSPV, no. 408: http://www.british-history.ac.uk/cal-state-papers/venice/vol1/pp92-126 [accessed 27 November 2017]; 'Vitellius A XVI', Kingsford, *Chronicles of London*, p. 179; McGovern, C. J. M. *Lancastrian Diplomacy and Queen Margaret's Court in Exile, 1461–1471*, unpublished BA diss., Keele University, 1973, pp. 43–4.
19 CSPM, no. 169: http://www.british-history.ac.uk/cal-state-papers/milan/1385-1618/pp122-128 [accessed 27 November 2017]; 'Vitellius A XVI', Kingsford, *Chronicles of London*, p. 180; Gregory, pp. 236–7; Annales, pp. 789–90; Warkworth, p. 5; Hicks, M. A., 'The case of Sir Thomas Cook, 1468', *English Historical Review* 193, no. 366 (1978); Pollard, *Warwick the Kingmaker*, pp. 63–4; Scofield, Cora L., 'The Early Life of John de Vere, Thirteenth earl of Oxford', *English Historical Review* 29, no. 114 (1914), p. 231.
20 Warkworth, p. 2. For discontent at English poverty and unrest see ibid., p. 4; Gregory, p. 227; *Great Chronicle*, p. 207; Dupont, *Waurin*, III, p. 193; CSPM, nos. 137, 160, http://www.british-history.ac.uk/cal-state-papers/milan/1385-1618/pp110-114 [accessed 27 October 2017];

http://www.british-history.ac.uk/cal-state-papers/milan/1385-1618/
pp122-128 [accessed 27 November 2017]; Annales, pp. 788–9; 'Short
English Chronicle', *Three Fifteenth-Century Chronicles*, p. 80.

21 Ingulph, p. 445; Gillingham, *Wars of the Roses*, p. 161.

22 Lord Audley and Sir John Fogge were also named in the articles. Vale,
pp. 212–15.

23 The Croyland Chronicle claimed the rebel army was 60,000 strong,
three times the size of Edward's; the Milanese ambassador heard
Robin of Redesdale had 40,000 followers; and Warkworth 20,000.
The former reports almost certainly inflate the numbers involved
but suggests the alarming size of the rebellion. Ingulph, pp. 445–6;
Warkworth, p. 6; CSPM, no. 173, http://www.british-history.ac.uk/
cal-state-papers/milan/1385-1618/pp128-134 [accessed 27 February 2018].

24 Warkworth, p. 6; Pollard, *Warwick*, p. 65.

25 Warkworth, pp. 6–7; CCC, pp. 115, 117; Ingulph, pp. 446–7; CSPM,
nos. 173, 176, http://www.british-history.ac.uk/cal-state-papers/
milan/1385-1618/pp128-134 [accessed 27 February 2018]; 'Vitellius A XVI', Kingsford, *Chronicles of London*, p. 180.

26 Warkworth, p. 7; CCC, p. 117; Gillingham, *Wars of the Roses*, pp. 164–6;
PR 1470, Introduction, http://www.british-history.ac.uk/no-series/
parliament-rolls-medieval/november-1470 [accessed 25 November
2017].

27 PL, II, p. 390.

28 Warkworth, pp. 8–9; CCC, p. 121; Scobie, *Philippe de Commines*, p. 188;
CSPM, no. 182, http://www.british-history.ac.uk/cal-state-papers/
milan/1385-1618/pp134-145 [accessed 25 October 2017]. For the
Lincolnshire rising and flight of Warwick and Clarence, Gillingham,
Wars of the Roses, pp. 166–78; Pollard, *Warwick*, pp. 67–8.

29 CSPM, no. 189, http://www.british-history.ac.uk/cal-state-papers/
milan/1385-1618/pp134-145 [accessed 25 October 2017]; Margaret's 'right difficult'-ness was dwelt on in 'Maner and Guyding', Vale,
p. 216. For the negotiations (which are misdated to 15 July–3 August)
see 'Maner and Guyding', Vale, pp. 215–18; CSPM, nos. 184–95,
http://www.british-history.ac.uk/cal-state-papers/milan/1385-1618/
pp134-145 [accessed 25 October 2017]; Scobie, *Philippe de Commines*,
pp. 187–9; Warkworth, pp. 9–10; CCC, p. 121.

30 'Maner and Guyding', Vale, p. 216.

31 Ibid., pp. 215–18; CSPM, nos. 184–95, http://www.british-history.
ac.uk/cal-state-papers/milan/1385-1618/pp134-145 [accessed 25
October 2017]; Scobie, *Philippe de Commines*, I, pp. 187–9; Warkworth,
pp. 9–10; CCC, p. 121.

32 'Maner and Guyding', Vale, p. 216; Kekewich, Margaret L., 'The Lancastrian Court in Exile', in Stratford, Jenny (ed.), *Proceedings of the
2001 Harlaxton Symposium: The Lancastrian Court* (Donington, 2003),
p. 105, Appendix 2; Pollard, *Warwick*, pp. 68–70.

33 CSPM, no. 190.

34 CSPM, no. 191.

35 'Maner and Guyding', Vale, p. 218.

36 Warkworth is the only source for the arrangement that Clarence
    would accede if the Lancastrian line failed. It is possible that such
    an eventuality was discussed – although it does not feature in the
    Lancastrian version of events nor is it mentioned by the Milanese
    ambassadors – but with a newly married Prince Edward, the probability
    of Clarence's accession was remote. Warkworth, p. 10.

37 Scobie, *Philippe de Commines*, p. 188.

38 'Maner and Guyding', Vale, p. 216.

Chapter 39. 'That puppet of a king'

1   CSPM, no. 78, http://www.british-history.ac.uk/cal-state-papers/
    milan/1385-1618/pp37-106 [accessed 26 September 2017].

2   For the events of September and October 1470, see 'Vitellius A XVI',
    Kingsford, *Chronicles of London*, pp. 181–2; Warkworth, pp. 10–11;
    CCC, pp. 122–3; CSPM, nos. 196–7, http://www.british-history.ac.uk/
    cal-state-papers/milan/1385-1618/pp134-145 [accessed 25 October
    2017].

3   'Tharticles of the proclamacion of the duc of Clarence and erle of
    Warrewic at their londing...', Vale, p. 220. For more proclamations
    see ibid., pp. 218–22.

4   Warkworth, p. 4.

5   'Vitellius A XVI', Kingsford, *Chronicles of London*, p. 181; Scobie,
    Philippe de Commines, p. 192.

6   See, for instance, *EHD*, IV, p. 306; CCC, p. 123.

7   CSPM, no. 204, http://www.british-history.ac.uk/cal-state-papers/
    milan/1385-1618/pp145-162 [accessed 27 November 2017].

8   Warkworth, p. 12; Wolffe, p. 342; PR 1470, Introduction, http://www.
    british-history.ac.uk/no-series/parliament-rolls-medieval/novem-
    ber-1470 [accessed 25 November 2017].

9   The records of this parliament did not survive the restoration of
    Edward IV. For Warwick's lieutenancy and the attainders of Edward
    and Gloucester see *Great Chronicle*, p. 213; 'Vitellius A XVI', Kingsford,
    Chronicles of London, p. 183.

10 Scofield, I, pp. 543–4; Rymer, XI, http://www.british-history.ac.uk/
    rymer-foedera/vol11/pp679–681 [accessed 14 November 2017].

11 'Tharticles of the proclamacion', Vale, p. 221; Hammond, P. W., *The
    Battles of Barnet and Tewkesbury* (Gloucester and New York, 1990),
    p. 44.

12 *Great Chronicle*, p. 212; Warkworth, p. 9.

13 'Vitellius A XVI', Kingsford, *Chronicles of London*, p. 182; Warkworth,
    pp. 9, 13; *Great Chronicle*, p. 213; PL, II, pp. 411–12; Scofield, I, p. 547.

14 See Jones, Michael K. and Underwood, Malcolm G., *The King's Mother:*

Lady Margaret Beaufort countess of Richmond and Derby (Cambridge, 1999), pp. 51–2 for the context to this meeting.

15 Polydore Vergil, 135.

16 *EHD*, IV, p. 306.

17 Some have claimed the marriage between Prince Edward and Anne Neville never took place, but Anne is consistently referred to in financial accounts and chronicles as his wife. They were probably married at Amboise in December 1470. See Laynesmith, J. L., *The Last Medieval Queens: English Queenship 1445–1503* (Oxford, 2004), p. 44, n.87; Lewis, Katherine J., *Kingship and Masculinity In Late Medieval England* (New York and Abingdon, 2013), p. 244.

18 CSPM, no. 198, http://www.british-history.ac.uk/cal-state-papers/milan/1385-1618/pp134-145 [accessed 25 October 2017]; Scofield, pp. 563–4.

19 *EHD*, IV, pp. 306–7. For wider context see Scofield, I, pp. 549–64, although I disagree with Scofield's contention that Margaret was the reason for delay; McGovern, C. J. M., *Lancastrian Diplomacy and Queen Margaret's Court in Exile, 1461–1471*, unpublished BA diss., Keele University, 1973, pp. 52–3.

20 Ibid., p. 53; Scobie, *Philippe de Commines*, pp. 198–9.

21 Scobie, *Philippe de Commines*, p. 199.

22 Ibid.; *Arrivall*, p. 2; CCC, p. 127; Warkworth, pp. 13, 17; CSPM, no. 210, http://www.british-history.ac.uk/cal-state-papers/milan/1385-1618/pp145-162 [accessed 27 November 2017]; Polydore Vergil, p. 134; Hammond, *The Battles of Barnet and Tewkesbury*, p. 48.

23 CCC, p. 124; Warkworth, pp. 13–14; Polydore Vergil, pp. 137–9; *Arrivall*, pp. 4–5.

24 Gillingham, John, *The Wars of the Roses: Peace and Conflict in Fifteenth-Century England* (London, 1990), p. 183.

25 *Arrivall*, p. 6.

26 PL, II, p. 423.

27 Scobie, *Philippe de Commines*, pp. 188–9; *Arrivall*, pp. 9–11; Hammond, *The Battles of Barnet and Tewkesbury*, p. 64.

28 'Vitellius A XVI', Kingsford, *Chronicles of London*, p. 184. Blue was the colour of royal mourning, worn by the king on All Hallows (1 November), for the burial of certain family members and other 'solemn days'. David Starkey, 'Henry VI's Old Blue Gown', *The Court Historian* 4, no.1 (1999), p. 2.

29 Hammond, *The Battles of Barnet and Tewkesbury*, p. 68; Scofield, I, p. 575.

30 Dupont, *Waurin*, III, p. 211. A transcription of a letter from Edward's sister Margaret, duchess of Burgundy, to her mother-in-law Isabella, dowager duchess of Burgundy, probably written April 1471. Ibid., pp. 210–15.

31 For the Battle of Barnet see 'English Heritage Battlefield Report: Barnet 1471', https://content.historicengland.org.uk/content/docs/

battlefields/barnet.pdf [accessed 1 November 2017]; 'Vitellius A XVI', Kingsford, *Chronicles of London*, p. 184; *Arrivall*, pp. 18–20; Warkworth, pp. 15–17; CCC, p. 125; CSPM, no. 213, http://www.british-history. ac.uk/cal-state-papers/milan/1385-1618/pp145-162 [accessed 27 November 2017]; Polydore Vergil, pp. 144–7; Scobie, *Philippe de Commines*, pp. 200–1; Dupont, *Waurin*, III, pp. 210–15; Kleineke, Hannes, 'Gerhard von Wesel's Newsletter from England, 17 April 1471', *Ricardian* 16 (2006), http://www.richardiii.net/downloads/ Ricardian/2006_vol16_kleineke_gerhard_von_wesel.pdf [accessed 1 November 2017].

32 Chastellain, V, p. 490.

33 Warkworth, p. 16.

34 Scobie, *Philippe de Commines*, p. 201.

35 PL, III, pp. 6–7 for a letter from Oxford to his wife in the wake of Barnet, asking her to send him money, men, armour and horses as he escaped through the country.

36 Warkworth, p. 17.

37 Kleineke, 'Gerhard von Wesel's Newsletter'; Warkworth, p. 16; CSPM, no. 213.

38 'Vitellius A XVI', Kingsford, *Chronicles of London*, p. 184; PL, III, p. 4.

Chapter 40. 'The shadow on the wall'

1 Chastellain, V, p. 490.

2 Warkworth, p. 17; *Arrivall*, pp. 22–3; CSPM, no. 210, http://www. british-history.ac.uk/cal-state-papers/milan/1385-1618/pp145-162 [accessed 27 November 2017].

3 Polydore Vergil, pp. 148–9; Hammond, *Battles of Barnet and Tewkesbury*, p. 81. The countess of Warwick remained in sanctuary until June 1473.

4 CCC, p. 127; CSPM, nos. 215, 216, http://www.british-history.ac.uk/ cal-state-papers/milan/1385-1618/pp145-162 [accessed 27 November 2017].

5 Polydore Vergil, p. 151; CCC, p. 128; *Arrivall*, pp. 23, 26. The Recorder of Bristol was killed fighting for Margaret at Tewkesbury. Benet, p. 233; Toulmin Smith, Lucy (ed.), *The Itinerary of John Leland in or about the years 1535–1543 Parts VII and VIII with Appendices Including Extracts from Leland's Colleactanea* (London, 1909), p. 163.

6 *Arrivall*, pp. 24–7.

7 Ibid., pp. 27–9; 'English Heritage Battlefield Report: Tewkesbury 1471', https://content.historicengland.org.uk/content/docs/battlefields/tewkesbury.pdf [accessed 1 November 2017]; Warkworth, p. 18; Hammond, p. 87.

8 Polydore Vergil, p. 151.

9 Gower was killed in the field. Toulmin Smith, *The Itinerary of John Leland*, p. 63.

10 *Arrivall,* p. 28.
11 Hall is the only source for this gory detail. Contemporary sources only tell us that Wenlock died on the field. Hall, p. 300.
12 Warkworth, p. 18; *Arrivall,* p. 30. A tradition developed within a few years that Prince Edward had been captured and brought before Edward IV after the battle. Giving insolent answers to the king's questions, the prince was struck across the face by the king then killed by leading Yorkists including Edward IV's brother Richard, duke of Gloucester (the future Richard III). Early Tudor chroniclers expanded on the rumours of the prince's murder and it became part of the 'black legend' associated with Richard III, most famously expressed in William Shakespeare, *Henry VI, Part III,* Act 5, Scene 5. However, closer contemporaries are unanimous in saying that Prince Edward was killed in the field, most likely in flight. See Hammond, *The Battles of Tewkesbury and Barnet,* Appendix III.
13 An unusually full record was kept of those who had been killed at Tewkesbury, whether in battle or by execution. The numbers of those beheaded varies in contemporary sources between fifteen and nineteen. Similar scenes played out at Didbrook parish church 10 miles (16 km) away. 'Chronicle of Tewkesbury Abbey' *EHL,* pp. 376-8; PL, III, pp. 8-10; Warkworth, p. 18; Benet, p. 233; Toulmin Smith, *The Itinerary of John Leland,* p. 163; *Arrivall,* p. 31.
14 *Arrivall,* p. 31.
15 'Chronicle of Tewkesbury Abbey' erroneously names a Sir *William* Whittingham among the dead. Warkworth, p. 19; *Arrivall,* pp. 31-2; Toulmin Smith, *The Itinerary of John Leland,* p. 163; 'Yorkist Notes', 'Chronicle of Tewkesbury Abbey', *EHL,* pp. 374, 377-8; Benet, p. 233.
16 'Yorkist Notes,' *EHL,* p. 375; 'Vitellius A XVI', Kingsford, *Chronicles of London,* p. 184; Polydore Vergil, p. 152.
17 Preparations to oppose Fauconberg are recorded in the Issue Roll for 11 Edward IV (PRO E403/844). My thanks to Dr Jeremy Ashbee for providing me with a transcript of this document. For Fauconberg's rebellion see Warkworth, pp. 19-21; CCC, pp. 128-9; 'Vitellius A XVI', Kingsford, *Chronicles of London,* p. 185; *Arrivall,* pp. 36-7.
18 *The Arrivall* was written in 1471 by one of Edward IV's servants, a highly partisan eyewitness to the events of Edward's restoration, and intended for widespread dissemination.
19 *Arrivall,* p. 38.
20 Warkworth, p. 21.
21 CCC, pp. 130-1; CSPM, no. 220, http://www.british-history.ac.uk/cal-state-papers/milan/1385-1618/pp145-162 [accessed 27 November 2017].
22 St John Hope, W. H., 'The Discovery of the Remains of King Henry VI in Saint George's Chapel, Windsor Castle' *Archaeologia* 62, no. 2 (1911), p. 537. By the time of the exhumation any evidence for stab

wounds – or, indeed, for violent death in general – would have been extremely difficult to trace. See below, p. 553.

23 A similar logic, of course, suggests that the order to kill Edward IV's two sons, 'the princes in the Tower' in 1483 could only have come from Richard III.

24 CCC, p. 131; Warkworth, p. 21.

PART V: AFTERLIFE
Chapter 41. 'Very dolorous and discomforted queen of England'

1   Chastelain, George, *Le Temple de Bocace: édition commentée par Susanna Bliggenstorfer* (Berne, 1988), p. 81.
2   Farcy, Louis de, *Monographie de la Cathédrale d'Angers. volume II: Les Immeubles par destination* (Angers, 1905), p. 313; 'Extrait d'un manuscrit de Megsire Guillaume Oudin, prètre-sacriste de l'abbaye de Notre-Dame-du-Ronceray d'Angers (xve siècle). — Deuxième partie', *Revue de l'Anjou et du Maine* 1, no. 3 (1857), p. 138.
3   PL, III, p. 33.
4   Scofield, II, p. 23.
5   Dunn, Diana, 'Margaret of Anjou, Queen Consort of Henry VI: A Reassessment of Her Role, 1445–53', in Archer, Rowena, ed., *Crown, Government and People in the Fifteenth Century* (New York, 1995), pp. 111–12; Laynesmith, J. L., *The Last Medieval Queens: English Queenship 1445–1503* (Oxford, 2004), p. 172.
6   Laynesmith, *The Last Medieval Queens*, p. 172; Radulescu, R. L., 'Preparing for her Mature Years: The Case of Margaret of Anjou and her books', in Niebrzydowski, Sue (ed.), *Middle-aged Women in the Middle Ages* (Cambridge, 2011), pp. 134–5; Chastelain, *Le Temple de Bocace*, p. 15.
7   Calmette, J. and Périnelle, G., *Louis XI et L'Angleterre (1461–1483)* (Paris, 1930), pp. 395–7.
8   My italics. Scofield, II, p. 159.

Chapter 42. 'Holy King Henry'

1   'A prayer to holy kynge Henry.' Blacman, p. xii.
2   Knox, Ronald and Leslie, Shane (eds. and trans.), *The Miracles of King Henry VI: being an account and translation of twenty-three miracles taken from the Manuscript in the British Museum (Royal 13 c. viii)* (Cambridge, 1923), pp. 149–56.
3   Ibid., pp. 57, 77–84, 89–98, 106–9, 127, 163–7, 177–80, 182–6. Votive items can be seen displayed around the shrine of King Henry in a woodcut of c.1490–1500, now preserved in the Bodleian, MS. Bodl. 277, f.370 5v, http://bodley30.bodley.ox.ac.uk:8180/luna/servlet/detail/ODLodl~14~14~76776~135161:Henry-VI,-King-of-England,-invoked-?sort=Shelfmark&qvq=w4s:/what/MS.%20Bodl.%20277;sort:

Shelfmark;lc:ODLodl~29~29,ODLodl~7~7,ODLodl~6~6,ODLodl~1 4~14,ODLodl~8~8,ODLo [accessed 28 November 2017].

4   Spencer, Brian, 'King Henry of Windsor and the London Pilgrim', in Bird, Joanna, Chapman, Hugh and Clark, John (eds.), *Collectanea Londiniensia: Studies in London Archaeology and History Presented to Ralph Merrifield* (London, 1978), p. 240; McKenna, John W., 'Piety and Propaganda: The Cult of King Henry VI', in Rowland, Beryl (ed.), *Chaucer and Middle English Studies in Honour of Rossell Hope Robbins* (London, 1974), pp. 73–4.

5   Piroyanski, Danna, *Martyrs in the Making: Political Martyrdom in Late Mediaeval England* (Basingstoke, 2008), pp. 74–98.

6   Scofield, II, p. 366.

7   St John Hope, W. H., 'The Discovery of the Remains of King Henry VI in Saint George's Chapel, Windsor Castle' *Archaeologia* 62, no. 2 (1911), pp. 536–7, 541; White, W. J., 'The Death and Burial of Henry VI, a review of the Facts and Theories', *The Ricardian* 6 (1982), pp. 75, 77.

8   Wright, Thomas (ed.), *Three Chapters of Letters Relating to the Suppression of the Monasteries* (London, 1843), p. 221.

9   McKenna, 'Piety and Propaganda', p. 76.

10 Marks, Richard, 'Images of Henry VI', in Stratford, J. (ed.), *The Lancastrian Court: Harlaxton Medieval Studies, X* (Donington, 2003), pp. 114–18.

11 Offerings were made at Windsor later in the year too. Nicolas, Nicholas Harris (ed.), *Privy Purse Expenses of Elizabeth of York: Wardrobe Accounts of Edward IV with A Memoir of Elizabeth of York and Notes* (London, 1830), p. 3. For further offerings see pp. 29, 42.

12 Piroyanski, *Martyrs in the Making*, p. 83.

13 Lewis, Katherine J., '"Imitate, too, this king in virtue, who could have done ill and did it not": Lay Sanctity and the Rewriting Of Henry VI's Manliness' in Lewis, Katherine J. (ed.), *Religious Men and Masculine Identity in the Middle Ages* (Woodbridge, 2013), p. 129; Anglo, Sydney, *Images of Tudor Kingship* (London, 1992), p. 71.

14 Stanley, Arthur Penrhyn, *Historical Memorials of Westminster Abbey* (London, 1876), I, pp. 570–9.

15 Wright, *Three Chapters of Letters*, pp. 221–6.

16 St John Hope, 'The Discovery of the Remains of King Henry VI', pp. 536–7.

Epilogue

1   'Gesta Henrici Quinti,' quoted in Curry, *The Battle of Agincourt: Sources and Interpretations*, p. 39.

2   John Lydgate's Troy Book and Siege of Thebes. BL, Royal 18 D II, f. 30v, http://www.bl.uk/catalogues/illuminatedmanuscripts/record. asp?MSID=8704&CollID=16&NStart=180402&_ga=2.64312687.

676   SHADOW KING

1390438930.1529398102–157633210.1495811005 [accessed 14 February 2018].

Appendix I: Where did Henry VI die?

1   The correspondence regarding Henry's memorial is in the National Archives, TNA, Work 14/982. My thanks to Jeremy Ashbee for bringing this file to my attention.
2   Ashbee, J. A., 'The Tower of London as a royal residence: 1066–1400', unpublished PhD diss., University of London, 2006; Keay, Anna, *The Elizabethan Tower: The Haiward and Gascoyne Plan of 1597* (London, 2001), pp. 37–8, 43–6.
3   *Ancient Monuments and Historic Buildings: Ministry of Works. The Tower of London* (London, 1948), p. 21.
4   *Great Chronicle*, p. 212.
5   PR 1461, item 15, http://www.british-history.ac.uk/no-series/parliament-rolls-medieval/november-1461 [accessed 2 November 2017].
6   BL Royal MS 16 F II, f.73, http://www.bl.uk/manuscripts/FullDisplay.aspx?ref=Royal_MS_16_f_ii [accessed 30 October 2018].
7   TNA, E403/844: Issue Roll 11 Edward IV.
8   CCC, p. 129; 'Yorkist Notes, 1471,' *EHL*, p. 375.
9   Warkworth, p. 21.
10 Ibid.; Fabyan, p. 662; Wegemer, Gerard B. and Curtright, Travis (eds.) *The History of King Richard the Third by Master Thomas More Undersheriff of London c. 1513* (Irving, TX, 2013), p. 5; Grafton, Richard, *Grafton's chronicle; or, History of England. To which is added his table of the bailiffs, sheriffs, and mayors, of the city of London. From the year 1189, to 1558, inclusive* (London: 1809), II; Holinshed, Raphael, *Holinshed's Chronicles Of England, Scotland, And Ireland* (London: 1808), III, p. 326; Polydore Vergil, p. 156.
11 My italics. Britton, John and Brayley, E. W., *Memoirs of the Tower of London: comprising historical and descriptive accounts of that national fortress and palace* (London, 1830), p. 335; De Ros, William Lennox Lascelles Fitzgerald, *Memorials of the Tower of London* (London, 1867), p. 10.
12 Thomas, John Wesley, *The Tower, The Temple and the Minster: Historical and Biographical Associations of the Tower of London, St Paul's Cathedral and Westminster Abbey* (London, 1873), p. 29.
13 For the disputed location of the princes, see Maurer, Helen, 'Bones in the Tower: A Discussion of Time, Place and Circumstance', 2 parts, *The Ricardian* 8–9 (1990–1). For Tower myths see Parnell, Geoffrey, 'Riddle of the Tower Ravens Almost Resolved', *Ripperologist* 124 (2012); idem, '1888: The Victorian Mutilation of the Tower Ends', *Ripperologist* 123 (2011).
14 Peers wrote this in an internal memo on 10 April 1923. The italicized portion was originally in Latin: *Populus vult decipi; decipiatur!* TNA, Work 14/982.

15 Younghusband, in a letter of 11 May 1923. Younghusband seems to have suspected that Henry was kept in the Lanthorn Tower, although he provides no sources for his theory. Ibid.

Appendix II: Key characters

1   Scobie, *Philippe de Commines*, I, p. 192.

Index

SHADOW KING

LAUREN JOHNSON is a historian and costumed interpreter with a first-class degree from Oxford University. She is the author of a novel, *The Arrow of Sherwood* (2013) and *So Great a Prince* (2016), a study of the accession of King Henry VIII.